AN A.K. RICE INSTITUTE SERIES

GROUP RELATIONS READER 2

edited by
Arthur D. Colman and Marvin H. Geller

AN A.K. RICE INSTITUTE SERIES

GROUP RELATIONS
READER 2

edited by
Arthur D. Colman and Marvin H. Geller

AN A. K. RICE INSTITUTE SERIES

GROUP RELATIONS READER 2

edited by
Arthur D. Colman and Marvin H. Geller

Group Relations Reader 2
Arthur D. Colman and Marvin H. Geller

Copyright 1985 A. K. Rice Institute

All rights reserved. No part of this book may be used or reproduced in any manner without written permission except in the case of brief quotations (not to exceed 1000 words) in a review or professional work. For information, address A. K. Rice Institute, P. O. Box 39102, Washington DC 20016.

Library of Congress Catalog Card Number 75-24569

International Standard Book Number 0-9615099-1-0
(Previously 0-9615099-0-2)

Published by the A. K. Rice Institute
P. O. Box 39102
Washington DC 20016

Printed in the United States by
Goetz Printing
Springfield VA

Cover design by W. Harold Bexton

First Edition

TABLE OF CONTENTS

Contributors i
Preface v
Acknowledgements vii

Part One—Theory 1

1. Our Adult World and Its Roots in Infancy 5
   Melanie Klein

2. Projective Identification in Dyads and Groups 21
   Leonard Horwitz

3. Recovering Bion's Contributions to Group Analysis 37
   Kenneth Eisold

4. Some Psychodynamics of Large Groups 49
   Tom Main

5. Leadership: The Individual and the Group 71
   Pierre M. Turquet

6. Regression in Organizational Leadership 89
   Otto F. Kernberg

7. The Group-as-a-Whole Perspective and Its Theoretical
   Roots 109
   Leroy Wells Jr.

8. Container and Contained 127
   Wilfred Bion

Part Two—Method 135

9. Collaboration in Small Groups: Theory and Technique for
   the Study of Small-Group Processes 139
   James P. Gustafson and Lowell Cooper

10. A Study of Very Small Groups 151
    R. Gosling

11. Men and Women at Work: A Group Relations Conference
    on Person and Role 163
    Laurence J. Gould

12. Advanced Learning in a Small Group 173
    Margaret J. Rioch

13. An Advanced Training Group Within the Group Relations
    Conference: Evolution, Design and Outcome 185
    Robert F. Baxter and Elizabeth Morgan Heimburger

14. Affect, Leadership and Organizational Boundaries 197
    Clayton P. Alderfer and Edward B. Klein

Part Three—Application 213

A. Systems Analysis 215

15. Family Dynamics and Object-Relations Theory: An Analytic
    Group-Interpretative Approach to Family Therapy 217
    Roger L. Shapiro

16. Management Development . . . some ideals, images and
    realities 231
    W. Gordon Lawrence

B. Consultation and Implementation 241

17. Organizational Development and Industrial Democracy: A
    Current Case-Study 243
    Eric J. Miller

18. The Assisted Independent Living Program: A New Model
    for Community Care 273
    Niles M. Medders and Arthur D. Colman

19. A Retrospective View of a Hospital-Wide Group Relations
    Training Program: Costs, Consequences and
    Conclusions 285
    Roy W. Menninger

20. Belfast Communities Intervention 299
    Edward B. Klein

C. Role Analysis 307

21. Women in Authority: A Sociopsychological Analysis 309
    Marjorie Bayes and Peter M. Newton

22. Dilemmas of Black Females in Leadership 323
    Rhetaugh Graves Dumas

23. The Psychodynamics of Taking the Role 335
    Larry Hirschhorn

24. Unconscious Process in an Organization: A Serendipitous
    Investigation 353
    Edward R. Shapiro

D. Evaluation 363

25. Why I Work as a Consultant in the Conferences of the
    A. K. Rice Institute 365
    Margaret J. Rioch

26. The Politics of Involvement 383
    Eric J. Miller

27. The Couch at Sea: Psychoanalytic Studies of Group and
    Organizational Leadership 399
    Otto F. Kernberg

Notes 413

Bibliography 419

Index 437

CONTRIBUTORS

Alderfer, Clayton P. Professor, Yale School of Organization and Management; Fellow, American Psychological Association

Baxter, Robert F., M.D. Member, Central States Center & Texas Center, A. K. Rice Institute; Director, Adolescent Psychiatry Service, Wyandotte General Hospital, Wyandotte, Michigan; Fellow, American Psychiatric Association

Bayes, Marjorie, Ph.D. Antioch/New England Graduate School, Department of Organization and Management

Bernard, Harold S., Ph.D. Member, Executive Board, New York Center, Board Member, A. K. Rice Institute; Clinical Associate Professor of Psychiatry and Chief, Group Psychotherapy Program, New York University Medical Center

Bion, Wilfred. Deceased

Colman, Arthur D., M.D. Board of Directors, GREX, Fellow, A. K. Rice Institute; Member and Faculty, C. G. Jung Institute, San Francisco; Clinical Professor, Department of Psychiatry, University of California, San Francisco

Cooper, Lowell. Member, GREX, A. K. Rice Institute; Associate Professor, California School of Professional Psychology, Berkeley

Dumas, Rhetaugh G., Ph.D., R.N. Member, Washington-Baltimore Center, Fellow and Board Member, A. K. Rice Institute; Dean and Professor, University of Michigan School of Nursing; Member, Institute of Medicine of The National Academy of Sciences

Eisold, Kenneth, Ph.D. President, New York Center, A. K. Rice Institute

Evans, F. Barton, III, Ph.D. Associate, Washington-Baltimore Center, A. K. Rice Institute; Assistant Director, Counseling Center, Georgetown University; Clinical Instructor of Psychiatry, Georgetown University School of Medicine

Geller, Marvin H., Ph.D. Associate, Washington-Baltimore Center, President, A. K. Rice Institute; Director, Princeton Counseling Center, Princeton University, Princeton, New Jersey

Gould, Laurence J., Ph.D. Associate, New York Center, Fellow, A. K. Rice Institute; Professor of Psychology and Director, The Psychological Center, Clinical Psychology Doctoral Program, City College of the City University of New York

Gosling, Robert. Past Chairman of the Professional Committee, Tavistock Clinic; Past Consultant Psychiatry, Tavistock Clinic (retired)

Contributors

Gustafson, James Paul, M.D. Board Member, Midwest Center, A. K. Rice Institute; Professor of Psychiatry, University of Wisconsin Medical School

Heimburger, Elizabeth Morgan, M.D. President, Central States Center, Board Member, A. K. Rice Institute; Associate Professor of Psychiatry and Behavioral Sciences, University of Texas Medical Branch, Galveston, Texas

Hirschhorn, Larry. Senior Researcher, Management and Behavioral Science Center, Wharton School

Horwitz, Leonard. Chief of Clinical Psychology, The Menninger Foundation; Training and Supervising Analyst, Topeka Institute of Psychoanalysis

Kernberg, Otto F., M.D. Member-at-Large, A. K. Rice Institute; Medical Director, New York Hospital-Cornell Medical Center, Westchester Division; Professor of Psychiatry, Cornell University Medical College

Klein, Edward B., Ph.D. President, Midwest Center, Board Member, A. K. Rice Institute; Visiting Professor, Yale School of Organization and Management; Professor, Departments of Psychology and Psychiatry, University of Cincinnati

Klein, Melanie. Deceased

Krantz, James, Ph.D. Associate, Washington-Baltimore Center, A. K. Rice Institute; Organization Consultant and Research Associate, Management and Behavioral Science Center, The Wharton School of the University of Pennsylvania

Lawrence, W. Gordon. Organizational Consultant, Shell International Petroleum Company, London; Consultant, Societe Internationale des Conseillers de Synthese, France

Main, T. F. Foundation Member, Tavistock Institute of Human Relations; Member, International Psychoanalytic Association

Medders, Niles M. President, GREX, A. K. Rice Institute; Director, Marin Assisted Independent Living Program, Buckelew Houses Inc., San Rafael, California; Member, Northern California Group Psychotherapy Society

Menninger, Roy W., M.D. President, The Menninger Foundation; Clinical Professor, University of Kansas Medical Center, Kansas City, Kansas

Miller, Eric J. Board Member, Honorary Fellow, A. K. Rice Institute; Director, Group Relations Training Programme and Consultant, Tavistock Institute of Human Relations, London; Policy Adviser, OPUS: An Organization for Promoting Understanding in Society, London

Contributors

Newton, Peter M. Professor of Psychology, Wright Institute, Berkeley, California

Rioch, Margaret J., Ph.D. President, Washington-Baltimore Center; Fellow and Board Member, A. K. Rice Institute; Professor Emeritus in Residence, The American University, Washington, D.C.; Member, Board of Trustees and Executive Council, Washington School of Psychiatry

Shapiro, Edward R., M.D. Board, Center for the Study of Groups and Social Systems (Boston Center), Associate, Washington-Baltimore Center, A. K. Rice Institute; Associate Clinical Professor of Psychiatry, Harvard Medical School; Director, Adolescent and Family Treatment and Study Center, McLean Hospital, Belmont, Massachusetts

Shapiro, Roger L., M.D. Associate, Washington-Baltimore Center, Fellow, A. K. Rice Institute; Clinical Professor of Psychiatry, George Washington University School of Medicine; Faculty, Washington Psychoanalytic Institute

Thompson, Verneice D., Ph.D. Member, GREX, A. K. Rice Institute; Core Faculty, The Wright Institute, Berkeley; Associate Clinical Professor, Department of Psychiatry, University of California Medical School, San Francisco

Turquet, Pierre. Deceased

Wells, Leroy, Jr., Ph.D. Associate, Washington-Baltimore Center, A. K. Rice Institute; Assistant Professor, The American University, College of Public and International Affairs, Washington, D.C.; Member, National Training Laboratory Institute, Rosslyn, Virginia

West, Kathryn L., Ph.D. Vice President, GREX, Board Member, A. K. Rice Institute; Clinical Psychologist, West Los Angeles VA Medical Center, Brentwood Division, Family Treatment Program; Clinical Assistant Professor, Department of Psychology and Department of Psychiatry and Biobehavioral Sciences, UCLA

PREFACE

This volume is the second in a series of *Group Relations Readers* published by the A. K. Rice Institute.

Reader 1 was published ten years ago and drew substantially on the now classic writings of Bion, Rice and Miller, who, together with other psychoanalysts and organizational consultants based at the Tavistock Institute of Human Relations in London, helped develop the Group Relations Conference model and its first applications. In addition, *Reader 1* traced the early development and use of this model after its export to the United States through the writings of Rioch and other Americans. *Reader 2* has continued the tradition of publishing "classics" by including the posthumous writings of Melanie Klein, Pierre Turquet and Wilfred Bion. However, the majority of the 27 articles in *Reader 2* represent the ongoing work of men and women actively committed to developing and deepening the Group Relations model as both an analytical tool applied to the study of groups and organizations and a powerful method for experiential learning.

The past ten years have witnessed steady growth in all aspects of Group Relations work, including the written word. Our general criteria for selecting among many relevant papers for *Reader 2* were to crystallize the important developments in Group Relations work since the publication of *Reader 1* in a form useful to students, teachers and practitioners interested in the psychology of group and organizational life.

Although this volume stands on its own, readers new to the Group Relations model may wish to refer to *Reader 1* for more introductory material.

We wish to thank the entire community of the A. K. Rice Institute and our international colleagues who have contributed to *Reader 2*. To Michele Newman we owe special praise for her dedication, nuturance and technical expertise through all phases of this book's production.

ACKNOWLEDGEMENTS

We wish to thank all those who contributed to *Reader 2*. In particular we wish to acknowledge the following:

The **American Group Psychotherapy Association**, for permission to reprint from the *International Journal of Group Psychotherapy*:

"The Couch at Sea: Psychoanalytic Studies of Groups and Organizational Leadership," by Otto Kernberg. Vol. 43, pp. 5-23, copyright 1984.

"Projective Identification in Dyads and Groups," by Leonard Horwitz. Vol. 33, pp. 259-279, copyright 1983.

The *American Journal of Psychoanalysis*, for permission to reprint:

"Recovering Bion's Contribution to Group Analysis," by Kenneth Eisold.

The **A. K. Rice Institute**, for permission to reprint from the *Journal of Personality and Social Systems*:

"Advanced Learning in a Small Group," by Margaret J. Rioch. Vol. 2, pp. 27-36, copyright 1980.

"Affect, Leadership and Organizational Boundaries," by Clayton Alderfer and Edward Klein. Vol. 1, pp. 19-32, copyright 1978.

"An Advanced Training Group Within the Group Relations Conferences: Evolution, Design and Outcome," by Robert Baxter and Elizabeth Morgan Heimburger. Vol. 2, pp. 89-99, copyright 1980.

"Dilemmas of Black Females in Leadership," by Rhetaugh G. Dumas. Vol. 2, pp. 3-14, copyright 1979.

"The Politics of Involvement," by Eric J. Miller. Vol. 2, pp. 37-50, copyright 1980.

"Why I Work as a Consultant in Group Relations Conferences," by Margaret J. Rioch. Vol. 1, pp. 33-49, copyright 1978.

Caesena Press, for permission to reprint from *Do I Dare Disturb the Universe?*, edited by James Grotstein, copyright 1981:

Acknowledgements

"A Study of Very Small Groups," by R. Gosling.

Jason Aronson, for permission to reprint from *Seven Servants: Four Works*, by Wilfred Bion, copyright 1977:

"Attention and Interpretation: Container and Contained," by Wilfred Bion.

and from *Internal World and External Reality: Object Relations Theory Applied*, edited by Otto Kernberg, copyright 1980:

"Regression in Organizational Leadership," by Otto Kernberg.

John Wiley and Sons, for permission to reprint from *Exploring Individual and Organizational Boundaries*, by W. Gordon Lawrence, copyright 1979:

"Men and Women at Work: A Group Relations Conference on Person and Role," by Laurence J. Gould.

Jossey Bass, for permission to reprint from *Analyses in Groups*, edited by Gibbard, Hartmann and Mann, copyright 1974:

"Leadership: The Individual and The Group," by Pierre Turquet.

Journal of Applied Behavioral Science, for permission to reprint:

"Women in Authority: A Sociopsychological Analysis," by Marjorie Bayes and Peter Newton. Vol. 14, pp. 7-20, copyright 1978.

MCB University Press, for permission to reprint from the *Journal of European Industrial Training*:

"Management Development...some ideals, images and realities," by W. Gordon Lawrence. Vol. 1, pp. 21-25, copyright 1977.

Peacock Publishers Inc., for permission to reprint from *The Large Group*, by Lionel Kreeger, copyright 1975:

"Some Psychodynamics of Large Groups," by Tom Main.

Petrocelli Books Inc., for permission to reprint from *Organizational Development in the U.K. and the U.S.A.*, copyright 1977:

"Organizational Development and Industrial Democracy: A Current Case Study," by Eric J. Miller.

Plenum Publishing, for permission to reprint from *Human Relations*:

"Collaboration in Small Groups: Theory and Technique," by James Gustafson and Lowell Cooper. Vol. 31, pp. 155-171, copyright 1978.

Acknowledgements

Psychiatric Annals, for permission to reprint:

> "Our Adult World and Its Roots in Infancy," by Melanie Klein. Copyright 1959.
>
> "A Retrospective View of a Hospital-Wide Group Relations Training Program: Costs, Consequences and Conclusions," by Roy W. Menninger. Vol. 38, pp. 323-339, copyright 1985.
>
> "The Assisted Independent Living Program: A New Model for Community Care," by Niles Medders and Arthur D. Colman. Vol. 15, copyright 1985.

University of Chicago Press, for permission to reprint from *Adolescent Psychiatry, Vol. VII*, edited by Sherman Feinstein and Peter Giovacchini, pp. 118-135, copyright 1979:

> "Family Dynamics and Object Relations Theory: An Analytic Group Interpretative Approach to Family Therapy," by Roger Shapiro.

William Alanson White Psychiatric Foundation Inc., for permission to reprint from *Psychiatry*:

> "Regression in Organizational Leadership," by Otto Kernberg. Vol. 42, pp. 24-39, copyright 1979.

PART ONE

THEORY

Section Editors: Marvin H. Geller
James Krantz

The work most centrally associated with the Group Relations tradition grew out of an optimism in post-war Britain that social science could be used in the construction of better social order (Trist, personal communication). To this end, researchers at the Tavistock Institute of Human Relations, using the integration of psychoanalytical thought and social systems theory, developed theories and methods aimed at the small work group, the organization as a whole as well as the larger social field.

The most influential psychoanalytic perspective was that of Melanie Klein and the object-relations school. It was from this vantage point that Wilfred Bion was able to develop his well-known ideas about group life. The central theorist in developing a systems approach to the field of psychology was Ludwig Von Bertalanffy. His work, too, can be traced to the intellectual climate in the post-World War II era in which scientists were moving away from a reductive view of physical reality to an approach that emphasized the study of the special properties of organized wholes. In psychology, this trend was marked by the emergence of new disciplines such as cybernetics, information theory, theory of games, and general systems theory. Despite differences between disciplines they were all generally concerned with "systems," "wholes" or "organizations."

Both elements contributed to the "group-as-a-whole" thinking, which is so central to Group Relations theory.

In selecting papers for this section, an effort was made to publish papers that have either significantly advanced or challenged the basic theory in the past ten years. While much has been written, and the work has been advanced, fundamental changes or challenges to the basic principles have not yet emerged. The past ten years have been a period of "normal science" in which the revolutionary breakthroughs associated with Wilfred Bion and Melanie Klein have been built upon and elaborated.

These two perspectives have become the central theoretical tools of the work represented in this book. The first article by Melanie Klein points to the persistence of infantile conflicts in our emotional and social life. Kleinian theory is the underpinning for Bion's work and establishes the foundation for understanding the covert and unconscious dimensions of group life that are central to the work of the A. K. Rice Institute.

Eisold's paper is an explication of Bion's work on groups. He develops the link between intrapsychic processes and the experience of group life.

Horwitz, in "Projective Identification in Dyads and Groups," attempts to clarify this often misunderstood but central concept. Bion has stated that without this concept, he doubted "if much progress could be made in understanding groups." Horwitz emphasizes both the intrapsychic and interpersonal aspects of the concept, as well as the universality of the phenomenon.

The following group of papers describes the relationship of basic theory to the understanding of group and institutional life. Kernberg's paper "Regression in Organizational Leadership" focuses on the problems in the personality of the leader and demonstrates how these problems can promote organizational regression. What is central to the paper is the necessity of considering the interaction between leader and follower if one is to find meaningful solutions to group and organizational dilemmas. Turquet's paper, "Leadership: The Individual and the Group," further develops the link between open-systems theory and Bion's ideas about group functioning. The concepts of open-systems, primary task and boundaries are tied to the view of leadership as a function, especially a boundary function. Main's paper, "Some Psychodynamics of Large Groups," is a further elaboration of the concept of projective identification. Main contends that large as contrasted with small groups provide fewer opportunities for reality testing and the retrieval of projections and provide greater opportunities for the transmitting and receiving of projections, making large group life more anxiety provoking than the dyad or small group. Well's paper is a comprehensive examination of the basic theoretical concepts that ties together group-as-a-whole thinking within a systemic socio-analytic framework.

Bion's paper, "Attention and Interpretation: Container and Contained," is included in this section since it deals directly with the import and challenge of introducing new ideas into established ways of thinking, a metaphor for the novel aspects of Group Relations theory, with its emphasis on unconscious processes, as it impacts on organizational life. His creativity, even in this short essay, makes it clear that since *Group Relations Reader 1* was published in 1975, no new "great masters" have appeared on the scene, nor have there been any major or systemic revisions in the work of the "old masters."

M.H.G.
J.K.

Part One—Theory

Our Adult World and Its Roots in Infancy 5
Melanie Klein

Projective Identification in Dyads and Groups 21
Leonard Horwitz

Recovering Bion's Contributions to Group Analysis 37
Kenneth Eisold

Some Psychodynamics of Large Groups 49
Tom Main

Leadership: The Individual and the Group 71
Pierre M. Turquet

Regression in Organizational Leadership 89
Otto F. Kernberg

The Group-as-a-Whole Perspective and Its Theoretical Roots 109
Leroy Wells Jr.

Container and Contained 127
Wilfred Bion

1.

OUR ADULT WORLD AND ITS ROOTS IN INFANCY

Melanie Klein

EDITORIAL NOTE

This paper, originally delivered by Melanie Klein on 11th May 1959 before the members of the Departments of Social Anthropology and Social Studies in the University of Manchester, is a brief but comprehensive statement of her findings and theories in psychoanalysis in a form specially prepared for a wider social-science audience.

In considering from the psychoanalytic point of view the behaviour of people in their social surroundings, it is necessary to investigate how the individual develops from infancy into maturity. A group—whether small or large—consists of individuals in a relationship to one another; and therefore the understanding of personality is the foundation for the understanding of social life. An exploration of the individual's development takes the psychoanalyst back, by gradual stages, to infancy; and I shall first enlarge, therefore, on fundamental trends in the young child.

The various signs of difficulties in the infant—states of rage, lack of interest in his surroundings, incapacity to bear frustration, and fleeting expressions of sadness—did not formerly find any explanation except in terms of physical factors. For until Freud made his great discoveries, there was a general tendency to regard childhood as a period of perfect happiness, and the various disturbances displayed by children were not taken seriously. Freud's findings have, in the course of time, helped us to understand the complexity of the child's emotions and have revealed that children go through serious conflicts. This has led to a better insight into the infantile mind and its connection with the mental processes of the adult.

The play technique that I developed in the psychoanalysis of very young children, and other advances in technique resulting from my work, allowed me to draw new conclusions about very early stages of infancy and deeper layers of the unconscious. Such retrospective insight is based on one of the crucial findings of Freud, the transference situation, that is to say the fact that in a psychoanalysis the patient re-enacts in relation to the psychoanalyst earlier—and, I would add, even very early—situations and emotions. Therefore the relationship to the psychoanalyst at times bears, even in adults, very childlike features, such as over-dependence and the need to be guided, together with quite irrational distrust. It is part of the technique of the psychoanalyst to deduce the past from these manifestations. We know that Freud first discovered the Oedipus complex in the adult and was able to trace it back to childhood. Since I had the good fortune to analyse very young children, I was able to gain an even closer insight into their mental life, which led me back to an understanding of the mental life of the baby. For I was enabled by the meticulous attention I paid to the transference in the play technique to come to a deeper understanding of the ways in which—in the child and later also in the adult—mental life is influenced by earliest emotions and unconscious phantasies. It is from this angle that I shall describe with the use of as few technical terms as possible what I have concluded about the emotional life of the infant.

I have put forward the hypothesis that the newborn baby experiences, both in the process of birth and in the adjustment to the post-natal situation, anxiety of a persecutory nature. This can be explained by the fact that the young infant, without being able to grasp it intellectually, feels unconsciously every discomfort as though it were inflicted on him by hostile forces. If comfort is given to him soon—in particular warmth, the loving way he is held, and the gratification of being fed—this gives rise to happier emotions. Such comfort is felt to come from good forces and, I believe, makes possible the infant's first loving relation to a person or, as the psychoanalyst would put it, to an object. My hypothesis is that the infant has an innate unconscious awareness of the existence of the mother. We know that young animals at once turn to the mother and find their food from her. The human animal is not different in that respect, and this instinctual knowledge is the basis for the infant's primal relation to his mother. We can also observe that at an age of only a few weeks the baby already looks up to his mother's face, recognizes her footsteps, the touch of her hands, the smell and feel of her breast or of the bottle that she gives him, all of which suggest that some relation, however primitive, to the mother has been established.

However, he not only expects food from her but also desires love and understanding. In the earliest stages, love and understanding are expressed through the mother's handling of her baby, and lead to a certain unconscious oneness that is based on the unconscious of the mother and of the child being in close relation to each other. The infant's resultant feeling of being understood underlies the first and fundamental relation in his life—the relation to the mother. At the same time, frustration, discomfort and pain, which I suggested are experienced as persecution, enter as well into his feelings about his mother, because in the first few months she represents to the child the whole of the external world; therefore both good and bad come in his mind from her, and this leads to a twofold attitude toward the mother even under the best possible conditions.

Both the capacity to love and the sense of persecution have deep roots in the infant's earliest mental processes. They are focused first of all on the mother. Destructive impulses and their concomitants—such as resentment about frustration, hate stirred up by it, the incapacity to be reconciled, and envy of the all-powerful object, the mother, on whom his life and well-being depend—these various emotions arouse persecutory anxiety in the infant. *Mutatis mutandis* these emotions are still operative in her life. For destructive impulses towards anybody are always bound to give rise to the feeling that that person will also become hostile and retaliatory.

Innate aggressiveness is bound to be increased by unfavorable external circumstances and, conversely, is mitigated by the love and understanding that the young child receives; and these factors continue to operate throughout development. But although the importance of external circumstances is by now increasingly recognized, the importance of internal factors is still underrated. Destructive impulses, varying from individual to individual, are an integral part of mental life, even in favourable circumstances, and therefore we have to consider the development of the child and the attitudes of the adults as resulting from the interaction between internal and external influences. The struggle between love and hate—now that our capacity to understand babies has increased—can to some extent be recognized through careful observation. Some babies experience strong resentment about any frustration and show this by being unable to accept gratification when it follows on deprivation. I would suggest that such children have a stronger innate aggressiveness and greed than those infants whose occasional outbursts of rage are soon over. If a baby shows that he is able to accept food and love, this means that he can overcome resentment about frustration relatively quickly and, when gratification is again provided, regains his feelings of love.

Before continuing my description of the child's development, I feel that I should briefly define from the psychoanalytic point of view the terms *self* and *ego*. The ego, according to Freud, is the organized part of the self, constantly influenced by instinctual impulses but keeping them under control by repression; furthermore it directs all activities and establishes and maintains the relation to the external world. The self is used to cover the whole of the personality, which includes not only the ego but the instinctual life that Freud called the *id*.

My work has led me to assume that the ego exists and operates from birth onwards and that in addition to the functions mentioned above it has the important task of defending itself against anxiety stirred up by the struggle within and by influences from without. Furthermore it initiates a number of processes from which I shall first of all select *introjection* and *projection*. To the no less important process of *splitting*, that is to say dividing, impulses and objects I shall turn later.

We owe to Freud and Abraham the great discovery that introjection and projection are of major significance both in severe mental disturbances and in normal mental life. I have here to forgo even the attempt to describe how in particular Freud was led from the study of manic-depressive illness to the discovery of introjection, which underlies the superego. He also expounded the vital relation between superego and ego and the id. In the course of time these basic concepts underwent further development. As I came to recognize in the light of my psychoanalytic work with children, introjection and projection function from the beginning of post-natal life as some of the earliest activities of the ego, which in my view operates from birth onwards. Considered from this angle, introjection means that the outer world, its impact, the situations the infant lives through, and the objects he encounters, are not only experienced as external but are taken into the self and become part of his inner life. Inner life cannot be evaluated even in the adult without these additions to the personality that derive from continuous introjection. Projection, which goes on simultaneously, implies that there is a capacity in the child to attribute to other people around him feelings of various kinds, predominantly love and hate.

I have formed the view that love and hate towards the mother are bound up with the very young infant's capacity to project all his emotions on to her, thereby making her into a good as well as dangerous object. However, introjection and projection, though they are rooted in infancy, are not only infantile processes. They are part of the infant's phantasies, which in my view also operate from the beginning and help to mould his impression of his surroundings; and by introjection this changed picture of the external world influences what goes on in his mind. Thus an inner world is built up that is partly a reflection of the external one. That is to say, the double process of introjection and projection contributes to the interaction between external and internal factors. This interaction continues throughout every stage of life. In the same way introjection and projection go on throughout life and become modified in the course of maturation; but they never lose their importance in the individual's relation to the world around him. Even in the adult, therefore, the judgement of reality is never quite free from the influence of his internal world.

I have already suggested that from one angle the processes of projection and introjection that I have been describing have to be considered as unconscious phantasies. As my friend the late Susan Isaacs put it in her paper on this subject "Phantasy is (in the first instance) the mental corollary, the psychic representative of instinct. There is no impulse, no instinctual urge or response which is not experienced as unconscious phantasy . . . A phantasy represents the particular content of the urges or feelings (for example, wishes, fears, anxieties, triumphs, love or sorrow) dominating the mind at the moment" (Isaacs, 1952).

Unconscious phantasies are not the same as day-dreams (though they are linked with them) but an activity of the mind that occurs on deep unconscious levels and accompanies every impulse experienced by the infant. For instance, a hungry baby can temporarily deal with his hunger by hallucinating the satisfaction of being given the breast, with all the pleasures he normally derives from it, such as the taste of the milk, the warm feel of the breast, and being held and loved by the mother. But unconscious phantasy also takes the opposite form of feeling deprived and persecuted by the breast that refuses to give this satisfaction. Phantasies—becoming more elaborate and referring to a wider variety of objects and situations—continue throughout development and accompany all activities;

they never stop playing a great part in mental life. The influence of unconscious phantasy on art, on scientific work, and on the activities of every-day life cannot be overrated.

I have already mentioned that the mother is introjected, and that this is a fundamental factor in development. As I see it, object relations start almost at birth. The mother in her good aspects—loving, helping, and feeding the child—is the first good object that the infant makes part of his inner world. His capacity to do so is, I would suggest, up to a point innate. Whether the good object becomes sufficiently part of the self depends to some extent on persecutory anxiety—and accordingly resentment—not being too strong; at the same time a loving attitude on the part of the mother contributes much to the success of this process. If the mother is taken into the child's inner world as a good and dependable object, an element of strength is added to the ego. For I assume that the ego develops largely round this good object, and the identification with the good characteristics of the mother becomes the basis for further helpful identifications. The identification with the good object shows externally in the young child's copying the mother's activities and attitudes; this can be seen in his play and often also in his behaviour towards younger children. A strong identification with the good mother makes it easier for the child to identify also with a good father and later on with other friendly figures. As a result, his inner world comes to contain predominantly good objects and feelings, and these good objects are felt to respond to the infant's love. All this contributes to a stable personality and makes it possible to extend sympathy and friendly feelings to other people. It is clear that a good relation of the parents to each other and to the child, and a happy home atmosphere, play a vital role in the success of this process.

Yet, however good are the child's feelings towards both parents, aggressiveness and hate also remain operative. One expression of this is the rivalry with the father that results from the boy's desires towards the mother and all the phantasies linked with them. Such rivalry finds expression in the Oedipus complex, which can be clearly observed in children of three, four, or five years of age. This complex exists, however, very much earlier and is rooted in the baby's first suspicions of the father taking the mother's love and attention away from him. There are great differences in the Oedipus complex of the girl and of the boy, which I shall characterize only by saying that whereas the boy in his genital development returns to his original object, the mother, and therefore seeks female objects with consequent jealousy of the father and men in general, the girl to some extent has to turn away from the mother and find the object of her desires in the father and later on in other men. I have, however, stated this in an over-simplified form, because the boy is also attracted towards the father and identifies with him; and therefore an element of homosexuality enters into normal development. The same applies to the girl, for whom the relation to the mother, and to women in general, never loses its importance. The Oedipus complex is thus not a matter only of feelings of hate and rivalry towards one parent and love towards the other, but feelings of love and the sense of guilt also enter in connection with the rival parent. Many conflicting emotions therefore centre upon the Oedipus complex.

We turn now again to projection. By projecting oneself or part of one's impulses and feelings into another person, an identification with that person is achieved, though it will differ from the identification arising from introjection. For if an object is taken into the self (introjected), the emphasis lies on acquiring some of the characteristics of this object and on being influenced by them. On the other hand, in putting part of oneself into the other person (projecting), the identification is based on attributing to the other person some of one's own qualities. Projection has many repercussions. We are inclined to attribute to other people—in a sense, to put into them—some of our own emotions and thoughts; and it is obvious that it will depend on how balanced or persecuted we are whether this projection is of a friendly or of a hostile nature. By attributing part of our feelings to the other person, we understand their feelings, needs, and satisfactions; in other words, we are putting ourselves into the other person's shoes. There are people who go so far in this direction that they lose themselves entirely in others and become incapable of objective judgement. At the same time excessive introjection endangers the strength of the ego because it becomes completely dominated by the introjected object. If projection is predominantly hostile, real empathy and understanding of others is impaired. The character of projection is, therefore, of great importance in our relations to other people. If the interplay between introjection and projection is not dominated by hostility or over-dependence, and is well balanced, the inner world is enriched and the relations with the external world are improved.

I referred earlier to the tendency of the infantile ego to split impulses and objects, and I regard this as another of the primal activities of the ego. This tendency to split results in part from the fact that the early ego largely lacks coherence. But—here again, I have to refer to my own concepts— persecutory anxiety reinforces the need to keep separate the loved object from the dangerous one, and therefore to split love from hate. For the young infant's self-preservation depends on his trust in a good mother. By splitting the two aspects and clinging to the good one he preserves his belief in a good object and his capacity to love it; and this is an essential condition for keeping alive. For without at least some of this feeling, he would be exposed to an entirely hostile world that he fears would destroy him. This hostile world would also be built up inside him. There are, as we know, babies in whom vitality is lacking and who cannot be kept alive, probably because they have not been able to develop their trusting relation to a good mother. By contrast, there are other babies who go through great difficulties but retain sufficient vitality to make use of the help and food offered by the mother. I know of an infant who underwent a prolonged and difficult birth and was injured in the process, but when put to the breast, took it avidly. The same has been reported of babies who had serious operations soon after birth. Other infants in such circumstances are not able to survive because they have difficulties in accepting nourishment

Our Adult World and its Roots in Infancy

and love, which implies that they have not been able to establish trust and love towards the mother.

The process of splitting changes in form and content as development goes on, but in some ways it is never entirely given up. In my view, omnipotent destructive impulses, persecutory anxiety, and splitting are predominant in the first three to four months of life. I have described this combination of mechanisms and anxieties as the paranoid-schizoid position, which in extreme cases becomes the basis of paranoia and schizophrenic illness. The concomitants of destructive feelings at this early stage are of great important, and I shall single out greed and envy as very disturbing factors, first of all in the relation to the mother and later on to other members of the family, in fact throughout life.

Greed varies considerably from one infant to another. There are babies who can never be satisfied because their greed exceeds everything they may receive. With greed goes the urge to empty the mother's breast and to exploit all the sources of satisfaction without consideration for anybody. The very greedy infant may enjoy whatever he receives for the time being; but as soon as the gratification has gone, he becomes dissatisfied and is driven to exploit first of all the mother and soon everybody in the family who can give him attention, food, or any other gratification. There is no doubt that greed is increased by anxiety—the anxiety of being deprived, of being robbed, and of not being good enough to be loved. The infant who is so greedy for love and attention is also insecure about his own capacity to love; and all these anxieties reinforce greed. This situation remains in fundamentals unchanged in the greed of the older child and of the adult.

As regards envy, it is not easy to explain how the mother who feeds the infant and looks after him can also be an object of envy. But whenever he is hungry or feels neglected, the child's frustration leads to the phantasy that the milk and love are deliberately withheld from him, or kept by the mother for her own benefit. Such suspicions are the basis of envy. It is inherent in the feeling of envy not only that possession is desired, but that there is also a strong urge to spoil other people's enjoyment of the coveted object—an urge that tends to spoil the object itself. If envy is very strong, its spoiling quality results in a disturbed relation to the mother as well as later to other people; it also means that nothing can be fully enjoyed because the desired thing has already been spoiled by envy. Furthermore, if envy is strong, goodness cannot be assimilated, become part of one's inner life, and so give rise to gratitude. By contrast, the capacity to enjoy fully what has been received, and the experience of gratitude towards the person who gives it, influence strongly both the character and the relations with other people. It is not for nothing that in saying grace before meals, Christians use the words, 'For what we are about to receive may the Lord make us truly thankful.' These words imply that one asks for the one quality—gratitude—that will make one happy and free from resentment and envy. I heard a little girl say that she loved her mother most of all people, because what would she have done if her mother had not given birth to her and had not fed her? This strong feeling of gratitude was linked with her capacity for enjoyment and showed itself in her character and relations to other people, particularly in generosity and consideration. Throughout life such capacity for enjoyment and gratitude makes a variety of interests and pleasures possible.

In normal development, with growing integration of the ego, splitting processes diminish, and the increased capacity to understand external reality, and to some extent to bring together the infant's contradictory impulses, leads also to a greater synthesis of the good and bad aspects of the object. This means that people can be loved in spite of their faults and that the world is not seen only in terms of black and white.

The superego—the part of the ego that criticizes and controls dangerous impulses, and that Freud first placed roughly in the fifth year of childhood—operates, according to my views, much earlier. It is my hypothesis that in the fifth or sixth month of life the baby becomes afraid of the harm his destructive impulses and his greed might do, or might have done, to his loved objects. For he cannot yet distinguish between his desires and impulses and their actual effects. He experiences feelings of guilt and the urge to preserve these objects and to make reparation to them for harm done. The anxiety now experienced is of a predominantly depressive nature; and the emotions accompanying it, as well as the defences evolved against them, I recognized as part of normal development, and termed the 'depressive position.' Feelings of guilt, which occasionally arise in all of us, have very deep roots in infancy, and the tendency to make reparation plays an important role in our sublimations and object relations.

When we observe young infants from this angle, we can see that at times, without any particular external cause, they appear depressed. At this stage they try to please the people around them in every way available to them—smiles, playful gestures, even attempts to feed the mother by putting a spoon with food into her mouth. At the same time this is also a period in which inhibitions over food and nightmares often set in, and all these symptoms come to a head at the time of weaning. With older children, the need to deal with guilt feelings expresses itself more clearly; various constructive activities are used for this purpose and in the relation to parents or siblings there is an excessive need to please and to be helpful, all of which expresses not only love but also the need to make reparation.

Freud has postulated the process of *working through* as an essential part of psychoanalytic procedure. To put it in a nutshell, this means enabling the patient to experience his emotions, anxieties, and past situations over and over again both in relation to the analyst and to different people and situations in the patient's present and past life. There is, however, a working through occurring to some extent in normal individual development. Adaptation to external reality increases and with it the infant achieves a less phantastic picture of the world around him. The recurring experience of the mother going away and coming back to him makes her absence less frightening, and therefore his suspicion of her leaving him diminishes. In this way he gradually works through his early fears and comes to terms with his conflicting impulses and emotions. Depressive anxiety at this stage predominates and persecutory anxiety lessens. I hold that many apparently odd manifestations, inexplicable phobias, and idiosyncrasies that can be observed in young children are indications of, as well as ways of, working through the depressive position. If the feelings of guilt arising in the child are not excessive, the urge to make reparation and other processes that are part of growth bring relief. Yet depressive and persecutory anxieties are never entirely overcome; they may temporarily recur under internal or external pressure, though a relatively normal person can cope with this recurrence and regain his balance. If, however, the strain is too great, the development of a strong and well-balanced personality may be impeded.

Having dealt—though I am afraid in an over-simplified way—with paranoid and depressive anxieties and their implications, I should like to consider the influence of the processes I have described on social relations. I have spoken of introjection of the external world and have hinted that this process continues throughout life. Whenever we can admire and love somebody—or hate and despise somebody—we also take something of them into ourselves and our deepest attitudes are shaped by such experiences. In the one case it enriches us and becomes a foundation for precious memories; in the other case we sometimes feel that the outer world is spoilt for us and the inner world is therefore impoverished.

I can here only touch on the importance of actual favourable and unfavourable experiences to which the infant is from the beginning subjected, first of all by his parents, and later on by other people. External experiences are of paramount importance throughout life. However, much depends, even in the infant, on the ways in which external influences are interpreted and assimilated by the child; and this in turn largely depends on how strongly destructive impulses and persecutory and depressive anxieties are operative. In the same way our adult experiences are influenced by our basic attitudes, which either help us to cope better with misfortunes or, if we are too much dominated by suspicion and self-pity, turn even minor disappointments into disasters.

Freud's discoveries about childhood have increased the understanding of problems of upbringing, but these findings have often been misinterpreted. Though it is true that a too disciplinarian upbringing reinforces the child's tendency to repression, we have to remember that too great indulgence may be almost as harmful for the child as too much restraint. The so-called 'full self-expression' can have great disadvantages both for the parents and for the child. Whereas in former times the child was often the victim of the parents' disciplinarian attitude, the parents may now become the victims of their offspring. It is an old joke that there was a man who never tasted breast of chicken; for when he was a child, his parents ate it, and when he grew up, his children were given it. When dealing with our children, it is essential to keep a balance between too much and too little discipline. To turn a blind eye to some of the smaller misdeeds is a very healthy attitude. But if these grow into persistent lack of consideration, it is necessary to show disapproval and to make demands on the child.

There is another angle from which the parents' excessive indulgence must be considered: while the child may take advantage of his parents' attitude, he also experiences a sense of guilt about exploiting them and feels a need for some restraint that would give him security. This would also make him able to feel respect for his parents, which is essential for a good relation towards them and for developing respect for other people. Moreover, we must also consider that parents who are suffering too much under the unrestrained self-expression of the child—however much they try to submit to it—are bound to feel some resentment that will enter into their attitude towards the child.

I have already described the young child who reacts strongly against every frustration—and there is no upbringing possible without some unavoidable frustration—and who is apt to resent bitterly any failings and shortcomings in his environment and to underrate goodness received. Accordingly he will project his grievances very strongly on to the people around him. Similar attitudes are well known in adults. If we contrast the individuals who are capable of bearing frustration without too great resentment and can soon regain their balance after a disappointment with those who are inclined to put the whole blame on to the outer world, we can see the detrimental effect of hostile projection. For projection of grievance rouses in other people a counter-feeling of hostility. Few of us have the tolerance to put up with the accusation, even if it is not expressed in words, that we are in some ways the guilty party. In fact, it very often makes us dislike such people, and we appear all the more as enemies to them; in consequence they regard us with increased persecutory feelings and suspicions, and relations become more and more disturbed.

One way of dealing with excessive suspicion is to try to pacify the supposed or actual enemies. This is rarely successful. Of course, some people can be won over by flattery and appeasement, particularly if their own feelings of persecution make for the need to be appeased. But such a relation easily breaks down and changes into mutual hostility. In passing, I would mention the difficulties that such fluctuations in the attitudes of leading statesmen may produce in international affairs.

Where persecutory anxiety is less strong, and projection, mainly attributing to others good feelings, thereby becomes the basis of empathy, the response from the outer world is very different. We all know people who have the capacity to be liked; for we have the impression that they have some trust in us, which evokes on our part a feeling of friendliness. I am not speaking of people who are trying to make themselves popular in an insincere way. On the contrary, I believe it is the people who are genuine and have the courage of their convictions who are in the long run respected and even liked.

An interesting instance of the influence of early attitudes throughout life is the fact that the relation to early figures keeps reappearing and problems that remain unresolved in infancy or early childhood are revived though in modified form. For example, the attitude towards a subordinate or a superior repeats up to a point the relation to a younger sibling or to a parent. If we meet a friendly and helpful older person, unconsciously the relation to a loved parent or grandparent is revived; while a condescending and unpleasant older individual stirs up anew the rebellious attitudes of the child towards his parents. It is not necessary that such people should be physically, mentally, or even in actual age similar to the original figures; something in common in their attitude is enough. When somebody is entirely under the sway of early situations and relations, his judgement of people and events is bound to be disturbed. Normally such revival of early situations is limited and rectified by objective judgement. That is to say, we are all capable of being influenced by irrational factors, but in normal life we are not dominated by them.

The capacity for love and devotion, first of all to the mother, in many ways develops into devotion to various causes that are felt to be good and valuable. This means that the enjoyment that in the past the baby was able to experience because he felt loved and loving, in later life becomes transferred not only to his relations to people, which is very important, but also to his work and to all that he feels worth striving for. This means also an enrichment of the personality and capacity to enjoy his work, and opens up a variety of sources of satisfaction.

In this striving to further our aims, as well as in our relation to other people, the early wish to make reparation is added to the capacity of love. I have already said that in our sublimations, which grow out of the earliest interests of the child, constructive activities gain more impetus because the child unconsciously feels that in this way he is restoring loved people whom he has damaged. This impetus never loses its strength, though very often it is not recognized in ordinary life. The irrevocable fact that none of us is ever entirely free from guilt has very valuable aspects because it implies the never fully exhausted wish to make reparation and to create in whatever way we can.

All forms of social service benefit by this urge. In extreme cases, feelings of guilt drive people towards sacrificing themselves completely to a cause or to their fellow beings, and may lead to fanaticism. We know, however, that some people risk their own lives in order to save others, and this is not necessarily of the same order. It is not so much guilt that might be operative in such cases as the capacity for love, generosity, and an identification with the endangered fellow being.

I have emphasized the importance of the identification with the parents, and subsequently with other people, for the young child's development and I now wish to stress one particular aspect of successful identification that reaches into adulthood. When envy and rivalry are not too great, it becomes possible to enjoy vicariously the pleasures of others. In childhood the hostility and rivalry of the Oedipus complex are counteracted by the capacity to enjoy vicariously the happiness of the parents. In adult life, parents can share the pleasures of childhood and avoid interfering with them because they are capable of identifying with their children. They become able to watch without envy their children growing up.

This attitude becomes particularly important when people grow older and the pleasures of youth become less and less available. If gratitude for past satisfactions has not vanished, old people can enjoy whatever is still within their reach. Furthermore, with such an attitude, which gives rise to serenity, they can identify themselves with young people. For instance, anyone who is looking out for young talents and who helps to develop them—be it in his function as teacher or critic, or in former times as patron of the arts and of culture—is only able to do so because he can identify with others; in a sense he is repeating his own life, sometimes even achieving vicariously the fulfillment of aims unfulfilled in his own life.

At every stage the ability to identify makes possible the happiness of being able to admire the character or achievements of others. If we cannot allow ourselves to appreciate the achievements and qualities of other people—and that means that we are not able to bear the thought that we can never emulate them—we are deprived of sources of great happiness and enrichment. The world would be in our eyes a much poorer place if we had no opportunities of realizing that greatness exists and will go on existing in the future. Such admiration also stirs up something in us and increases indirectly our belief in ourselves. This is one of the many ways in which identifications derived from infancy become an important part of our personality.

The ability to admire another person's achievements is one of the factors making successful team work possible. If envy is not too great, we can take pleasure and pride in working with people who sometimes outstrip our capacities, for we identify with these outstanding members of the team.

The problem of identification is, however, very complex. When Freud discovered the superego, he saw it as part of the mental structure derived from the influence of the parents on the child—an influence that becomes part of the child's fundamental attitudes. My work with young children has shown me that even from babyhood onwards, the mother, and soon other people in the child's surroundings, is taken into the self, and this is the basis of a variety of identifications, favourable and unfavourable. I have above given instances of identifications that are helpful both to the child and to the adult. But the vital influence of early environment has also the effect that unfavourable aspects of the attitudes of the adult towards the child are detrimental to his development because they stir up in him hatred and rebellion or too great submissiveness. At the same time he internalizes this hostile and angry adult attitude. Out of such experiences, an excessively disciplinarian parent, or a parent lacking in understanding and love, by identification influences the character formation of the child and may lead him to repeat in later life what he himself has undergone. Therefore a father sometimes uses the same wrong methods towards his children that his father used towards him. On the other hand, the rebellion against the wrongs experienced in childhood can lead to the opposite reaction of doing everything differently from the way the parents did it. This would lead to the other extreme, for instance to over-indulgence of the child, to which I have referred earlier. To have learnt from our experiences in childhood and therefore to be more understanding and tolerant towards our own children, as well as towards people outside the family circle, is a sign of maturity and successful development. But tolerance does not mean being blind to the faults of others. It means recognizing those faults and nevertheless not losing one's ability to cooperate with people or even to experience love towards some of them.

In describing the child's development I have emphasized particularly the importance of greed. Let us consider now what part greed plays in character formation and how it influences the attitudes of the adult. The role of greed can be easily observed as a very destructive element in social life. The greedy person wants more and more, even at the expense of everybody else. He is not really capable of consideration and generosity towards others. I am not speaking here only of material possessions but also of status and prestige.

The very greedy individual is liable to be ambitious. The role of ambition, both in its helpful and in its disturbing aspects, shows itself wherever we observe human behaviour. There is no doubt that ambition gives impetus to achievement but, if it becomes the main driving force, cooperation with others is endangered. The highly ambitious person, in spite of all his successes, always remains dissatisfied, in the same way as a greedy baby is never satisfied. We know well the type of public figure who, hungry for more and more success, appears never to be content with what he has achieved. One feature in this attitude—in which envy also plays an important role—is the inability to allow others to come sufficiently to the fore. They may be allowed to play a subsidiary part as long as they do not challenge the supremacy of the ambitious person. We find also that such people are unable and unwilling to stimulate and encourage younger people, because some of them might become their successors. One reason for the lack of satisfaction they derive from apparently great success results from the fact that their interest is not so much devoted to the field in which they are working as to their personal prestige. This description implies the connection between greed and envy. The rival is seen not only as someone who has robbed and deprived one of one's own position or goods, but also as the owner of valuable qualities that stir up envy and the wish to spoil them.

Where greed and envy are not excessive, even an ambitious person finds satisfaction in helping others to make their contribution. Here we have one of the attitudes underlying successful leadership. Again, to some extent, this is already observable in the nursery. An older child may take pride in the achievements of a younger brother or sister and do everything to help them. Some children even have an integrating effect on the whole family life; by being predominantly friendly and helpful they improve the family atmosphere. I have seen that mothers who were very impatient and intolerant of difficulties have improved through the influence of such a child. The same applies to school life where sometimes only as few as one or two children have a beneficial effect on the attitude of all the others by a kind of moral leadership that is based on a friendly and cooperative relation to the other children without any attempt to make them feel inferior.

To return to leadership: if the leader—and that may also apply to any member of a group—suspects that he is the object of hate, all his antisocial attitudes are increased by this feeling. We find that the person who is unable to bear criticism because it touches at once on his persecutory anxiety not only is a prey to suffering but also has difficulties in relation to other people and may even endanger the cause for which he is working, in whatever walk of life it may be; he will show an incapacity to correct mistakes and to learn from others.

If we look at our adult world from the viewpoint of its roots in infancy, we gain an insight into the way our mind, our habits, and our views have been built up from the earliest infantile phantasies, and emotions to the most complex and sophisticated adult manifestations. There is one more conclusion to be drawn, which is that nothing that ever existed in the unconscious completely loses its influence on the personality.

A further aspect of the child's development to be discussed is his character formation. I have given some instances of how destructive impulses, envy and greed, and the resulting persecutory anxieties disturb the child's emotional balance and his social relations. I have also referred to the beneficial aspects of an opposite development and attempted to show how they arise. I have tried to convey the importance of the interaction between innate factors and the influence of the environment. In giving full weight to this interplay we get a deeper understanding of how the child's character develops. It has always been a most important aspect of psychoanalytic work that, in the course of a successful analysis, the patient's character undergoes favourable changes.

One consequence of a balanced development is integrity and strength of character. Such qualities have a far-reaching effect both on the individual's self-reliance and on his relations to the outside world. The influence of a really sincere and genuine character on other people is easily observed. Even people who do not possess the same qualities are impressed and cannot help feeling some respect for integrity and sincerity. For these qualities arouse in them a picture of what they might themselves have become or perhaps even still might become. Such personalities give them some hopefulness about the world in general and greater trust in goodness.

I have concluded this paper by discussing the importance of character, because in my view character is the foundation for all human achievement. The effect of a good character on others lies at the root of healthy social development.

POSTSCRIPT

When I discussed my views on character development with an anthropologist, he objected to the assumption of a general foundation for character development. He quoted his experience that in his fieldwork he had come across an entirely different evaluation of character. For instance, he had worked in a community where it was regarded as admirable to cheat other people. He also described, in answer to some of my questions, that in that community it was considered as a weakness to show mercy to an adversary. I inquired whether there were no circumstances in which mercy would be shown. He replied that if a person could place himself behind a woman in such a way that he would be up to a point covered by her skirt, his life would be spared. In answer to further questions he told me that if the enemy managed to get into a man's tent, he would not be killed; and that there was also safety within a sanctuary.

The anthropologist agreed when I suggested that the tent, the woman's skirt, and the sanctuary were symbols of the good and protective mother. He also accepted my interpretation that the mother's protection was extended to a hated sibling—the man hiding behind the woman's skirt—and that the ban on killing within one's own tent linked with the rules of hospitality. My conclusion about the last point is that fundamentally hospitality links with family life, with the relation of children to one another, and in particular to the mother. For, as I suggested earlier, the tent represents the mother who protects the family.

I am quoting this instance to suggest possible links between cultures that appear to be entirely different, and to indicate that these links are found in the relation to the primal good object, the mother, whatever may be the forms in which distortions of character are accepted and even admired.

2.

PROJECTIVE IDENTIFICATION IN DYADS AND GROUPS

Leonard Horwitz

A frequent occurrence between two or more persons is the projection of certain mental contents from one person onto and into another with a resulting alteration in the behavior of the targeted person. The mechanism of projection alone is not sufficient to explain the event, since it describes only the process occurring within the projector and does not deal with the effect on the target person. That complex of processes has been termed projective identification, a concept introduced by Melanie Klein in 1946, when she described the paranoid-schizoid position. It is both a defense mechanism and an object relationship that occurs in the earliest stages of development, the first year or two of life, before a firm differentiation between self and other has been achieved. Expanding on Klein (1946), Wilfred Bion (1961), in a series of penetrating observations on the mental life of groups, made the concept into a cornerstone of group behavior.

Despite the apparent usefulness—indeed, the necessity—of that concept, it has failed to gain wide currency in either the psychoanalytic or the analytic group psychotherapy literature. In psychoanalysis, the concept has been confined mainly to Kleinian writers like Rosenfeld (1965), who made extensive use of the process in their interpretive work with psychotic patients. Kernberg's (1975) conceptualization of borderline pathology has relied heavily on that and other object relations concepts. Searles (1963) has used an aspect of the concept in his work with schizophrenics, particularly in his emphasis on the therapist's being willing to become a receptacle for his patient's distorted projections. Malin and Grotstein (1966) have suggested that projective identification is both a normal and a pathological mechanism that may be used to conceptualize the therapeutic action of psychoanalysis. But those contributions have not entered the mainstream of analytic literature.

In group psychotherapy, since Bion's (1961) original contribution, there have been only two articles (Masler, 1969; Grinberg, Gear, and Liendo, 1976) in the literature specifically focused on the topic. Recently, Ganzarain (1977) expanded on the dynamic in his article on the application of object relations theory to groups. The group relations conferences initiated at Tavistock and introduced into the United States by the A. K. Rice Institute have applied the concept extensively in their study of the dynamic processes in groups (Rice, 1965; Rioch, 1970). But only the field of marital and family therapy has begun to incorporate such thinking through its key concepts of role assignment and role collusion among family members, particularly marital pairs (Dicks, 1967; Mandelbaum, 1977).

How may we understand the failure of projective identification to gain wide currency as a basic explanatory concept in the psychotherapy literature? One possible explanation may be that it usually refers to early preverbal phases of development, when self and object are still relatively undifferentiated. Hence, the contents may be archaic and bizarre and often evoke deep-seated reactions against regression to primary process modes. Projective identification refers to efforts by persons to rid themselves of certain mental contents by projection and to the anxiety that those contents arouse when they are returned in kind, pushed back into them in the context of weak ego boundaries. The resistance that most people experience in accepting the existence of those primitive processes may be compared to the revulsion to Freud's ideas about infantile sexuality when they burst on an unprepared and unwilling Victorian society at the beginning of this century.

But even for those prepared to accept the discomforting reactions associated with oscillating transfers of mental contents in a setting of blurred ego boundaries, there are genuine conceptual unclarities that emerge in formulating the processes. During several years of studying and teaching the concept, I have found it more elusive and confusing than any other psychodynamic concept I have encountered. Despite their extensive writings on the subject and their own intramural understanding of the complex processes involved, the Kleinians have failed to make a comprehensive and lucid explanation of the concept. Those unclarities seem to be based on the following factors: (1) Unlike projection, the defense of projective identification stems from a variety of motivations and not just the wish to rid oneself of unwanted impulses like aggression and sadism. Wishes to dominate, devalue, and control—based on primitive envy and the wish to cling parasitically to the valued object—are among the other motives. (2) The identification part of the concept requires special clarification, since its usage differs from most psychoanalytic definitions, and one is frequently at a loss to know who is the subject and who is the object in the process. (3) Because the discovery of projective identification occurred in the context of very early development and was studied mainly in psychotic populations, a number of writers have failed to understand it as a universal phenomenon that is not confined simply to the functioning of psychotic persons. (4) Probably the basic unclarity is the fact that projective identification is not simply a defense mechanism involving internal or intrapsychic transformations, as is true of most other defenses; rather, it is both an intrapsychic mechanism and an interpersonal transaction that involves transformations in both the projector and the external object.

Bion's application of Kleinian concepts to group mentality and group behavior alerted group therapists to a number of seminal and provocative ideas. A brief resume of Bion's main line of thinking cannot do justice to the richness of his ideas and can only suggest the direction of his thinking.

He believed that groups tend to arouse fears and wishes of a primitive regressed nature; in particular, the group-as-a-whole stirs archaic fantasies about the contents of the mother's body. Although such reactions can be most easily observed in groups composed of regressed persons, said Bion, they may also be uncovered and shown to occur in groups of well-integrated people. The primitive fantasies operate not only on group members but on the therapist as well. When projective identification occurs, the group therapist has the experience that he is being manipulated to play a part in someone else's fantasy. Bion (1961) concluded that the ability to shake oneself out of "the numbing feeling of reality" that is a concomitant of that state is a prime requisite of the group therapist. Bion left no doubt that projective identification is the cornerstone conception in the functioning of groups and that the group therapist must observe its occurrence within himself, be able to distance himself from it, and rely on his affective experience as a major source of his interpretations.

Bion's description of projective identification puts its major emphasis on the interpersonal, as opposed to the intrapsychic, aspects of the transaction. Although the process starts with a person projecting a part of his self onto and into one or more other persons, it is the impact of the projected contents affecting the other person that is of special interest. In other words, projective identification may be divided into two general processes. The first deals with the vicissitudes of the projected material as it affects the subject himself, in which the external object is not the focus of interest. The second important aspect is the effect of the projected material on the external object itself. The other person or target undergoes an identification or fusion with the projected content and its unconscious meanings and thus has the experience of being manipulated into a particular role.[1]

In discussing those two facets of the process, I shall first describe the behaviors in which they were first discovered—that is, in a dyadic relationship—and then elaborate on their occurrence in a group context.

EFFECT ON THE SELF: THE INTRAPSYCHIC REACTION

The subject projects good or bad parts of the self or the whole self onto an external object. In contrast to straight projection, a variety of other motives are involved in the process, over and beyond ridding oneself of unacceptable impulses. Another motive, for example, is based on primitive envy of the object's idealized qualities, with a consequent urge to destroy, spoil, or devalue by filling the object with the subject's bad, corrosive qualities. Still another drive is that of parasitism or the wish for refusion with the object. In the course of developing differentiation between self and object, the subject's separation anxieties and symbiotic needs lead to regressive fusion wishes and the fantasy of once again becoming unified with the maternal imago.

The subject's projections often lead to persecutory anxieties concerning retaliation by the external object; hence, the process may be accompanied by a heightened need to control and dominate the object. A frequent fantasy is that parts of the self are intruding into alien territory and, therefore, run the risk of becoming entrapped, much like a spy dropped behind enemy lines. In other words, the projection of the impulse, frequently but not always aggressive in nature, is accompanied by a complex set of fantasies about the fate of the self that is projected and the reaction of the recipient of the projection. When the bad, aggressive self is projected, the subject may, for example, experience a depletion of energy and a loss of assertiveness as he rids himself of those impulses. And a further fantasy is that he is now subject to attacks by the targeted person; therefore, he must attempt to manipulate and control him in order to neutralize those dangers.

After the initial projection onto the subject, the subject identifies himself with the projected material; that is, he reintrojects the aggression or other content attributed to the external object. That process has been characterized as an empathic response (Kernberg, 1975) and becomes the prototype for later, more advanced forms of empathy. In this instance, the subject experiences his own projected aggression, which he has taken back into the self. Because the projected content returns to the self, projective identification has been referred to as unsuccessful projection and is another distinguishing difference from projection per se.

One may well ask why a person, adult or infant, would reintroject material that he or she has sought to be rid of. Why engage behavior that essentially undoes the primary defensive motive? The first consideration is that the permeability of ego boundaries, the relative lack of differentiation between self and object, associated with regression to the earliest stage of development permits and encourages a rapid oscillation of projection and introjection, so that contents are moving back and forth with relative lack of resistance. Hence, successful projection cannot occur. One may use the analogy of a leaky heart valve that permits some of the blood to circulate in the wrong direction.

But even more cogent is the fact that a frequent motive is to be at one with the object of one's projection. That is another difference from projection proper, in which the subject experiences the object as distant and alien to himself. The projected content is often held ambivalently and is both desired and feared—too conflicted to be contained within oneself but also containing a positive valence that draws the subject toward it. For example, a young married woman in analysis consistently avoided discussion of her sexual life; when the analyst encouraged her to describe such material in greater detail, he was experienced as an intrusive, voyeuristic man who was seeking vicarious gratification. With her husband, there was similar reluctance to indicate an interest of her own in sexual activity, and she consistently waited for him to initiate it. She gradually overcame her self-righteous attitude in the transference, and we were able to see more clearly that her discomfort with her "crude animal wishes" made it necessary to put those needs into the analyst. At the same time, there was a sufficient awareness of her own sexual desires to acknowledge that she was at one with the analyst as she perceived him; she, too, was as primitively sexual as he seemed to be. She had, in effect, reintrojected the projection, motivated by the part of her that wished to make such impulses her own, despite the discomfort they engendered in her.

The processes described in this section are best summarized in a quotation from Hannah Segal (1973): "Projective identification is the result of the projection of parts of the self into an object. It may result in the object being perceived as having acquired the characteristics of the projected parts of the self but it can also result in the self becoming identified with the object of its projection" (p. 126). Segal was referring only to the aspect of projective identification that had an effect on the self and not on the external object. She was referring to the intrapsychic side of the process, not the interpersonal. Her failure to make that distinction clear is an example of how conceptual unclarity surrounding the concept has developed.

EFFECT ON THE EXTERNAL OBJECT: INTERPERSONAL TRANSACTIONS IN DYADS

The second phase of projective identification, its effect on the external object and on the relationship between the two or more persons involved, is of special importance, since it underlies a variety of interactional phenomena in both dyads and groups. The content projected by one person upon or into another begins to influence the behavior of the other person insofar as the target person becomes the repository of the unwanted contents. The identification aspect of the process is one in which the projections emanating from the subject become fused with the characteristics of the object; thus, the external object begins to take on characteristics that have been "put into" him.[2] That is the reason Bion described the target person as having the experience of being manipulated in somebody else's fantasies. Segal (1973) defined this aspect of projective identification as follows: "Parts of the self and internal objects are split off and projected into the external object which then becomes possessed by, controlled, and identified with the projected parts" (p. 27).

In a penetrating analysis of marital interaction, Henry Dicks (1967) of the Tavistock Clinic made extensive use of projective identification as not only the cement that binds marital partners in their love-hate interactions but also the material that supplies the potential for the conflicting tensions that impinge on marital pairs. Typically, in accordance with the well-known principle of the attraction of opposites, A selects B as a spouse because of B's potential for acting as the container of A's internal objects that A cannot tolerate as part of his or her conscious self. A then strives to induce B to become the embodiment of the fantasied other in order to complement an identity that A cannot sustain. A permeability of ego boundaries between the two persons develops, so that each becomes a representative of the other's self (or parts of self) that are ambivalently held. With the blurring of ego boundaries that occurs to some degree in all marriages, each partner feels the other to be a part of himself or herself. Insofar as those projected qualities are unacceptable, A proceeds to scapegoat B, and the intensity of the hostility is proportional to A's ambivalent investment in those rejected qualities. The wife who is strongly attracted to and at the same time repelled by her authoritarian, domineering husband both encourages him toward a strict parental role and undercuts his controlling behavior. Thus, she not only projects her ambivalently held object representation onto her spouse but encourages and manipulates him to assume the desired role.

Even though the concept evolved in the context of studying primitive psychological processes, it is also useful in understanding certain kinds of higher-level functioning. Indeed, projective identification is a prevalent aspect of the psychopathology of everyday life, particularly in regard to intimate relationships like marital and family transactions and interactions among close friends. In those situations a permeability of ego boundaries occurs, and the conditions are ripe for well-integrated persons to transfer a whole range of mental contents, be they primitive or mature and well-differentiated.

In a good marriage, for example, it is common for a spouse to experience vicarious gratification of a motive with which he or she is not entirely comfortable or is perhaps unskilled in expressing. Such situations often reflect neurotic trends of a relatively benign kind. The wife who is uncomfortable with her own competence in intellectual activities may find gratification by encouraging her husband to act for both of them in such matters. Of course, if it is an area of great intrapsychic conflict for one or both of them, there is danger ahead. But if the activity is only mildly conflicted, a stable and mutually gratifying arrangement may be formed. Here we have projective identification of a relatively normal kind in which behavioral needs are complementary and roles are mutually adaptive. In fact, said Henry Dicks (1967), a marriage without such reciprocal involvement is a crippled and stunted relationship. It is the basis for the sage observation that the opposite of love is not hate; it is indifference. Projective identification grows only in the soil of intimacy and intense involvement.

Such instances of healthy, adaptive emotional interchange illustrate another source of difficulty and misunderstanding concerning the concept of projective identification. It was first described as characteristic of the first few months of life, before the achievement of self-object differentiation, and has been studied most extensively among schizophrenic patients and, recently, as a characteristic of borderline persons. Some writers (Meissner, 1980) have interpreted the concept as applying only to the realm of psychotic functioning and, thus, have unduly narrowed its meaning. But psychoanalysis has a long tradition of pathological states unlocking the door to a better understanding or normal and neurotic functioning. We are now aware that temporary regressive actions within a sound ego structure are important aspects of psychic functioning, like creativity, empathy, humor, and, in the present context, intimacy. The processes laid bare in psychoses among persons with defective ego boundaries may be seen to operate among healthy persons who are in intimate contact with each other.

The differentiation between healthy and pathological projective identification depends mainly on the strength or the weakness of the ego structures of the parties involved. If the projective identification derives from fragmented or split ego states, in which the intensity of aggression is high and the ego defenses are primitive, one expects the projector or the subject to experience increased self-other confusion and heightened distortions of reality testing. A similar result may ensue for the target person who is vulnerable and poorly able to defend against the intrusion and manipulation of the other person and who, in addition, may be inclined to collude with his partner in the process.

In the marital interaction of one disturbed couple, for example, their most common pattern consisted of a see-saw response to each other in which one tended to be healthy and the other sick at any given time. Despite their obvious conscious efforts to encourage better functioning in the partner, each had a strong unconscious need to drag the other down because of envy, fear of abandonment, and other motives. When the wife was able to make a clear step forward and take on increased job responsibilities, the husband overtly supported her but covertly attempted to undermine her confidence by emphasizing her anxieties and her need for his help and by subtly taunting her with her failures in her new position. He was, in effect, attempting to reestablish the old equilibrium in which two relatively handicapped people leaned on each other and found gratification and security in lending strength to the other. From her side, she colluded with his manipulation by readily experiencing temper tantrums and disabling depressions. The husband unconsciously wanted a sicker wife, and there was enough regressive potential in her to comply with his pressure. When the equilibrium was thus established, a new cycle was begun in which both partners attempted to reverse the sick and healthy roles that had previously been assigned and adopted.

At the other extreme is the healthier person who is capable of temporary suspension of ego boundaries in the interest of intimacy and empathy. That person is able to project and introject without a significant loss of stable identity and tends to experience an enrichment of relationships to significant others.

Turning to another dyad, the therapist-patient pair, Racker's (1968) contributions in the area of countertransference have made extensive use of a process akin to projective identification. He described two kinds of countertransference responses, one based on concordant identifications and the other on complementary reactions. The concordant identification results from the analyst's effort to understand and empathize with his patient, to be in tune with various aspects of the patient's personality. To some extent an identification process occurs in each part of the analyst's personality with the corresponding part in the patient; his id with the patient's id, his superego with the patient's superego, and his ego with the patient's ego. Ideally, those identifications occur at a conscious level. But to the extent that the analyst fails in his concordant identifications and rejects them, complementary identifications become intensified; that is, the analyst's ego becomes identified with the patient's internal *objects*. Thus, if the analyst is unable to empathize concordantly with the patient's aggression, the patient will begin to experience him as a rejecting and punitive figure, and a process of manipulation occurs in which the analyst begins to take on the characteristics of the patient's rejecting superego. In that way the analyst becomes the embodiment of the patient's internal object, and a complementary identification has occurred.

Grinberg (1979) contributed a useful distinction between Racker's complementary countertransference and what he referred to as projective counteridentification, another form of deviant reaction to a patient's behavior in the psychotherapeutic situation. Racker (1968) was describing the usual countertransference situation in which the patient's productions touch on the analyst's own unresolved conflicts and thus elicit a neurotic response. The emphasis here is on the analyst's potential for an antitherapeutic, conflict-determined response to the patient. Grinberg (1979), on the other hand, emphasized the primacy of the patient's manipulation in producing projective counteridentification. In a number of well-chosen examples he demonstrated how the intensity of the pressure on the analyst may, indeed, elicit the patient's wished-for response in a manner that is fairly independent of the analyst's idiosyncratic neurotic make-up. Of course, those two modes, complementary countertransference and projective counteridentification, are two polar points on a continuum, and the countertransference response in the real therapeutic arena consists of some contribution from both factors.

It should be clear by now that the identification processes referred to in projective identification apply to both the subject and the object, to the self and the external object, to the intrapsychic and the interpersonal aspects. The subject identifies himself with his own projection, which returns to him as a reintrojection. On the other hand, the external object is manipulated to behave in accordance with the subject's self-representations or object representations and identifies himself with those projected contents. Another confusion that surrounds that complex of processes is that identification is alternately used to refer to one aspect or the other, the self or the external object, without always making clear the locus. Furthermore, the accepted definition of identification is that it is a transformation in a subject's ego or superego in accordance with certain characteristics of an object (Kernberg, 1976). But in contrast to introjection, identification occurs in the context of relatively well-differentiated boundaries between self-representation and object representation. Thus, projective identification would have been more accurately named projected *introjection*.[3]

A GROUP DYNAMIC TRIAD

Only when we are aware that persons in interaction may transfer mental contents one from the other and back and forth may we appreciate the full complexity of behavior in a group setting. We may then understand Bion's (1961) observation that each individual contribution adds to the reservoir of the group mentality. One of the fascinating experiences in group work is to find that the key to understanding fully one person's contributions is to hear later associations and reactions of other members. The dynamics of A's quarrel with his boss, for example, often become more comprehensible later in the session when B and C engage in a heated interaction between themselves or with the therapist. The therapist often undergoes an "Aha" experience as he attempts to piece together the contributions of various members. That kind of unitary functioning in a group has been described by such hypotheses as Bion's (1961) basic assumptions and Ezriel's (1952) common group tension. It is possible that the mechanism underlying those shared fantasies of group members is their capacity to put into each other certain mental contents.

But there is little doubt that three significant and interrelated group dynamisms are energized by projective identification, particularly its interpersonal aspect. I am referring here to (1) the phenomenon of role-suction, (2) the use of a member as spokesman, and (3) the pervasive occurrence of scapegoating.

Role-suction was first introduced by Redl (1963) and is related to an earlier conception called billet proposed by Arsenian, Semrad, and Shapiro (1962). Those authors observed that there are necessary roles to be filled in a group and that the group in its wisdom selects or drafts its most likely candidate to fulfill a particular function. The term "suction" graphically suggests the idea, nicely illustrated by Redl (1963), that group forces may sometimes act in powerful ways to pressure a person into a needed role. Projective identification adds a further dimension to the process by introducing the idea that the person who is thus suctioned has also become the repository of the projections of others and is being manipulated to engage in needed roles and behaviors.

With regard to the second phenomenon, a spokesman is one who assumes a leadership role in expressing the dominant theme of the group at any given time. As suggested in the above description of role-suction, there is always a collusion between the person's conflicts and character style on the one hand and the group's dominant needs on the other. Groups quickly learn which members are best able to express anger, who can deal most comfortably with closeness and libidinal attraction, and who can experience dependency with a minimum of conflict. There are varying degrees of consciousness on both sides regarding the relative contributions of the group and the individual to the role taken by the patient; more often than not, the group is content to disown the spokesman and vice versa. In fact, the most common error committed by the neophyte group therapist is his failure to recognize that a given member's behavior is not only a product of his own individual propensities but carries some degree of group freight as well. I have been impressed by the frequency with which the group therapist experiences the feeling that there is one particularly noxious and abrasive member, often a monopolist, who is interfering with the functioning of the group, and, so the fantasy goes, "All would be well if I were not burdened down by that member." In most instances, the extrusion of the recalcitrant member does not really improve matters, since the group quickly finds a new recruit among its ranks and promptly installs him as a replacement.

It is appropriate to ask how one may differentiate between the occasions when a member serves as spokesman and when he primarily speaks for himself. Resistant behavior that is persistent and that the group expects the therapist to deal with is most often being actively or passively encouraged by the whole group. Whether the behavior is produced by a monopolist, a silent member, or a chronic help-rejecting complainer, the group's failure to deal with it usually indicates that the member is expressing an important feeling for all. By contrast, the member who truly speaks for himself often finds little encouragement from his fellow group members, and the group's associations tend to move into other issues that resonate better with the group's central preoccupations.

The third dynamic, scapegoating, is perhaps the most commonly observed and accepted of all group dynamic processes.[4] Whether a therapist is more group-centered or more individually oriented, he has great difficulty in ignoring the process of scapegoating except, of course, when under the pressure of a strong countertransference response. The most frequent form of scapegoating is the displacement of a patient's aggressive or libidinal impulses from the therapist onto another member, toward whom such feelings do not elicit the same fear of punishment or retaliation. Projective identification, however, suggests that there is another form of scapegoating that may not be quite as obvious but occurs with considerable frequency. Those members who become the carriers of unwanted affects, the spokesmen for desired but threatening impulses, are particularly prone to end up as victims of the group's active effort to repress and reject such ideas and feelings. Those patients are often castigated, ridiculed, and even sometimes extruded from the group. Unless the therapist recognizes that the group is enacting a drama in which they are symbolically flailing themselves for their own unacceptable desires, in that instance projected onto the victim, he may very well participate himself in the cruel sacrifice. That kind of scapegoating was poignantly illustrated in the classic short story "The Lottery" by Shirley Jackson (1968), in which a community engages in a ritual stoning of one of its members, selected by lottery, in order to rid itself symbolically of its unwanted impulses.

My thesis is not that the three aforementioned processes—role-suction, spokesman, scapegoating—are entirely dependent for their operation on projective identification. We have seen, for example, that scapegoating may simply be a process of displacing an impulse from one target to another. By the same token, role-suction and the spokesman phenomena may theoretically occur without members' forcing their unwanted ego states into another member in such a way that the targeted person begins to undergo a manipulation and transformation. Probably all three of those dynamisms tend to be affected by projective identification to some degree. The group therapist who fails to appreciate the profound reverberating effects of those intense affective exchanges is neglecting a highly important determinant of group behavior.

ILLUSTRATIVE EXAMPLES OF GROUP BEHAVIOR

Two vignettes on group functioning, one from a Tavistock study group and the other from an ongoing therapy group, illustrate the operation of this dynamic triad. The study group is one of the events in the Tavistock (or A. K. Rice) Group Relations Conferences and consists of an unstructured small group experience. About a dozen participants meet with a consultant with the primary task of studying the dynamics of their group.

In one study group, which met daily over a period of almost two weeks, Don was extremely hostile and critical toward the consultant from the outset. At first, he made minor jibes at the consultant's interventions, and later he made more biting and sarcastic criticisms of his personal characteristics, like his haughty, aloof manner in the group. Ordinarily, the consultant (like the therapist) would have dealt with those attacks as manifestations of negative feelings toward authority figures and would have attempted to uncover such feelings as they existed in others, as well as Don. Instead, the consultant incorrectly began to show obvious signs of irritation with Don, glared at him unappreciatively on a few occasions, and flushed and bristled with annoyance when he was being ridiculed. Since the consultant was obviously reacting on a personal level and countertransference was interfering with his task, the group became increasingly inhibited about expressing their negative feelings toward the consultant, with the result that Don became even more the carrier of the negative affects. As the process continued, Don became alienated and scapegoated, with the other participants becoming greatly annoyed with him, at least on a conscious level. They experienced his attacks as unfair, crude, and tasteless. Finally, near the end of the conference, Don left the group prematurely but only after he had made a farewell speech in which he went around the room and picked apart each member, describing their Achilles's heels with telling accuracy. One of the more dramatic aspects of the episode was that, at the conclusion of his speech, he proceeded to commit a symbolic suicide by throwing open the tall French windows in the room, dropping a few feet to the ground, and exiting with a memorable flourish.

The triad of role-suction, spokesman, and scapegoat emerged clearly in that incident, particularly inasmuch as the consultant failed to deal actively with the contributions of the entire group. The group had put their aggression into Don; as a result, he not only experienced his own transference reactions but also was carrying the group's hostility.

The second example is from a therapy group that had been going for about a year. The therapist announced that he was bringing in a new member in a few weeks, and there was no immediate, visible response. However, in the next session, Ken, a potentially troublesome patient, began to resume some of his previously difficult and annoying monopolizing behavior. The therapist and the group had worked hard during the year to help Ken control his annoying and endless obsessional ruminations, and now it was reappearing, as though none of the previous work had been done. In the session Ken launched into a long, ruminative, free-associative monologue about himself, showing no intention to interact with the group and rather obviously imposing himself in an irritating way. He created in the therapist a feeling of helplessness and revived the therapist's fantasies that the group could function more effectively without this troublesome member. At one point the patient launched a tirade about his supervisor's incompetence and his inability to perform the job properly, whereupon the therapist attempted to interpret the barely disguised metaphoric attack on the therapist's skill. The interpretation was blithely ignored as Ken proceeded in characteristic fashion to continue his monologue as if the therapist had never spoken. At that point the group howled in amusement as they watched their therapist being treated with disdain and helplessly floundering to find a way of stemming the onslaught. It was now clear that the group was enjoying their spokesman, and, in contrast to the first example, they were at least partly conscious that Ken was expressing the anger that they also were experiencing about the therapist's imposing a new member on them. After the therapist had overcome his "numbing feeling of reality" (Bion, 1961) that it was Ken alone who was acting destructively, his interpretation about the entire group's resentment was effective in helping to bring the monopolist under control.

In effect, an unconscious collusion between Ken and the group had been established in which his characteristic behavior was used to express what the group was experiencing. The therapist was not getting his usual help from the group in controlling the man because their partly conscious wish was that he should, indeed, be the spokesman for their negative feelings. When the therapist helped to undo the projective identification involved in the process, when he redistributed the mental contents that had been put into that particular member, the group's anger could be uncovered and dealt with, and the therapist's countertransference toward the annoying member had come under control. It is manifestly clear that the major technical device for dealing with that kind of problem is to interpret the group's exploitation of the scapegoated member in getting its needs expressed.

TOWARD A DYNAMIC EXPLANATION

The phenomenon of projective identification, its effect on the interaction of dyads and groups, seems well established as an observable fact. The target of the process does, indeed, experience a change in his psychic functioning due to the intrusion of mental contents from another person. Most authors describe that process by saying that certain material is being "put into" the person. Projection per se is described with the preposition "onto" to indicate that the projected content does not necessarily penetrate the recipient, that it only affects the projector's perceptions of the target. In contrast, projective identification is more appropriately described as a projection *into* to indicate that it sinks below the surface of the target and, indeed, modifies the target's behavior. Those terms may be graphic and descriptive, but they fail to explain the actual process whereby a person experiences the feeling of being manipulated by someone else's projected contents. In my view, we do not have an adequate causal explanation of that important aspect of mental life.

Masler (1969), in his paper on the interpretation of projective identification in groups, proposed that a patient initiates the process by training others in the group to react in a manner complementary to his projections. Thus, a patient who exhibits abrasive behavior that has the effect of evoking criticism and censure from his peers is training the group to react to him as his own superego does. In effect, the patient has projected his superego into the other group members and has manipulated them into punitive reactions toward him. In Masler's (1969) illustration the patient provokes a wished-for superego reaction and thus externalizes an internal conflict, with the result that a complementary identification does indeed occur. The implicit explanation is that the mental contents, in that instance a punitive superego, are projected into the group through the subject's provocative behavior.

Racker's (1968) description of the process involved in countertransference reactions may bring us closer to an understanding of the mysterious event whereby one person puts mental contents into another. With regard to the relationship between patient and analyst, the usual process is that the boundaries between the two begin to merge to some extent, and there arises an approximate union or identity between various parts of the subject (the analyst) and the object (the patient), giving rise to a concordant identification. However, the interferences that occur as a result of the analyst's own blind spots and transferences interfere with the ideal situation, and the patient begins to treat the analyst as one of his internal objects. In consequence of feeling treated as such, according to Racker, the analyst begins to identify himself with the object.

To carry it one step further, we may think of two distorting mirrors facing each other and producing increased distortions as the reflected images bounce back and forth. Thus, the patient feels angry at the therapist and has the conviction that the therapist is cold and indifferent. The therapist, in turn, feels unfairly accused and begins to get irritated. The patient then not only reintrojects his projected anger but begins to sense the therapist's real irritation, feels more justified in his accusations, and experiences a heightened sense of mistreatment that he directs at the therapist. The therapist, on his part, experiences increased countertransference and, hence, a greater identity with the patient's views of him. Thus, an escalating cycle is set in motion. That series of provocations and reactions leads to ever-increasing distortions and pressures that ultimately push the therapist toward identifying himself with the patient's internal object, and eventually he begins to feel similar to the way the patient was perceiving him.[5]

Such a formulation is certainly consonant with the experiences of all clinicians, particularly those who have worked intensively with borderline or psychotic patients, in whom the intensity of primitive transferences promotes a blurring of ego boundaries. Therapists are often left by their patients with the disturbing feeling of having become the angry, punitive, withholding parent, for example, and such reactions may vary from fleeting and transitory to more long-lasting experiences. Under ideal circumstances, the therapist is able to use those reactions in the service of better understanding the dominant transference situation prevailing at a given time and can usually shake himself free of those disturbing introjections.

Important additions concerning the growth-inducing effects of projective identification were made by Malin and Grotstein (1966) and amplified by Ogden (1979). Not only does the therapist resonate with the emotional impingement of his patient and then free himself from its effects, but he also processes the received contents in such a way that the material becomes integrated at a more mature, realistic, and adaptive level. Thus, the projected fantasy of parental disapproval for successful assertive behavior should ideally be processed by the therapist and become toned-down or even corrected. The patient may be unconsciously attempting to provoke criticism or punishment, but the therapist's capacity to distance himself from the patient's manipulations enables the therapist to respond with a growth-inducing response that indicates that his attitude is different from the expected reaction of the bad internal object. The processed content then becomes the material that is reintrojected by the patient. That theory of therapeutic action is similar to Strachey's (1934) view that a part of the analytic process is based on the introjection of the therapist's more benign superego. It also resembles the views of several other writers who subscribe to the view that internalization of some aspect of the therapist or the therapeutic relationship promotes change and growth (Bion, 1961; Loewald, 1960; Winnicott, 1965; Horwitz, 1974).

In therapy groups, even in a collection of well-functioning and well-integrated patients, a number of strong regressive forces propel members into acting and reacting with developmentally early layers of their psychic functioning. The contagion effect of group emotion, the threats to the loss of one's individuality and autonomy, the revival of early familiar conflicts, and the prevalence of envy, rivalry, and competition—all contribute to the regressive reactions in a group. Small wonder, then, that Tavistock group relations conferences in which unstructured groups, both large and small, are a prominent part of the format sometimes induce temporary psychotic reactions in some members. Usually, they result from those members' becoming the carriers of the group's feelings of chaos and disorganization, victims of projective identification. Such instances, however painful, are instructive lessons in the regressive potential of the unstructured group and, in particular, the impact and potency of projective identification.

Thus, the intensity and the primitiveness of the projection are capable of eliciting in the target person varying degrees of transformation. Such changes may involve the recipient's beginning to feel and act as though he were like the projected object.

CONCLUSION

I have attempted to explain why projective identification has been a source of considerable confusion among dynamically oriented psychotherapists. Unlike most other mental mechanisms, it is a concept that is both intrapsychic and interpersonal. Like the quality of mercy, it is twice processed; it affects him that gives and him that takes. Projective identification has been defined alternatively with a focus on the effect of the self and, at other times, in terms of its impact on the external object. Confusion has often resulted from not making clear which aspect of the process was being described. The identification part of the term refers both to the self that projects and reintrojects and to the external object that introjects the projected content. It is a concept that elucidates the behavior of regressed persons but is equally important in the understanding of intimate relationships within the normal range, like transference and countertransference phenomena and family and marital interactions. It plays a major role in the dynamics of a group insofar as mental contents of one part of the group are put into another part and underlies such occurrences as role-suction, the spokesman phenomenon, and scapegoating. An understanding of those dynamic processes is essential to a full appreciation of the complexities of both group and dyadic relationships.

3.

RECOVERING BION'S CONTRIBUTIONS TO GROUP ANALYSIS

Kenneth Eisold

Bion is clearly acknowledged as a pioneer in group theory and practice. His book, *Experience in Groups* (1961), in which he wittily recounts his baffling early experiences in group therapy and attempts at theoretical explanations, has become a classic, frequently cited alongside Freud's (1921) paper on group psychology. He is the first to have approached the group-as-a-whole and to have called attention to the central role of pre-oedipal dynamics in the unconscious life of groups. Moreover, with his phenomenological descriptions of the "basic assumptions" he provided a tool for categorizing the central events of group life that many group workers continue to find indispensable. In what sense does this work have to be "recovered"?

To be sure, his actual practice—what we might loosely call his "method" has come under considerable fire. For him, the term "group therapy" referred not to therapy that takes place in the context of the group but, rather, therapy that is directed at the group as a whole, therapy that attempts to make a poorly functioning group more effective. Thus he typically did not direct his interpretations at individual group members but at the group entity, and this was consistent with his fundamental attempt to establish contact with the emotional life of the group as a whole, to observe what was being referred to when group members said, "we," for example, how this group entity made attempts to establish a consistent relationship with him, and how individual members fit into and were used by this entity as well.

In so doing, he did not posit a new force or a different kind of psychic reality manifesting itself in group life. Following Freud's disavowal of the need to posit a group or herd instinct, he sought to understand behavior in groups as expressions of collective, shared or parallel fantasies, and, in so doing, he took account of individual behavior only in so far as it was expressive of developments in the group as a whole. That is to say, if a group member attacked the leader, for example, he would attempt to interpret why this was being done on behalf of the group at a given moment—neglecting, although he was fully aware of the fact, that this behavior was also meaningful to the individual in the light of his own particular history.

To put it another way, he took as the object of his analysis all the evidence produced by group members that they believed they belonged to a group: the common fantasies, the concerted behaviors and tacit agreements that pointed to the existence of a shared group mentality. In a sense—and this is a point I will elaborate on later—he allowed himself to be taken in by the fiction of a group that the group members seemed to share, allowing himself to experience the conscious and unconscious manifestations of this fiction or set of assumptions, including his own fantasies of belonging. Thus while he did not in fact believe that something new—some distinct group reality—came into existence when individuals joined together, he attempted to observe all the evidence for the belief and reflect back to the group what he observed. And, in so doing, he strove not to undermine or distort the sense of groupness by establishing contact with individual members. He directed his comments at group members in general about what he could observe to be their overt as well as covert common beliefs about the group they seemed to feel and act as if they belonged to.

This "method" has been severely criticized and is now, I think, quite unpopular. Yalom (1974), in his highly influential textbook on group therapy, attacked this approach and cited an outcome study that questioned the therapeutic benefits of such groups. More recently (Gustafson & Cooper, 1979), Bion's method has been criticized as inflicting too great a narcissistic injury on individual group members; if members are not responded to personally by group leaders, it has been suggested they cannot experience the trust that is essential to disclosure, risk taking and change.

Off-shoots of Bion's method continue to be nurtured at the Tavistock Clinic (Heath and Bacal, 1972; Gosling), but in this country, group therapy still refers by and large to therapy taking place in a group rather than therapy for the group. The method has survived primarily as an educational tool, in group relations conferences designed to explore group and organizational dynamics (the so-called "Tavistock model") and in university courses. And even in these applications, emotional stability is sought as a prerequisite for participation. Clearly a consensus has emerged in this country that Bion's pioneering method of working with groups is dangerously stressful, of questionable therapeutic value, only for the hardy.

In seeking to recover Bion's contribution to group analysis, thus, I will not attempt the task of combatting the consensus. I will try instead to side step the question of method and practice entirely and focus on his theory and, more broadly, on his understanding of the dimensions of the problems posed by group membership. I think this effort will be warranted even in the eyes of those who reject Bion's method. For one thing, some of the criticisms leveled against the method affirm the power and potential destructiveness of the forces he attempted to chart. For another, being the first to point out the pre-oedipal dynamics of group life, he has had a significant impact on the thinking of many group workers who do not consider employing his methods.

Recovering Bion's Contributions to Group Analysis

In what sense, then, does Bion's contribution to group analysis have to be recovered? I'd like to focus on two related aspects of his theory. First, I will attempt to reformulate his account of the group's regression—a regression that makes belief of the group possible—in more contemporary and, I think, more acceptable object relations theory. As a Kleinian analyst, at least at the point when he wrote *Experiences in Groups*, he attributed to the level of infantile experience to which group members regressed a concreteness and specificity of fantasy most of us now have difficulty accepting. Second, I would like to attempt to express some of the fundamental implications—and dilemmas—of group life that Bion was able to see clearly, uncomfortable and disconcerting thoughts that, nonetheless, I think, require our attention.

Bion's theory of group dynamics takes as its point of departure the simple and obvious question—so obvious no one seems to have asked it before: what kind of an object is a group? It is, of course, a collection of individuals, an aggregate; but what makes it appear to be an entity? Let me quote Bion's well known sentences on this point: "The adult must establish contact with the emotional life of the group in which he lives; this task would appear to be as formidable to the adult as the relationship with the breast appears to be to the infant, and the failure to meet the demands of this task is revealed in his regression. The belief that a group exists, as distinct from an aggregate of individuals, is an essential part of the regression" (Bion, 1961, pp. 141-142). The problem thus is one of adaptation, establishing emotional contact with the group members, an adaptation that cannot take place without regression because we lack other means of relating to an aggregate. A regressive process thus enables us to experience a loosely assembled collection of vaguely differentiated parts of an entity that has the potential to include us as well. In other words, to see the group as a group, consisting of members or part objects rather than separate whole objects, is to regress in our object-relatedness to that point in development prior to the "depressive position," in Klein's term, where the defense of splitting predominates and the maternal object is an unstable and loosely assembled collection of part objects with whom we still had the capacity for merger. To put it crudely, the group is mother, but before mother was experienced as a person entirely distinct from other significant members of the family constellation such as grandmother, father or big brother, and before that vaguely shifting entity, that "other," was established clearly as separate from the perceiving child. With this recollected object world to draw upon from the depths of early experience, the person wishing to join the group can perceive the group as a group and he can hope for the condition of being joined to it.

But, according to Bion, he must also suffer the consequences of unleashing other primitive fantasies as well, characteristic of the "paranoid-schizoid position": fantasies of personal fragmentation and disintegration, of persecution by "bad" breasts and penises as well as their poisonous substances, of tantalization by unstable "good" objects, of unbounded greed and envy, in short, that terrifying, phantasmagoric world of infancy Klein has described, without order or security. It is to combat these fantasies that the group's basic assumptions come into play, as common strategies that stem the regressive process and structure the group world to defend against these sources of anxiety, "psychotic anxiety," Bion calls it, following Klein, to emphasize its chaotic, overpowering intensity. Basic assumptions, in effect, create group leaders, through the mechanism of projective identification; that is to say, the group members agree to designate individuals who are thus seen as distinct objects, separate from the amorphous mass, who become receptacles for projections and around whom somewhat more developmentally advanced and stable fantasies can crystallize. Thus in the basic assumption of dependency, for example, the group creates a leader on whom it believes it can depend for nurturance and comfort. In so far as the assumption can be sustained that such a leader exists in the group, that person becomes a focus. In the basic assumption of fight/flight, the group leader is seen by the group to embody either the evil that must be fought against (concretizing all the sources of danger felt to exist in the group) or the power needed to fight the evil. In the basic assumption of pairing, the group establishes a pair of leaders that embodies its hope of producing a new solution. In all cases, the level of anxiety is reduced to more managable proportions as external, "real" objects are established that serve to limit to some extent the chaotic turbulence of infantile fantasy. But, Bion points out, the stability is only relative as ever new sources of anxiety arise, given the regressed nature of the group and the variety of its real threats produced by the group's fantasy life. Thus the basic assumption activity of the group is itself unstable and continually shifting.

Let me give two examples to illustrate how groups act as groups—that is, with concerted actions that point to the existence of common fantasies. First, I'll refer to an episode Bion himself described in *Experiences in Groups* and then to one I encountered in my own work.

The group Bion describes consisted of four women and four men, including himself. He writes:

> The prevailing atmosphere is one of good temper and helpfulness. The room is cheerfully lit by evening sunlight.
>
> Mrs. X: I had a nasty turn last week. I was standing in a queue waiting for my turn to go to the cinema when I felt ever so queer. Really, I thought I would faint or something.
>
> Mrs. Y: You're lucky to have been going to a cinema. If I thought I could go to a cinema I should feel I had nothing to complain of at all.
>
> Mrs. Z: I know what Mrs. X means. I feel just like that myself, only I should have had to leave the queue.
>
> Mr. A: Have you tried stooping down? That makes the blood come back to your head. I expect you were feeling faint.
>
> Mrs. X: It's not really faint.
>
> Mrs. Y: I always find it does a lot of good to try exercises. I don't know if that's what Mr. A means.

Mrs. Z: I think you have to use your will power. That's what worries me—I haven't got any.

Mr. B: I had something similar happen to me last week, only I wasn't even standing in a queue. I was just sitting at home quietly when...

Mr. C: You were lucky to be sitting at home quietly. If I was able to do that I shouldn't consider I had anything to grumble about.

Mrs. Z: I can sit home quietly all right, but it's never being able to get out anywhere that bothers me. If you can't sit at home why don't you go to a cinema or something?

Reflecting on this exchange, Bion comments that it is becoming increasingly clear that anyone in the group suffering from a neurotic complaint is going to get only advice that everyone already knows is perfectly futile and that the prospects for cooperation in this group are nil. A slogan to characterize the group's futility occurs to him: "Vendors of quack nostrums unite!" But no sooner does this strike him that it becomes clear he is expressing his feeling of the group's unity. Indeed the point is that beneath the surface of inattention and random complaints, the group is organized against him and purposefully sabotaging the task he represents.

In this instance, he has been identified as the enemy, the danger the group is attempting to exclude. Bion does not attempt to account for this, but it may well be that the group's hostility towards him has arisen out of their frustration and disappointment that the professional expertise they attribute to him has not resulted in any magical improvements, much less comfort in his presence. The hostility of group members is thus projected onto him, permitting the group to bask in an aura of good temper and helpfulness while it remains in flight from the menacing object it persists in shutting out. This is its primary activity, that which makes it cohesive. But at the same time, one can also observe a loss of differentiation among group members. Though members make efforts to refer to different outside experiences and remind themselves that some are lucky to have problems different from their own, there is, in fact no real acknowledgment of different problems requiring different solutions, no listening to each other as if those differences were real. Indeed, they act as if they shared a common identity as helpless victims of obscure complaints who are trying as ineptly as they must feel Dr. Bion is ineptly trying to offer help. They provide a vicious parody of helpfulness.

The second example I want to describe occurred in a therapy group also of four men and four women that included a male/female pair of therapists. The third meeting of the group began with members drifting in late, making a few casual remarks as they sat down, and then lapsing into fifteen minutes of tense silence. Nothing seemed to be happening as members stared glumly at the floor, except that a statement of sorts was being made in the seating arrangement and postures of the members that just seemed randomly to have occurred. The male therapist was flanked by two male members whose legs were outstretched in a seemingly casual posture as they slumped in their chairs, but their legs formed a barrier, splitting him off from the female therapist sitting opposite. On her right, a chair was left empty, the only vacant chair in the circle, obviously left for the one member who had not yet arrived, the third male member of the group who had expressed angry feelings towards the female therapist the previous week. Again, a seemingly random collection of individual decisions by group members suddenly provided evidence of a hidden unity of purpose, an unconscious plot to isolate the female therapist and pair her with a substitute who then could attack her, giving vent to the group's fear of her malevolent power and rage at their frustrated expectations of nurturance.

The silence was broken by the female therapist with a comment about the seating arrangement and the "plot" it suggested, a comment that appeared to cause consternation among members because it both exposed their disavowed intention and confirmed their worst fears of the female therapist's omniscient power. Shortly after, the male member arrived who had been given the role of the group's fight leader in his absence. Only now, the covert plot having been exposed, the group proceeded to make him into a scapegoat by projecting onto him their feelings of rage and fear, and attempting to expel him from the group. They did this, first, by utterly failing to explain to him what had transpired before he entered the room, though they referred actively to the uncovered "plot" and one member even spoke of her wish to inform him as he could not possibly know what they were talking about. Thus, they rendered him confused, helpless, isolated and enraged. Second, they entered into a lengthy discussion about his selfishness in having joined the group with what he had referred to in the opening session as a "personal agenda," as if no one else might have personal goals or motivations in joining the group or, indeed, should have such reasons for seeking help in therapy. Thus they further confused, isolated and enraged him, making him into a suitable object onto whom they could project their own feelings of vulnerability and rage as they cast him out from the group that could then sit back and congratulate itself on its selflessness, generosity and unity.

In this maneuver, the group attempted two methods of defending itself against the anxiety aroused by its fear and rage, both of which broadly speaking exemplify the basic assumption of fight. First designating the female leader as the danger to be combatted by the late-arriving male member, the group members projected their hostility into a fight pair and sat back as seemingly innocent bystanders. Failing in that and more convinced than ever of the female leader's power, it turned to fight the male member, contemptuously rendering him impotent and confused, projecting their feelings of anger and vulnerability onto him and drumming him out of the group.

I can't describe these examples without being aware of the skeptical observer, of course, who will doubt my observations, much less my analysis of such events. And this is a concern Bion himself frequently expressed, telling his reader that the phenomena he inadequately tried to describe could only be experienced and seen in actual groups. But even seeing itself is inadequate unless the observer is able to employ what Bion called "binocular vision." That is, one eye has to be trained on the surface, the level on which individuals maintain their discrete identities and interact in a random manner, the level on which the first group acted as an assortment of inattentive, uncooperative members and the second group experienced itself as not even having begun its meeting. The other eye, however, must be trained on the group purpose, the hidden unity, the level on which nothing is more important to members than the need to belong and to find a common method of defending against their anxiety through the creation of leaders, leaders who paradoxically in the very act of being attacked and excluded can reveal the value of their membership.

To my knowledge, Bion's discovery of this binocular view of group process is an unparalleled contribution to the understanding of group life. Moreover, his account of the regressive process his binocular vision attempts to expose is also profound and true. That is, the regressive perception of the group as a maternal entity allows the group to be perceived as a collective entity that can be joined. This is a point that has impressed many subsequent theorists (Colman, 1975; Durkin, 1964; Foulkes, 1957; Gibbard & Hartman, 1973; Saravay, 1975; Scheidlinger, 1974; Schindler, 1966) and it is the starting point for any attempt to go beyond Freud's account of oedipal dynamics centering on the group leader. It is also, I think, a point for which our language provides convincing evidence as the fundamental analogy between our thinking about the body and about groups is expressed in so many parallel terms. Thus the term "member" refers to a body part as well as a part of a group. We also speak of deliberative or legislative bodies, the body politic. Bion's description of the phenomena of basic assumption behavior in groups also has proven an enduring, and appreciated, contribution, an accurate guide to the unrealistic and fickle forms leadership takes, particularly in relatively unstructured groups. But I think we can recast his account of the regressive process in terms of more recent developments in object relations theory and, in so doing, provide a fuller description of the variety of anxieties group membership arouses.

I don't want to over-emphasize this point, because Bion was too fine an observer of events and had too much integrity as a thinker to substitute explanations for facts. But the theoretical framework of object relations he employed led him to view the extreme—"psychotic"—anxiety group members experienced, which caused them to cohere defensively in the unstable and infantile forms of basic assumption behavior, as a response to paranoid fantasies of early part-object relationships. Thus, for example, in the fragment of behavior he described, the members attempted to shut him out because that activity helped them to put aside the terrifying, persecutory fantasies aroused by the psychological act of joining themselves to mother's body. Nowhere does he spell this out, but it is a reasonable conjecture that in his view, members relieved themselves of the anxieties aroused individually by this act of joining through a common agreement that was then acted upon in fleeing from him: projecting some of their terrifying fantasies on to him and denying some of their others, they were able to agree he was a kind of poisonous penis (I'm guessing) who embodied the threat all members felt. In the second example, similarly, one could view the agreement to fight the female group leader as a defensive strategy to attack the "bad" breast, making this fantasy common and pervasive over the multifarious individual fantasies aroused in members by their regressed state of attachment.

Instead of viewing the infant's early object world as consisting of sharply visualized part objects, however, we can, I think, adopt in general the view of Jacobson, Mahler, Kernberg and others that the infant's perceptual world only gradually achieves distinctness and organization in response to the maturation of perceptual and cognitive abilities as well as to its own affectively charged experience. That is, gradually a sense of good maternal object as well as a bad one is organized out of the recurring fragments of experience. Thus the regressive-adaptive process that group members go through as they search for analogs in their experience that would allow them to establish a relationship with the group as a whole brings them in touch with preambivalent "good" and "bad" objects of this earlier object world as well as part objects that are defined with varying degress of distinctness and associated with varying degrees of firmness to larger entities. Almost certainly such primitive object worlds would vary considerably for each person, based upon each person's early experience of the object world encountered in his family of origin. And we would expect these objects to be linked with a variety of fears: abandonment by good objects, destruction of good objects, persecution by bad objects, etc. But we would also expect that in most instances where childhood development was not severely pathological, such fears were more or less successfully defended against in ways that are not totally inaccessable to the regressed ego. That is to say, it seems unlikely that a regression in object relationships would arouse in all or even most individuals the intensity of "psychotic anxiety" associated with Klein's view of the chaotic and menacing part-object world of early infancy. But we do need to account for the arousal of intense anxiety through the regressive-adaptive process in order to explain, in the context of Bion's theory, the desperate defensive maneuvers of basic assumption behavior.

An additional and, I think, greater degree of anxiety comes about from another source: the disintegration of psychic structures in the ego and superego. That is to say, if we draw on the contributions of Jacobson (1964) and others in elucidating the reciprocal development of the self and the object world, we can readily see that a regression in object ties is likely to be linked with the loosening of structural identifications incorporated in the self-image and the ego-ideal.

The disintegration or dedifferentiation of the super-ego in group settings has, of course, frequently been observed since Freud called attention to it (1955a). In his view, the group leader is incorporated by group members as a replacement for more highly developed and individualized super-egos, leading often to a combination of behaviors both more permissive and more harsh. But the effect on individual psychic structures is even more catastrophic, as the self-image also begins to come apart under the influence of regressive object ties. Thus as the mature object world gives way, earlier self-representations are activated, including some that have been discarded in the developmental process. And they are given validation and support as impulses previously repressed gain expression in the group and as more primitive defenses become activated. All these archaic aspects of the self tend to gain validation and support in the group because, of course, all members are subject to similar repressive processes and engaged in a collaborative effort to establish a consensus about the nature of the group object they compose. And yet, at the same time, members cannot completely forget the mature object ties that link them with the world outside and the self-images validated in that world. Thus the situation in the group poses continual threats to self-esteem, making members vulnerable to confusion, embarrassment and shame.

But perhaps most distressing of all is the threat this adaptive process poses to the ego's synthetic function. The continual effort that the ego makes to integrate its self-image with its ideals and actual behavior, and reality with fantasy and impulse, cannot easily be sustained when the materials it has to work with are as disparate as in the group setting and from such different levels of functioning. And because the ego's ability to integrate and synthesize is its source of strength and self-confidence, the core element in the sense of identity, group membership thus necessarily disrupts and undermines the member's very sense of a stable and functioning identity. This, I think, is the greatest source of anxiety: a kind of panic arising out of a faltering, disintegrating self that is losing its very capacity to right itself.

Observational data available to anyone who works in groups will lend some support, I think, to this view. Not only are primitive impulses unleashed in group settings but more often than not it is with conviction and support from others. We have seen that in the examples described earlier where intense and cruel pressure was exerted by members who, were they to be granted a moment of objectivity, would recoil in embarrassment from the meanness they casually uttered out of the security of membership. And membership makes people complacently stupid, as we witnessed by the offering of "quack nostrums" Bion observed, in the first example, and the inability of group members in the second example to acknowledge that they all had, or might consider the value of having, "personal agendas" in joining a therapy group. How quickly and fully members embrace common and extremely narrow identities, as well-intentioned victims or altruistic contributors, even in the face of evidence to the contrary. But also, how fragile and fleeting such identities are shown to be as the focus of the group and its defensive needs begin to shift.

Thus, I think, we can understand the sources of anxiety aroused by the process of joining somewhat differently from the way Bion did: as arising not only from the liberation of primitive impulses but also from the fragmentation of the self and the loss of the ego's capacity for flexible and integrative behavior. And these sources of anxiety are, I think, quite sufficient to account for the degree of restless desperation necessary to produce basic assumption behavior as well as for the naivete to explain basic assumption beliefs.

Thus it seems to me that Bion's fundamental contributions to group analysis can be integrated into more recent object relations theory, with a full appreciation of the disruptive power of group forces, which brings me to the second topic I wish to address in the paper: in essence, why it is important to understand these forces in the first place; what the implications of this theory are that we would do well to bear in mind.

Group membership necessarily involves us in a number of irreducable dilemmas. We cannot join a group without entering a process that overthrows, if only temporarily, we can hope, vital achievements of maturity. The very nature of the task of joining demands a regressive immersion in primitive levels of experience that sets aside our highly developed capacities for discriminating object relationships as well as threatens our differentiated identities. To belong is to regress.

This is, of course, not news to those who work with therapy groups. Indeed the very effectiveness of group treatment has often been seen to require such a regression, but then, it has also often been seen as a benign process. Scheidlinger (1955), for example, has written about the regressive processes of adaptation to the pre-oedipal "mother group" but as an essentially nonconflictual process in which the group becomes a "good" maternal object fostering a sense of basic trust. This has become a rationale for group treatment as members thus are seen as being able to risk change because they come to trust the group as a matrix for corrective emotional experience. The group leader becomes the recipient of "bad" or hostile projections.

This view does not seem warranted in the light of Bion's theory and the examples cited above. The group entity as regressively perceived can take many forms and, indeed, usually does in rapid succession. Moreover, it would be surprising if the group, which demands as a condition for joining the overthrow of higher level functioning, were not perceived as the threat it truly is. No amount of leadership can evade this reality.

This raises a second, sobering point: as Bion points out that leaders emerge in the group as part of the group members' strategy to stem the regressive process and defend against anxiety, he implies that leaders are the creature of the group. That is to say, they serve only because they serve the group's purpose and only as long as they do. This is very much the opposite of conventional wisdom, not to mention our own often cherished beliefs in the power of our or others charismatic leadership ability. We foster the value of leadership; we neglect the role of follower.

It is entirely true, of course, that individuals vary enormously in their suitability and availability for different leadership roles. In the second example I gave earlier, the group member who was designated with the job of fighting the female leader and ended up by being extruded across the group's emotional boundary was familiar with the role of the angry outsider from his childhood on. Note that he arrived late for that meeting and that he himself did not ask for clarification about what had happened in his absence. Thus from the start he saw himself and acted in a way that perfectly suited the group's need for someone to occupy that role. And most of us carry with us a capacity for specific roles that were acquired in our families of origin, which is to say, our groups of origin, internalized roles that provide the stock from which subsequent groups may draw upon in their search for leadership. And talent for leadership is also often the possession of narcissistic personalities (Kernberg, 1979) who are less vulnerable to the disintegrative threat of regression and more mercurially suited to pick up the subtle currents of group feeling and exploit them in the service of seeming important and influential.

According to Bion, no group leader can afford to neglect the question of what defensive service his leadership is providing the group, a message that need not be lost on therapists familiar with the defensive uses of transference. But because of the depth of the regressive phenomena in groups and, thus, the intensity and variety of the anxieties aroused, leadership takes many subtle and shifting forms. It is often not easy to see all the ways in which group members offer themselves up or are offered up to be used in the service of the group's defensive needs and how that relates to the uses the group makes of its formal leadership.

For group therapists, Bion's message can be easily summarizied, I think: ignore these forces at your peril. Regardless of whether one chooses to do individually focused therapy in a group setting, focus on interpersonal interactions in a group, or approach the group as a whole, the group itself is always alive in the unconscious of its members and its leaders. The amorphous entity is continually being shaped and tested out for validation by members, its boundaries continually being redrawn, and its power is being confirmed in every statement and thought that testifies to the existence of a group, that is to the existence of the regressive fantasy that a group exists, rather than a collection of individuals who want and need to belong.

I'd like to add a final word about the implication of Bion's work on groups for the world at large. The forces he describes are at work in all groups: committees, staffs, faculties, jurys, units, classes, teams, etc. And all groups have a reason for being called into existence, a job to do. Thus all groups are simultaneously what Bion calls "work groups," often with formal structures, traditions, procedures for establishing membership, as well as basic assumption groups. And thus we belong to groups in two senses: we have been formally admitted or assigned to it and given a work role to perform and we come to feel as if we belong to it and have an accepted place.

But again this need to feel we belong places a constraint on our ability to work: we serve two masters, the group task and the group itself. The one requires all our intelligence and skill and the other requires our regression and "valency" (Bion's term for an individual's predisposition to be subject to unconscious group processes). It is an essential, that is to say, inescapable conflict. Social stability and institutional achievement are built upon the basis of work groups, that is, collective collaborative efforts in which individual members can be replaced, work roles can be re-assigned. It is fair to say that civilization depends on our ability to function in work groups at the same time that our ability to join in work groups impairs our capacity to function at our maximum capacity. It is, I think, a tragic dilemma we can only engage again and again and attempt to understand.

In a work Bion (1977) wrote some years after *Experiences in Groups*, when in fact he had seemed to give up his interest in groups, he commented on the relationship between what he called the "mystic" or the "genius" or the "messiah" (which he considered interchangeable terms—but note that he did not use the term "leader") and the institution or "Establishment." The truly creative individual exists in an essential but antagonistic relationship with the established order. The established order exists to preserve the wisdom of the past and make possible the future vision of the truly creative individual, yet it is endangered by the emergence of that vision. It is a container threatened with explosion by what it does not know how to contain, the reality or truth, the "O," which only the creative individual can approximate.

This is, I think, a special case of the universal dilemma of group membership. Society is an association of diverse groups, and our need to belong to at least some of these groups is as profound as our need to sleep and dream. And yet, what we give up to belong! Some of us have more to give up than others, to be sure—certainly from the perspective of society that stands to lose precious contributions of wisdom. We cannot evade the dilemma involved in joining. But I think Bion's message can be expressed as the thought that we can make it conscious. It's possible to analyze experiences in groups.

I conceded at the outset of this paper that Bion's "method" of group analysis has been discredited in this country. But can we afford to neglect any means of acquiring binocular vision into so central an aspect of our experience? Perhaps the point is that his method needs to be exercised with those who attempt to work in groups, in organizations, who occupy assigned leadership roles and find themselves mysteriously enabled or thwarted in their attempts with others to achieve their tasks. Maybe group therapy as Bion conceived it—in a society of groups—is too important to be wasted on patients.

4.

SOME PSYCHODYNAMICS OF LARGE GROUPS[1]

Tom Main

PROJECTIVE PROCESSES IN SOCIAL SETTINGS

Although projective processes are primitive attempts to relieve internal pains by externalising them, assigning or requiring another to contain aspects of the self, the price can be high: for the self is left not only less aware of its whole but, in the case of projective identification, is deplenished by the projective loss of important aspects of itself. Massive projective identification of—for instance—feared aggressive parts of the self leaves the remaining self felt only to be weak and unaggressive. Thereafter, the weakened individual will remain in terror about being overwhelmed by frightening aggressive strength but this will now be felt only as belonging to the other. Depending on the range of this projective fantasy the results will vary from terrified flight, appeasement, wariness and specific anxieties about the other, even psychotic delusions about his intentions.

The above instance concerns only the projector's side of the projective relationship: but projective processes often have a further significance. What about the person on the receiving end of the projection? In simple projection (a mental mechanism) the receiver may notice that he is not being treated as himself but as an aggressive other. In projective identification (an unconscious fantasy) this other may find himself forced by the projector actually to feel and own projected aggressive qualities and impulses that are otherwise alien to him. He will feel strange and uncomfortable and may resent what is happening, but in the face of the projector's weakness and cowardice it may be doubly difficult to resist the feelings of superiority and aggressive power steadily forced into him. Such disturbances affect all pair relationships more or less. A wife, for instance, may force her husband to own feared and unwanted aggressive and dominating aspects of herself and will then fear and respect him. He in turn may come to feel aggressive and dominating towards her, not only because of his own resources but of hers that are forced into him. But more; for reasons of his own he may despise and disown certain timid aspects of his personality and by projective identification force these into his wife and despise her accordingly. She may thus be left not only with timid unaggressive parts of herself but having in addition to contain his. Certain pairs come to live in such locked systems, dominated by mutual projective fantasies with each not truly married to a person, but rather to unwanted, split off and projected parts of themselves (Bannister and Pincus, 1965; Main, 1966). Both the husband, dominant and cruel, and the wife, stupidly timid and respectful, may be miserably happy with themselves and with each other, yet such marriages although turbulent, are stable because each partner needs the other for pathological narcissistic purposes. *Forcible projective processes and especially projective identification are thus more than an individual matter: they are object-related and the other will always be affected more or less.* The results are a variety of joint personality deplenishments and invasions and interpersonal disturbances.

Projective processes are also observable in *group* behaviour. Half a century ago in *Group Psychology and the Analysis of the Ego* (1972) Freud pointed out that a leader can occupy the role of super-ego for members of a group, who are thus freed not only of responsibilty for decisions but also of burdens of self-criticism and doubt. But it is a costly freedom; the group members actually lose individual moral sense and the capacity to think and to judge as individuals. In the light of this observation alone we can understand something of the plight of the Nazi leaders at the Nuremberg Trials who knew themselves only as decent family men and innocent of responsibility for the criminal acts they had loyally carried out. Having early projected away and into Hitler their capacity for moral judgment they (with few exceptions) had lost the capacity to know that they had behaved viciously and could not understand the present censure. They were psychically impoverished, morally blinded, by projective processes.

Freud's discovery of mental splitting and the projection of the super-ego in group life, coupled with Melanie Klein's later discoveries of projective-identification fantasies have allowed studies of other group-roles than that of leader. It has often been observed in studies of *small-group* life that certain individuals may be unconsciously forced by the group to feel certain things and to carry out particular roles. This one may be unconsciously appointed and required as a sinner, to feel and act accordingly, that one as the giver of wisdom, others as saboteur of the work, buffoon, invalid, etc., with various degrees of personal discomfort.

There is little discomfort for the receiver if he has some capacity that matches the projections fairly well, in a good 'role-fit.'

Example

In a working group one member was observed to be used as the repository of all projected financial meanness. He was kept in this role so that the others could safely feel free not to think about financial matters but he was steadily stimulated to be strict and watchful by their regular financially reckless ideas or behaviour. But he did not mind this *because he actually had character tendencies to be financially strict.*

The unconscious forcing of feelings and abilities into another in a small group will, however, create observable discomfort in the receiver if his relevant character-tendencies are few. He may respond as he is required to yet his loss of freedom to behave otherwise will create strain for him, perhaps breakdown, resignation or illness. Instances of group projection with role comfort and discomfort in the members are easy to observe in play groups, discussion groups and work groups. But whether the role-fit be good or bad the penalty for all in personality restriction loss or invasion should be noted.

In *large* unstructured groups—with memberships of over 20 or so—projective processes may be wide-spread and can lead to baffling, even chaotic situations, which can bring the groups' work to a standstill. The members will sit in long uneasy silences with even the most resourceful apparently lacking the capacity for contributing usefully. It seems that many individuals at such moments actually do not have their full thinking-capacities at their own disposal. For various reasons—which I shall later discuss—they have denied, split off and projected much of their mental vigour outside themselves, occasionally into particular individuals but more often into a vague nonpersonal creation which they call 'the group.' In the presence of this mysterious powerful 'group' they will actually feel stupid, helpless and afraid of what it may do to them if they speak or move incautiously.

Projection and projective identification as interpersonal concepts have value for the understanding of the behaviour of large unstructured groups as well as small groups, pairs and individuals.

They can also aid the understanding of structured groups, and shed light on how far the procedures, beliefs, organisational structures and activities of an enterprise are reality-orientated and how far they are the result of anxieties, powerful fantasies and defences (Menzies, 1961). Projective processes in the service of relief from intrapersonal pains in industrial situations are powerful factors of major industrial inefficiency and conflicts (Jaques, 1961). Those of us who work in hospitals need, however, look no further than under our noses.

In the literature that has followed my proposition (Main, 1946) that a total hospital community could be therapeutic or anti-therapeutic, there has been good agreement that one benefit of therapeutic community technique derives from the staff's readiness to offer patients and staff reciprocal adult roles with participant powers and responsibilities for various aspects of institutional life, and further that it can be beneficial if there is open study, by all, of the problems of sustaining these roles. A therapeutic community is one of on-going inquiry about personal and group anxieties and defences and of endeavour to create adaptive thought-out roles, relations, structure and culture geared to reality tasks and relevant to the capacities and needs of the individuals within the community. This is in contrast to the classical medical organisation model in which only roles of health or illness are an offer; staff to be only healthy, knowledgeable, kind, powerful and active, and patients to be only ill, suffering, ignorant, passive, obedient and grateful; and with a corresponding staff structure and a culture of kindness and discipline.

Now to create adult roles for all in a hospital, adaptive to individual capacity and relevant to efficiency is—quite apart from the time required for on-going studies—easier said than done. Not only is present hospital tradition against this but all of us concerned always carry within ourselves personal attitudes more or less neurotic that hamper such a development. It is of course the insightful laying bare of these very attitudes that allows community therapy to proceed, but this is never easy. In most hospitals the staff are there because they seek to care for others less able than themselves, while the patients hope to find others *more* able than themselves. The helpful and the helpless meet and put pressures on each other to act not only in realistic but also in fantastic collusion and in collusive hierarchical systems. The actively projectively helpful will unconsciously *require* others to be helpless while the helpless will *require* others to be helpful. Staff and patients are thus inevitably to some extent creatures of each other. Therapeutic community technique, which seeks insight for all, is a useful check on institutional collusive projection, but if the mutual projective system is accepted blindly and is institutionalized without reality-testing then it carries dangers to the personality integration of all concerned.

Temporary patient/staff mutual collusive projection of socially split strength and weakness *may* be highly effective, for instance in an acute surgical unit where the illnesses are short and the regression that accompanies illness is temporary and self-limiting; but it is clearly not useful in any psychiatric unit where human behaviour rather than organ performance is under active study and in which regression is not so much the secondary accompaniment of a temporary illness as a primary and permanent part of one.

Requirements of only health for staff and only invalidism for patients are, however, neither socially inevitable nor truly practicable, for human states are never absolute. Stable healthy people contain elements of instabilty and ill health, and unhealthy unstable people contain elements of health and stability. Indeed there is something strainfully collusive about those psychiatric hospitals that are managed so that one party comes to regard the other as being in an absolute state, either of health or ill health, and they offer us paradigmatic questions for all similar large groups. Why are certain roles (bosses and workers, teachers and pupils, experts and ignoramuses, staff and patients, police and criminals, etc.) so often collusively required to be *absolute*? How does it come about that one party is content to notice its differences from the other but uneasy at recognising the similarities? What are the implications, benefits and dangers when human beings cling to absolute categories?

These questions may in part be answered by a revealing but unpublished study made at the Cassel Hospital by my colleague, Malcolm Pines, of patients who had been nurses. All had had traumatised childhoods with grossly inadequate nurturing and all had developed a similar way of dealing with needy but untended parts of themselves. From childhood onwards they had striven to overcome these by disowning, denying and projecting them into others; and had then sought to nurse these aspects of themselves 'out there' in attempts at vicarious satisfaction. In their adulthood they had done significant work nursing *others*, but in each the projective endeavours to keep suffering 'out there' had eventually failed. All were now unusually humiliated; breakdown was all right for 'patients,' but not for 'nurses.' In hospital they presented special problems of which I select one: sometimes each sought to be treated *only* as a resourceless patient but at others *only* as a nursing colleague of the staff, helpful to 'the patients.' One role *or* the other. It was most painful for them to contain both parts of themselves at one time, i.e., to be *sick/nurses*, and any such attempt at integration was quickly followed by further splitting and projection of one or other part. *Absolute states seemed preferable because integrated ones contained unbearable conflict and pain.*

This last finding, well known in individual psychoanalysis, has implications for all social and international situations in which we/they beliefs arise. The common defences against personal mental pain, of denial, splitting and projection into others have immense social consequences when used by whole groups of individuals.

PROJECTIVE PROCESSES AND REALITY-TESTING

It must be emphasised that externalising defences and fantasies can involve positive as well as negative aspects of the self; and that projection of impulses and projective identification of parts of the self into others are elements in 'normal' mental activity. *When followed by reality-testing* trial externalisations of aspects of the self help an individual to understand himself and others. For instance if we are to *sense* (as distinct from notice the signs of) the distress in a crying child, we can do so only if there is within us a former experience of having been a distressed child ourselves. An experimental projection of this into the child before us, followed by reality testing, can help us decide whether our understanding of the child's distress is more or less appropriate. Similarly, if we are to sense another's joy we can only do so by the experiment of projecting former joyous states of our own, *followed by a reality test* to decide how far our projection fits the facts; i.e., we 'put ourself in his place.'

It is when projective processes are massive and forceful that they are difficult to test or reverse. In malignant projective identification this difficulty arises not only because of the forcefulness of the projection but also because, with the ego impoverished by loss of a major part of the self, reality-testing becomes defective. Thus unchecked and uncheckable pathological judgements may now arise about oneself and the other, quasi-irreversible because of the pains of integration.

Malignant projective processes are to be found in both neurotic and psychotic patients, and may be temporarily observable also in 'normal' people suffering major frustration. Grossly in such delusions as, 'He has stolen the thought-radio and listens to my thoughts' or, 'They whisper filthy accusations that I'm a queer.' Less psychotic but still pathological are *absolute* judgements such as, 'You are an incorrigible thug, without a *single* redeeming feature,' or, 'I can *always* count on your help,' or 'As *usual*, the boss is thinking only of himself.' 'Dr X will *never* understand this.'

With less forceful projection systems followed by reality-testing the present is usefully tested against the past, and external events against internal ones; the individual maintains his individuation, re-finds out who he is and who he is not, what he feels and thinks, who others are, and who they are not, what they feel and think. Where a reality test confirms that a trial projection fits the other one learns positively about him; and where it shows the projection to be *only* a projection the individual can re-own the projected part, and grow a surer awareness of the distinct identity of himself and the other. Trial projection and *reality-testing* are thus essential preliminaries to real as distinct from narcissistic relationships. By contrast, in malignant projection systems the self is impoverished, reality-testing fails, the other is not recognised for what he is but rather as a container of disowned aspects of the self, to be hated, feared, idealised, etc., and relations are unreal and narcissistically intense up to the point of insanity.

DEPERSONALISATION AND PERSONALITY INVASION

When major parts of the personality are subject to compelling fantasies of projective identification the damaged powers of thought and diminished identity-sense in the remnant self lead to various degrees of *depersonalisation* accompanied by bizarre object-relations. When the superstitious person projects into an object (or a person) his own denied areas of, say, malice, he will experience that object not only as malicious but uncannily *alive*, with himself only as magically weakened and in danger. In such nightmarish situations appeasement, flight, warding off the magic by desperate counter-magic, the seeking of allies, or a leader, and so forth, may take place. This is the world of psychosis and of extreme industrial and civil strife.

Where positive aspects of the self are forcefully projected similar degrees of depersonalisation occur, with feelings of personal worthlessness and with dependent worship of the other's contrasting strengths, powers, uncanny sensitivity, marvellous gifts, thoughts, knowledge, undying goodness, etc. This is the world of the devotee, cults and hero-promotion.

But what of the recipient of projection? I have pointed out that in *benign* forms where the projection does not 'fit,' the receiver will feel some discomfort at something being inaccurately attributed to him. Sensitivity to this discomfort is an important attribute of all therapists because it is a clue to what is occurring, but this discomfort can be met in daily life. A person may treat us as if we are more clever than we truly are, we may even begin to feel unusually clever, and if we are thoughtless we may try to avoid contention by trying to justify the other's good opinion, by rising to the occasion and straining to be as clever as possible; and so collusively intensify and prolong the 'take-over' that *we* are clever while he is *not*. (He may now actually become stupid and adoring and thus intensify our plight.) Such thoughtless acceptance of a projection means that we are no longer quite ourselves, for we are filled up and dominated by a part of somebody else. If we can recognise the discomfort and think about it we will not however feel unduly clever but simply misjudged or invaded; and so we can remain ourself and indicate by behaviour or protest that the other's beliefs are not justified by fact. In individual *treatment* we would hope to deal with it in another way; show the patient what he is doing and why. My example concerns a positive aspect—cleverness; but similar events can occur with negative aspects—say, confusion, rage or stupidity.

Where projective processes are malignant the recipient always experiences severe discomfort. If rageful confusion is forcibly projected into him he may now feel a strange rage and confusion and may join in ignoring and devaluing his best qualities; and with his rage and confusion preyed upon and stimulated he may over-estimate these and come to feel that they are his essence. Lacking any confirmation of his true self from the other, his own reality-sense will be further threatened. Badly invaded by alien feelings he will have difficulty in thinking calmly, clearly or helpfully. Therapists of severely disturbed patients know well this strain of sorting out inside themselves what belongs to them and what does not. Searles (1961) has well described the effort needed to extricate oneself regularly from crazy relationships with schizophrenic people and to regain touch with one's own intra-psychic world and to recover the capacity to think and feel authentically.

PROJECTIVE PROCESSES IN GROUPS

The creation of realistic relations in *small groups* depends upon its members being able benignly and regularly to project experimentally their various attributes and to undertake reality-testing. Thus regularly confirming themselves and each other, they can carry out joint work realistically. If a member is ill-fitted for an attempted projection the group will withdraw it, because of reality-testing, helped by the member who will resist the projection. If the recipient has appropriate properties to make the projection a good enough 'fit' he may by words or behaviour confirm that they exist in reality, he may feel better recognised and can recognise more of himself. His relations with the group may thus be deepened.

With forcible malignant projection where the projectors are depleted and reality-testing is impaired, all recipients will be unhappy, with their *true* selves devalued and in a strain because of having to sort out various confusing projections thrust into themselves. All may become so invaded by projections that reality-testing and judgement become flawed and relations only fantastic.

In *large groups* the multiplicity of relations puts thorough reality-testing at a discount; projection systems and personality invasion may thus run rife in networks of unchecked and uncheckable fantasies. In my experience—mostly limited to hospitals—in any unstructured group of 20 or more members, projective systems alone are liable to produce major difficulties.

Unfantastic recognition of one's self and of others is a dynamic process, not a static once-and-for-all event. Experiments in sensory deprivation have shown vividly that fidelity to one's internal mental life and past experiences are not enough to maintain sanity or the sense of self; the regular confirming of oneself in a continuing relation with the reality-tested external world is essential.

In a group everyone does what he can to understand the many people, to maintain his thinking capacity in the face of many viewpoints and to retain his sense of self. His confirmation of himself by the others is liable to be slow and slight but given fair identity-sense and freedom from mental splitting he can use benign projective processes and reality-testing to confirm who he is and who he is not, and to learn where and where not his projective fantasies fit others. But this takes time, and meanwhile relations with the others are much influenced by the inner world and little by reality-tested sureness.

If he can maintain his own sense of self he can offer his distinctive thinking to any discussion and so can help others to test their fantasies about him. Knowing him better they in turn may offer their more realistic thinking and benign cycles of awareness may thus arise.

In large group discussions it is easy to discern such processes of reality-testing with members responding variously to projections, accepting this one, then that one only after modifying it and now rejecting a third.

Most formal large groups are structured with chairman, agenda, orders of precedence, rituals, rules and procedures that discipline, more or less wisely, spontaneous personal interchange. Such groups keep formal order but at a cost, and they are well known to give ultimate dissatisfaction to their members and to fragment into splinter-groups and factions. They are well worth study but they do not offer the best opportunities for studies of the primitive mechanisms in large-group life. It is in experimental situations, such as total meetings in therapeutic communities, where structuring is at a minimum, that unfettered group behaviour can best be studied.

My own observations were made in such groups at the Cassel Hospital, and I have valued there the most 'difficult' group occasions when phenomena of disturbance were in their crudest form. For reasons of tact alone, I must stress that they were not necessarily typical meetings, that they occurred several years ago and that since then I have had the opportunity of studying less disturbed large group meetings. But the data in the rest of this contribution were observed there.

LARGE-GROUP MEETINGS

Politicians involved with complex human issues—even at a distance—often escape from the huge problem of trying to understand everybody by resorting to single generalising thought-models—'the housewife,' 'the young,' 'the property owner,' 'the working man,' each of which he invents and endows with more or less plausible stereotyped needs, powers and desires. These may bear little relation to the varieties of the actual people and his statements may reveal more about the politician than about those he attempts to encompass. Something of this escape from human complexity into generalisation and simplification is liable to occur when many people meet together to study each others' contributions; a single entity is liable

Some Psychodynamics of Large Groups

to be invented—'the group,' 'the meeting,' etc.—and to be endowed with various qualities. These group qualities may be plausible but are inevitably much derived from the internal life of the individual, and until reality-tested they contain much projection. They too may tell us more about the speaker than about the various others in the group.

Nonetheless, 'the group,' this single invented object, however fictive, no matter how much endowed with projected properties, has an important defensive value for the individual—it allows escape from the danger of being frustrated and overwhelmed by the variety of half-tested interacting others. The simplification allows him to relate to *one* simplified object—'the group'; to study 'it,' to formulate general laws and expectations about 'it' and to make remarks to 'it' and about 'it.' Now he need not think about the many others, nor risk becoming so invaded, occupied and confused by them, that contact with the self might be lost.

By relating to 'the group' the individual of course renouces major attempts to relate to many of the individuals present as well as any prospect that they can make personalised relations with him. This withdrawal from *personal* relations means that the individual is alone in the group and much in resort with his inner world. In this state of increased narcissism he is now liable to use projective processes to rid himself of unwanted aspects of his personality, and because he relates now not to individuals but to 'the group' it is mostly into 'the group' as a single entity that these unwanted and aggressive aspects are projected. 'The group' that is somewhere around but not located in any persons thus becomes endowed with unpleasant aspects of the self. It is felt as uncannily alive and dangerous, while the individual, weakened and depersonalised, is no longer in possession of his full mental resources. The perception of the group can eventually get so distorted by cycles of projective processes that all the *others* may become felt to be the authors of a developing group malignancy, in vague inexplicable fashion. The dreadful belief may arise that in some inexplicable way all have collectively created an intangible monster to be appeased or hidden from.

Many individuals because of projective loss now become 'not themselves.' Awed by 'the group' they are unusually quiet, modest, deferential, and may have noticeable difficulty in thinking or in making unprepared or unwritten statements. The self may now be felt as too ordinary, motives not noble enough, abilities too few. In timid isolation from the others, the behaviour of each is cautious, unspontaneous, conventional. Early contributions tend to be quiet, slow, equivocal or tentative, and are often about those *not* present; perhaps out of envy or in reluctance to engage with those actually present. Discomfort is controlled, disowned or expressed impersonally or indirectly, perhaps disguised as an innocent nonpersonalised question or generalisation (e.g., 'I wonder if people feel these meetings should finish earlier?'). Some large groups have initial formalities that, whatever their other functions, postpone personal commitment or revelation; recruiting an agenda, requesting news about a former decision or reports from sub-groups, seeking and making administrative arrangements, etc. Almost any communication *except* personalised thinking about individuals and relevant to the *immediate* situation tends to be seized and dwelt on for initial defensive safety. A member may make a personal statement. It is less likely to concern his thoughts about any present individual or the present setting than to be derived from the past or from outside, but in any event is likely to be made tentatively. Often the timid others will remain silent and nonresponding, and noticing his fate, other potential contributors may retreat further into narcissism. A second member may venture another remark, but it is noteworthy how often this too will be narcissistic, and heedless of and unrelated to the previous contribution. Individuals are not addressed nor named. 'People,' 'members,' 'the group' are addressed.

In an on-going group of fair sophistication, someone will eventually address a remark not to 'people' or 'the group' but directly to one or more persons, and may be responded to by that person or persons more or less sincerely. By the institution of other remarks that relate to individuals, dialogue may grow and others may join in. It usually takes about twenty minutes, however, before reality-testing is sufficient to show the majority that 'the group' is a fiction and that the others are not just collective 'people' but separate individuals comparable with oneself, singular but mortal. By now others will contribute and respond more authentically and less fantastically to named individuals and less to that single unit, the projectively aggressivised 'group.' An initial period of reality-testing of projective fantasies and defences seems to be necessary before collaborative discussion in large unstructured groups can occur. This seems to be true even for those groups in which members know each other fairly well, and it has been well, if imprecisely, described as the 'warming-up' period. Thereafter contributions can be responsive to individuals, agreement and disagreement can be less based on fantasy and more on fact, others can be related to for what they are and say and do, and now the fuller exploration of thoughts and reality-testing of the self and the other can proceed.

This is not to say that a group that proceeds fast to reality-tested individuation and to attempts to understand, respect and relate to the complexities of its members will always remain so; depending on events, individuals will tend regularly to withdraw into fantasy viewpoints and to receive these from others.

It is the projection into 'the group' of ego-ideals as well as other personality deplenishments that makes the individual feel that his everyday thinking is not good enough for the group. It may lead him to silent humility, but another individual may try to be only at his best and strive to contribute more profoundly and ably than is his wont. This may result in contributions that are truly useful but, insofar as they are aimed at impressing the ideal-endowed 'group' rather than at relating to individuals, they usually lack the sincerity that furthers relations. Many a group member addressed by another will be embarrassed that his answer is so mundane and will attempt mere rhetoric to match the fantasied high stands of the 'group.' This 'Nobel-Prize thinking' and its effects are in contrast to the warm pleasure felt by all when a member breaks such a cycle by confessing to a thought that is low-level and ordinary.

Some meetings never develop reality-tested relations but remain gripped by an immovable collusive system with contributions and responses so dominated by mutual projective fantasies that good reality-testing is impossible and a general retreat into narcissistic mental models blocks all progress. The anger arising from such frustrating situations is constantly split off and projected into 'the group' and individuals become further involved in cycles of narcissism, projection of rageful aspects of the self into the group, further personality deplenishments, loss of abilities, and fears. Feeling stupid, even badly depleted by such cycles, many individuals may now have serious difficulty in thinking and fear exposure and humiliation about this.

The task of understanding the complicated surrounding reality still remains for the weakened and deplenished individual, as well as the task of finding and reaffirming himself amid the multiple projections forced into him. He may hear others confusedly trying to resist projections, e.g.,

'I did say something like that but not the way you took it. I was thinking of something quite different.' Or,

'When I said "X" activity was useful I meant it honestly not sarcastically.'

'It was only an idea, I thought it might be interesting. I meant it to be helpful, *not* for the reasons *you* seem to think.'

'Why do you treat me as if I was always trying to stop things.'

'I'm all for action.'

The withstanding and sorting of multiple and collusive projections in a fantasy-ridden large group, now very difficult for an integrated person, are impossible if the personality has been depleted in ways described above. The depleted individual may find it impossible to sort out what is truly him and what is being attributed to him and projecting this very confusion into the group will further fear it and hate it. Hopelessly unable to understand what is going on, some may now deliberately cut themselves off from perception and take to day-dreaming; one or two may become explosively hostile and abusive to 'the group'; occasionally one may declare that 'the group' is driving him crazy and will walk out slamming the door; but the majority usually remain in confused silence.

Sometimes everyone may sit silent, withdrawn and motionless for long periods. The longer the silence the more cycles arise of frustration, projected hostility, personality depletion, stupidity and fears of something awful. The loss of the members' capacity to think or relate calmly leads to a dread of everything lest matters get worse. Progress stops and nothing is allowed to occur.

The painful phenomena of long silences are familiar and worrying to all large-group convenors. The general tension, the withdrawals shown by staring out of the window, inspection of shoes or ceiling or fingernails, the occasional cautious looks at other members, one member remarking fearfully that he feels anxious in a voice so unassertive that he cannot easily be heard so that everyone ignores him, the platitudinous comments that get no response, the staff members equally uneasy, stupid and platitudinous, the convenor himself having difficulty in thinking, uneasily waiting and letting sleeping dogs lie but feeling both responsible and confused, many sitting in corners or near the wall or the exit, one member ostentatiously opening a newspaper, another sighing histrionically, another impulsively walking out swearing, the surreptitious glances at the clock, everyone far now from recognising that all are fellow-human beings, all in dread of 'the group' and fearing that the next thing will only be worse; all these are familiar.

On such occasions the projective expectation of being attacked by the others now acquires some validity, because few are now free from the hostility that comes from frustration and many are in addition containing alien hostility projectively forced into them. With stupidity, suspicion and fear of hostility widespread, even matters such as lighting a cigarette or uncrossing legs now become matters of courage in the face of expected attack, and this is not wholly delusional, for anyone who does anything may be treated as hostile. Innocent contributions are now liable to be greeted with inquisitions. Anyone who seeks to understand by asking a question may be challenged and questioned in turn. Here are some actual replies to members of such silent groups who have cautiously voiced discomfort.

> 'What do you *mean* you're anxious? What are you trying to indicate?'
> '*I* don't feel tense, what's wrong with you?'
> 'You seem to be only drawing attention to yourself.'
> '*Everybody* is feeling uncomfortable, what's so special about *you*?'

Anyone who identifies himself as a singular person is liable to be attacked, and pushed back into silent mindlessness. The staff equally depleted, frustrated and projective are equally liable to criticise anyone who moves or speaks.

In endeavours to recover both abilities and intellect certain individuals, especially staff, may seek to assert themselves, but less by making thoughtful personal statements than by ill-aimed and vaguely hostile theoretical generalisations not about themselves but about the difficulties of 'people' or 'the group.' But just as *any* contribution, innocent or critical, personal or general, is now in great danger of being treated only as hostile, such interventions have little chance of being simply received. The staff is always liable to be used by patients as the chief container for projected hostility and when they actually offer lofty interpretations about 'the group' they only make the situation worse. In any event absolute judgements run rife and hostile we/they situations abound. If staff remain silent the patients in turn will attack them for that. Total responsibility for the group's difficulty is liable to be projected into the staff.

> '*You* started it.'
> 'It's *your* meeting.'

'We are only patients.'
'*We* did not arrange this, etc.'

Sections of staff—perhaps all—may be felt by patients to be stern, contemptuous, waiting to pounce, and whatever they do or say may be regarded only as confirming their hostility or duplicity. In turn they may hate the patients or their fellow staff absolutely, as only hostile and destructive. In these we/they situations, judgements are absolute, each side claims innocence and feels the other as willfully destructive. The recipients of the projections of hostility resent their goodness being ignored. Those accused may become helplessly possessed by the very qualities (e.g., contempt, aggressiveness) attributed to them.

ANONYMISATION AND GENERALISATION

A regular feature of disturbed large-group situations that have not proceeded to terrified silence is the loss of personalisation of relations and the growth of anonymity. Nobody is recognised as a whole person or is addressed by name. Even people who may know each other quite well may address each other only as innominate members of a class, and speak in vague impersonal terms:

'Why doesn't *somebody* say something?'
'Some *people* seem to enjoy making things awkward.'
'The *group* is a waste of time.'
'The *administration* doesn't seem to be interested in people.'
'The *nursing staff* aren't aware that some *people* prefer to be by themselves.'
'I don't agree with the last *speaker*.'

Personal identities are thus not recognised, the very identity of the speaker is veiled, and views are general and unspecific. Vivid personal views, feelings and experiences about actual others are denied, no individuals exist, only 'people' and only moral platitudes or intellectual generalisations remain.

In this anonymous climate individuals often hide behind the class they belong to.

'The medical staff are fairly sure that people are . . . .'
'Many patients have found that the . . .'
'The married people feel that bed-time should be . . . .'
'This is very confusing for the nursing staff.'

Personal viewpoints are concealed in statements from one class about another. This hiding of identity arises especially when an individual imports into the group a personal disagreement with another whom he is afraid to confront directly. In the group it can be made into an impersonal general issue. But it can also arise when personal disagreement arises in the group

61

itself. The result is the same—the group is presented with disembodied general issues of principle and class.

These general class statements allow the individual and his hostility to remain unidentified. The disownment of personal hostility and its projection into one's own class averts personal attack from others (because one is lost in a class) and avoids retaliation from any other because he too is lost in a class. Many remarks in a large group thus appear to come from nobody in particular, to be about nobody in particular and to be addressed to nobody in particular. This avoidance of asserting the self and others' selves in personal interchange, together with the accompanying projective processes, is liable to lead now to paranoid class wars and heated moralisings. These can only be ended if the initiating highly personal issues can be brought to light, and seen as important for certain individuals but irrelevant to the larger group. If they are not brought to light but remain as general matters, the issues may become used as containers for all sorts of other hidden and undeclared personal disagreements. Anonymous class wars over plausible general principles are now seized upon to pay off old personal scores that have not been voiced in the 'dangerous' group. Vehement discussions about abstract principles, and class behaviours thus often develop a baffling unreal quality where the passion, produced by projection and displacement, is out of all proportion to the manifest issues. Certain individuals may usefully identify both the underlying *personal* issues and the few involved; but such meetings often end in high feeling with each class feeling righteous, misunderstood, and angry, while endowing other classes with stupidity and malice.

But even if class wars do not occur, anonymisation creates a 'safe' but stultifying stasis in which nobody exists and nothing much gets done. The gain is that the fantastically 'hostile' group cannot attack anybody for nobody exists as a person or speaks as one. The cost is that personal thought, discussion and interchange are crippled.

ENVY AND DEMOCRATISATION

If the large group is endowed with projected positive aspects of the self, the projectors will be depleted and relatively ineffective, but will be in awe of and dependent on the abilities now lost and now attributed to the idealised group. But whereas most members actively resist negative aspects being forced into them, so that the invented 'group' is needed and used as the single container of these, the fate of positive aspects is somewhat different. Because of human narcissism some people do not resist positive qualities being attributed or forced into them and do not make appropriate reality tests; some even enjoy being idealised and try to collude with high qualities being attributed to them. A few may even view prominently for idealising projections and seek to be regarded by the depleted majority as 'the only people who make the group worthwhile.' Such members usually have some suitability as containers of positive projections but a good 'role fit' is not inevitable and the correspondence of their gifts with those now attributed to them may be indifferent. Those who embark on 'high-level' competition may get admiration and envy of the depleted others; but this leads in turn to the others becoming doubly passive and ineffective so that group discussion is replaced by 'prima donna' displays. The 'prima donnas' in turn project ineffectiveness and invalidism into the group. The single entity of the 'group' may itself become the sole repository of projected positive qualities and itself become idealised and worshipped by its depleted members, and when so endowed with magical status its real activities and its members' functioning may actually be of a low order.

The projection of positive abilities not only leads to mental poverty, awe, tutelage and worship of selected others; more painfully it may result in envy of these others for their abilities, real or fantasied. Those who retain the capacity to think and relate with assurance may thus be privately belittled as too clever, conceited, ambitious and competitive, etc., and at times even attacked in public.

'There we go again. More clever ideas.'
'Why do you try so hard? The group is quite happy being quiet.'
'What gives you the right to think that you know better than the rest of us.'

Envy is a disease of poverty and also of impoverishment by projective identification, but envy is itself often denied and projected, so that others come to be feared as dangerously envious. The resultant *fear of being envied*, as well as the demonstrated attacks on those who retain their individuation and abilities, gives further cause for the hiding of abilities and thoughts from the 'malignant' group and for outbreaks of safe generalisations.

In this overdetermined state of anonymity[2] even talented individuals may be careful to remain undistinguished nonentities; nobody dare be original or unique in thought or capacity. Everybody collusively seeks similarity to others and all are regarded as having identical needs and rights. All patients have the same amount and kind of distress and out of 'fairness' none should be given less or more consideration than others. All staff have the same status and aims, all nurses are equally skilled (or unskilled), all doctors are equally useful (or useless). All treatments are equal in effectiveness, by equal staff to equal patients, and should last an equal time. The rights of minorities are sunk, and the word democracy now acquires magical values and is in common usage. The normal processes of externalisation with subsequent reality-testing that help the individual to find out, differentiate and maintain himself and others come to a stop. The recognition of the variety of talents becomes lost. Truly democratic processes, the creation of a social structure with election to distinct roles of authority and responsibility matched to the special skills of individuals, and with sincere consideration of the different capacities and needs of individuals, are brushed away as 'undemocratic.' Candidates for significant posts and elected positions declare themselves unfit for election or uninterested, so the group loses the benefits of their ambitions and gifts. Indeed the general fear of enviable distinction may lead to the election of harmless nonentities to important posts.

In the face of projectively enhanced fears of group hostility and envy, staff have particular problems because of their inescapable distinct position. Some may now minimise these in placating statements to the group. Others may seek to be on first-name terms with each other and with patients or make other anxious attempts at 'democratic' bonhomie. Others will blur or renounce their roles, authority and responsibilities, and emphasis their powerlessness and goodwill in attempts to escape from envious attack.

Placatory actions of this kind hinder analysis of the fear of envy and prevent the growth of sincere reality-tested relations. Painful problems are evaded in anxious democratic goodwill; and the brake of appeasement is put on discussion, argument and decision-making.

THE RECOVERY OF THE SELF

After a large unstructured group meeting has ended, no matter whether it has gone 'well' or 'badly,' many members gossip with each other. In twos and threes they rapidly seek to recover lost parts of themselves and to re-experience others also as whole personalised individuals, and they no longer act or use these others only as containers of projections. Critical faculties and abilities become re-owned and no longer denied, and simultaneously comes to re-assertion of the self and the capacity to think freely and to relate again to others as asserting individuals. An open shared sense of relief at the break-up of the large group is common in this 'post-mortem.' Many who were silent, paranoid, anonymised, depleted, depersonalised, baffled and stupid in the large group will now, after a short period of feeling dazed and unsure, begin to chatter and to seek feelings and ideas within themselves and explore and express these with increasing confidence with their fellows; and now interchange with and the exploration of the feelings and views of fellows proceed apace. It seems that in the different, less complex setting the individual can take back into himself much of the aggressive energy he had projected and lost into the larger setting; and can rid himself of elements projected into him by others while he was in the large group. And he will now find others of his kind, also recovering and freer also to *be* again and to allow others to *be*.

In therapeutic communities it is also common now for staff 'after-groups' to meet and discuss with each other the large group events that a few minutes before had perhaps puzzled or confused them. Somewhat formally they do what the patients simultaneously do informally, reviewing the large-group events and recovering and rediscovering themselves and others. These 'after-groups' are not inevitably successful for they too carry the potential anxieties of any sizeable group; and there is an added danger that the 'outsiders' (the patients) may be used as suitable depersonalised receptacles for continued or new projections. Staff after-groups, being relatively small, can usually preserve individual reality-testing but they are not inevitably immune from relational chaos.

A CONTRAST WITH SMALL GROUPS

Certain differences between small and large groups make for different experiences in the two settings. Benign projective identification, with reality-testing, can certainly proceed faster and more surely in small groups; and the affirming of oneself and the findings of others, and acceptance, modification or rejection of others' projections are faster. The individual has fewer receptacles for his own projections and has fewer others seeking to intrude theirs into him; all are in less danger, both of being overwhelmed and of being seriously depleted by very many others. The individual's ability and need to find himself through relating to others is not so confounded, lost, overlaid or ignored in the simpler matrix of the small group. Retirement from frustrated attempts at relations is therefore less common in the small group, and retreat to personal models, narcissistic experiences, and denial of and projection of self-hatred are less used, and when used are less vigorous. Because the situation is less frustrating, hostility is less, and projective identification is neither so massive nor forced. Because personality depletion is less, the individual has more of his faculties for use in reality-testing.

SOME TECHNICAL OBSERVATIONS

How can one help reduce the complex of anxieties that hinder the large group's work task—which in the case of a psychiatric hospital is the examination of the disturbances in working alliances that result from insufficient awareness of the self and of others?

Whereas in personal or small-group psychotherapy interpretation is *sanctioned because sought* it has no such sanction in large groups. Interpretation in large groups is therefore liable to be viewed only as a model of unengaged observer-behaviour and the others may gladly follow this model because of its defensive nonrevelatory safety. As a result general talk about what 'the group' is doing may become epidemic. Then nobody is *in* the group, for all become observers of it 'out there,' interpreting 'it,' exchanging Nobel-Prize thoughts about 'it,' and addressing 'it,' but not interacting as and with personalised individuals. Moreover, unsanctioned 'group' interpretations are often the result of unease in an interpreter at feeling himself confused, insignificant and lost; they may simply be his attempt to assert a threatened thinking capacity about an 'it' rather than a personal engagement with individuals present. The nonpersonalised interpreter may thereafter become irrecoverably used as a container for projected positive or negative aspects of others. He may be felt as containing magical abilities to be submitted to in passivity and indeed may continue to be projectively stimulated to be prominent and clever while all others maintain innocence and stupidity; or he may come to be enviously attacked; or be regarded as full of malignities to be feared and hidden from. Many of the complications in large groups outlined earlier may thus be unchanged, and indeed 'group' interpretations may simply confound confusion. The 'therapeutic alliance' of psychoanalysis is not available in work with large groups.

The complexities of large-group life mean that any accurate interpretation about 'it' is at best a part-truth. Large groups rarely behave as wholes moving only in one direction, indeed the individuals in it may be moving in several different directions, and interpretations about group form or content, or themes are therefore almost always incomplete. This is not to say that the understanding of total processes in which many persons are involved can never be attempted, but the interpreter should be fairly sure of his observations, his understanding of these and his motives before he speaks, together with the result he expects. But it remains difficult for the group interpreter to avoid offering a model of me/you-all thinking, with the dangers of ensuing ambivalent dependence on him.

The convenor or convenors cannot of course escape their task, which is to listen, understand, intervene and observe the effects of their interventions. But not all interventions need be interpretive, and in large groups *noninterpretive therapeutic interventions* have major merit. Like interpretations in individual treatments, such interventions should be carefully timed and phrased, but, unlike interpretations about 'it' out there, should be highly *personalized* statements about *one's own* sincerely felt position in the face of specific contributions by individuals or groups of individuals; they are distinguished from mere personal revelations, however, in that they are offered only if the declared personal position has been thought out as being revealing also about the situation of others.

Noninterpretive therapeutic interventions are not easy to formulate but are often simple in themselves. They are difficult because they require tolerance of and fidelity to the self and to others in the face of all the group's projective processes, hostilities, confusions, anonymisations, Nobel-Prize thinking, narcissistic withdrawals, generalisations, etc. Of course the better the pathological group-processes are understood the easier it is to remain a whole person relating to well-perceived others and thus to offer models of personalised thinking. Non-interpretive therapeutic interventions rarely concern the whole 'group' however; for they are attempts to help *individuals* recover and rediscover themselves and each other in it and from it. They offer a model of an individual relating not to 'the group' but to individuals present. The following is an example of such an intervention on a not very troubled group. It seems ordinary and elementary *because* it was thoughtful and skilled.

Example

Discussion became taken over by a dozen teenage patients. They addressed only each other and used private slang and nicknames and discussed a complicated set of relations and feelings about an event they had obviously created the previous evening. It was friendly and yet it was private and excluded many present. The older members listened politely but at least some began to feel envious, curious and guilty over being so ignorant, as if they ought to have known about the event. (Staff were able to check this at an after-group.) Afraid of disclosing his remiss ignorance to the large group (and to the other older ones) many an older member sat in uneasy solitude, hiding and trying to disown his uncomfortable feelings from all others. None of this was clear to the members at that time; they took part in it but were not aware of it, only of their various discomforts.

Group interpretations would have been possible perhaps about group splitting, age-rivalries, denial and projection of guilt over enjoyment, denied hatred of younger people, secret delinquency, fear of retaliation, etc. with all the dangers of being both chancy and me/you-all.

One of the staff said, 'I'm feeling left-out of this, and fed up. And I notice I'm ashamed I didn't know about last night and I'm ashamed to say I'm curious. It sounds good—what went on?'

Some older members made immediate noises of agreement. All stopped looking down and looked towards the younger people, who at once began to talk to the older people. Last night they had invented and played a new intelligent game and they explained this. Then one said and the others agreed that they had been disappointed no older people had seen them— 'You'd have been impressed. Honestly, we didn't know we were so good.' Now there was general laughter and much goodwill. A general discussion now took place over details of the evening and then moved on to other incidents in which shyness between older and younger people had limited their relating to each other. Resentments by all at being misunderstood were discussed insightfully and a few plans for the future were made.

It is obviously not possible to make a list of noninterpretive therapeutic interventions for all occasions. It can be said, however, that any that help individuals to feel easier about owning and declaring more of themselves and their situations are therapeutic for all. Not only do they reduce mental splitting and increase personality integration for the individual, but they also allow others to know him (and therefore themselves) less fantastically and more surely. All can therefore better reaffirm themselves and each other, and can grow aware of how, in group settings, personal integration can be maintained.

It is possible, however, to indicate in aphoristic form a few samples of opportunities for noninterpretive therapeutic interventions; they are obvious, even trite, and anyone familiar with large groups will add many more; yet they are difficult to remember and use in the pressures of large-group disturbances. Behind statements of class views is an individual with a recent painful experience with someone in the other class: personal feuds tend to be expressed as a 'group' matter: early generalising statements often indicate a personal carry-over from a particular recent experience; every question conceals personal thoughts and wishes and is never 'innocent': absolute judgements are the result of recent personal pain; statements about 'people' usually hide thoughts about one person: steady presentation of various grumbles are a displacement from one concealed matter—sometimes a good one felt to need protection from others' envy.

The *manner* of intervening is not, however, thus indicated, and it hardly needs stating that aphoristic interventions would be merely non-personal, lofty and generalising. The intervener's manner should be of an ally to those in difficulty and what he says about himself should help them sort out and declare themselves.

Example

A woman patient cautiously asked the group to formulate a view about behaviour at night in the corridors. Perhaps all felt both attacked by this question and glad of the generalising defence it contained, for it was accepted at face value and steadily discussed as a general issue. What *were* the group's views? The group split into those who were and were not in favour of making rules. Ideas and arguments about designating 'quiet' areas arose. Respecting the rights of others and society's needs for defences against anarchy took the topic into abstract levels. Projection processes led to vicious arguments about law-giving and law-breaking with examples. The original speaker and her request became ignored. Many grew silent. Eventually an intervener addressed the first speaker, and said surely hers was not just an academic question. What had happened at night to lead to the question? Could it be spoken about?

Well, the speaker's child had been woken by 'people' talking on the corridor at 10 o'clock last night and it had taken an hour to get him to sleep. People? Could she mention names? Well she didn't want to cause trouble. Others murmured their support of her keeping the issue anonymous. Now several speakers declared their personal innocence and indignant sympathy for the mother. Eventually a pressurising silence arose as if in wait for a sinner to confess. The intervener said if she had been one of the night-time talkers she couldn't possibly say so now, because the group was somehow now making a Federal offence out of a bit of ordinary carelessness. She had herself sometimes forgotten to keep quiet outside a child's room and she couldn't promise to be perfect in the future, but she'd try. Was it a hanging matter? One or two others said that they too had sometimes forgotten to be quiet in corridors. Two patients said they thought it must have been them. They'd forgotten about the child and hadn't realised it until this meeting. The mother smiled grimly and said she knew it was them but hadn't liked to say so (although she'd met them that morning). She'd been furious last night. There was some laughter and more apologies. Individuals had emerged. The group's heat about general moral issues vanished and discussion moved on to another topic, with members again in possession of themselves, and relating to others.

CONCLUSION

Projective processes affect not only individuals but others related to them, and are therefore stuff of multibody psychology. Mutual projective processes not only impoverish and distort experience of the self and the perceived world; they also affect the behaviour of this world towards the self. Human organisations inevitably create projection systems; some are rife with them and where they enshrine and perpetuate them they create personal and interpersonal impoverishments and ineffectiveness.

Therapeutic two-somes and small groups offer the internally divided individual a chance of resolving in some depth the anxieties and fantasies observable in those settings. The problems for the individual of maintaining himself and others in large-group settings are allied but distinct, and together with the behaviour of large groups in using collusive projective systems merit separate study.

At present our best-tested therapeutic technique and most fruitful observations rest on the classic two-body situation. Comparatively little is yet known about multibody psychology and very little about the multibody psychology of large groups. Therapeutic communities therefore offer important observational and technical opportunities.

5.

LEADERSHIP: THE INDIVIDUAL AND THE GROUP[1]

Pierre M. Turquet

By way of introduction, I would like to make three preliminary points.

First, I shall be describing, from personal experiences, small group behavior; that is, the behavior of groups with eight to twelve members, with sixteen as the extreme upper limit. There is nothing mysterious about such numbers. Many a committee is so composed—the board of directors of a company, a selection committee for a post, the senior faculty of a university department, or a committee to plan and organize some event. Slightly larger groups—say, with a membership of twenty to thirty, the typical honorary committee for some event, or the board of governors of an institution—seem to get little or no work done. In my experience, they live up to their "honorary" title all too easily. My advice to anyone invited to join such a committee is to recognize that he is being invited for his name, rank, or whatever, but not for work. If he has a taste for work, then he had better refuse this signal invitation to futility. In fact, such moderately large committees tend to split into small executive committees; but then we are back to our original smaller numbers of eight to twelve. When groups reach even larger numbers (say, fifty to eighty, and eighty is the largest group that I have studied in detail), and so because of their size can no longer remain face-to-face groups, the presence of other phenomena intrude on the characteristics of the small group.

These new phenomena are of a different order from those of small groups and in part center around the question of the institutionalization of the individual as a means of saving the single person from annihilation, which constantly threatens. In part, the observable phenomena seem also to stem from the need of individual members to search for and find an encompassable whole. Another reason, it would seem, for preferring to work in a small group is that it is encompassable by each individual member, as well as being face-to-face. Hence a membership of twelve seems to be getting near the upper limit of a single member's capacity to encompass and take in, with sixteen as the extreme limit. It is perhaps relevant to point out that chess has sixteen pieces. But role differentiation on an institutional basis—that is, a large-group phenomenon—has already begun to crystallize out. On the other hand, and at the other extreme, if membership numbers are five or six, again phenomena of a different order appear—phenomena more directly related to the field of family dynamics and family fantasies.

My second introductory point is that a small group, if it is to be alive and active, must have a *primary task* (Rice, 1963)—a task that the group must carry out if it is to survive. Thus, a factory must produce goods, a businessman must make profits, a bank must show a return on its investments, a hospital must cure a visible number of its patients, a school must teach the subjects on its curriculum, a university must produce graduates from undergraduates. A functioning small group must therefore seek to know its primary task, both by definition and by feasibility. Failure in these matters inevitably leads to the dismemberment of the group, and hence to its final dissolution, or to the emergence of some other primary task unrelated to the one for which it was originally called into being.

Even though some groups or institutions may have more than one primary task, nevertheless, at any one moment in time they must decide which primary task to pursue. A surgeon can teach while operating, but teaching has to go by the board when the patient shows signs of vascular collapse, at least if the surgeon wishes to be able to continue to operate on a live patient—a matter of taste if you like. If the sales department of a factory is unable to sell the factory's goods, further attempts on the part of the personnel department to solve the local unemployment problem can lead to the bankruptcy court, which is no way of solving unemployment. In my opinion, universities, especially in England and the United States—the former less so than the latter—appear to have got themselves into a difficult situation by attempting to carry out two of the main contradictory primary tasks, to teach and to do research; or at least they appear to have failed to distinguish between them. They are different in that, for instance, each requires its own method of work, its own group membership, and its own leadership. To the research worker, the undergraduate is a chore, and the able teacher a second-class citizen, a mere "vulgarisateur" who waters down, if he does not actually distort, the research worker's valuable and fine ideas. For the teacher, the research worker is an ivory tower specialist, demanding more and more facilities and time for his own work, requiring more specialized and highly expensive equipment, thereby starving the departmental library of basic textbooks for the students, and increasingly making claim to professorial teaching chairs. In such a conflict situation it is no wonder that the undergraduate feels more and more disaffected.

Consider our prisons. If in recent months there has been an increase in prison escapes, it is perhaps because prison administrators are uncertain about which of their diverse primary tasks to implement. In a reformist prison, the uniformed disciplinary staff feel undervalued or unneeded. In a no-escape prison, the socializing reformer experiences the impossibility of his task. Thus the staff members become easy victims for the escaping prisoner. Only by drawing clear boundaries between conflicting primary tasks can a group resolve tensions and confusions. The implication here is that structure and primary task are internally linked, and that primary-task fulfillment requires an appropriate structure.

Leadership: The Individual and the Group

The first signs of group institutional failure can be sought in an examination of primary task "products": the ratio of satisfied to dissatisfied undergraduates in a university or of cured to dead patients in a hospital, the escape rate from prisons, the balance sheet of a commercial enterprise. That is, the groups or institutions that I have mentioned are *open-system groups*, interacting with the environment in which the group has its being. Hence, their primary-task products are to be found in their external environment. If no such products are externally detectable, then the group in question is probably a closed-system group (one of the basic-assumption groups discussed later). Because a group's primary task involves interactions with the environment, there will be a surface of interaction between the group and the environment. Such an interaction surface leads to the formation of a boundary between group and environment. Furthermore, because there is a boundary, there will be transactions across the boundary; and such transactions will require mechanisms of control—in particular, and in individual terms, the presence of a leader. A fundamental aspect of leadership, therefore, is boundary control at this interface.

Furthermore, the clearer the boundary, the easier it is for these transactions to be studied and, indeed, for the fact of their existence to be acknowledged. In the debate that took place in the House of Commons after World War II on the rebuilding of the House following its destruction by German incendiary bombs, Winston Churchill eloquently argued for a rectangular House on the grounds that such a House would inevitably highlight the act of "crossing the floor" as an open, deliberately taken decision—and he himself was well experienced in such political tergiversations—as against a semicircular House modeled, for instance, on the Continental or American examples where all that is required is a shifting movement of the bottom, the boundaries being so structurally indeterminate.

Open-system groups are involved not only in an internal/external world of differentiation but also in an internal-world differentiation, in the setting up of the internal processes of intake, conversion, and output. Such internal processes help in turn to strengthen the boundary between the internal and external worlds and thereby to support the exercise of the leadership function of boundary control. The complication for leadership is that, like the psychoanalytic model of the ego, it has to be Janus-like, looking both internally and externally, becoming both participant and observer. If the leader allows himself to become an observer gliding above the fray as a nonparticipant, he will deprive himself of knowledge of certain vital aspects of the group's activities. Hence, he will lose much of his evidence about the state of the group and especially the group's expectations with regard to his leadership. Indeed, there will be times when the only evidence available to him as to the state of the group's health will be his own personal experience of the group, what he feels the group is doing to him, and how he feels the group inside himself. Equally, of course, total immersion or loss of self in the group is destructive to leadership as a boundary function. It follows, too, that leadership has to act as a projection receptacle and to bear being used. As a motto for leadership, I would offer a saying attributed to Socrates: "It is never right to return a wrong or to defend ourselves against a wrong by threats of retaliation," for groups are beset by fears of such retaliations.

Furthermore, if I have in one and the same breath talked of groups and institutions, it is because more and more institutions are controlled and directed by small groups, as Galbraith for one points out in his recent book, *The New Industrial State*. Leadership of an institution is therefore apt to have two faces. On the one hand there is the leadership exercised by a small group, and so it becomes possible to think of group leadership. But there is also the personal leadership of an individual—a chairman, or director, or president—and hence it is possible to think in terms of the personal leadership of a small group. These two aspects can become disconnected, however, especially if the personal leadership is charismatic in quality.

Because in open systems there are interactional surfaces with exchanges across boundaries, and because primary-task products are detectable outside the group or institution, there is no place in such groups for secrecy. Leadership of a group or an institution, either as a group or as an individual function, is therefore a public function. Leadership that is not public belongs to a different order of phenomena, a point I will come back to later. Secrecy, like charisma, may be appropriate for a particular moment in the life of a group or an institution, but such moments are for obedience rather than for learning, more for the creation of beliefs than the establishment of demonstrable facts, more for the greater glory of one person than for the healthy development of the whole.

To illustrate, with an example from business: A family firm was profitably manufacturing and marketing a product that was sold under the family name, mostly by small retailers. The chairman and founder of the business, upon learning that several large distributing stores were interested in marketing the product under trade names of their own choosing, suggested to his fellow directors that they accept this departure from tradition, to seek greater profits. His suggestion was rejected: "Our unique product under somebody else's trade name? Allow control over our processes? Never." The chairman had done his charismatic job too well. Eighteen months later the firm was the object of a successful takeover bid; the directors lost their seats on the board, and the product is now being sold under new trade names. The directors had made their primary task the protection of a name, rather than the pursuit of profits through manufacture and selling.

My third and last introductory point relates to the work of Bion (1959)—specifically, his notion that a small group can exist in two states: as a sophisticated work group and as a basic-assumption group. The primary task of these two groups is different, and hence also the quality of the leadership required for primary-task implementation.

The sophisticated work group is a group called into being for a predetermined, clearly defined primary task that has been openly accepted, at least at the conscious level, by its members and at which, again consciously, they have agreed to work. *Ab initio*, therefore, such a group will be

Leadership: The Individual and the Group

concerned with trying to define its primary task or, as work progresses, whatever discrete aspects of its primary task are on hand at that particular moment. Such a group is therefore concerned not only with definition but with a high level of self-awareness—an awareness concerning impingements between itself and the external world in which its work is taking place. Later, as "work" develops, the group will seek to maintain its relationship between its primary task and the external milieu, especially as this relationship undergoes change following on work. In this sense a work group behaves like an open-system group.

In its attitude to primary-task implementation—that is, to work—the work group is activated by a desire to know: to acquire insights, to discover and understand explanations, and to form hypotheses that can be tested. It will also be concerned with the consequences of its own behavior and actions—not only between individual members of the work group but also with the group's external milieu.

The members cooperate freely in primary-task implementation through the skills each brings to his task; indeed, each member is valued for the skills brought to its implementation. Furthermore, as part of the initial definition of the primary task, the work group will examine the skills present among its members to ensure at least the possibility of its fulfillment. A surgical team will require a surgeon; it may or may not need a physician. A society may or may not need a treasurer, depending upon the number of subscriptions and financial transactions involved. This preliminary examination of skills in relation to primary-task definition is especially crucial with regard to leadership. It is not self-evident that a chemical plant requires the leadership of a chemist, particularly if sales or profitability is its immediate current primary task.

Furthermore, a very important distinguishing feature of a work group is the freedom to associate enjoyed by its members. They are also free to resign, and resignation is not necessarily a threat to their personal existence; also, the work group is free to dissolve. Furthermore, the members of a work group assume responsibility for the group's interactions—both internally as between members, and externally as between themselves and the environment—and their consequences. The assumption of responsibility is a collective one, somewhat like the doctrine of collective responsibility that guides the British Cabinet, and is not left to become the sole responsibility of an individual. The notion of the leader, of a single member being solely responsible, is not only derogatory of the individual skills of the other members of the group but is also inimical to the task of inquiry. Particular experts may be necessary for specific functions, but their expertise has to be assessed by the group if the group is to flourish as a sophisticated work group and not to behave as something else. A board of directors may need an accountant, but disaster will ensue if he is the only member of the board who can read a balance sheet.

If a work group has structure—chairman, secretary, minutes, and the like—this structure is related to the needs of the primary task. Minutes of a meeting are not ends in themselves but are there to refresh memories of decisions taken and the reasons for those decisions being taken at that time. If there is a chairman, the implication is that there is a particular aspect of boundary control that requires such a role. When structure becomes an end in itself, it is most probable that we are dealing with a basic-assumption group. Similarly, if a group seeks to include some particular function without relating that function to the group's primary task, without taking into account the consequences of the inclusion for group functioning, or without investigating the skill contribution offered to primary-task fulfillment, then again we may find ourselves in a world other than that of the work group.

Work groups are not mutual admiration societies. Though they may contain friends, they can and should be able to tolerate and contain disagreements. Implicit, too, in the notion of freedom of association is freedom for disassociation, for work-group dissolution. A classical illustration—to put the point the other way round—is the tendency of research teams to perpetuate themselves. Initially a research team will come into being for some clear-cut purpose, perhaps at the request of another research group. Though it may take time, the purpose for which the group was formed is accomplished. But because its members have been successful, perhaps also because they are now familiar with each other's quirks, are now "friends," there is a marked tendency for such groups to perpetuate themselves by finding another project to work on. It is seemingly easier for them to carry on "as before" than to consider self-dissolution or to examine the skill requirements of the further project. Under these circumstances it is more than likely that the second project will not be as successful as the first, particularly if the primary-task requirements for the second project favor a different member composition.

BASIC-ASSUMPTION GROUPS

Let us now turn to the basic-assumption group and its way of life, which is very different from that of the sophisticated work group. In the first place, its primary task arises entirely from within its own midst and is pursued solely for the satisfaction of the internal needs of the group. The *basic-assumption dependency group* (the BD group), seeks to obtain security for its members, who are to be looked after, protected, and sustained by a leader and only by that leader. The *basic-assumption fight/flight group* (the BF group) pursues the aim of fighting or of flying from somebody or something—with the leader to ensure this necessary action, and the members to follow. The *basic-assumption pairing group* (the BP group) strives to create something, some hope, some new idea or Messiah, to reproduce itself through a pair in the group, with all other members vicariously participating in this paired relationship. To these three basic-assumption groups described by Bion, I would add a fourth—the *basic-assumption oneness group* (the BO group), whose members seek to join in a powerful union with an omnipotent force, unobtainably high, to surrender self for passive participation, and thereby to feel existence, well-being, and wholeness.

Basic-assumption groups (hereafter referred to as Ba groups) require leaders, but it is a personified leadership located in one person, who is expected to do "all that is necessary" for accomplishing the group's basic-assumption primary task. The group may have to adopt special methods to persuade the leader to act accordingly. Thus, a member of a BD group may offer himself or herself as a sick person to be looked after and thereby seek to move the leader to providing succour. Similarly, a BF leader, if he cannot find enemies to fight or fly from for himself, will be offered suitable candidates to stimulate the necessary paranoid qualities through "atrocity stories" of the stupidity of a therapeutic colleague in another hospital, the iniquitous sales campaign techniques of a rival firm, the alleged absence of the necessary culture in another group or nation, and so on.

Here I must emphasize four points.

First, in such Ba groups it is entirely a question of leader and led, with a collusive interdependence between the two. It is never a question of equals, nor is the leader a "first among equals." He is there by kind permission of the group and will survive as long as he fulfills the primary task of the Ba group. However, since this task contains impossible elements—to be omnipotent; to know without being told; to find and lead into a promised land; to be constantly active with regard to potential enemies; to foster new hopes and ideas, which in themselves are doomed to die; to face impossible unfriendly odds—failure is his future and his replacement is inevitable. (It is true that he may be deified for worship, or changed into a book, or become the subject of much textual exegesis, as Freud was; but appreciation of such consolations is not easy from beyond the grave.) Such groups are therefore often unstable because of changes in leadership; a new leader must be found to replace the old failing one, but the new leader fails too and is replaced, and so it goes.

Second, such groups are not primarily interested in interactions with their environment. They are self-contained, closed systems and, as such, are not like the sophisticated work group, which is interested in predictions and consequences. Hence, they have little or no desire to know, since knowledge might be an embarrassment, might cause disturbance in the internal harmony or "groupiness" of the group. Their motto might be "Don't confuse me with facts; I have my own ideas." Their attitude toward knowledge is very similar to Goebbels' attitude toward art. Being fearful of and aggressive toward knowledge, lacking the necessary predictive techniques, scornful of hypotheses, hence uninterested and unaware of consequences, they have little or no sense of collective responsibility. In the main, responsibility is left to the leader. External reality is regarded as a potential source of sudden unpleasantness and therefore to be avoided. All coldness is outside; all warmth is inside, with members huddling together like so many babes in the wood, especially in BD. Outside is death; inside is life.

Third, such groups appear to come into existence spontaneously, with no preparatory formulation, no expectations to be fulfilled. Hence they act on an "as-if" basis—as if things will come to pass because they are so and so; as if their leader has but to act, which as a good leader he obviously will do. No effort seems to be required for their emergence, and they have a full dynamic energy of their own. Such groups are indeed lively affairs. Equally, the group seems to know what to do, and no previous training of its members seems to be required. In addition, the assumptions on which the members act are rarely formulated, certainly not by one particular member. Intellectually, their task is neither troublesome nor thought-provoking. Their primary task is simply to be carried out, not developed and not the object of adaptive processes.

Fourth, these leadership concepts, brought into being by the interpersonal relations between the members of the group, contain a mythical quality. As myths they have such universality that major sections and institutions of a community—hospitals, church, and clergy for BD, army for BF, aristocracy or ruling intellectual families for BP, the "mysteries" for BO—represent and embody those myths on behalf of society. These institutions often have the characteristics of closed systems—their leadership recruitment, for instance, comes from within, their sense of time is oriented toward the past or an out-of-time timelessness, and their failures at crisis moments, when called on to fulfill their primary tasks, are notable. But the further point, both theoretical and technical, is that our attention is drawn by the presence of such myths to the dynamic, myth-making quality of interpersonal, interface relations.

For instance: For the dyadic relationship, there are the myths of Penelope, of "marriages made in heaven," of marriage as an exposed, eternally available breast, and the myth of the birth of a savior. For the triadic relationship, there is the oedipal myth. For the family groups, there is the revengeful "Urvater" who watchfully encourages sibling self-destruction, or the all-embracing succouring mother. For the small group, there are the Ba leader myths already described. For the large group, there is the errant mob so aptly displayed in Goya's painting of Rumor. For the individual seeking his identity in group situations, there is the myth of Odysseus. And for each situation there are others. Technically these myths have to be elucidated because by their binding together quality, they contribute to the perpetuation of fruitless nonadaptive systems.

The members of such Ba groups are both happy and unhappy. They are happy in that their roles are simple, requiring little skill and no great soul-searching. In BD the role is to be looked after, to be the "casualty" for the exercise of the leader's thoughtful expertise in caring and the object of the group's concern. Though there may be competitiveness for such a role, the criterion for success—command of the leader's attention—is simple. In BF it is to be a member of a combat team for courage and obedience; though casualties—to be neglected and treated as malingerers—may abound, they are compensated for by the great sense of camaraderie, of action, of doing something, even though it may be over the cliff or into the mouth of the cannon. (Watching such a group in action, I have often sympathized with the French general in the Crimean War who, on observing the famous Charge of the Light Brigade at Balaklava, is reported to have said, "C'est beau, mais ce n'est pas la guerre"—It is nice, but it is not war. Clearly for him war was a matter for a sophisticated work group.) In BP the member is either one of the pair or part of the vicarious participating audience, in either case lost in the ongoing activity, buoyed up by hope, like the characters in a Chekov play expecting that "spring will come," the total atmosphere being of bated breath, as in a Flemish picture of the Adoration. In BO the group member is there to be lost in oceanic feelings of unity or, if the oneness is personified, to be part of a salvationist inclusion.

With these levels of simplicity, there is little need for personal assessment of whether individual members possess the skills needed for task implementation. Throughout, the member gets his task from the group, and his social role is defined by the group. It may not always be pleasant to be the objector, the interpreter, or the buffoon. But better such roles than none at all, which may be a consequence of membership of a work group. In such a role a member may be missed. Thus, in committee, when the objector is absent, confusion ensues, so that a decision is postponed until he returns, when the matter is quickly settled and the objections promptly overcome.

On the other hand, there are difficulties and unhappinesses. Participation in Ba groups results in individual members' becoming deskilled in varying degrees. Memories become poor. Time sense is impaired: "Some time back somebody said so and so." Living in the here and now seems very difficult, and there is a marked tendency to go back over past events: "What did we do last time?" There is a disturbed location of speaker: "Somebody over there, I forget who, said. . . ." Sentences, especially if they seek to convey an explanation or insight, have to be simple and relatively short. The preference is for the leader to act without the group's having to indicate its action wishes: "How clever he is; see, he knew it all along." Indeed, in a BD group so strong is the wish for magic that all disasters are treated as signs of the most thoughtful planning. If I go to America and leave a group with my assistant, the comment is "See how thoughtful he is? It is all for our own good."

The deskilling of the individual member can be great. Thus, a group of analysts, psychologists, and social workers, all well versed in psychoanalytic theory, meeting for the primary task of studying group processes, on one occasion decided that one of my wrists was swollen, and perhaps my ankles also, and expressed concern. When I suggested that there might be some oedipal significance to this discussion, I was greeted with looks of frank amazement. Very painfully and slowly they gradually reestablished the fact that they had been talking about swollen ankles. Then a member remembered that there was a link between Oedipus and swollen ankles. But they were quite insistent that it was the father who had killed the son. Such deskilling can be in favor of group cohesiveness. For instance, a member of a similar study group commented, "Why is the group wearing black ties?" Only with difficulty did they discover that of the ten people present only three seemed to be wearing black ties and that one of these ostensibly black ties was not black, since it had a dark-purple stripe. The black ties were clearly wanted—in the name of cohesiveness and uniformity.

An additional cause of pain is the concreteness of the situation in these groups. It is not that there is a picture of an angry Dr. Turquet, but that Dr. Turquet is in fact angry. An interpretation from a consultant is often treated as a rebuke: "we have got it wrong again." It may also be treated as a specific instruction to do something. Thus when a whole conference membership of fifty or so, assembled to study intergroup relations, heard the statement, "It seems that in order to carry out this exercise some process of small group formation will have to be thought about," it was taken as an instruction to divide, and the room cleared itself in a matter of seconds. Army commanders of small units are well aware of the dangers arising from the concrete interpretation put on orders. Thus when a platoon pinned down on a machine-gun swept beach, unable to move, was given the order "forward march," the men all stood up and marched, and were killed to the last man. In addition, this concreteness makes the assumption of responsibility particularly difficult and painful.

Nor is the individual member there for his own sake. Like the leader, he is given his role for the fulfillment of the group's purpose, and only for that purpose. If the member oversteps the mark and behaves idiosyncratically, then he is out. Thus, in a psychotheapy group a patient was encouraged to tell her story in the hope that the consultant would demonstrate his skill and do something about her pain. At first she was very inhibited and apologetic, particularly at taking up the group's time, but the group encouraged her to talk. Finally she told the group that after many hesitations because of her sexual shyness, she had accepted an invitation from a man in her office to meet him for a drink. She had arrived a half hour late—which the group accepted as a woman's privilege. Then she said she had been seized by fear, and claiming that she had to make a telephone call, she had slipped out by another door, leaving the man stranded. This proved too idiosyncratic for the group, and she was left for the rest of the session neglected and crying in her corner. Equally, in BF anyone who gets sick is treated as a malingerer, as asserting individual values over and against the group's supremacy. One member, with the group's approval, tried to form a pair with me. He got much encouragement from the group in this new plot, despite my interpretations. The matter turned sour on him when he asked me for a private consultation. Gods can be public but not private. Such groups can be ruthless toward their members; and members can avoid receiving such treatment only by fitting in with the group's roles and requirements.

Consolation for each member would seem to come from the group's undoubted action nature. There is no time for pausing or thinking and no sympathy with such activities. Thinking is referred to as "introspective nonsense," particularly in the BF group, where "Rome is always burning and the work group fiddling." There are frequent statements such as "We are getting nowhere" and "Where does that get us?" Although a group may ostensibly be seeking to understand itself, the consultant's explanations in these circumstances are described as "Our consultant is always blocking us," leading to "We've got to do something." This kind of phenomenon may become acute, as in the general practitioner's surgery with the anxious wife questioning the husband after his visit: "Well, what did he do?" Indeed, often the general practitioner, while having diagnosed his patient's condition as psychological, and after having discussed with him the relevant emotional problem, finds himself forced to give him a bottle of medicine in the name of having done something. To talk is not to do anything.

Such basic-assumption groups, then, are very cohesive and coherent, full of energy and life. They are helped in this by having a structure, though the structure becomes an end in itself. The committee has a treasurer even though the budget is very small. Minutes become laws rather than aids to memory; often the minutes seem written to provide a "full record" rather than a summary of actions taken. The chairman directs and the members rubber-stamp. Members seem to be required to sit in the same chairs. The chairs of absent members are removed to close the ranks, on an "out of sight out of mind" basis, a further example of concreteness. Structure and cohesion are also reinforced by the tendency of these groups to use broad generalizations and cliches. There are to be no divergencies.

WORK GROUPS VERSUS BASIC-ASSUMPTION GROUPS

What then is the relationship between the work group and the basic-assumption group? Here I would suggest the dream as a paradigm. Just as the manifest content of the dream is suffused with latent content, so the work group is constantly suffused with basic-assumption elements. Just as it is impossible to have a dream of manifest content alone, so a pure work group is very rare. On the other hand, it is possible to have a dream of latent content only. So, too, a pure basic-assumption group can come into being and remain in being for some time.

The question of the relationship between the two groups, especially how a work-group atmosphere can be sustained with few lapses into basic-assumption modes of behavior, can be further explored through an examination of the phrase "sophisticated work groups." The sophistication of work groups is expressed in four principal ways.

First, a work group is sophisticated in the use it makes of leadership. The leader of a work group is a "first among equals," having, like the other members of the group, skills for primary-task implementation; he is not the only member of the group who has skills. In Ba groups the leader is believed to be the only one who matters, and is in fact the only one who is listened to; and though other members can be insightful, their contributions remain virtually ignored. The work-group leader's primacy is in defining and maintaining the primary task in relationship to the environment. As new and different facets of the primary task emerge, changes in leadership may be required. For instance, in an operating team, under normal conditions the surgeon is probably in charge. If, however, respiratory embarrassment occurs, the anaesthetist may take over while the surgeon packs the operating site and perhaps acts as assistant to the

Theory: Turquet

anaesthetist. When the respiratory crisis is overcome, the surgeon will again assume the leadership role and continue his operation. Thus, in a sophisticated work group, though there may be shifts in leadership, the nonoperant leader does not become a discarded and rejected member of the group. In contrast, in an Ba group his nonuse amounts to defeat or annihilation—as, for instance, is the case with politicians voted out of executive office. The work group will indeed be anxious to preserve the leader's skills since they are not pure leadership skills but have another component that initially was concerned with the group's primary task, as with the anaesthetist in the operating team. In the Ba group it is a question of sacking and dismissal; in the work group it is a question of shift of emphasis. Furthermore, the need for such shifts is not the responsibility of the leader alone. Members of a work group have also to assess the nature of the leadership required at any particular moment in relation to the discrete aspects of the primary task on hand at that moment. In addition, an outside observer will be able to detect some of the reasons for this shift in leadership in the work group. This is not so with the Ba group, whose leaders come and go for no externally discernible reason, the reasons being purely those of failing to satisfy internal needs.

Second, in contrast to the Ba group, the work group seeks in a sophisticated way to protect the skills of its individual members. Moreover, each member must constantly assess and reassess himself in skill terms for primary-task implementation. Such a reassessment may require the painful decision to withdraw from the work group on the grounds of lack of skill; this is bound to be painful because no one can easily accept the rupture of member-to-member continuity that group life contains. Because of role simplicity, no such self-evaluation is required in Ba groups, and hence that kind of life is less painful. It is a function of the work-group leader to help group members in this type of assessment.

Perhaps, however, the most important area of skill preservation in leadership is over the leader's inalienable right to executive action. The nature and grounds of his decision-making may be questioned, but not his right to make decisions or to ensure their implementation. Ideally, the decision-making process should center around predictions and their testing. In practice no group can afford to wait for definitive certainty, and decisions have to be taken on incomplete knowledge. One aspect, therefore, of the work leader's skill is his capacity to tolerate anxiety and doubt. In this connection very noticeable efforts are often made to deskill the leader by various members of the group, who fill him up with their anxieties and their fantasies. As a result, his threshold for anxiety and doubt may become so lowered that his skill for taking executive action becomes impaired, resulting in his becoming a leader by permission of the group. That is, a Ba group leader may become so involved in the group's internal life that he is no longer able to preserve the necessary boundary between himself as an individual and the group as a whole. He then becomes the prey of the group's action requirements, pausing and thinking together, with work going by the board. Of course, what can happen to the leader by way of filling up can also happen to other members of the group. It is therefore in the mutual interest of all that the skills of all should be preserved. The sophisticated preservation of the leader's skill therefore involves self-containment by each member. Each work-group member has to learn to think in "appraisal" terms and not in "discharge" terms; to extract and appraise the relevant information rather than give an excited discharge through a detailing of all the minutiae of the event. This latter process is Ba-group behavior; in essence, it leaves appraisal to the group leader, and by using "discharge" rather than "appraisal," treats him as akin to a bottomless wastepaper basket. Appraisal requires skill and familiarity with the primary task as well as the exercise of personal responsibility, but without these safeguards, survival of member and leader can be in doubt.

Third, a work group is sophisticated in that it uses predictions. That is to say, the leader furthers the work of the group around testable hypotheses. All successful businesses have predictive aspects—what stocks of which raw materials will be needed when, sales expectations, preparation of budgets, rate of personnel replacement, and so on. Hospitals will develop notions about bed occupancy rates; general practitioners are interested in seasonal morbidity rates and the like. Similarly, in training seminars the leader of the seminar says in essence: "If you do or say so and so, such and such will follow." The most important predictive leader statement is the "because" clause, since the statement that so and so *is*—because of this or that—enables the leader's sense of reality, his "intouchness," to be seen and tested. In the absence of such predictions, a group lapses into hunches or is ruled by one experience. In extreme cases of absence of testable hypotheses, and many an example can be found, Ba ways of life come to dominate such groups. Here universities could be quoted. Predictions at admission are in the main rarely related to the results three or four years later. Worse, little is know about the rejectees—what proportion might have done better than those accepted. In these circumstances, Ba ways of life—with more and more insistence on higher intake standards—tend to take over, with schools accused of not giving these young people the right grounding, though little work is done to demonstrate that universities know how to use the material that is offered them, and little predictive testing is carried out to support their contention that higher standards are needed. Much of the trouble between the so-called schools of psychiatry stems from the absence of testable predictions, so that psychiatric clinics oscillate between BD development toward their patients—trying to give better and better care to more and more sick patients—and BF development toward other clinics, who are treated as foolish rivals who have not seen the light. Indeed, it is not too much to say that the degree of arbitrariness with which a point of view is held, particularly in medicine, is directly related to the extent to which it can be, or has been, tested.

A further essential point here is the time span of predictability; that is, how soon in time can predictions be verified? In a sense, the shorter the time between prediction making and verification, the better placed the group is to adapt and correct its behavior. The longer the time span, the more likely Ba ways of thinking are to develop. Most sales departments have not only annual forecasts but also monthly checks. And similarly, with annual budgets, most firms have cash flow accounting or similar systems. Psychotherapy presents the contrary picture. A time span of three years or more between taking in a patient and thinking about discharge allows the psychotherapeutic institution to go its own way unchecked, so that it becomes more and more devoted to a BD way of life. In fact, it has nothing else.

Fourth and last, the work group seeks to make a sophisticated use of the relevant Ba group for the implementation of its primary task. It seeks to mobilize the relevant Ba group in support of its work, and to keep any Ba group that would be inimical to its primary task, at bay. For instance, a surgical team will seek to mobilize BD through its ward structure, the efficiency of its organization, the calm routine it provides, the detailed preliminary knowledge the doctors, nurses and auxiliaries have of the patient and his circumstances, so that the patient can give himself over to the situation in a trusting, dependent way. Often the BD is reinforced by BP, the patient pairing with a nurse or ward orderly. So, doubly fended off, BF is kept at bay.

There also have to be sophisticated changes in Ba-group mobilization to meet shifts in primary-task implementation. Thus, in schools, too much fighting against the teacher hampers learning. BD is mobilized, as is BP, through individual attention from teacher to single pupils. Most schools in England try to get away from the large classroom teaching situation in favor of smaller groups, where the BD content of the situation can be more adequately controlled. Hence, too, the development of the seminar system in universities. But BD is of no use in the examination situation. It is not realistic to expect the examiner to look after the candidate—or such has been my experience. With medical examinations, for instance, there is a sophisticated mobilization of BF. Back papers are gone over, the pet subjects of the examiners are discovered, and in general the examinations are treated as an enemy offensive, which must be turned back by a strategy based on counterintelligence. BP may also be mobilized through two candidates examining each other.

In addition, the mobilization of Ba-group ways of life helps give to the work group its liveliness, warmth, and sense of cohesion. The inevitable suffusion by Ba elements is thus used constructively by the work group. But only a work group can do this, the sophisticated use of basic-assumption ways of life being an outstanding characteristic of work groups.

A classic example of the sophisticated use of basic-assumption ways in the service of work can be found in Thucydides' *History of the Peloponnesian War*, in connection with that shattering event, the defeat of the Spartans by the Athenians at Sphacteria. The Athenians held the mainland shore at Pylos and the Spartans the island of Sphacteria. The Spartans are about to force a landing and Demosthenes, the Athenian general, addresses his troops thus: "Soldiers, all of us together are in this: I do not want any of you in our present awkward position to try to show off his intelligence by making a precise calculation of the dangers which surround us. Instead we must simply make straight at the enemy and not pause to discuss the matter, confident in our hearts that these dangers too can be surmounted.

For when we are forced into a position like this one, nice calculations are beside the point." Needless to say, he was addressing the intellectual elite of the ancient world; it is to be presumed that Spartans neither needed nor would have understood such language.

THE INDIVIDUAL AND THE GROUP

Essentially, the single individual who joins a group is in a dilemma. He wishes to be part of the group and at the same time to remain a separate, unique individual. He wants to participate, yet observe; to relate, yet not become the other; to join, but to preserve his skills as an individual. He wants the Ba-group way of life for the satisfaction of his own basic-assumption needs, for the security such groups afford, for their simple ways of living, for their recuperative contribution to man's ultimate aim—to establish his uniqueness while maintaining his relatedness to others.

Initially, the individual achieves a sense of belonging through his identification with the leader. The leader helps the joining member to reality-test his perception of the primary task. Joining will be reinforced by the new member's personal affinity for one of the Ba-group ways of life. Therefore, the work group's implicit Ba culture must coincide with the individual's preferred interrelational method of work. Doctors must have an affinity for BD, physicians more so than surgeons. But woe betide the prison governor who expects his prisoners to look after him. He requires a strong "valency" (Bion's term) for BF. A salesman should have a strong liking for BP, since both he and his client have to pair to create the myth that the article is worth buying. The individual's later belongingness depends on work-group satisfactions, the development of his skills in primary-task implementation, and on the satisfaction of his group needs. Moreover—and this is the dangerous element—if his work-group skills are not satisfied, or if he lacks the necessary skills for the primary task, he may be tempted to remain because of this satisfaction of his Ba-group needs.

The individual's apartness from the group is brought about through splitting and projection, projection into an individual group member or into the group as a whole. Hence we see the development of a "nothing to do with me" attitude and a group's capacity to offer the individual opportunities for opting out. The use of these two mechanisms—splitting and projection—has important consequences. They tend to increase the absence of responsibility; responsibility is elsewhere linked to the disowned parts of the self, which are also projected elsewhere. They increase the power of, and hence the dependency on, the leader. For, by projection, the leader becomes the sole repository of power, skills, and reality testing. They also increase the cold, unfriendly, even persecutory nature of the world outside the group, leading to various fears (Will the boundary hold? What will happen when that which has been projected returns?), fears that again increase the strength of the centripetal forces within a Ba group.

And so the single individual struggles. As he leaves the Ba-group way of life, he experiences loss: loss of satisfaction of his needs to belong; loss of a sense of unity, cohesiveness, camaraderie, of being a part of something bigger than himself; loss of a determined, unargued role; and loss of opportunities for action, to "feel" that he is doing something, together with a sense of vitality and excitement. Confronting these losses, he is attracted back into Ba-group ways. And so he oscillates, first leaving Ba-group life and then returning to it, returning to fraternize with death by exclusion from the group, or by nonfulfillment, or idiosyncratic use of a group role, or by attempting to lead—and inevitably dealing with death in ways fit not for high tragedy but more for low comedy, expiring "Not with a bang but a whimper."

And so he pulls out again, to meet loneliness and isolation, to face alone Camus' "Absurdo"; to know things that cannot be shared, to search for what cannot be found; to be solely responsible for his actions, and even more for his knowledge and what he does with it; to have constantly to reassess himself vis-a-vis others, and perhaps to withdraw; to face relatedness with consequences for pain and pleasure; and to experience a future over which he has little control. And so back to the Ba-group life, where the one for whom the bell tolls never seems to be him, and where there is a myth of life and no mention of death. Basic-assumption groups are defenses against death, but like all psychological defenses, Ba-groups have a content, which in fact *is* death. All nonconforming members die of exclusion in the cold outside world. Failure in flight or in fight is death. The not-looked-after group member dies. The Ba-group leader dies, martyred or otherwise, crushed by the impossibility of his task.

What lives on for the support of future generations are the myths the group creates. Bruno Snell has aptly written of the Greek myths: "The reflection which the Greek myths are designed to assist usually produces a greater sense of humility. The majority of paradigms teach men to realize their status as men, the limitations upon their freedom, the conditional nature of their existence. They encourage self-knowledge in the spirit of the Delphic motto 'Know thyself,' they extol measure, order, moderation." Such knowledge and experience, offered through myths, are the ultimate contribution of the Ba group's way of life to man's endeavor.

Many words dominate Greek Tragedy—Sophia, Hubris, Sophrosuno, Time, and Aristeia—but not least in importance is Anake, or necessity: all these unalterable, inescapable facts that constitute the human conditions of living, the double yoke of man's own nature and a world he never made. As Arrowsmith writes: "Necessity is first of all death; but it is also old age, sleep, the reversal of fortune and the dance of life: it is thereby the fact of suffering as well as pleasure, for if we must dance and sleep, we must also suffer, age, and die."

It is Oedipus' necessity—he is Anake—to strive stubbornly, to know and to face the consequences of his knowledge and "by asserting his total, utter responsibility for his own fate, to win victory over a necessity that would have destroyed another man." Thus, Hamlet and the duel scene: "Ripeness is all." The victory is the broadening and deepening of compassion (so Oedipus at Colonnus), compassion experienced as shared suffering that makes men "endure with love in a world which shrieks at them to die," which gives dignity to the human struggle and thus saves it from futility. The Ba group way of life, however brief its occurrence, is a reprieve in this struggle. It gives man a breathing space and enables him to return refreshed by the strength of fraternity to face his aloneness. So refreshed, he endures and survives to demonstrate "the dignity of significant suffering" that alone gives a man his crucial victory over his Anake, his fate—a victory impossible without opportunities for the basic-assumption way of life. Hence man is a "political animal," a fact that, as Bion points out, we neglect at our peril.

6.

REGRESSION IN ORGANIZATIONAL LEADERSHIP

Otto F. Kernberg

The choice of good leaders is a major task for all organizations. Information regarding the prospective administrator's personality should complement questions regarding his previous experience, his general conceptual skills, his technical knowledge, and the specific skills in the area for which he is being selected. The growing psychoanalytic knowledge about the crucial importance of internal, in contrast to external, object relations, and about the mutual relationships of regression in individuals and in groups, constitutes an important practical tool for the selection of leaders.

In an earlier study (Kernberg, 1978) I described the effects of regressive pressures in psychiatric institutions on the administrators of these institutions. There, I pointed out that while crises in organizations often appear at first to be caused by personality problems of the leader, further analysis reveals a more complex situation. Quite frequently, a breakdown in work effectiveness stemming from various internal organizational factors and relationships between the organization and the environment induces regressive group processes first, and regression in the functioning of the leadership later. If these group processes remain undiagnosed, only their end product may be visible, in the form of what appears to be primitive, inadequate leadership and, more specifically, negative effects of the leader's personality on the organization. Thus, leadership problems are not always the real cause of the crisis. In what follows, I turn to the consideration of regressive pressures stemming from within the administrators themselves. At every step I will emphasize the importance of distinguishing between regressive organizational components and regression in the leader.

My approach is intermediate between two positions: (1) the traditional approach, according to which leadership is "inborn"—particularly "charismatic" leadership; (2) the opposite, more recent theoretical thinking, which considers leadership as derived mostly or exclusively from learned skills and understandings. My approach is based on the findings of various authors (Bion, 1961; Dalton et al., 1968; Emery and Trist, 1973; Hodgson et al., 1965; Levinson, 1968; Main, 1957; Miller and Rice, 1967; Rice,

1963, 1965, 1969; Rioch, 1970a,b; Sanford, 1956; and Stanton and Schwartz, 1954). This approach combines (1) a psychoanalytic focus on the personality features of the leader; (2) a psychoanalytic focus on the functions of regressive group processes in organizations, and (3) an open-systems-theory approach to organizational management. All three aspects interact dynamically, and the origin of failure or breakdown of functioning of individuals, groups, or the organization at large may lie in any one or several of these areas.

THE PSYCHOANALYTICALLY TRAINED CONSULTANT TO ORGANIZATIONS

Consultants are usually called at times of crisis, but the nature of their task is not always clear: an organization may use a consultant to escape from full awareness and resolution of a problem as much as to diagnose realistically the problem and its potential solutions (Rogers, 1973). The consultant's first task is to clarify the nature of his contract and to assure himself that the resources to carry it out are adequate. This means not only sufficient time and financial support, but necessary authority to examine problems at all levels of the organizational structure.

It goes almost without saying that support from the top leader of the organization is essential. The consultant needs to be sufficiently independent from the organization to be able to reach his conclusions without excessive fears of antagonizing the leader; therefore, he must not be too dependent on any one particular client.

One main question that needs to be formulated is whether a certain conflict within the organization represents a problem stemming from: (1) "personality issues"; (2) the nature of the task of the organization and its constraints; or (3) "morale"—that is, group processes within the organization. The nature of the problem is often described in such confused and confusing terms that a translation into these three domains is difficult.

It is helpful to focus first on the nature of the organizational tasks and their constraints, for only after task definition has been achieved, the respective constraints have been outlined, and priorities have been set up regarding primary and secondary tasks and constraints, is it possible to evaluate whether the administrative structure does, indeed, fit with the nature of the tasks, and if not, how it should be modified. This analysis requires the clarification of the organization's real tasks in contrast to its apparent ones. In one psychiatric hospital, the apparent task was to treat patients and to carry out research, but the real task seemed to be to provide the owners of the institution with an adequate return on their investment. In actuality, the interest in research represented wishes to obtain funding from external sources with which to cover part of staff salaries, and the treatment of patients constituted a constraint on the real task.

Once tasks and constraints have been defined, questions regarding the administrative structure required for task performance can be examined. Does the organization have effective control over its boundaries, and if not, what administrative compensating mechanisms can be established to

Regression in Organizational Leadership

restore boundary control? One psychiatric organization depended on one institution for its administrative-support funding, and on another for its funding for professional staffing. Chronic fights between administrators and professionals throughout the entire organization reflected the lack of resolution of boundary control at the top. The consultant's recommendation that all funding be channeled into a central hospital administration, directed by a professional with administrative expertise, became acceptable to both funding institutions and to the staff at large, and provided the organizational solution to the "morale" problem that had prompted the request for consultation.

Once boundary control seems adequate, the nature of delegation of authority in the institution and each task system can be studied. Inadequate, fluctuating, ambiguous, or nonexisting delegation on the one hand, and excessive, chaotic delegation on the other, are problems that have to be solved as part of the redefinition of the administrative structure in terms of task requirements.

Having diagnosed the overall task and its constraints, and, it is hoped, corrected the respective administrative structures, it is possible to focus on the nature of the leadership, and more concretely, on the qualities of the leader himself. The consultant should attempt to diagnose the personality qualities of the administrator that influence the organizational functioning (which will be elaborated in the third section of this paper), the regressive pulls that the leader is subjected to from group processes in the organization, and his own contributions to such regressive group processes. What kind of intermediate management has the leader assembled? How much understanding in depth does he have for people, their assets and liabilities? How much tolerance of criticism, strength and yet warmth, flexibility and yet firmness and clarity, does he have in his relation to staff? The accuracy and quality of the leader's judgment of those around him is a crucial indicator, not only of his administrative skills, but of his personality as a whole. What are his reactions under stress? In which direction does his personality regress under critical conditions? The strength of his convictions, the presence or absence of his envy of staff, the extent of his moral integrity and courage—these are usually surprisingly well known throughout the organization.

The psychoanalytic exploration of group processes in the organization may become a crucial instrument for the evaluation of problems in both the administrative structure and the personality of the leader. The regressive nature of group processes in psychiatric organizations—"morale"—may reflect conflicts in the organizational structure, the impact of the leader's personality, the regressive pull directly induced by the pressure of patients' conflicts, or combinations of these factors. The closer the observed group processes are to the actual work with patients, the more the patients' conflicts will directly influence the development of regressive group processes within staff and the staff/patient community generally. The closer the observed staff groups are to the final decision-making authority at the top, the more the conflicts of top leadership and of organizational structure will dominate. However, it is impressive how the conflicts affecting the total organization are reflected in actual group processes at all levels. Therefore, the careful observation of group processes at various administrative levels constitutes a kind of "organizational projective test battery," which may give the direct information needed to clarify problems at the levels of task definition and constraints, patients, administrative structure, and leadership, all in one stroke.

The accuracy of the diagnosis arrived at by the consultant can be tested when measures geared to restore a functional administrative structure to the organization are instituted. For example, the shift in functioning of the administrative leadership when there is a redefinition of primary tasks and constraints should improve morale throughout the organization in a relatively short period of time. The restoration of a functional structure—in contrast to an authoritarian structure brought about by distortions of the hierarchical network of power—may effect almost immediate positive changes.

For practical purposes, the consultant usually obtains most helpful information from the active participation of senior and intermediate management in a free and open discussion of issues, within a group atmosphere that permits some exploration of group processes as well as of the actual content of the administrative problems under examination. The consultant's diagnosis of the problems of top leadership and intermediate management should include an evaluation of the human resources in the organization. Because human resources are the primary potential assets of organizations, the degree of intactness of senior leadership has an important prognostic implication.

When the conclusion reached is that the leader's personality problems or his general incompetence resulting from lack of technical knowledge, conceptual limitations, or administrative inadequacies are involved, the question arises of whether he can be helped to change, or whether he should be helped to leave his job. There are no obvious answers to this question. Leaders may sometimes be helped to improve their functioning by reducing the regressive pulls on them stemming from group processes in the organization. Improvement in task definition, task performance, boundary controls, and the administrative structure as a whole, may all bring out the leader's positive assets and reduce the negative impact of his personality characteristics. Increase in gratification of his emotional needs (in the areas of aggression, sex, or dependency) outside of the organizational structure may sometimes help. At other times, the best solution seems to be to help him step down by either changing his professional functions or moving him geographically within the organization—if such alternatives are available.

Although such a recommendation—that he resign—is always a serious narcissistic blow, it often happens that deep down the administrator knows that he has not been able to do his job well, and he may feel relieved when someone from the outside confronts him with that reality. On the other hand, when the consultant arrives at the conclusion that the organization has a bad leader at the top, the consultant might discreetly withdraw (or be discreetly asked to withdraw).

The situation is different, of course, when the problem involves an administrator at some lower hierarchical level. When this is the case, top leadership needs to be helped in understanding that firmness in eliminating bad situations is indispensable for the health of the organization at large. To help a man who cannot do his job to leave may seem aggressive or even sadistic to his superior; but it is usually more sadistic to leave a bad leader in charge of an organizational structure than to ask him to change his functions. The suffering induced in staff by a bad leader should be a primary concern of the top leader. Optimal leadership sometimes implies hard decisions, and at times, unfortunately, the leader must be able to be very firm and decisive with somebody who may be a close personal friend.

There are times when the problem can be diagnosed but for some reason cannot be resolved. Some organizations function as if they were geared to self-destruction, unable and unwilling to accept positive change. This is a dramatic situation for a consultant and, of course, much more dramatic for the staff of the organization. One important use of an understanding of organizational structure and conflict may be the possibility for staff, particularly senior staff who are able to obtain an overview of the situation to diagnose the organizational conflicts and even their sources, and reach realistic conclusions about the prognosis and, therefore, their personal future.

There are certain situations that are so bad that the only solution is for self-respecting staff to leave; in other words, there is such a thing as a "poisonous" organizational environment that is bad for everybody in it. It is impressive how often staff developing within such a destructive environment deny to themselves the insoluble nature of the problems of the organization and obtain gratification of pathological dependency needs by denial and failure to admit the need to move on. Understanding organizations in depth can be painful; at times, awareness does not improve the effectiveness of staff members; but understanding always makes it possible to gain a more realistic, even if painful, grasp of what the future probably will be. The parallel to the painful learning about some aspects of one's unconscious in a psychoanalytic situation is implicit here: there are pathological defenses against becoming aware of what the reality is about the place where one works. At some point, the individual has a responsibility to himself that transcends that to the organization; and knowledge of organizational conflicts may permit him to reach more quickly an understanding of what that point is and where his personal boundaries are threatened by an organization from which he should withdraw.

Under less extreme circumstances, there is much that an educated, task-oriented staff can do to help its leadership correct or undo distorted administrative structures and reduce the effects of pathology of top leadership. The staff in positions of intermediate management may be of particular help to the organization and the top administrator in preserving functional administrative relationships by open sharing of communication and of analysis of the situation. In this regard, the responsibility of followers in not perpetuating and exacerbating the problems of the leader cannot be over-emphasized.

Disruption of functional administration always brings about regression to "basic group assumptions." I refer here to Bion's (1959) "basic assumptions" groups: "dependency," "fight-flight," and "pairing," which become activated when groups—and organizations—do not function adequately. Such regressive phenomena in groups involving intermediate leadership and staff at large may reinforce the personality difficulties of individual staff members and reduce their awareness of the need for change or their willingness to fight for it. If individual staff members courageously spell out what the situation is, it may have a positive therapeutic effect in increasing rational behavior throughout the organization; in such instances, helpfulness emerges from a functional attitude of criticism based not upon "fight-flight" assumptions but upon a genuine interest in helping the leader and staff generally to improve their understanding and functioning in the organization. Open communication among the intermediate management group may also help reduce their mutual suspicion and distrust and their fear of speaking up. An alliance for the sake of the functional needs of the organization is a good example of political struggle in terms of the task, rather than in terms of perpetuating the distortions in the distribution of authority and power.

For the top administrator, particularly at a time of crisis when uncertainty is increased for him and everyone else, the availability of senior staff who are willing to speak up openly and responsibly, without excessive distortion by fear or anger, can be very reassuring. A mutual reinforcement between staff who are able and willing to provide new information to the leader and a leader who encourages such staff action may strengthen the task group throughout.

"Participatory management" as a general principle is an important protection against regressive effects of the leader's personality on the administrative structure. A variety of factors affect the general question of what degree of participatory management, or what degree of centralized decision-making is required. When a distortion of the administrative structure has occurred under the impact of regressive pulls on top leadership, from whatever source, increasing participative management is indicated. Such an emphasis on participatory decision-making does not mean a replacement of a functional by a "democratic" structure. Flexibility is necessary regarding the extent to which the organization shifts back and forth from centralized to participatory management; at periods of rapid environmental change, of crisis or "turbulence" in the external environment, there may be a need for increased centralized decision-making. At times of external stability, increased decentralization and participatory management may be helpful. Internal change often requires participatory management, especially in the preparatory or early stages of change. A centralized, simplified administrative structure may become functional in times of internal consolidation or stability.

AUTHORITARIAN PERSONALITY AND AUTHORITARIAN ORGANIZATIONAL STRUCTURE

Adorno and his co-workers (1950) have described the "authoritarian personality" as follows: He tends to be overconventional, rigidly adhering to middle-class values, and oversensitive to external social pressures; he is inappropriately submissive to conventional authority, and at the same time, extremely punitive to those who oppose such authority and to those under him; he is generally opposed to feelings, fantasies, and introspection, and tends to shift responsibility from the individual onto outside forces; he is stereotyped, thinking rigidly and simplistically in terms of black and white; he tends to exercise power for its own sake and admires power in others; he is destructive and cynical, rationalizing his aggression toward others; he tends to project onto others—particularly "out-groups"—his own unacceptable impulses; and finally, he is rigid with regard to sexual morality.

While Adorno and his co-workers applied psychoanalytic concepts to study the metapsychological determinants of such a personality structure, in their methods and clinical analyses they combined both personality and sociological criteria: their authoritarian personality structure seems to me a composite formation, which reflects various types of character pathology exacerbated by authoritarian pressures exerted by social, political, and cultural systems. In my view, within the restricted frame of reference of the study of leadership of psychiatric institutions, the social, cultural, and political issues may be relatively less important than the mutual reinforcement of authoritarian pressures derived from the institutional structure and from various types of character pathology that contribute to authoritarian leadership behavior. In what follows, I explore the pathological contributions of specific personality characteristics of the leader to the development of authoritarian pressures throughout the organizational structure. However, I wish to emphasize again that a leader's authoritarian behavior may stem from features of the organizational structure, and not necessarily from his personality.

Sanford (1956) has pointed out the necessity to distinguish between authoritarian behavior in leadership roles and authoritarianism in the personality, and that the two do not necessarily go together. An authoritarian administrative structure is one that is invested with more power than is necessary to carry out its functions, whereas a functional structure is one where persons and groups in position of authority are invested with adequate—but not excessive—power.

The adequate power invested in the leadership in a functional structure usually receives reinforcement from social and/or legal sanctions. Authoritarian behavior that exceeds functional needs must be differentiated from authoritative behavior that represents functionally adequate or necessary exercise of authority. In practice, authority—the right and capacity to carry out task leadership—stems from various sources (Rogers, 1973). Managerial authority refers to that part of the leader's authority that has been delegated to him by the institution he works in. Leadership authority refers to that aspect of his authority derived from the recognition his followers have of his capacity to carry out the task. Managerial and leadership authority reinforce each other; both are, in turn, dependent upon other sources of authority, such as the leader's technical knowledge, his personality characteristics, his human skills, and social tasks and responsibilities he assumes outside and beyond the institution. The administrator is responsible not only to his institution but also to his staff, to his professional and ethical values, to the community, and to society at large: responsibility and accountability represent the reciprocal function of the administrator to the sources of his delegated authority. In addition, because of his personality characteristics, or because he belongs to special groups or to political structures that invest him with power unrelated to his strictly technical functions, the leader may accumulate power beyond that required by his functional authority—the excessive power that constitutes the basis for an authoritarian structure.

In contrasting an authoritarian administrative structure with a functional administrative structure, I am emphasizing the opposition between authoritarian and functional structure, not that between authoritarian and democratic structure. This point is important from both theoretical and practical viewpoints. A tendency exists in some professional institutions—and psychiatric institutions are no exception—to attempt to modify, correct, or resolve by means of democratic political processes problems created by an authoritarian structure. Attempts are made to arrive at corrective decisions in a participatory or representative decision-making process. Insofar as those involved in actual tasks should, indeed, participate in the decision-making process, such "democratization" is helpful; but where decision-making veers toward being determined on a political rather than on a task-oriented basis, distortions of the task structure and of the entire administrative structure may occur. These are extremely detrimental to the work being carried out, and eventually may even reinforce the authoritarian structure they are intended to correct. In addition, the attempt to correct authoritarian distortions by political means leads to the neglect of a functional analysis of the problem. This is certainly a temptation for top leadership: by means of political management or manipulation, they may be able to dominate the negotiations across task boundaries. If so, they may come to rely more and more on the exercise of political power, eventually focusing almost exclusively on the increment or protection of their power base and neglecting the functional interests of the institution.

SOME FREQUENT PATHOLOGICAL CHARACTER STRUCTURES IN THE ADMINISTRATOR

Schizoid Personality Features

Schizoid personality features may, in themselves, protect the leader against excessive regression—his emotional isolation makes him less pervious to regressive group processes. However, the proliferation of distorted fantasies about him is hard to correct because of his distance and unavailability. An excessively schizoid leader may also frustrate the appropriate dependency needs of his staff; usually, however, schizoid leadership at the top tends to be compensated by the warmth and extroversion of managerial figures at the intermediate level.

A very schizoid head of one department of psychiatry conveyed the impression that "no one was running the place"; most authority for daily operations had been delegated to the director of clinical services, who was seen as the actual leader of staff, and who, because of his excellent capacity for carrying out the boundary functions between the department head and the staff, did indeed fulfill important leadership functions. However, the needs of the senior staff for mutual support, warmth, and understanding were not met, and the atmosphere of each being on his own was transmitted throughout the entire institution. Although this department was considered a place with ample room for independent, autonomous growth of staff "if one had it within oneself," a considerable number of staff members were not able to work in this relative human isolation and decided to leave.

In another institution, a markedly schizoid hospital director was insufficiently explicit and direct in the decision-making process, and this created ambiguity with regard to delegation of authority. Nobody knew for sure how much authority was vested in any particular person, and nobody cared to commit himself to anything without repeated consultations with the director. This produced excessive cautiousness, hypersensitivity, and politicization about making decisions throughout the organization. Eventually, the message was conveyed that one had to become a very skilled and tactful manipulator to get ahead in that department, and that direct emotional expression was very risky. Thus, the leader's personality characteristics, through group interactions, filtered down and became characteristic of the entire organization.

Obsessive Personality Features

Obsessive personality features in top leadership are quite frequent. On the positive side, the focus on orderliness, precision, clarity, and control may foster good, stable delegation of authority and clarity in the decision-making process. Contrary to what one would expect, there is usually very little doubtfulness in obsessive personalities in leadership positions; severely obsessive personalities usually don't reach top positions when excessive doubt and hesitation are their predominant characteristics. Chronic indecisiveness in the administrator may have obsessive origins; however, chronic indecisiveness at the top is most frequently really a consequence of the leader's narcissistic problems. Obsessive personalities, then, usually function rather efficiently from an organizational viewpoint. Their clear stand on issues and commitment to values have important creative functions for the institution at large.

On the negative side, some dangers are the leader's excessive need for order and precision, his need to be in control, and the expression of the sadistic components that often go with an obsessive personality. An inordinate need for orderliness and control may reinforce the bureaucratic components of the organization—that is, encourage decision-making on the basis of rules and regulations and rather mechanized practices, all of which may interfere with the creativeness of staff and with appropriate autonomy in the decision-making process at points of rapid change or crises. Excessive bureaucratization may at times protect the organization from political struggle, but it reinforces passive resistance in the negotiations across boundaries and fosters misuse of resources.

Because pathological defensive mechanisms and, particularly, pathological character traits of the leader tend to be activated in times of stress, an increase in obsessive perfectionism and pedantic style may characterize the obsessive leader at critical moments. This may create additional stress for the organization at a time when rapid and effective decision-making is required. An educated awareness in the staff that under such conditions it is necessary to protect the security system of the leader in order to get the work done may be very helpful. This, of course, is true for the effects of pathological character features of any kind in the leader, and to know how to help him in times of crises is a basic skill demanded of intermediate management.

A major problem created by some obsessive personalities in leadership positions is that of severe, unresolved sadism. The need to sadistically control subordinates may have devastating effects on the functional structure of the organization. Whenever there is strong opposition among staff to a certain move by the administrator, he may become obstinate and controlling, revengefully "rubbing the message in," and forcing his "opponents" again and again into submission. Such behavior reinforces irrational fears of authority and the distortion of role-perception in the staff; it also fosters a submissiveness to hierarchial superiors, which reduces effective feedback and creative participation from the entire staff.

The end result may be the development of chronic passivity, a pseudodependency derived from fear of authority rather than from an authentic "dependent" group, and a transmission of authoritarian, dictatorial ways of dealing with staff and patients in the whole institution. In one department of psychiatry, the appointment of an obsessive and sadistic director drove the most creative members of the senior professional leadership away from the institution within a year and brought about consolidation around the leader of a group of rather weak, inhibited, or mediocre professionals who were willing to pay the price of sacrificing their autonomous professional development for the security and stability afforded them by submission to the leader. The repetition of these conflicts approximately a year later at the next lower level of organizational hierarchy, however, created such a combination of general "fight-flight" grouping and overall breakdown in carrying out organizational tasks that the administrator was finally removed by the combined efforts of staff at large.

Paranoid Personalities

Paranoid personalities always present a serious potential danger for the functional relationships that administrators must establish with their staff.

The development of "fight-flight" conditions in the group processes throughout the organization—a development that may occur even in the most efficiently functioning organization from time to time—may propel into the foreground a "leader of the opposition." With the silent tolerance or unconscious collusion of the majority of staff, a violent attack on the administration by this opposition leader may induce the top leader to regress into paranoid attitudes, even if he does not have any particularly paranoid traits. In other words, there is always a potential—particularly in large organizations with several levels of hierarchy—for suspiciousness, for temptations to exert sadistic control, and for the projection of the administrator's rage onto staff. When the administrator also has strong paranoid character features, the danger of paranoid reactions to "fight-flight" conditions is intensified, and he may perceive even ordinary discussions or minor opposition as dangerous rebelliousness and potential hidden attacks. The need to suppress and control the opposition, which we saw in the obsessive leader with sadistic trends, becomes paramount in the paranoid leader. Because of the ease with which the leader may interpret what "they say" as lack of respect, mistreatment, and hidden hostility toward him, staff now may become afraid of speaking up. Staff's fearfulness, in turn, may increase the administrator's suspiciousness, thus generating a vicious circle.

Because paranoid personalities are particularly suitable to take on the leadership of basic-assumption groups in a "fight-flight" position, the "leader of the opposition" is often a person with strong paranoid tendencies. This does not mean that all leaders of revolutions are paranoid personalities, but that because of the nature of their psychopathology, paranoid personalities may function much more appropriately under such revolutionary conditions. The fighting "in-group" that they represent becames "all good," and the external groups or the general environment they fight becomes "all bad." The successful projection of all aggression outside the boundaries of the group he controls permits the paranoid oppositional leader to function more effectively within the boundaries of his group, even though at the cost of an important degree of distortion of perception of external reality. But when such a paranoid leader takes over control of the organization, the very characteristics that helped him gain leadership of the "fight-flight" group may become very damaging to the institution. The tendency to project all hostility outside—that is, to see the inside of the institution as good and the environment as bad—may temporarily help to protect the good relations between the leader and his followers; in the long run, however, the price paid for this is institutionalization of paranoid distortions of perceptions of external reality, distortions in the boundary negotiations between the institution and its environment, and the possibility that the leader's capacity to carry out his organizational tasks will break down. Within the organization, the revengeful persecution of those the paranoid leader suspects of being potential enemies may eliminate creative criticism to a much larger extent than in the case of obsessive personalities with sadistic features.

Theory: Kernberg

The director of one psychiatric institution that functioned closely with several other psychiatric institutions felt chronically endangered by what he saw as the power plays of the directors of the other institutions against him. At first he appealed to his own staff for help and support, and temporarily morale improved as they all felt united against the external enemy. Eventually, however, by constantly antagonizing leaders and representatives of the other institutions, the director became less able to carry out his functions in representation of his own institution, and started to blame subordinates within his own system for his difficulties in obtaining the necessary space, staff, funding, and community influence. He began to suspect some of the members of intermediate management of his own institution of having "sold out to the enemy," further reducing the effectiveness of his institution vis-a-vis its professional environment. The situation reached a final equilibrium by a protective transformation of the boundaries of the institution into a true barrier, behind which it isolated itself from the local community and redefined its task in terms of a regional chain of institutions to which it belonged.

The following example, in contrast, illustrates the resolution of paranoid regression induced by "fight-flight" conditions in an organizational leader without paranoid personality characteristics. The director of one hospital was very suspicious and upset over a senior member of his staff, Dr. B, who seemed to challenge him at all professional meetings. The director saw Dr. B as a severely paranoid character whose group behavior was splitting staff and potentially damaging the organization, and who perhaps should not continue on the staff. He nevertheless accepted other staff members' judgment that Dr. B was a good clinician and was providing valuable services to the hospital. A consultant recommended to the director that he meet privately with Dr. B and discuss his group behavior. The director did so and discovered that Dr. B was much more open and flexible in individual meetings than in group situations. But the challenging behavior continued in groups and the director now concluded that regardless of the personality characteristics of the "leader of the opposition," a group process must be fostering his contentious behavior and that a study of this particular organizational area was indicated. In the course of the ensuing study, it became apparent that there were serious conflicts within the institution that had reduced the effectiveness of the professional group to which Dr. B belonged, so that "fight-flight" assumptions chronically predominated among them and induced Dr. B into the role of their leader. Analysis of the organizational problem involved led to resolution of the conflicts concerning the entire professional group; Dr. B, finding himself no longer supported by the "silent consensus" and actively discouraged by the group itself, finally stopped dominating group discussions.

Narcissistic Personality Features

Of the dangers to institutions stemming from the leader's character pathology, narcissistic personality features are perhaps the most serious of all. I must stress that I am using the concept of narcissistic personality in a restrictive sense, referring to persons whose interpersonal relations are characterized by excessive self-reference and self-centeredness; whose grandiosity and overvaluation of themselves exist together with feelings of inferiority; who are overdependent on external admiration, emotionally shallow, intensely envious, and both depreciatory and exploitative in their relations with others (Kernberg, 1970, 1974).

The inordinate self-centeredness and grandiosity of these persons is in dramatic contrast to their chronic potential for envy of others. Their inability to evaluate themselves and others in depth brings about a lack of capacity for empathy and for sophisticated discrimination of other people, all of which may become very damaging when they occupy leadership positions. In addition, when external gratifications fail to come forth, or under conditions of severe frustration or failure, they may develop paranoid trends, rather than depression and a sense of personal failure. Such paranoid tendencies reinforce even further the damaging impact on the organization of the leader's narcissistic character structure.

Because narcissistic personalities are often driven by intense needs for power and prestige to assume positions of authority and leadership, individuals with such characteristics are found rather frequently in top leadership positions. They are often men of high intelligence, hard-working and eminently talented or capable in their field, but with narcissistic needs that dramatically neutralize or destroy their creative potential for the organization.

Pathologically narcissistic people aspire to positions of leadership more for their power and prestige—as a source of admiration and narcissistic gratification from staff and from the external environment—than because of commitment to a certain task or ideal represented by the functions carried out by the institution. As a consequence, they may neglect the functional requirements of leadership, the human needs and constraints involved in the work, and the value systems that constitute one of the important boundaries against which administrative and technical responsibilities have to be measured. Leaders with narcissistic personalities are unaware of a variety of pathological human relations that they foster around themselves and throughout the entire organization as their personalities affect administrative structures and functions at large.

In contrast to leaders with pathological obsessive and paranoid features, the narcissistic leader not only requires submission from staff, but also wants to be loved by them. He not only fosters but artificially increases the staff's normal tendency to depend on and idealize the leader; as staff become aware how important it is for the administrator to receive their unconditional, repetitive expression or demonstration of love and admiration, adulation and flattery become constant features of the process of communication with him.

Before proceeding further, it must be emphasized that the negative influence of pathological narcissism has to be differentiated from the normal narcissistic manifestations that are part of the gratifications of any position of responsibility and leadership, gratifications that may be the source of increased effectiveness in leadership as well as a compensation for administrative frustrations. I have examined the differences between normal and pathological narcissism in earlier works (Kernberg, 1970, 1974) and will limit myself to outlining some of these differences as they apply to the person in the leadership position.

Administration and leadership positions in general provide many sources of gratification for narcissistic needs for success, power, prestige, and admiration. Under optimal circumstances these needs have been integrated into mature ego-goals and the need to live up to a mature ego-ideal and superego standards. Normal narcissistic gratifications have mature qualities; for example, the nature of normal self-love is enlightened and deep, in contrast to childlike and shallow self-aggrandizement; normal self-love goes hand in hand with commitments to ideals and values and the capacity for love of and investment in others.

Under optimal circumstances, the leader of a psychiatric institution may obtain normal narcissistic gratification from being able to develop an ideal department or hospital, opportunities for professional growth and development of staff, scientific progress, organizational and administrative effectiveness, and above all, the best possible treatment for the patients in the institution's care. Narcissistic gratifications also come from the administrator's awareness that he can help to provide gratification with their work for the people involved in his institution, which fosters their self-respect, and can contribute to broad goals representing social and cultural value systems. In other words, striving for a position of leadership may involve idealism and altruism intimately linked with normal narcissism.

With pathological narcissism, in contrast, the narcissistic leader's aspirations center around primitive power over others, inordinate reception of admiration and awe, and the wishes to be admired for personal attractiveness, charm, and brilliance, rather than for mature human qualities, moral integrity, and creativity in providing task-oriented, professional and administrative leadership. Under conditions of pathological narcissism, the leader's tolerance for the normal, unavoidable frustrations that go with his position is low, and a number of pathological developments take place within him, in his interactions with staff, and throughout the entire organizational structure.

Above all, the preeminence of unconscious and conscious envy has very detrimental consequences for the relations between him and his staff. Insofar as he cannot tolerate the success and gratification that others obtain from their work, and cannot accept professional success of others that he sees as overshadowing or threatening his own, the narcissistic administrator may become very resentful of the most creative of his staff. Narcissistic personalities may often be very helpful to trainees or junior members of the staff, whose development they foster because they unconsciously represent extensions of the leader's own grandiose self. When these younger colleagues reach a point in their development in which they become autonomous and independent, however, the leader's previous support may shift into devaluation and relentless undermining of their work.

For example, a narcissistic mental health professional who assumes administrative functions that interfere with his clinical or research interests may envy those of his colleagues who continue developing their clinical identity. One solution in such instances—which are fairly common—is for the senior administrator to obtain his narcissistic gratification from developing administration as his theoretical or practical specialized expertise, or to have some professional area other than his administrative work where he can continue doing creative work on his own.

It is part of normal narcissism to be able to enjoy the happiness and triumph of those one has helped to develop; enjoyment of the work and success of others—a general characteristic of the normal overcoming of infantile envy and jealousy—is an important function that is missing in the narcissistic personality. The narcissistic administrator may also envy some on his staff for the strength of their professional convictions; it is one of the tragedies of narcissistic personalities that their very lack of human values in depth brings about a chronic deterioration of those value systems and convictions that they do have.

Another consequence of pathological narcissism stems from the encouragement of submissiveness in staff. Since narcissistic leaders tend to surround themselves with "yes men" and shrewd manipulators who play into their narcissistic needs, more honest and therefore occasionally critical members of the staff are pushed onto the periphery and eventually may constitute a relatively silent, but dissatisfied and critical opposition. The dependent group of admirers further corrodes the administrator's self-awareness and fosters in him additional narcissistic deterioration.

The narcissistic leader might depreciate those he perceives as adulating him, but he cannot do without them; and his respect for the integrity of those who criticize him gradually erodes into paranoid fears. In terms of internalized object relations, it is as if the narcissistic leader induces in the human network of the organization a replication of his internal world of objects populated only by devalued, shadowy images of others and by images of dangerous potential enemies.

The narcissistic leader's inability to judge people in depth is a consequence of his pathology of internalized object relations. It stems both from the narcissistic personality's tendencies to achieve "part object" rather than "total object" relations (Kernberg, 1967, 1970) and from his lack of commitment to professional values and to value systems in general. The narcissistic administrator therefore tends to judge people by superficial impressions of their behavior, in terms of their past "prestige" or out of political considerations, rather than by a mature judgment of the nature of the task, the nature of the person required to carry it out, and the personality and knowledge of the one involved. The inability to judge people in depth and the reliance on people who play into the administrator's needs for admiration reinforce each other and bring about the danger that eventually the narcissistic leader will be surrounded by people similar to himself, people suffering from serious behavior disorders or cynically exploiting their awareness of his psychological needs.

Paradoxically, in large institutions the worse the distortion of the administrative structure by the leader's narcissistic pathology, the more compensating mechanisms may develop in the form of breakdown of boundary control and boundary negotiations, so that some institutional functions may actually go "underground," or in more general terms, become split off from the rest of the organization. It is as if a parallel existed here to what happens in some cases of severe psychopathology, when generalized splitting or primitive dissociation of the ego permits the patient to maintain some semblance of adaptation to external reality at the price of fragmentation of his ego identity. However, the general thesis still stands that the overall creativity of the organization suffers severely under such excessively narcissistic leadership. Although in the short run the grandiosity and expensiveness of the narcissistic leader may transmit itself throughout the organization as a pressure to work or as "charismatic" excitement and bring about a spurt of productivity, in the long run the deteriorating effects of pathological narcissism predominate. They tend to drown creativity in sweeping dependency or in the cynicism that develops among those in the organization with the greatest knowledge and strongest convictions.

When the institution directed by a narcissistic leader is small, the negative effects may be overwhelming from the beginning, for everybody is directly affected by the leader's problems. The development of understanding is hampered by the leader's constant doubts and uncertainty over everything—doubts derived from unconscious envy, devaluation, and lack of conviction—and by his need to change constantly his interests as he loses the enthusiasm for what is no longer new and exciting. The narcissistic leader's incapacity to provide gratification of realistic dependency needs of staff—in the simplest terms, his incapacity really to listen—frustrates staff's basic emotional needs and at the same time strengthens the negative consequences of the distortions in group processes: the submissive and dependent in-group and the depressed and angry out-group mentioned before.

Severely narcissistic leaders whose ambition is frustrated by the external reality of the organization may require so much additional support from their staff that most energy is spent in attempts to restore the leader's emotional equilibrium. In one department of psychiatry, the chairman had reached this position at an early stage of his career, when he seemingly was one of the promising members of his generation; however, he had progressively lost his professional leadership functions and had become chronically embittered and depressed. After a number of years, those senior staff members who remained saw it as their principal organizational task to protect the leader from unnecessary stress and narcissistic lesions, and to stimulate his capacities by ongoing applause and rewards. As a result, the general productivity of the department decreased noticeably.

At times, it is amazing and really encouraging to observe how staff members of institutions directed by a narcissistic leader may keep up their personal integrity, autonomy, and independence in spite of the corrupting influence of their immediate environment. These isolated members may provide an outside consultant with the most meaningful information about the organization's "hidden agendas" and preserve the hope for change in the midst of general despondency. It is as if the social situation of the institution were reflecting the intrapsychic life of narcissistic personalities—with fragments of healthy ego floating in the midst of a sea of deteriorated internalized object relations. Although narcissistic leaders often irradiate a quality of personal prominence and of messianic suggestibility, and have the capacity to stimulate the group's identification with the leader's confidence in himself, not all narcissistic leaders are charismatic and not all charismatic leaders are narcissistic. Personal charisma may stem from a combination of various personality traits and may be imbedded in strength of technical, moral, and human convictions. Sometimes staff accuse a strong and committed leader of being "narcissistic" when in reality they are projecting onto him their own frustrated narcissistic aims and expressing envy of the successful man. The "consensus" leader—whom Zaleznik (1974) has contrasted with the "charismatic" one—may also present either severe narcissistic or normal personality characteristics. One has to differentiate the mature "consensus" leader, who has the capacity to explore the thinking of his staff and to use creatively the understanding and skills of his administrative group for carrying out the task, from the power-oriented, smoothly functioning, politically opportunistic, narcissistic "consensus" leader, who shrewdly exploits group phenomena for his narcissistic aims.

There is a special kind of narcissistic leader whose gratifications come mostly from keeping himself in the center of everybody's love, and at the same time in the center of the decision-making process, while he coolly sacrifices any considerations regarding value systems or the organization's functional needs to what is politically expedient. The typical example is the leader who is a "nice guy" with no enemies, who seems slightly insecure and easily changeable, and who at the time is extremely expert in turning all conflicts among his staff into fights that do not involve himself. The general narcissistic qualities of shallowness, inability to judge people sensitively, inability to commit oneself to any values, are dramatically evident in his case, but what seems to be missing is the direct expression of grandiosity and the need to obtain immediate gratification from other people's admiration. At times this kind of leader obtains the gratification from his position by using it as a source of power and prestige beyond the organization itself. He may let the organization run its own course, trying to keep things smooth, so long as his power base is stable.

A somewhat similar outcome may stem from a different type of personality structure—namely, that of individuals with strong reaction formations against primitive sadistic trends. In this case, the direct friendliness of the leader in his relations with his immediate subordinates is in contrast to violent conflicts within the level below that of his immediate administrative group. Still another type of consensus leader has achieved his position on the basis of his technical or professional skills, and has been willing to accept the position without ever fully assuming the responsibilities it entails. This is one of the conditions leading to an essentially leaderless organization: the man at the top is really more interested in a particular work of his own than in developing authentic leadership, and for that reason stays away from the painful process of making hard decisions. In summary, both charismatic and consensus leadership may stem from various normal and pathological sources.

One major question that can be affected by pathological narcissism is the perennial one of when to compromise and when to stick to one's convictions in any particular conflict. At one extreme, the rigid, self-righteous person who has to have his own way and cannot accept any compromise may reflect pathological narcissism; at the other extreme, the person willing to sell his convictions—and his staff—down the river for any opportunistic reason may equally reflect severe pathological narcissism. Somewhere in between are the realistic compromises by which the leader's essential convictions are respected and effective boundary negotiation is carried out in achieving a creative balance among conflicting priorities, tasks, and constraints. In other words, intelligent political maneuvering may protect the task and distinguish between what is essential and what is not. Sometimes it takes very long-range vision indeed to separate the immediate political implications of a certain move from its value in terms of the overall, long-range organizational tasks and goals. Pathological narcissism dramatically interferes with the leadership function that differentiates the expedient from the constructive.

THE CHOICE OF A NEW LEADER

When choosing a leader for an organization, it is necessary to explore intensively the broad area of human or interpersonal skills so that those skills are not inferred from what may be only surface adaptability and social charm. As we have seen, skill in judging immediate situations, skill in negotiating conflicts on a short-term basis, the fact of "not ever having had any enemies," and driving ambition are not necessarily good indicators for high quality leadership. The following are some illustrative questions that should be formulated at times of selection of leadership.

How much creativity has the candidate shown in his area in the past? How much investment does he have in a professional source of gratification that would continue to be available to him in addition to his administrative functions? How much gratification will he obtain from actual creativity as an administrator, in contrast to the need for external applause and admiration? Implied here is the depth of identification of the prospective administrator with professional values and with value systems in administrative theory, and his capacity to identify with the goals of the organization. As a general rule, if the future administrator is judged capable of giving up his new administrative functions without a major loss of his professional self-esteem, he has an important source of security that would be an asset in his position.

A major issue is the extent to which the administrator is aware of and invested in basic professional values, in contrast to an opportunistic involvement with issues that are fashionable to bring about short-term returns. Particularly during times of rapid change, a number of basically uncreative and even mediocre professionals rise to the fore because they quickly shift to publishing or working in the areas of growing interest.

Another question is to what extent the candidate has shown the courage to fight openly for his convictions, in contrast to giving evidence of skills in manipulation of conflicts in terms of power and prestige. The courage to stand up for his beliefs, to fight for his staff, to challenge the established powers—obviously in terms of the task, rather than in terms of immature emotional rebelliousness—is an important asset. One has to differentiate here courage stemming from strength of conviction from that representing paranoid querulousness, obsessive stubbornness, or narcissistic ruthlessness, but in practice it is not too difficult to make that distinction. Strength and decisiveness are of course crucial for the painful decision-making process that is the main task of the administrator.

The extent to which the candidate obtains authentic enjoyment from the growth and development of other people is one more important consideration in the selection of leadership. The implication is that the creativity and success of those who will work under him should not be threatened by excessive conflicts around envy in the leader.

Those in charge of evaluating potential leaders are usually aware of the importance of the leader's moral integrity, in addition to purely professional skills and assets; my stress has been on the additional importance of the leader's relations in depth with values—including professional values—and with internal as well as external objects.

I mentioned earlier that there are normal narcissistic gratifications in leadership functions that realistically should contribute to the prevention of pathological regressions in the administrator's personality and help to compensate for the regressive pulls that may be coming from group processes throughout the organization. In addition, an adequate resolution of his oedipal conflicts may permit the leader to protect himself from regressive group processes and may contribute to his ability to take the position of leadership, to enjoy success, to triumph over rivals, and to combine assertiveness with tolerance and humanity—all important aspects of administrative work. Similarly, sufficient gratification of his sexual and dependent needs outside the organizational structure will also help the leader to resist regressive group pressures. However, I am not saying that these issues are practical considerations that should enter the selective process for leadership. Regardless of its important role in his functioning, the administrator's personal and intrapsychic life, in contrast to his behavior, should be protected by boundaries of privacy. His character structure and moral integrity are part of his public domain.

Finally, under the best of circumstances there will be certain built-in organizational constraints related to the "human condition" of social organizations, to the limitations of the personalities of all the individuals involved; some battles need to be fought over and over again, endlessly so. The "ideal" administrator, like the "ideal" organization or the "ideal" group, reflects regressive fantasies of groups and individuals.

7.

THE GROUP-AS-A-WHOLE PERSPECTIVE AND ITS THEORETICAL ROOTS[1,2]

Leroy Wells, Jr.

INTRODUCTION

This paper describes some theoretical roots of the group-as-a-whole perspective. Emphasis is given to concepts and constructs that elucidate group-as-a-whole (group level) phenomena. Several case vignettes will illustrate how the group-as-a-whole perspective can be applied, in an organizational context, to better understand, interpret and intervene in interpersonal and group relations.

THEORETICAL CONTEXT

Groups as Multilevel Systems

The group-as-a-whole perspective emerges from an open system framework applied to the understanding of group and organizational processes. Alderfer (1977), using a systems framework, defines a human group as:

> ... a collection of individuals: a) who have significantly interdependent relations with each other; b) who perceive themselves as a group by reliably distinguishing members from nonmembers; c) whose group identity is recognized by nonmembers; d) who have differentiated roles in the group as a function of expectation from themselves, other members and nongroups; and e) who as group members acting alone or in concert have significantly interdependent relations with other groups.

In the context of this definition, group and system processes refer to actual working activities, i.e., formal and informal relations as well as unconscious and conscious psychosocial dynamics that occur among individuals and groups in organizations. Five levels of group processes are graphically represented in Figure 1 and summarized in Table 1.

FIVE LEVELS OF ORGANIZATIONAL PROCESSES
(FIGURE 1)

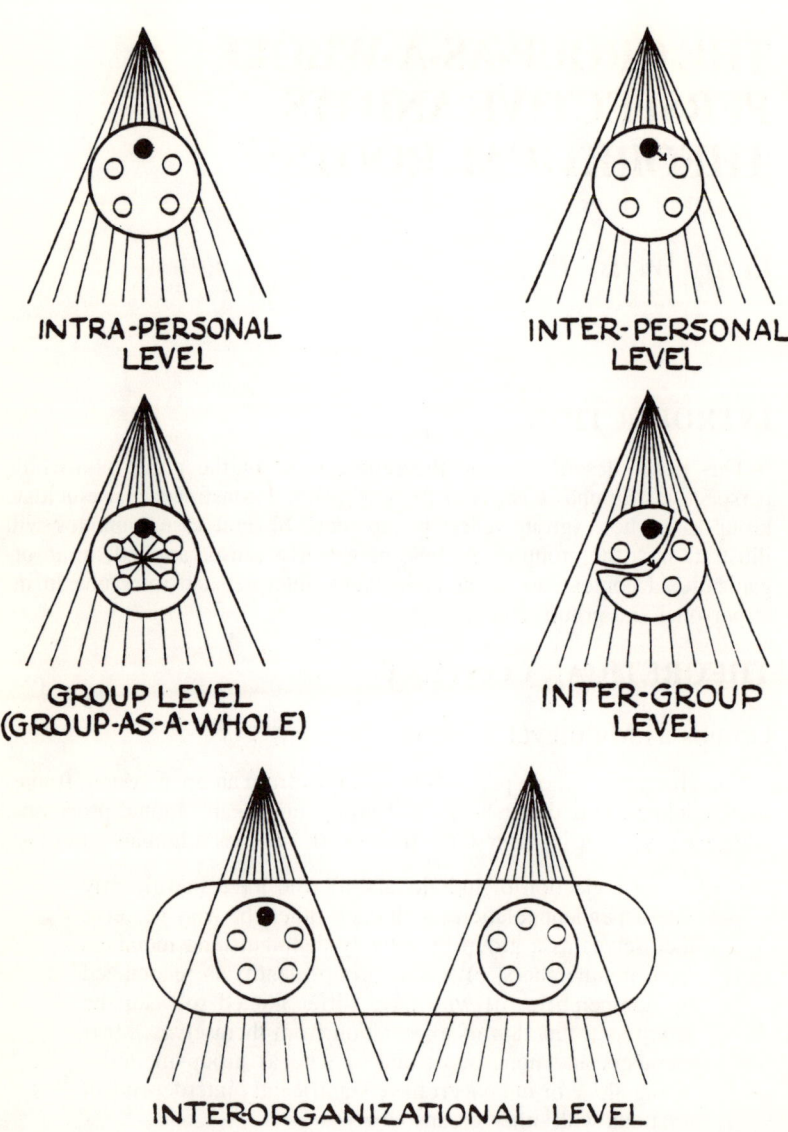

Table 1. FIVE LEVELS OF GROUP PROCESSES

Level and Unit of Group Processes	Definition	Assumptions About Group Behavior	Experiential Learning & Teaching Method	Applications
1. INTRA-PERSONAL	Involves analyses of individuals' relatedness to themselves. Focus on the individual's 'personality needs', 'character structure', constellation of object representation.	Individual behavior in groups is primarily a function of individual's character and represents the internal life and dynamics within the group member.	Gestalt therapy, personal growth groups, EST training, self-differentiation labs use intrapersonal level of group processes as the foundation of their work.	Personnel departments, assessment centers typically examine intrapersonal characteristics in an organizational context. Meyer-Briggs, PACE, SAT, GRE, TAT, IQ are among tests used to explain the behavior of individuals in group and organizational settings.
2. INTER-PERSONAL	Involves analyses of relations and dynamics between individuals in a group context. The foci are on type and quality of member-to-member relations, communication patterns, information, levels of cooperation and conflict.	An interpersonal level analysis assumes individuals are social beings and difficulties in relations emerge from social style and orientation.	Typically, T-group encounter, PET, and sensitivity training focus on interpersonal processes and dynamics between members. Symlog analyses focus on interpersonal processes.	Most supervisory and management development training focuses on interpersonal processes and skills. Emphasis is placed on how to listen and to give constructive feedback.

Table 1. FIVE LEVELS OF GROUP PROCESSES—(Continued)

3. GROUP-AS-A-WHOLE	Refers to behavior of group as a social system and the individuals' relatedness to that system. The focus is on supra-personal relations. Groups are considered more or less than the sum total of their individuals. Individuals are considered interdependent subsystems co-acting and interacting via an 'unconscious group mind'. 'Group mind' may be defined in Batesonian tradition as a pattern of organization or a set of dynamic relationships in which the individual co-actor functions as a vehicle through which the group expresses its life-elan vital.	When a person behaves in a group context that represents aspects of the group's unconscious mind, individuals are then considered living vessels through which the unconscious group life can be expressed and understood.	Tavistock Group Relations Conference and Yale School of Organization and Management group on group design.	Sociotechnical analyses work redesign for groups, semi-autonomous work groups use the group-as-a-whole as a foundation in their approach.

The Group-as-a-Whole Perspective

Table 1. FIVE LEVELS OF GROUP PROCESSES—(Continued)

4. INTERGROUP	Refers to relations and dynamics among various groups or subgroups. Intergroup processes derive from the various group memberships that individuals carry with them into a group and their behavior toward other groups. Intergroup dynamics can develop from hierarchical, task, position, gender, race, age, ethnic identities and ideological differences.	Intergroup forces bring meaning and profoundly color our perceptions of the world and how in part, we treat and are treated by others. Assumes when a person speaks or acts, they may be representing or be treated as if they are representing a subgroup to which they are felt and/or perceived to belong.	Oshry Power labs, Star Power, CARS (class, age, race/ethnic, sex) Labs, "Getting to Yes" Workshops.	Managing conflicts at the organizational interfaces, labor/management negotiation, reducing destructive conflict among departments.
5. INTER-ORGANIZATIONAL	Refers to relationships that exist among the organization, environment and other organizations. The organization is comprised of sets of groups which form an entity called an organization. Interorganizational analyses focus on organization's relations with their organization set and the texture of the markets.	That an individual represents large organizational unit and must when behaving. When individuals are interacting, they may be representing those institutional traditions in which they were socialized and have sentiences.	Strategic management training. War and disarmament games.	Stakeholder analyses, environmental scanning, and strategic planning and management, creating mergers and acquisitions.

Each of the five levels described in Table 1 and depicted in Figure 1 refers to behavioral systems conceptually different from, but not unrelated to, each other. Hence, for a comprehensive analysis and understanding of group processes, each level of the process should be considered. Since behavior is multidetermined, group processes can be examined and understood in terms of any or all of these levels.

GROUP-AS-A-WHOLE PHENOMENON

The group-as-a-whole is a level of analysis that represents processes that are more and less than the sum total of the individual co-actors and their intrapersonal and interpersonal dynamics. The group-as-a-whole is then conceptualized to have a life different from, but related to, the dynamics of the individual co-actors. From this vantage point: "Groups are living systems and group members are interdependent co-actor and subsystems whose interactions form a gestalt." Wells (1980, p. 169) This gestalt and its motif form the 'elan vital' and becomes the unit of study from the group-level perspective.

The group's gestalt is related to the concept of group mentality that connects and bonds the group member in ". . . an unconscious tacit agreement" (Bion, 1961). Gibbard (1975) notes that a group's mentality is best understood as:

> ". . . a process of unconscious cohesion. . . . . . a machinery of intercommunication which is at once a characteristic of groups and a reflection of the individual's ability or even his propensity to express certain drives and feelings covertly, unconsciously and anonymously."

In sum, the group-as-a-whole phenomenon assumes that individuals are human vessels that reflect and express the group's gestalt. Individual co-actors are bonded together, into an interdependent, symbolic, tacit, unconscious, and collusive nexus in which their interactions and shared fantasies and phantasies[3] create and represent at once the group-as-a-whole.

It is from this premise that an individual speaking or acting in a group is perceived as expressing aspects of the group's tacit, unconscious and collusive nexus. What follows is an attempt to excavate the central theoretical roots from which the group-as-a-whole perspective grows.

GROUP-AS-MOTHER: THE THEORETICAL ROOTS OF GROUP-AS-A-WHOLE PERSPECTIVE

At its core, the group-as-a-whole perspective is derived from a theoretical analog that conceptually treats and, in part, equates individual behavior in groups with the unconscious reactions and maneuvers of infants in relation to the ambivalently held mothering object. Bion (1961) first stated that the group-as-a-whole:

The Group-as-a-Whole Perspective

". . . approximates too closely in the minds of individuals comprising it, very primitive fantasies about the contents of the mother's body."

Many other group scholars also affirm this conceptualization. (See Gibbard, 1975; Horwitz, 1983; Scheidlinger, 1964; and Wells, 1980.) Figure 2 provides a synoptic and heuristic description of the theoretical components upon which the group-as-a-whole perspective is built.

Theoretical Root

The 'group-as-mother' analog fundamentally draws the parallels between 'infant-in-relation-to-mother' and 'individual-in-relation-to-group.' Figure 3 delineates the same shared experience between the infant's relationship with the mothering object and the individual's relationship with the group.

The central thrust here is that the group situation creates such ambivalence and anxiety that it unconsciously returns the group members to earlier relationships with primal mother and evokes all of the psychosocial mechanisms involved.

In sum, groups, like the mothering objects, create strong, conflicting, ambivalent feelings of love and hate, bliss and despair, dread and joy. (See Klein, 1959, for more details.)

Derivative 1

Primitive ambivalence, anxiety and regression are generated as a consequence of the group's representing the primal mother. In regard to this primitive ambivalence, Gibbard (1975, p. 33) aptly remarks:

> "The natural psychological habitat of man is the group. Man's adaptation to that habitat is imperfect, a state of affairs which is reflected in his chronic ambivalence towards groups. Group membership is psychologically essential and yet a source of increasing discomfort."

Moreover, Bion (1961, p. 131) in a penetrating way declares:

> "The individual is a group animal at war not simply with the group, but with himself for being a group animal and with those aspects of his personality that constitute his 'groupishness.'."

The central notion is that individuals are always managing the tension created by their own 'groupishness.' The battle is to come to terms with their contempt for and dependence upon groups for a sense of well-being. The group as an object of both contempt and desire certainly creates a psychologically paradoxical and troublesome situation.

Figure 2. THE ROOT AND DERIVATIVES OF THE GROUP-AS-A-WHOLE PERSPECTIVE

Derivative 5 — The group gestalt and mentality (based on the lattice of projective identification shared among group members) canalize and compartmentalized 1) affective, 2) symbolic, 3) instrumental, and 4) other special functions into group members. These compartmentalized functions result in role differentiation, role suction, and the prevailing quality of group relations and culture.

Derivative 4 — As a result of projective identifications, group members evolve into a tacit, interdependent, symbolic, unconscious, and collusive lattice which gives rise to the group's gestalt and mentality, i.e., the group wholeness.

Derivative 3 — A changing motif of projective identification is created where group members function as receptacles for each other into which they can deposit split-off parts of themselves. This shared pattern of projective identification forms a pattern that tends to canalize group members' behaviors.

Derivative 2 — Splitting as a defense is evoked to 'solve' the ambivalence and anxiety generated by the group.

Derivative 1 — Primordial ambivalence, anxiety, and regression are generated as members participate in the group.

Root — 'Group-as-mother' analog provides the theoretical root and anchor from which the group-as-a-whole perspective grows.

The Group-as-a-Whole Perspective

Figure 3. PARALLELS BETWEEN INFANTS WITH MOTHERS AND INDIVIDUALS WITH GROUPS

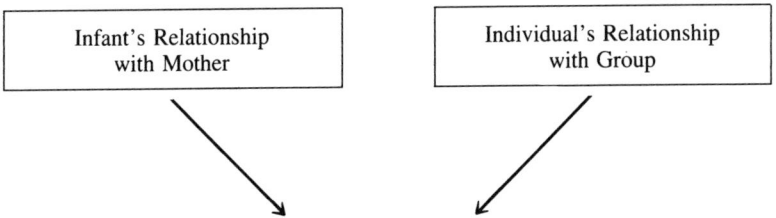

- Struggles with fusing/joining and separating/isolation.
- Experiences both nurturance and frustration.
- Experiences strong ambivalent feelings.
  —Experiences both love and hate simultaneously.
  —Elicits defense mechanism of splitting and projective identification to cope with ambivalence.
  —Struggles with tension between engulfment and estrangement.

(Wells 1980)

Derivative 2

Splitting[4] is a defense that is evoked to cope with the ambivalent feelings toward the object and concomitantly aims to quell the anxiety and reduce the psychological complexity that the group creates. Splitting is a developmentally early defense that enables the individual to divide and segregate negatively and positively held feelings toward the object. In short, splitting reduces the complex and contradictory affects associated with an object. In this regard, individuals in groups (as do infants in relationship to the mothering one) use splitting to reduce the contradictory effects and chronic ambivalence that characterize this nexus. Often the central aim of the individual in the group is to dissipate anxiety and manage the regression in order to make group participation more comfortable and palatable.

In short, for group members who effectively utilize splitting, participation in group life becomes less demanding and dreadful. Having split off the various aspects of the group (the object), the group members then look to other authority figures or outside objects (out of group) to reduce their ambivalence and anxiety. There is an insatiable need to extinguish the anxiety of ambivalence and inner conflict.

Derivative 3

A changing motif of projective identification is created when group members function as repositories for each other in which they can deposit split-off parts of themselves and concomitant feelings.

If splitting dynamically separates ambivalently held objects, then projective identification is the process by which split off feelings and thoughts are expelled to the outside world. Splitting divides and segments the object and its associated feelings. Projective identification expels split-objects and locates proxies outside the self to which objects and associate feelings can be placed.

Projective identification is a psychosocial process that operates at intrapersonal, interpersonal and intergroup levels.[5] It is a process whereby individuals and groups expel parts of themselves and unconsciously identify with those parts as seen in others. The phrase 'unconscious identification with projected content' is appropriate here because subjects consciously 'dis-identify' with the projected attributes (especially if it is a devalued aspect of the self) seen in the object. Kaplan (1982) suggests that, via fission, group members consciously differentiate themselves from the projected material, but at once unconsciously identify with the material. Malin and Grotstein (1966, p. 27) remark:

> "A projection of itself seems meaningless unless the individual can retain some contact (identification) with what is projected."

More explicitly, projective identification has two dimensions:

1. Projective identification involves intra-psychic processes in which the subject projects internal material onto an object and, at the same time, unconsciously identifies with the projected material. But, consciously the subject dis-identifies with the projected part seen in the object.
2. Projective identification involves the effects and impact of projected material on the object. In this case, the object becomes a receptacle being filled up with projected material. At some level the object identifies with or introjects the external projections expelled by the subject(s) that then modifies the behavior of the object.

This identification with or introjection of external projective content transforms the object's internal life and subsequent behavior.

In the group, members are both objects and subjects for one another, with each being the others' symbolic receptacles in which to place projections and at once consciously dis-identifying (denying) with, but unconsciously introjecting or identifying with, the projected content. In this regard, each group member becomes a symbolic object for the others in which each 'cues' and 'draws' particular types of projective identification and attribution. Personality valences or predispositions, gender, racial/ ethnic identity, and status of group members are among the major 'cues' that evolve particular attributions and projective identifications. Shared attributions and projective identification among group members form a collective pattern or motif that shapes relationships—whence group behaviors emerge.

Put literally, if a group member 'cues' and draws particular attributions and projective identification that are at variance with the group members' self-perceptions or felt predisposition, the group's attributions and projective identifications prevail in shaping intragroup relations. Thus, as a result of these group dynamics, individual group members may often be unable to change successfully their behavior in the group. As an analog, the shared pattern of projective identification (which is precipitated by what 'cues' and 'draws' each group member evokes) forms a set of 'forces' or 'fields' that then tends to 'canalize' (see Sheldrake, 1982) group members behavior and group culture.

Derivative 4

As a result of shared projective identification, group members evolve into an interdependent, symbolic, tacit, unconscious, and collusive lattice (an organized set of connections). This lattice gives rise to a group's gestalt and mentality.

Each group member, via projective identification, becomes a symbolic object represented in each of the others' minds, which then governs how each behaves toward the other. For instance, if a black member of a predominantly white group symbolically represents aggressiveness and anger to the white members, then he/she may be treated accordingly. Being treated as if one is angry and aggressive often leads one to display anger and aggression—even if the experience of oneself is at variance with the group's attribution. Additionally, if a member tends to be introverted, shy and reserved, he/she may be symbolically treated as impotent. Hence, that person's comments in the group are largely ignored, and he/she is pushed back into the role of silence and impotence. In short, each group member becomes a symbolic representation for each of the others. These symbolic representations are mostly comprised of transference reactions, parataxic distortions, and attributions that group members exchange.

The exchange and interaction of group members' symbolic representations via projective identification form a nexus or a lattice among group members that give rise to group gestalt and mentality. The essence of this group gestalt and mentality results from the pattern of organization formed in the exchanges and interactions via projective identification among group members. This pattern of organization serves to connect and, simultaneously, govern relations among those who comprise the group system.[6] Changes in projective identifications among group members can alter the group lattice and hence, its gestalt and mentality. Additional changes can also occur by alteration in task design and fluctuations in the group's environment (Trist and Branforth, 1951).

Derivative 5

The group gestalt and mentality (based on the lattice of projective identification shared among group members) results in role differentiation and role suction and often determines the prevailing quality of group relations and culture.

The group's gestalt and mentality canalize and compartmentalize specialized functions based on the kinds of projective identifications that group members exchange. The prevailing group needs that are represented by the lattice of projective identifications will give rise to specialized roles. If the group members are employing excessive splitting and projective identification (e.g., as in the case of pathological narcissism and ethnocentrism [see Wells, 1982]), then an intense unconscious search for appropriate candidates ensues. Under this condition, the scapegoat role is often produced.

The function of the scapegoat, as in the ancient ritual, is to take away all of the iniquities, sins, and unwanted devalued parts of the group (i.e., the tribe). The group hopes (as did the 12 tribes of Israel) that the devalued parts of themselves, deposited in the scapegoat who is banished, will never return. Indeed, the scapegoat continuously returns and the ritual is repeated. Clearly, it is an imperfect solution to group problems and destructive to the person or group chosen as the scapegoat. Often functions that are distributed to group members are split between affective vs. cognitive, hero vs. villian, process concerns vs. task concerns, fight vs. flight, hope and despair, and competence and incompetence. If there is an unmet need among group members for a specialized function such as defending against uncertainty, ambiguity and authority, a group member may be asked or sucked into (role suction) filling this need.

Consider, for example, the Carter administration's Iranian hostage rescue attempt. It appears that Secretary of State Vance was asked to carry the negative side of the ambivalence about the proposed rescue mission. He raised many objections to the plan and embodied the side of caution and restraint. This allowed the parts of President Carter and others that were against the mission to identify projectively with Vance's caution. With Vance carrying the caution about the mission, he became a receptacle into which the Security Council members could deposit their own doubts about the rescue plans. Since the ambivalence was such an intolerable experience, an unconscious pressure mounted to scapegoat Vance and force his resignation. Knowing about his possible resignation, the Security Council members could pursue the mission straightaway—unencumbered by their own ambivalence. Indeed, it was hoped that once Vance (the scapegoat) had resigned, what he represented would also disappear. The magnitude of the mission's failure points to poor planning and insufficient forecasting.

The group's gestalt and mentality distributed and compartmentalized the mixed sentiments about the rescue primarily into Vance and Brzezinski with Carter finally being drawn into the ranks of the 'hawks.' (For details, see Brzezinski, 1983; Carter, 1982; and Vance, 1983.)

The Group-as-a-Whole Perspective

The excessive projection identification among those on the Security Council led to, as in the Kennedy Bay of Pigs decision, a poor policy and strategic error (see Janis, 1972). No group is exempt from the power of group gestalt and mentality and distributive functions.

The theoretical roots and derivatives upon which the group-as-a-whole perspective is based needs further empirical investigation. Such investigation would require a methodology sensitive to unconscious manifestations. This theoretical treatment of group-as-a-whole may begin to advance our understanding, in a more precise way, about group-level processes. Yet, many issues are left unanswered about group-as-a-whole phenomena that can be addressed with further empirical inquiry. Nonetheless, we turn to some applications of group-as-a-whole analyses.

CASE VIGNETTES

This section briefly describes two case fragments using the group-as-a-whole analyses.

Case: Incompetent Team Member Preventing Team Effectiveness

Setting: A highly specialized research and development unit of 10 white male engineers in a hi-tech organization is under urgent pressure to solve some unpredicted technical problems in a new computer hardware product that is scheduled to 'hit' the market in 12 months.

Dynamics: A management consultant has been invited by the unit head to conduct a team diagnosis and team-building intervention. His decision is endorsed by top management. The consultant's initial data collection via interviews revealed:

1. The majority of the team members felt that Mr. W. (who, at age 56, was the oldest team member) interfered with the productivity of the team as it attempted to solve technical problems. They accused him of being uncooperative, abusive, and disruptive to team planning and technical meetings. Recently, however, Mr. W. had been taking sick-leave and was often tardy to work and began missing important team meetings. In short, the team members considered Mr. W. to be a block to the team's functioning. Mr. W., however, had 15 years with the company and at times was very creative.
2. Although the majority of team members felt negatively toward Mr. W., they never publicly or directly informed him of their concerns. However, team members would constantly complain to the team leader and to each other about Mr. W.'s incompetence. They wished that he would be removed from the team. Some threatened to quit if something was not done to 'get rid of' Mr. W. Under pressure, the team manager covertly called an executive search firm and asked the firm to call Mr. W. about possible positions. This would be done without Mr. W. knowing about his manager's or company's involvement. The manager also sought to transfer Mr. W. Moreover, there

was a strong company norm against terminating long-term, loyal employees. Since Mr. W. was at times technically very creative (which was well known to top management of the corporation) and had logged 15 years with the firm, termination was prohibited.
3. Mr. W. reported that he was comfortable with the team. He thought the team was not exceptionally friendly, yet he felt comfortable with the relationship. At times, however, he felt isolated and did not interact socially with members of the team. Nonetheless, he felt that he was valuable to the company and to the team. He mentioned in the interview with the consultant that executive search firms had been calling him during the last several months. Mr. W. interpreted the calls as confirming his competence and his marketability. He told neither his team members nor his manager about the calls from the search firm. Moreover, Mr. W. felt that the company had been good to him during the years. Mr. W. also reported that the manager had cancelled his last performance appraisal meeting and that it had not been rescheduled. He had received moderate salary increases and felt that he was performing at a satisfactory level. (He was 'vested' and had longevity with the company, so he was very secure financially.) Yet, in recent months he had not been 'feeling great'; he experienced chronic back pain and felt tired.

Analysis: It appears that Mr. W. has been unconsciously asked to carry or feel the incompetence for the team. Perhaps, being the oldest team member contributed to Mr. W. being in this role. R&D work by its nature can be frustrating. The pressures of solving technical problems for the company's new products increased the frustration and pressure. Evidence also exists that the team and the manager felt anxiety about their ability to solve the problems before the new product reached the market. Perhaps their covert concern was their own incompetence. The team, via projective identification, could use Mr. W. as a receptacle for their own dreadful concerns. The manager also contributed to this collusion by inviting an executive search firm that had the net effect of having Mr. W. stay with the company. Moreover, in some ways the team wanted and needed Mr. W. to stay because they could then blame him for team failure. However, the time and resources spent on Mr. W.'s problem could be better spent examining technical solutions. This motif of projective identification was creating a potential scapegoating of Mr. W. (a human offering, as it were) but was an imperfect solution to the problem of the team's ineffectiveness and anxiety about the task. Yet, the team and manager assumed an intrapersonal understanding of the dynamics surrounding Mr. W. They then sought to remedy the problem by consciously wanting to remove Mr. W., but unconsciously identifying with and needing Mr. W. to remain to serve as a receptacle for their shared split-off feelings of incompetence and anxiety.

Case: "It's Their Fault"—The Group Conflict

Setting: A small, urban child health care facility with support staff of six black women.

Dynamics: The executive director invited an external consultant to assist in "doing something about relations among my staff." It was reported that two intake clerks, Ms X and Ms Z, who registered patients were consistently in intense conflict. The conflict often erupted between them in the presence of patients. This conflict resulted in delays and mistakes in requesting patient charts and making appointments. Moreover, the clinic was steadily losing patients to a local HMO. Thus, patient relations was of utmost importance. The facility was also experiencing a financial deficit, and a staff reduction or facility shutdown was threatening.

Other staff members consistently complained to the executive director about the behavior of Ms X and Ms Z. Both Ms X and Ms Z would come to the executive director to report the other's transgressions. During lunch time, the other staff members would get together and deplore the behavior of Ms X and Ms Z. Yet no staff member intervened publicly when conflictual episodes erupted.

Analysis: It appears that Ms X and Ms Z were unconsciously being asked to carry conflict and anxiety on behalf of the staff. A collusive relationship had developed between the dyad and the rest of the staff. By complaining to the executive director about Ms X and Ms Z, the staff created and maintained a pattern of conflictual relations. The staff projectively identified with the conflict and anxiety expressed by Ms X and Ms Z. Moreover, there was underlying fear and anxiety about the viability of the facility and staff jobs. Structurally, Ms X and Ms Z were in the lowest status positions and were physically located at the intake and export boundaries. They acted as buffers for the facility. Hence, they were structurally vulnerable to express the staff's anxiety and conflicts. Moreover, the more emphasis and attention given to the conflict between Ms X and Ms Z, the less attention was given to the question of the facility's survival. Perhaps this was even more troublesome and dreadful for the staff.

In sum, Ms X and Ms Z were asked to carry the conflicts within the system. They were convenient objects upon which split-off parts of others could be placed. Certainly there was a collusion between the dyad, the staff and the executive director.

These case illustrations represent how the group-as-a-whole analysis can help better understand a work situation that often is presented as interpersonal and intrapersonal problems. To intervene in a work relationship, based on the intra- and interpersonal framework without consideration of group-as-a-whole perspective, can be insufficient and lead to cursory and ineffective solutions. Moreover, evidence and experience show that group-level analysis should be pursued first. This would allow for the 'group-level solution' that can prevent and protect the individual from, at the extreme, being terminated or devalued that can lead to much pathos and despair in the work place. To see dynamics initially as a function of how the group-as-a-whole operates, shift the foci of the problem and solution frame from the individual. The pervasive managerial strategy is to locate problems inside individuals as opposed to discovering what is being 'put into' the individual by the group via the projective identification motif.

These case illustrations are just two examples among many of how group-as-a-whole can cast a different light on relationships and dynamics at work.

IMPLICATIONS

A Shift in the Paradigm

This section describes some implications of the group-as-a-whole perspective. The group-as-a-whole perspective takes a radical view of group and individual behavior. It implies that individual behavior in groups is largely a result of group 'forces' that 'canalize' individual action. This group force is generated from the changing pattern of shared splitting, projective identifications, interactions, and task demands. The perspective assumes that when a person speaks, he/she does so not only for themselves, but in part, speaks via the unconscious for the group. Moreover, what may be understood as individual initiative and behavior in a social setting may well be the distribution and expression of the "group's force" that has 'canalized' individual action.

The group-as-a-whole perspective is at variance with the prevailing intrapersonal and interpersonal perspectives that dominate group process consultations and team-building approaches. The group-as-a-whole perspective mandates that the individual is not seen as an isolate in a social vacuum, but rather as an interdependent social creature bond-connected, inspired, and in part, governed by the collective forces.

In this regard, the individual cannot, then, be completely understood as an 'independent' or 'free-willed' being acting solely on his/her own volition and recognizance. Such conceptualization runs straightaway into western tenets that emphasize the unique individuality of humans and the primacy of individuals' volition and responsibility to determine their own behavior and to chart their own courses. To wit, the group-as-a-whole perspective draws attention to the concept of humans as interdependent creatures, in part governed and unconsciously and inextricably bound together into a collective community. This perspective is consistent with the directions of the new sciences, like quantum physics, the holographic paradigm, second-order cybernetics, and Sheldrake's hypothesis of formative causation. (See Berman, 1984; Capra, 1982; Sheldrake, 1982.) These new shifts in understanding all view humans as interdependent (at least) entities influenced and, in part, governed by 'forces,' 'fields,' and 'frequencies' above and beyond what may be considered individual volition. Further theoretical development and empirical investigation of group-as-a-whole phenomena may reveal greater ties with the current paradigm shift and the new sciences.

Group-as-a-Whole Competence for Managers and Organizational Consultants

For managers and organizational consultants committed to excellence, interpersonal competence is no longer a sufficient skill, but in addition, group-as-a-whole competence as a skill is now required. Merely understanding individual differences and interpersonal relations in organizations is too myopic and limited.

Since the group-as-a-whole exerts such a profound influence on human behavior, managers and consultants should begin to recognize how shared patterns of splitting and projective identifications may be operating within the group with which they work. Adopting the group-as-a-whole perspective evokes the following questions in working with groups:

1. What have the group members been asked to carry on behalf of the group?
2. What may be being deposited into each member on behalf of the others?
3. Is a group member who is identified as incompetent, inept, too aggressive, or too passive merely unconsciously being asked to carry these projected split-off parts and attributes for the group-as-a-whole?

Without these questions being asked, the individual actor may be accused and held solely responsible for playing out roles that have been primarily ascribed and distributed by the group-as-a-whole. Through exploration of these questions, greater understanding of the dynamics surrounding the group member can be achieved. The exploration and explanations may reveal solutions that focus on the group-as-a-whole.

From a manpower perspective, group-level solutions to process problems may be more cost effective than solutions sought at individual levels of analysis. More often than not, solutions derived from individual (i.e., intrapersonal and interpersonal) levels result in group members being held solely responsible, in need of 'fixing,' blamed, scapegoated, transferred or terminated. Moreover, if the real issues reside in the group-as-a-whole, an individual-level solution is imperfect, at best. At its worst, the individual-level solution to a group-as-a-whole dynamic may contribute to:

1. scapegoating of the individual;
2. human pathos widely experienced in organizations; and
3. decline in task performance.

Without the group-as-a-whole analysis, it may remain unknown if, indeed, an individual is being unconsciously ascribed functions on behalf of the group. To assume an individual perspective typically creates an individual-oriented solution such that the individual actor is at risk of being victimized.

Requirements and Responsibility

Employing the group-as-a-whole perspective dictates an examination of how one 'uses' and is 'used' via projective identification in the group in which he/she grows up, lives and works. This perspective also focuses attention upon how human beings are unconsciously and inextricably bonded to each other via our collective community, despite our preferences and/or conscious wishes. For instance, the contempt that we may have for others, may be, in part, the contempt we have for ourselves. The other may be asked to carry that devalued part of ourselves. To face parts of ourselves openly as seen in the other requires courage and grace; courage to embrace those disowned parts of ourselves, and grace to accept ourselves and the other with all of our human fragility and potentiality.

8.

CONTAINER AND CONTAINED

Wilfred Bion

An advantage of believing that observations are the foundation of scientific method is that the conditions in which they are made can be stated and then produced. The simplicity of this has its appeal for the psychoanalyst: an analytic situation is presumed to exist and interpretations of the observations made in that situation are then reported. It is possible to believe that the analysis has a location in time and space: for example, the hours arranged for the sessions and the four walls of the consulting room; that at such times and in such a place the analyst can make observations that he cannot do if the domain has not these limitations, or if 'psychoanalytic observations' do not conform to the conventional view of an observation. If I pictorialize the statement 'the conventional view of an observation' to be a container, like a sphere, and the 'psychoanalytic observation' as something that cannot be contained within it, I have a model that will do very well not only for the 'conventional view,' to represent my feelings about a 'psychoanalytic situation,' but also for the 'psychoanalysis' that it cannot contain. It will also serve as a model for my feelings about certain patients: I cannot observe Mr. X because he will not remain 'inside' the analytic situation or even 'within' Mr. X himself.

I have found theories of acting-out enlightening, but not enlightening enough; none of the theories known to me 'contains' the 'facts' by which I seek to be enlightened. My 'facts' gird against the framework of definition and theory that I seek to erect around them. The patient who is acting out cannot be 'contained' within existing formulations.

This is a characteristic of the mental domain: it cannot be contained within the framework of psychoanalytic theory. Is this a sign of defective theory, or a sign that psychoanalysts do not understand that psychoanalysis cannot be contained permanently within the definitions they use? It would be a valid observation to say that psychoanalysis cannot 'contain' the mental domain because it is not a 'container' but a 'probe'; the formulation that I have tried to further by using the symbols ♀ and ♂ minimizes this difficulty by leaving ♀ and ♂ as unknowns whose value is to be determined.

I would pursue this train of thought further by discussing something more practical and particular. It is a matter where action[1] seems to be called for, namely, the institutionalization of psychoanalysis comprising publication, selection, training, and qualification.

Theory: Bion

In recent years, there has grown up the use of the term Establishment; it seems to refer to that body of persons in the State who may be expected usually to exercise power and responsibility by virtue of their social position, wealth, and intellectual and emotional endowment. (This list is not an order of priority of attainments.) I propose to borrow this term to denote everything from the penumbra of associations generally evoked, to the predominating and ruling characteristics of an individual, and the characteristics of a ruling caste in a group (such as a psychoanalytical institute, or a nation or group of nations). Because of my choice of subject it will usually be used for talking about the ruling 'caste' in psychoanalytical institutes.

The Establishment has to find and provide a substitute for genius. One of its more controversial activities is to promulgate rules (known in religious activities as dogmas, in scientific groups as 'laws,' e.g. of nature or perspective) for the benefit of those who are not by nature fitted to have direct experience of *being* psychoanalytic (or religious, or scientific, or artistic) so that they may, as it were by proxy, have and impart knowledge of psychoanalysis. Group members will not through incapacity be denied a sense of participation in an experience from which they would otherwise feel forever excluded. At the same time these rules (or dogmas) must be such that they attract rather than repel, help rather than hinder, the membership of genius, which is essential to the group's continued existence and vitality. A Freud can discover and establish psychoanalysis, but it must be maintained by a continued supply of 'genius.' This cannot be ordered; but if it comes the Establishment must be able to stand the shock. Failing genius, and clearly it may not materialize for a very long period, the group must have its rules and a structure to preserve them. Thus an environment exists ready, as Nietzsche said of the nation, to fulfill its proper function, namely, to produce a genius. Similarly, it may be said of the individual that he should be ready to produce a 'flash of genius.' Let us therefore consider this phenomenon.

The term 'genius' does not carry the associations I want, so I propose to use the term 'mystic,' leaving it to be supposed that the mystic has characteristics usually associated with genius and that the person represented by the term 'genius' or 'mystic' may with equal propriety be described by the term 'messiah.'

The mystic is both creative and destructive. I make a distinction between two extremes that coexist in the same person. The extreme formulations represent two types: the 'creative' mystic, who formally claims to conform to or even fulfill the conventions of the Establishment that governs his group; and the mystic nihilist, who appears to destroy his own creations. I mean the terms to be used only when there is outstanding creativeness or destructiveness, and the terms 'mystic,' 'genius,' 'messiah' could be interchangeable.

The problem posed by the relationship between the mystic and the institution has an emotional pattern that repeats itself in history and in a variety of forms. The pattern may appear in the relationship of a new phenomenon to the formulation that has to represent it. It appears in the relationship of widely dissimilar groups to their mystics; it reveals itself in the history of the Christian heresies, the heliocentric theories, the relationship of the rabbinical directorate of the Kabbalah to revolutionary mystics such as Isaac Luria, the political reformer, and the Establishment. My object is to show that certain elements in the development of psychoanalysis are not new or peculiar to analysis, but have in fact a history that suggests that they transcend barriers of race, time and discipline, and are inherent in the relationship of the mystic to the group. The Establishment cannot be dispensed with (though this may appear to be approximately achieved in Sufism and in the theory of Marxism) because the institutionalized group, the Work group (see Bion, 1961), is as essential to the development of the individual, including the mystic, as he is to it. Homeric psychology indicates a stage of mental development in which the distinction between man and god is ill defined; in the individual psyche, little distinction between ego and superego is recognized. The Work group, under the religious vertex, must differentiate between man and god. Institutionalized religion must make man conscious of this gulf in himself and in the counterparts of himself in the group of which he is a member.

The institutionalization of psychoanalysis requires a psychoanalytic group that has 'Establishment' as one of its functions. It is itself a replica, in the external world, of an object in which the desired separation has been effected. But its function is then to effect this separation in the personalities of its members. It is thus both a model of a state that is desired and an institution whose function it is to make the individual aware of the gap between himself (his idealized, super-egoized self) and himself (his unregenerate, unpsychoanalyzed self).

One result of separation is no direct access of the individual to the god with whom he used formerly to be on familiar terms. But the god has undergone a change as a part of the process of discrimination. The god with whom he was familiar was finite; the god from whom he is now separated is transcendent and infinite.

To restate the above in terms appropriate to a background of human experience: Freud and his associates mix on terms of equality such as exist between any human colleagues in a common venture. Freud, merely by being a person of outstanding statute, stimulates the tensions and emotional drives appropriate to a primitive group and stimulates them still further by his work. The primitive stages of the analytic group contribute to the obtrusion of tensions and emotional drives appropriate to the primitive group, as Freud observed through his study of the individual. I doubt that he appreciated the force of the messianic hopes aroused. The primitive stage makes way for the stage of discrimination described in the religious group: a distinction is made, otherwise there will not be recognition of the real distinction that exists between a mystic (in my sense) and ordinary human beings.

This distinction cannot be achieved adequately by saying that it is inseparable from idealization. Idealization in the group is a reality-based activity that is essential for the growth of discrimination in the individual. The individual himself must be able to distinguish between himself as an ordinary person and his view that he is omniscient and omnipotent. It is a step towards recognition of a distinction between the group as it really is and its idealization as an embodiment of the omnipotence of the individuals who compose it. Sometimes the separation fails and the group is not only seen to be ideally omnipotent and omniscient but believed to be so in actuality. The individual's realization of a gulf between his view of himself as omnipotent and his view of himself as an ordinary human being must be achieved as the result of a task of the group itself as well as in individual analysis. Otherwise there is a danger that a state of mind is transferred (by projective identification) to the group and *acted out* there—not altered. Some details of this situation must be described.

In the first stage, there is no real confrontation between the god and the man because there is really no such distinction. In the second stage, the infinite and transcendent god is confronted by the infinite man. When the function of the group is to *establish* the separation there is no question of reunion. In the third stage the individual, or at least a particular individual—the mystic—needs to reassert a direct experience of god of which he has been, and is, deprived by the institutionalized group. Before I turn to this it is necessary to glance at some peculiarities of the group that has been institutionalized and of life in it.

The individuals show signs of their divine origin (just as the gods of the previous stage show signs of human origin). The individuals may be regarded as being incarnations of the deity; each individual retains an inalienable element that is a part of the deity himself that resides in the individual. He can be regarded as constantly attempting to achieve union with the deity, or he can be regarded as divine in a somewhat low-grade way. This last shows signs of being related genetically to the stage where no real distinction exists between god-like human beings on the one hand and very human gods on the other. Finally, the individual strives for reunion with the god from whom he feels consciously separated. This is reflected in the actualities of the human relationship and contributes to the hatred of the group for a state in which individuals cannot have direct access, or even a sense of direct access, to the great man (as they might once have had to Freud). Individuals cannot reconcile themselves to a discrimination that means conscious separation of themselves from a belief in their Freud-like qualities and recognition that Freud, a genius (mystic), no longer exists. Another Freud cannot be created no matter how essential he may be.

The group and mystic are essential to each other; it is therefore important to consider how or why the group can destroy the mystic on whom its future depends and how or why the mystic may destroy the group. I shall indicate the nature of the questions at issue since it is vital that the problem should be seen to exist. It is inherent both in the nature of man as a political animal and in the nature of psychoanalysis as the explosive force.

The relationship between group and mystic may belong to one of three categories. It may be commensal, symbiotic or parasitic. The same categorization may be applied to the relationship of one group with another. I shall not trouble with the commensal relationship: the two sides coexist and the existence of each can be seen to be harmless to the other. In the symbiotic relationship there is a confrontation and the result is growth-producing though that growth may not be discerned without some difficulty. In the parasitic relationship, the product of the association is something that destroys both parties to the association. The realization that approximates most closely to my formulation is the group-individual setting dominated by envy. Envy begets envy, and this self-perpetuating emotion finally destroys host and parasite alike. The envy cannot be satisfactorily ascribed to one or other party; in fact it is a function of the relationship.

In a symbiotic relationship the group is capable of hostility and benevolence and the mystic contribution is subject to close scrutiny. From this scrutiny the group grows in stature and the mystic likewise. In the parasitic association even friendliness is deadly. An easily seen example of this is the group's promotion of the individual to a position in the Establishment where his energies are deflected from his creative-destructive role and absorbed in administrative functions. His epitaph might be 'He was loaded with honours and sank without a trace.' Eissler (1965), without mentioning the general principle involved, shows the dangers of the invitation to group or individual to become respectable, to be medically qualified, to be a university department, to be a therapeutic group, to be anything in short, but *not* explosive. The reciprocal attitude in the mystic is that the group should thrive or disintegrate but must *not* be indifferent. The attitudes are not conscious and deliberate; they are essential. Without them the group is not a group nor the 'mystic' a mystic. An analytic parallel is the psychoanalytic interpretation that is death to the existing state of mind, the state of mind that is being interpreted. Worse than being right or wrong is the failure of an interpretation to be significant, though to be significant is not enough; it merely ensures that it exists. It must also be true. The parasitic group can be primarily concerned to destroy the mystic, or mystic (messianic) ideas, but if it fails to do so it must 'establish' his or their truth.

Eissler discusses 'applied' psychoanalysis. I suspect that applied psychoanalysis, even if 'applied' to curing people, is a method of bringing psychoanalysis under control and rendering it harmless to the Establishment. I have expressed this in another context and in a different approach by a rule that the analyst should not permit himself to harbour desires, even the desire to cure, since to do so is inimical to psychoanalytical development. Development itself is not an object that can be 'desired.' The painful nature of the dilemma is essential.

The recurrent configuration is of an explosive force with a restraining framework. For example, the mystic in conflict with the Establishment; the new idea constrained within a formulation not intended to express it; the art form outmoded by new forces requiring representation.

It is essential that the language should be preserved. To this end, rules are produced under which words and definitions are to be used. The *Oxford Dictionary*, linguistic philosophy, mathematical logic, are tributes to the work that is incessantly proceeding for this purpose. On this work ordinary men and women with ordinary ability depend to do work that otherwise would be done only by exceptional people. Thanks to Faraday and other scientists ordinary people can illuminate a room by the touch of a switch; thanks to Freud and his co-workers ordinary people hope by psychoanalysis to be able to illuminate the mind. The fact that the world's work has to be done by ordinary people makes this work of scientification (or vulgarization, or simplification, or communication, or all together) imperative. There are not enough mystics and those that there are must not be wasted.

The more successfully the word and its use can be 'established,' the more its precision becomes an obstructive rigidity; the more imprecise it is, the more it is a stumbling block to comprehension. The new idea 'explodes' the formulation designed to express it. Sometimes the emotion is powerful but the idea weak. If the formulation survives it can be repeated. If it can be repeated under severe conditions it becomes stronger until it communicates meaning without disintegration. Conversely, the formulation may destroy its content. In his play *Major Barbara*, George Bernard Shaw describes the apotheosis of the dictum 'No man is good enough to be another man's master' as a method of rendering the emotional content ineffectual.

It may be that the distinction between creative and nihilistic mystic is no more than a temporary expedient depending on the need to express one view of the mystic rather than the other. The most powerful emotional explosion known so far, spreading to many cultures and over many centuries, has been that produced by the formulations of Jesus. The effects are still felt and present grave problems of containment even now, though some measure of control has been established. Jesus at first expressly disavowed any aim other than fulfillment of the laws of his group. The rabbinical directorate failed to solve the problem of containment, a failure associated with disastrous consequences for the Jewish group. The disaster attributed to Christian teachings did not terminate at any finite point, as for example at the crucifixion; after Alaric had sacked Rome four hundred years later St. Augustine felt the reproaches against the Christians to be sufficiently serious to require refutation in his 'City of God.'

The problems of mystical revelation that centre on having, or claiming to have, a direct relationship with the deity remain. The need for the Establishment to do what the rabbinical directorate had failed to do soon became evident. Complaints by the disciples that miracles were being done by unauthorized or, as we might say, 'lay,' people, suggest awareness that we expect to find associated with an Establishment. That, and evidence of a need to establish a structured hierarchy ('who shall sit at the right hand'), is too slender to be more than a starting point for conjecture. Something must have contributed to the efflorescence of structure, hierarchy and institution. The institution is evidence of the need for the function that the rabbinical directorate had failed to provide. Although in many respects the Church was more successful, the long history of heresy (see Knox, 1950) shows that the structure required to contain the teaching of Jesus was, and still is, subjected to a great strain. It has not, however, been without its successes, and even today complaints can be heard, which are really a tribute to the success of the institutionalizing process, of the lack of enthusiasm, drive and 'spirituality' of the Church.

Though we may contrast the success of the Church favourably with the failure of the rabbinical directorate, the force of the mystical revelation has not yet spent itself. There are signs that the Oedipus myth, and the elements that in the Christian religion touch on paternity and sonship, both have a configuration suggesting an underlying group of which these elements are representative. I have used the sign O to denote this 'ultimate reality.' Any formulation felt to approximate to illumination of O is certain to produce an institutionalizing reaction. The institution may flourish at the expense of the mystic or idea, or it may be so feeble that it fails to contain the mystical revelation.

A formulation may approximate to 'illumination' of O. Many mystics express their experience of direct access to the deity in terms of light, but light is not the only model used. Jewish mystics in particular find the voice a telling representation of the experience. St. Paul found light *and* voice necessary to represent the experience. It is significant that psychoanalysts seeking direct access to an aspect of O, thought it is not only to that part of O that informs god-like characteristics, conduct their affairs through language. To be confined to one medium of communication only is too restrictive even if it has the flexibility and capacity for development of language. Psychoanalytical observation certainly cannot afford to be confined to perception of what is verbalized only: what of more primitive uses of the tongue?

The suspension of memory and desire promotes exercise of aspects of the psyche that have no background of sensuous experiences. Paradoxically, the release of these aspects of the psyche enables them to reveal elements such as the nonverbal muscular movements of the tongue, as in stammer. The dominance of sensuous experience promotes expressions such as 'seeing' or 'hearing'; the falseness introduced by such formulation contributes to those differences that seem so significant but are in fact unimportant. Intuitive power cannot develop because it is hindered by such obtrusions of 'sense.' The institutionalizing of words, religions, psychoanalysis—all are special instances of institutionalizing memory so that it may 'contain' the mystic revelation and its creative and destructive force. The function of the group is to produce a genius; the function of the Establishment is to take up and absorb the consequences so that the group is not destroyed.

PART TWO

METHOD

Section Editors: Harold Bernard
Barton Evans III
Margaret J. Rioch

There have been substantial advances in methodology since the first *Group Relations Reader* was published in 1975. The Tavistock method is ten years older now and the papers included in this section illustrate some significant areas in which growth and change have occurred.

The Gustafson and Cooper paper could have as easily been placed in the Theory Section. We chose to include it in the Method Section to emphasize technique issues in taking up the role of a small group consultant. Gustafson and Cooper believe that the basic assumption described by Bion results from the abandonment and intrusion fostered by the technique typical "Tavistock Group" consultant. They suggest that an entirely different kind of small group (collaborative in nature) emerges when the consultant is neither abandoning nor intrusive, but is available when needed.

The remaining five papers represent a cross-section of thinking that advances the method by which work in the Tavistock tradition is carried out. Gosling's paper on Very Small Groups (VSG) explicates the unique features of this new conference event. He describes how the VSG compares and contrasts with other conference events, especially the small group.

Gould's paper describes the "special theme" conferences that have been offered most often in recent years: namely, those that focus on issues of gender. He describes the unique features of these conferences, which have been the progenitors of a burgeoning variety of special theme conferences including role relations and the impact of age.

Rioch describes a unique model that she and her colleagues have developed to train experienced conference participants in small group consultancy. The paper conveys the flavor of these training experiences, as well as some of their complexities. Baxter and Heimburger trace the evolution of a training model they have developed, in which the trainees constitute a junior staff group separate and distinct from the senior staff, the administrative staff and the "regular" membership. The issue of how to train people for conference staff roles and consultation in this model continues to evolve.

Finally, Alderfer and Klein describe the analysis of a particular organization by a team of consultants from the Tavistock and National Training Lab "schools" in order to compare these models of organizational analysis.

H.B.
B.E.
M.J.R.

Part Two—Method

Collaboration in Small Groups: Theory and Technique for the
    Study of Small-Group Processes 139
James P. Gustafson and Lowell Cooper

A Study of Very Small Groups 151
R. Gosling

Men and Women at Work: A Group Relations Conference
    on Person and Role 163
Laurence J. Gould

Advanced Learning in a Small Group 173
Margaret J. Rioch

An Advanced Training Group Within the Group Relations
    Conference: Evolution, Design and Outcome 185
Robert F. Baxter and Elizabeth Morgan Heimburger

Affect, Leadership and Organizational Boundaries 197
Clayton P. Alderfer and Edward B. Klein

9.

COLLABORATION IN SMALL GROUPS: THEORY AND TECHNIQUE FOR THE STUDY OF SMALL-GROUP PROCESSES

James P. Gustafson and Lowell Cooper

THE PROBLEM

Little is known about how consultants work with study groups.[1] Bion (1961) describes many of his interventions, but this is quite unusual, since most reports bracket "the group process" as an entity unto itself, as if it were not in fact a relation between a particular consultant and a group. Mann (1975) writes frankly when he suggests that each consultant he has known has had his own favorite phenomena that he is apt to elicit, yet the usual reader is left to infer this possibility and scientific progress in clarifying this relation is hindered.

Recording would not necessarily provide intelligibility. As Lewin (1948) argues, the social field of a small group is complex and quite uneven in dynamic importance. Psychological variables, which may seem very powerful in abstraction, in fact often may have little dynamic importance in a group if the social field is not organized to bring them out. For example, the consultant's apparent difficulty with intimacy is not material if the group is pushing in other directions. Lewin attempted to solve this problem of how the unevenness of the social field might be adequately described in his concepts of "quasi-stable equilibria," "channels," and "gate" functions. Our argument in this paper is that the social field is shaped very powerfully by whether or not the working relation between consultant and group is collaborative or noncollaborative or in transition between these extremes.

What do we mean by "collaboration"? The dictionary reveals a bright and a dark side to this word, which is of great importance to the phenomena we are considering. On the one hand, "collaboration" means working together cooperatively on a project of common concern and benefit. On the other hand, "collaboration" means to work along with opposition or enemies in betrayal of one's own kind or class. In fact, the word can be used to contain a spectrum of meanings from the bright to the darkest. In the middle of this range, for instance, is the meaning that emerged in the early work of the Tavistock Institute of Human Relations with industrial firms after World War II. Jaques (1948) uses the term explicity to describe the kinds of relations his research group attempt to establish with all parties concerned in a client firm, from top management to supervisors to labor union representatives. The terms of the research group were those of being acceptable to all parties, of making known within the firm the results of all meetings with subgroups, of joint responsibility for the final report. Later (Miller, 1976d) this task was conceptualized by Rice in the concept of "primary task," that each party had a common, collaborative interest in the primary task, which was that task that had to be performed for the firm to survive. We would summarize this as "collaboration for production." Its meaning is, however, quite ambivalent: on the bright side, the success of production and of some work satisfaction, yet, on the dark side, the realization that more fundamental working demands are usually lost in the priority that production takes or is allowed.[2]

This spectrum of political meaning in the collaborative relation is of greatest importance in the work of a small study group, where a consultant indicates an interest in working "collaboratively" with a group by his remarks or interpretations.[3] In our view, what issues is a testing process in which the group tries to find out what shade of "collaboration" the consultant, in fact, means to establish.

The two extremes in meaning of collaboration are reflective of quite different group atmospheres that evolve. On the one hand is a group that is organized around having either an internal or external enemy. In a conference situation this might be the staff or the consultant to the particular small group. There is the feeling that to work with the consultant is to collaborate with the enemy; consultant suggestions are used begrudgingly and there is a continuous underlying feeling that one must be on guard against vulnerability to withdrawal by or assault from leadership. The other side of the coin seems quite a bit more difficult for the group to get at developmentally and relates to some capacity for intimacy: being able to feel that it is possible to work well in cooperation with other members and leadership without having to defend against this mode by either developing a culture of overinvolved oceanic fusion in which all are part of one big happy family, or having to have more distance between the self and others (as in a more highly competitive situation). It involves modulation of distance and comfort with cooperation, and is no doubt based on what a consultant seems to want and encourage by his/her style of intervention.

Our paper is, principally, about this unfolding relationship and process and its vicissitudes. The plan of the paper is as follows. First, we consider the collaborative situation in psychoanalysis for comparison, in the light of recent contributions, from which we borrow. This leads to our formulation of the major initial sources of resistance to collaboration in small groups. Second, we outline the two basic sets of small-group phenomena inherent in the previous small-group literature, those of noncollaborative and collaborative groups, and their relation to the leadership offered. Third, we illustrate these phenomena in practice. Finally, we summarize our concept of collaborative leadership, passing tests of its intentions and capabilities in the light of the usual resistances.

THE ADEQUATE HOLDING ENVIRONMENT

Early psychoanalytic writing emphasized the overcoming of resistance in the patient. A parallel point of view with respect to groups is forcefully carried through by Bion in *Experiences in Groups* (1961), where the pedagogy consists of trenchant descriptions to the group of their irrational patterns of thinking that interfere with cooperation. Bion notes frequently that describing resistance seems to have little effect on it, even when described ever so sharply, but he persists in his efforts to secure cooperation this way nevertheless. In our experience, this method of consultation continues much the same in the traditions fathered by Bion, the Small Study Group Event in the Group Relations Conference, as sponsored in England by the Tavistock Institute of Human Relations and in America by the A. K. Rice Institute.[4] Not only is the oral tradition intact, but there has not been a single article in these traditions that reconsiders the method of taking study groups.

Psychoanalysts seemed to have learned more in the meanwhile from their experience concerning collaboration in the two-person situation of analysis. As children and more disturbed adult patients were taken into analysis, analysts began to appreciate what little cooperation might be gotten from the patient, what were the essential elements in this cooperation, and what the analyst could do to foster it. When it could not be taken for granted and relegated to the background, it became an object for consideration. This is the literature on the "therapeutic alliance" and on the analytic setting as containing elements of the mother-child relation. We will emphasize the contributions of Modell (1976), Balint (1959), and Klein (1959) as the most pertinent to our reconsideration of the group situation. In general, the line of thought is as follows: For the patient to tolerate the painfulness of exploration of old injuries and maintain a lively curiosity to learn from these experiences, the patient must feel adequately "held" by the treatment. Although the reference to being held is a metaphor for the security of the infant held securely by the mother, in fact this security of the patient extends from literally being supported by the couch in a pleasant room through a wide range of further protections. The patient feels held by the understanding of the analyst of matters the patient cannot hold in his own mind, by the calm of the analyst who is unprovoked, by the provision of environment in which reality is not overintrusive, but where fantasy is allowed its own sway (Modell, 1976; Winnicott, 1965). The patient may range freely between the cozy dark comfort of curling up on the couch, if the larger domain is too much for him, to ranging about the room or in his mind on wide-ranging adventures in the open spaces, if enclosure is threatening (Balint, 1959). In all, the adequate or "good enough" holding environment provides the conditions or background of safety (Sandler, 1960; Weiss, 1971). This background is necessary even to the healthiest of neurotic patients for them to spin out the substance of their neurosis into the patterning of the transference neurosis that then can be recognized and learned from. More disturbed patients, as Modell (1976) and others have shown, may remain in a "cocoon" transference, as it were, for many months even in the best of facilitating environments.

To be fruitful, study groups, like analysis, require their members to play out the patterns in their minds. What kind of "holding environment" is necessary and possible in groups? In the early days of study groups, it seems as if study group members were buoyed by their identifications with one another in the somewhat heroic pioneering venture of group self-study (Slater, 1966). Missing was the literal security of the couch, being understood individually, having the latitude of movement described by Balint (since the group could be so constraining), but the fixity of purpose of the consultant and his ability to follow and hold the group as a whole in his mind over a great range of its travels could be sustaining enough for some members. Given these conditions as background, the foreground of theorizing about the business of the consultant could be devoted to overcoming resistances to specific understandings. Participation was counted on and needed no theory of its own.

We are in different days and with different members for whom the above conditions are not sustaining enough. In the first place, many people are not personally suited to be pioneers of the group unconscious. In the second place, the social conditions that are the context of the study group intrude upon it so unceasingly that it is no longer the kind of preserve from reality that is possible in the psychoanalytic consulting room. Racial and class antagonisms remain literal in the study group. The boundary between street or bureaucratic life and the possibility for allowing illusions to unfold in a protected space is lost.

Let us look more closely at each of these kinds of shortcomings of the study group holding environment—the personal or depth-psychological first and the sociological second. To involve oneself in archaic relationships in a group for purposes of study is, to follow Michael Balint (1968), a kind of "new beginning," in the freshness and inarticulate possibilities that emerge. To allow oneself this kind of regression is to proceed backwards beyond what Melanie Klein (1959) called the "depressive" and "paranoid" positions. The "depressive position" is the fear of the total indifference of others and the "paranoid position" is the fear of retaliation. Each position is taken up out of concern for the force of frustrated individual needs, of greed, envy, and hatred. It seems, in groups, that contributions of inner experience cannot be made when the individual is preoccupied with the possible indifference or retaliation of others. This tends to result in singleton ("cocoon") status in the group. A similar finding from the larger context of organizations is that of Jaques (1974), who shows how apparently rather small changes in social organizations are interfered with by massive anxiety about how depressive and paranoid anxieties will be contained in the new arrangements. Balint (1959) describes the related phenomena of the need for primitive relationships to the environment, either of the clinging type or the thrills type. Individuals who must cling do so because of the dread of open spaces. Individuals who must continually range abroad in thrill-seeking fear being trapped in enclosures. The parallels to these in group would seem to be the necessity for some to be affiliated with basic assumption (Bion, 1961) groupings continuously, for others to be above and separate from the groups as singletons. Of course, such restrictions would be antithetical to the necessary flow of the mind necessary for learning about groups.

What is essential about the recognition of these failures of the group holding environment for the individual is to understand what makes them more likely to be magnified or diminished. It is clear that study groups can bring out these primitive anxieties to the extent that the members feel in danger of falling into very bad early or primitive situations, or they can feel adequate or good enough protection from such misfortunes. We think that Sartre (Laing and Cooper, 1964) goes to the core of the matter when he argues that (felt) scarcity is the fundamental disturbance in group life: scarcity of attention, honor, love, or whatever is wanted. This makes sense theoretically, when we consider, following Melanie Klein (1959), how scarcity could engender anger, greed, envy, and hatred in large measure, and foster either the paranoid or defensive positions. Klein suggests further that identification and gratitude are what tend to make all of this bearable. Scarcity tends to be less acute when members participate by identification in one another's fortunes, and gratitude begets more helpfulness. We shall examine the nature of the collaboration between consultant and group in the next section, to see how it may strengthen or exacerbate the inherent scarcity problems in the group. We should hardly expect that a group preoccupied with scarcity issues would provide much of a holding environment for the play of illusion and learning.

Members of a new small study group come into such a group usually from a variety of previous social experiences. Given the conditions in institutions in which the study group members have had most of their experience, these previous experiences are not apt to have been collaborative in the deepest and best sense. Why should they then expect anything different than they have been used to? No matter the promise of collaboration that is held out to them. False promises may be the rule. Educational institutions generally tend to be directed heavily from above, as Freire put it (1970), with the students as repositories in the "banking" method of education. Study group members sit back then waiting for valuable experiences and formulations to be deposited in them. Bureaucratic institutions may be interested strictly in the letter of regulations to the exclusion of the spirit. As a number of our students once put this matter, "We enter your course via the slot in our schedule which indicates we are to be here."
As described in a previous paper (Gustafson, 1976a), study group members may be primarily adherents of other task groups that have assigned them to the study group, which they relate to then as they would to a bus or any other assigned vehicle, as numbers in a series, as passengers holding tickets. An even more dire perspective, as if the previous ones were not sufficient, considers the inherent alienation of membership in capitalist institutions. A worker who uses manual dexterity may function simply as manual dexterity in the abstract sense in a factory, or a bureaucratic ad-

ministrator may be reduced to being an auditor of other people's miscalculations. The whole person is reduced to be part (alienation) in his or her institutional role (Ollman, 1971). What preparation is this for collaboration in depth in a study group? Even further, persons with highly complex talent that has considerable value and allows a great expressiveness for the individual are habitually pulled by the capitalist market into evaluating and calculating and planning their own exchange value, in order to command resources for work (Schneider, 1975). This forced preoccupation with exchange value easily may erode the individual's actual concentration upon the work itself, and again is poor preparation for collaboration with others in depth. The small study group can become reduced as well to an opportunity not for learning, but for impressing and allying oneself with other important people. We have seen study groups completely immobilized by such preoccupations, as if each member were a kind of common stock and the process that of a stock exchange in which values rose and fell.

In summary, the good enough holding environment for learning in the study group is apt to be vitiated in advance by deep concerns about scarcity and previous average social experience. We turn now to how the consultant initiates relations with group members who meet him in these conditions.

CONDITIONS OF SCARCITY AND CONDITIONS OF SAFETY

The literature of small-group phenomena is not very large. We think that the previous findings may be organized roughly into two broad categories: (a) the phenomena consequent to conditions of scarcity; (b) the phenomena consequent to conditions of safety. We start with the first class of phenomena, most brilliantly described by Bion (1961) and Slater (1966), but confirmed by many others.

We do not contest the accuracy of Bion's findings, but rather the failure to specify the limiting conditions under which they occur. This is no great matter to discover, if one considers Bion's own text (1961) carefully with some theoretical perspective. In the first paragraph of his account, Bion notes that the Professional Committee of the Tavistock Clinic asked him to take therapeutic groups. Bion's wry comment, "It was disconcerting to find that the Committee seemed to believe that patients could be cured in groups such as these," as refreshing as it may be in its candor, still conveys the contradictory situation he allowed his groups to be placed in, namely, of expecting something from someone who made no claim to be offering what they wanted. Indeed, his very first interpretation to the group he describes conveys his abdication: "It becomes clear to me that I am, in some sense, the focus of attention in the group. Furthermore, I am aware of feeling uneasily that I am expected to do something. At this point I confide my anxieties to the group, remarking that, however mistaken my attitude might be, I feel just this" (Bion, 1961, p. 30). He continues in this vein in a series of ten interpretations, not only to abdicate, but also to intrude, which he concedes he feels himself to be doing, exposing ever more mercilessly the wish of the group to idealize him despite his abandonment of them.

In the light of our previous considerations concerning the maternal aspects of early holding enviornments in groups, nothing could be more traumatic than abandonment and intrusion, the cardinal characteristics of very primitive images of the bad mother.[5] It is under these conditions that Bion elicits with remarkable clarity the so-called basic assumption groups. Bion evinces several explanations for these tenacious and primitive group formations, foremost of which is the need to preserve the group, which would otherwise be dispersed, for example, where Bion states: "Reproduction (basic assumption pairing) is recognized as equal with fight-flight in the preservation of the group" (p. 64). In our study group and clinical group therapy experience, such abandonment and intrusion errors as made by Bion do indeed regularly lead to basic assumption groups of great tenacity, or, on the other hand, to group dispersion, or group rebellion (Gustafson, 1976a; Slater, 1966). According to Yalom (1970), from the context of group therapy, group therapists who cannot be confronted with their limitations, because they are frighteningly formidable or weak and distant, develop groups that never become cohesive and responsible. This finding as well could be explained by the hypothesis that an adequate holding environment is prevented by abandonment or intrusion by the leader.

That there is an alternative way to take study groups is our main practical purpose to demonstrate, but the previous literature is helpful chiefly when findings from events other than the study group are considered. Consider, for example, how different is the relation between leader and members in the following account by Michael Balint of his method for collaborating in group seminars with general practitioners to understand their working problems: "As long as the mutual identifications of the members are fairly strong, any individual member can face strains because he feels accepted and supported by the group. His mistakes and failings, although humiliating, are not felt as singling him out as a useless member; quite on the contrary, he feels that he has helped the group to progress, using his failings as stepping-stone. *It is a precondition of our technique to establish this kind of atmosphere in the group, and it is only in such an atmosphere that it is possible to achieve what we term 'the courage of one's own stupidity.'* This means that the doctor feels free to be himself with his patient, that is, to use all of his past experiences and present skills without much inhibition'' (1954, p. 40).[6] In brief, we have another world of small-group phenomena here, which, as Balint astutely points out, depends *as its "precondition"* on the leader being able to establish the right conditions (of safety). Balint even goes on to explain how the group norms follow from his own (collaborative) relation to the group: "Perhaps the most important factor is the behavior of the leader in the group. It is hardly an exaggeration to say that if he finds the right attitude he will teach more by his example than by everything else taken together. After all, the technique we advocate is based on exactly the same sort of listening that we expect the doctors to acquire. By allowing everybody to be themselves, to have their say in

145

their own way and in their own time, by watching for proper cues, *i.e., speaking only when something is really expected from him* and making his point in a form which, *instead of prescribing the right way of dealing* with the patient's problems, *opens up possibilities* for the doctors to discover some right way of dealing with the patient's problems, the leader can demonstrate in the 'here and now' situation what he wants to teach'' (p. 41). Again, we discover through Balint the cardinal importance of being there when needed (not abandoning), but not being intrusive and prescriptive. With these conditions of safety, we get an entirely different kind of small group than under the conditions of scarcity provided by Bion.

The distinction being drawn between the Bion method of group analysis and the work done in Balint's groups involves a substantial conceptual issue: How can covert processes that inevitably occur in groups be worked with so as to create collaborative work atmosphere?

The mechanism of projective identification is probably inevitably in operation, particularly in groups structured as study groups. In this projective process members unconsciously imbue leadership and often each other with important thoughts and feelings that have powerful influences on their (member) behavior. Partly members do this because of the regressive power of the group situation, partly they do this as a communicational device that is intended to make leadership aware of covert forces that cannot be verbalized (for a variety of reasons, such as their being out of the awareness of the members involved) by inducing the warded-off attitudes in the consultant. For example, a group unable to handle its own contempt may take actions that induce contempt for them in the consultant. They thus communicate the problem to him and have the opportunity to learn from him how to manage it.[7]

Bion makes it quite clear that this projective identification is occurring and in fact uses whatever data he has of these projections as the substance of his interpretation. It is as if the kind of work that members do with consultation in a Bion-type group is to provide the data for exposing basic assumption functioning. This kind of uncovering almost inherently encourages an increase of such functioning since, it becomes either explicitly or implicitly what the work contract is between leader and member. *It is the end to which the projective data is used that is the crucial difference in the Bion and Balint situation.* It is possible to use the more covert, projective data about basic assumption life in a very different way, to foster a more collaborative work contract.

In a more limited conference situation, it seems to be assumed that what members are least able to sense explicitly, and what the function of consultation should be, is openly dealing with their fantasy and impulse life. Within this context it is possible to exaggerate such behavior. We are assuming that behind this basic assumption functioning, or along with it, is an equally difficult kind of work collaboration that doesn't involve a mutual admiration and mutual protection atmosphere, but rather the use of the covert process material to focus on difficulties with and fantasies about a more mutual and reality-based work relationship. This is not to deny or try to bypass the difficult underlying material, but not to use it only for the exposure of the infantile side of group behavior. We are suggesting that the material be used both in its meaning as a resistance and as an expression of difficulty in experiencing one's strength, skills, and competence, taking responsibility for these experiences, and functioning in a collaborative way in the face of strong irrational desires and needs. That is, members not only resist collaboration, but may also *make prominent* what their difficulties are in collaborating in order that the difficulties may be clearly grasped and overcome.[8] Balint's method seems to accept the members' contributions in this spirit, which, we think, allows members to be more able to continue showing what they need help with.

Very much related to Balint's way to taking groups is that advocated from an entirely different context by Freire in his *Pedagogy of the Oppressed* (1970), in which he describes his "culture circles" and projects to teach literacy to peasants in Latin America. Freire adds to Balint's appreciation of the depth-psychological conditions of safety his own grasp of countering the sociological or political tendencies that would interfere with the right relationship of the leader to the group. Freire describes the so-called "director culture," in which powerful people from the cities enter the rural areas to prescribe and proscribe, to define the terms of the conversation, which are then the terms used by the peasant participants, who themselves remain in a "culture of silence" concerning their own actual experience. Problem-posing technique, as used by Freire, completely avoids formulation by the leader, because of the endemic tendency of the participants to then become lost in using the leader's terms. Freire poses problems, often nonverbally with pictures, asking the participants to find their own expression for what concerns them about the situations. From the depth-psychological perspective, this is brilliant avoidance of inflicting the intrusion trauma that is chronic for these peasants. From the sociological or political perspective, it represents the clearest signal of a new situation for these participants from what they are used to, so as to minimize the carryover of expectations from noncollaborative oppressive social institutions. The reader may, at first glance, take Freire's practice as peculiar to extraordinary circumstances of oppression. Our experience is contrary, in that we find students, bureaucrats, doctors, and housewives entering study groups trying to grasp the right terms of the leader to manipulate for themselves. This tendency must be countered, as by Freire, if true collaboration is to emerge.[9]

IN PRACTICE

The weaknesses of a tradition are often painfully obvious in its neophyte practitioners. Their earnest imitations of classical practice not only reveal their own clumsiness, but also can remind observers of the classical practice itself, which is revealed through the exaggeration (caricature). To illustrate our thesis about the difficulties of collaboration, we have chosen a rather simple dynamic, in which the needed intervention is clearcut, as a series of seven neophyte consultants tried to grapple with it. The context was a special type of Small Study Group event devised by Rioch (unpublished), in which the seven members of the group took turns being the consultant. Each had the opportunity to take this role for a period of an hour and a quarter, following which the individual had an opportunity to discuss his/her interventions with the staff observers. The ordinary difficulty in any study group of obtaining collaboration was enhanced by the competition of the members to do the best job and earn further opportunities to consult in Group Relations conferences.

Each of the seven consultancies began with lively expectation, even excitement, which in every instance but one went dead. The six consultants who allowed this to happen very early showed to their colleagues their discomfort, insecurity, and lack of confidence. They were then not attacked directly, and gradual withdrawal ensued. The seventh consultant (actually fifth in sequence) began very aggressively by pointing out the attempt of the group to subdivide into cozy parties as an avoidance of dealing with the end of the event. She indicated by her demeanor as well as her intepretation that she was prepared to deal directly with their hostility to the task and her leadership. Excitement continued as the members felt free to bring forward their rivalry with her without fear of injuring her, without the depressive anxiety that they would later have to live with serious guilt about their actions. In this depth-psychological sense, she provided an adequate holding environment for the expression of what the group members were full of, namely, their own fierce competitiveness *and* their wish to collaborate in exploring it.

Once the other six consultants had signaled their need to be protected by showing obvious weakness—not making an interpretation for a half hour despite many opportunities, mumbling the first interpretation, sitting away from the chair previously reserved for the consultant—the collaboration was in serious difficulty, unless the consultant could show some clear ability to recover strength that would reassure the members that they might bring forward their hostilities safely. The obvious move (to the staff observers) was to confront directly the dramatic change in climate from excitement to deadness, the most straightforward and explicit process. This would be reassuring at a depth-psychological level to the other members, because his/her equanimity in facing early difficulty would signal strength that could be safely challenged, which is what they wanted to express. None of the six could bring up this dramatic process. One showed some later vigor and secured some involvement with his consultation that was marred by heavy undertones of depressive anxiety, as the fear of injuring him could not be relieved when he could not face directly their first loss of faith in his dominance.

In the conference discussion between the observing staff and the seven member-consultants, the dramatic change in climate in six of the consultations was soon identified, and the question was posed to them by the staff: What made it difficult for them to confront that process directly? Their replies were intense and thoughtful and confirm our major theses about the difficulties in collaboration. All of the six consultants sensed the change in the group during the time that it occurred, but felt helpless to discuss it with the group. Some felt that only full interpretations of what was wrong would be acceptable, and since they could only acquire a partial understanding while it was happening, they did not feel free to bring this forward and ask the members to meet them halfway. They conceived of their role as having to be oracular. Some felt that direct discussion of one's first interpretation as inadequate was to invite disaster, in the form of the group's pleasure in that, or one's own anger at them for wanting one to fail. These personal responses were greatly feared by the six consultants, who were desperately trying to hold onto a professional role. They reported they felt they could not think about the significance of these strong emotions because they feared them as merely personal and idiosyncratic, i.e., not signifying some general relevance to the situation, because they were desperately preoccupied with maintaining the right external professional visage, because they then had to cut off their own fantasy, fearing to go inside themselves to get in touch with it, because they needed to keep an eye on the group members continually. Their solace was that "the respect" for the consultant and his chair, however formalized and dead a religion, was better than none at all.

In summary, the difficulties of these neophyte consultants reflect both a sociopolitical resistance and a depth-psychological resistance. The first is straightforward, in that the social role of the consultant is conceived of as having to be oracular, i.e., which is an impossible idea when the consultant is dependent on his colleagues for the data to work with and must secure their collaboration. The second resistance to taking a collaborative stance is the depth-psychological (primitive) dichotomy between being all-powerful or totally helpless, where one inept intervention equals a completely inept consultant. What was needed in these difficult situations was neither pronouncement nor invulnerability. Had the staff attempted either in the conference discussion, more deadness would have ensued. What was needed was for someone to *pose the problem* (Freire, 1970) of the dramatic change in process and encourage participants to have the "courage of their own stupidity" (Balint, 1954), which when supplied in the conference discussion, resulted in the outpouring of collaboration (about what had gone wrong) which has been just described. One might wonder about the selection of the members for this conference, whether they were well-suited for consultant work. It is possible that some of them were not, but we take another point of view as well: namely, that they were *making prominent* (Sampson, 1976) their difficulty with collaboration—a difficulty the tradition of Group Relations Conferences had left them in, all having had several previous memberships in these conferences—in order to be helped with it. When the difficulties were received in this spirit in the conference discussion they began mastering it.

OUR MODEL OF COLLABORATION IN STUDY GROUP CONSULTATION

We may now summarize what we take to be the essential points of technique in consultation to study groups that will bring out collaboration in depth. The abandonment-and-intrusion model of Bion (1961) leads to collaboration only under the very special circumstances of having exceptionally hardy or pioneering members who are able to overthrow the leader and establish their own cooperative arrangements (Slater, 1966). It is otherwise overly traumatic in the depth-psychological sense, and overly dominating and defining in the political sense, to constitute an adequate holding environment for learning.[10] Balint's emphasis on being there for the members "when something is really expected" but not otherwise, and in a "problem-posing way" so as to avoid the director culture, as demonstrated by Freire, is entirely in the right direction for the study group consultant.

Balint's method is very similar to that recommended by Weiss (1971) and Sampson (1976) in the context of psychoanalysis as conditions for the emergence of deeper concerns. The provision of "the right relationship," that is, supplying the missing ego function and/or the analysis of the resistances to the first emergence of that functioning in the patient, leads to the emergence of new themes from the patient. This is again a case of being there in the right dose and with the right function that is missing, but not being too much there when the patient can be helped to supply it himself. Again, the opposite of abandonment and intrusion is providing the right relationship. In our view, the "emergence of new themes" in the group occurs under these conditons of safety described by Weiss and Sampson from the individual psychotherapy context. If the group members can supply the function themselves but are having trouble maintaining it, the consultant's task is to help them see their interference with their own work. If they are entirely missing a sorely needed function, he may provide it but then step back to let them use it themselves.

Finally, we would emphasize, with Jaques (1948), that the intention thus to provide the right relationship to foster the capabilities of the members of the group will be continually *tested*, both from the depth-psychological and political perspectives. The consultant is invited to be intrusive or to be neglectful of critical matters. He is invited to take over formulation and direction. Only when he passes these tests continually can the conditions for collaboration in depth securely hold the members in a group culture, that is, a "new beginning," that is thereby acquired and distinguished from the dreaded internal dangers and average social oppression.

10.

A STUDY OF VERY SMALL GROUPS

R. Gosling

INTRODUCTION

In 1948, or thereabouts, after some years as an Army Psychiatrist, Wilfred Bion had the disconcerting experience of finding himself surrounded by a small number of patients expecting treatment from him in the setting of a Psychiatric Clinic that had a reputation for harbouring some experts in psychotherapy. Furthermore, Bion had been made to realize that the Professional Committee of the Clinic held to the idea that he had become something of an expert in "taking" groups, though just what the Committee Members thought his "taking" them would consist of he had no means of knowing. It goes without saying that they had also made the assumption that these groups that he was to "take" would have a therapeutic effect on the patients that composed them. To be caught up in such a nexus of expectations and to feel stimulated to see what can be made of the situation is a not uncommon experience. What was uncommon, however, was to have an alert and thoughtful man such as Bion to do it and then to describe some of his experiences.

His open-eyed and somewhat startled approach has had a widespread influence on the understanding of the social dynamics of small groups, particularly to the extent that the dynamics are the product of powerful fantasies that have become shared by those composing the groups as a result of various kinds of communication that to a large extent go unnoticed or unacknowledged. The fantasies that have become shared in this way are experienced as self-evidently reasonable assumptions. As each member's contribution to their formation has been made anonymously, no one seems to be responsible for them.

The stance that Bion tried to adopt in relation to his experience of being a "staff member" among a small number of "patients" in a clinic was similar to the stance that a psychoanalyst might try to adopt in relation to the events taking place in his consulting room. In trying to articulate his experience, however, he was careful not to slip into using the images and metaphors of infancy and childhood that abound in psychoanalysis, but turned instead to the language of wider social experience, namely, history and mythology.

Method: Gosling

This approach, particularly insofar as it gave pride of place to unconscious processes, gave a particular emphasis to the work done subsequently by his colleagues in the Tavistock Institute of Human Relations in the fast developing field of Group Relations Training. Following the seminal work of Kurt Lewin, the study of small group dynamics flourished in a variety of ways in the USA under the auspices of the National Training Laboratory until it exploded into a veritable shower of adventures of the present day encounter movement and beyond. The preoccupations of a small number of Tavistock workers, following in the direction first suggested by Bion, led them to develop the human relations laboratory method of learning along a somewhat different channel. This resulted in a series of experiential conferences held at Leicester, England, by which name they are widely known. Their design and the thinking that lies behind the design have been described by Trist and Sofer (1959) and by Rice (1965).

Over time the central preoccupation of these conferences has shifted considerably. For instance, in 1960 the conference was entitled "A Training Conference in Group Relations" and its stated task was "to provide members with learning experiences which can enable them to become aware of the main problems of leadership and especially of the deeper and frequently unrecognised forces at work in modern organisational life and inter-personal relations." By 1971 the title had changed to "Authority and Leadership—A Working Conference" and the task was "to provide members with opportunities to learn about the nature of authority and the interpersonal and inter-group problems encountered in its exercise." Five years later the title had come to be "Authority, Leadership and Organisation—A Working Conference" and the task had come to include opportunities to learn about "the institutional problems encountered in exercising authority within the conference organisation."

For such undertakings, conference members are recruited from a wide variety of backgrounds, professions and disciplines: industrialists and social workers, psychiatrists and educators, clerics and social administrators; both sexes and all ages. The aim of the conference is reflected in its setting, namely a university hall of residence. The aim is educational and not therapeutic; members come to study and learn and not as patients to find treatment; such therapeutic gain as there may be is a chance by-product, though an acceptable one. The design of the conference and the tone of the various meetings reflect a belief in the value of learning from experience; any teaching in the conventional sense is provided only incidentally; the aim of the staff is to help the membership to come to grips with its own behaviour in the "here and now" through the offering of interpretations of that behaviour. Some of the experiences commonly encountered in such conferences in the setting of small groups (numbering about ten members and one consultant) and large groups (numbering from 40 to 80 members and two or three consultants) have been described in detail by Turquet (1974; 1975).

This approach to learning has been elaborated further as a result of working in conjunction with other similarly interested organisations beside the Tavistock Institute of Human Relations, in particular, the Grubb Institute for Behavioural Studies in London, the Department of Education of Bristol University and the A. K. Rice Institute in Washington, DC. It is a pleasure to acknowledge my indebtedness to colleagues in all these institutions. To anyone who has read Bion's book, "Experiences in Groups" (1961), my great indebtedness to Bion will be obvious. Fundamentally, however, I am indebted to the various conference members whose uncertain capacities for cooperation have been linked to my own in exploring the phenomena of very small groups (numbering five to six members and one consultant); it is they who have provided me with the raw material for the reflections that I can now present.

Before doing so, however, my position within the sequence of these conferences should be made clear so that my reflections on the very small groups may be put into their context. For some years I had taken the role of consultant to a number of different events in these training conferences, in particular, the small groups set up to study their own experience as the conference proceeded. In 1975 it bore in upon some of us that many members coming to these training conferences spent much of their working lives engaged in groups consisting of five or so people, and that although the conference offered them opportunities to explore the phenomena occurring in small groups of about ten members and large groups of from 40 to 80, they did not do so for groups of the size they most commonly encountered in their work settings.

Consequently, at the next conference, in parallel with the on-going examination of small groups (SGs) and large groups (LGs), members were offered an opportunity to study the events in groups consisting of only five members and one consultant (VSGs), the members being selected in such a way as to avoid so far as possible their coming together with either members or a consultant from their small group experience. Naturally, as the large group experience included all the membership, they had inevitably met each other during that event. Furthermore, there were other concurrent formal training events, to say nothing of numerous informal meetings of a "social" kind, in which members were free to choose their own companions, such as an event to study inter-group processes and another to study the impact of the institution of the conference itself on the individual and of the individual on the institution. Although members of the very small groups (VSGs) might therefore have relations with each other of their own making outside the group, the conference management in its design of the program had kept them down to a minimum.

During the conference, the consultants working in their first VSGs had opportunities for comparing notes, refining some of their emerging ideas and sharpening their awareness. It was commonly known that this particular experiment had not been carried out before in such a conference and so in their temper they had a needle of excitement to them that sometimes verged on a point of outrage. Believing there was ever only one first time, I was glad to be able to test out some of my first impressions in a second series of VSGs scheduled for a conference in the following year. It is from my experience of this second conference that most of my reflections are drawn.

It should be recognised that just as members of such a conference move from one episode to another, sometimes dragging with them hang-overs of feelings and expectations, sometimes determined to differentiate one event from another and to let by-gones be by-gones, and very frequently suffused with such a sense of deja-vue that the whole series of events seems to be one long drawn out relearning of what has always been dimly known, so too the staff members are inevitably caught up in analagous trajectories through the experience of the conference, a conference that in some respects is unlike any conference that has ever gone before. My reflections on the VSGs, therefore, are an aspect of my own particular trajectory through this particular conference (following upon the particular conference that went before it and so on). The VSGs that I refer to took place concurrently with a series of SGs and LGs, as well as some other training events, according to the program given below. With the SGs and LGs they shared certain features: as well as being events that depended strictly on studying the "here and now" experience of the group, they were in addition groupings that had been designated by the conference management and were bounded in their work by this membership and by a designated place and duration. In the other training events there were more options open to the membership as to how they went about their learning.

CHARACTERISTICS OF THE PSYCHOLOGICAL FIELD

The simplest way for members of a VSG to dispose themselves so as to study the group's behaviour is to arrange themselves in a circle. This means that for each person present the others fall within his field of vision. No turning of the head is needed to take in a neighbour's fiscal expression, gestures or posture as is usually the case in a SG of ten or so members. Even less is it like a LG in which it is virtually impossible to take in what most of the other members are up to. There is therefore, in comparison, a plentiful and detailed nonverbal feed-back. Members less commonly get confused with other members, and statements are only rarely attributed to the wrong member. When a member starts to tilt his chair backwards and to balance on its back legs, to the other members it speaks loudly of his momentary anxiety, his wish to take up a mid-position in the matter that is being considered, his wish to be half in and half out of the group, or whatever else; in a SG although the same event would certainly have an impact, its precise message might, as it were, be just out of hearing. In a SG, opportunities are plentiful for conducting transactions that escape some members' notice and that quickly produce an atmosphere of not knowing what is happening or quite where one is in it all. Although recall of recent events is often inaccurate and statements are often wrongly attributed, there is usually a not too remote possibility of putting them right and so reconstituting for the members concerned a boundary to their own individuality. In a LG, by contrast, the depersonalising processes are continual and are often only countered by differentiating oneself from one's neighbour or by engaging actively with the consultants.

In the VSG each member can give roughly an equally personal account of all the others; it is relatively difficult to hide behind another member successfully or to remain virtually anonymous. In a SG, inevitably there are prominent characters at any one time, and opportunities abound for others to remain hidden while yet having an effect on the group. If a member is absent from a VSG his or her identity is instantly recognised by all the others; in a SG it may take a moment or two to work out who the empty chair belongs to; in a LG it is often impossible to know for sure whether or not anyone is absent and if so who it is. In this sense the boundary of the VSG in respect to membership is easily perceived and feels firm. This firmness is further attested to by the way a sense of familiarity soon builds up that stands in contrast to the uncertainties of the other conference events; indeed the reality of these past and future other events gets very attenuated indeed and the VSG can spend long periods absorbed in its own experience as if nothing else in the world existed.

This intense personalisation of each member of a VSG, as well as of the consultant, precludes some of the adventurous splitting, stereotyping and unashamed use of other members as vehicles for projection that wax and wane in a SG. In a VSG, it is as if some other thread of experience of a member demanded recognition before the previous one had been fully grasped and shared; no sooner have the members identified the consultant's behaviour, say, as the cause of their present disarray than someone remembers that he made quite a useful remark only a short while ago. It is therefore more difficult to encounter and explore in a VSG some of the enormities of archaic convictions that soon become apparent in a SG, let alone what happens in a LG. A further feature of this brake on splitting tendencies in a VSG is that the very prominence of the nonverbal communications keeps them perpetually linked to what is being said in words; a member tends therefore to be experienced as someone sending a complex, even contradictory, message, but one representing a relatively whole and ambivalent person. In a SG, however, there often grows up a culture that pays almost exclusive attention to what has been put into words and does its best to ignore all that is being expressed by other means. This tendency is doubtlessly reinforced by the consultant's behaviour as he is seen struggling to put into words his impression of what the group is up to. The extreme form of this culture occurs when a group colludes in propounding the view that you only need to be silent to be sure you communicate nothing.

Another prominent characteristic of the psychological field is related to the physical proximity of members to each other, i.e., to all of the other members, not just to one's neighbours. This characteristic is manifested in the self-consciousness of members about how close their hands are to those of their neighbours, whether their feet are likely to touch those of a member opposite, how big a shift backwards of their chair they can make without appearing notably hostile. Your neighbours' breathing becomes a prominent feature of your awareness; if you want to cough you must do

Method: Gosling

Figure 1. PROGRAMME: SEPTEMBER 1976

Time	Thurs 9th	Fri 10th	Sat 11th	Sun 12th	Mon 13th	Tue 14th	Wed 15th	Thurs 16th	Fri 17th	Sat 18th	Sun 19th	Mon 20th	Tue 21st
8:15 Breakfast													
9:00–10:30		SG	SG	SG	SG	—	—	LG	LG	LG	LG	LG	P
10:30 Coffee													
11:00–12:30		MG/VSG	MG/VSG	MG/VSG	MG/VSG	—	LG	SG	SG	SG	IE	OG	OG
1:00 Lunch	P 2.00												
2:30–4:00*	OG	IG	IG	—	2.3.30 IG	—	SG	—	IE	—	IEP	—	
4:00 Tea*					3:30 Tea								
4:30–6:00*	SG	IG	OG	IG	4-5:30 OG	—	IE	IE	OG	IE	OG	P	
6:30 Dinner													
7:30–9:00	SG	MG/VSG	—	MG/VSG	—	—	IE	IE	—	IE	—	OG	

P = Plenary Session   MG = Median Group   IG = Intergroup Event
OG = Orientation Group   VSG = Very Small Group   IE = Institutional Event
SG = Small Group   LG = Large Group

Note: At this conference members were given the option when applying to take part in either a VSG or a MG—a Median Group of about 20 members.

it into someone's face unless you make a deliberate manoeuvre not to. Eye contact is telling when present, awkward when absent and always under keen surveillance as to its intensity and duration. It would seem that in this way the VSG is constantly faced with the problems of intimacy, particularly intimacy as a danger to be avoided, as if the bodily proximity of other members were sexually so exciting as to threaten an explosion. Although at the start of the series of meetings, members may comment on their sense of safety and the promise of intimacy, as time goes on, revealing or forthright statements are prominent by their absence. Members' behaviour suggests that intimacy is an impending danger that must always be guarded against. Open recognition of sexual feelings for each other, for instance, that at some point is a comment event in a SG, is embarked on in a VSG with great caution. My impression is that in a SG it is felt that all that might take place is a sexual orgy with little personal commitment, whereas in a VSG it felt as if it could alter the whole course of one's life, like wife-swapping. But this remains little more than a personal hunch and I find myself not at all well informed about the nature of the menace that intimacy is felt to have in a VSG.

Yet another characteristic of the psychological field that influences events is related to the number of people present and to the nature of the mental work that this requires of members. I suggest that for most of us it is possible to have simultaneous relations with several people at once, allowing each person moderately full recognition, provided the number is small. Empathy, or coenaesthetic perception (Spitz 1965) is effected by putting oneself in the other person's shoes, i.e., by splitting one's self into a part that stays at home and another that is exported imaginatively to feel out what the other person is experiencing. Now splitting one's self up into parts is obviously potentially damaging to one's sense of integrity; exporting these parts, furthermore, is obviously potentially depleting. To recognise another person fairly fully requires the exported part of the self to be a sizeable segment of one's own self, containing a fair mixture of both good and bad objects and a coherent sub-ego that experiences them. Although people vary in the number of simultaneous fairly full relationships they can sustain, I suggest that at some point the splitting and projective processes required become more threatening to the individual than the advantages experienced from the multiple relationships.[1]

To engage affectively with the membership of a VSG therefore, though it does not promise plain sailing, is not immediately felt as a divisive and impoverishing undertaking. A SG, however, at once poses questions of alliances, the prospect of being rejected by everyone else, a mass attack, the strong and the weak, the parts and the whole, fragmentation and homogenisation and so forth. The individual's sense of his own identity can come in for some fairly rough handling through being set up to play a part on behalf of the group or being used as a vehicle or repository for impulses that are generally unwanted to deplored. Engulfment, disturbing and intrusive attributions and scapegoating are in the forefront of the picture when joining a SG, whereas in a VSG more benign expectations can be entertained. As one member put it, the interchanges of the VSG felt less "grabby" than those in her SG. Threats to an individual's sense of his identity are even greater and more perpetual in a LG (see Turquet, 1975).

Finally, a fifth characteristic of the psychological field is that of perceived symmetry. With only six or seven people in the room, pairing continually reappears. Another member is nearly always experienced as being either next to you or opposite you. Although remarks may be made by a member as if they were addressed to the group as a whole, within a short time the responses tend to be coming from one other member. For a while some issue may be tossed around as of general concern, but before long it seems to get captured by a pair of members. Whereas in a SG this capturing of a theme by a pair is usually tolerated for a long time and even enjoyed as a vicarious experience, in a VSG the pairing quickly becomes exclusive and the fact that the theme being developed does not tally with the experience of one of the other members becomes obtrusive. The pairings are therefore short-lived but continually recurring, often with a sense of surreptitiously continuing something that had had to be abandoned prematurely or at least carrying overtones of what had taken place earlier. Indeed, the simple dyadic gestalt that seems to be hard to resist puts distinct limitations on what takes place in a VSG. One member remarked on the fact that in the VSG he missed the "power politics of the SG and all the attendant archaic and crazy events."

PSYCHOLOGICAL MODELS

Within this field, some characteristics of which have been adumbrated above, the members of the VSG have a variety of experiences. In an attempt to give meaning to these experiences various psychological models are offered using memories of analagous experiences of the past. Of course, none fits exactly and the work of the group in coming to grips with the uniqueness of its experience lies in bringing into conjunction fragments of memory in a novel, apt and suggestive way. No one person is in a position to do it all, though for periods of time the belief that there is such a one may take root. In fact it is a never ending interactive process in which the search for meaning itself creates new conditions that in turn require new meanings to be found for them.

Nevertheless, as each member has limited experience to draw upon and a modest capacity for inventiveness, I have so far been able to identify only four clusters of past experience from which psychological models appear to be drawn:

1. The Confessional. On entering a VSG ideas about greater intimacy, getting to know people "better," confession, letting one's hair down, dropping one's facade, honesty etc. usually abound. In such states I, as the consultant, have been experienced as some kind of bishop, a psychotherapist or a somewhat oversized friend acting as host.
2. The Family. In the shifting configurations of the group, notions concerning the nuclear family return time and time again. Moreover these notions are usually expressed with pleasure as if something

reassuring had been discovered, this despite the fact that it later transpires that at least some of the members have had anything but reassuring experiences in their actual families. In this state I tend to get cast in a parental or grand-parental role, adoptive or generative, or as an enfant terrible, or occasionally as a suitor from another family.
3. Negotiation. The ebb and flow of individual differences and the commonalities of membership, of what is private what is public, of what is idiosyncratic and what is shared are sometimes construed as negotiations. The notion of negotiation, however, touches on a wide spectrum of experience from political negotiations of power, to commercial negotiations of value, to the kind of negotiation of personal realities that takes place in a marriage or in a therapy group. Here I tend to get cast in the role of a negotiator with an unfair advantage, an adjudicator or a landlord.
4. The Balloon or Lifeboat. The fourth model that I think I have identified is related to an experience few of us have had in actuality but that seems to be very familiar in psychic reality; it is that of a balloon in which someone has got to be jettisoned and who is it going to be? This model is so scaring that it appears only momentarily and I am not at all sure of its validity for anyone but myself.

By contrast, in a SG the culture of dependency is likely to be more like that met with in the body of a church or an evangelical chapel than in a confessional, and more like that of a classroom than a tea-party. If it comes to be felt as a safe place to return to from other exciting and divisive events in the conference, it is likened to a home rather than a family, defined by territory, rules and a tradition rather than a set of relationships. The roles created from the matrix of a SG resemble the figures of the Comedia del Arte more than they do members of a nuclear family. In a SG there are frequent periods of preoccupation with issues of control over threatening explosions or rivalrous chaos; these are not prominent in the VSG and may be represented more by issues concerned with having to regulate a threatening intimacy.

A particular manifestation of the characteristic of a VSG whereby the members are highly personalized is that when some member is mobilised to perform an important group task, such as to stand up to the consultant's authority, the person's known outside role may be taken into account in his selection. In one VSG it was a parson set up to embroil me in a "psychoanalysis versus religion" conflict; in the other it was a family therapist to embroil me in arguments about individual versus family therapy. My experience in SGs suggests that selection for such an important role usually gives greater weight to relevant personality characteristics such as a notably argumentative, authoritarian or courageous person, than to his actual role in the outside world. Similarly a member who is to carry bewilderment and incomprehension on behalf of the group, the dunce or the ingenue, can come from quite a range of candidates in a SG. In both the VSGs of my experience an actual difference of cultural background and native language was used for much of the time.

No sooner had these thoughts of mine got to the stage of being expressed as above than I was confronted with the experience of yet another VSG to which what I thought I had learned so far seemed to have only the vaguest relevance. This was a VSG experience in 1977 provided for members of a Training Group numbering 13 in conjunction with a Working Conference membership of 45 and a Conference Staff Group of 12. Training Group members had each had experience of being a member of a Working Conference on at least two occasions before. The aim of the Training Group was to provide them with the experience of assuming the role of consultant to groups of Working Conference members later in the conference. In this setting the two VSGs, one of six members and the other of seven members, remained firmly sub-groups of the 14; it was the Training Group as a whole that held the predominant sentience.

There was much nostalgia for the raw experiences of the SGs of yesteryear; there was some pressure to demonstrate expertise in identifying some small group phenomena that had become familiar; notions of "doing things on behalf of the group" were so quickly mobilised and so firmly ensconced in the orthodox jargon of the group that there was little room left for testing things out in the light of members' personal experience. For my part I had, by accepting a staff role in relation to the Training Group, come to put a premium on the fact that I had worked in two VSGs before and so was more "experienced" than most others. I was constantly hoping that some of the psychological models that had seemed to be fruitful in the past would turn out to be so again. It is unclear how much time was wasted by us all trying to recreate circumstances that would have vindicated the idea that we all had "experience." In fact the salient affective issues in the VSG were of a depressive kind, in particular how one is one's own most dangerous saboteur and how one's public stance on the side of learning turns out to be a determination to repeat what one already knows and to learn as little that is new as possible. This was affectively related to the "middle age" position of one's life-span and the members' experience of being in the middle of a sandwich between the Working Conference members and the Conference staff.

This experience left me with two vivid realisations:

1. How much the events I was trying to get to grips with were defined, predicated or determined by their social context and therefore how empty of meaning it was to refer to VSGs, SGs or LGs as if they were reproducible objects or even that there was such an identifiable category as what I have heard referred to as "conference learning." The initials VSG refer to events that have a certain amount in common, such as number of participants and the fact that they take place in a tradition of exploration called the Leicester Conference, but that are profoundly influenced by what is going on round them in time and place. So much is this the case that any generalisation about

VSGs that can fairly be made is likely to be so modest as to be of very little use or interest.
2. How quickly a formulation, a concept or a theory loses its enabling quality and becomes a barrier to the possibility of making further observations. This is a topic that has been greatly enriched by Bion of recent years. An experience of a VSG is deepened or led on to a further and new experience only at the moment that a theory about it is being fashioned. The theory may then lie around for a while to be applied occasionally and enjoyed in a way that is neither productive nor harmful. Sooner or later, however, it becomes a barrier to new experiences, a Procrustean bed and a downright blight. Psychoanalytic practice is also replete with this phenomenon. Using Bion's (1977) notions of the *container* and the *contained,* the relationship between them is either symbiotic, commensal or parasitic: productive, uneventful or destructive. Perhaps the most that can be hoped for is that this cycle of degeneration, if there is one, is accomplished in as short a time as possible.

At this point I am reminded of the fact that the theory of Oedipus Complex remains for me a recurrently enlivening one. It is a theory that I seem constantly to have forgotten only then to have to discover it all over again and each time as if I were doing so with great originality; the shock of the event confronts me with my rivalry and hatred of Freud and is something that my patients quite often don't get over all that easily either. It occurs to me therefore that the theory (and set of images) of the Oedipus Complex must lie for the most part (for good and obvious reasons) just on the boundary of what I must repress and what I can acknowledge. This instability of what is known, or thought to be known, seems to be required if it is to be rediscovered repeatedly always in a new context and so always for the first time.

I am therefore led to think, and reluctantly to believe, that while any reader or any author of an essay entitled "A Study of Very Small Groups" might reasonably search its pages for some clarity of exposition and firmness of conclusion, to the extent that he claims to have found it he may be headed for disaster. It seems that the most he can expect are a variety of suggestive comments any one of which can become an albatross hung about his neck if it is taken at its face value. It is as if learning has always to take place on the edge of exasperation. In these matters there can be few authors more stimulating to one's inclination to re-examine one's experiences yet once again than Wilfred Bion. His writings are rich in suggestiveness. At the same time there are few authors whose obliquity is more exasperating—unless the present author has unwittingly outdone him!

11.

MEN AND WOMEN AT WORK: A GROUP RELATIONS CONFERENCE ON PERSON AND ROLE[1]

Laurence J. Gould

INTRODUCTION

The exploration of issues related to gender, sexuality, and age seem particularly germane in our current work and personal situations. In recent years, we have witnessed the dramatic upsurge of many sorts of incipient revolutions. Certainly one among these has been in the sexual realm—not only in the intimate and narrow sense of sexual, but in the broader areas concerning the nature of the family unit itself, and role shifts or changes in the world of work. However, there is much to suggest that the ability of men and women to work together effectively is still often seriously impaired by deeply held gender-related issues. And finally, the loosening of sexual constraints, both internally and externally, confront us continually with the dilemmas of temptation, choice, and action that cross traditional boundaries. This constellation of gender, sexuality, and age may be viewed, therefore, as an increasingly salient aspect of group and organizational work settings as it influences or interacts with issues of authority and leadership.

The 'Men and Women at Work' group relations conferences to be discussed in this paper are specifically designed to provide opportunities to study the ways in which collaboration among and between men and women in group and organizational work settings is affected by attitudes and beliefs, both conscious and unconscious, related to gender, sexuality, and age. The aim is to further the exploration and understandings of these attitudes and beliefs as they are manifested behaviourally in the various conference events and in the conference as a whole.

CONFERENCE ORIGINS

Initially, heightened awareness of the issues noted above were stimulated, of course, by the developing 'women's movement'—so towards the end of the 1960s a number of my colleagues and I began to think about new conference designs that would hopefully provide more sustained and direct opportunities for exploring various aspects of male/female interactions. While such study seemed to be timely, on a more personal level I was deeply influenced by a number of women who were involved in the 'movement' including some colleagues, women graduate students in my programme and, most directly, by the woman with whom I live. If anything was needed to convince me of the importance of these issues, it was the continual and often disturbing experience of living with a woman and working with women who had begun the painful and exhilarating struggle to redefine themselves, personally and professionally. For my part, I had all of the awkward and self-conscious responses of a man with 'liberal' convictions—I assiduously practiced saying Ms until it smoothly rolled off my tongue, tried to deny my anxiety, attempted as best I could to support the efforts of the women that I knew to change, and I tried to change aspects of my own behaviour.

The confluence of these forces led eventually to my participating, in a bit of a role reversal charade, as administrator (I made the coffee, ran errands, etc.) at a conference, staffed entirely by women colleagues, called 'A Working Conference on Women in Authority.' This conference was designed to provide both men and women with opportunities to explore their attitudes towards women in authority roles. Our explicit rationale was as follows: a large gap existed for most men and women between their earliest experiences with women in authority—namely, mothers and elementary school teachers—and adult experiences with women in authority roles; we also felt that, increasingly, both men and women were going to be working with women in positions of authority and leadership; and finally, we believed that women needed opportunities to explore models offered by women taking authority and leadership roles as a means of facilitating their own development in such roles.

This conference, held in New York City, attracted 30 women and 20 men. I and the women who comprised the professional staff group had all worked in many conferences on authority and leadership, but none with an explicit focus on gender and a design that included a professional staff group composed entirely of women, single-gender events (the small group), and a professional man in the administrator's role. Today, we take such configurations for granted—especially work groups composed of women—but in early 1970, as I vividly recall, sitting in the staffroom on the first day of the conference, we were terribly anxious and excessively constrained.

In all, however, we were sufficiently excited by this conference to plan another. For the second such conference 75 women and only three men applied! While we considered an all-women's conference an interesting option (Taylor et al., 1979), we felt that it would not be a substitute for men and women working together around these issues. Therefore, a conference with 75 women and three men was clearly not the ideal learning environment. As a result, I had the rather awkward task of trying to entice some of my male graduate students to participate. I finally did manage to cajole about seven or eight of them into the conference, and as of this writing most, I believe, have forgiven me. I think that the very small number of male applicants, and the experience of the men who did attend, say a great deal about the fantasies and feelings that men have about women in authority. The anticipation of being 'surrounded by women' in an organizational environment where the authority structure is composed entirely of women apparently was just too disturbing, and as such, it was an experience to be avoided. I might also add that for the men who did participate, injury was added to insult, since the only man with whom they could identify, namely myself, was 'wearing an apron' and making coffee. If these men, therefore, experienced the conference as a symbolic harbinger of the future (as I believe they did), their distress was indeed understandable.

The paucity of male applicants and the experience of the men who did attend led us to modify almost entirely the structure of these conferences. Their successor had a different design, a staff group composed of both men and women, and was called 'Male-Female Work Relations in Group and Organizational Settings.' These conferences, of which there were about ten during the next five years, did attract a sufficient number of men, although with few exceptions, and until recently, they attracted considerably more women. Almost all of these conferences, which were in weekend formats, went through a series of successive changes and modifications as our experience in them accumulated, and our thinking developed. In 1976 we felt ready to hold a full-scale residential conference (Gould, 1976), and during this past year (Gould, 1977) we held the second such conference, described in detail below.

CONFERENCE ORGANIZATION

Introduction and aims

When authority is vested in a person, he or she thereby assumes a work role that in a formal sense is the same regardless of sex, age, race, or personal characteristics. However, the way in which he or she performs in role, the difficulties encountered in filling the role, and the way he or she is perceived by others, are all influenced by such personal and demographic factors. In the 'men and women at work' conference, the focus is on an exploration of how attitudes and fantasies about sexuality and gender in relation to age (more specifically, in relation to particular stages of adult development) influence the ways in which men and women exercise authority and leadership in their roles, and how their roles are perceived and influenced by others. It is in this context that conference participants have opportunities to study their own and others' behaviour in situations in which the characteristics of the person or persons in authority, as well as the other members of the group, vary. A major aim is the heightened awareness of issues related to sexuality, gender, and age that may have a significant influence in work situations, often unnoticed or not consciously experienced by the persons involved.

While the behavioural sciences are extending our understanding of gender, sexuality, adult development (e.g. Levinson *et al.*, 1974), and of group and organizational processes, a gap exists between such understanding and the day-to-day problems encountered by those who must exercise authority and leadership. Often intellectual formulations are too generalized to be applicable to a particular set of relationships. In addition, the pressures and involvements of the immediate work situation often make it difficult to stand back and attempt a dispassionate analysis. It is the further aim of this conference, therefore, to bridge this gap by providing a means through which experience can be studied, and at least partially understood, as it occurs.

Although the aims noted above are in general the same as those underlying other group relations conferences (e.g. O'Connor, 1971; Rice, 1965; Rioch, 1970), the special emphasis of this conference entails some change in design and in the definition of the primary task.

The primary task

The primary task of the 'Men and Women at Work' group relations conference is to explore the exercise of authority and leadership as it is influenced by gender, sexuality, and stages of adult development.

Conference design

The conference is designed to provide opportunities for participants to study relations among and between men and women in group settings that vary in task, size, composition, and staff presence, as well as in the conference as a whole.

The various group events, described below, are viewed as an integrated system of activities, which together with the staff and participants who engage in them, comprise the formal work organization of the conference institution. The conference, therefore, can be viewed as a temporary educational organization designed specifically for the performance of the primary task.

The conference begins with an *opening plenary* session in which the conference and staff are introduced to the participants, and proceeds through the following events (see Figure 1 for the schedule of events):

Small groups consist of from 10 to 14 participants of the same gender. The task of the small group is to study its own behaviour. Each group has the services of a consultant of the same gender as the members to help it in its task.

In the *large group* all of the men and women in the membership meet together. The task of the large group is to study male/female dynamics in a group consisting of more people than can comfortably meet face to face. In the large group, participants have the opportunity to experience the ways in which the constellation of gender, sexuality, and age influences a situation in which sides appear to be taken spontaneously, subgroups form and dissolve, and myths emerge. Consequences for the individual with regard to gender, sexuality, and age as these influence the nature of roles taken, and of group support or its absence, are experienced and seen. The

Figure 1. Schedule of events for the 'Men and women at work' group relations conference (Gould, 1977)

TIME	DAY 1	DAY 2	DAY 3	DAY 4	DAY 5	DAY 6
8:00 Breakfast						
9:00–10:30		SG	SG	SG	SG	RRCG
10:30 Coffee						
11:00–12:30		LG	LG	LG	RRCG	TCP
12:30 Lunch	2:00 p.m. PCO					2:00–3:30
2:30–4:00	SG	—	IE	IE	—	RRCG
4:00 Coffee						
4:30–6:00	LG	IE	IE	IE	GCP	
6:30 Dinner						
8:00–9:30	SG	IE	GCP	—	RRCG	

PCO—Plenary conference opening
SG—Small group
LG—Large group
    Break
IE—Institutional event
RRCG—Role relations consultation group
GCP—Gender conference plenary
TCP—Total conference plenary

large group has the services of a male and a female consultant to help it examine its own behavior.

The *institutional event* has the task of studying relationships among and between men and women in the conference membership, and between the participants as a total group, and the staff group within the context of the conference institution. The membership has the services of the entire staff to help in this task.

Three *conference plenaries* provide participants with opportunities for reflecting upon the experiences of the conference. In the first two *gender conference plenaries*, men and women meet separately with all staff members of the same gender. Their respective tasks are to review the role of the men and the role of the women—both members and staff—in the conference up until that point in time. In the third and final *total conference plenary* the entire membership and staff meet together to review the experience of the conference as a whole and in its various parts.

Role-relations consultation groups have three related tasks:

1. To provide opportunities for each conference participant to examine his or her personal and social relatedness to the conference institution, and the varying experiences—both gratifying and frustrating—the institution has offered.
2. To consider the relevance of the conference experiences to participants' own work settings and their roles in them.
3. To provide a forum in which to explore the dilemmas of leaving the conference and returning home.

The membership of these groups is mixed, and each group has a staff consultant to assist in its task.

The staff role

The task of the staff members acting as consultants in the various events is to help the groups with which they are working to carry out the task of the event. They seek to behave in such a way as will, in their view, provide the best opportunities for participants to learn about the nature of authority and leadership in relation to sexuality, gender, and stages of adult development, as well as how participants' experiences relate to the conference institution as a whole. Staff consultants intervene only when they believe that their interventions will facilitate the work of the group.

Since the focus of the conference is on the nature of authority and leadership, the behaviour of the men and women on the staff, who represent the management of the conference, is explicitly available for study in relation to gender, sexuality, and age.

Membership

There is no special prerequisite for participation except serious interest. The intention, so far as possible, is to draw together an equal number of men and women of all ages and from a variety of backgrounds and work settings.

A major value of the residential conference is the challenge provided by an unfamiliar situation. In order to obtain maximum benefit, we suggest that not more than one member of an immediate family apply. However, in the interests of applying conference learning to one's work setting, there is some advantage if participants attend with colleagues from the same institution, and preferably with colleagues of the other gender.

TECHNICAL ISSUES IN DESIGN AND INTERPRETATION

The basic conference method (e.g. Rice, 1965; Rioch, 1970) is to construct situations in which conventional defences, both personal and institutional, against recognizing or acting upon attitudes, beliefs, and fantasies are reduced. This facilitates an examination of the covert forces that continually influence interactions at all levels, from the interpersonal to the organizational. In this conference, these interactions focused on age and gender, as they relate to authority and leadership, occur within the context of the various events that are group situations that differ on a variety of dimensions (see 'Conference design' section, above).

Further, there are two particular aspects of the design of this conference that should be highlighted. First, the conference is not designed to address itself to questions about the origins of attitudes, beliefs, and fantasies in the realm of gender, sexuality, and age—whether, or the extent to which, for example, gender differences do, or do not have, biological bases. Rather, the conference is designed to illuminate experience and behaviour in the 'here and now,' and it does make the assumption that attitudinal and behavioural differences (as well as similarities) do exist between men and women whatever their original source. Why else have a 'Men and Women at Work' conference? This relates to the second point that I would like to make about the conference design. In a number of the conference events, men and women, both participants and staff, are in separate groups (e.g. the small group and the gender conference plenaries). It may be argued that such groupings create dilemmas, stimulate feelings, and exacerbate a divisiveness that would not exist if the groups were structured otherwise. Within the confines of this paper, I can only suggest, on the basis of experience in these conferences, that I do not believe this to be the case. Rather, I view this feature of the conference design as a structural vehicle for highlighting various dimensions of male/female interaction. By creating these group boundaries (e.g. Miller and Rice, 1967) rich material is elicited for study and examination. For example, participants have opportunities to experience the sorts of gratifications, anxieties, and defences that are stimulated by the different settings. That is, this design feature allows participants to experience differences and similarities in behaviour, affect and process in single-gender settings as contrasted to mixed-gender settings. It is useful, therefore, to have these settings juxtaposed. The partial structural separation of men and women has the further advantage of making more manifest gender-linked aspects of sentient bonds—that is, the nonrational aspects of affiliation or loyalty, as distinct from rational or task groupings (Miller and Rice, 1967). What, for example, is the quality and emotional strength of 'sisterhood' as compared to 'brotherhood'? What is the fate of these ties in mixed-gender situations? How do such ties either facilitate or hinder the development of appropriate task groupings or forms of task organization? Or yet, how do these ties influence the assessment and attribution of competence? If the conference design, in fact, raises these questions for the participants, as I believe it does, it is serving the aims of the conference.

A parallel issue to the above concerns the nature of interpretation. This conference specifically focuses on how a person's characteristics, namely, his or her gender, sexuality, and age, interact with his or her work roles as a member of a group and an organization. If interpretations are focused on these aspects of the person/role boundary and group processes, it may be argued that issues relating to gender, sexuality, and age are exaggerated or are spuriously created. Again, I can only say that I do not believe this to be the case. Rather, I would suggest that this situation is more adequately conceptualized as a 'figure/ground' phenomenon. In other group relations conferences, person characteristics tend to be 'ground,' while role, group, intergroup, and organizational processes are 'figure.' By contrast, the emphasis in the 'Men and Women at Work' conference is on how various dimensions of these unfolding processes are accounted for by the gender, sexuality, and age of the participants. In practice, this means that certain other aspects of these processes are either neglected or simply noted in passing. Put another way, the staff are continually faced with choices in providing interpretations. If the primary task is adhered to, some learning opportunities will be forsaken or minimized. However, it should be noted that the pursuit of any task necessarily constrains the pursuit of others—no less so in this than in any other enterprise.

CONFERENCE PROCESSES AND CULTURE

It is beyond the purpose and scope of this paper to provide an analysis of the specific processes and dynamics that develop in relation to the exercise of authority and leadership as it is influenced by gender, sexuality, and stages of adult development. Rather, I will attempt to provide an overview of the 'Men and Women at Work' conference from the perspective of the general processes it sets in motion, and aspects of the culture that develop during the life of the conference.

The appropriate starting-point is, I believe, the particular person/role focus of this conference. That is, this conference, more than others, directly touches very intimate and personal concerns and anxieties in ways that compared to other group relations conferences, are more difficult for the individual to defend against. While we do, in fact, believe that issues of authority, leadership, and work are quite personal, in other conferences there are somewhat greater possibilities for splitting off concerns about work relationships from what we ordinarily think of as personal relationships (with loved ones, family, friends, etc.). In this conference, however, the participant can be viewed, and may experience himself or herself, for example, as being as much an implicit representative of the family as he or she is explicitly a representative of a work organization. Therefore, the issues and anxieties around gender, sexuality, and age that are mobilized in this conference can be as intimate and personal, in the ordinary sense, as they are work-related. Hence, the boundary between the personal sphere and the realm of work, in whatever manner it may be conceptualized, is at best extremely tenuous. By implication, this aspect of the 'Men and Women at Work' conference raises anew the issue of training *v*. therapy (see Rice, 1965, Chapter 12, for a complete discussion), and the appropriate boundaries between these activities. While I do not believe that the 'Men and Women at Work' conference is in fact a therapeutic enterprise, the 'pull' in this direction is none the less generally somewhat stronger than in other group relations conferences. In practice, therefore, the staff must remain alert if the appropriate tasks boundaries are to be maintained, lest they inadvertently go into collusion with the participants to shift these boundaries subtly towards a therapeutic, as distinct from an educational, stance.

One other aspect of the conference culture requires elaboration, and that is the immediate emergence of quite powerful nonsexist and nonageist norms. This is not surprising given the ideology and conscious convictions of the majority of both participants and staff. That is, while participants attempt to collaborate in an exploration of nonrational and nonconscious aspects of attitudes and beliefs about gender, sexuality, and age, there is, at the same time, often massive denial, since everyone also tends to be quite self-consciously on 'good behaviour.' The resulting culture of non-sexism and nonageism and the suppression of sexist or ageist attitudes and behaviours make new learning, of course, quite difficult. The staff for their part struggle with the same dilemmas. They also attempt to be nonsexist and nonageist, and as a result they may initially engage in a collusive avoidance with the membership, or project their own unconscious attitudes and beliefs onto the membership, making them the repository of all gender-linked and age-linked 'badness.' The participants may in turn engage in similar sorts of projections in an attempt to avoid their own dilemmas. It is often remarkable what details are used as a basis for these projections. The fact, for example, that the conference brochure was blue became, in the view of one participant, *de facto* evidence of staff sexism. In addition to a collusive avoidance, and the fight stance (Bion, 1961) and defensiveness that may ensue when powerful mutual projections dominate the group process, a third type of collusion may develop and alternate with the above to provide a social defence system (Menzies, 1967). This process is characterized by subtly shifting the appropriate 'figure/ground' emphasis of this conference, noted in the preceding section, to the more familiar emphases of other group relations conferences. This process tends to develop when, as is often the case, a substantial number of prticipants have attended other group relations conference, and are, therefore, able to use such familiarity defensively. Further, since most of the staff have also had considerably more experience in other conferences as well, the likelihood that they will collude in this process is exacerbated for similar reasons. As a result, the 'Men and Women at Work' conference may, at times, have its particular focus in name only. Therefore, as with the boundary between the training enterprise and the therapeutic enterprise, noted previously, the staff must struggle against these collusive internal and external pulls if the requisite task boundaries of a 'Men and Women at Work' conference are to be maintained.

SUMMARY AND CONCLUSION

By way of a summary, I would like to enumerate several aspects of the 'Men and Women at Work' conferences that are implicit in the foregoing discussion.

First, the emphasis on work-related processes in these conferences continues to provide unique learning opportunities compared to other types of groups such as encounter and sensitivity training. For the most part, these tend to focus almost exclusively on the more narrowly intimate, personal, explicitly sexual and/or interpersonal aspects of male/female relationships.

Second, the focus on group and organizational aspects of male/female relationships in these conferences provides a perspective that is markedly different from the large body of research on the male/female dyad. That is, this perspective may help us to understand aspects of dyadic relationships in a new light (whatever the personal and demographic characteristics of the pair). What, for example, are the forces that influence the nature of the boundary that defines a dyad, and hence the quality of the relationship, whether these originate in the larger family, the social network, or the organizational environment? After all, the problem for Romeo and Juliet was that they were members of groups!

Third, these conferences can be conceived as a laboratory in which the emergent behaviours provide an enormous amount of data and stimulate almost endless hypotheses about gender-related and age-related aspects of authority and leadership, group functioning, and organizational behaviour. Many of these can then be more carefully investigated under controlled conditions. Numerous instances are available in which the conference experience led, directly or indirectly, to a variety of systematic formulations and empirical investigations (e.g. Bayes *et al.*, 1977; Bayes and Newton, 1976; Beauvais, 1976; Chandler, 1975; Gould, 1975; Wright, 1976; Wright and Gould, 1977). These in turn have enriched our ability to conceptualize aspects of the conference, as well as provided an opportunity for retesting the validity of these formulations and research findings in subsequent conferences.

Finally, while the above are important, these conferences have the primary task of helping men and women in their struggle to collaborate more effectively and with greater satisfaction. The hope is, therefore, that the conference setting will provide opportunities for an authentic and passionate engagement of issues related to gender, sexuality, and age in mode that will facilitate continued learning and change for the individual's personal, social, and institutional roles in the 'back-home' environment.

12.

ADVANCED LEARNING IN A SMALL GROUP

Margaret J. Rioch

This paper concerns a form of training or learning, especially for Small Group Consultancy, which I first developed in 1974. In 1976, at the First Scientific Meetings of the A. K. Rice Institute in Minneapolis I gave a preliminary report on this method that I had already used three times. Since then I have been one of two supervisors in this event about eight more times; about four times in Washington with Marvin Geller, twice in Los Angeles with Lars Lofgren and twice in San Francisco with Arthur Colman. In addition the method has been used in Houston by Glenn Cambor and others, and in Sweden by Lars Lofgren and Imre Szesody. During my illness it was used in Washington by Marvin Geller and Donald Boomer. In other words, it has been thoroughly tried and developed since its inception.

The method is essentially very simple. A small group of approximately seven or eight students is formed. Each of them is given a turn at being the consultant to the rest of the group for one session in a series of "here and now" sessions. The group is observed by two senior consultants or supervisors. Following each session the two observing supervisors provide individual supervision to the student who has just consulted to the group. There are also opportunities, spaced at various intervals, for general discussion by the whole group including the observers.

The first and second time it was used occurred in the Learning Center of the American University. Dr. Charles Ferster, the Director, instituted this Center in the University about 1970 as a place where students could have the freedom to learn without the restrictions of traditional courses. He found that "process groups," which were very much like our conference "Small Groups," running once or twice a week over a part or whole semester seemed to contribute to the students' understanding of their own "authority to learn." A culture developed in the Learning Center that was very consonant with A. K. Rice Conferences. A number of the students and instructors came to our conferences and were interested to learn more. The Learning Center was also in need of people to conduct its process groups since funds were not always available to hire outside consultants in sufficient numbers. Thus there was a need for both training consultants and advanced learning.

173

Method: Rioch

In the fall of 1974 there were easily seven takers when we offered this opportunity to graduate students and young instructors who were involved in the activities of the Learning Center. The prerequisite for the course was that persons had to have attended at least two A. K. Rice Conferences, one of them residential. At the last moment, because someone had to drop out, we had one member who had attended only one conference. Charles Ferster (who had at that time been a consultant at several weekend conferences and one residential conference) and I were the observers.

We scheduled the sessions for a weekend, Saturday and Sunday, so that it would be possible to run through all seven members as consultants within the two days with 1 1/2 hour consulting sessions. The announcement of the course, "Advanced Learning About Small Groups" as it was called, stated that the series of sessions had a double purpose. The first was learning for the members. The second was selection of persons to conduct process groups in the Learning Center. It will be obvious to you that the second purpose would be likely to obscure the first in the minds of most, if not all, of the members. The fact of the matter was that two or three persons *were* going to be chosen and it was clearly more honest to say so than to come up with it later, even if it had not been known to some of the members that this would be the case. I think you can imagine that the competition was severe, since, for obscure reasons, people seem to want to become consultants.

The group consisted of five men and two women all in their 20s or thereabouts. Two of them had their Ph.D.s and were employed as instructors in the Learning Center. The rest were graduate students, either in the Department of Psychology or employed part-time in the Learning Center. All of them knew each other, some very well indeed; others only slightly. Two of the men were very close friends. One member of the group was my Teaching Assistant that year; one of the others had been my Teaching Assistant the year before. In other words all of them were dependent in the "real world" on either Charles Ferster or me or both of us, either for their jobs or for letters of recommendation that could make or break their futures. It is really hard to imagine how one could arrange a more stressful situation. And indeed it was.

The procedure for these groups is to draw lots for turns. The person who draws the first lot has the advantage of not having to wait. On the other hand he does not get the advantage of the experience of the others and the experience of becoming familiar with the group. The last one gathers a lot of experience but it is extremely stressful to have to wait till the end, and often the last cannot pay much attention because he is waiting for his turn. He also does not have the experience of being reintegrated into the group since his is the last session.

The only room available for the meetings was very small. The usual circle was formed by the group. The two observers sat in opposite corners and of necessity were close enough to the circle to be able literally to breathe down the neck of whichever member sat closest to them. At least one of us took notes during all the sessions.

As you would expect, the observers were the subject of much of the talk in the here and now sessions. They were referred to, at first inadvertently, as "the consultants." And when this was noticed, the members agreed that they were indeed the "real consultants."

The difficulties inherent in this situation were worked with to a fair degree. Not unexpectedly, the resentment against the observers was soft-pedalled. We were a bit too close and a bit too powerful. In fact our power and expertise were magnified beyond recognition. There were fantasies about the relationship between Charles Ferster and me. Sometimes one was seen as benevolent and one as destructive. These roles shifted. Since Dr. Ferster deferred to me in the discussions as the more experienced and senior consultant, my power was sometimes seen as greater. The members then had to remind themselves that in the "real world" it was Dr. Ferster who gave half of them their jobs.

He and I were often seen by the members as parents looking on critically while the children played. They sometimes thought of themselves as engaged in sexual play of which the parents would certainly disapprove. One of the women members mentioned that she had often listened from the second floor while her children were playing house with their dolls and with each other downstairs. She had been struck by the seriousness and intentness with which they played. But when she appeared on the scene, the seriousness suddenly vanished and they became giggly, silly little kids. There could be no better description of one way in which the members viewed themselves.

When this weekend was over, the members of the group met together for a discussion of the experience. They decided that it had been a very extraordinary learning experience. There was a general feeling that they would like to have another try at it. We offered them the possibility of meeting for one session a week over a period of seven weeks. In order not to bring more group pressure than necessary upon anyone, we agreed not to come to any decision during the meeting, but to leave it to each individual to make application for the session if he or she wished. They all applied and we started on a second round.

This time it was easier to wait. Some of the intensity of the first experience was gone. It took longer in the initial phase of each session to warm up and get going. People experienced a feeling that the agony was a bit too drawn out since it went on for seven weeks. But toward the end of the period there emerged a consensus that the learning was perhaps even greater than the first time because it had time to sink in. It is difficult, of course, to measure such things, but my impression, confirmed by Dr. Ferster, was that practically all of the members did better the second time around. You will remember that the members of this group were told that in addition to the primary purpose of the exercise, namely learning, there was a secondary purpose that I am sure added to the competition that occurs in a group anyway. The secondary purpose was the selection and training of a few people to conduct process groups in the Learning Center. For the spring of the year Dr. Ferster and I selected two members who seemed to have done a competent job in both the first and second series.

I believe our judgment in this proved to be correct as both members did reasonably well, at least so far as I could judge as their supervisor in the process groups that they ran. I think that the people who were chosen gave evidence of having learned quite a bit in the training sessions.

I should like now first to outline how this method has been developed and perfected up until now, in 1979, and then to mention what I think have been the main issues in the event.

First, the development: soon after I first reported this method in 1976, Dr. Geller and I made an important change. Partly at the request of students or members and partly because we ourselves judged it to be an improvement, we gave each member two chances at consultancy, one on Saturday, one on Sunday. This meant that the sessions had to be much shorter. We have most recently (in California) scheduled 45 minute sessions for each of seven consultants, a 15 minute supervisory session immediately thereafter, and 5 minutes for us and the student-consultant to get coffee, go to the bathroom, and get from one room to another. Although this means cutting the time for each session in half, we find it more desirable for everyone to have two chances, especially since there is no opportunity to run a second series as there was in the Learning Center. Almost everyone is significantly better the second time; and there is clear evidence that learning has taken place from the first supervisory session, as well as a night's sleep and from other people's experience. The lots are made up so that the person who goes first the first time is tucked well into the middle the second time; and the person who goes last the first time also has a "safe" place toward the middle the second time. These two places are unusually exposed. The person who goes first on the first morning is especially in an anxiety producing spot and should not have to do this twice, even though the second morning is not as bad for anyone.

Whether one schedules slightly longer or shorter supervisory sessions and group sessions depends on whether one takes seven or eight students and also on how long, how early, or how late one is willing to work.

We made one other major change after running the first two series, in the middle of the third, i.e., the first one that Marvin Geller and I conducted. In the sessions in the Learning Center we had scheduled a 15 minute discussion after each group session, in which Dr. Ferster and I took part. The students made lively and eager use of these, but in the third series, these discussions were desultory, inhibited and not especially valuable. We soon abandoned them in favor of a one hour discussion period at the end of each day, which has seemed to all of us (Drs. Geller, Lofgren, Colman, and me) to be very valuable. My sense of it was that the student group wanted to use these periods to integrate the one who had just been a consultant back in the friendship or working colleague group from which he had been temporarily separated by his different role. In the third series, since there was essentially no friendship group to begin with or to end with either, this need was not felt and the short sessions fell flat.

In the discussion sessions we have been able to do some much needed teaching. The fact that it has often been so much needed points up in my mind the need for more theoretical orientation and discussion possibilities for consultants than we provide at present. In the discussions there usually has been observable on the part of members a wish, as in conference discussions, to turn them into question and answer sessions in which we would provide the answers, particularly to the ever present question: "Have we been a good group?" as well as "Have we been a good conference?" But once that is past, we are able to address questions about the rationale for making group, rather than individual, interpretations, technical questions about closing the door or leaving it open at the end, leaving a chair for absent or late members, etc. It sometimes seems to come as a surprise to members that these things have been thought about, that there is a reason for doing them in a certain way, and that rules have not been laid down arbitrarily from on high for doing them in the "Tavistock" method. In fact, there might be differences of opinion about what one should do. It is often quite possible to identify whose Small Group a particular member has been in from what he does or how he behaves, since certain manners or words are taken over by simple imitation. This is not necessarily bad, for probably all of us learn more or less by identification, but it is sometimes quite surprising for members to become aware of what they are doing and to hear that it is possible to do it another way. Often the idea members have that a "Tavistock" consultant is by definition enigmatic and sphinx-like needs to be brought to awareness and questioned.

Another point we often find ourselves making in supervision as well as in the discussions, and that often seems to come as a surprise to members, is that it is possible to use one's own feelings, one's own reactions to the group as data one can share verbally with the group. In fact it is not only possible but also desirable. It is necessary, of course, to separate one's reactions to the group, which are relevant to the group process, from idiosyncratic feelings left over from breakfast with one's spouse, etc. Members have to learn, it seems, that consultants use what the group is doing to them as important data for the group. Consultants are not, as members sometimes suppose, unfeeling, impersonal machines upon whom they can have no effect.

Another difference between the first two and the third series had to do with the physical set-up. Series III was held in the Group Therapy room of the Washington School of Psychiatry, which has a one-way mirror. After an initial orientation, Marvin Geller and I disappeared behind the screen. This was quite different from the cramped quarters Dr. Ferster and I occupied in the first two series.

I have now conducted about four groups in Washington with Marvin Geller and me observing behind a one-way mirror. The set-up that Lars Lofgren and I have used in Los Angeles also makes possible the presence of the observers behind a one-way screen. But in San Francisco, Arthur Colman and I have used his quite spacious office. We sit in the room with the group, but we both sit on a sofa off to one side. It clearly can be done either way, although my preference is for the screen. I think that whether the group focuses on us as the "real consultants" depends more upon the group and how the members relate to us and to each other than upon the one-way screen or lack of it.

Method: Rioch

To come now to the main issues that are addressed in this exercise.

1. First is the anxiety members experience because they are judged as to whether they should be selected as consultants. This is sometimes a very hot issue, as it was in the Learning Center when some people, but not all, were actually selected. However, we all know that the number of conferences that can use new consultants is diminishing. Some people have come as students, i.e., group members, who have already been appointed as consultants at least once and whose position in this respect is not in any doubt. These are very brave souls and I wish there were more of them. I have a strong hunch that it could be very valuable to all of us to do this. But as the need to train new conference consultants diminishes, we have changed the emphasis of the sessions from "training and selection" to "advanced learning." Whether or not there is cause and effect in this or merely coincidence, I do not know. But since we have done this I have seen some of the best groups with which I have ever worked, not only as consultants but as group members.
2. Second, I should like to speak of other sources of anxiety. Of course, one can easily say that there are as many sources of anxiety as there are or will be members. However, what are the factors making for anxiety and tension in *this* particular situation?

The members are on display to each other as well as to the two supervisors. One need only imagine oneself in that situation to understand how anxiety producing it can be. The members are in competition with each other, if not for a place on a conference staff, then merely to do "well" whatever that is thought to be. We know, or should know, about this from ordinary conference small groups. This competition can destroy the skills of fellow students as members or as consultants. It may occur with or without direct attack. In the very first group, one of the most anxiety producing sessions occurred when there was not only no direct attack at all but on the contrary a surfeit of protection of the consultant who was the youngest of the group. He was also one who could fairly make claim to being a protege of Dr. Ferster and certainly well thought of by me as well. He was generally liked and respected by his peers. In his session the members outdid themselves to be nice while he became more and more selfconscious and tense, so that the perspiration was standing out on his forehead, but his behavior was controlled. He made only three interpretations during the whole session. He was known to have worked with autistic children and somehow this was introduced into the conversation by one of his good friends. And then the group could not drop the subject of autism as the consultant became more self-preoccupied, so it seemed, while the group tried to draw him out. I have rarely seen so clear an example of the conscious good intentions of a group of people being subverted by the unconscious impulse not to allow this young "fair-haired boy" to have any better time as a consultant than any of the rest of them had had. I think

Advanced Learning in a Small Group

they were all really shocked as they began to realize what they had done. It would be hard to arrange a more striking lesson of the victim producing tendencies of groups. Fortunately, the young man in question was not only resilient but extremely thoughtful and capable of learning, so that after a rather bad period of several days, he integrated a good deal of what he had experienced in such a way that he could use it.

It is common that an awareness develops in the group that the members are all unwilling to let anyone else appear to be "best" as consultant. In fact, that turns out often to be an inhibiting factor in the group. A kind of *quid pro quo* morality develops. "If you will be nice to me, I will be nice to you." This seems to ensure that the members will not do terrible things to each other, at least not consciously. It also ensures, alas, that they will not bring up matters that are significant but that would be hurtful to one another. They would not hesitate to bring them up to a "real" consultant. Sometimes quite sophisticated conversations occur in which these matters are discussed and questions are raised as to whether there is any way out of this predicament, whether they could compete and still collaborate. One group recently envisioned the possibility and actually did some work in which they collaborated with one another, building upon each other's interpretations in recently past sessions, much the way Large Group consultants may build upon each other's interpretations in the Large Group of a conference.

3. And third, I should like to mention the intergroup aspects of this method emphasized in recent years. There are sub-groups present in the weekend event that become quite clear, just as there are sub-groups present in an intergroup event and in conferences in general. One is the supervisory pair who have a different role and different task from that of the members. The second is the student or member group. And third is the student-consultant by himself, a role that rotates among different people each session. The unique aspect of this method, which no one who has not been in it has experienced, is the relatively quick and frequent change of role required from the students. This is a unique aspect of the method, not unusual in real life, and very useful, but also very difficult. I think most students find correctly that being the consultant is a very lonely role. We have frequently pointed out in discussion sessions that at a conference the consultant has his staff group, his own reference group, to which he returns between sessions and to which he may return in his head many times. But the student-consultant has no such group. The other people confronting him are in a different role as members. He is uniquely *alone*, even though everyone else has a turn at this.

This is not an easy role. In fact, I think that being a conference consultant for the first time is in many ways easier. I remember one time a student-consultant missed commenting on what (to the observers) was obviously occurring in the group, namely the increasing anger at and scapegoating of one of its members *by the group*. When asked about this in a supervisory session, the student-consultant replied, I think correctly, that he had been so much a part of the group that he could not pull himself out enough to comment on this. This is one of the ways a group has, quite unconsciously, of seducing the consultant out of his consultant role and back into a member role.

The problem of reintegrating the past consultant into the group as a member is often felt and spoken of, especially at the beginning or end of a session when he has just been or is about to be consultant. An individual may make this especially easy or difficult for himself. If he is the only person from another city, or the only black woman or man, it is, of course, especially easy for him to feel isolated and for the other members to feed into this.

The role of the supervisory pair is a subject of great interest to the members. So far, when I have been one of the supervisors, there has always been a man and a woman. This gives rise, in spite of my advanced age, to lots of fantasies about what we are doing behind the screen or after hours. It also gives rise to the fantasy of the supervisory sessions taking place in the parents' bedroom, which by exception, the consultant is allowed to enter when he has done his job. There are extraordinarily different attitudes that individuals and groups have toward telling what happened "in the bedroom." There is often a tendency at first for people to clutch what happened there to their hearts, as if it were a secret they should not or do not want to see.

This is felt to be a rule, so much so, that it comes as a surprise when we question it in supervision, and even suggest the unconscious motive of holding something secret for oneself rather than sharing it as a bit of knowledge or insight that others might use. Sometimes, as a result of our prodding, it may become at least an open question whether it should or should not be shared.

Often one of us is from the same city in which the event is held and in which most of the members live; and one is from farther away. This, of course, makes for different realities and fantasies. It is important how much or how little the real relationships to us are explored. Sometimes the members are our friends, sometimes our students. There is almost certain to be some kind of relationship of greater or lesser connection to one or both of us either that is kept secret or that becomes an object of scrutiny, even anger, or the like. Occasionally the two of us are merged as, for example, in Los Angeles, when Lars Lofgren and I were referred to inadvertently as "Mars." Sometimes we are separated with one being good, one bad, or one known, the other unknown, though in the course of the weekend, both of us are visible and audible and, so far, usually consciously thought of as helpful and supportive but sometimes as frustrating. Sometimes one of us is known simply by reputation. Bits of information or fantasy almost always emerge, sometimes painfully.

The relationship of the members to the supervisory pair is spoken about a great deal in the group and heard, of course, by the supervisors

Advanced Learning in a Small Group

either through the one-way screen or directly in the room. The members are impelled by themselves and by each other to be as honest as they can about their attitudes. The supervisors, on the other hand, although they try to be honest in their supervision, are under no obligation to express their personal feelings about the members to them. In fact, I think this would be a disservice. The attitudes of members vary depending on their personal relationships and their attitudes toward authority. Occasionally someone says that he or she finds it distressing to find himself in a student role after being out on his own in the "real" world. We are surely familiar with this in conferences where members are forced to look at their attitudes toward authority. It is not surprising but rather sad I think, to see again how hard it is to take the role of learner, of student. We mouth pious phrases about learning all of one's life, but it is a different story when one really feels in the position of learner. It is important, I think, for us all to see over and over again, how hard this is once one is out of school.

I recently teased out of a group of graduate students how it feels now that they are finally coming to the end of their student days. They expressed very ambivalent feelings akin I think to adolescence, where one yearns to be still a child, protected by the family, and at the same time one cannot wait to be grown up, independent and out on one's own. Surely members in these events and in conferences have similar attitudes.

4. Fourth, the question of authority in the group is an important and interesting one. We have solved it, at least tentatively, by assuming (and stating the assumption) that by signing up for the course, the students have given us, the supervisors-instructors, the authority to conduct the course along the lines put out in the announcement or brochure or whatever document is circulated. We authorize each student in turn to become consultant to the group. And we assume that the group as a whole agrees to this authorization. We also authorize the other members to become a small group like a conference small group. We announce what arrangements are made about coffee and lunch. We usually make coffee and see to it that cups and cookies are provided. Members are on their own for lunch. We sometimes provide them with the names of restaurants since they may be in a place with which they are not familiar. The student-consultants are told that when it is their turn, they are responsible to see that the chairs are in a circle and that ash trays are emptied, as consultants do at conferences. One time we had a sort of emergency. The Washington School, where we were holding the event, was supposed to be opened on Sunday morning by a young man who had seemed very reliable. I did not have a key since there are all kinds of security measures familiar only to the people who work in the building. The reliable young man did not show up and we were standing, freezing, outside the building, while telephone calls were made to our administrator and finally to the young man who, it seems,

had overslept. The overblown fantasies of how powerful we were, which had emerged the day before, suddenly collapsed, and the group, which had been rather inhibited, came vividly to life. Administrative changes in schedule had to be made since we were significantly late in starting. The supervisors took responsibility for making them. We came out of our place behind the screen and became active participants. This whole matter became a subject for discussion and disagreement in the group and was food for thought not only in the group sessions but also in the general discussion at the end of the day.

One significant point associated with the issue of authority is the question often raised by students as to whether they really have authority as consultants or whether they are just puppets in the hands of the *real* power sitting behind the screen or outside the circle. They have felt both ways since, not only as consultants but also as members, they are very aware of the authority of the supervisors.

I should now like to mention three possible variants on this design that we have considered but never used for reasons I shall give.

1. First, students have sometimes suggested the possibility that the supervisory sessions be open to everyone so that all could learn rather than just the one person having a private session with us. Although I can imagine a situation in which this is feasible, I am opposed to it as a general thing. I think it would be feasible if all the members were roughly equal in experience and in talents, and if all had working supervision with each other so that they were used to sharing supervision and other kinds of learning. But I am opposed to it when the students are a group of strangers who do not know each other and may never meet again. One consideration is that one or more of them may be very much poorer at the job of consultancy than the rest. Then, no matter how kind and supportive the supervisors may be, it is sure to be humiliating to the student, especially because the supervision, kind though it may be, is also honest. If something has been grossly overlooked or mismanaged by a student-consultant, one may point this out to an otherwise gifted consultant without his feeling terrible. But if one points out many things like this in front of the whole group to a student who is already felt by his fellow members to be incompetent and stupid, it is not only painful, but it will have an adverse effect on group functioning. Both supervisors and students can be more open and honest if they are not performing in front of a group. Generally not all the members who sign up for such a weekend are known to the supervisors. And there is no good way to screen them, unless the event can be held by invitation only. Even so there may be some surprises. I am convinced that in general the advantages of private supervision of each individual far outweigh the presumed advantages of general learning. Students, being human, are bound to spend much of the supervisory time, if it is shared,

making comparisons with themselves. And supervisors, also being human, are often not at their best when "giving a performance."
2. One other variation we have considered is for either both supervisors or one of them to take the group for one session. I am also opposed to this. We have never tried it, although many students may have seen one or both of us at conferences. It is much too much like saying "This is the way it should be done" and "Model yourselves upon me." Inviting criticism and discussion sounds very nice, but it would probably not occur usefully or with any openness.
3. We have considered whether one person might be used as a supervisor-consultant rather than two as supervisors. I think this is possible, and where circumstances dictate the need for this, I should think it might be done. Certainly, however, it is more pleasant to have a pair. I also think it is more useful. Not only is it desirable to have someone with whom one can talk over the event at lunch, on Saturday evening, and in the brief pauses, if any, but also it is certain that two pairs of eyes see more than one or for that matter two pairs of ears can hear better. And two people can perform better supervision, in that one may at times be more able to find a way to relate to a given student than another. One person can also be more easily sucked in to a group than a pair who give each other support. I really can see no reason other than financial need why one person should do the job if two are available.

In conclusion I should like to say that I think this method is useful primarily in the work of the A. K. Rice Institute. But I see no reason why it should be limited to that. If one wants to teach some other form of group work, this method could very well be used.

In any case, I think that this event is an extraordinarily intensive and valuable learning experience in membership and, in consultancy in a small group, and in changing roles.

13.

AN ADVANCED TRAINING GROUP WITHIN THE GROUP RELATIONS CONFERENCE: EVOLUTION, DESIGN AND OUTCOME

*Robert F. Baxter and
Elizabeth Morgan Heimburger*

In a recent review of the literature, Klein (1978) reported multiple and diverse applications of the Tavistock method of group study in the United States, all of which have been developed since the first group relations conference at Mount Holyoke College in 1965. Yet his review included no papers on advanced training opportunities for individuals interested either in exploring issues at a level beyond that generally available to members in conferences or study groups or in preparing themselves to take staff roles in these conferences.

The failure to include such papers was not an omission. Rather, it reflects that few such training opportunities are currently available in the United States. Rioch and Geller (1977) and Rioch (1979) have described a specific training technique that they and others have used to prepare people to take the role of small group consultant, but these reports have been the exception.

This paper will describe the development of another advanced training experience that has evolved as a part of a series of group relations conferences held at the University of Missouri-Columbia. Since 1974, the University has sponsored (and more recently, cosponsored with the Texas Center of the A. K. Rice Institute) a series of nine conferences based on the Tavistock method of group study. These conferences were first reported in 1976 (Heimburger & Baxter) and have been described more fully in a recent paper (Heimburger & Baxter, 1979).

Although the conferences have been three-day nonresidential conferences, beginning on Friday at noon and closing in the early evening on Sunday, they have been designed to include all traditional Tavistock events (Rice, 1965). For example, the most recent conference was structured to include six small group events, four large group events, five sessions of the institutional event, a conference discussion and two application group meetings. With only minor variations, this model, with a total of eighteen events, has been utilized in the last several conferences.

This series of group relations conferences was begun within an educational institution as a supplemental, elective learning experience for students enrolled in ongoing training programs. While the majority of the membership has come from academic programs in the health care field, students from other schools in the University and from other regional colleges and universities also have participated, as have faculty and, more recently, people unaffiliated with academic institutions. Nonetheless, these conferences remain today, as they began, as learning opportunities supported by an educational institution primarily for the benefit of its own students.

From the beginning, it was hoped that this series of conferences would provide the opportunity to learn about issues in group relations for people who were in various stages of career training and development and who, likewise, had varying levels of knowledge about, and experience with, group relations work. Therefore, consideration was given to providing some kind of advanced experience for selected participants as early as the second conference.

Further impetus for developing an advanced training experience came from the recognition that these conferences were being held in a region of the country outside of the areas where the A. K. Rice Institute has traditionally concentrated its work. Few people could be identified locally to serve on conference staffs; yet a local, or at least regional, pool of consultants and administrators needed to be available if expenses were to be minimized, thereby supporting a membership fee within the limited financial resources of a student population. Therefore, in response to both an interest in providing varying learning opportunities and an awareness of the necessity for developing a local staff, the early conference design, which was used with only minor modifications for several conferences, included nonparticipant observers in all events.

Consistent with their roles, the nonparticipant observers were offered an essentially passive learning experience. Without specifically defined learning objectives or a conference structure designed to support more sophisticated approaches to learning, the observers were, in essence, merely a small collection of extras, "tacked on" to learn whatever they would, however they could. That learning did occur under these conditions is not, and was not at the time, questioned. However, in the interest of tracing the evolution of the current training program, the less-than-satisfactory aspects of this early experience will be emphasized here.

Basically, the nonparticipant observers, most of whom were already very experienced in other types of work with groups, were placed in highly dependent positions. Paired with staff consultants, they had little opportunity to utilize their own skills beyond the level of observing and attempting to understand the behavior of groups and the consultants' interventions. Not surprisingly, therefore, their dependency, in one way or another, invariably became an issue that demanded considerable attention from the staff. At the same time, however, it was thought to interfere with the staff's primary task of providing an opportunity for conference members to learn.

Dependency issues were manifested by the nonparticipant observers in two general ways: 1) initial acceptance and identification followed, ultimately, by disappointment or 2) counterdependent resistance and social withdrawal from the staff. The former, actually observed more frequently, usually began with the development of a cordial, pleasant relationship between the pair, consultant and observer. Much of the preconference exchange between them combined activities appropriate for establishing superficial social bonds with work-related discussions about the ways in which they would take up their respective conference roles, the times they could identify for discussing their impressions of the small group's work, etc.

Once into the conference, however, the relationship most often changed rapidly. The earlier sense of collaboration diminished. In its place there evolved a "perfect," nonquestioning teacher-student pairing characterized by "good feelings" on the part of the consultant and by receptive passivity and identification on the part of the observer.

Inevitably, however, under the pressure of an intense work schedule, dictated by the conference structure, and the consultant's commitment to the primary task of the conference institution, reality demands began to intrude on these observer-consultant relationships. As often happens in situations in which dependency is not a mutual phenomenon, consultant staff soon came to experience the observers as "draining," "overly demanding" and even "insatiable." Meanwhile, as the conference progressed, the observers sometimes had occasion to witness the staff take diverse positions or become involved in dissent and disagreement among themselves. As a result, they became less awed and enchanted by the consultants and increasingly were disappointed with the role models they provided.

Subtly provocative questioning, complaining and outright irritability became more and more apparent on the part of both staff and observers; and despite resistance, the staff found itself increasingly drawn into focusing its attention on the relationships between the observers and themselves. To compound matters, as noted above, this was experienced by the staff as inconsistent with its primary task. So repeated work on this issue, essential as it may have been under the circumstances, only served to isolate further the staff from the primary work it had committed itself, individually and collectively, to do.

While the experience described above was repeated, in one form or another, in each of the conferences in which this training model was employed, several nonparticipant observers over the years resisted assuming a dependent position, even within reasonable and potentially useful limits, from the beginning. Thus, these few individuals were unable to establish any kind of paired relationship with their respective consultants in the interest of their own learning. At the same time, they had difficulty relating to the other observers who were actively engaged, either by identification or through frustration, with the appropriate consultants. Likewise, the staff itself was not readily available to these occasional "deviant" observers. Thus, they were left with little support for their learning, and they essentially remained isolated and disengaged through their training experience.

Initially, the complications presented by the nonparticipant observers were tolerable, in part at least, because the conferences were small, with thirty-six members. Thus, the staff itself was relatively small; and even with the nonparticipant observers, it was a readily manageable group. However, over time the conferences expanded to forty-eight and then sixty members; and as the conferences and the conference staff grew in size, the dilemmas surrounding the nonparticipant observers seemed more cumbersome, time-consuming and intrusive on the primary work of the staff. At the same time, however, there was recognition that the program had provided a significant learning opportunity despite the problems it engendered. It was also clear that a training program needed to continue if more potential conference staff were to be developed in the local area.

Thus, an attempt was begun to restructure the training experience in ways that would decrease the dilemmas for the staff and that, additionally, would ensure that it would be something more than an addendum to the conference itself. As an initial step, the Conference Director (Dr. Heimburger) authorized the Associate Director (Dr. Baxter) to develop and manage a training program that would utilize the resources of the staff while not overtaxing them. The intention was to develop a training experience that would be integrated into, and make use of, the conference structure, at the same time leaving the conference staff relatively free to concentrate on providing optimal learning opportunities for the membership.

The training program that has resulted from this initiative has continued to evolve from conference to conference. However, from the broader perspective, it has gone through two major phases to date. The first phase encompassed conferences six and seven in this series, while the second phase involved the eighth and ninth conferences, the two most recent ones.

During the first transitional phase, the staff-in-training (as they came to be called) continued to serve as nonparticipant observers, paired with consultants during the small group events; and they also functioned as nonparticipant observers during the large group events. However, unlike the situation in earlier conferences, few opportunities were made available for consultant-observer pairs to meet between scheduled conference events. This freed the consulting staff from the pressures to teach actively the nonparticipant observers that they had experienced in earlier conferences.

Instead of meeting with their respective consultants, the staff-in-training met, as a group, twice daily with the Associate Director, who was serving as director of the training program. These staff-in-training meetings provided the trainees with an opportunity to examine and compare their separate observation experiences. Thereby, they were able to enrich their own experience while supporting the learning of others. They were able to utilize their own skills, individually and collectively, in furthering their understanding of the phenomena under study; and they utilized the training director as an additional, but by no means only, resource. In this way, they actively processed some of their own experiences, thus avoiding some of the personal deskilling inherent in the passive-dependent posture adopted by most of the earlier trainees.

In addition, these meetings supported the development of sentient relationships among the staff-in-training; and somewhat unexpectedly, they also provided an opportunity for minimal exploration of intragroup issues such as competitive strivings, task definition and role boundaries. This exploration of their own group dynamics was considered to be particularly useful by the staff-in-training. Therefore, in the next conference, the training group was actively encouraged to examine its own behavior during these sessions.

In these same two conferences, the staff-in-training were paired with consultant staff during both the intergroup event and the application groups. These pairings differed, however, from those related to small group events in that the trainees were authorized to take the role of co-consultant rather than that of nonparticipant observer. Thus, in yet another way, the staff-in-training were being encouraged to take a more active and interactive role in their own learning.

However, while this change certainly offered additional learning opportunities for the staff-in-training, it also produced considerable discomfort and some open conflict between and among the training group and the senior conference staff during the first of these two conferences. Specifically, the conflict was related to the lack of clarity involved in establishing consultant teams. Naively, in order to avoid addressing the varying levels of experience and competence between the senior staff and the trainees, the Conference Director and Associate Director had paired and listed application group co-consultants alphabetically, suggesting that no differences existed in authority or responsibility.

This, of course, threw the entire staff into a dilemma. For the staff-in-training, it offered the seduction of abandoning their primary task of learning, clearly perceived as a lower status task, in favor of taking up the senior staff's primary task of facilitating members' learning. At the same time, the staff-in-training were anxious about the opportunity and resented being ejected, as they perceived it, from their learning role.

Meanwhile, confusion was only compounded by the senior conference staff, a group that reasonably might have been expected to bring some clarity to this authority issue. However, their ambivalence about the training group prompted them to act otherwise. Freed of much of the pressure experienced with the earlier training model, the staff felt disconnected and isolated from the staff-in-training and, at times, openly envious of their opportunity to review leisurely (a staff fantasy!) their conference experience during their own mealtime meetings. In response, the conference staff seemed eager to join with the staff-in-training as a total, cohesive staff group. Differences among individuals tended to be blurred, and considerable discomfort attended any discussion of the different tasks assigned to senior conference staff and staff-in-training.

Ultimately, of course, the issue was resolved. The Conference Director authorized the senior member of the consultant team to determine the way in which the team would function, thereby making him or her responsible for the work carried out by that team. However, the issue itself and the work done around it have had a lasting impact on the design of this particular training program. They emphasize the necessity for a program design that is totally consistent with the trainees' authorization to learn and that makes it clear that their authority is distinctly different from the authority delegated to the senior conference staff.

Despite the problems, it was apparent that this model had stimulated considerably more active involvement and, presumably, greater learning than had the earlier nonparticipant observer program. Emphasis on modeling behavior and identification had been decreased, while increased opportunities were provided for staff-in-training to apply their own skills, both old and new. The changes also produced an enlivened interest in the total conference institution, replacing the earlier, unbalanced preoccupation with the work of the small group consultants. Furthermore, these changes were accomplished with an appreciable decline in the amount of stress and fatigue experienced by the conference staff.

At the same time, however, it had become obvious that the training program remained only vaguely defined and that a clear, total commitment to having an advanced training group within the conference had yet to be made. Therefore, consideration was given either to dropping the training program entirely (a possibility since more potential staff were now available locally and more money had been identified to support out-of-town staff) or to revising it, recognizing it as a major component of the conference institution.

In support of the latter alternative, interest in the advanced training experience remained high. Locally, inquiries continued from people interested in conference work; but even more individuals, without a particular interest in taking on staff roles, were asking about the training experience as another opportunity to increase their learning for application in other areas. At the same time, people from other regions of the country began to express an interest in the training program, and there was encouragement to open it for national application. Paradoxically, the people outside of the immediate area generally were interested in increasing their experience in order to prepare for Center membership in the A. K. Rice Institute or, if they were already members, to advance their chances for conference work.

Because of this continuing and even increasing interest, it was decided to continue the training program, in modified form, and to solicit nationally applications for appointment to the staff-in-training. In modifying the program, it was decided that experiential learning would be emphasized and passive learning, dependent on nonparticipatory observation, would be further de-emphasized. The training program also would be designed to provide some opportunity for staff-in-training to negotiate their own work and to apply their learning within the conference setting. Finally, specific learning objectives would be defined and explicitly stated so that people with diverse interests and varying needs could decide responsibly whether to pursue this particular activity.

Therefore, in the announcement for the most recent training program (March 1979), the following objectives were stated specifically:

1. To provide staff-in-training with the opportunity to study the conference institution as a whole from the perspective of the staff.
2. To provide staff-in-training with an experience in which they might study the dynamics of their own and others' behavior, both as members of the staff group and as members of a smaller subgroup, the training group.
3. To provide staff-in-training with an opportunity to focus on the work of facilitating the learning of conference members.

It should be noted that nowhere in these objectives was a statement made indicating that this particular program was specifically designed to prepare people to take up staff roles in group relations conferences. In fact, in the announcement, the list of objectives was followed by this statement: "Whatever use will be made of the various training experiences, of course, will be the ultimate responsibility of each participant in the training program."

The specific training events, modified slightly from those of the preceding year, also were described briefly in the announcement. People were then invited to apply for appointment to the staff-in-training by letter, indicating their prior conference experience and stating their personal objectives in seeking further training in this model.

Appointments were made by the Associate Director on the basis of this information and a reference letter obtained for each applicant, and the selected applicants were offered appointments by letter. This letter described the training events more fully, contained a limited bibliography of recommended readings and closed with the following statement: "If you should accept this appointment, it is understood that you have authorized me, as Associate Conference Director, to conduct the training program as described above and, furthermore, have confirmed Dr. Heimburger's role as Conference Director." This final sentence was intended to clarify, as much as possible, issues of authority and responsibilty before the conference opened.

During the actual training program, the staff-in-training participated in all staff work sessions and was involved in seven other types of activities. Each of these is described below:

1. *Preconference Activities.* On the afternoon prior to the conference opening, the seven members of the staff-in-training met for an hour and a half with the Associate Director. This time provided the trainees a limited opportunity to become acquainted before the entire staff assembled later in the evening. It also was utilized to review, together, the planned training program and to share individual hopes and expectations that had brought these people together.

During this time, it became apparent that people had arrived with diverse interests and expectations. For example, one trainee indicated that he applied primarily to learn to work with female authority figures and that he intended to devote considerable attention to the anticipated relationship that would evolve with the Conference Director. Inasmuch as this goal was inconsistent with his earlier written statement of personal interest in the training program, it produced considerable discussion. More importantly, however, it led the trainees to consider what impact one's personal agenda, worked outside of the negotiated contract, might have on one's ability to carry out his agreed upon task and on the ability of others to support him in that work. Thus, the topic of one's commitment to work as authorized, and only as authorized, was explicitly introduced early in the training experience.

Later in the evening, the total conference staff (including the staff-in-training) assembled for dinner and some initial conference work. During this time, the trainee subgroup tended to become solidified, recognizing that its members were part of the staff while, at the same time, having a primary task that clearly differed from that of more senior staff members. By the time that the staff assembled the next morning for its formal preconference work session, the cohesiveness of the staff-in-training subgroup was even more apparent and was well-utilized in the interest of work. Staff-in-training participated actively in that planning session, and it seemed clear that they felt fully authorized to comment and question in ways that supported their own learning.

2. *Small Group Events.* During this conference, the staff-in-training constituted its own small group with the Associate Director serving as consultant to the group. This aspect of the program was introduced during the preceding conference as an outgrowth of the staff-in-training meetings of earlier conferences. Its introduction was given further impetus, however, by the increasing levels of sophistication and experience of the trainees in recent conferences. The nonparticipant observation experience, which this small group replaced, had seemed less useful than it had before. Furthermore, it had been clear that concerns about competence, experience, status, competition, gender, special relationships, etc., had emerged with considerable force in the training groups in the past; and it was thought desirable to provide an opportunity, outside of the total staff work setting, for the staff-in-training to explore these issues and the ways in which they influenced their own work and learning within the training program.

While this small-group experience recapitulated the experience of conference members in small groups in many ways, important differences were also apparent. Members of this group were already well acquainted and, most significantly, perhaps, they were relatively familiar with their consultant, his position on the conference staff, his style in taking up his work in other settings and his social relationships and habits. These factors tended to focus early and repeated attention on: a) role definition and role boundaries, especially as these topics related to changing roles within the conference setting; b) special relationships and sentience as they might support, or interfere with, work and the assessment of competence; and c) the individual's commitment to learning, involving, as it does, one's responsibility for allowing himself not to know something already. This third topic, which was prominent during both conferences in which this model was used, seemingly appeared in specific response to the reality that the consultant also filled the role of director of the training program, a role that often became confused with the role of an evaluator in the small group setting.

In total, the staff-in-training group met with its consultant five times during the conference. While no specifics about this small group were revealed to the conference staff by the consultant, the general themes that emerged were reported at the same time that other small group reports were given. The staff-in-training, of course, heard these reports. Therefore, they had the opportunity to compare their perceptions with those of the consultant.

3. *Nonparticipant Observer Activities.* Staff-in-training each observed two of four large groups, teamed with senior members of the conference staff. During the large group events they did not observe, opportunities were available for discussion of their earlier observations.

In addition, the staff-in-training served as nonparticipant observers during the initial session of the institutional event. This single session was designed as an IG 1 with consultants assigned to various rooms to consult around issues such as group formation, task definition and membership criteria.

4. *Institutional Event.* In the preceding conference, staff-in-training were paired with senior conference staff during the institutional event. As before, however, there had been confusion over their specific authorization to work. In addition, such pairings again seemed to foster dependency, so it was decided to abandon this format in the most recent conference.

Instead, following the opening session of the institutional event, the staff-in-training were told merely that a room had been reserved for their use, should they want it, and that they were free to define or negotiate their own work, as it related to their primary task of learning, within the institutional event. Again, this reflected an interest in allowing the staff-in-training to assume responsibility for determining their own goals and for defining ways of achieving them within the boundaries of the conference.

Interestingly, the staff-in-training seemed to experience considerable difficulty around the issues of leadership, delegation of authority and representation during the institutional event. They seemed, at times, almost immobilized by their anger over the fact that their subgroup was working in isolation from the other subgroup of the staff, the senior conference staff, even though they recognized that this isolation was intended to support each group's work on distinctly different tasks.

Ultimately, the staff-in-training proposed negotiations designed to allow them to pair with senior staff consultants during the remainder of the institutional event. However, great confusion surrounded this proposal, and their representative failed to appear at the agreed upon time. It can be speculated (with a modicum of confirmatory data) that negotiations broke down primarily because the training group recognized that their proposal was motivated, in large measure, by sentient interests rather than by a desire to work further on their own learning task. By proposing an activity that exactly duplicated an earlier training model (which had been abandoned because it fostered dependency and was thought nonproductive for learning) the staff-in-training seemed to be expressing their regressive wish for reunion with the conference staff rather than an interest in learning more about consultancy.

This event offered the training group the opportunity to study and struggle with issues that emerge for subgroups in any larger work group. It also gave them the chance to work with the dilemmas encountered when one negotiates, rather than accepts assignment of, one's work, whether that is in the conference setting or elsewhere.

For the conference staff, too, considerable learning was achieved during this aspect of the training program. The senior staff entertained many fantasies about the activities of the staff-in-training; and they also had to acknowledge their wish to reunite, to blur the task boundaries that separated them from the trainees, and to work together rather than separately.

Furthermore, the senior staff, and most particularly the Associate Director, came to appreciate, more fully than ever before, the remarkable commitment to task that is required if one truly allows trainees the freedom to assume personal responsibility for their own learning. The temptation to intervene in one way or another, to offer a suggestion or to sanction their work by discussing it between events, was resisted only with difficulty.

5. *Application Group Experiences.* During the two application group events, staff-in-training were paired with senior consultants. It was explicitly stated that the team member from the senior staff was authorized to head the consultant team, but no other attempt was made to prescribe how these teams might work together. Rather, each pair had the option to negotiate its own working relationship; and in fact, the teams functioned quite differently as the result of individual negotiations.

6. *Conference Plenary Experiences.* Seated as a group but somewhat separated from the senior staff, the staff-in-training participated in the Conference Opening and Conference Discussion as they consistently have in the past. Rarely, however, have the staff-in-training contributed any thoughts or ideas during the conference discussion.

7. *Review Activities.* Two review sessions were held for the staff-in-training. The first, scheduled just prior to the initial application group on the last day of the conference, offered the staff-in-training an opportunity to review their experiences and perceptions with the Conference Director. It also provided a forum for discussing the actual conference design and for examining the rationale behind that design.

The second review session was held with the Associate Director on Monday morning, following the Sunday evening closing of the conference itself. This time was utilized to review the conference experience together and, in the mode of more traditional application groups, to begin to apply learning to situations outside of the training experience.

These seven activities, together with the trainees' participation in staff work sessions, constitute the latest model for advanced training in this series of conferences. This complex training program has evolved from one that originally served merely to expose nonparticipant observers to the behavior of both groups and consultants. Over time, it has emerged as an opportunity for trainees to examine their own behavior and the behavior of others in work group and task-specific subgroup settings; to negotiate their own work and learning; and to experience and study further some of the difficulties and dilemmas inherent in the commitment to work within and among groups. Having begun as an addendum to an established conference structure, it now has evolved into a carefully structured program in its own right.

Nonetheless, this particular advanced training experience remains closely related to the conference structure itself and highly dependent on both the conference staff and, indirectly, the conference membership for support. Yet to date there has been no evidence that either group has experienced itself as unduly deprived by the presence of a training group (current model) within the conference institution. The senior staff has been aware that their commitment to the training program has required extra work and the management of extra relationships, but it has not been an intolerable or generally disagreeable burden.

The current training program has been integrated relatively successfully into the conference institution, in large measure because it has been directed by a single, appropriately authorized member of the senior staff rather than being parceled out to several individuals as it was in the early conferences. Furthermore, the fact that the role of director of the training program has been taken by the Associate Director has seemed significant inasmuch as it reflects the Conference Director's commitment to, and support of, the staff-in-training within the larger conference institution.

It is, of course, more economical to offer a training experience that utilizes the skills of various staff members during their "free" times, but it is questionable whether this is in the best interest of the trainees. Earlier experiences suggest that it is not. Therefore, since the introduction of the current training model, a fee has been charged sufficient to support an additional member of the senior staff and, thereby, free the Associate Director to work with the staff-in-training program.

Not only has this training experience been integrated successfully into the conference structure and been manageable within the limitations imposed by that structure, but the results have been gratifying, too. Some of the former trainees have applied their learning in conference settings. For example, two consultants and both administrators in the most recent conference had participated in earlier training experiences. Others have made use of their experiences in areas outside of conference work, such as organizational or departmental administration and organizational consultation; and one former trainee, who has sought no further conference experience, has maintained an active interest in the ongoing development of techniques for assessing conference learning.

Therefore, despite the complexities and problems encountered in providing multilevel learning opportunities within the framework of a single conference institution, it appears worth doing. The advanced training group has provided useful opportunities for participants, according to their own reports, and it has, in the authors' opinions, enriched the conference experience for the senior staff as well.

14.

AFFECT, LEADERSHIP AND ORGANIZATIONAL BOUNDARIES

Clayton P. Alderfer and Edward B. Klein

Since the late 1940s, two institutions have played a prominent role in group and organizational training. In the United States, the NTL Institute of Applied Behavioral Science pioneered in the development of the T-Group as a key element in laboratory education, while in Great Britain, the Tavistock Institute of Human Relations refined the study group as the major building block in leadership conferences. Similarities and differences between these two approaches have been explored conceptually (Alderfer, 1970; Klein and Astrachan, 1971) and empirically (Harrow et al, 1971; Joseph et al, 1975).

While both "schools" developed methodologies for intensive group learning experiences, writers associated with each also conducted research and consultation in formal organizations (NTL: Argyris, 1962, 1970; Marrow, Bowers and Seashore, 1967; Tavistock: Jaques, 1961; Rice, 1963; Miller and Rice, 1967). But unlike *group training*, comparisons between NTL and Tavistock *organizational consultation* are virtually nonexistent. While some of the comparisons that have been identified for small group training may generalize to organizational work, there is no reason to assume a parallelism between them. One method for providing greater insight would be for a team of investigators representing both to study the same organization. This paper reports such an effort, and, in contrast to previous work, the authors represent both approaches.

This work grew out of a sustained and problematic effort to compare and combine the two traditions. In 1971, a seminar of six Yale faculty was formed with an equal number of NTL and Tavistock oriented members: the authors and Boris Astrachan, Portia Bowers, Alvin Fitz and James Miller. This group decided to study an industrial enterprise in interaction with its complex environment. In the next section, the major conceptual issues focused upon will be identified, and in the following portion data from the field study will be reported and linked to theoretical concerns.

THEORETICAL ISSUES

Three topics were chosen for analysis in this paper. They were: (1) assumptions about human nature; (2) the relationship between social structure and process; and (3) the nature of leadership and power.

Assumptions about Human Nature

In general, the Tavistock tradition is associated with a relatively pessimistic view of human nature, while the NTL position is viewed as more optimistic with regard to human potential. Back (1971), analyzing the social conditions promoting the rise of group training, quotes Margaret Rioch as follows:

> One of our colleagues said once, again in a grossly simplified *bon mot* that the NTL is concerned with love and we are concerned with death. Well, I should say that we are not 100% grim and we even laugh occasionally, but still there is something in it.

Maslow, a strong influence in NTL, spoke for a decidedly positive outlook toward human nature. After observing a bold experiment in Theory Y management, Maslow subsequently titled his book *Eupsychian Management* (1965):

> I've coined the word Eupsychia and defined it as the culture that would be generated by 1000 self-actualizing people on some sheltered island where they would not be interfered with. . . . Eupsychia can also . . . mean 'moving toward psychological health' . . . or it can mean the far goals of therapy, education, or work.

The differences in emphasis in the quotations readily lend themselves to sharper polarization than a careful reading of the literature supports. In fact, NTL recognizes the more unpleasant elements of the human condition, and Tavistock writers express ideals that have much in common with Maslow's wishes.

McGregor's (1960) well-known distinction between Theories X and Y is an application of the self-fulfilling prophecy to the work setting. McGregor's point is that *assumptions* made by leaders about followers determine a great deal of what managers experience as employee behavior. To the extent that leaders assume that material reward is what motivates employees, they will get followers who dependently seek economic satisfactions from work. But, when conditions permit motivation through higher order needs, managers will find employees exhibiting self-directed intrinsically motivated behavior. Maslow noted that his Eupsychian principles held "primarily for good conditions, rather than for stormy weather."

> The healthy individual can be expected to be flexible and realistic; i.e., able to shift from growth to defense as circumstances may demand. The interesting theoretical ex-

trapolation to an organization would be to expect it, also, to be flexibly able to shift from fair weather efficiency to foul weather efficiency whenever this became necessary.

While not commonly recognized, Tavistock writers also make a prominent place for the more positive qualities of human beings. Melanie Klein (1960), writing on leadership and team work, said:

> The ability to admire another person's achievement is one of the factors making successful team work possible. If envy is not too great, we can take pleasure and pride in working with people who sometimes outstrip our capacities, for we identify with these outstanding members of the team. . . . The influence of a really sincere and genuine character on other people is easily observed. Even people who do not possess the same qualities are impressed. . . . For these qualities arouse in them a picture of what they might themselves have become or perhaps even still become.

Another feature of Tavistock theory is the concept of "good group spirit," originally proposed by Bion (1961, p. 25). The qualities include: a common purpose; recognition of the group's boundaries; the capacity to absorb and lose members; flexible internal subgroup boundaries; individuality being recognized; and a capacity to face and cope with dissent among members.

Overall both NTL and Tavistock recognize the decidedly mixed quality of human nature. But this basic similarity should not blur some real differences. Humanistic psychologists minimize concern about physiological or psychological existence. For Maslow it is a society of self-actualizers, cut off from other struggles. For McGregor it is management oriented toward higher order needs. These writers project bad objects (nonself-actualizer's) and feelings (the severe tensions associated with struggles for basic survival) outside their desired social organization. In a somewhat complementary fashion, Tavistock theorists give less attention to the more admirable qualities of human nature. Sincerity, integrity and support for others are uncommon and likely to emerge authentically only after extensive working through of negative affects in an individual whose earliest relationship with mother was especially gratifying (Klein, 1960). Tavistock assumptions do evoke the more disturbing aspects of human nature.

Social Structure and Process

In the area of social structure and process, the *simplified* difference between the two positions gives Tavistock the structural orientation and NTL the process focus. More careful examination reveals that both schools concern themselves with structure and process, but in somewhat different ways. Tavistock writers proposed the concept of a sociotechnical system and the autonomous work group as a useful organizational innovation (Trist et al, 1963). Theorists who have influenced NTL have also been concerned with the dynamics of social structures. Several writers identified the difficulties associated with lower ranks in the system (Argyris, 1957; 1964). They have placed relatively more emphasis on the solution of process problems leading to structural alterations, while the Tavistock emphasis has been toward seeking congruance between tasks and structure.

Both perspectives give extensive attention to the role of feelings in social systems. But, a crucial difference lies in the Tavistock emphasis on unconscious motivation. Several researchers have proposed hypotheses for relating organizational structures to individual ego defensive processes. Menzies (1961) studied a nursing setting and found that the organizational structure formed a social defense system that operated to eliminate activities and relationships that evoked anxieties. Jaques (1974) proposed that the renegotiation of wage rates in the Glacier Metal Company was affected by unconscious mechanisms for dealing with paranoid and depressive anxieties.

NTL researchers have generally not dealt with unconscious processes *as phenomena for intervention*. At the individual level, Argyris (1968) distinguished between competence acquisition and therapy. He argued that persons in need of individual therapy were not good candidates for interpersonal competence training, and depth oriented therapy was not useful to competence oriented individuals. The closest he came to dealing with unconscious processes in social systems was to note that some individuals became "externally closed" (i.e., defensive) in response to social system pressures.

A major Tavistock concept is the *primary task*, the work that a system must do *to survive* in its environment (Rice, 1963). Tavistock consultants work on identifying the primary task and examining forces that interfere with its effective accomplishment. There is no comparable focus defining a crucial variable in relating a system to its environment among NTL writings. The sociotechnical approach emphasizes the primary task with *group* level intervention (Trist et al, 1963; Rice, 1958, 1963). In this way of organizing work, employees form autonomous groups to accomplish total tasks. Within groups, workers exchange assignments according to interests and abilities. The group is paid according to its total production—rather than individual contributions. The literature suggests that there are many desirable outcomes of this approach. Production and satisfaction are higher and absenteeism is lower. Workers report greater cohesion, use of skills and jurisdictional battles tend to decrease.

Leadership and Power

In 1964, when both the economy and laboratory education were expanding, Warren Bennis and Philip Slater wrote "Democracy is inevitable." They argued not that the environmental conditions permitted democratic leadership, but that given a desire to *survive*, democracy is the most effective means to achieve this end. Six years later, after serving as an educational administrator, Bennis (1970) distinguished between macro and micro systems:

In short, interorganizational role set of the leader, the scale, diversity, and formal relations that ensue in a pluralistic system place heavy burdens on those managers and leaders who expect an easy transferability between the cozy gemutlichkeit of a Theory Y orientation and the realities of macropower.

Bennis changed his views of leadership as a result of his administrative experience during one of the most turbulent periods in American academic history. A similar change is reflected in the ideas of Douglas McGregor (1944) who wrote about leadership as a *relationship*. Followers needed certain qualities from their leaders, among which were an atmosphere of approval, knowledge of what is expected, forewarning of changes, and consistent discipline. Ten years later, after service as a university president, McGregor (1954) had learned that a leader must exercise authority, absorb hostility and displeasure, and protect his institution from a hostile environment. The Bennis and McGregor writings indicate a similar pattern. Initial concerns were with internal matters, including "democracy" and the provision of support and nurturance to followers. Later works demonstrated a broader conception of leadership by dealing with external "boundary-crossing" activities.

Tavistock theorists have consistently focused on external boundary management. Rice has symbolized the leader as a "Janus-like" figure who must look inward and outward and contend with the stresses between the two perspectives. Recognizing that internal and external demands may not always be easily compatable, he tended to focus on the problems generated for external affairs by internal conditions. "It is unfortunately true," he wrote (1963), "that an established relationship between leaders and followers can be an inhibiting factor in allowing a leader to take effective action to adapt to change" (p. 210).

Another difference in emphasis between McGregor and Rice is the explicitness of leader-follower relations. McGregor's early writings proposed dealing with dependency in a supportive fashion. Rice (1965), on the other hand, recognizing the mutual dependency between leaders and followers, identifies the potential mutual hostility between the roles. He makes explicit that hostility resides in both leaders and followers.

The difference between early McGregor and Bennis and Rice probably lies in the level of leadership being observed. Attending to the emotional needs of subordinates is easier for lower ranking managers in micro-systems that it is for leaders in macro-systems. Executives generally manage more external boundaries with greater incipient chaos than lower ranking leaders. Bennis (1970) makes the point:

> In macropower situations, the leader is almost always involved in boundary exchanges with salient interorganizational activities which inescapably reduce, not necessarily interest in group members or activities, but the amount of interaction he can maintain (p. 606).

Logistics make it difficult to have mutually supportive and trusting relations. To develop a climate where it is possible to identify and work through negative and positive feelings requires time for interaction. The pulls on higher level managers from external events increase the costs of finding this time. The magnitude of issues at stake makes it risky for sensitive issues to be discussed openly. As Rice (1965) noted, a leader must be able to make decisions on behalf of his followers, with or without their collaboration.

A difference in emphasis in leadership tasks can be identified between the two approaches. Initially, McGregor and Bennis addressed themselves to internal issues in leadership development in order to create conditions that permit leaders and followers to reduce the social distance between themselves. As life experiences brought them to top management, their perspective changed to include more attention to external affairs. Rice's analysis was consistently to emphasize dealing with the external environment. He tried to enable leaders to develop insight into individual and social processes to allow them to stand amid the multiple cross pressures contained in their role. There has been a tendency in Rice's writing to minimize supportive interpersonal processes internal to the organization. Although he developed the notion of sentience late in his career, this concept is less formed than many of his other contributions (Rice, 1970).

THE OBSERVATIONAL STUDY

In the following section we report empirical observations in terms of assumptions about human nature, social structure and leadership as outlined above. A manufacturing plant of a national company was found for study, and a combined model of investigation was followed. The group decided to look at the internal, management, and community relationships via subteams represented by one NTL and one Tavistock researcher at each location. Thus, two members of the group studied the internal functioning of the plant, two observed its relationship to national headquarters and the present authors studied the relations between the plant and the surrounding community. We then show how the three concepts developed in the introduction (management assumptions, social structure, and leadership) influence the internal, corporate and community relationships of the plant.

Background

The plant was designed during the late 1950-early 1960 period, an expansive time when executives in an old factory within the corporation were schooled in the writing of Maslow and McGregor. The region was personally selected by the plant manager for reasons having to do with geography, availability of a labor force, and desirability on the part of the town fathers to have a "clean, progressive" plant in the community. Although there were Irish, Italian and Afro-American ethnic groups and the area was known as a center for crime in the mid-1940s, economic control of the community rested with a predominantly white Anglo-Saxon Protestant group.

The managerial philosophy fit with many norms. The new managers strongly believed in the merits of cross training to provide employees with the skills to do many tasks in the plant. Visiting the community, we saw many signs of people valuing self-sufficiency as a life style. A foreman proudly took us by his own home to see his nursery business. The widely developed system of participation in the plant required a high level of involvement from employees. Many voiced a similar kind of commitment to the local community. The plant reflected a high degree of identification with the national corporation and its products, a phenomenon that was matched locally by a high degree of loyalty to the community and the area. The plant manager had sought the location in part because of his feelings for the people and place.

After several initial years of severe stress, the plant was now marked by sparkling success. The technology and management philosophy was implanted in new soil, had grown, and achieved. Indeed, the plant was so robust that executives from many parts of the system came to visit and learn about its functioning. It was used as a showcase for many young executives in the larger system in order to experience working in a futuristic setting. The positive elements included a successful technical operation, high worker involvement, low turnover, cross training, good profit margin, pleasant environment, and an unlimited future. The plant also lacked a variety of problematic elements (unions and organized minority groups) that are part of urban, industrialized America. Therefore, the plant, from the perspective of executives, met job and career needs. This plant was different from many others within the national system because of the management philosophy and technical success. In addition, we suggest that the factory also served a special symbolic function for the total system. It represented hope for the future. It had the qualities of a "star," a showcase for company executives, visiting dignitaries, and academic researchers.

INTRA-PLANT DYNAMICS

Within the plant the way boundaries were managed supported sharing and cooperation. Informality was the rule; everyone was called by first name, and people did not punch time clocks. There was a high degree of involvement and a team approach. Workers report, "There is nobody looking over my shoulder." Individuals in most of the departments readily communicated with each other and attempted to understand the problems of other groups. Employees also saw top management as sympathetic, concerned, and knowledgeable about them and their work.

According to McGregor (1960), management philosophies reflect leader attitudes and underlying assumptions about human nature. There was a relatively high degree of congruence among the executives in the plant on matters of managerial philosophy. They assumed that workers would behave responsibly, with self-direction and creativeness, if treated as mature adults. In addition, the operating philosophy seemed to imply that there were no unresolvable issues between managers and workers. Our observations were that within the plant morale was high, people got along well and there was a great deal of collaboration. Workers were well-treated. They were made to feel welcome and part of the total enterprise and had extremely amiable relations with managers. Opportunities to obtain cross training were utilized by workers. They reported feeling skilled and competent. Much of the work activity within the plant was organized on a team system, an innovation leading to positive work attitudes and a peer group atmosphere. It was not unusual for a team to redesign their own jobs to find more efficient ways to utilize their time. In addition, when machinery broke down, members of the team as well as managers rolled up their shirt sleeves and repaired, on the spot, extremely sophisticated and expensive machinery, often from foreign manufacturers.

These relatively autonomous task groups are consistent with the sociotechnical system associated with the Tavistock approach (Rice, 1958, 1963; Trist et al, 1963).

Foremen, the first line of management between the task teams and executives, reported that they often felt redundant in such a setting. As the enforcers of company rules in a setting that prided itself on not having very formal authority, foremen often felt covertly attacked by both workers and management. Foremen reported that they sometimes were not backed by management, and workers "got away" with many things. Even though teams cooperated and boundaries between them were permeable, the men on the boundaries received negative feelings from both sides.

In terms of leadership and power, workers in the teams shared their leadership and experienced themselves as collaborators for specific work activities. Some skill differences were acknowledged and efforts made to produce the most effective strategies for efficient task performance. On the other hand, foremen felt that their leadership was often undermined, and they were made to feel less than fully competent. Though paid more than team workers, they did not experience themselves as highly effective. In addition, the foremen were local men, and the higher levels of management were staffed primarily by college graduates from out of town. Therefore, foremen seemed to be in a more tenuous position than other managers in this organization. We hypothesize that this phenomenon occurred because of the strong emphasis on Theory Y management philosophy with its positive assumption about human nature, the indirect nature of expressing negative feelings, and the need to dilute the authority structure within the plant.

Within the plant there was one major exception to the pervasive Theory Y management philosophy: the Finishing Department. Job applicants went through the State employment agency that screened them. They then had a personal interview at the plant, and if accepted for employment, were placed in the Finishing Department where they spent a probationary period. While working there the individual learned particular skills and demonstrated his work capacity. Simultaneously, the foreman and others made an appraisal of how the individual fitted into factory life. Therefore, one can view the Finishing Department as providing an acculturation process in which successful performers were rotated out to other parts of the system, questionable ones remained for longer periods and failures were dropped.

Finishing Department workers, in comparison to teams, had duller, simpler and more repetitive tasks organized more like a production line. But they also had a total view of the products produced by the factory, since all items were finally assembled in this Department. Structurally there was much more of a hierarchy with foremen delegating tasks and supervising work. There was also close checking for quality control since this was the last function performed before products were sent out of the plant.

This department had the lowest morale, often felt picked on, and complained more about working conditions than any other group. Retrospectively, we noted that the department had one of the highest rates of female employees, blacks and long-haired, "hippie-looking" young men. Therefore, it may be no accident the plant had difficulty promoting black workers, women, and youth, given this introduction to company life. The Finishing Department was located on the boundary between the community and the plant. It was the entry system for people and the exit system for products. Being on the boundary, it contained the most Theory X attitudes and behavior within the plant. One of the tasks of the Finishing Department was to make new employees congruent with the value system of the factory. Until new employees became like "us," and moved into other parts of the plant, they were treated in a relatively authoritarian, rigid manner.

MANAGEMENT DYNAMICS

When turning to middle and upper management we noted important social differences that distinguished managers from workers and foremen. Managers tended to be from middle and upper-middle class backgrounds with college educations and often advanced degrees in management. Below the top level many were younger men in training who were highly mobile within the national company and primarily from other parts of the country. Workers and foremen, on the other hand, came from working class backgrounds, usually had a high school education and were somewhat older natives of the local community who were less mobile in their occupational world. One may draw a parallel, particularly for the younger managers who were getting advanced training, to "colonialists" who were in leadership positions over the "natives." This tendency no doubt was present but attenuated by the fact that a number of middle-level managers had been fired in the past for not being able to behave according to Theory Y principles. There was pressure on managers to endorse and to behave in a fashion consistent with the models demonstrated by the top two executives (although, as noted above, this was not always consistent).

Top leadership demonstrated a particular division of labor with associated symbols. The plant manager, in addition to starting the factory and making it a viable economic concern, was seen internally as a socioemotional leader. His family was from the local area, and he knew all of the employees by first name. He had a leadership style that took into account the human factors involved in running a successful business. He also knew all the technology intimately and could solve mechanical problems as well as anyone in the plant. Some aspects of the feminine role were carried by this number one executive. At one time he was referred to as Mrs. Brown, suggesting the caring, giving qualities of leadership. The task leadership was carried by the number two executive who was more concerned with running the plant. His style tended to stress structure over process, and power rather than sharing. The number two manager was seen as a taskmaster, a somewhat more distant "father-like figure" than number one, although both were highly regarded as extremely competent managers and viewed in a positive fashion. Between these two men, who worked well together, both the work and sentient tasks were carried out with regard to the internal functioning of the plant and its relationship to the national company. The number three manager, in charge of community relations, was the only executive whose position was problematic in nature and to whom negative affect was directed. In many ways, he was least Y-like. His X behavior was consistent with managing the plant/community boundary, whereas the Y behavior of the other two executives was in accordance with internal functioning. That is, nondemocratic behavior was more acceptable, perhaps even necessary, when directed outside as opposed to within "the family."

This executive was on the boundary in charge of community relations and personnel. He dealt with the outside, "uncontrollable world" where there was always the danger that unfamiliar people and ideas would get in. For example, he had stopped telling people rejected for employment why they were refused because he had once been threatened by a lawsuit. This X behavior went with the attitude that outsiders could not be controlled and things might get out of hand. It is not surprising that he was viewed in an ambivalent fashion by those inside the plant. In many ways he was seen as the receptacle for many negative intramanagement feelings. We posit that this was not only due to his personality, but also to his role for the system. When difficulties with the community were maximal, his position was most problematic. Although relations with the parent plant and national headquarters were well managed, those with the community were much more ambiguous. The community relations manager was not the most frequently named executive by community respondents when commenting on plant-community relations. This top manager, like the foremen, suffered from a lack of clearly delegated authority.

Theory Y attitudes and behavior extended to relations with the parent plant. Though there was some rivalry between the two, we were surprised that relations contained a great deal of cooperation. Managers from the older plant came for advanced training. In general, the boundary between the two plants was well managed and sharing of information, techniques and news was a common norm.

When we move to a corporate level, however, more X-like behavior prevailed. The boundary to national headquarters, though well managed, had some problematic aspects to it. The subteam studying plant-headquarters relations was discouraged from visiting corporate headquarters. In general, the plant-system relationship was a positive one, but X behavior did occur when there seemed to be some threat implied. As part of the contract between the research group, national headquarters and the plant, feedback was given at the end of the study. During the session, the presence of one of the executives from national headquarters reduced the ease of communication. As a result, the research team was more cautious about exposing conflicts within the plant. Exposure might have been dangerous before somebody who had real power to affect the plant and its special position in the organization.

PLANT COMMUNITY DYNAMICS

In many ways the pair investigating plant-community relations had the most difficult time. From the outset we made unexpected demands on plant management. Since the original invitation from top management was to investigate the extent to which Theory Y management was operational *in* the plant, the request to interview community people deviated from management's major objectives. We also made specific requests that drew further on plant resources. A list of key roles in the community was provided, and plant staff were asked to arrange interviews. On arrival, we learned that most of our requests for interviews had been met. Meetings had been arranged with suppliers, the past president of the council of churches, president of the Chamber of Commerce, mayor, chief of police, editor of the local newspaper, and the head of the State Employment Service. Additions were made to the list at our request, but omitted were meetings with the state labor council, a local college ecology group, and representatives from minority groups (e.g., NAACP, Urban League). No amount of pressure succeeded in getting access to these additional perspectives on community relations. To us, the omissions were a decidedly nonrandom sample. Other researchers thought that excessive concern for getting access to the community people would jeopardize the whole team's "guest" relationship with plant management. Thus, we not only faced resistance from management in obtaining certain kinds of information, we also experienced conflict within our own team on this matter.

Among the parties whom we contacted, conversations with high ranking members of the community were typically open, relaxed and spontaneous. Generally, we learned that the plant was perceived as a "good" corporate citizen in the community—contributing stable, well paying jobs, clean work, no labor problems, and a fine national reputation. Several of the top executives were significant community leaders. The one complaint on which there was some concensus was that the plant might contribute more of its talent toward the solution of community problems. State Employment Office personnel and suppliers held a decided sense of awe for the plant, which had high and discriminating standards for potential employees.

Some suggested that plant leaders had not actively encouraged the entry of another nationally known corporation into the community. One point of view was that the other firm did not enter the neighborhood because their own labor market survey revealed an inadequate supply of talent. Another view (not necessarily contradictory to the first) was that the plant did not utilize its considerable resources for aiding entry because it was not in its interest to do so. A second highly regarded company would have increased competition for labor and made the area more attractive to national unions.

It was also learned that the manager once brought in corporate specialists to conduct a seminar for other industrial leaders after an organizing attempt at the local hospital. The plant manager acted after he learned that hospital administrators unknowingly violated National Labor Relations Board regulations in trying to prevent employees from organizing. He wanted to prevent other large companies in the area from making similar mistakes.

As noted above, the managerial philosophy was not just passed by word of mouth. There was a plant handbook that stated overall practices in quite explicit terms. Because there was considerable proselytizing about Theory Y management internally, we wanted to see how well this new ideology was understood outside the plant. We found no evidence of articulate understanding of the management philosophy among community members. Respondents used words like "good conditions, cleanliness, progressive management, no labor problems," but when pressed to explain what these meant operationally, no one was able to cite anything like the contents of the handbook. Apparently knowledge of Theory Y management stopped at the external boundary of the plant.

Management was not the only group who engaged in organized efforts to influence the community. Nonmanagement employees had recently organized a "Community Action Committee" to provide a forum for discussion of political and economic concerns. Generally, this group functioned for informational and educational purposes but in reviewing the minutes we noted a marked departure from this philosophy. One subcommittee defined its aim as "getting the mayor out of office." This information was especially noteworthy because an interview with the mayor showed him happily reporting what fine support he got from plant employees.

The emerging picture of plant-community relations contrasts markedly with other sectors of the organization. During this part of the study there was active and successful resistance on the part of plant management to prevent us from obtaining data from certain sectors of the community. Groups over which management had no direct control and which might conflict with plant objectives were barred from study. Easy access was granted to people who were dependent on the plant (e.g., suppliers) or whose interests were associated with management's. Among those respondents who were contacted we found predominantly positive attitudes toward the plant. Indeed there were times when we sensed we were being treated as conveyors of good tidings to management from parties outside the system. Perhaps management felt they could not risk initiating contact with potential adversaries because it would provide a form of legitimation that might hinder plant objectives. Knowledge about the operating managerial philosophy was scarce in the community, and there were significant discrepancies on perceptions of political matters. The use of Theory Y management did not extend to community relations as it did in other sectors of the plant.

DISCUSSION

All of us were impressed by the amount of cooperative behavior that was observed in the total system.

But Theory X attitudes and behavior were also observed in all three sectors: within the larger system in the relationship to corporate headquarters; in the plant by attitudes expressed toward foremen, the Finishing Department, and the community relations executive; and toward the community by negative feelings about unions, minority and ecology groups. There was a gradient of affect going from most negative attitudes toward community groups (particularly unions), then to corporate headquarters and finally to selected sections within the plant. Groups "like us" were reacted to in the most positive manner. Unions were most disliked because they represented another power base. They were unfamiliar, uncontrolled, had different values, were outside, and represented a real conflict. Management specifically feared that with unions, employee roles would be limited and work options would be restricted. It might be difficult to have a program of cross training. Unions might lead to a lack of loyalty on the part of employees. The ecology group was not "like us" (possibly academic, nonpractical, college based troublemakers), made alternative demands (clean up waste disposal systems), were outsiders, but were in less conflict with management. Minorities, in an organized sense, were not "like us." They represented a potential threat, but less than the ecology group and certainly less than the unions.

The executive in charge of community relations had negative feelings directed to him because he had an ambiguous plant-community boundary to manage with questionable authority.

Within the plant there was negative affect involving the Finishing Department because it too contained people not "like us" (unacculturated, women, blacks and hippies who did not yet have the values of the company family), although some *individual* blacks and women in the plant were "like us." These minority groups potentially represented sentient ties that were a threat to the plant philosophy and the rather informal nature of employee/manager relationships. The unions, on the other hand, might formalize differences between workers and managers and therefore be a threat to both the task and sentient systems. Some of these issues were highlighted in the Finishing Department because it was on the boundary to the community both in terms of the input of people and the export of products.

Negative feelings about foremen had to do more with the ambiguity of their being on the boundary between management and employees than with dealing with an unknown or foreign group, except in the Finishing Department.

There were also negative feelings and X attitudes towards corporate headquarters, since they could impose their authority.

In general, the further away the group, the more negatively it was viewed; the more unlike *management* the harsher the stereotype. The good groups were those who looked like them, were familiar, and might even be considered part of a comfortable extended family, with shared values. These groups were also clearly defined in an equal or lower position in the authority structure and related with a greater sense of mutuality.

One can conceptualize the plant in its internal, corporate, and community relations as a system taking into account the theoretical notions explicated in the introduction. Assumptions about human nature were determined by whether individuals and groups under consideration were inside or outside the plant. The structural aspects were highly related to management's anxieties (Menzies, 1961) and developing paranoia (Jaques, 1974) about deviant individuals and groups that were experienced as threatening to the enterprise. Leadership and power were differentially displayed according to whether the managers were working within the plant or dealing with outside groups that could not be as easily controlled. In addition, there was a group psychology that underlay each sector within the larger system. Within the plant itself a psychology of growth predominated. Local management was clearly in control, optimism prevailed, negative affect was minimized, and there were great hopes for the future. With regard to the larger system, there was a mixture of X and Y philosophy, and a group psychology of being a star in the national corporation. In general, the more positive aspects were demonstrated in collaborative efforts with the older plant and the occasional X-like behavior was displayed toward national headquarters when under threat. In terms of the community, there was more of a psychology of survival. The most negative aspects were directed toward groups seen as economic threats or as endangering the plant's functioning and growth. The positive side of the ambivalence toward community was carried by other like-minded community groups.

In combining NTL and Tavistock approaches, it appears that different parts of the system were more interpretable in one view than the other. Overall, each tradition provided insights not available through the other alone. Theory Y management seems most viable for secure internal issues and least operative in external relations. But internal stresses can lead to Theory X behavior and certain external conditions can promote cooperative exchanges. Theory X behavior occurs internally when one of the following is present: a dual power source (unions, an alternative philosophy, pressure groups); strangers among us (Finishing Department); people on unclear boundaries (foremen, executive in charge of community relations); or an authority group that is external and more powerful (corporate headquarters), i.e., whenever there is a potential threat to survival. If it is internal and management controls, the relationship will be more positive and Y. If it is external with people whose value base is similar, it will also be Y oriented. One must therefore conclude that no single variable (e.g., management philosophy, social structure, leadership, group psychology and expression of affect) explains the complexities of what was observed, but rather a multidimensional analysis is needed to understand X and Y behavior in the plant, community and the corporate system.

The research approach used in this study contributed to a more differentiated view of Tavistock and NTL theory and application. The methodological innovation of one NTL and Tavistock researcher at each of the three boundaries (Intra-Plant, Plant-Corporation and Plant-Community) aided in developing a balanced view of the phenomena. One observer from each orientation provided correctors for tendencies to move in extreme directions and facilitated more shared perceptions. This principally involved interpretation of observations, not the data itself. Having the two orientations represented at each of the three locations parallels the analysis and keeps the intergroup nature of the research team in the foreground.

PART THREE

APPLICATION

Section Editors: Arthur D. Colman
Verneice Thompson
Kathryn West

The practical value of the Group Relations model as both an analytic and design tool in social systems seems amply confirmed by the many papers describing its investigation and effective use in a variety of clinical, educational and organizational situations. For example, there is now documentation of its value in nursing homes, in-patient psychiatric wards, adolescent treatment units, drug abuse programs and industrial projects to name just a few (Miller, 1972; Trop, 1980; Menzies, 1979; Braxton, 1983). Similarly the use of group relations conferences, either in standard or modified form, as an experiential mode of education and training in different work and social settings, also seems well established. Thus there are papers in the literature describing programs designed specifically for different professionals, such as social workers, psychiatric residents, psychologists, medical residents, health care professionals, management personnel, and teachers (Beck, 1983; Benson and Lundgren, 1982; Cooper and Gustafson, unpublished; Gustafson, unpublished; Gillette and Van Steenberg, 1983; Heimburger and Baxter, 1979; Johnson and Fleisher, 1980).

The papers included in the Application Section of *Group Relations Reader 2* are divided into four sections. The first section, System Analysis, includes Shapiro's analysis of the family system and therapy intervention, and Lawrence's discussion of the metapsychology of management development. Both papers begin to define a general methodology of applied analysis that could be used in a wide range of complex systems. In the second section, Consultation and Implementation, each paper starts with an analysis of a specific system and then develops appropriate interventions, training and program modification based on what was learned. Miller, in his work on organizations in developing countries, takes us through his analysis of a factory and then goes on to describe how he transformed his findings into specific training procedures designed to foster organizational development and provide data for further analysis and development. Medders and Colman also begin with an analysis of a task system, in this case care of the chronic mentally disabled, and then use their findings to develop a new system of care better suited to the task. The paper by Menninger is a ten-year outcome study of an institution-wide consultation that includes analysis, training and evaluation, while Klein's description of his team's work in Belfast is an example of the innovative marriage of Group Relations and other experiential training modes to a national crisis. What these and

213

other papers are beginning to define is a general model for action-based consultation that integrates different aspects of the Group Relations training model as they apply to a specific situation.

The last two sections deal with a newly developing area in group relations that extends the English origins of application work—with its early focus on task and hierarchy in organizations—to the more personal dimensions of work role reflecting the American social experience. In the Role Analysis section, the papers by Bayes and Newton and by Dumas discuss the relevance of gender and ethnicity to institutional work settings, while those by Hirschhorn and E. Shapiro consider the intersection of personal psychological processes in the consultative roles. The papers in the last section, Evaluation, extend these personal dimensions even further. Evaluation here utilizes data derived not from objective measurement but from intensely personal considerations. Thus Kernberg and particularly Rioch and Miller address the relevance of group relations work in their life and work. They each ask the question that Rioch poses overtly: Why do I do this work? and find three very different answers, each with deep meaning for themselves, their relations to professional sentient groups, and ultimately to the readers. In doing so, they model self-study of their own person/role interphase and define in new directions for all of us interested in applying Group Relations work to internal as well as external boundaries.

A.D.C.

Part Three—Application

A. Systems Analysis 215
B. Consultation and Implementation 241
C. Role Analysis 307
D. Evaluation 363

A. Systems Analysis

Family Dynamics and Object-Relations Theory: An Analytic
  Group-Interpretative Approach to Family Therapy 217
Roger L. Shapiro

Management Development . . . some ideals, images and realities .. 231
W. Gordon Lawrence

15.

FAMILY DYNAMICS AND OBJECT-RELATIONS THEORY: AN ANALYTIC GROUP-INTERPRETATIVE APPROACH TO FAMILY THERAPY

Roger L. Shapiro

Psychoanalysis became an object-relations theory when Freud proposed the structural hypotheses in *The Ego and the Id* (1961). Prior to that, in psychoanalytic theory, interest in objects was limited to their role in affording need gratification through drive discharge, and identification was conceived of as a mechanism of defense. Freud's increasing recognition of the role of identification in mental life led him to propose that identification was a crucial factor in the formation of ego and superego. This was a change in his conceptualization of the role of object relations development.

In structural theory, internalizations of object relations were crucial constituents in the formation of psychic structure (Loewald 1966). The structural theory established psychoanalysis as a developmental theory. Subsequent contributions to psychoanalytic theory in ego psychology and the work of the British school of object relations were built on the foundation of structural theory. These contributions continued the effort to comprehend the relation of the individual to reality through conceptualizing processes of internalization of object relations during development and their persistence and state of organization in both conscious and unconscious mental processes (Shapiro 1978).

This position is consistent with that of Kernberg (1976), who states: "In the broadest terms psychoanalytic object-relations theory represents the psychoanalytic study of the nature and origin of interpersonal relations, and of the nature and origin of intrapsychic structures deriving from, fixating, modifying and reactivating past internalized relations with others in the context of present interpersonal relations. Psychoanalytic object-relations theory focuses upon the internalization of interpersonal relations, their contribution to normal and pathological ego and superego developments, and the mutual influences of intrapsychic and interpersonal object-relations."

Psychoanalysis was established as a personality theory and as a therapy before the structural theory was formulated. The methods of psychoanalysis as a therapy were based upon prior topographic theory. Although the structural theory soon led to important changes in analytic technique—specifically, the methods of defense analysis (Settlage 1974)—other modifications of technique, derived from developmental considerations and from the role of object relations in personality formulation, have evolved more slowly in the years since the structural theory was formulated. These modifications have been particularly significant in the treatment of children and adolescents. The methods of child analysis are one example of such technical development.

This chapter is concerned with another technical development that addresses specific problems in the treatment of adolescent disturbances. In it, I will discuss methods of analytic assessment and treatment of the family of the disturbed adolescent. I believe treatment of the family may be required because of the body of findings, predicted by structural theory, relating pathology in children and adolescents to disturbances in relationships within the family.

First, I will discuss the need for an analytic framework for the assessment of families of disturbed adolescents and indications for the application of such a framework to the group-interpretive treatment of certain of these families concurrent with the individual psychoanalytic psychotherapy of the adolescent. I will then outline an analytic theory of family functioning that conceptualizes family regression and is derived from Bion's (1961) theory of small groups. Finally, I will describe findings in families of adolescents with borderline conditions or pathological narcissism that are indications for combined individual and family treatment.

ASSESSMENT OF FAMILIES OF DISTURBED ADOLESCENTS AND INDICATIONS FOR CONCURRENT FAMILY THERAPY

In one of Freud's (1963a) last discussions of theory of the therapeutic effect of psychoanalysis, he says that most of the failures of psychoanalytic treatment are due, not to unsuitable choice of patients, but to unsuitable external conditions. He notes that, while the internal resistances to therapy, the resistances of the patient, are inevitable and can be overcome, the external resistances to therapy that arise from the patient's environmental circumstances are also of great practical importance. Freud writes:

> In psychoanalytic treatment resistances due to the intervention of relatives is a positive danger, and a danger one does not know how to meet. One is armed against the patient's internal resistances, which one knows are inevitable, but how can one ward off these external resistances? No kind of explanations make any impression on the patient's relatives; they cannot be induced to keep at a distance from the whole business, and one cannot make common cause

with them because of the risk of losing the confidence of the patient, who—quite rightly, moreover—expects the person in whom he has put his trust to take his side. No one who has any experience of the rifts which so often divide a family will, if he is an analyst, be surprised to find that the patient's closest relatives sometimes betray less interest in his recovering than in his remaining as he is. When, as so often, the neurosis is related to conflict between members of a family, the healthy party will not hesitate long in choosing between his own interest and the sick party's recovery.

Freud says in conclusion that he followed the rule of not taking on a patient for treatment unless the patient was not dependent on anyone else in the essential relations in his life.

Clearly, the conditions Freud recommends as optimal for psychoanalysis are by definition not possible in the treatment of adolescents. The shift from the adolescent's dependency on his primary objects (the parents) to the finding of new objects is a central aspect of personality reorganization throughout adolescence (Jacobson 1961; Shapiro 1963). Difficulty in this process is among the important causes of disturbance in the adolescent. It is therefore essential to design a therapy that helps the adolescent to manage difficulties in family relationships that interfere with the transition from preadolescent dependency on parents to a new level of autonomy in relationships inside and outside the family in late adolescence. Such a therapy requires work with the external resistances to analytic therapy described by Freud. The nature of the adolescent's dependence on his parents dictates a redefinition of the task of his treatment to include management of the external resistances. The boundaries of adolescent therapy have expanded, then, to include methods for the maintenance and repair of a working alliance with the parents.

Adequate assessment of an adolescent patient involves careful evaluation of the internal resistances, of his defensive organization, and of the causal relation between the state of ego functioning, defenses, and symptomatology (Laufer 1965). Assessment of the adolescent must also include evaluation of the external resistances, the nature of the adolescent's dependency on his parents and the nature of evidence in the family of the parents' interest in and conflict over the adolescent changing or remaining as he is. I believe this assessment is best done through interviews with the parents and adolescent together (conjoint family interviews), in addition to individual interviews with the adolescent (Shapiro 1967; Shapiro and Zinner 1976). In addition to their value for assessment of external resistances, conjoint family interviews have the goal of forming a beginning working alliance with the parents as well as with the adolescent. It is important that this alliance be established and general goals of treatment agreed upon. Family interviews establish a working situation that can be held in reserve and, in the most favorable cases, may not be needed again.

If, however, the situation is one where neurosis in the adolescent is related to conflict between members of the family, change in the adolescent may lead the parents to define the situation in a way that assumes their interests are opposed to the adolescent's; they may choose their own interests over his, and new external resistances may arise. This possibility should be anticipated in the assessment phase. A reconvening of family interviews is then indicated to attempt to manage the external resistances interpretively in a way analogous to management of internal resistances through defense analysis. In conjoint family interviews, exploration of the nature and the sources of the impasse between parents and adolescent is possible. The therapist is aided in his effort to maintain a stance of neutrality because he can orient himself to the goals of therapy the family has agreed upon. He may then proceed to examine the interferences with the accomplishment of these goals. The framework of conjoint family interviews established during the assessment phase is the foundation that authorizes the therapist to work interpretively on this task. He attempts to understand and interpret unconscious assumptions activating resistances in the family to change in the adolescent, both from the side of the parents and from the side of the adolescent. The psychotherapy of adolescents with severe neurosis or higher-order character pathology may then be preserved through analysis of external resistances to treatment when they arise in the family.

The more severe disturbances of adolescence, the borderline conditions and pathological narcissism, present a specific indication for ongoing treatment of the family, concurrent with individual psychotherapy of the adolescent, because of the severe pathology in the family in the area of separation-individuation.

Interest in problems of separation-individuation in early childhood has led to new recognition of their links to processes of individuation during adolescence, which Blos (1967) has called the second individuation phase. Disturbances in separation-individuation, studied by Mahler in childhood (Mahler 1971; Mahler, Pine, and Bergman 1975), have been shown to determine borderline and narcissistic pathology in the adolescent in the work of Kernberg (1975), Masterson (1972), and my research group (Berkowitz et al. 1974a, 1974b; Shapiro et al. 1977; Shapiro et al. 1975). These disturbances are seen both in the parents and in the adolescent and are treated most effectively in concurrent individual and family therapy.

THE THEORY OF UNCONSCIOUS ASSUMPTIONS

Our research into the origins of adolescent disturbance has utilized evidence from direct family observations to explore the family contribution to pathologic outcome in adolescence (Berkowitz et al. 1974a, 1974b; Shapiro et al. 1975, 1977; Shapiro and Zinner 1976; Zinner and Shapiro 1972, 1974). This evidence leads us to conclude that, during the course of his development, and depending upon his particular emotional meaning to his parents, the adolescent who is disturbed has not been supported by his parents in his efforts to accomplish phase-appropriate life tasks. On the contrary, his parents have responded to his development with anxiety and repudiation of change in their relationships with him. In the face of progressive individuation in the developing child and adolescent, characteristic defensive behaviors are mobilized in these parents that distort their perceptions of the child and adolescent and dominate their responses to him. We find that the nature of disturbance in the adolescent is related to and in part determined by the characteristics of regression and the nature of defenses that dominate his parents' behaviors with him. Furthermore, our evidence suggests that these episodes of regression and related defenses in parents are activated by their unconscious fantasies regarding the child.

Our findings from observations of family interaction indicate that the nature of character pathology in the adolescent is related in specific ways to the characteristics of defenses, regression, and consequent distortions in the relationships between the parents and the developing child. In order to specify what characteristics in families are related to specific adolescent character pathology, we assess the level of regression and characteristics of defense in family transactions and the nature of unconscious fantasies that are the motives for defense. We find evidence within families for an organization of shared or complementary unconscious fantasies and related higher-level repressive defenses or lower-level defenses including denial, splitting, and projection. These shared or complementary fantasies and related defenses serve to maintain equilibrium among family members and constitute external resistances to change. The underlying assumptions of the family based upon unconscious fantasies are conceptualized as the unconscious assumptions of the family as a group. We observe repetitive behaviors in families that appear to militate against change, development, and individuation of the child and infer that shared unconscious assumptions in family members motivate and organize these repetitive behaviors. These unconscious assumptions are assumed to derive from the internalized developmental experience of both of the parents in their families of origin. An organization of motives and higher- or lower-level defenses evolves, then, in the marriage, conceptualized as the unconscious assumptions of the family. These are operative throughout the development of the adolescent. Depending upon their centrality and coerciveness as the family develops, unconscious assumptions are powerful determinants of disturbance in the maturing adolescent.

The concept of unconscious assumptions of the family group is a construct that originates in clinical observation. It derives from the small-group theory of Bion (1961) and facilitates an integration of family-systems theory and psychoanalytic concepts of individual psychology. It has proven useful both in the differentiation of families of neurotic, borderline, and narcissistic adolescents and in the clinical understanding and treatment of these families in conjoint therapy.

The small-group theory of Bion derives from psychoanalysis and is a conceptualization of both the conscious functions and tasks that define groups and the unconscious motives that are also present in group members and that may dominate group behavior. Our effort to conceptualize family behavior has been facilitated by using a similar framework, that of family functions and tasks and of a variety of unconscious motives that interfere with their accomplishment. From the point of view of adolescent development, we conceive of the family as having an important function in promoting specific developmental tasks. These include the promotion of individuation and relative ego autonomy, resulting in an integrated identity formation in adolescent family members that leads to a substantial alteration in the quality of their relationships to parents and to peers (Blos 1967; Erikson 1950, 1956; Jacobson 1964; Shapiro 1969). Adolescent development is interfered with by unconscious assumptions in the family that militate against these changes. Unconscious assumptions inimical to the task of adolescent individuation activate states of anxiety and defense in family members in response to manifestations of individuation. Regression and symptomatic behavior are then seen in the family, often most markedly in the adolescent member.

A brief review of Bion's small-group theory will help us to clarify its application to family process. Bion proposed a group theory that articulated two levels of group functioning, a mature and a regressed level. In Bion's terminology, the mature level of group functioning is called the work group, the regressed level is the basic-assumption group.

Bion brought the concepts and framework of Kleinian theory to his work with groups. The Kleinian concept of positions facilitated a conceptualization of the two levels of group functioning as being present simultaneously in all groups. Depending upon the relation of the members to leadership in the group, either the mature or the regressed level of functioning might be the chief determinant of the group's behavior. This framework is also useful in conceptualizing mature family functioning and family regression, two levels of family functioning present as potentialities in any family situation.

Through the concept of position, Klein emphasized that the phenomena she was describing in individuals as belonging to the paranoid-schizoid position or the depressive position were not simply a passing stage or phase. Her term implies a specific configuration of object relations, anxieties, and defenses that persists throughout life. The depressive position never fully supersedes the paranoid-schizoid phenomena, so that the individual at all times may oscillate between the two. Some paranoid and depressive anxieties always remain active within the individual, but, when the ego is sufficiently integrated and has established a relatively secure relation to reality during the working through of the depressive position, neurotic mechanisms gradually take over from the psychotic ones (Segal 1973).

Bion applied Klein's concept of position to groups in his conception that in every group two groups are present, the work group and the basic-assumption group. The work group is the mature group, defined by its work task. But the work group is only one aspect of the functioning of the group; the other aspect is the regressive level of group functioning, the basic-assumption group. We postulate that mature and regressive aspects of family functioning are present in any family, just as both aspects of group functioning are present in any group and primitive positions of mental functioning are present along with mature functioning in the individual. Bion's capacity to effect a shift in perspective from the individual to the group as a whole was crucial to his method of working with groups and to his articulation of shared levels of regressed functioning, as well as mature functioning, within groups. This same shift in perspective from the individual to the family as a group is crucial in analytic family treatment.

In the work of Bion, a group is defined by the task it is gathered to perform. Consciously motivated behavior directly implementing this task in reality terms is called work-group functioning. The group is behaving at a mature level in that it is working at its task, its relation to reality is good, and communication among group members is logical and clear. In contrast, Bion observes that much behavior in groups appears to have some other organization and motivation. This is behavior that suggests a level of regression dominated by unconscious assumptions on the part of members that the group is gathered for quite different purposes than the realistic accomplishment of the work task. Bion postulates unconscious mechanisms in group members that are mobilized in group interrelationships and that result in behavior unconcerned with the considerations of reality such as task implementation, logical thinking, and time. He calls these regressive states, where group behavior appears to be determined by wishful and nonrational unconscious considerations, basic assumptions. In such states a group appears to be dominated and often united by covert assumptions based on unconscious fantasies. Bion outlines three general categories of basic assumptions, which he frequently sees dominating the regressive behavior of groups. One is the unconscious assumption that the group exists for satisfaction of dependency needs and wishes; another is the assumption that the group exists to promote aggression toward or to provide the means of flight from real tasks, issues, and objects; the third is an assumption of hope and an atmosphere of expectation that is unrelated to reality considerations and is frequently seen in relation to pairing behavior in the group. The basic-assumption mode of group behavior is, then, regressive behavior that implies covert and often unconscious assumptions in group members about the purpose for which the group is gathered. These assumptions, which have little to do with considerations of reality, have powerful unconscious determinants and are conceptualized as expressions of shared unconscious fantasies in group members. Shifts in direction and power of basic-assumption fantasies and behavior, and work, are observed in groups; it is important to investigate the conditions under which these shifts occur.

Turquet (1974) has emphasized that basic-assumption group behavior is mobilized for defensive purposes having to do with the difficulties of the work task and disturbance in relation to the work leader. The work of the group, its functioning and task performance, is impaired with deterioration of the ego functioning of the members. The realities of the situation and the task are lost sight of, reality testing is poor, secondary-process thinking deteriorates, and more primitive forms of thinking emerge. There is a new organization of behavior that seems to be determined by fantasies and assumptions that are unrealistic and represent a failed struggle to cope with the current reality situation. Thereby the group survives as such, though its essential functioning and primary task are now altered in the service of a different task.

Application: Shapiro

We derive a framework from Bion, then, an orientation to clinical observation of the family. States of anxiety, defense, and regression in the family are conceptualized as consequences of unconscious assumptions, in which an organization of meanings and motives is inferred. These assumptions are in opposition to the developmental tasks of the family with respect to its children and adolescents. Family-group behavior now appears dominated by assumptions that particular meanings of childhood and adolescent individuation represent a danger to family requirements, cohesiveness, and even survival. These assumptions are generally unconscious and may be denied by family members.

The family group is different in essential ways from the "stranger" small group conceptualized by Bion. In considering the family as a group, the fact that its members have a shared developmental history and have specific role relationships through development results in a differentiation and specificity of shared assumptions, motivations, and defenses that cannot exist in the randomness of the stranger group. In this sense the complexity and differentiation of family process is much closer to individual psychodynamics than it is to group process. However, the study of the family is greatly facilitated through observing the shifts from family behavior implementing reality tasks to family behavior dominated by unconscious assumptions. It is possible to characterize the level of family regression, to define shared unconscious fantasies and assumptions with precision and to describe the characteristics of shared and complementary higher-level or lower-level defensive behaviors between and among family members. In contrast, Bion's formulations about basic-assumption behavior in stranger groups are global and generalized conceptualizations of group regression and of regressive group wishes in relation to the leader.

Let us now consider the evidence in family interaction that leads us to infer that unconscious assumptions are dominating family behavior. When the family is in a situation of anxiety as a consequence of mobilization of unconscious assumptions, we find clear analogies to small-group basic-assumption behavior. Behavior showing conflicting motivations, anxiety, and higher- or lower-level defenses is seen in family members, with evidence of ego regression. Behavior in the family appears to be determined more by fantasy than by reality. Work failure is evident in the family situation, similar to basic-assumption functioning. There is emergence of confused, distorted thinking, failure of understanding and adequate communication, and breakdown in the ability of the family to work cooperatively or creatively in relation to developmental issues and tasks. It becomes impossible to maintain a progressive discussion in which family members understand each other or to respond realistically to the problems under discussion. In short, when the family is in a situation in which unconscious assumptions are mobilized, associated anxiety and higher- or lower-level defensive behaviors are seen, and there is disturbance in the family's reality functioning. In contrast, in the absence of mobilization of unconscious assumptions, the family does not manifest anxiety and prominent defensive behavior, is clearly reality oriented, and relates well to tasks facilitating the maturation of children and adolescents.

UNCONSCIOUS ASSUMPTIONS, DEFENSIVE DELINEATIONS, AND PROJECTIVE IDENTIFICATION

In order to characterize the family contribution to adolescent disturbance, we study episodes of family regression determined by unconscious assumptions carefully. We observe behaviors of the parents with the adolescent and behaviors of the adolescent with the parents in order to define the defensive meanings of their relationships to each other that are implicit in their behaviors. And we infer from these defensive behaviors unconscious meanings of the adolescent to the parents and parents to the adolescent from which we formulate unconscious assumptions of the family as a group.

We use the concept of delineation to formulate the dynamics of the parents' relationship to the adolescent and the adolescent's relationship to the parents. This is a concept closely linked to observable behavior. Delineations are behaviors through which one family member communicates explicitly or implicitly his perceptions and attitudes—in fact, his mental representation of another family member—to that other person.

Delineations may communicate a view of the other person that seems to be predominantly determined by his reality characteristics. Or delineations may communicate a view of the other person that appears to be predominantly determined by the mobilization of dynamic conflict and defense in the delineator. We call the latter defensive delineations. For example, let us consider parental defensive delineations of the adolescent. When parental delineations are observed to be distorted, stereotyped and overspecific, contradictory, or otherwise incongruent with the range of behaviors manifested by the adolescent, we make the inference that these delineations serve defensive aspects of parental personality functioning. That is, they are not simply realistic characterizations of the adolescent. Further, we find that the parents, through their defensive delineations, seek to hold the child and adolescent in relatively fixed roles throughout development, in the service of avoiding their own anxiety.

The predominant mechanism underlying parental defensive delineations is projective identification. The concept of projective identification provides a highly useful means of conceptualizing phenomena of regression and elucidating dynamics of role allocation in families. In family regression there is rapid reduction in usual ego discriminations. Dissociation and projection are increased, with confusion over the ownership of personal characteristics that are easily attributed to other family members. When one individual assumes a role compatible with the attributions of others in the family at the regressed level, he quickly becomes the recipient of projections that tend to fix him in that role. Family members project this aspect of their own personal characteristics onto him and unconsciously identify with him. The power of these projections, with their accompanying unconscious identifications, may push the individual into more extreme role behavior and into feelings that are very powerful and may be experienced as unreal and bizarre.

Bion (1961) observes that Freud's view of identification is almost entirely a process of introjection by the ego. To Bion, however, the identification of group members with the leader of the regressed group depends not on introjection alone, but on a simultaneous process of projective identification as well. The leader is as much a creature of the basic assumption as any other member of the group. Group members project onto the leader, on the basic-assumption level, those qualities required and mobilized in shared basic-assumption fantasy. This is also true in families where projective identification results in the projection onto a child or adolescent of those qualities required and mobilized by the unconscious assumptions of the family.

These parental projections have a critical effect on the individual child maturing within the framework of family-group assumptions. Developmental theory emphasizes identification processes as internalizations that are major determinants of structure formation in the child. In addition, we believe that the child internalizes through development characteristics of parental relationships with him. His dynamic meaning to his parents, attributions made to him, and attitudes toward him are delineations that modify the child's self-representation and are determinants of structure formation. Parents' delineations of the child and adolescent, where the parents' regression is at a level of impaired self-object differentiation and primitive projective identification, are particularly coercive. Behavior in the child that counters these parental delineations leads to anxiety in the parent. The child is then motivated to behave so as to mitigate this parental anxiety. Internalization by the child of the parent's defensive delineations of him moves the developing child and adolescent into a role that is complementary to parental defensive requirements. Defensive delineations are, consequently, dynamic determinants of role allocation in the family. The role allocated is necessary to maintain parental defense and mitigate parental anxiety. The dynamics of role allocation operate in a broader framework of unconscious assumptions of the family as a group. Over time, these establish a pattern of internalizations within the self-representation. Unconscious assumptions within the family, and related experience of defensive delineations, impinge upon the reorganization of internalizations required by ego-id maturation during adolescence. These influences may interfere significantly with individuation and the consolidation of identity in the adolescent.

In the families we have studied we find evidence that each family member participates in the regression we have described. It is through the participation of all family members in these regressive episodes that the level of family regression and higher- or lower-level defensive organization achieve their stability and their power.

In family assessment and family therapy we attempt to articulate the unconscious assumptions of the family as a group and to discern the participation, contribution, and collusion of each family member in the episodes of family regression, dominated by unconscious assumptions and higher- or lower-level defensive organization, which we consider to be decisive for the developmental disturbances we are discussing.

FAMILIES OF ADOLESCENTS WITH BORDERLINE CONDITIONS OR PATHOLOGICAL NARCISSISM

In families of adolescents who manifest borderline or narcissistic disturbances, we consistently find evidence of a powerful cluster of unconscious assumptions that equate separation-individuation with loss and abandonment. Thinking and actions of family members that are not in accord with these assumptions are then perceived and reacted to as destructive attacks (Shapiro et al. 1975; Shapiro and Zinner 1976).

There are important areas of similarity in the characteristics of regression in these two types of families. In both types of families, regression is activated by behavior in family members signaling separation-individuation and loss; in these circumstances there is clear evidence of anxiety in the family and efforts to restore the previous equilibrium. There is regression to an organization of lower-level defenses, of denial, splitting, and projection, and an active splitting of aspects of self and objects. These split self and object representations are then distributed by projective identification. There is, however, a difference in the nature of the split in the self and object representations found in these two types of families, and, consequently, there is a difference in what is projected onto the separating and individuating family member.

In families of borderline adolescents, individuation, manifested in either autonomous or needful behavior in one family member, activates unconscious assumptions in other family members about the nature of relationships containing good experiences. Such behavior is unconsciously perceived as a threat to the survival of the family as a group, leading to anxiety and projection of destructiveness onto the individuating family member.

In these families a structure of internalized object relations is found in family members in which there is splitting of all good and all bad self and object images. Family members split off those bad aspects of themselves, which are associated with painful and aggressive experiences with objects in the past. In particular, painful responses to autonomous strivings within individuals, or to needs for nurture and support, give rise to shared unconscious assumptions in the family about the dangers of such behavior. Through projective identification, they relate to the separating and individuating adolescent as they would to a repudiated part of themselves and rebuff him in episodes of aggressive turmoil and withdrawal. The result in the adolescent is an identity formation dominated by negative self and object images, a continuation of splitting of positive and negative internalized relationships, and a clinical picture of identity diffusion.

In contrast, in families of narcissistic adolescents the unconscious assumptions focus on the specific meanings of a narcissistic relationship between parent and adolescent (Berkowitz et al. 1974b). If a parent projects valued aspects of himself or herself onto a child or adolescent and utilizes him as a self-object, the narcissistic equilibrium of the parent is disturbed when, during the individuation, the child or adolescent moves into a position no longer complementary to the parent's narcissistic need. This disruption of a central narcissistic relationship in the family disturbs the self-regard of other family members, whose narcissistic equilibrium depends on the parent who is now suffering an abrupt disturbance in self-esteem.

In families of narcissistic adolescents we find a structure of internalized object relationships in which there is an active splitting of grandiose and devalued self and object images. Real, ideal, or devalued images of self and object are not integrated in family members into a self-concept with stable internal regulation of self-esteem. An effort to stabilize self-esteem is seen in the activation of a narcissistic relationship within the family. In these families such a differentiated narcissistic relationship is found between a narcissistic parent (grandiose self) and the adolescent (idealized self-object). This external relationship helps maintain the split in both parent and adolescent. The adolescent, who is utilized by the parent as a self-object, also evolves a pathological narcissistic self-structure and requires the relationship to an omnipotent parental image to maintain narcissistic equilibrium. Separation-individuation produces narcissistic disequilibrium in both parents and adolescent, with episodes of narcissistic rage and projection.

Family regression militates against further differentiation of the adolescent from the family. Instead, through projective identification, boundaries between family members become even more blurred, with parents and siblings projecting onto the adolescent who is attempting to individuate those feelings of devaluation denied within themselves.

These findings lead to combine psychoanalytic psychotherapy for the adolescent with analytic, group-interpretive family treatment in borderline conditions or pathological narcissism of adolescents. In family treatment the continuing problems of projection and loss of differentiation between parents and adolescent are interpreted, and there is an opportunity for working through the meaning and experience of separation over time. Less bound by the projections of his parents, the adolescent has a new possibility for individuation that he is able to explore more fully in his individual therapy (Berkowitz et al. 1974a; Shapiro et al. 1977).

CONCLUSIONS

In the treatment of adolescents, unconscious assumptions in the family lead to external resistances to analytic therapy. The parent's family relationships frequently interfere with therapy more than the patient's own internal resistances. This is a central problem in treatment. Methods of conjoint family interviewing have been described for the management of external resistances in the treatment of adolescents. Such interviews should be part of the initial assessment of the disturbed adolescent as they help to establish a working alliance not only with the adolescent but also with his family.

I have presented concepts and methods that we have used to study families of disturbed adolescents. An organization of shared or complementary unconscious fantasies and related higher- or lower-level defenses within family members that maintain equilibrium among them is postulated. Anxiety and intensified defensive activity are activated by behavior that challenges or contradicts the underlying assumptions determined by these unconscious fantasies. These unconscious assumptions of the family as a group are evidenced in repetitive behaviors in families that appear to militate against change, development, or individuation of children. Shared unconscious assumptions in family members that motivate and organize these repetitive behaviors derive from the internalized developmental experience of both of the parents in their families of origin. An organization of motives and higher- or lower-level defenses evolves, then, in the marriage. These are operative throughout the development of the children and adolescents and have critical effects on their personality development.

For neurotic adolescents, conjoint family interviews should be resumed when the external resistances interfere seriously with treatment.

For adolescents manifesting borderline conditions or pathological narcissism, where serious disturbances over separation-individuation, found in both adolescents and parents, are profoundly interfering with adolescent development, concurrent psychoanalytic psychotherapy for the adolescent and group-interpretive family treatment is indicated.

16.

MANAGEMENT DEVELOPMENT . . . SOME IDEALS, IMAGES AND REALITIES

W. Gordon Lawrence

INTRODUCTION

Management development, in common with terms such as democracy and participation, has its meaning suffused with a sense of goodness; it is difficult to find a negative connotation. When, however, the activities, roles and organisational systems of management development are examined, it is possible to differentiate among the ideals, images and realities of management development that brings us closer to the various meanings the term can have. Such an analysis may give insight into some important covert social processes of business enterprises.

An attempt at such an analysis is possible as a result of a study of the role of the management development adviser carried out by a team of researchers from the Tavistock Institute of Human Relations. This study was funded by the Training Services Agency and has been reported under the title *Towards Managerial Development for Tomorrow* (Lawrence, unpublished). In this article I shall only focus on the central ideals, images and realities of management development that have been highlighted by the study.

I present these in the form of *working hypotheses*. Because human behaviour is so complex, a researcher can never be certain that he has captured the truth of a social situation. Indeed a valid and reliable statement of "the absolute truth" is an impossible attainment because the data of a social researcher are phenomena. From identifiable phenomena it is possible to conjecture what ultimate reality might be, but it will never be known absolutely (Bion, 1977). The working hypothesis is, then, a sketch of the reality of a social situation. It is the outcome of a disciplined attempt to process subjective experiences of phenomena. Because the attainment of what is commonly known as "objectivity" is essentially the result of the clarification of subjectivity (Lawrence and Miller, 1976), the validity and reliability of a working hypothesis can be judged by others using their subjective experiences of the same events and phenomena. In that process of evaluating a working hypothesis it can be accepted and elaborated or rejected and another substituted. Through this method a more accurate approximation and representation of the truth may be made.

SOME IDEALS

The ideals of management development were imported to Britain in the post-war years from America. At first, the American concept was executive development, by which was meant "the planned improvement of high-level management in those understandings, attitudes and activities that enter into or influence their work and work relations" (Planty and Freeston, 1954). Understandably, given the political climate in America in the late 1940s, executive development was linked with national survival. As one writer put it:

> "Development of executive leadership is in my opinion the greatest opportunity facing American businessmen . . . it is also a challenge, for failure to develop greater and more effective participation of business leadership in the management of public affairs will greatly diminish the ability of democracy to succeed in the conflict with totalitarianism." (Bower, 1949).

Other writers were to democratise executive development by substituting management development. An executive from Standard Oil, writing in 1949, explained the shift in emphasis thus:

> "Some companies have adopted the title "management development" (rather than executive development) which, in many respects, I like better. Management implies organisation as well as personal leadership. Besides there are usually more managers than executives; therefore, the target is larger and more easily recognised by the men down the line." (Lawrence, 1975).

As management development evolved, it became equated with the realisation of the ideals of advanced industrial societies. Peter Drucker saw business as a source "for the fulfilment of the basic beliefs and promises of society, especially the promise of equal opportunity" (Drucker, 1955) and thus saw management development as a way thereby "management discharges its obligations to make work and industry more than a way of making a living. By offering a challenge and opportunities for the individual development of each manager to his fullest ability the enterprise discharges, in part, the obligation to make a job in industry a way of life." (Drucker, 1955).

Drucker also saw management development as having architectonic qualities in that it discharged a three-fold responsibility "to the enterprise, to society, to the individual" and, presumably, integrated the manager into larger social structures. Others, on the other hand, held more pragmatic views and suggested that management development ought to be concerned with giving managers quite specific skills to enlarge their capacities to be more effective managers.

Early British writers on management development reflected some of these divergent ideals. There were those who suggested that, ideally, management development ought to be concerned with preparing individuals to cope with change in an increasingly complex environment. The other view was less liberal and aimed to develop managers' capacities to do profitable work that was relevant to company objectives. Hence the management development activity ought to be directed at identifying managerial talent, developing it as a resource and deploying it within the enterprise.

The translation of these ideals of management development into practice becomes an almost intractable problem. While management development may be idealised as in the ways just shown, when it is operationalised it appears to come out as an attempt to reconcile the tension, even conflict, between organisational development (the needs of the enterprise) and professional development of managers (the needs of the individual). This conflict is felt and perceived by people involved in their various institutional roles in the business enterprise. This is particularly so in Britain because there are few adequate concepts of organisation being used to allow for organisational development and the development of the individual in his, or her, institutional role to be seen as being mutually supportive processes. Here we find ourselves at the centre of the drama of management development activities: the acting out of resolutions to this perceived conflict. Until new metaphors of management development are found, this tension will continue to define consciously and unconsciously, the various tasks, activities and roles associated with management development.

In the meanwhile, one way around this felt conflict is to create an image of management development. An image is a pseudo-ideal that is planned to create a certain kind of impression. An image has to be "believable, passive, vivid, simplified and ambiguous" (Boorstin, 1963). When management development statements of policy are examined, it can be seen that they have some, if not a good many, qualities of an image. The thrust of the image is to render management development palatable to the manager as consumer and to bring about his participation in its activities.

THE SALIENT IMAGE

The salient image presented through some management development practices is of an ordered set of activities contained within an enterprise within which the individual manager can find a place and fulfilment. The image is of a developmental activity that resolves the tensions between the individual and the enterprise. The image is presented through such a diagram as shown in Figure 1.

Here the objectives and tasks of the enterprise appear to be realised through the organisation and the various arrangements for assessing and training people so that they will become motivated managers within it. Similar images may use language such as strategic plans, tactical plans, unit objectives, management objectives, assessment and training for the

Figure 1. The "Image"

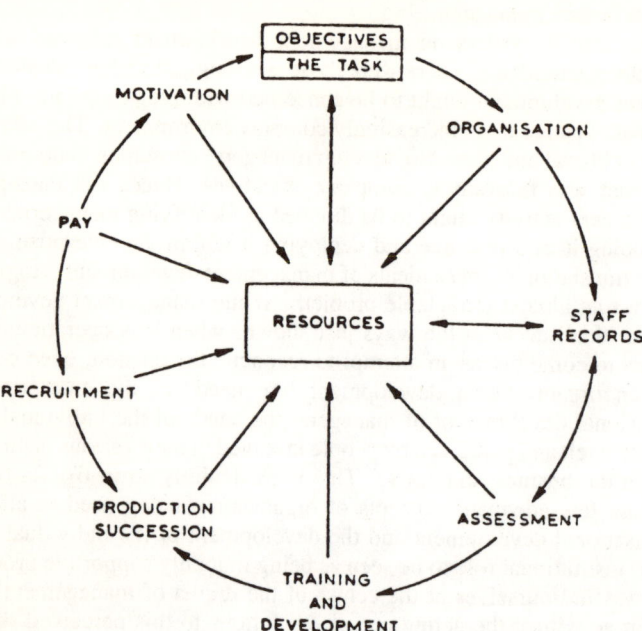

correction of faults and the development of skills to attain objectives. The image is of an enterprise that is a rational, bounded universe that can operate almost in a military fashion to gain objectives; to win. The image owes much to ideas about scientific management and related ideas that the organisation of enterprises is analogous to the mechanics of the machines they contain. Hence management development unwittingly is presented as a sophisticated form of "lubricant" for the better maintenance of the enterprise. The manager, therefore, is placed neatly in this context somewhat like a "cog," to pursue the analogy.

Even with, and perhaps because of, such well-regulated plans, managers are highly ambivalent about management development. On the one hand they believe that it must benefit them, but on the other that it may be an indirect exploitation. And yet few managers would disrupt whatever the system of management development in which they take part for reasons that I give below.

The credibility of management development is nevertheless always under question, but usually indirectly. The evidence for this can be found in the experience of management development advisers who have to spend time in persuading managers to take part in the activity when a new management development scheme is mounted. The ambivalence, even hostility, to management development, and therefore suspicion of its credibility, is expressed through tardiness in completing appraisal forms and in giving "feed-back" to participants. Consequently, management development ad-

Management Development

visers who may be responsible for collating data have to devise elaborate time-tables for appraisal procedures thereby, unwittingly, exacerbating the ambivalence.

The image, then, with its rhetoric of rationality, and its resultant practices of management development, brings about a number of consequences not all of which are intended consciously.

PRIMARY TASK ANALYSIS

The realities of management development can be more systematically analysed if we identify its various *primary tasks*. The concept of primary task is a tool of inquiry to understand the realities of organisations and other social arrangements of men. Enterprises are open-systems interacting with their environment. They are open-systems because imports are taken in, transformed in some way, and whatever is produced is exported back into the environment. Clearly, there are a range of imports such as materials, men, and capital, just as there are a variety of outputs apart from whatever is produced in the dominant transformation process. An enterprise has a *boundary* across which inputs and outputs flow to and from the environment. The definition of boundaries is always within the province of the management of the system as a whole. Within the total boundary of the enterprise that differentiates the inner world of the enterprise from its external environment, there will be a variety of sub-systems each with its boundary.

The dominant transformation process will be an arrangement of men and machines concerned with, for example in a production enterprise, the processing of raw materials into finished products. The primary task of the enterprise can be defined in terms of this dominant throughput process. Similarly, each sub-system of an enterprise, each with its bounded import-conversion-export process, can be defined in terms of its primary task in relation to the whole enterprise. In a complex enterprise there will be a series of related task systems alongside the dominant task system. Each of these task systems can be seen as a socio-technical sub-system within the enterprise as a system. Within each such task system there will be roles and sets of activities and relationships that are available for individuals who cross the boundary of the enterprise to take up employment. To understand the activities of an enterprise and any of its sub-parts, and therefore of the roles that are offered by the enterprise, we use the concept of primary task as a tool of exploration.

As Miller and Rice have described it:

> "The primary task is essentially a heuristic concept that allows us to explore the ordering of multiple activities (and of constituent systems of activities where these exist). It makes it possible to construct and compare different organisational models of an enterprise based on different definitions of its primary task; and to comprise the organisations of different enterprises with the same or different primary

tasks. The definition of primary task determines the dominant import-conversion-export system . . ." (Miller and Rice, 1967).

Enterprises are only buildings with plant until people take up their roles and subscribe to the organisation. Hence, the definition of primary task is not a given but belongs to the people engaged in the activities. From the examination of an enterprise and its various task systems with allocated roles we find that different kinds of primary task are pursued by people, individual and collectively. These primary tasks can be distinguished as follows:

> "The *normative* primary task that is the task that people in an organisation ought to pursue (usually according to the definition of a superordinate authority,
> The *existential* primary task that they believe they are carrying out, and
> The *phenomenal* primary task that it is hypothesised that they are engaged in and of which they may not be consciously aware." (Lawrence and Robinson, 1975).

Primary task analysis can be seen as being directed at understanding and clarifying what meaning individuals place upon themselves in their roles in relation to their enterprise as a system and the discrete task system in which they are located. It is also a tool for individuals and groups within an organisation to clarify, interpret and define their tasks, activities and roles in relation to the changing circumstances in their environments. This process is clearly important at a time in history when environments have never been so uncertain.

SOME REALITIES OF MANAGEMENT DEVELOPMENT

The *normative* primary task of management development ought, it is generally agreed by practitioners and managers, to be directed towards ensuring that there is a supply of trained and motivated managers to ensure the long-term survival of the enterprise. Alongside this there is also the stated aim that managers ought to develop themselves. This commonly held public definition of management development reflects the central conflict of management development; person and organisation are juxtaposed not related. The image of rational order begins to fall apart. When the existential and phenomenal tasks are identified we can see that much of the effort is directed both consciously and unconsciously at taking the strain of or denying the perceived central conflict.

The two main *existential* primary tasks of management development are to be a "civilising" influence in the enterprise and to represent the enterprise as neutral in selecting and promoting talent. The "civilising" influence can be defined in different ways depending on what managers are thought to be lacking. The "civilising" at one level is about educating the manager about budgetary control, for example, or giving him exposure to behavioural science. The manager is usually sent to a country house staff college for these kinds of instruction. "Civilising" can also be realised through, for example, courses in how to give "smoother interviews" ending with a "good atmosphere." The thrust is towards the creation and maintenance of "good" relationships within the enterprise. The "civilising," at another level, can also be brought about through the use of counsellors ("grandfathers") who induct the young into the ways of the enterprise by giving them professional advice. The culture of the enterprise is thus maintained.

The fostering of the myth of the neutrality of management development is critically important. Despite the evidence of commonsense, it has to be believed that the management development activity can transmute subjective data into objective facts. Hence the elaborate, scientific-looking forms, the procedures and rituals that the management development function surrounds itself with. The point is that managers have to make themselves publicly believe in the neutrality of management development in order to comply with it. The notion of neutrality helps to foster the ideal of equality of opportunity but also that the enterprise is a rational order that will select the best of talent.

These two existential primary tasks take us further into the dynamics of management development, and they can be elicited from what people say about management development. These hypotheses about primary tasks are derived from the meaning people consciously put upon their activities and roles in both the management and management development systems.

The third set of primary tasks—the *phenomenal* tasks—are inferred from behaviour. They are hypotheses about what takes place at partly conscious and unconscious levels.

There is, as has been said, a tension, even conflict, in the normative primary task between organisational development and individual development that no amount of image-building can quite overcome. Hence a phenomenal task is to avoid this conflict. A good many firms do this by concentrating on manpower audits and planning. They attempt to tie their management development activities as closely as possible to the image. The notion that managers can develop themselves slips out of ken. When this happens management development comes to be used as "a controlling device for restricting the development of managers in order to further group interests" (Skertchley, 1968). And in this control the conflict being alluded to merely is made covert.

As a further defence against the possibilities of the conflict becoming overt the management development activity comes to be used as a buffer to absorb the tension between manager and management development. The mere fact that a management development function is present demonstrates to the manager that there is hope for his development and eligibility for promotion. It offers promise that there will be an examination of performance. All this brings about a sense in the individual that he is not lost to or in the enterprise. Somewhere in the enterprise, perhaps the management development office, there is a record of his capabilities. His identity is thus felt to be extended beyond himself and lodged somewhere in the enterprise. With these hopes and promises around it becomes possible to swallow or hide one's feelings of ambivalence and hostility and to avoid the full implications of the unexamined tension. Essentially, then, management development comes to be a buffer between the enterprise with its organisational demands and the individual with career aspirations in his job.

Management development carries other phenomenal primary tasks that are to do with much larger issues of work and life. The management development activity can provide an institutional system for defending individuals against the anxiety of death. The "deaths" I have in mind here are of life, career, and the enterprise. The enterprise is experienced as being immortal. It will exist beyond the career and life-span of an individual manager. It is experienced as having an existence of its own. The fact that the viability of an enterprise is contingent upon the quality of the managers, among other factors, gets lost. The management development activity fosters the fantasy that the immortality of the enterprise also belongs to the individual. The two become fused. Management development with its connotations of progress, its implicit promise of a career trajectory, helps to postpone the acknowledgment of career death.

Some realists point out that this is a major flaw in management development as it is at present practised, because participation and involvement in its activities raise expectations that cannot always be fulfilled. (What happens, for example, in times of recession and redundancy to the image of management development?) The postponement of the realisation of career death is also a postponement of the acceptance of the fact of real death. And the avoidance of that reality must have repercussions on the quality of living (Freud, 1957b) and, presumably, on the qualities individuals bring into their managerial roles.

Related to the theme of immortality is that of inheritance. Another phenomenal primary task of management development is the encouragement of the belief in an inheritance. Earlier it was said that an existential primary task of management development was that of "civilising" and that counsellors were used, among other methods, to bring this about. This could be called the Pygmalion model of management development. The metaphor is of the old and wise transforming the young and raw into their own image. It is an induction or socialising—perhaps conditioning—process. It is designed and entered into with the best of intentions: the preparation of young managers to emerge as leaders capable of continuing to manage the business into an uncertain future.

There are, however, some flaws in the plot. Top management and management development advisers *unconsciously* lead other managers to believe that all have an equal chance to inherit. In reality top positions are few. Nevertheless younger managers have to collude with the idea of inheritance and participate, however ambivalently, with management development schemes irrespective of their quality. Outspoken critics of management development schemes become a minority voice and for the purposes of managing a career it is better to keep silent. Paradoxically, it is just those people who attempt to manage their career and their role relationships and activities who are least likely to need management development.

Given the scenario for inheritance, managers feel they have to "make out" in the management development activity just as they feel they have to "fit in" to some abstract, reified thing called the enterprise. The question is whether or not such behaviour is a constraint on the long-term effective task performance of the enterprise in an uncertain environment.

The final working hypothesis about the phenomenal primary tasks of management development takes us to the mutual interpenetration of the activity of management development and the culture of the enterprise. It is a working hypothesis that relates to other phenomenal primary tasks and attempts to link them in relation to the enterprise and its organisation. It is one that allows us to contemplate a number of related unconscious phenomena.

At times a dominant collective paranoid fantasy of the people in any enterprise is that disorder and chaos will either disrupt the inner world of the enterprise or obtrude from the outer world and rupture all the known boundaries. Hence, a good deal of effort is directed at ensuring that there is order. It is always a puzzle to clarify whether the order created within an enterprise through the managerial structures is for the pursuance of tasks on a reality basis or whether it is a defensive system to keep generalised anxieties about disorder at bay. It can be that the systems that are so developed become so effective that the realities of turbulent and uncertain external and internal environments are denied. Hence management ceases to be able to transact across the boundary of the enterprise on a reality basis, i.e., exercising an appropriate leadership function on behalf of the organisation.

The management development activity has, then, the phenomenal primary task of maintaining order. In particular, it can be an organisational defence system against the disorder and chaos it is fantasied would break out if open competition, and rivalry among managers, with attendant feelings of envy and jealousy, were allowed. So each year, or at regular intervals, the "objective" management development activity of appraisal etc. is mounted. Order is maintained.

The fantasy of disorder and chaos—which is construed as being destructive—is a powerful motivating force that leads people to support the management development activity, irrespective of its form.

A consequence of this is that some people unconsciously come to look at the management development activity, and therefore to the enterprise and its senior management, for the satisfaction of their primitive, dependency needs. This arrogation of responsibility for developing oneself in relation to the enterprise is exacerbated by the experience of management development with its penumbra of existential and phenomenal primary tasks that have been described above. Some management development schemes "adopt" the manager as a "child-in-business" and develop and nurture him till he is ready for top management as an "adult-in-business." Earlier it has been said that managers "make out" in the systems. Managers accept management development schemes and activities unquestioningly in public—just as an "obedient child" might—but in private, they do so guardedly and with limited conviction. It therefore becomes a collusive arrogation. This hidden process continues over time and from one generation of managers to another and so we can describe the phenomena as a cycle of collusive arrogation.

Clearly, this cycle will be more salient in some enterprises than in others, but it can be said that the more salient it is the more likely will the enterprise be mobilising in its managers an unsophisticated dependency orientation to the enterprise and its organisation. In such cases management development will have quite opposite results from those overtly intended.

CONCLUSIONS

The diffuse ideals of management development are difficult to operationalise. Management development highlights the tension, even conflict, between the ideals of enterprise and individual development, at least that is how it is construed and experienced by people taking part in development activities. Consequently, an image of management development comes to be fashioned in enterprises. The image attempts to bring these perceived conflicting ideals into a whole that can be understood and subscribed to by those being "developed" and their "developers."

The public image, however, can often mask a number of other realities of management development. Essentially, the activities of management development can bring about a quality of unsophisticated dependency in managers that cannot in the long term serve the best interests of any enterprise that has to stay in business in an environment that is increasingly characterised by uncertainty and turbulence.

Until these factors are identified, explicated and understood within an enterprise by individuals in their roles, the translation of ideals of management development into practice can only continue to be constrained by realities such as have been indicated. The paradox is that a collective exploration of these factors by individuals in their institutional roles might well bring about the redundancy of management development as an activity—at least as often as currently practised.

The question now, however, has to be: what would be the best model of management development that would enable the individual manager to take responsibility and authority for his own professional development and, at the same time, serve the best interests of the enterprise? Fundamentally, the evolving of such a model requires that current notions about the nature of the relationship between the individual and his organisation be reconceptualised. This might bring about a different kind of involvement of people in organisations than the kind of unquestioning dependent compliance that currently appears to be fostered unconsciously.

B. Consultation and Implementation

Organizational Development and Industrial Democracy: A Current
    Case Study 243
Eric J. Miller

The Assisted Independent Living Program: A New Model for
    Community Care 273
Niles M. Medders and Arthur D. Colman

A Retrospective View of a Hospital-Wide Group Relations Training
    Program: Costs, Consequences and Conclusions 285
Roy W. Menninger

Belfast Communities Intervention 299
Edward B. Klein

17.

ORGANIZATIONAL DEVELOPMENT AND INDUSTRIAL DEMOCRACY: A CURRENT CASE-STUDY

Eric J. Miller

INTRODUCTION

'What do rural development in Mexico and studies of health care systems have in common with organizational change and development in industry?' The person who asked that question was looking at a list of Tavistock Institute projects. One thing they have in common is that they are all fields in which for some time I have been personally committed in a consultancy-research role. Beyond that, I brought to this work, partly from a background in social anthropology, and more specifically through the influence of other Tavistock colleagues, a set of concepts, values and methods, which in turn have been developed and modified in the course of my experience. Indeed, I have been struck by the extent to which insights gained in one field illuminate another situation that on the face of it may seem quite dissimilar. How far, however, is the similarity something imposed by me? It is inevitable that to some extent I must be re-defining 'reality' in order to defend myself from more dissonance than I can cope with. For that reason, I propose in the first part of this paper to describe briefly some of the thinking I brought to, and have derived from, certain of these experiences, especially those outside industry, so that the reader may form his own judgments about the preconceptions and biases that may be structuring my picture of reality. This will set the scene for an account, in the second part, of an ongoing piece of work in a manufacturing company.

Still by way of introduction, however, I want first to say a few words about the title of this paper. Neither 'organizational development' nor 'industrial democracy' has a single, widely accepted definition, though both terms are very much in vogue. In Britain, the Government recently set up the Bullock Committee to make recommendations on mechanisms for a narrowly defined version of industrial democracy: the appointment of trade union members to boards of directors. But the term also has a wide extension, which includes, at one end of the spectrum, devices for employee participation (another term that is heavily used and quite im-

Application: Miller

precise) in managerial decision-making at shop-floor, factory and company levels, and, at the other end of the spectrum, notions of worker control, through collectives, co-operatives and other organizational forms. Associated with these different meanings are, often, divergent ideologies and strong emotions. Much the same applies to 'organizational development.' Inherent in every definition is an explicit or implicit view of man, of organizations and of the nature of the relationship between them—which includes assumptions about the nature of authority. Goals range from the idealistic, such as egalitarianism, to the pragmatic, such as improving efficiency. Interventions made by OD practitioners may be consistent with stated goals, but quite often they are more consistent with different, unstated and perhaps unintended goals. Commonly, for example, OD is concerned to temper the instrumental view of employees as components in an organizational machine with the more liberal notion that employees are human individuals with drives, attitudes and emotions that the organization must allow space for and, indeed, put to positive use. In the process, however, OD may become unwittingly involved in the rather different task of displaying that bosses are human too—and, perhaps, suppressing evidence to the contrary. Understandably, this leads OD to be viewed with suspicion by those who interpret the boss-employee relationship in class terms and perceive an irreconcilable conflict of interests between the two groupings in capitalist societies: from this standpoint OD is a cunning palliative. Suspicions of manipulation are sometimes justified by the avowed intentions of OD practitioners and not just by inadvertent side-effects of pursuing more creditable goals. Thus I have met those who see OD as something to be applied on behalf of their clients, top management, to the rest of the organization—top management itself being exempt from the process. Among these practitioners are some for whom this is a calculated exemption, on the principle of not biting the hand that feeds you. Others, astonishingly, have not even considered that there might be alternative stances.

Plainly, therefore, the terms 'industrial democracy' and 'organizational development' can be used to denote only a broad area of work and concerns. They are open to widely differing interpretations, some of which are political interpretations. In fact consultancy in this area cannot but be a political activity, at least insofar as it promotes some values and not others. Professional status, despite the claims often made for it, does not place the practitioner beyond the realm of values. Even in medicine, where the myth of purity and disinterest dies hard, values intrude in crude and subtle ways. The doctor who decides to give one patient better treatment than another is thereby engaging in a political act—regardless of whether his motives are economic or humanitarian. Less obviously, the decision to treat both patients equally, on the premise that all lives are equally important, is also a political decision, since it implements one particular set of values. If even the treatment of individuals has political connotations, in the 'treatment' of organizations they are patently much more significant. Hence my contention that the responsible professional has to try to make explicit the values that, consciously and perhaps less consciously, bear upon his role. Although we are intellectually aware of the problem, social scientists in general do not pay enough attention to the way in which values enter into the selection of conceptual frameworks and measuring instruments. It is not only the consultant who is in the game of political intervention. As I hinted earlier, frameworks and instruments that appear to be objective and scientific nevertheless favour certain interpretations of 'reality' and preclude others. The 'pure' research worker too is affecting the organization he is studying simply by being selective—unavoidably so—in the people he addresses and in the assumed roles in which they are addressed: he is not neutral. As Heisenberg pointed out, a sub-atomic physicist can demonstrate that electrons have wave-like properties; but another, taking another perspective and using different measuring instruments, can show that electrons behave as particles. Out of the range of properties of a situation, we see those that we are predisposed to look for. Hence we have an obligation to try to specify our predispositions.

PART I: VALUES, CONCEPTS AND METHODS

Ten years ago, a colleague and I concluded a book with these words: 'Long-term solutions to the problem of maintaining adaptiveness to change cannot...depend on manipulative techniques. On the contrary, they must depend on helping the individual to develop greater maturity in controlling the boundary between his own inner world and the realities of his external environment' (Miller and Rice, 1967, p. 269). This theme and the values implied in it have continued to be dominant in my own work and thinking, and also for a number of colleagues in the Tavistock Institute and Clinic and associates outside. If I were rewriting that paragraph now, I would want to reword it in a couple of places. The phrase 'adaptiveness to change' might imply that change is an extraneous—almost superhuman—process and that all we ordinary mortals can do is to make less or more satisfactory adjustments to it; hence I would prefer now to speak of 'management of change,' so as to imply that we ourselves by our decisions and actions create the future: we can be proactive, not merely adaptive. Secondly, 'controlling the boundary. . .' could sound negative, as if the impulses and fantasies of the inner world should be inhibited; whereas my concern is with making the most fruitful use of one's internal resources: some are appropriately held out of one situation and brought forward in another. Consequently, 'understanding and managing the boundary. . .' might be a better formulation. But these are clarifications and refinements: I remain committed to the essence of the earlier statement. A major preoccupation of mine, therefore, as of many colleagues, has been the relationship—indeed the tension—between individual and group, individual and organization: 'An individual has . . . no meaning except in relation to others with whom he interacts. He uses them, and they him, to express views, take action and play roles. The individual is a creature of the group, the group of the individual' (Miller and Rice, 1967, p. 17). At times he is swallowed by the group, at times struggling for separateness.

This has demanded a conceptual framework within which the relationship can be examined. Here Kurt Lewin had a significant influence on my early Tavistock colleagues in the late 1940s. His application of topology to the study of psychological and social systems, his field theory (Lewin, 1936, 1950) and in general his insistence that conventional modes of scientific analysis could not uncover the 'Gestalt' properties of complex human systems—one had to conceptualize groups as wholes—fitted and extended my colleagues' own developing views. As Lewin pointed out, whereas in the history of physics the reality of wholes was taken for granted and it was 'the reality of the atom, the electron, or whatever else was considered at that time to be the smallest part of physical material' that tended to be called into question, 'in the social sciences it has usually been not the part but the whole whose existence has been doubted.' And again: 'In the social as in the physical field the structural properties of a dynamic whole are different from the structural properties of subparts. Both sets of properties have to be investigated. . .' (Lewin, 1947, p. 8).

At about the same time, Wilfred Bion was pursuing his own studies of groups as wholes (Bion, 1948-51), which also made a lasting impact on Tavistock thinking. Bion's postulate is that at any given time the behaviour of a group can be analysed at two levels: it is a *sophisticated group* (or *work group*) met to perform an overt task; and it is at the same time a *basic group*, acting on one, and only one, of three covert *basic assumptions* (fight-flight, dependence and pairing), to which its individual members contribute anonymously and in ways of which they are not consciously aware. It is a function of the basic assumption operating at any one time to keep at bay emotions associated with the other two assumptions— emotions that may be inconsistent with the overt task. Thus it may well be appropriate for the hospital patient to accept total and uncritical dependency on the doctors and nurses, rather than to fight them; and, anyway, he has little choice. On the other hand, a subordinate who accepts total and uncritical dependency on an incompetent superior is storing up trouble for himself and his organization. Therefore, the basic group modifies— often detrimentally, sometimes positively—the goals and activities of the work group. Bion's framework was extended by others (e.g., Rice, 1951, 1969; Turquet, 1974).

Bion's approach was derived from psychoanalytic concepts, which themselves had a profound influence on early Tavistock thinking and which continue to be important to myself and a number of my colleagues today. Psychoanalysis, besides suggesting that explanations for human behaviour might be found in unconscious processes and not merely in stated intentions, also provided an important role-model for Tavistock staff working not with individual patients but with groups and organizations. Nearly all Tavistock work at that time (and much of it still today) was a form of action research in which the research worker was also a consultant, taking a professional role in relation to the client system; and indeed consultancy was the method through which research data were generated. Individuals and groups interact in order to find ways of giving meaning to their experience and also to develop mechanisms that defend them against uncertainty and anxiety (cf. Jaques, 1953; Menzies, 1960); these defences, often unrecognized and deeply rooted, are jeopardized by prospects of change; hence it is an important aspect of the professional role to serve as a container during the 'working through' of change. Also directly derived from the psychoanalytic model has been a belief in the importance of examining the transference and counter-transference within the professional relationship; that is to say, the way in which the consultant is used and experienced, and also the feelings evoked in him, may provide evidence about underlying issues and feelings about them within the client system. In so far, then, as the consultant uses himself as a measuring instrument, means are required for calibrating that instrument, so that he has a better chance of distinguishing between feelings that belong to him and feelings projected into him. Personal psychoanalysis became a favoured method for attempting this calibration.

I would argue that adoption of this particular action research role directly influenced the types of theoretical formulations that were produced. For example, an important feature of the consultant's method is to propose working hypotheses (the equivalent of psychoanalytic interpretations) that are tested by the client. Therefore, models for understanding organizations have been a product of the consultant-client relationship and have correspondingly been particularly attentive to sources of resistance to change (Miller, 1976a, 1976b).

A further major and continuing influence on Tavistock thinking about organization was the concept of *open systems*, derived from von Bertalanffy (1950a, 1950b). Systemic thinking was not, of course, novel: Lewin's thinking has already been mentioned. Already too there had emerged, mainly from the Institute's early students of coal-mining (Trist and Bamforth, 1951), the concept of the *socio-technical system*. This provided a way of examining, and possibly reconciling, the relationship between the psycho-social and the techno-economic elements of purposeful organizations. Classical organization theory had subordinated the human element to technological imperatives (a view that still persists in much contemporary 'scientific management'); countering this 'structural universalism' the so-called 'human relations school' had responded by an equivalent 'psychological universalism' (cf. Lupton, 1976), which sought to demonstrate that organizations could be changed and performance improved by manipulating only the psycho-social variables, such as leadership style (and again this assumption has persisted in the work of writers such as McGregor, Likert and Blake and of many contemporary OD practitioners). The concept of the socio-technical system, therefore, opened up possibilities of jointly optimizing the two types of variables and thus of organizational choice (cf. Trist, et al, 1963; also Rice, 1958 and 1963; Miller, 1959 and 1975; Emery and Trist, 1960). But its immediate application was at the level of the primary work-group rather than the wider organization. The notion of the open system made it possible to look simultaneously both at the relationship between social and technical and also at the relationships between the part and the whole, the whole and the environment. *Inter alia*, it provided a further way of conceptualizing the relationships that especially

Application: Miller

preoccupy me—between individual and group, individual and enterprise. And, despite the assertion by Lewin quoted above, it showed that 'the structural properties of a dynamic whole' might not be so different from 'the structural properties of subparts'; both could be seen as having similar systemic characteristics.

A key connecting concept, derived from open system thinking, is that of *boundary*. It has become a statement of the obvious to say that an enterprise or institution can survive only through a continuous interchange of materials with its environment. There are the materials that the enterprise distinctively exists to process—thus a manufacturing company converts raw materials into saleable products (and waste), a college converts freshmen into graduates (and drop-outs)—and there are the other resources that are required to bring about the processing—the production workers, the teachers, the machinery, the supplies, etc. The boundary across which these materials flow in and out both separates the enterprise from and links it with its environment. It marks a discontinuity between the task of the enterprise and the tasks of those other systems in its environment with which it transacts. Because these relationships are never stable and static, because its behaviour and identity are subject to perpetual renegotiation and redefinition, the boundary of the enterprise is best conceived not as a line but as a region. The inner boundary of this region interfaces with the internal subsystems through which the conversion work of the enterprise—the transformation of intakes into outputs—is conducted, the outer boundary with the related external systems. Thus the boundary region may be seen as the location of those roles and activities that are concerned with mediating relations between outside and inside. For example, the leadership exercised in this region can protect the internal subsystems from the disruption of fluctuating demands from the outside; but it also has to promote those internal changes that will enable the enterprise to be adaptive and indeed proactive in relation to the environment. Survival is therefore contingent on an appropriate degree of insulation and permeability in the boundary region.

This conception is equally applicable to a subsystem within an enterprise, such as a production department. In this case, the rest of the enterprise constitutes a major part of the environment.

If we turn now to the individual, who provides a basic component in the enterprise (a statement on which I shall expand presently), the open system and psychoanalytic conceptions, taken together, allow us to construct a very similar model. In the individual, the boundary region may be equated with the ego function. The inner world of the individual includes experiences, emotions, attitudes and skills of which he is largely conscious and which, through the ego-function, can be appropriately mobilized or suppressed in the service of whatever goal he is pursuing and role he is taking at a particular moment of time. The inner world can also be conceived as being populated, as it were, by a set of 'objects' and 'part-objects,' which are the residual representations of earlier—including infantile—experiences of relations with others (cf. Klein, 1959). Thus the individual, when he engages in adult life with, for example, a new boss, will not simply respond in a rational way to what the boss actually says and does, but he will bring forward, from his internal repertoire of objects and part-objects, his experience of earlier authority figures, including mother and father. These will underlie the new relationship and so affect his perceptions.

Both enterprise and individual, therefore, can be conceived as open systems, engaged in continuing transactions with an environment; each has a boundary region exercising a regulatory function mediating between the inner world and the environmental systems with which it interacts. (A group, of course, may also be thought of in similar terms.) I now want to turn to the relationship between individual and enterprise.

For any given description of its primary task we can construct for an enterprise an organizational model, or perhaps more than one. Building such models and using them as a tool of exploration with members of the client organization has been a common method of working at Tavistock (cf. Rice, 1963; Miller and Rice, 1967). The *primary task* defines the through-put and the kind of relationship with the environment—e.g., in terms of sources of intakes and customers for outputs—that is necessary to keep the enterprise in business. This identifies then the *activities* that will be required—by people, by machines or by both—to convert the intakes into outputs and to transact with environmental systems. Boundaries between sets of activities identify *task systems*, around which organizational boundaries may potentially be drawn. These are socio-technical subsystems within the enterprise as a system. (In a large complex enterprise, further differentiation into sub-subsytems, etc., may be appropriate.) People—the human resources of the enterprise—are then needed to carry *roles* through which they contribute the requisite activities to the task of the subsystem.

Recently, Lawrence has suggested a distinction between:

1. the *normative* primary task as the task that people in an organization *ought* to pursue (usually according to the definition of a superordinate authority),
2. the *existential* primary task as that which they believe they are carrying out, and
3. the *phenomenal* primary task that it is hypothesized that they are engaged in and of which they may not be consciously aware (Lawrence and Robinson, 1975).

Now what the normative primary task requires from people is only their contribution of activities, their roles. The roles that individuals bring to the task belong inside the boundary of the enterprise; the individuals who provide the roles belong outside: they are among the more important elements in the environment with which the enterprise has to interact. This implies, therefore, that the appropriate perspective for examining the relationship between the enterprise and the individuals who supply roles within it—and, indeed, whose role-taking gives the enterprise its existence—is an *inter-systemic* perspective: it is a relationship between the

Application: Miller

enterprise as a system and individuals (and groups of individuals) as systems.

This perspective is difficult to hold on to. As Goffman puts it succinctly: 'every institution has encompassing tendencies' (Goffman, 1968, p. 15). The group or the enterprise draws upon, and the individual colludes in supplying, more than the requisite role. The individual requires group membership to give meaning, to confer status, to confirm his picture of himself, his identity; and also, as Bion demonstrated, he uses the group to express what appear to be quite primitive feelings in the areas of dependency, aggression and hope. The individual is usually unaware of this process: these basic emotions slip under the guard, as it were, of his ego function. He thus finds his supports and defences in what have been called *sentient groups*, which may or may not correspond to the boundaries of the task-groups—the socio-technical subsystems—in which he exercises his work-role (Miller and Rice, 1967). Although his role in the enterprise does not predetermine the relative *sentience* for him of the various groupings to which he belongs, which will be located both outside and inside the enterprise, these memberships are nevertheless relevant to effectiveness of task performance, supporting or opposing it.

As a consequence, the relationship between individual and enterprise is usually not seen, by either party, as a relationship between two systems, one of which supplies a role for the other; much more commonly it is seen from both perspectives as a relationship between part and whole—as if the individual were a subsystem of the enterprise as a supra-system. For the interdependence of the inter-systemic relationship there tends to be substituted the dependence of the subordinate—superior relationship. It is a necessary condition for the survival of the enterprise that the leadership function—the regulation of the boundary between outside and inside—should be credible to those who contribute roles to it (as well as to the external systems). Indeed, an enterprise as such is no more than the product of the shared beliefs, of those outside and inside, that it exists and that the organizational boundaries of the enterprise as a whole and of its parts are located in particular places. Its survival is therefore contingent on the sanctioning of the role-holders on these boundaries by the role-holders inside them. Consequently, some degree of dependence is realistic. But the encompassing tendency of institutions exaggerates this dependency. Those on the boundary tend to receive and assume power and prestige that go beyond the sanctioned authority for the boundary role. Correspondingly, those inside are surrendering power and prestige to those in the boundary positions. The reciprocal dependence of the boundary role-holders on the role-holders inside goes unrecognized; it gets forgotten that there can be no leaders without followers.

Following Bion's formulation, we may ask what happens in this situation to emotions associated with 'fight.' Often they are deposited in the trade union. The employee can use his union to express his aggression and hostility by contesting with an undifferentiated 'management,' and this preserves the dependency of the individual superior-subordinate relationship. 'Unofficial' actions, such as wild-cat strikes, evoke considerable anxiety because they threaten to impinge on and to question the unassailability of the dependent relationship.

If I may now refer back to the opening of this paper, one thing that patients in long-stay hospitals and sub-subsistence rural communities have in common is lack of union membership or its equivalent as an outlet for 'fight.'

I will mention here only one of the studies of health care systems that colleagues and I have been involved in over recent years—a study of residential institutions for the physically handicapped and chronic sick (Miller and Gwynne, 1972, 1973). Analysis of these institutions in input-output terms suggested that a significant characteristic of the inmates admitted to them was that they were not merely severely handicapped and unable more than partially to look after themselves; they were also rejected. Often they had been personally rejected by parents and spouses who were no longer willing or able to take care of them; but all in effect had been socially rejected by the outside community, in which they were defined, at least implicitly, as no longer having a valued role. Moreover, once cripples are admitted to these institutions, it is unusual for them to be discharged back into the community: in other words, the normal output consists of dead inmates. All these realities are painful to face, for staff and inmates alike. Consequently, such institutions are especially prone to develop forms of organization that will defend their members from anxiety (cf. Jaques, 1953; Menzies, 1960). In the institutions studied, two patterns repeated themselves so consistently that it became possible to identify two opposed models of residential care. Much the more common was the 'warehousing model,' in which staff related wholly to the dependency of inmates. The phenomenal primary task could be defined as: 'to prolong physical life.' Attempts by inmates to assert individuality or to display independence were constraints on task performance and therefore discouraged. Staff controlled the boundary of the individual, effectively taking over his ego-function and removing his areas of discretion. The prevailing fantasy was that staff were omnipotent, inmates wholly dependent. Emotions associated with 'fight,' having no permissible outlet, could be seen as turned self-destructively inwards on the individual, who characteristically displayed depression, apathy, listlessness, withdrawal. In the less common 'horticultural model,' by contrast, the emphasis was on the unsatisfied drives and unfulfilled capacities of the inmates. The phenomenal primary task was to promote their independence and, by implication, to rehabilitate them for re-export to the community outside. This approach seemed so much more in tune with our own liberal values that at first we found it difficult to recognize that this too was inadequate. We noticed, however, that the prevailing culture was one of 'fight'—of inmates against staff identified as oppressive and sadistic, or of staff and inmates together against a management committee or other perceived external enemy. The fight was invigorating— although there was a great deal of frustration, there was also much more aliveness among these inmates —but expression of dependency needs seemed to be taboo. Thus while the warehousing model related to inmates' dependence and denied their independence, the horticultural model related to their independence and denied the reality that for most of them rehabilitation was a mirage: the prognosis was increasing dependence, deterioration and death. By making these defences explicit and working through the implications with staff and inmates, it was possible in one institution to develop a form of organization within which inmates could choose and move between multiple roles—an organization that both accommodated the dependent needs of inmates and used their independent capacities.

Lack of choice also characterizes what we call 'poverty' and 'underdevelopment.' These are terms to be used with caution. If certain social groups are defined as underdeveloped by the criteria of the developers, rather than by the criteria of the people themselves, one is drawn into a 'top-down' philosophy. It suggests a distinction between, on the one hand, the benefactors, the superiors, those who do not need to change, and, on the other, the beneficiaries, the inferiors, those who need to be changed. The objective of development, tacitly if not explicitly, is then to make 'them' more like 'us.' With these qualifications, it is nevertheless possible to give operational meaning to such terms. Underdevelopment can be defined as relative lack of control over relations with one's environment, where that includes both the local physical environment and the external environment of the wider socio-economic-political system. Development, then, implies a change in such relations in the direction of influencing and controlling the environment, instead of being controlled by it—a shift from impotence towards potency. (This is not dissimilar to Paolo Friere's formulation (Friere, 1970a, 1972b.) Hence my work on rural development in two Latin American countries has led me to the proposition that one needs to define the primary task of a development programme as to help the client system bring about such a change. An important aspect of the development task is to help the client system to make fuller use of, and to exercise greater control over, recognised and unrecognised resources in its local or internal environment. Thus improved health can release greater energy, and education can lead to new skills and techniques. It becomes possible for the client system to enlarge its resources by improving the productivity of the soil, bringing new land into cultivation or changing land use; drinking water is delivered to the house instead of having to be collected from the spring; and so on. In this way the people shift their boundary with their physical environment. But these have to be seen only as means, not as ends in themselves. Experience suggests that such changes cannot be achieved or, if achieved, will not be sustained, unless they are also accompanied and reinforced by changes in relations with the external environment: the client system needs to become more autonomous and influential in managing these relationships. Obviously, a major element of the changed relationship, and thus an important criterion of development, will be economic: for example, the client system sells produce instead of manual labour; it sells its produce in a processed form instead of selling it unprocessed (e.g., cheese instead of milk); it diversifies its economic relations; it extends its control over distribution and so commands higher prices, etc. But there are also other elements, such as increased power within the political system; and in addition there are more subtle qualitative changes in the image of the client system held by bodies in the environment and in the client system's image of itself. If changes in the relationship with the external environment are a condition for development, then it follows that there must also be changes in the bodies that constitute that environment. Development requires a change in the wider system that includes both the 'underdeveloped' and the 'developed.' In very general terms, therefore, we can say that a process of development occurs through a relationship between a 'development agency' (which might be anything from a government department to a political agitator) and a client system as a result of which the client system—probably first through making fuller use of its human and physical resources—acquires greater control over its external environment. And that external environment includes, of course, the development agency itself. Discussion of the appropriate role for the development agency in this process deserves far more space than can be spared here. Very often the starting-point is a collection of people displaying the symptoms of inmates in a 'warehousing' institution—impotence, apathy, lack of self-esteem—and there is a need to help them discover an identity as a client system. One approach is through political education: they learn that their condition is not the result of inherent inferiority but the consequence of perhaps generations of oppression and exploitation. Dependency gets transformed into fight. However, this needs to be accompanied by improved social and economic capability. A community that relies too much on fight as its basis of identity and organization is placed at risk not only by defeat but by victory. The other approach is the transfer of dependency to the benign leadership of the 'developer.' He guides his protégés along new paths of economic development and secures their commitment to new activities and methods. Here the risk is that the client system will not have been allowed to learn through making mistakes and it will have been protected from adjusting and developing its internal organization to cope with the changes. Hence, if the benign leadership disappears, the system is likely to collapse. Very few development efforts in Third World countries have been able to navigate a course between this Scylla and Charybdis.

In this account of values, concepts and methods, I have left until last a discussion of a particular approach to group relations training that has perhaps been the most direct forerunner of the work to be described in Part II. This approach derives much from the pioneering work of the late A.K. Rice and P.M. Turquet at the Tavistock Institute in the early 1960s (see especially Rice, 1965) and has been carried on by Turquet, myself and other colleagues in recent years both at the Tavistock and in other institutions (including, in the United States, what is now the A.K. Rice Institute). Bion had established a mode of working with groups in which individual behaviour was explained in the context not of personality variables but of processes occurring in the group as a whole. The interpretative focus, by analogy with psychoanalysis, was the relationship between the group and Bion as consultant. This method was established as having not only therapeutic but educational relevance. Early group relations training conferences organized by the Tavistock Institute in the 1950s were primarily devoted to using the method to give participants experience of the behaviour of small groups (of ten to twelve members) and to reflect on its applications to their own roles (Trist and Sofer, 1959). In 1959, Bridger extended the method to the study of inter-group behaviour (Higgin and Bridger, 1964). Subsequently, other events were added to the conferences. These included the 'Large Group,' which explores the processes that occur in a group of between forty and eighty members with perhaps four consultants. This is not an unstructured group, since there is at least the role differentiation between members and consultants, but it is a good deal less structured than most groups of this size, which in a work organization, for example, might include several different sections and hierarchical levels; and hence it probably displays dynamics that underlie formally structured groups, including anxieties against which structures provide some form of defence (cf. Turquet, 1975). (At the other end of the scale, some conferences now also provide for study of the potentially intimate relations within a 'Very Small Group' of five to six members.) A further extension from the 1960s onwards has been to provide opportunities to experience and study organizational relationships of a more complex kind: the focus in certain events is the 'here and now' relationship between the total membership and the total staff group within the conference as a whole, which is conceived as a temporary institution.

The conferences as they are operated today therefore offer a variety of settings within which to explore the interplay—or, as I called it earlier, tension—between individual and group, individual and organization. Except for some sessions set aside for review and application work, all the events are devoted to experiential learning from behaviour as it occurs. In contrast to certain other group methods (and there are many of them), the consultant in these conferences does not purport to be an uninvolved commentator or individual and inter-personal behaviour. On the contrary, what the members make of the role and authority of the consultant, and what he in turn experiences of their projections into him, constitute primary data for the elucidation of group processes. Correspondingly, the member has a chance to explore the part he plays in different kinds of authority relationships—for example, how far he is responding to what the other person is actually saying and doing, and how far he intrudes into the relationship primitive images of a benign or punitive authority that belong to his own internal world. What he learns, therefore, is unique to him. He cannot be told what he 'ought to have learned': indeed, that phrase itself is an expression of dependence on authority. Other people, including the consultant, may offer their views of a situation; but only the individual member is in a position to understand, in light of the role he has, the relationship between what is happening around him and what is happening inside him; hence it is on his own authority that he accepts what is valid for him and rejects what is not.

Fig. 2.1 illustrates the kind of systemic framework that I have in mind when I take a consultant role in such a conference. (The double line around individuals and groups depicts the boundary region, described earlier,

Organizational Development and Industrial Democracy

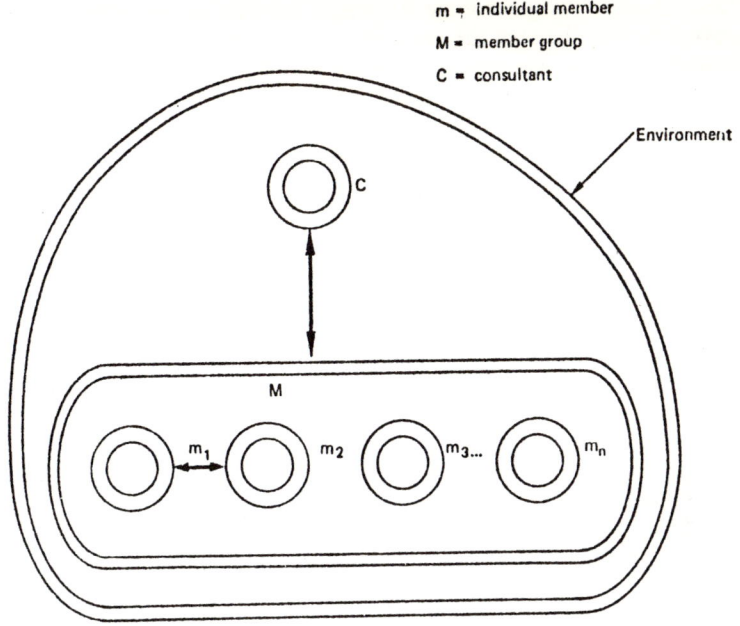

FIG. 2·1

between the inner world and the environment.) Transactions between individual members, $m_1 \leftrightarrow m_2$ are to be understood in terms of a hypothesis about the relationship between the member group and the consultant, $M \leftrightarrow C$. The relationship, $M \leftrightarrow C$, in turn implies some image or fantasy of the wider system that includes both—the group or institution—and its relation to its environments. The same basic model can be extended to include the more complex situation, in which, for example, m may itself be a subgroup of members, M the total membership group, C the staff of a conference, and thus the outer boundary is that of the total conference as an institution. Application of this method to 'in-house' conferences—i.e., where the members are all drawn from the same institution—has demonstrated repeatedly that assumptions about $M \leftrightarrow C$ and about the containing system reflect significant, though often not overtly recognized, aspects of the culture of the institution from which the members are drawn. These group relations trainings conferences, therefore, epitomize the main concepts, methods and values that I have attempted to describe. Conceptually, they use an open systems framework, together with propositions derived from psychoanalysis, to explore the relationship between individual, group and organization. They suggest that important elements of the intakes and outputs of these systems are not merely material objects but images, fantasies and projections. The method too is derivative from psychoanalysis, in that it makes use of the various forms of transference in the client-consultant relationship as a means of illuminating dynamics within the client system. Finally, in terms of values, I see the conferences as vitally concerned with 'helping the individual to develop greater maturity in understanding and managing the boundary between his own inner world and the realities of his external environment.' It is on his own authority that he decides what to do with this understanding in his roles in other institutions, whether as manager or managed. However, I acknowledge that I personally hope that he will acquire greater potency to question and perhaps change his relationship with his working environment.

PART II: DEVELOPMENT IN A MANUFACTURING COMPANY

I would reiterate that Part I describes where I stand: I do not claim that the statement would be wholly shared by my colleagues or by the client system in the work I am about to describe. Secondly, I do not want to give the impression that I personally came to this system with a ready-made theoretical framework, which I proceeded to apply in order to procure some kind of transformation. On the contrary, my involvement has been relatively marginal. The main architect of this particular piece of work was Andrew Szmidla (hereafter referred to as 'AS'), who, with Olya Khaleelee ('OK'), had already achieved a good deal before I came on the scene in January 1975; and I am sure I have learned at least as much from them as they have from me. Thirdly, this does not purport to be a success-story, with proven lessons ready to be applied elsewhere: it is still ongoing, and neither we nor the client system know what the outcomes of our relationship will be. I am presenting it because it illustrates what I believe to be an innovative approach in the industrial democracy/organizational development area—and I see this as an area in which innovation is badly needed if industry is to keep pace with the changing structure and values of contemporary British society.

The company, which I shall call 'Omicron,' manufactures equipment widely used in the engineering and construction industries. Its main factory is about twenty miles from Central London and it employs eight hundred people. Historically, by all accounts, it had been a successful company. It had an international reputation for the quality of its products, many of which were tailor-made for specialist applications; and it was profitable. In the middle 1960s it was taken over by a large British-based group ('Omega'), which itself owned a company ('Kappa') manufacturing similar equipment. Omicron's name was retained (presumably because of its higher reputation); Kappa was merged into it; sales were incorporated into a large Omega sales department that covered other types of production; and Omega put its own men into senior managerial positions. Other changes followed. Manufacturing processes in the two companies were rationalized. A two-shift system was introduced. This led to the loss of a large part of Omicron's female labour force and to their replacement by inexperienced male labour. Profits turned into increasing losses; redundancies became necessary; and a series of general managers appointed by Omega attempted to introduce their own solutions without success. Omicron was seen in Omega as a major problem.

Towards the end of 1973, the most recently appointed general manager sought advice from AS, a psychologist. As an internal consultant employed by Omega, AS's services were available to companies within the group. As a starting-point, AS designed a diagnostic questionnaire that was distributed to all employees of Omicron during February 1974. It was based on Levinson's approach to organizational diagnosis (Levinson, 1972). Many questions were open-ended and some were projective: for example:

> 'Tell me about Omicron. What do you think is its greatest strength and greatest weakness?'
> 'What kind of people would be likely to apply for a job here?'
> 'If you were to make changes that would make the company a better place for you to work, what would you change?'
> 'Make believe Omicron is a person. Think about that person for a minute. Describe the person to me so that I can get a good idea of the picture you have in mind.'

The response rate was high—seventy percent—though, of course, not all the respondents tackled every question. The results were analysed over the next four months and presented for discussion in a series of six open meetings. These were attended by about a hundred of the employees.

The ways in which members of the organization saw Omicron were in many respects a direct consequence of the history I have outlined. Omicron was perceived as having four potential strengths: its membership of the large Omega group; the technical excellence and the reputation of the product; its social amenities (its active social club being an important focus not only for the main factory site but for the local community outside); and the workers. But these potentialities were not being used. Externally, there was a lack of co-operation and communication between Omicron and Omega. The core employees of Omicron saw Omega as having grossly violated the boundary of their organization by, on the one hand, foisting Kappa on them and, on the other, by depriving it of an essential element—its sales force. Related to this were several internal splits. There was rivalry and antipathy between the old Omicron and Kappa factions. Omicron staff saw the old company's distinctive competence for specialist applications being whittled away by emphasis on Kappa's standard 'bread-and-butter' lines: in recollection, differences between the two companies were much greater than they had been in reality. To some extent this split fed into interdepartmental relations, which were characterized by isolationism and back-biting. There was also a worker-management split, 'experienced by the individual worker as an isolation and detachment from the management of the site and symbolized by the roadway running between the factory and the offices, so that although management actually worked on both sides, they were perceived as only working on one side.[1] Management was seen as top-heavy; there were too many management changes, which deprived the organization of stability and continuity; and there was a feeling that Omicron was being exploited by serving as a stepping-stone for Omega managers on their way to senior positions in the group. Additionally, management's preoccupation with union relationships—which were said to be good—left staff employees feeling neglected and unappreciated.

Overall, there was a sense of inefficient use of resources, both material and human: the scrap rate was excessive; people felt themselves treated as numbers; and departure of experienced people was seen as having created a dearth of expertise.

> ... Both individuals and departments within the organization were extremely confused as to what their objectives were and how they related to the organization's objectives.
>
> Omicron thus presented itself to us as an organization split up into departments, each trying to exist as a separate entity, each having little awareness of corporate objectives, each apparently expending energy in competition with other departments within the organization rather than in competition as an integrated entity with the outside world. This internal competitiveness seemed to take up so much time that Omicron often appeared to be out of touch with aspects of its environment such as its competitors or knowledge of market share. Overall, either very little mention was made of outside factors, or else a grossly distorted view of certain parts of the environment, such as Head Office, was presented to us.
>
> Thus the fragmentation of the site seemed to operate at all levels; at the level of the individual relating to other individuals; at the group level, where departments needed to relate to other departments; and at the level of the totality—that is, the relationship of the organization to its environment.

I have quoted at some length from the conclusions that AS and OK drew from their survey, because these led directly to the strategy of intervention that was adopted. They conceived Omicron as a system. Inefficient and precarious though it was, it was nevertheless surviving. Its behaviour as an organization had to be seen as the result of a collective belief—by no means explicit—on the part of the people in it that it was necessary to behave in this way in order to achieve organizational and personal survival. And I think it is worth reiterating here a point that sometimes gets forgotten: that an enterprise has no independent existence as an entity: it is a product of the actions and interactions, beliefs and assumptions, of people located inside it and outside. Before any change was possible, therefore, it was necessary to discover the implicit 'rules' that were guiding people's behaviour. 'Because the rules were in the minds of the people who worked at Omicron, it was only with their help that they could be discovered and only with their co-operation that they could ever be altered.' A further related conclusion was that the work to be done at Omicron would eventually have to involve the whole organization. The question was: how?

Out of this emerged the idea of what came to be called the 'People Programme' in Omicron. As one element in this, the General Manager formed an Employee Consultative Group (ECG), consisting of elected and appointed representatives from the principal levels and areas of the organization. He envisaged this, or a successor body, as potentially taking on more than a consultative role and assuming at least some of the responsibility conventionally regarded as the prerogative of 'management.' That was an open question. But it is worth noting that the General Manager conceived it at the time not as a carefully controlled device for providing token worker participation, but as an open-ended experiment that might have unknown and quite radical outcomes.

The other main element of the People Programme was designed to give as many employees as possible an educational experience akin to that of the group relations training conferences described earlier:

> Our thinking at this stage was that in any system which had more than a small number of people, there are three quite distinct boundaries at which interaction takes place and work gets done: between individuals; between groups; and between systems (i.e., across the external boundary and with the outside world). The People Programme was designed to provide members with an opportunity to examine these boundaries, in order to learn about themselves in relation to other people, in order to learn about the underlying dynamics of groups, and finally in order to look at the way the organization as a whole related to the outside world; and overall, to be able to distinguish form from content so that employees of the company would be able to stand back from their situation and look at *processes* which were operating as distinct from merely acting out the work role. In this way we hoped that a self-consciousness or self-awareness would develop, initially on the individual level and later on a departmental and organizational level, so that the process of fragmentation could be replaced by more meaningful interconnections between the different parts, and this in turn would lead to improved effectiveness of the system as a whole.

But there was a problem of numbers. I recall that my first meeting with AS was at a Tavistock Conference in September 1974 (he and OK had also attended a conference in the previous year), and the question he put to me there was essentially this: 'How does one consult to a Large Group of up to 1000 people?' OK had left the project in May 1974 and, although she was to rejoin later in the year as a research officer on the Omicron payroll, for the time being AS was single-handed. If one accepted the logic that one had to start by giving people an opportunity to study the first of the three boundaries identified—that between individuals—then the appropriate medium was the Small Group (of about 12 members); but to provide small-group experience for 800 people would occupy more time, consultancy resources or both than seemed reasonable. A further constraint was the size of the Large Group that was the selected medium for working at the third (inter-systemic) boundary: practically and technically the upper limit of membership was around 100. Hence a critical decision was made in the autumn of 1974 to limit participation in the initial stages to a group broadly defined as 'management' at the main site—a group of about 120 people from general manager to supervisors and including some specialists in nonmanagerial roles. Participation would be voluntary. Given that this was the largest number that could be encompassed at that stage, an alternative strategy would have been to make the programme accessible to a cross-section of the total organization. That might have helped in working at the split between management and workers. However, the selected strategy had two strong arguments in its favour: the 'management' group constituted a meaningful sub-set of the total system and it was potentially the most influential sub-set in terms of the possibilities of change.

For the Small Group exercise they were formed into nine groups, each meeting for one and a half hours weekly over twelve weeks.

I myself became involved in the design and operation of two residential weekends, held at Omega's management college, for the study of inter-group relations. Other outside consultants were also introduced for these events. I mentioned earlier the way in which this type of exercise can illuminate the culture of an institution: here one pervasive characteristic of Omicron managers—one of the tacit 'rules' of the organization—seemed to be a sense of their own powerlessness in influencing their individual and collective futures. The 'real' management was somewhere else; because it was ignorant of local factors its decisions would probably be bad; but there was nothing that Omicron managers could do about it except to acquiesce and obey. The notion that they themselves by default were bestowing power on this 'senior management,' through failing to exercise their own authority, was discomfiting.

Following the inter-group weekends, participants returned to their small groups for four more weekly sessions, in which they reviewed and consolidated the learning that had taken place and began to apply it to their understanding of Omicron and their own roles within it.

The Programme then moved into its third phase at the end of March 1975 for the study of inter-system relationships. For this, six weekly meetings were arranged, open to the whole of the management in a 'Large Group' configuration, with AS and myself in the role of consultants. Whereas in the small group and inter-group exercises the task was defined as the study of the actual processes occurring in the 'here and now,' the Large Group was asked to examine the relationship between Omicron and its environment. A seventh working session was added with the explicit task of discussing a review document prepared by OK, as follows.

At the time, the Large Group was not a wholly satisfactory experience and we wondered whether we had the design right. We felt some uncertainty about the consultant role. The task required us to act as consultants to the Omicron management group as they engaged in their task of examining their boundary with the environment, and we were able to make some comments about their perceptions of each other and of external systems; but we found it hard to discover and to use as data what they were projecting into us, who could be perceived as representatives of the environment actually present in the room. For participants, too, the experience seemed disappointing. At the first session attendance was substantial and there was an air of high expectancy; subsequently absences increased. We were therefore somewhat surprised by the outcome of the final session. The ending of the Large Group marked the end of the formal educational phase of the People Programme that AS had initiated in the previous October. The stance we had taken was that if there was to be any continuation or extension of the Programme, its leadership could come only from the client group. They had been given their opportunity to learn and reflect: what they now did as a result was up to them. No doubt the discomfort of both members and consultants in the Large Group was partly attributable to anxiety about this impending transition. Throughout the final session the mood suggested that the Programme was going to end 'not with a bang but a whimper.' Only in the concluding minutes did a few participants recognize that our statement that it was the last session was not binding on them—that they could exercise their own authority to continue. They rapidly appointed a convenor and agreed to meet the following week. And in fact the group has continued in existence up to the time of writing.

OK, who had a role in monitoring the Programme, was at this time interviewing a sample of one-third of the group who had been, as it were, on the books of the Programme since the previous October, including the small minority of persistent non-attenders. OK's interviews and report (which was distributed to all participants in the People Programme) were not, however, focused only on the Programme, but included the state of the organization as seen through their eyes. Thus it was a partial follow-up of the survey a year previously.

One impression that emerged was that many of the dissatisfactions that the survey had exposed were still very much alive: the Omicron/Kappa split, interdepartmental rivalries, the loss of expertise, the scrap problem. There was a good deal of frustration around these issues. The following comment summed up some of the feeling:

> The frustration is due to banging one's head against a brick wall. When you talk to people they look around the room and don't really listen. Even if they say it's a good idea nothing is ever done about it. Or they say they are too busy now, but will see you this afternoon, tomorrow, next week, but they never do. So you have to keep chasing them and never get any satisfaction.

Against that had to be set comments on the People Programme (in which at the time of the survey the small groups were still the dominant experience). About a quarter of the responses were quite negative; half were positive, and the remainder equivocal. But OK reported that the most significant outcome in general was said to be better communications:

The people I talked to think that they themselves and other members have become more perceptive, more observant, more willing to listen to other people, more self-examining and less dogmatic. The sessions were seen as an opportunity for people to get to know each other and as a stimulus for better communications across departments. The groups are seen to have provided a beneficial environment for exchanging information and are said to have created a greater awareness of what is going on in Omicron and a greater willingness to check out information before accepting it.

Other reported effects of the group experience were that: it had given greater confidence to speak out; it had provided some insight into the operation and power of groups; it had brought to the forefront the issue of the supervisory role—resulting in some appropriate action; some people had been made more dissatisfied and critical; it had made the organization damagingly introspective; and it had caused a good deal of resentment among those excluded from the Programme.

Thirdly, and in some respects most interestingly, the survey report focused attention on the number of new problem-solving groups that had begun to emerge during the preceding six months. Most of them straddled conventional departmental and hierarchical boundaries. At least some of them were formed as a direct outcome of the People Programme, either at the initiative of a head of department (perhaps partly in response to pressures from his subordinates for greater involvement) or spontaneously among a group of colleagues.

An example of the latter was the Project Engineering Group (PEG), its aim being defined as 'to examine the structure of the department and the roles of individuals within it in order to be better able to meet the objectives of the department.' It was set up without the participation or even permission of more senior managers in the engineering department—a fact which rankled for a time. But PEG persisted in its weekly meetings, it invited AS to act as its consultant, and by the spring of 1976—a year later—it was sponsoring a miniature People Programme of its own for some fifty engineering employees.

Let me return now to the decision by the Large Group to continue to meet on its own initiative after the initial programme of experiential learning had been completed. The mounting of the People Programme had relied heavily on the personal leadership of the general manager, who himself had participated as a member of the Programme through all its phases. By doing so, he had demonstrated the possibility of role-changes: the notion of superior and subordinate need not pervade all organizational relationships; it could be appropriate for some tasks and not for others. At the same time there were pressures on him, sometimes very powerful, to give up the role of fellow-student and to provide instead a leadership on which they could depend. As in the case of rural development, he had introduced Omicron to new ideas and methods, for which there was a fair degree of support, but there was the same kind of risk that it was more

Organizational Development and Industrial Democracy

comfortable to go on following him—almost to the extent of going through the motions in order to please him—than to exercise one's own independent authority, with the attendant anxiety of actually re-examining safe assumptions about the superior-subordinate relationship. The spontaneous decision by the Large Group to continue its existence, which was followed by its appointment of a chairman and co-ordinating group, represented a belief in the possibility that leadership did not have to come only from the top. (The chairman was not a member of the senior management group and the co-ordinators came from different levels.) The Large Group became a forum in which issues such as the objectives of the company, the processes of management, the meaning of the managerial role and the whole question of industrial democracy and participation were explored. AS continued as its consultant. The co-ordinators successfully applied to the general manager for a small budget, part of which they spent on sending two of their number to a course on participation in industry, on which they reported back fully to the Large Group. One of the speakers on the course was Lord Brown (formerly, Wilfred Brown, Chairman of the Glacier Metal Company and an authority on organization, especially the creation of representative systems in industry), and they invited him to present his ideas to the Large Group. Of the original 120 participants, about 60 were fairly frequent attenders at the regular weekly meetings, with the average attendance being about 30. There was—and is—continuing uncertainty over whether participation in the Large Group should be seen as part of one's work role or as something of an indulgence, the 'real work' being elsewhere.

The Large Group was just one of the new forms that the People Programme took after May 1975. For the half-dozen members of the senior management group AS gave a series of weekly seminars on concepts relating to individual, group and organization. The high intellectual standard he set—which included reading and discussing journal articles from the psychoanalytic and organizational literature[2]—was fully justified by the response. He also acted as a consultant to them in regular 'state of the organization' meetings. Later he gave a similar series to the Large Group co-ordinators, to whom he was also a regular consultant. (Some of these found the material more difficult to grasp.) Several senior managers and a trade union convenor were financed to attend group relations training conferences run by the Tavistock Institute. AS continued as a consultant to PEG, to the Employee Consultative Group (ECG) and, from time to time, to other groups and individuals. And, of course, as this implies, the continuing commitment of Omicron to the People Programme—or at least the commitment of the general manager—was evidenced by continuing payment for the services of AS and OK, and of myself, from January 1975 onward, primarily in the role of external consultant to the internal consultants.

My picture of developments in Omicron is therefore derived from my regular discussions with AS and OK in this role, from their records and other documents, and from such documents from within the company—such as minutes of Large Group meetings—which they passed on. In our discussions, we worked on the proposition that the way in which the organization related to them might illuminate current dynamics within Omicron, such as underlying attitudes towards senior management and to the general manager in particular; and that their relationship to me was likely to reflect the relationship between the client system and themselves.

Undoubtedly, our dominant concern in the second half of 1975 was the continuing precariousness of the Programme—how far its survival was still dependent on the personal leadership of the general manager. He was a fairly regular attender of the Large Group, and we were struck by the frequency with which the group, when in difficulty, would mobilize him in the role of general manager instead of fellow-member and therefore, in a sense, regress. There were subterranean rumours—which turned out to be well-founded—that he would be leaving before the end of the year. Associated with the rumours was an anxiety, explicit in AS's and OK's discussions with me, that if Omega replaced him with a new general manager, members of the organization would surrender their precarious assertion of authority, revert to dependency on the new leadership, and all traces of the People Programme would quickly disappear into the sand.

In the event he nominated Omicron's manufacturing manager as his successor; a little later a new manufacturing manager was appointed from outside; and, despite all the fears, the transitions occurred with scarcely a hiccup and indeed, in January-February 1976, the People Programme seemed to be more firmly entrenched than ever.

My impression at the time was that the departing general manager had presented his nominee to Omega management almost as a *fait accompli* that it would be difficult for them to resist. Certainly, Omicron was in a much stronger position than it had been a year previously in relation to Omega. Results for the recently ended financial year had shown a dramatic turn-around. Omicron was moving from a loss to a healthy profit in a period when many fellow-subsidiaries of Omega were moving in the reverse direction. But Omicron managers were becoming perceptibly more confident, buoyant and assertive in their transactions with Omega long before the figures had been added up and published—a phenomenon commented on by some Omega visitors to the site. Cause-and-effect relationships are notoriously difficult to establish within complex systems. It is not even clear whether confidence 'caused' profitability or profitability 'caused' confidence. *Prima facie*, however, the People Programme is likely to have been associated significantly with the increased confidence. The contribution of the Programme to profitability is not established; OK is currently seeking methods to explore the null hypothesis—i.e., that it had no effect.

The actual change of general managers, therefore, contradicted the mood of precariousness that AS and OK often (though not perpetually) communicated to me in our discussions. Their feeling came mainly from the experience of the Large Group. It was thus possible to speculate that the Large Group, including AS as its consultant, was a container into which managers were depositing some of their uncertainties and anxieties about the unknown future into which the Programme was taking them, while in their other roles, both within the established departments (where some organizational boundaries were being re-aligned) and within the newer working groups, they were tackling their tasks with greater energy and effectiveness. I am not suggesting that it functioned only as a container: it was certainly seen by at least some of its members as a crucible where new ideas and also new values were being forged and tested for application in their other roles. I am in no doubt, however, that an innovative developmental programme of this nature requires the formation of new and separate sub-institutions, such as the Large Group, which have a degree of insulation from the 'real work,' in order to provide a legitimate forum not only for the debate of major issues, such as the forms of industrial democracy, but for the voicing of either 'crazy' ideas or doubts and anxieties that, if left unexpressed, get in the way of the 'real work.'

Throughout this period, direct participation in the Large Group and the People Programme generally was largely restricted to the 'management group' of about 120 people (though there had been some leavings and joinings), and the ECG remained the only forum for the rest of the organization. The ECG was kept informed of the Programme. Indeed a progress report by AS and OK from which I quoted earlier was prepared at the request of the ECG in August 1975 and urged the importance of extending the work done with the management group to include all members of the organization. The ECG discussed this but reached no conclusion. What it did, however, was to ask AS and OK to carry out a survey of the way in which the ECG was perceived within Omicron. They conducted interviews with all ECG representatives and deputy representatives (20 in all) and a further 40 with constituents selected at random. Additionally a stratified random sample of 184 employees received a questionnaire: on this there was a 60 percent return.[3] The findings were not comforting. Among the main points to emerge were:

1. There is considerable diversity of opinion within the ECG itself as to what its function is on site.
2. There is lack of information available for constituents to assess the performance of the ECG.
3. There appear to be gross failures of communication between the representatives and the constituents that makes it difficult for the representatives to fulfil the expectations of the constituents.
4. In some instances there is a clear divergence between the way the representative sees his role on the ECG and the way the constituents see the role of the ECG.
5. There appear to be certain omissions in the representational structure.
6. Correctly or not, many people are worried that representatives may use their position on the ECG to obtain privileges denied to others.

Thus the ECG was faced with basically re-examining its objectives and method of working. It proceeded to do this in a series of five special meetings between January and March 1976.

I have said that at this time the People Programme seemed more firmly entrenched than ever. However, this is not to be taken as implying that the Programme was static: on the contrary. Overall management of the

Application: Miller

company had for some time been vested in a group consisting of the general manager and five executive managers. This Executive Management Team (EMT) operated on the cabinet model of collective responsibility, the general manager being roughly equivalent to prime minister. Careful distinctions were drawn between actions taken by members on behalf of the EMT collectively, and actions taken in their departmental roles. Management of the People Programme was plainly in the former category. (Thus when PEG wanted to sponsor its own 'People Programme' for members of the Engineering Department, the negotiations were between PEG and EMT—as distinct from other possibilities, such as between PEG and the manufacturing manager or the personnel manager.) Probably, in fact, the confidence with which the new general manager and his EMT were operating made possible the surge of new developments that occurred between March and May 1976. Here I will only record the main events, without elaboration, in order to give a flavour of the internal life of Omicron at that time:

1. After the fourth special meeting of the ECG, the stewards of the three major unions met as a Combined Trades Unions Select Committee (CTUSC) and resolved not to participate in the ECG in its present form; but they were prepared to take part in a form of participation with higher management.
2. The ECG decided to disband and to re-form, with the same membership but a different task, as an Employee Participation Discussion Group (EPDG), this being seen as a transitional body that would disband when an appropriate representative system had been created.
3. CTUSC was equivocal about taking part in the EPDG and began a direct dialogue with the EMT to discover senior management's view of participation. The EMT also agreed to a request from CTUSC for observers to attend EMT meetings 'as a learning experience.'
4. EPDG and CTUSC agreed to send out a joint document to all employees on participation. A document was drafted but not sent.
5. Representatives of the Large Group (LG) were invited to a CTUSC meeting and it was agreed to send out a joint letter to all employees on participation. A letter was drafted but not sent.
6. The LG established a separate Research Group. (An initial list of eleven potential research topics was prepared. Examples were: 'the nature of authority in a representative system of management'; 'what part does scrap play in the dynamics of the site?'; 'the place of myth in understanding the development of organization'; and, of most immediate concern, 'how to develop a representative system for participation at Omicron.')
7. The LG, with some qualms, opened its membership to all employees on site. The half-dreaded, half-hoped-for inundation did not occur, but a few faces appeared and two newcomers were drafted as Coordinators.

That list of events demonstrates the active search by various groupings in the company to find new ways of engaging with each other and with the site as a whole. It also illustrates the difficulty of risking change. However, it should be noted that amidst this evident ferment, the 'real work' of Omicron was continuing unimpaired.

The consultants were not unaffected by the ferment. As the external consultant, I had experienced, from the previous autumn onwards, increasing difficulty in occupying an effective role in relation to the internal consultants. One interpretation of this was that there was increasing uncertainty about their role in relation to the client system. Who was the client? AS and OK were working with a variety of different groupings and saw themselves as actually, or at least potentially, consultants to the entire organization. From the outset they had seen this as the requisite position from which to help the people of Omicron to re-examine the implicit 'rules' that they had collectively adopted. On the other hand, an alternative view could be that the client was the departing general manager. It was he who had negotiated the original contract with them and who authorized the spending of money on the consultancy. (One can see that such a view would be comforting for those with doubts about committing themselves to the People Programme.) In this construction, the client system was certainly no broader than the senior management group—the EMT. Meanwhile, increasing demands were being made on the time of AS and OK; yet it was by no means clear whether the determination of priorities rested on their professional authority or on the EMT's managerial authority. In either case, what kinds of mechanisms were required to sanction the authority? In my judgment, it was therefore made extremely difficult to hold on to a notion of the organization as a whole and to interpret events and processes in the context of that overall dynamic. From the technical point of view, therefore, the consultants' role needed to be redefined in order to make that more possible. A further point was that there was a recognized need to develop some of Omicron's own staff to take on part-time consultant roles, as a means of making the experience of the original management group of 120 more widely available. Who was to be responsible first for their training and subsequently for the work they did in the consultant role? For this quite distinct task it seemed more appropriate that their authority should be derived from membership—albeit temporary—of a professional group, rather than from the management of the company.

In March 1976, we therefore proposed to the EMT that the consultancy resources currently available to Omicron for the People Programme—i.e., OK, AS and, on a part-time basis, myself—should be brought together as a quasi-independent Consulting Resource Group (CRG), separate from, but available to, the Omicron organization as a whole. One image used later was of the CRG as a man-made satellite of Omicron, thus potentially, at least, having a perspective on the company that would not be available from a consulting position within the boundary. We postulated that from the position outside we should be better able than we had been as Large Group consultants to help the organization to explore the interrelationship between the internal dynamics of Omicron and its transactions across the boundary with systems in its environment. Given that the CRG would be analogous to these external systems, we inferred that the behaviour of the organization towards CRG would reflect significant aspects of these other transactions across the boundary. This can perhaps be illuminated by reference back to Fig. 2-1. Assume that M represents Omicron, that m_1, m_2, m_3 ... m_n represent sub-systems within the organization, and that C represents the CRG. We would expect the CRG's experience of its relationship to M to throw light on the $m_1 \leftrightarrow m_2$ relationship. But the dynamics would be more complex than in a conference, where M is a temporary group formed for the purpose of learning and C (the consultant) is the most significant system in its environment. In the model we were proposing, M (Omicron) was a system with its own established transactions with external systems, while C (the CRG) was to be a more temporary system, though in a special relationship to the client system. In this context we postulated that the relationship between M and C would shed light not only on $m_1 \leftrightarrow m_2$ relationships internal to M, but also on relationships between M and other systems in its environment (not marked in Fig. 2-1). In this way, M could begin to study how, *as a system*, it managed its main boundaries with its environment.

This account must end with the EMT's acceptance of our proposal in May 1976. The following extract comes from the EMT's announcement of its decision:

> The People Programme at Omicron was set up in 1974. Its aim was to help all of us, as individuals and collectively, to broaden and deepen our understanding of this organization and our various relationships to it. By examining how the organization actually functions—more fully and openly than is normally done—we are well on the way to achieving not only enhanced business performance but also increased individual learning and personal growth.
>
> In normal day to day situations the opportunity to do this does not present itself very often. Yet without such opportunities, learning cannot take place.
>
> In order to pursue this aim further, the EMT has created the Consulting Resource Group. The CRG has, as its primary task, the creation of opportunities for learning that, if taken by the organization, will lead to a progressive and cumulative gain in the ability of employees to understand the processes that operate within the organization in terms of relations between individuals in their various roles at work, between groups, and between the organization and the outside world.

CONCLUDING COMMENTS

Perhaps a better heading for this closing section would be 'Interim Comments,' since what has been reported is very much work in progress. And the direction of the 'progress' is unknown.

Organizational Development and Industrial Democracy

That open-endedness, however, to me is one of the most crucial features of this approach. In our role as consultants, we can give people an opportunity to extend their personal and conceptual understanding of relations between individuals, between groups and between systems. We can help them to reflect on what they are doing as they apply this understanding in their work-roles and relationships. We can draw their attention to assumptions they are making and to choices they may not have recognized, and in this way they can acquire greater consciousness of the organization as a system and of their own actual and potential contributions to the shaping of that organization. We can offer them greater scope for managing themselves in their roles. But what we cannot do is to predetermine what use they will make of these opportunities. Perhaps one of our more important functions, as they set about their task of managing themselves, is simply to be available.

Open-endedness is often found frightening by managers (and also by some OD consultants) who therefore often seem to impose limits on the development of participative processes: thus far and no further. Part of managers' fear, I think, is that their competence will come under close scrutiny; part, too, is that if the managerial role and authority are called into question, this poses a threat to all the trappings of 'management'— the assumption of power, status, privileges, the sense of self-importance, and so on. Such fears are not without foundation. Unbridled participation certainly does invite scrutiny of the ways in which roles are performed. But what tends to be forgotten is that appraisal of superiors by subordinates does not originate with participation. Judgments are constantly being made; and corresponding patterns of behaviour are developed as a means of exploiting weaknesses or expressing contempt. Sometimes these take the form of adjustments to the work-role itself; sometimes the union role is used as the vehicle. Participative mechanisms, therefore, do not provoke appraisal of superiors as a new phenomenon; they are much more likely to sanction the overt expression of views that have hitherto been covert.

Notwithstanding the immense gulf between the affluent industrial worker in western society and the Third-World peasant living in squalor and poverty, the industrial worker in his relationship to his work-place has something in common with the underdeveloped or the handicapped, in that within his work-role as such he is frequently in a dependent and relatively impotent position. To be sure, he may invent devices to cope with his situation, but they do not basically alter the typical posture of inferiority and subordination. He often has to rely on union membership to redress the balance. Hence, as I indicated earlier, the union becomes the vehicle for expressing the fight that in the work relation has to be suppressed. The People Programme at Omicron makes room for more than one set of roles and role-relationships within the work-setting. On some issues, such as the optimum product-mix, the general manager can properly be expected to proffer an expert opinion; but on others, such as the values that the organization of the company should be pursuing, the shop-floor worker and the general manager are fellow-employees and it is difficult to argue that one should expect to impose his values on the other. Thus it is possible for the individual to take on more than one kind of role within the work-setting and in this way exercise greater control over his environment.

However, even in the work-role itself that the individual occupies within the task system, there is the possibility of exercising greater or lesser influence in relation to his environment. Every individual employee may be conceived as being a 'manager' in two senses. First, there is management of the boundary between person and role: the individual determines what skills, attitudes, feelings, etc., he will devote to the role and what he will withhold. Secondly, there is management of activities within the role and of transactions with other role-holders. These two elements are included in the term, 'managing oneself in role.' In practice, therefore, the individual will act as a manager in these two senses: the issue is whether room will be made for him to do this in the service of the task of the organization or, alternatively, perhaps, to its detriment. The role that we more conventionally think of as managerial is located on the boundary of a system or subsystem and is concerned with regulating the linkages between the internal activities of the system and its external environment. The task of this type of managerial role can be defined as: 'To provide the boundary conditions within which members of the organization manage their roles and relationships in such a way as to produce effective performance of the task.' Thus the People Programme, by legitimating the notion of 'managing oneself in role,' leads to that somewhat austere, task-oriented definition of managerial roles and calls into question other kinds of behaviour associated more with power and status than with task. These are no longer available as covers for incompetence in task performance.

If this kind of shift is threatening to some managers, it may also be threatening to trades unions, since the employee who is managing himself in role, and who is not tied to a posture of dependency in relation to superiors, has less need of the union to carry 'fight' on his behalf. But this in no way implies that unions become redundant, any more than managers cease to be necessary. What it does mean is that union leaders, like managers, have to adjust to the demands of more sophisticated constituents, who may be looking not for a body to conduct a vicarious fight against management at a basic assumption level, but for advice and support in negotiating opportunities for participation that make more space for individual development and responsibility.

In general, therefore, the approach I have been discussing assails established dependency relationships, between managers and managed and between union leaders and their constituents, as well as assailing 'fight' relationships between unions and management. Authority, by becoming detached from rank and status, and attached instead to task and role, is available to each member of the organization. Conflict partly moves out of the well-known channels into new and shifting configurations. Hence it is not only to managers and trades union representatives that open-endedness is frightening; its consequences affect everyone. When I speak, therefore, of the importance of consultants' availability, I have in mind their function of receiving some of the dislodged dependency during these transitions. Beyond that, they have the task of trying to interpret such shifts in the dependency structure as a further way of helping the client system to understand these internal processes.

To sum up: the essential feature of the People Programme at Omicron, in my view, is that it aims to give each employee, regardless of role or level, a greater opportunity to consider what is happening in the relationship between himself and the organization and, if he so wishes, to seek new or modified roles within which he can exercise his authority. By extension, the same opportunity is available to groups within the organization and to the organization as a collectivity in relation to its environment. The primary task of the consultants in this setting is to try to clarify, as rigorously and uncompromisingly as they can, processes as they occur, the proposition being that this is the best way of helping members of the client system to discover their own authority. Attempts either by company management or by consultants to pre-structure new roles and mechanisms, and to ordain who is entitled to discuss what issues and when, are a negotiation of participation. Just as my experience of rural development suggests that it is not enough for a community to gain greater control over its internal or local environment—such changes have to be accompanied also by acquisition of greater control over the external environment—so in the case of 'industrial democracy' or 'organizational development' I postulate that significant developments will not be sustained unless participants also extend their authority into management of the external boundary of the relevant client system, whether that is a primary work-group, a production department or the enterprise as a whole.

18.

THE ASSISTED INDEPENDENT LIVING PROGRAM (AIL): A NEW MODEL FOR COMMUNITY CARE

Niles M. Medders and Arthur D. Colman[1]

INTRODUCTION

In San Francisco, as in other areas across the country, agencies are experimenting with a variety of new models to find programs capable of filling the gap between full and partial treatment facilities and independent community living for the chronic patient (Faulkner et al, 1983; Maux et al, 1973). Most notable are the satellite programs that provide reduced levels of clinical services in living environments that approximate, but do not require, fully independent functioning (Beard, 1978). In this model, a residential program leases or buys an apartment or a house in the community to be sublet to individual patients or groups of patients. The residential treatment program then provides a variety of counseling services in practical living skills such as shopping, house maintenance, cooking, etc., in addition to continuing work on interpersonal skills. The patient continues to be connected to the residential program from which he had "graduated" while learning to live more on his own. Satellite programs have been successful in helping patients move on from residential treatment programs with less stress and recidivism (Lamb, 1981). However, they have been less effective in helping patients to make the more difficult transition to true independence in the community. The formal and informal links of the patients to the residential treatment programs often seem to foster dependence on that system rather than promoting autonomy in the "outside" world.

The program presented in this paper was developed as a nondependency oriented model to provide opportunities for patients to learn how to make the transition from the clinically intensive 24-hour care programs to independent functioning in the community.

PROGRAM DEVELOPMENT: THEORY

The AIL program had its beginnings in 1976 in San Francisco's Mandala House, a residential treatment program that was part of Baker Places, Inc.,

273

a agency that runs several treatment facilities for chronic mental patients. One of us (N.M.), then director of Mandala, had become interested in the use of "Tavistock" group relations theory, specifically the relationship between formal authority structures and unconscious group life in organizations, to clarify the treatment task of the program (Rioch, 1975; Colman, 1975). Focusing on excessive dependency as a central intrapersonal and institutional impediment to effective functioning in clinical settings, the program was reorganized to transfer authority gradually from staff to patients (Bion, 1961). Over several years, staff learned to delineate and modify more accurately their authority and responsibility in the treatment system. For example, by the end of a patient's stay, staff tried to become an additive rather than a limit-setting resource as patients took more responsibility for their own behavior in most areas of their lives. It was distressing, therefore, to see so many patients still unable to use either Mandala House or a satellite program as a way station to full return to the community.

Our efforts to understand the difficulty in transferring and maintaining newly acquired skills to community living resulted in identifying two problems: first, the need to improve the methods by which daily living skills taught at Mandala House were applied to living in the community; and second, the formal authority structure of both residential treatment programs and satellite housing programs. Thus, although entry into Mandala House was voluntary, its patients often had little real choice about agreeing to come. Once in, they could exert little formal authority except to leave prematurely through a variety of routes—most labeled maladaptive. Despite determined efforts to elicit "patient involvement," none of the program elements belonged to them. Of course, they felt far more responsible for their behavior and had more options than in a hospital setting, but their actual authority had not changed; they still lived as dependents in a system designed, operated and ultimately controlled by others. The staff might act as if they were delegating some of their authority to the patients, but the patients could never, in reality, take that authority from the staff.

The formal constraints in the satellite housing facility were similar. While it was true that staff allowed patients to take more responsibility for their own lives by reducing clinical services, in a formal sense as long as the facility was *owned and operated by the treatment facility, the patients have no real authority of their own except to leave.*

We recognized that dependency systems of this kind are appropriate for many learning tasks, including the treatment and rehabilitation of individuals with severe mental illness (Cumming and Cumming, 1967). However, we came to believe that such systems can never approximate independent living where authority is, by definition, vested in the individual and not the caretaker. From this viewpoint, the transition from a residential treatment facility to satellite housing is not on a continuum between dependence and independence at all but rather falls between greater and lesser degrees of dependence. For the patient, the real transition to independent living is not bridged.

Since the symptomatic onset of their illness, and often before, most of our patients had never experienced themselves as successfully functioning independent persons (Goldman et al, 1981). Most could look to few if any successful independent accomplishments. They had moved from one dependent setting to another. The self image engendered by continuing perceived inadequacy and incompetence was both pessimistic and, eventually, highly resistant to change. In residential and satellite programs, they correctly perceived themselves as functioning successfully in a system in which they had no formal authority and upon which they were, in fact, totally dependent. While they moved from one such system to another, their experience of independence remained anchored in fantasy. Viewed from an organizational perspective, in order to break this cycle, it would be necessary to design a transitional program in which actual authority, not conditional authority, was with the patients, a program in which staff did not delegate authority because they never had it.

The AIL program was developed with both requirements in mind. Patients would live in their own homes, a setting in which _they_, not the clinical staff, had formal (legal) authority and in which _they_ could take the opportunity to learn skills that enhanced independent living. This would be accomplished by allowing clinical staff to operate as consultants, professionals whose skills were for hire—and fire—to individuals and groups with chronic mental illness who wanted to live independently in the community. Clients requesting consultation from the AIL program would be helped in all ways possible to attain their goals. Skills necessary to choose roommates, to find an appropriate apartment or house, to negotiate with landlords, setting up the home, as well as interpersonal and living skills—in essence, whatever was needed to establish and maintain a successful independent living situation—were areas in which the consultant would aid the client. Independence would become a reality, not an illusion. The program would be organized so that the bottom line was always clear: if the clients decided to fire a consultant, the consultant left and the client stayed home!

The critical concept in the program design was changing the formal staff role from caretaker to consultant. When first presented, this concept was not an easy one for staff to grasp, particularly those trained in conventional residential treatment settings where authority is never actually relinquished. A far different conceptualization of role and function was required, somewhat akin to a voluntary outpatient clinic. For most staff, the role of consultant was new, particularly the notion that their clients, not they, held authority over treatment and living space. In fact, the staff had to be retrained to see their roles differently. They needed to learn how to support the client's taking the concrete steps necessary to establish independent households without deviating from their consultancy framework. Clients also found it difficult to accept this concept, for real independence required a return to, or development of, their own authority and a retreat from blaming "the system" for their difficulties. Perhaps the most difficult part of the program was establishing this concept in the development of the first few households. Once that was accomplished and anxiety allayed, program growth was rapid.

PROGRAM DEVELOPMENT: PRACTICE

Screening and Referral

Clients are referred to the AIL program by crisis services, day treatment programs, residential treatment programs, private practitioners, state hospitals and by themselves. All diagnostic categories of mentally disabled are accepted; most clients fall into chronic schizophrenia, manic depressive, or severe borderline disorders. Additionally, the program works with a few households of higher functioning developmentally disabled clients and two families with young children in which the parents' psychiatric difficulties had resulted in the children being abused. Staff attempts to screen out those individuals who do not fulfill most of the following minimum levels of functioning:

1. Ability to plan, purchase ingredients for, and prepare three simple meals with minimum staff support.
2. Ability to use public transportation.
3. Ability to manage money with staff support.
4. Sufficient impulse control to contact staff, their therapist or crisis services when needed.
5. Motivation to live independently with at least two other people.
6. Sufficient money to cover the expenses of living independently, about $450.00 per month.

The program serves clients between 18 and 65 years of age. It does not serve clients who pose an imminent risk of doing physical harm to themselves or others, or clients with a primary problem of drug or alcohol abuse.

An intake interview of the applicant is conducted to obtain a psychiatric history. Following acceptance into the program, the client is seen individually for at least three sessions. The purpose of the individual meeting is focused on answering the question: "Given the difficulties you've had in the past, what would need to be true of your home for it to be a stable and supportive setting?" The client then develops a list of criteria he or she will use in selecting housemates and in finding housing. Typical criteria include cost of housing, desired locale, proximity to transportation, type of relationship desired with housemates, personality characteristics of housemates and household management structures. Clients at the lower end of the functioning scale are frequently not able to answer these questions directly and staff needs to help them formulate goals and criteria. Additionally, the individual meetings address the development of an individual treatment contract. The contract deals generally with the clinical commitment of the program to the client and the client's responsibility to the program. In its initial phases, before the household is formed, the contract focuses on the client's long-term goals such as comfort and assertiveness in groups, finding a stable living environment and moving towards volunteer or paid employment. In addition, it identifies individual problem areas that have, in the past, hindered achievement of these goals. Once the household is formed, this general contract becomes a frame for more specific areas of work for the individual. In the course of consultation, when problems surface the client is reminded of his contract and held accountable to work towards realizing the goals outlined in it.

Consulting to a New Household

Once the client's individual program has been developed, he is referred to the group interview to meet other program members who are seeking roommates. Staff facilitates sharing of individual criteria and discussion of areas of agreement and difference between interviewees. Following the group interview, staff meets individually with participants to help them evaluate the potential housemates. Generally, after two to four group interviews, clients will have found appropriate partners to form a household group, usually of four people.

At this point, staff shifts to a more consultative role in working with the household group. The groups meets with staff two to three times weekly, and together they review individual goals and renegotiate a household contract common to all members. A household management structure is agreed to, differences are reviewed—will people eat dinner together, will there be a regular social outing—and compromises effected. Once the household has developed its household contract, the focus of meetings shifts to the primary task at hand: finding a house or an apartment.

Now the group must assess its resources and decide on the price range, location, size, etc. Staff teaches clients how to fill out rental application forms and how to talk to landlords and rental agents. The sources of rental information are identified and the group begins to delegate tasks. One roommate will check the local newspaper, another the rental library, and a third the local real estate company specializing in rental property. Staff strongly encourages the group to meet together, not less than three times weekly, to look at and submit applications for houses. The group is advised that they must commit to this process generally and not become emotionally invested in acquiring any particular house. They must face being rejected because they don't have jobs, are receiving government money or "look different." The household will usually look for three to five weeks before finding housing. Meetings with staff focus on supporting them during this difficult stage. Staff occasionally accompanies lower functioning clients when they look for housing.

Once a house has been found, plans are made for the move to their new home. The group has now become a household. A schedule for meetings with staff is established when clients have moved in. This schedule will vary depending on the level of functioning of the household and will involve more support during the first few months until the household feels relatively secure in their new home and with one another. At the minimum, a new household will meet twice weekly, always at the clients' home. These meetings will focus on practical household management problems: how will the rent be paid, who will pay it, when will it be done, how will others get their share to the rent payer? Payment of all other household expenses, such as utilities, telephone, and food, as well as practical housekeeping tasks like cooking and cleaning, will be clarified in the same detail.

In general the program is designed to adjust the amount of support to the need of a household. For example, households requiring higher levels of clinical support will receive up to fifteen hours per week of additional staff time. At the most intensive level of support, a typical schedule might be three one-hour consultative household meetings per week, one hour with each individual, and three to four hours three days per week of practical support such as preparation of dinner and food shopping.

As a household develops the capacity for management of the physical environment, the consultant's emphasis naturally shifts to interpersonal concerns. This work differs from individual or group therapy—for which the consultants have no contract with their clients—because the focus is on the way behavior might improve or interfere with successful independent living. Now the consultant's task is to support development of the skills of living together: relating, empathizing and problem solving.

In general, households develop through three stages of maturation that affect program operations. Stage one is characterized by a primary concern with the physical survival and the stability of the household, focusing on details such as ensuring that bills get paid and that food is in the refrigerator. Stage two is primarily concerned with the emotional needs of the household members, issues such as—how can I get what I want from my roommates, how much do they want from me and what can I afford to give, and can I accept that my roommates may not be able to meet all of my needs? In stage three, the focus shifts to the future and members' relationships with the outside world, to issues such as returning to school or getting a job. The consultant must be sensitive to these changing stages and support both individual and group growth and development as they progress.

Developing a Community

The final component of the AIL model is the development of a larger peer support network (Tolsdorf, 1976). Cluster Meetings composed of three to five households meet monthly with a consultant to share information, experiences and ideas. Attendance at this meeting is one of the requirements for remaining in the program. The content is <u>in the hands of the clients</u>; the staff acts as consultant to the group. Semi-annually there is a meeting of the entire program—the Community Meeting—usually about eighty to one hundred people. This meeting combines committee reports and a party.

These Cluster and Community meetings have given birth to a number of different offsprings, such as a weekly women's group, a bi-weekly philosophy group, an activities committee of elected representatives that plans monthly activities for the entire program, and an AILP monthly

The Assisted Independent Living Program

newsletter, "Rave Reviews." There is also a client-owned and operated credit union (gross assets = $700.00) where clients save $2.00 per month (at 5% interest) and loans are made for household start-up costs (security deposits), emergency loans (a lost SSI check), and home improvements (a vacuum cleaner).

Staff

Staffing organization and structure resemble an out-patient department or a consulting unit more than a residential treatment program. Each staff member serves as a consultant to several households, the number varying depending on the functioning level of the households. Typically a staff member works with individuals until they form a household group, and continues consulting to that group as they find and develop a functioning living environment in the community.

In 1984, the program staff consisted of one director, one clinical supervisor, one consultant, and seven clinicians. The Director was responsible for overall administration, personnel management and budget operation and negotiations. The Clinical Supervisor was responsible for direct supervision of staff, monitoring general service delivery, coordination of linkages with other units and overseeing documentation of clinical services (charting). The Coordinators provided direct services to clients and carried a caseload of twelve to twenty clients living in three to five households. The Consultant (A.C.) worked with the director and staff in a variety of roles including consultation to the director and/or clinical supervisor as well as clinical and organizational consultation to staff on a weekly basis. He also was involved in program design and staff training. Most importantly, the consultant's mode of functioning provided an ongoing model for staff as a mirror image of the way staff worked with their clients.

Results and Discussion

A pilot program was started in August 1976, with a half-time staff person (N.M.) serving ten clients in three households. Over the next 6-1/2 years, the program was expanded to its current operational level of about 105 clients in 21 households. Overall, 250 clients have been served in 35 households.

Who were served? Almost all clients carried long-standing chronic psychotic diagnoses, the majority schizophrenia. The age range of clients was between 18 and 67 with 60 percent falling between 25 and 35. Sixty-two percent were male and 38 percent were female. Most had been totally dependent on the residential services sector of the mental health sytem for many years. An index of this chronicity is reflected in the fact that prior to entering the program, clients averaged 3.8 hospital admissions per year, spending 32 days per year in the hospital.

How well were they served? On a pragmatic level, although the number of hospitalizations per year did not change significantly, the length of hospitalization decreased from 32 days per year to 7 days per year for clients who spent at least six months in the program. This probably reflects the greater motivations on the part of the clients to return to their own homes. Another important measure of benefit is financial. In San Francisco an inpatient bed costs approximately $400 per day. The cost of intensive Community Mental Health System residential treatment programs is $40 to $100 while other forms of satellite housing programs cost $15 to $35. The AIL program costs $8 per day (exclusive of rent paid by clients) (San Francisco CMHS Budget). Clients receive no financial subsidies from the AIL program; there are no capital or overhead costs for housing or maintenance. The only expense is the cost of an office for staff—thus AIL is an extremely cost effective program.

The most important benefits measure of any mental health program must, of course, be on a human level, the quality of life of the mentally disabled people involved. Objective measures here are far more difficult and beyond the scope of this program.[2] It could be argued that the AIL program reduced the comfort level of its clients by requiring a degree of independence most previously felt unable to achieve. In fact, approximately 60 percent of the clients who met the criteria for admission either dropped out or failed to form households and were discharged within the first six months. It is important to note, however, that many of these returned to try again and were successful on their second or third try.

We are not saying that it is easy for any of our clients to form and maintain independent living systems. Large amounts of practical and emotional support are required, and provided, at every stage of the process. The clients are accustomed to failure and to mental health professionals taking charge of their lives. It is extremely difficult for staff to remain in the consultant role, for it implies continued rejection of the dependency assumptions that are such a basic part of the client's illness and interpersonal strategies and staff's professional stance. Our sense with most of our clients is that living independently as part of a community of households and receiving continued consultation of the kind AIL offered is not necessarily more difficult than dealing with other treatment systems and living environments. Independence is frightening for our client group, but it is also heady stuff with a positive dynamic of its own once the clients really understand that the AIL program staff believes that they can be on their own, are prepared to prove it, and only have the authority to consult to them while they do it.

Given the clients' chronic disabilities and the staff's inexperience with our consultative model, the development of an independent household is indeed a challenging endeavor. Our clients are referred primarily from protected environments such as residential treatment, inpatient settings or disturbed families. They all have major doubts, conscious and unconscious, about their ability to select appropriate roommates, find adequate housing and, most importantly, remain stable in the community. And for the most part, that skepticism is warranted. These individuals have few skills or achievements that they can point to with pride. The program has to offer a realistic hope that their future can be better than their past. And staff needs to deliver on that promise by directing clients to look to themselves and, most importantly, to their household group to solve problems.

Assuming Authority

One household of three men with long (5 to 10 years) histories of institutionalization confronted a typical issue of independent living when, after moving into an apartment, they were deluged with freeloading guests. At a household meeting a few days after moving in, they were discussing how to say no to "friends" dropping by for dinner or to spend the night. It became apparent none of them had ever been in a position of having the authority or the responsibility of controlling the boundaries to their home. In their lives, that role had been filled by parents, halfway house counselors or board and care home operators. With the help of consultation, an agreement was made that before anyone was invited over or allowed into the apartment all three of the house members would discuss and decide whether or not they wanted that guest. While no single individual was strong enough to protect themselves from intrusion, as a group they seemed far more capable of exercising that authority. Over a period of four months of work reinforcing their procedure, individuals in this household felt more clear about the criteria of the household in relation to guests and more authorized to enforce that criteria on their own initiative.

Locating authority and accountability in the household group for day-to-day problem solving provides opportunities for change that may not be possible when problems are routed through the clinician. For clients with histories of long institutionalization—whether it be in the community, residential treatment programs, board and care homes or on inpatient or state hospital wards—there is little opportunity to exercise real control over their lives. While they have learned various living and social skills, it has always been in a protected setting. Making the transfer to the world outside is a process approached with much anxiety and ambivalence.

Developing Accountability

In one group this ambivalence showed up in their inability to save enough money to move to their own home. They confidently sat down with staff and planned their individual budgets and then proceeded to spend all their money on nonessentials. Discussions of this problem resulted in expressions of guilt, despair, astonishment and pleas for help, in the form of a loan from the program; in other words, they were asking staff to take over for them. Instead, staff suggested this potential household establish a joint checking account that required the signature of any two of the household members in order to cash a check. This meant the individuals would have to confer and agree before any of the money allocated to saving for the house could be spent. The group was forced to address their commitments to one another and to themselves individually rather than struggling with staff over authority issues, in this instance, as an avoidance mechanism.

All of the problems of living encountered in work with households offered opportunities for the development of individual and group problem-solving skills and the increased sense of confidence that comes with a new sense of competence. In an increasingly complicated and automated world, all of us are confronted with perplexing situations in our day-to-day lives. Given the range of disabilities, the shortage of real skills and the deficiencies in self-confidence in our clients, it is not surprising that they perceived their inability to manage difficult challenges of day-to-day living as more proof that they are failures.

Dealing with a Complex World

A recent illustration of this occurred with a group of five clients who recently moved into their own home. At the end of their first month, they received the phone bill—a twelve-page document. They had attempted to calculate their individual phone calls (in fact, had actually done so) but there was still a sizeable amount unaccounted for. The fear of everyone (unstated) was that somebody had not been honest, either one of the household or, less probably, the phone company. Something they had not considered was that the bill itself was difficult to understand. It consisted of regular monthly service charges, amortized start-up costs, local county user fees, etc. The forty-five minutes spent by staff working with the household as they tried to calculate their fair shares was frustrating for everyone; what was learned was that some things are just hard to figure out and not necessarily someone's fault or because of their illness.

Once a group has settled into their home they are certain to experience periods where one member is in a state of distress including making suicide threats, overt psychoses and hospitalizations. The group's ability and their commitment to deal supportively with these periods is often more effective than interventions by staff.

Dealing with Decompensation

In one household where a client had stopped taking her Lithium, the other residents expressed their concern about her not sleeping and acting in bizarre ways such as shouting back at her voices. One resident expressed the concern and the household's commitment and expectation when he said, "Mary, when I am going through what you are, I want my roommates to tell me, 'Go to the hospital and get back on medication.'" Everyone else nodded saying, "Yes, me too." In this context staff had only to supply technical assistance, i.e., transportation; there was no question of being "forced to go to the hospital by my counselor."

Over time, it is the community of households, as much as each separate household, that has the greatest potential of supporting clients living relatively normal lives on their own time (Pattison et al, 1975; Sokolvsky et al, 1978; Hammer, 1981). It provides a secure social base that transcends the individual turmoil—hospitalizations, depression, withdrawal—that is so much a given in chronic mental illness. In fact, we came to see the ability to rely on the larger community support as a major predictor of long term success in, and eventual graduation from, the AIL program. Thus an individual might progress from dependence on the consultant staff, to reliance on roommates, to the ability to trust and share in the larger community.

In 1983, one of us (N.M.) was asked to develop an AIL program in Marin County as part of Buckelew Houses, a social rehabilitation agency serving that community. This has given us a chance to see how much of the ethos and design of this program is transferable to a more affluent and suburban community, and how well the San Francisco program would withstand a critical change in leadership. It is still too early to tell just how well the old program will survive and the new one develop. Thus far, however, the San Francisco AIL program has continued to function and is on the verge of a new expansion.[3] The program in Marin has grown to five households and three staff in its first year. Marin is a community that has developed a sophisticated residential treatment system that provides fairly long-term care to clients. The addition of an AIL type program there has presented clients and treaters with new options. It has become clear that introduction of this program involves considerable re-education of referers, staff and clients. We suspect that the introduction of an AIL model into other communities will require a similar readjustment, highlighting the power of belief systems, shared by clients and therapists alike, to determine the limits of function and futures of the mentally disabled.

CONCLUSION

The Assisted Independent Living (AIL) Program fills a perceived gap—between the clinically intensive CMHS residential treatment programs and full independent living in the community—in the treatment/rehabilitation of the chronically mentally ill. Mental health staff, acting solely in the role of consultants, aid clients drawn from residential programs and other components of the mental health system in an urban environment, in establishing their own living places within the community and joining these households into a community that supports and rewards independent living. A total of 105 clients in 1984 were maintained in a dynamic community of 21 such households each consisting of three or more residents, most of whom have been incapable of sustained independent living outside of treatment facilities. The success of this program is reflected in its adoption by another Bay Area County mental health system.

The AIL program offers an effective and humane model for aiding the chronically mental disabled to live independently in the community.

19.

A RETROSPECTIVE VIEW OF A HOSPITAL-WIDE GROUP RELATIONS TRAINING PROGRAM: COSTS, CONSEQUENCES AND CONCLUSIONS[1,2]

Roy W. Menninger

This article retrospectively examines the impact of an organization-wide group relations conference experience for professional staff training on a private mental hospital. More than a decade later, the residual assessment of the experience by a large majority of participants is strongly positive, both in regard to personal and professional benefits, and the impact on the organization itself. The conferences provided the organization with an approach to the trials of transition through a difficult period, and led to the development of several important new programs. The experience, however, was not entirely positive. Enthusiasm for the new knowledge of group dynamics led to an inappropriate use of groups as a procrustean method for managing hospital administrative issues, solving personal and professional problems and treating psychiatric patients. These problems were intensified by the simultaneous introduction of a therapeutic community concept into the hospital. The indiscriminate application of conference methods to the many tasks of a psychiatric institution reflected a failure to recognize that group relations training is a method of learning, not treatment nor management. Its limitations notwithstanding, the experience was undeniably positive.

INTRODUCTION

Eleven years ago, the author described how A.K. Rice (Tavistock) Conferences (Rice, 1965; Miller and Rice, 1967; Rioch, 1970b; Rioch, 1977) had influenced the professional staff of the Menninger Foundation

Application: Menninger

(R. Menninger, 1972; also Colman and Bexton, 1975). This article updates those comments and looks at the group relations conference (GRC) experience from a greater distance.

In 1972, the author described the crisis that abruptly confronted the organization in the mid-1960s when one founding brother died and the other partially retired. The organization's staff were deeply shaken by the loss of these charismatic leaders, as they had long depended upon them for leadership and direction. However the founders' paternalistic and authoritarian style had generated unexpressed resentment and suppressed rebellion. With the end of their era, therefore, feelings of relief and a new sense of freedom emerged.

Along with this new status came the need for organizational self-governance, a task for which its management groups lacked confidence, experience and guidance. Initially, however, they responded with enthusiasm, establishing a committee to provide effective direction and to maintain organizational cohesiveness while a new president was selected.

Shortly after the author was installed as president, latent anxieties within the organization became manifest. Resentments and disappointments generated by the previous administration became "bills due," and staff demanded that the president settle old scores, seemingly unaware that this was an impossible task. Departments sought special favors from the new president (as they had with the previous administration); rumors that many "private arrangements" were in place were widespread; competitive struggles for power and influence became more visible and more intense. Some staff were afraid that the president would not apply policy equally and fairly. Open splits developed, not only interdepartmentally but between professionals and administrators as well. Professional staff had long depreciated the nonclinically trained administrators, believing they had been too influential, were exclusively concerned with finances, and had no commitment to the idealistic goals of mental health professionals.

But perhaps the gravest anxiety arose because some members feared that the past would reassert itself in the form of another authoritarian leader. This anxiety was an ambivalent one for it also contained the unspoken hope that a strong leader would return to rescue an organization seemingly headed for decline and mediocrity.

Staff members responded to these concerns by holding evening meetings, establishing committees and "task forces," creating a professional organization, and meeting repeatedly with the president. Their objective was to create a reliable structure where all individuals would have an opportunity to contribute to organizational decision-making and that would protect them from the depredations of a potentially autocratic leader.

Although he understood these objectives and the feelings that stimulated them, initially the president unrealistically tried to listen to *every* concern by *every* person and *every* group. Urged and encouraged by staff, the president sought to create a series of participative structures, only to abandon them as each modification seemed inadequate to the tasks of channeling energies into the many challenges that faced the organization. At that point he was struggling with the long and difficult transition from his role as an empathic psychotherapist who dealt with the organization as if it were a patient, to the new and quite unfamiliar executive role.

Those were turbulent years, marked by considerable tension, arguments, episodic outbursts of hostile and paranoid feelings, and fragmentation of the staff into competing constituencies. As noted earlier (R. Menninger, 1972, p. 416; also see Colman and Bexton, 1975, p. 266), "a climate [of the organization was one] of anxiety and helplessness, punctuated by crises focusing on part of the organization with intense scapegoating attacks on the 'integrity' or 'pathology' of the individuals most prominently identified with the crisis group or issue."

The fortuitous exposure of several staff to the Tavistock Group Relations Conference in the late 1960s brought attention to an experiential program that seemed to offer a new understanding of organizational behavior. Soon after this initial contact, the president attended a group relations conference. He became enthusiastic about the possibility that this approach might enable the organization to manage divisive group phenomena and examine new styles of management while augmenting the traditional individual orientation with a better understanding of group behavior. He saw that this program had the potential capacity to bridge the gulf between "traditional" hospital management and therapeutic process, and might therefore assist in the vital task of integrating the two (Kernberg, 1982). Because the program was consonant with the president's participative management style and the evolving managerial patterns in the organization, he was willing to make the substantial financial commitment that would enable many staff members to participate in subsequent conferences.

During the six years between 1968 and 1974 that the GRC model was used by the Menninger Foundation as a major training device for staff, the administrative structures gradually stabilized and a sense of growth and movement was reestablished. Anxieties about power, control, and helplessness attenuated, and a new sense of individual autonomy and organizational strength emerged. Some discontented staff left and others more identified with the new president and his philosophy of participative management became department directors. At the same time administrative personnel within operating departments and in finance and human resources developed a higher level of managerial competence. Most importantly, the president became a more effective executive.

Identifying accurately the roles of the various influences that played a part during a difficult transition is obviously impossible. Ascribing all responsibility for the changes to a single influence such as the group relations conference training program would be inaccurate. Yet, the GRCs came at a propitious time and were undeniably helpful and supportive. In the author's view, they increased the momentum of a process that was already underway.

Though a relatively well-established program, the group relations conference as a method of learning about groups and institutions is still unfamiliar to many mental health professionals as well as executives and managers in business and industry. As background for this article, a brief description may suffice.

In a study of the training benefits of the group relations conference for mental health professionals, Correa et al. (1981) observed that group relations conference emerged from a

> "unique integration of the psychoanalytic theories of the British object relations school as characterized by the work of Melanie Klein (Segal, 1973) and Wilfred Bion (1959) and the sociotechnical approach to open systems illuminated by the work of Eric Miller and A. Kenneth Rice (Miller and Rice, 1967). This approach provides a depth view of the psychological dynamics of individual and group within the context of social and political realities . . . [with a special] focus . . . on the boundary between the individual and the group or organization."

Describing the conference structure, they noted that

> "the Tavistock training conference forms a temporary learning institution, a laboratory, in which participants are relatively free to study through experience as well as conceptualization, the covert dynamics within groups, the political mechanisms between groups, and the impact of authority and its exercise on the individual, the group, and the institution.
>
> "Conferences generally include two major kinds of events. "Here and Now" exercises are predominantly experiential events in which participants are faced with the task of learning about dynamics as they unfold. The staff function in a consultative role commenting on the unfolding process when they feel such comments will facilitate the work of the group. The refusal of staff to teach or lead in conventional ways by providing content or structure is generally experienced by the participants as frustrating. The freedom of individual members to explore the situation in which they find themselves is quite often constrained by the number of friends or colleagues who are sharing the experience. Thus, to the extent that a conference is made up of members and staff with significant outside relationships, there may be repercussions of the participant's behavior in the conference vis-a-vis these continuing relationships. To this extent then, the conference becomes less of a laboratory and more "real life." "Here and Now" exercises include small face to face groups, large groups, intergroup exercises (IGEs) and/or institutional events. These latter two exercises have an explicitly organizational focus.
>
> "The second type of events are discussions such as the review or plenary sessions, application groups, role analysis groups or lectures. These events focus on the content of particular topics in a conventional way. Although this is

much more familiar ground to most of the participants, the shift from the compelling experience of here and now exercises to the more cognitive mode of the discussion sessions is usually quite difficult and in itself provides learning."

With its focus nominally on "the nature of authority and the interpersonal and intergroup problems encountered in its exercise," (Rice, quoted in Rioch, 1970, 1975), considerable attention in actual practice is given to the social systems concept of boundaries of and between groups and between roles, and the responsibility of leadership to manage these boundaries (Singer, et al. 1975).

The nature and aim of the learning process in a group relations conference experience has received increasing attention since Bion's initial theoretical propositions about the forces governing group behavior (Bion, 1959) and the application of these concepts to group relations conferences by Rioch (1970a and 1970b) and Rice (1965). Palmer (1979) suggests that the learning shifts the participant's focus of attention and the way he or she construes social and institutional situations. He identifies five such changes:

As a result of this experience, the participant is:

1. Developing a habit of attention to his own ongoing experience;
2. Learning to recognize fantasy as a mode of experience, and to distinguish between fantasy and reality;
3. Learning to recognize the influence of shared fantasy in groups and organizations;
4. Becoming alert to the influence of fantasy in relations between leaders and followers;
5. Gaining facility in using some key theoretical concepts for describing the unconscious structuring and conscious organization of working groups.

As Klein suggests (Klein, 1983; Klein et al., 1983), participants in such conferences learn more when the teaching experience has strong sponsorship, strong authority linkages between members and staff, and strong sentient ties. Unquestionably, there was powerful reinforcement of such learning in this organization by virtue of the president's strong ideological and financial support for the program. His role as a member of the Board of the organization sponsoring the GRCs further enhanced this support.

By February 1972, 70 staff had attended at least one conference. Before the largest segment of participation ended in late 1974, a total of 132 staff had attended at least one conference and 50 had attended more than one. Subsequent to 1974, 10 more members participated in group relations conferences.

Summarized by levels of management and profession, the breakdown for the 142 staff members who participated is shown in Tables I and II.

To help with a difficult retrospective assessment, questionnaires were sent to the 76 professional staff at the Menninger Foundation who participated in one or more GRCs. Thirty-nine people responded (51%). These questionnaires were supplemented by selected interviews with sophisticated members and former staff who were an important part of that period. These remarks are a personal reassessment of the experience and in no sense a scientific study.

Table I. Number and Percentage of Staff Attending GRCs by Level of Administrative Responsibility

	Number attending	Percentage
Top management	18	13%
Middle management	44	31%
Professional staff	80	56%

Table II. Number and Percentage of Staff Attending GRCs by Discipline

	Number	Percentage of attendees	Percentage of discipline
Psychiatrists	52	37%	46% (113)[a]
Psychologists	23	16%	47% (49)
Social workers	22	16%	37% (60)
Nurses	16	11%	31% (51)
Administrators	12	8%	60% (20)
Unclassified	17	12%	
Totals	142	100%	44% (293)

[a] Total number of staff in each discipline.

NEAR-TERM RESULTS OF THE GRC TRAINING

As reported earlier (R. Menninger, 1972), staff who participated in the GRC were impressed with the power of the experience and with its relevance to their work. They reported a sharp increase in awareness of the importance of group processes, both within and between groups.

As the numbers of participants grew, efforts to apply the GRC in the organization appeared, generating new dynamics of stabilization and change. Increasingly the small group became the locus of therapeutic work within the adult hospital and the locus of organizational administration. Subdivisions moved away from decision making by one or two senior staff members to more broadly representative councils. New concepts appeared and the jargon changed; there were more references to "plenipotentiaries," IGEs (intergroup exercises), and "managing the boundaries." One department even formally identified administrative sessions as "Doorkeeping Meetings," using them to control departmental input.

In this climate, several important programs were started. Sensing a need for a shorter-term treatment than had been available, four senior staff—

all GRC participants—visited several psychiatric centers and returned to establish a group-interaction inpatient treatment unit. Shortly thereafter, the director of the adult hospital instituted a hospital-wide therapeutic community treatment program, building on the growing interest in group process.

These new programs further reinforced the organization's use of group process. Unrealistic enthusiasm infected some units, and group process came to be seen as the way for doing everything, from treating patients and managing administrative issues to handling personal problems. Meetings rapidly escalated in both number and frequency, and attendance grew to unwieldy proportions. Increasingly, leadership passed to those who had GRC experience, even though these group leaders were sometimes the least experienced professionals.

Rather early, the new perspective of group behavior added a dimension to an organizational culture that had been largely committed to an intrapsychic (psychoanalytic) theory of pathogenesis and treatment. Prior to GRC exposure, groups were considered to be little more than aggregations of individuals and without much therapeutic potential. For example, the outpatient group psychotherapy program failed to achieve high visibility and influence because individually oriented psychotherapists discounted its worth and consequently made few referrals.

Many psychoanalysts who participated in the GRC found it to be moving and instructive. One noted that next to his personal analysis, the GRC was the most powerful learning experience he had ever encountered. He and others, whose theoretical perspective was psychoanalytic, became more sympathetic to this new perspective.

Unfortunately, this new interest of the psychoanalysts coincided with the growth of a "True Believer" mentality among many GRC participants. This zealousness intensified the inherent conflict between individual and group approaches.

Since the adult hospital is the largest unit in the organization and had supplied the majority of GRC participants (80/142, or 56%), the group/individual tension became acutely manifest in the interactions between senior psychoanalysts (who served as consultants) and hospital personnel, who thought "outside consultants" simply did not understand inpatient work. The "limited" view of the consultants along with ambivalence about a perceived decrease in the relevance of intrapsychic perspectives to hospital treatment caused a bipolar splitting of the hospital staff from the psychoanalytic consultants similar to that described by Gustafson and Hausman (1975). Resistance to the individual psychodynamic input of consultants increased further as the GRC-induced preoccupation with groups reinforced the "here-and-now" orientation of the therapeutic community.

Developing a manageable group-individual balance was an ongoing task for the organization. Not until the mid-1970s did the organization achieve an integrated position that utilized both perspectives more appropriately.

One of the most dramatic benefits of the GRC was a marked reduction in the attacking/scapegoating/backbiting conduct so prominent during the late 1960s. Tendencies to use others as targets of blame were sharply checked by an awareness that such behavior was "just like the Group Relations Conference," and was therefore inappropriate. The GRC provided an understanding of the normative nature of such defensive but destructive behaviors, and helped moderate previously endemic attitudes and behavior.

The Intergroup Exercise added another dimension to understanding the distortions that can be generated in one group about the motivations of other groups, and a more objective understanding of the prevalence of myth and fantasy in "normal" intergroup relations. One discipline director commented that after the GRC, he became sensitized to the destructiveness of rumors generated by one group about another; when he returned home, he checked out all stories about his discipline, no matter how wild or unreasonable, and conscientiously sought the facts from whomever, up to and including the president.

During this time, the use of group processes in corporate administrative procedures also increased. In the president's Interdepartmental Council, all administrative issues—from the budget to matters affecting only several people—had been placed on the agenda, discussed, reviewed, and commonly postponed without decision. The emphasis then was on the quality and intensity of participation rather than on outcome. The realization that decisions *must* be made forced a gradual change in how organizational business was done.

The first step occurred when the president recognized that the department directors, all competent mental health professionals, needed expert help in setting priorities and fiscal planning. The Interdepartmental Council could identify various interdepartmental issues, but their decisions were not consistently good, and the participative process obscured the fact that the department directors had difficulty with decision-making.

To correct this problem, the management structure of each department was reorganized around a team of two: a senior administrator who was to supply data about resources (money, space, time availability, staff) and a senior mental health professional who served as department director. His responsibilities were to assess and maintain program quality. Although a variant of this plan had been used intermittently for many years, effective collaboration between mental health professionals and administrators was not achieved until the GRC had moderated interdisciplinary tensions. Although these additional managers doubled the size of the Interdepartmental Council, the organization's capacity to deal with economic and administrative issues improved.

Such considerations of administrative effectiveness illustrate a characteristic of the organization that may have contributed to the positive impact of the group relations conferences: a recognition that managerial theory *is* relevant to the processes of treatment (Kernberg, 1983). Apparently the GRC facilitated an incorporation of this perspective by mental health professionals.

LASTING EFFECTS

In the light of the foregoing comments, it was a surprise to learn from questionnaire responses just how positively the GRC continues to be regarded by virtually all those earlier participants still employed at the Foundation. The vast majority of respondents spoke appreciatively of the experience for what it had taught them personally and professionally. At least a quarter could think of no disadvantages from the experience. However, an unexpected pattern of difference in retrospective enthusiasm surfaced. Impressionistically, the level of enthusiasm was related to the respondents' disciplines, and diminished as follows: psychiatrists and psychologists > social workers > nurses > administrators.

While the reasons for these variations are not clear, several possibilities come to mind. The greatest enthusiasm for the GRC came from those whose previous perspective was largely dyadic; the discovery of new dimensions of behavioral dynamics both relevant to professional work and congruent with the psychoanalytic framework was powerful and exciting. At the other extreme were administrators who do not operate with a theoretical perspective that emphasizes unconscious forces. Therefore, an experience that demonstrates these elements had no special appeal for them. Moreover, their work within organizations is largely group rather than individually based. As a consequence, several administrators commented that they learned little that was new; on the contrary, the GRC was a great deal like their normal working experience (Sheffel, 1951).

One might speculate that for nurses and, to a lesser extent, social workers, the GRC was less novel because their normal work is substantially group oriented. Neither discipline, but particularly nurses, found the primitive dynamics of group process as helpful to their work tasks as did psychiatrists and psychologists.

Those who were less enthusiastic helped to define some of the limitations noted above and elaborated on below. But even those people guardedly acknowledged some tangible benefits.

Three General Effects

The diverse consequences of the GRC cannot be summarized simply. There were three general effects—two positive, one not.

1. The first has to do with changes in attitudes about authority of two kinds: (a) those directly affecting individuals in their leadership roles (in a treatment team, a discipline group or task force), and (b) those affecting individuals' perceptions of their roles as members of a staff group *vis-a-vis* "management."

(a) The GRC dramatically demonstrated the consequences of a leader's failure to manage the boundary of the group (Miller and Rice, 1967; Klein and Gould, 1973) or to provide a clear definition of the task. The resulting confusion was reminiscent of committees back home, for the organization had indeed offered many examples of these consequences: unproductive meetings, diffident participation, erratic attendance, poor morale, and abundant criticism.

In an earlier period, these problems would have been blamed on "administration," or inappropriately cited as examples of pathological or character-disordered motivation (Kernberg, 1978). But after the GRC, these problems were recognized as common group experiences that reflected covert conflicts as well as failure of the leaders to discharge their responsibilities.

The GRC also helped those in leadership positions to do a better job by providing them with models and encouragement to overcome the reluctance to exercise authority that is endemic to mental health professionals. They were better able to recognize that it is an illusion to think that "authoritarianism in institutions can be successfully overcome by democratization of them, rather than by a functional analysis of task requirements and the functional administrative structures corresponding to them" (Kernberg, 1978), i.e., by the exercise of appropriate leadership.

Several leaders commented that after GRC training they had acquired a new awareness of the importance of providing support to their colleagues. Such remarks illustrated a new understanding of the leader's responsibilities and reflected the steadily growing competence in professionals' administrative skills that the GRC program had helped to catalyze.

(b) As attitudes about authority changed, so did those about management. As staff members began to appreciate the role of authority, their tendency to scapegoat "management" for all the ills—real or imagined—affecting the system diminished (Kernberg, 1978). One colleague noted that although the intensity and frequency of irrational attacks on "administration" did diminish, power and authority will always be challenged, no matter how effective the leadership. After additional staff gained experience with GRCs, staff-management interactions focused more on tasks and issues and less on affects of a transferential nature (Klein, 1977).

Another important corollary was a new awareness that many individuals have strong but unacceptable dependency needs. When such needs are in conflict with a personal image of self-reliance, they are denied and projected onto others, especially "the administration." By disowning individual responsibility, staff members are able to keep intact a protective denial that minimizes and depreciates their dependent relationship to the organization while permitting them to sustain it. The cost, however, appears in the inhibition of individual initiative and in covert feelings of diminished self-worth.

Several respondents noted that GRCs stress the point that each individual ultimately contains his own authority and has the responsibility of exercising that authority. When this individual dimension of authority is accepted, the tendency to shift blame upward is reduced, and a concept of "responsible followership" emerges. One respondent thought this trend was an important consequence of the GRC and suggested that a strong sense of individual responsibility has helped the organization stay financially afloat in a shrinking economy.

Also contributing to lessening staff-management tension was a renewed awareness of the importance of timely information. In the absence of sufficient data about decisions, rumors based on fantasy are generated to fill the gap. As the GRC so well illustrated, these fabricated substitutes for reliable information feed the potential for paranoid thinking that arises in information-hungry groups. The increase of participative groups in the organizational structure enhanced the flow of information, but it also underscored the importance of continuing to provide regular communication.

2. The second positive effect involves those structural and programmatic developments that resulted from, or were markedly strengthened by, the GRC. For example,

(a) In the adult hospital, rigid adherence to a psychoanalytic model for long-term treatment has diminished. There is a greater openness to new ideas and greater ability to utilize self-examination without inducing destructive self-criticism. Alternative approaches (therapeutic community, psychopharmacology, short-term therapy, biofeedback and cognitive educational methods) have been introduced into the treatment system.

Increased use of groups within the hospital catalyzed a shift away from an exclusive reliance on the doctor, to a greater emphasis on the therapeutic potential of the milieu. Concurrently, new ideas about patients' responsibilities to the community and to each other emerged. This process reflects a move from an exclusive dependence on the dyad as the locus of treatment, to a model that more adequately acknowledges the potential therapeutic powers of groups and the environment itself.[3] The introduction of a therapeutic community model did, however, bring problems as well as benefits.

(b) Middle-level councils were introduced as a part of the formal organizational structure. These councils mirrored the role of the top management council and reflected a new emphasis on the use of participative decision-making at all levels. These councils provided staff members with a broad participation in the governance of the organization that they had so eagerly sought.

(c) After years of neglect, there was an increased interest by staff in the group psychotherapy program. One colleague noted that ". . . conference attendance heightened my interest in groups, [so] I took group psychotherapy training and am doing it now. I no longer think in the one-to-one mode only, but consider how whatever I am doing could be applied to a group setting."

Responding to the same influence in the late 1960s, the Karl Menninger School of Psychiatry shifted the group dynamics training program for psychiatric residents and other professional trainees from an NTL T-group to the Tavistock/Group Relations model, still in use at the present time.

(d) An awakened interest in family therapy led to establishing a training program. The organizer, encouraged by his GRC experience, developed the program in spite of minimal support from his colleagues. He found the GRC invaluable and noted strong parallels between family systems concepts and those of small and large groups.

(e) In June 1982, the adult clinical services and associated support systems moved from the original structures to 22 new buildings on a campus

3 miles away. The complexity of the task was enormous: how to plan and execute such a move while maintaining an effective therapeutic program for 160 patients.

The move required a high degree of clarity in task definition and countless hours of consultation and planning. People at many levels had to work together to accomplish a great many interlocking tasks. The moving plan was published well in advance and special task-focused meetings were held with staff. As a result, people were able to continue their normal work responsibilities while carrying out the time-limited tasks of moving. The smoothness of the move was cited by several as a measure of the capacity of the organization to manage its intergroup boundaries effectively.

The success of the move was perceived as exemplifying the vital importance of structure, adequate communication, and clearly stated expectations. One observer contrasted the move with the more ambiguous, ongoing issues in patient-management, where "the task" is often difficult or impossible to define. In such circumstances, he noted, staff tend to emphasize the group examination of interpersonal feelings rather than to address the primary task.

3. The third general effect concerns a group of negative consequences that reflect distortions of group dynamic concepts and an inappropriate transposition of the GRC to the work setting.

This inappropriate transfer was apparent in a variety of ways. Treatment teams would appropriately use group dynamics to deal with problems of countertransference that threatened the progress of the therapeutic work. But the seductive nature of this process and the tendency for seriously ill patients to split the team often led to a profusion of meetings devoted to examining the team's own process, largely ignoring patients. The capacity of a team to provide vitally necessary nurture and support to its members sometimes encouraged the development of sentient groups more concerned with their own welfare than with the therapeutic tasks.

The GRC training was a powerful catalyst in the development of the therapeutic community in the institution. This program amplified hospital treatment by exploring individual aspects of group conflicts and the relationship of these issues to the structure of hospital management (Kernberg, 1973). But the therapeutic community program had adverse effects as well. Staff members often felt deskilled, reduced to roles of limited scope, and imprisoned by a swelling tide of paralyzing egalitarianism that insisted that staff members (as well as patients) had equal rights, authority, and voice in all decisions. The use of groups for both treatment and administration seemed to express an idealistic fantasy that wise decisions could be made by large groups of good-hearted, well-intentioned, undifferentiatedly equal people.

This denial of difference in competence, experience, and responsibility contributed to a reduction in productivity, heightened anxiety, turgid decision-making, diffusion of responsibility, and widespread ambiguity about who was accountable for what and who had what kind of authority. One physician, a team leader, said he could not write orders for a patient without first getting a consensus from his treatment team; he justified his refusal to act authoritatively as a "necessary step to support the work of the team" and did not see his inaction as a failure to take responsibility.

Potentially damaging to the therapeutic process was a tendency, during the immediate post-GRC period, to equate "group process" with treatment. The powerful effects of expressing primitive feelings and the instructive experience of group-induced regression led to a natural but mistaken view that such experiences were the essence of therapy. In some cases, achieving a high emotional intensity was the unspoken objective of the staff in their work with patient groups, displacing the primary tasks of learning and understanding.

This perspective seemed to assume that the GRC was a *model of treatment* rather than a *method of education*. Group process is compelling and deeply involving, but it is not psychotherapy nor is it a substitute for a dynamic understanding of the patient. Such confusion led to many instances of inappropriate use of GRC techniques as therapeutic tools and strongly reinforced a misperception that process is an "end-in-itself."

Coupled with this pattern was a tendency to use group process to "manage" a patient's deviant or pathological behavior. Emphasis on the "here-and-now" diminished attention to the dynamic roots of the symptom. Rather than seeking to understand the psychological function of aggressive behavior in a patient, the team colluded with the community to suppress it. Although such pressure was often successful in controlling a patient's socially undesirable behavior, it added little to the patient's comprehension or his successful assimilation of the improved behavior. Such a management approach to pathology seemed to be little more than psychodynamically empty behavior modification.

Of course, such examples are not the fault of the GRC alone. The concurrent introduction of the therapeutic community model confounded the picture. But there is a high probability that the enthusiasm for group process contributed to the confusion. Put otherwise, hospital directors planning to utilize the GRC should be aware of the strong likelihood that participants may get carried away by their enthusiasm and should be sure that specific cognitive measures (such as well-designed application groups) are included in the program.

CONCLUSIONS

That most of the respondents remain strongly positive about their GRC experience after nearly a decade, and believe that it has had a substantial, valuable, and lasting impact on the organization was a pleasant surprise. Whether the benefits ascribed were actually due to the GRC may be less important than the perception that they were. All things considered, the program clearly has been of great value.

There are several important observations that may be relevant to the use of GRC by other mental health professionals.

1. The excitement of discovering the power of group process can mislead participants into a set of unrealistic expectations:

Application: Menninger

(a) the GRC is essentially a *method of learning* not a system of treatment, and the two modalities must be *clearly* distinguished.

(b) by itself, group process has no special capacity to solve the substantive problems that afflict every organization; there is no substitute for attention to the primary work tasks of the system.

2. The major strength of such a program is its dramatic ability to illustrate the proclivities of "normal" groups under conditions of inadequate structure, poorly defined tasks, and/or inadequate leadership. GRC participants become quite able to recognize these symptoms in groups of which they are a part or for which they are responsible, and are then in a better position to correct the problems.

Finally and *most* importantly, there is more to leadership than setting the agenda, managing the boundaries and delegating tasks; ultimately, the most important role of the leader is to create a vision, a sense of purpose with which followers can identify and claim as their own. This *sense of commitment* to a commonly defined task is a special form of sentience deserving special emphasis.

Editor's Introduction to Belfast Communities Intervention

In the past ten years, a number of attempts have been made to apply the theory and methods of group relations work to situations where external conflicts seem to overshadow unconscious and covert issues. We say "seem" because, as in individual therapy, the focus on external conflicts may be both diversions and metaphors for more internal difficulties.

Most of the applications that are represented in this volume reflect work in areas where difficulties are consciously acknowledged to be, at least in part, psychological in origin, where participants are not holding the reins of power in major institutions in our society and where the external issues are rarely life-threatening to subgroups involved and represented. Less has been written about the ventures of group relations consultants into more explosive and uncharted arenas. For example, Dr. Colman directed a conference for police chiefs of major U.S. and foreign cities and U.S. Congressmen focused on "law and order" in which issues of politics and the ethics of terror and counter terror either drowned out psychological consultation, or when heard, further inflamed those involved in ways that did not always support individual and group learning. Dr. O'Connor directed four Group Relations Conferences in Dublin, Ireland involving important representations from warring factions in that war-torn city. Life and death issues were all too real; the concept of the conference as a "temporary learning institution" with control of external boundaries, usually thought of as necessary for meaningful learning, became more fantasy than reality. Many other such conferences have been tried in terribly difficult situations with mixed and often chaotic outcomes.

Dr. Klein's paper is an example of a carefully planned and executed collaboration of Group Relations and National Training Laboratory techniques. Despite its technical clarity, it was ultimately experienced as an ambivalent intervention.

As Group Relations work grows as a discipline, consultation in situations of national and international significance and to groups with power and influence may become more usual. It is an area we desperately need to know more about.

A.C.

20.

BELFAST COMMUNITIES INTERVENTION[1]

Edward B. Klein

This articles describes a training program that provided group and organizational skills to enable people living under extreme conflict to be more effective leaders. The training was held for Belfast citizens and has been briefly reported (Doob and Foltz, 1974; Miller, 1977); with more distance, it offers a way of conceptualizing an intervention in a conflict situation that still attracts international headlines.

The program grew out of the work of Doob (1970) who first used experiential group events in an international conflict situation with representatives of Somalia, Ethiopia and Kenya. Somewhat later, a Yale team met and decided that a training conference was the most effective way citizens of Belfast could obtain leadership skills.

METHOD

There are two major views of groups and organizations: the Tavistock analytic-systems approach and the NTL human relations orientation. Both use unstructured exercises that focus on interpersonal, group and systems behavior and assume that effective learning involves both thought and emotions. The primary task of Tavistock is the study of authority while NTL highlights interpersonal competence.

The most dramatic difference between the two approaches is seen in the small group leader's behavior. Tavistock consultants emphasize group behavior rather than individual reactions. NTL trainers minimize authority by giving "nonevaluative" feedback and promote a peer-group situation (Klein and Astrachan, 1971).

PHASE I

We met in New Haven during 1971-72 and designed a 14-day conference to train leaders in two working-class Protestant and Catholic districts, with the hope that local administrators would carry on the work. We viewed the year as a planning phase, including a trip to Belfast. Stirling University in Scotland agreed to make its facilities available to us, and Yale offered to finance the project. Our foremost question was: would any plans developed 3,000 miles away match the realities of Belfast?

Application: Klein

The city of Belfast was ugly, crowded and old, in marked contrast to the beauty of the Irish countryside. We found ourselves in the middle of a funeral, a death march, surrounded by the military moving side-by-side with civilians. We were amazed that the civilians never consciously acknowledged the presence of the military.

Our first step was to meet with mental health professionals, all of whom endorsed training for Protestants and Catholics in a relatively safe environment with professional leaders. None, however, wanted to participate, demonstrating their own ambivalence. We spoke with psychiatrists, who told us of the indiscriminate prescribing of tranquilizers to mothers, children running wild, husbands hiding from violent groups, and a lack of family and community authority structures. We were made aware of the people's despair over their attempts to bridge "the great divide" between two warring groups.

After numerous attempts, we finally obtained local sponsors and two administrators. We discussed their roles in recruiting members, obtaining informed consent, confidentiality and follow-up in Belfast of the work begun at Stirling.

We announced a training conference for 60 men and women of various religious and political interests who wished to learn about leadership, authority, group and organizational issues. The sponsors were three local institutions: Protestant and Catholic religious groups and a department at Queens University. Funding was provided by Yale University. The conference was scheduled for nine days, in order not to interfere with people's work schedules, and would be held in August at Stirling University. Transportation would be provided and money given to participants for time lost from work, babysitting and other personal expenses.

The administrators were American expatriates who had strong roots in the academic/political/community development subgroup within Belfast. We impressed on them the stressful nature of the training and explicitly excluded as members people with a psychiatric history. The administrators' activist commitment boded well for recruiting a membership, but one more directed toward community development than a group relations conference. This difference in outlook was to have untold consequences.

PHASE II

Upon returning to New Haven, it became clear that we needed both women consultants and NTL group leaders since only the Tavistock orientation was present in the original team.[2] We shortened the original 14 day to a 9 day training schedule. Day 1 consisted of introductory discussion groups; each member was assigned to three groups, which were arranged by age, sex and religion. Days 2 through 5 consisted of Tavistock Small, Large and Intergroup events focused on the dynamics of different sized groups and issues of authority and leadership. Days 6 to 9 involved T-group skill building exercises, and member-selected planning groups for implementation back in Belfast.

We arrived in Scotland August 1972, one-and-a-half days before the members, and prepared for the Conference with one administrator. On the second night, 56 tired Belfast citizens arrived at Stirling University after a long trip with the other administrator. There were 60 percent men, 40 percent women, 60 percent Protestant, 40 percent Catholic, varying in age between 16 and 60. Over three-fourths were members of the working class.

The discussion groups were held on the first day. Most members disliked participating in groups that were segregated by religion. The women enjoyed participation in the all-female groups, while in contrast the men in the all-male groups tended to complain and to split by religion. The members of the youth group were excited about the Conference and developed a peer culture among themselves that minimized religious differences.

On the second day, Tavistock training began. There was a clear delineation between staff and members. The Director stated the contract, training objectives and roles of staff and members. The first event was the small group, which allowed members to experience small group interactions and study their authority relations with the consultant. In general, the groups were similar to those conducted with Americans except for the cross-cultural difference (Irish members and American consultants). For many members, a woman in a role of authority was a completely new experience. The interaction with consultants alternated between working on understanding the group and flight from the task (Bion, 1961). What distinguished these groups was the absence of the expression of fantasy, because Belfast reality concerns took greater precedence in each small group. The Large Group was considered fascinating and illustrative of the difficulties of being a member in a large committee.

The last event was the Intergroup exercise. The design called for the staff to be a separate group, which was assiduously avoided by members. There were few requests for consultation; staff was treated in many ways like the English government—aloof and powerful, in short, upper class staff vs. working class members.

During the four days of Tavistock training, several trends were noted: 1) women tended to be excluded and ridiculed; 2) youth were chastised for showing "disrespect for their elders." In general, women, youth and Catholics were more emotionally involved, paralleling training events in the United States, where people who identify most with staff are minorities, women and lower status professionals. This occurs because individuals are stripped of their outside roles and are thus made equals. If one is in a lower power position, it is not too negative an experience, but if on top, the drop is precarious and painful.

The Tavistock training ended Wednesday, and a transition to a new training phase began. There were two announced purposes for NTL training: planning and skill acquisition. Staff diagnosis was that members wanted help with public speaking, assuming the chairman's role, negotiating skills and specific project interests.

To meet these needs members formed four groups. There were 1) 10 individuals led by a Protestant minister, who were politically centralist and considered irrelevant by others; 2) 10 members in their twenties equally divided by religion who planned to get financing for a nonsectarian community center on the boundary between two Protestant and Catholic ghettos; 3) a group of older Protestant and Catholic women formed to work on housing and redevelopment, who were dismayed by the lack of responsiveness on the part of Belfast governmental agencies. The fourth group included 20 individuals from labor relations and political organizations, which included all of the IRA, UDA and labor leaders. This group was equally divided by religion and chose to work on stopping unauthorized assassinations—e.g., sectarian killings where responsibility is not publically taken within 48 hours. They felt that these activities were psychopathological in nature. Consultation was concerned with the contradictions in social structure that prompted individual acts of destruction. The group discussed rumor control, and meeting back in Belfast with a woman chairperson, but the power lay with the extremist men.

A number of additional events were held. A labor-management role-play was enacted in which Protestants played Catholic workers agitating for more jobs in the shipyards, while Catholics role-played Protestant management using a hard line stance to keep Catholics in their places. Members found this activity very exciting. Another exercise was the money tree game. Members were randomly assigned as haves and have nots: groups that had money and those that did not. This exercise was an all-too-realistic portrayal of Belfast society.

On the last day, there was a general review that everyone attended, and the possibility of a future weekend workshop, 3 months hence, was discussed. The final event was a houlie—a community party with singing, dancing, drinking, story-telling, laughing and crying.

In sum, the Stirling conference membership was primarily Irish working class, whereas the staff was American middle class. The membership, therefore, symbolically represented the <u>victims</u> of the conflict, not its perpetuators. While social class was a major factor separating members and staff, it was only indirectly addressed. Because it was difficult to attack staff directly since they were funding the conference, a member newspaper was started, which gently ridiculed staff actions. Therefore, the first line of systems defense was sectarianism. Whenever the going got tough, people defended themselves by reverting back to their religious subgroups. Catholics were the more emotionally involved of the two groups, the Protestants more withdrawn. Catholics were thus more likely to be psychological casualties since they displayed more emotion than Protestants. Of the six members who experienced the greatest inner turmoil, five were Catholic.

The next major systems finding involved the effect of age on the Conference. From the first day, youth identified their issues and voiced their grievances. Given the war-torn city, it is not surprising that the youth should be the bearers of idealistic expectations about the future. The staff helped the youth culture to develop, since we identified with them in their goals.

One of the most critical outcomes of the Conference pertained to the role of women. Due to the administrators' recruitment efforts, women comprised a higher percentage of the membership than had been expected.

It was, in fact, the women who organized a follow-up conference 15 months later in Portrush, Northern Ireland. After the Stirling conference, five participants, including two women, ran for election. All were defeated, but for three of them this was a new act showing political and personal development.

PHASE III

There was no three-month follow-up conference, because the administrators defected from the staff for political/philosophical reasons (Boehringer et al., 1974). Nine months later, in June 1973, Doob and Foltz (1974), personally interviewed 40 of the 56 participants. They had learned much from the conference, particularly about organizational dynamics, leadership and authority. None were dramatically affected negatively by the conference, although some were upset. There were some outstanding examples of work started at Stirling. These included 1) the group of older women who drove extremists out of their community, 2) a woman who obtained $750,000 for the purpose of developing nondenominational youth centers, and 3) the political planning group that was instrumental in decreasing the violence around a Protestant run factory in a Catholic ghetto. Other participants felt that the conference had been less worthwhile. While in Belfast, Doob and Foltz asked if members wanted a follow-up. A Protestant woman, with the help of some Catholic women, organized a two and one-half day Portrush follow-up conference in November 1973. At Portrush, half of the membership were women. Both staff and member women became more militant and held consciousness-raising groups that were ridiculed by male staff and members.

DISCUSSION

Klein, Correa, Howe and Stone (1983) suggest that three social system factors help account for member learning in group relations conferences: 1) sponsorship, legitimacy and support of training activities; 2) heterogeneity of learning opportunities, an indication of systems openness; and 3) authority and sentient (socio-emotional) linkages between members and staff. The Stirling conference had relatively weak sponsorship (since Yale was paying for it); it was hard for members to be open given the realities of the stresses in Belfast, and there were no authority or sentient connections between consultants and members. The administrators had sentient ties with the members but left the project. In many ways, this act might have been predicted given the administrators' role conflicts. Consultants spent considerable time preparing the administrators for the Conference, but it was still not done as well as it could have been (Alevy, et al., 1974). It is now clear that the administrators carried too great a burden and could not work out their issues well enough at Stirling so that they could fulfill their contract to keep the work going in Belfast. Members maintained contacts among themselves and organized the Portrush conference. One can take a social systems viewpoint on the intervention program and suggest that it was experienced by all concerned in an ambivalent fashion. The administrators represented the impossibility of applying the knowledge gained at Stirling, while the members' organization of Portrush symbolized hope for the future.

Members, we hope, learned about group scapegoating and how system defenses are constructed by religion, age and sex. In the chaos of Belfast, members applied new learning within their own religious groups. For instance, one munitions expert for a Protestant military group obtained permission to spend time on youth work. The collaboration across the religious divide was minimal. The long-term effect of these interventions will only be tested in the future in, hopefully, a more peaceful society. The story is not over; we hope our contributions have been worthwhile for the forgotten community leaders in Belfast.

C. Role Analysis

Women in Authority: A Sociopsychological Analysis 309
Marjorie Bayes and Peter M. Newton

Dilemmas of Black Females in Leadership 323
Rhetaugh Graves Dumas

The Psychodynamics of Taking the Role 335
Larry Hirschhorn

Unconscious Process in an Organization: A Serendipitous
    Investigation 353
Edward R. Shapiro

21.

WOMEN IN AUTHORITY: A SOCIOPSYCHOLOGICAL ANALYSIS

Marjorie Bayes and Peter M. Newton

Recent studies of the role of women in work settings outside the home typically emphasize the inequality of opportunity for women in work organizations and advocate increasing high-level positions for women (e.g., Ginzberg & Yohalem, 1973; Huber, 1973; Willett, 1971). Only a few studies (e.g., Hennig & Jardim, 1977) consider the problems that arise for organizations and individuals when women actually secure positions of authority. While women are now more often considered for leadership positions, there is little evidence of careful thought being given to the social psychological repercussions of this type of social change. We will discuss here several issues related to authority and sex roles, using as case material a woman unit chief and her staff working within a mental health center.

Discrimination against women in work organizations is being reduced first at lower levels, but much more slowly at higher levels of authority. Although women represent about 40 percent of the labor force, only 20 percent of persons classified as managers and administrators are women (U.S. Bureau of the Census, 1976), and only 2.3 percent of high-level administrators, earning over $25,000 per year, are women (Women's Bureau, U.S. Department of Labor, 1975).

Why is there such vast inequality at management levels? The first level of explanation must emphasize economic competition for precious resources and the monopolization of privilege by white males. In addition, however, there are psychological barriers. Women are often perceived, and perceive themselves, as unsuited for positions of authority; many capable women do not aspire to high-level management positions. The supposed reluctance of both men and women to be subordinate to a woman manager has often been cited (e.g., Special Task Force, HEW, 1972; Women's Bureau, U.S. Dept. of Labor, 1974), although many people have never actually been subordinate to a woman in an adult work setting. When a woman does reach a management position, she and her staff may behave in ways that deskill her, deny her authority, and sabotage the work task.

Men and women are socialized in a culture that both explicitly and implicitly defines sex roles as total roles and that trains individuals in these roles. A total role is one that defines a sense of self and a set of appropriate behavior, including the level and kind of authoritativeness; it permeates all aspects of life and takes precedence over other more situation-specific work or social roles if they are incompatible. Dominance and independence are linked with the masculine role, while submissiveness, passivity and nurturance are linked with the feminine (Broverman, Broverman, Clarkson, Rosenkrantz, and Vogel, 1970). These sex-linked role conceptions are learned through socialization, primarily within the nuclear family.

The view, pervasive in the culture, that women should be powerless, nurturant, and submissive, co-exists with, and is perhaps a response to, the fantasy that women are potentially more powerful and dangerous than men. Neumann (1955) presents substantial anthropological evidence that representations of female godesses preceded representations of male gods. He discusses various artistic and mythological representations of the archetype of femininity. This archetype, portrayed for thousands of years, has three forms: the Good Mother who is giving, nurturing, caretaking; the Terrible Mother who is aggressive, devouring, ensnaring; the Great Mother who combines all of these attributes.

Currently the essence of desirable femininity, culturally defined, emphasizes the Good Mother image, and the avoidance of the Terrible or Great Mother, requiring that women repress or suppress anger and aggressiveness. It seems important to society to keep women in a nurturing but otherwise powerless role; this role becomes established as a social fact (Lerner, 1974; Neumann, 1954), perpetuated in the basic social structure and process of the nuclear family.

A woman given primary authority for a work group (e.g., project team, treatment ward, consultation unit) or for an organization faces a basic incongruity between role requirements of the position and the sex-linked role conception she and her staff have learned. Subordinates will respond to her partly as an individual and partly according to the cultural stereotype of woman. *Our concern is for those instances in which the responses of the woman manager and her staff, based upon the sex-role stereotype, interfere with the work of the group.* When these social influences are not recognized, difficulties arise that are easily blamed upon individuals, who then become victims or casualties.

We will present our observation and analysis of the functioning of one woman manager, her staff, and their organization, as it was affected by the fact of female leadership. Our analysis draws upon the social system model of Miller and Rice (1967), concepts of work group functioning (Newton & Levinson, 1973), their extension to sex-role socialization in the family (Newton, 1973), and psychoanalytic theories of group behavior (Bion, 1961). As a basis for our discussion, we will first briefly consider the nuclear family as the prototype of sex-linked authority roles.

THE FAMILY AS A SOCIAL SYSTEM

Newton (1973) has adumbrated the social structure and process of the nuclear family in its traditional form. The family, like other social systems, has boundaries, major tasks, and social structural arrangements that include the definition and distribution of positions and roles. It is within the nuclear family that females and males learn socially generated, sex-typed role conceptions that permeate thought and action in adult life. Children observe the division of authority between their parents and begin to build assumptions, definitions, and models of authority, which tend later to be unconsciously and inappropriately applied to other groups. It is the linkage between sex roles and authority that concerns us.

Families are small groups whose primary societal function is childrearing. Parents form a leadership coalition to take responsibility for the family with father and mother typically in No. 1 and No. 2 levels of authority. The father's greater authority is related to his primacy in the economic system, derived from the monopolization by males of higher-paying jobs (c.f., Horkheimer, 1972). The father, as No. 1, traditionally has a position on the external boundary. As the executive of the enterprise he obtains resources, provides protection, and generally represents the family to the external world. An indication of the father's authority is the fact that all other members of the family take on his surname. Within the marriage and the family, the title of "Mrs." conveys the difference in authority between the man and the woman, and identifies the woman.

The mother, as No. 2, manages the internal boundary between parents and children in carrying out the internal work—the care and socialization of children—and the internal maintenance of the system. She has primary authority *only* over children, and interacts with them constantly. She is experienced as the earliest and most immediate authority. As the primary caretaker of a helpless infant, she has great power to destroy. To the child the mother seems to be highly powerful, the key to survival as well as the creator of life.

The mother enters into strongly erotic relationships with her children, engaging in contacts of great physical intimacy. At the same time, she is required to act as the agent of their frustration, depriving them of gratifications in order to socialize them appropriately (Parsons, 1954). Freud (1932) and Horney (1967) wrote that this role of women as primary socializers, controlling satisfactions and frustrations and thereby becoming a target for the earliest sadistic impulses, is a major factor in bringing about in males a "dread of women." Lerner (1974) agrees that our definitions of "masculine" and "feminine" behavior and the devaluation of women stem in large part from a defensive handling of the persistent affects of the early infant-mother relationship.

An important developmental step for children is to resist maternal authority. Prolonged subordination to maternal authority, particularly for males, is regarded with scorn and derision. This has special significance in adult life in men's reactions to being subordinate to a woman. Female responses to a woman in authority seem more complex and confused, probably because of the added factor of identification.

THEMES FROM A CASE EXAMPLE

We have chosen major themes from a case example of a professional woman, Dr. A., newly promoted to a position as chief of a community consultation unit within a mental health center. The case, we believe, involves a particular combination of organization, work group, and leadership characteristics in which issues of gender were highlighted. We will present a brief background as well as our understanding of the difficulties that arose for the work group and its female leader within the following categories: (a) the generation and use of power; (b) the leader's relationship to a subordinate No. 2, and (c) dependency in the staff group.

Background of the Case

The Consultation Unit (CU), a unit of the community mental health center, was created to provide program consultation to groups and agencies. The CU contained nine staff positions—a psychologist, two psychiatric nurses, two social workers, and four paraprofessionals.

Following the tenure and resignation of two successive male unit chiefs, a CU staff member, Dr. A., a female psychologist in her mid-30s, was proposed by staff as unit chief. The Director of the Center appointed Dr. A. as Unit Chief and combined the unit with another, creating the superordinate structure of the Community Division. Each unit within the division essentially maintained its own previous form. The leader of the second unit, Dr. S., a male psychologist, became Division Head.

Dr. A. inherited a group that had certain strongly marked characteristics. There was a continuing, confused struggle for task definition. The group described itself as a democratic, liberal, victimized group with no formal or philosophical connection to the organization of which it was in fact a part. It was a group, then, in which the ties to the real world of work had always been somewhat tenuous.

Because Dr. A. felt that the unit had a need for outside consultation about its social structure and process she approached one of the authors (PMN) who had consulted to other work groups in the Center. He agreed to serve as a consultant to the unit, and did so for a 2-year period. He attended the weekly staff meetings and met weekly with the unit chief alone. He also met with other staff members for individual consultation when they requested it.

After the conclusion of the consultation the authors of this paper collaborated in analyzing the consultation data. These consisted of minutes from staff meetings and the consultant's memoranda describing the ongoing process of the consultation. We began to notice the recurring importance of the unit leader's gender. We now present the emergent themes that we believe to be most closely related to the fact of female leadership.

THE GENERATION AND USE OF POWER

Levinson & Klerman (1967) wrote that an executive needs to be concerned with gathering and using power in order to meet organizational responsibilities. We will focus on two major aspects of this executive function: (a) management of the external boundary, and (b) locus of power within the work group to accomplish tasks.

Management of the External Boundary

An important aspect of the executive function is to maintain a position on the external boundary of the work group, importing supplies, exporting products or services, relating the group to the external world, and protecting the group from environmental stresses. Many aspects of the nuclear family's structure and process create for a woman an identity incompatible with functioning in a position with primary responsibility for managing the external boundary of a group. The position of mother, prototype of a woman in authority, is not located on the external boundary. Her traditional responsibility and authority are for people and events internal to the family group and for supporting the No. 1 position of the father.

The two aspects of boundary management most troublesome for Dr. A. were the tasks of sustaining ties with the total organization and protecting the group from intrusion.

> Throughout most of her tenure, Dr. A. was the only woman Unit Chief in the Center; there were no women Division Heads, no women in Central Administration. Therefore, many meetings of Center leadership were all-male groups, with the exception of Dr. A. and perhaps a female secretary to take minutes. Such meetings often opened with a discussion of current male sports events—the "locker room" kind in which Dr. A. was out of place. Her femaleness was a covert group issue. In one meeting, the joking comment was made that since Dr. A. was seated in a chair occupied the day before by the male Governor of the State perhaps she might be "impregnated by his aura." On another occasion, when she commented that it was too warm in the room, she was jokingly asked if she were having "hot flashes."

Linkages between male managers were often made informally, the men meeting socially or engaging in athletic pursuits together. Occasionally, committee meetings or dinners for visiting dignitaries were held at a social club that did not allow women members. Since a female manager was a rarity in this organization, she experienced an alienation directly attributable to her gender.

Dr. A. had particular difficulty in relating the unit to this total organization. Ties to other units were tenuous, and took the form of Dr. A.'s friendly but distant relationships with other Unit Chiefs and Division Heads, with little actual collaborative work. She accepted the fact of the organization's male dominance without question and regarded herself as appropriately dealt with when she was being subtly derogated or isolated on the basis of gender. Fabian (1972) has suggested that this is a typical response of professional women to such a situation.

Although not openly discussing this situation, Dr. A.'s staff behaved in various ways that indicated anxiety that her gender would lead to further isolation of their unit, already suffering from lack of ties. Staff frequently complained of feeling isolated, lacking coordination with the broader system. Subordinate male staff members who had no authority to take on external boundary functions anxiously displayed the need to do so. They often took a consulting role to Dr. A. around such issues. At one point, one male staff member began conducting some negotiations with another unit chief to plan interunit cooperation. No one noticed the inappropriateness of this action.

Finding it difficult to address the external boundary issues, Dr. A. spent a major portion of her time with internal issues, particularly her staff's interpersonal relations. She interacted with them in a kindly and supportive manner, and felt puzzled by the tenacity of their discontent.

As a second important boundary function, an executive protects the group by monitoring the forces that intrude upon it. In the traditional family the father is in charge of the physical safety of the group. With a woman group leader, incongruity arises between the need of the group to have its leader protect the external boundary, and the traditional cultural concept of a woman as object or possession, won and protected by a powerful male, and biologically vulnerable to bodily intrusion through rape, seduction, or pregnancy.

Dr. A. had difficulties in conceptualizing and carrying out the protective function. Some of these difficulties were symbolized by boundary problems of the weekly staff meetings.

> At first, Dr. A. allowed various persons—the Chaplain, the Public Relations Officer—to attend unit staff meetings for indeterminate lengths of time. At times they were present at discussions of sensitive unit issues, better handled within the confines of unit boundaries. Dr. A.'s closing of this boundary by disinviting extraneous personnel was the first step in recognizing her protective responsibilities. On several occasions, however, the Division Head showed up at unit staff meetings unannounced, without first conferring with Dr. A. about attending. This was accurately perceived by staff as a startling and threatening intrusion that Dr. A. was not able to prevent.

On these and other occasions, the staff seemed to feel that there existed an unalterable breach in the boundary that could not be adequately protected and that was constantly vulnerable to penetration.

Locus of Power and Authority to Accomplish Work

In our case example—and we believe it to be common—both the female leader and her subordinates acted in ways that kept her from using her authority. In the family the mother's power derives from her coalition with male authority, and is understood to be power to nurture and train. A family without a male leader is perceived as damaged, a "broken home," and incomplete. A woman achieves a No. 1 position in the family by default, by abdication of the male leader.

When a woman holds a position of authority the group may doubt if she can really *use* it. A primary, although never articulated or acknowledged, theme in the Consultation Unit was that only men can really use authority. Because the theme was never openly examined, it led to the expenditure of time and energy in what we term a *search for male authority*, a search for a male equal or superior in status to Dr. A. who would be the real leader and with whom Dr. A. might pair, but as a No. 2.

> Following Dr. A.'s appointment as Unit Chief, work within the unit all but ceased. Staff members were comfortable with their inactivity, believing that the major work of the unit was to be done by the male Division Head, with Dr. A.'s assistance. One staff member, Ms C., commented in a staff meeting that the group had "an absent leader" and was "run by remote control." Ms C. was referring to the Division Head who, it became clear, was not to be closely involved in unit work. Over time, staff alternated between hostility toward his remoteness and a wish to be closer to him. They sought contact by requesting that he attend all staff meetings, or by challenging him in ways that engaged his time and attention. When Dr. A. began to exercise more authority, the staff felt cut off from Dr. S. and sought him out even more. In general the staff put pressure on Dr. S. and Dr. A. to assume the traditional positions and roles of No. 1 and No. 2 for the unit, and tried to bring Dr. S. in to head the unit as well as the division.

Dr. S. was not the only male potentially available for unit leadership; the consultant was also male.

> The C.U. staff began to behave as if Dr. A. had brought in a potential male leader, and strongly tended to pair Dr. A. with the consultant. Initially he was welcomed with great respect and his comments went unchallenged. When his comments seemed critical, staff members asked for his advice and direction to rectify matters. Before long, however, as he maintained his consultant role and declined a leadership role, the staff, particularly the two senior male members, began to attack him.

Male staff members did not openly compete with Dr. A. for leadership, but seemed to display both a wish for external male leadership and competitiveness with the potential candidates. Although male staff challenged Dr. A.'s authority over them and their work (as will be discussed later) they did not usually compete with her for unit leadership and control of the work of others.

What was Dr. A.'s stance in regard to the search for male authority? At times she affirmed her own authority as unit chief. At other times she colluded with the group in their belief in male authority, and participated enough in the collective search to help keep it alive. Only gradually did she become aware of her own predilection for and readiness to take the supportive role of No. 2 to a powerful male.

When the search for a male leader failed, and Dr. A. became more successful at actualizing her authority, she was confronted with recurrent challenges. These seemed to take a different form than challenges to male authority, which are more often open confrontations. Challenges to Dr. A.'s authority were usually unacknowledged, subtle, and masked, occurring as instances of covert defiance, denial of subordinancy, or attempts to seduce her out of her role. The most direct challenges came from women.

Dr. A.'s response to these challenges was weak and uncertain, partly because she had difficulty recognizing and defining them as challenges. She was not able to mobilize her own aggression in the service of managing the enterprise. Her approach to staff was often as a supportive, helpful teacher. She attempted to be "nice," to make people feel comfortable and secure and discouraged conflict. Her responses seemed to reflect discomfort in taking an authoritative role vis-a-vis other adults without the support of a male superior.

> On several occasions Dr. A. delegated responsibility for work to various staff members, who would then decide that the work should be done differently or by different people. Dr. A. was greatly displeased, but did not respond angrily. There was then a very soft-spoken struggle, with no direct confrontation of this critical challenge to her authority. She was hesitant to exercise the legitimate power of her position, behaving in ways that obscured her authority and made for continued struggle.

When open conflict did occur, members of the group seemed to deny Dr. A.'s authority to bring weighty sanctions to bear.

> Ms C. at one point engaged in prolonged open resistance to Dr. A.'s delegation of tasks to her. Dr. A. told Ms C. that she might therefore be transferred or terminated. Ms C. expressed great surprise that such a thing might happen, as if it were inconceivable that Dr. A. would have the right to invoke such sanctions.

Male subordinates occasionally attempted to seduce Dr. A. out of her role, thereby negating her authority over them. For example, in the midst of an encounter with a male paraprofessional staff member whose work Dr. A. was criticizing, he began to compliment her on her style of dress and figure. Confused by his unexpected and inappropriate shift, she attempted to reinstate the work roles without direclty confronting the violation, and was not entirely successful in doing so.

Male staff were inclined to by-pass Dr. A. and to flout the organizational structure. When senior male staff spoke with her about their work, it was in the spirit of obtaining her consultation to them, thereby obfuscating their subordinacy. They struggled to be independent of her, to distance themselves from her authority. They had difficulties in accepting criticism from Dr. A. and would go to great lengths to defend their work. For her part, Dr. A. found herself being excessively cautious in offering a negative assessment of male staff members' work.

The important point is that a woman leader and her staff have no important previous social experience that enables them to perceive a woman as having legitimate power to control and protect the external boundary of an adult group, to stand alone as a figure of authority, to delegate authority, and to evaluate output of other adults.

THE FEMALE LEADER'S RELATIONSHIP TO A SUBORDINATE NO. 2

The most important internal boundary for a work group is typically that which separates the leader from its other members. A No. 2 level position of authority can have a crucial place in the structural space between leader and subordinates.

In a work group the responsibility is typically divided (as in the nuclear family) so that the No. 1 devotes primary attention to the external boundary and the No. 2 devotes attention to the internal boundaries. The latter manages not only many of the concrete details of the work task, but also the socio-emotional functions. Without this No. 2 position the leader is compelled to attend to all task and maintenance functions, and priorities may conflict (Newton & Levinson, 1973).

The No. 2 may protect the No. 1 from attack by the staff members. If such protection is available, the leader does not need to exert energy in maintaining defense against attack from subordinates and can concentrate energy on task functions. If there is no internal protection, the leader must continually seek out or verify the support of subordinates, or operate without a clear sense of unified support from staff members.

In contemporary society a male is typically No. 1, and a female may work comfortably as No. 2 to him, as in the prototype of the family. Special problems arise, we believe, in creating a leadership coalition in a unit led by a female.

The male Director of the Center had a male Associate Director, setting a model of a male No. 1 and also a male No. 2. Some of the male Division Heads and Unit Chiefs employed women to function in No. 2 level positions, but usually without a clear title of second-in-command; that is, women performed many important day-to-day functions but without commensurate authority, salary, or recognition, and without being in line for promotion.

Attempts to Establish a No. 2 Role

In the Consultation Unit Dr. A. wished to establish a No. 2 position; however, none of the senior staff members was able to develop a satisfactory No. 2 role relationship with her.

> Mr. Y., a senior professional staff member, seemed the most appropriate candidate for the No. 2 role. Despite the fact that he had held a strongly supportive No. 2 role in relation to the former male Chief, and had not himself wished to take the No. 1 position, he never developed such a coalition with Dr. A. He and Dr. A. had had a comfortable working relationship as peers; upon her promotion, however, he became much less active in unit work and within a short time left the unit.

Males tend to have difficulty in accepting the No. 2 position with a female No. 1, particularly if it is a unique situation within the organization. There is some evidence that a male No. 2 on the Consultation Unit would have felt particular discomfort in the presence of the Division Head and Dr. A.

> During a week in which Mr. Y. and Dr. A. were privately discussing the possibility of Mr. Y. taking a No. 2 position, a staff meeting was held at which Dr. S. was present. Throughout most of the meeting Mr. Y. remained silent. When Dr. A. asked him about his unaccustomed silence, he declared that he was taking the role of an observer. Dr. A. and Dr. S. had been seated at opposite ends of a table; when Dr. S. left the meeting early, Mr. Y. moved to sit in his chair and began to participate.

There were several instances in which male staff members specifically rejected the possibility of a coalition with Dr. A. and reaffirmed their membership in the staff group. They seemed to feel a sense of discomfort, possibly danger, in a coalition with her. We speculate that it seemed to present the threat of a return to maternal ties, and to the Oedipal situation of perilous competition with Dr. A.'s male superordinate.

Socialized to take the No. 2 position with a male No. 1, women find the situation very different in taking a secondary leadership role with another woman as leader. Women have been trained to compete with other women for favored positions with powerful men. It seems difficult for women to join in supporting or protecting another woman.

It may also be that males in the group are fearful of female coalition and act to prevent it.

> The next senior ranking woman, Ms C., not only did not attempt to take the No. 2 role, but engaged in a covertly competitive struggle with Dr. A. When Ms F. was hired in a senior position, she and Dr. A. agreed on major issues

and had similar work styles, but they had difficulty in defining a No. 2 role for Ms F., finding it confusing, uncomfortable, seemingly without substance. Both women had difficulty with open communication and collaboration with each other. An angry frustration and competition developed that was very difficult for them to acknowledge.

When they began to address these issues in a staff workshop, male staff members became highly anxious, changed the direction of the discussion, insisted that the two women were really already in coalition, and interchanged their names several times. The men effectively prevented the examination of feelings or fantasies about what might happen if the two women either formed a real leadership coalition or became openly competitive, and reduced the possibility of their working toward real collaboration. Shortly thereafter, Ms F. left the unit to accept a No. 1 position in another section of the Center.

Neither men nor women seem to feel comfortable in a No. 2 role under a female leader. In the absence of No. 2 a woman leader may either be isolated from staff or immersed in all the details and squabbles of the personnel, with profound effects on her ability to manage the overall enterprise.

DEPENDENCY IN THE STAFF GROUP

Bion (1961) theorized that members of a work group operate on two levels: one level involves the work task, and the other involves a basic assumption that the group has made about itself, but that remains largely outside of awareness. Bion identified three basic assumptions—dependency, pairing, and fight-flight. A group may behave as if it meant to depend upon its leader for all forms of nourishment and security, or to accomplish work only through the pairing of two members, or to fight or run away from somebody or something. When the group's behavior is primarily determined by basic assumptions, members may behave in ways that are inappropriate for the work task.

The individual's original experience with a woman in authority, the mother, teaches that her role is to supply nurturance and training; it is in these areas that her authority lies. The presence of a female leader in a work group appears to stimulate unusually strong dependency needs within the group and to lead directly to the formation of a basic assumption of dependency. That is, the staff is likely unconsciously to perceive the female leader's task as feeding and training, no matter what task has been designated to her in reality. Members of the group thereupon present themselves as though they were helpless children eager to be fed and taught.

When Dr. A. assumed leadership of the Consultation Unit, staff members almost automatically asked for further training whenever she made a demand for work. During the consultant's first session with the group, he noted that it had become unclear whether individuals were staff members or trainees. He cited the staff's demands for more in-service training, and asked why they did not attempt to obtain it in other ways, since they had access to a large number of training seminars. He noted that they were behaving as if there were no external source of supplies, as if all resources must somehow be obtained from the unit leader.

If the woman leader consistently directs her attention to the work task instead of to the dependency needs that have been evoked in part by her gender, she may enable the group to learn after a time that she will not play a primarily nurturant role. However, the woman leader, due to her own socialization, may relate to staff in various ways that keep alive and promote the fantasies of the giving, teaching mother.

Consequences of Failure to Satisfy

When dependent needs were not met, there ensued general feelings of emptiness, personal insufficiency, and covert rage toward the depriving leader. When Dr. A. made demands that staff give out rather than take in, she was confronted with passive-aggressive sabotage. A prototypic example involved an actual feeding of the group.

> For several months, Dr. A. provided coffee at staff meetings without requesting that expenses or responsibility be shared. When she ceased to provide the coffee, staff members attempted to provide supplies but in an ineffective way. Some significant part of the supplies (cups, instant coffee, spoons) was always omitted and no one could in fact obtain a cup of coffee. During the first week that she attempted to stop providing oral supplies in concrete form, two staff members brought food to her (homemade fudge, cookies) as a continuation—although a reversal—of the feeding transaction, as if to prime the pump. After resisting for several weeks Dr. A. finally resumed the work of providing, freely and unilaterally, all essential components of the morning coffee enterprise. She had real difficulty, in this situation as well as more generally, in perceiving the staff's dependency as inappropriate, and in trying to reverse the enduring basic assumption of dependency in the group.

Although Dr. A. tended to behave in ways that kept the dependent fantasies alive, in time she became less gratifying. As she attended more exclusively to the work task, she became transmogrified into a profoundly depriving figure. Subordinates responded with anger and hostility. At one point, the group seemed unwittingly to have put forth one staff member to voice its sense of cruel deprivation.

Ms C. clung tenaciously to a demanding, needy stance, expressing the group's dependent insistence that the Unit Chief's emphasis upon more work and less training was oppressive and unreasonable. This spokeswoman seemed to voice the collective appeal to the leader to be the Good Mother. In the name of "unit philosophy"—which was wistfully counter-cultural—she objected to Dr. A.'s attempts to exercise authority.

The fact that it was often impossible to determine who was responsible for a given project, and that numerous projects taken on by the staff actually disappeared forever, was not especially compelling for the staff. A dependent group process had developed so strongly that, in this context, otherwise competent people felt incapable of taking individual responsibility for projects.

In a situation of basic assumption dependency, a leader loses the ability to perform important functions. Through inducing guilt about being a depriving, withholding mother, the staff urge the woman leader to abdicate legitimate leadership. They can overwhelm her with greedy demands—more training, resources, supplies of various kinds. She is vulnerable to being made to feel authoritarian for being authoritative, ungiving and withholding for being realistic, unreasonable for expecting adult behavior and responsibility from staff.

SUMMARY AND CONCLUSION

Dr. A. became much more knowledgeable about her own, the group's, and the organization's contribution to her difficulty in exercising authority. She grew to behave in a more aware fashion over the course of the consultation and of her continuing tenure. Within a year after the conclusion of these observations, for reasons involving other organizational issues, a higher-level reorganization of the Center took place in which the Consultation Unit was terminated. Dr. A. was offered an administrative position in another section of the Center, which she accepted.

We have emphasized the areas of difficulty, which we believe to be gender-related, for this woman and her staff in the hope that we are identifying unrecognized but common problems in ways that will be useful to others, and that we are offering a theoretical view of the specific organizational implications of these problems. We suggest that, because of the fantasy and fear of women's power, both men and women are socialized to accept a strongly held stereotype of women as possessing legitimate authority only to nurture. Therefore a woman is likely to have difficulty exercising authority in those areas that are seen as inappropriate to her sex role, and for which she receives little or no early training: maintenance of a group's external boundary, mobilization of aggression in the service of work, establishment of a No. 2 position with her as No. 1. She is also

Application: Bayes and Newton

likely to stimulate and collude in the maintenance of dependency in her staff.

For these reasons a woman in authority should be prepared to counteract strong social forces in herself and in others that act to preclude competent leadership behavior. An understanding of such potential difficulties helps a work group and its female leaders to mobilize resources in more effective ways.

22.

DILEMMAS OF BLACK FEMALES IN LEADERSHIP

Rhetaugh Graves Dumas

From the time they first set foot in the New World, black females have struggled courageously to contribute toward a better quality of life in black communities and in society at large. From 1619 to the present, their struggles have been waged from the lowest position among black and white Americans, and they have labored under the hardest conditions. While their contributions have been significant in the development of this Nation and in the continuing fight against the oppression of its black citizenry, black females have yet to enjoy the full benefits of their suffering and arduous labors. Obstructed by the dynamics of racism and sexism in the groups in which they live and work, the full leadership potential of black females throughout their history in this country has remained a relatively untapped—or at best, underutilized—resource, not only in predominantly white institutions and organizations, but also in black communities.

During slavery, organizations often were not permitted among the slaves. Among the free, black women had limited opportunities, if any, to head the significant organizations that existed in the north during slavery or those that developed around the country after the Civil War. Organizations that included black and white males and females were headed by white males. Women's groups that were racially mixed were headed by white women. Outside the family, which was headed by males, the black church was the first major social institution fully controlled by blacks. As the critical training ground for black leadership, the vast majority of black leaders, including the post-war politicians, got their start in the church. Despite the fact that women comprised 62.5% of the membership and their dues provided the bulk of the financial support, their roles were facilitative and supportive (Woodson, 1921). Men held the top leadership posts and the power. Just a couple of years ago, for the first time in history, two black women were appointed to high posts in a black church organization. Whatever access the black community had to the powerful leaders in the larger community was achieved through the church. Black preachers were able to exercise more influence than others in the black community. Prior to emancipation and for some four decades to follow, black men had greater access to education. The first college degrees in the black community were earned by males. In higher education, the first black woman earned a

Application: Dumas

Ph.D. degree forty-five years after the first such degree was awarded to a black male in the United States. That woman was Sadie T. Mossell (Alexander) who earned her degree in Economics at the University of Pennsylvania in 1921. Edward A. Bouchet was awarded the doctorate from Yale in 1876.

Historically, due to their executive positions and training in the church and their access to formal educational institutions, men have been the most powerful and the most celebrated leaders in black communities. During the Reconstruction in the South, there was a great emergence of black men who provided political leadership. Men held the franchise for their communities; twenty served in the U.S. House of Representatives and two in the Senate. Others served as lieutenant governor, sheriff, prosecuting attorney, recorder of deeds in their localities. One woman served as postmistress in Indianola, Mississippi. The vast majority of black women leaders were limited to projects for the social uplift of the community, and their main followers were other black women and youth. It was only during periods of extreme stress that the value of the black woman's leadership outside of her women's groups could be realized. Even then the women not only had to struggle on the boundary between blacks and whites, but they also had to find ways to endure the frustration and hardships posed by the lack of support from black males. Existing circumstances and prior experiences made it difficult, if not impossible, to transcend what I call the hydraulic system principle of male-female relationships. That principle stipulates that black males can rise only to the degree that black women are held down. Black females were unable to submit to their dissatisfactions when survival in a hostile and increasingly violent environment, and a sense of community and togetherness seemed so essential. Therefore, women with leadership abilities concentrated their efforts on relieving the suffering imposed by illiteracy, poverty, and disease. This situation was still very apparent as late as the sixties. Earlier black female leaders realized the need for the strength and mutual support that would come from group effort, and they began in 1892 to organize local black women's clubs and thus planted the seeds that ultimately grew into a national movement still existing today. Under the motto "Lifting as we climb," the National Association of Colored Women provided the model for what became the most significant resource available to black women, not only for mutual support and social uplift, but also as a training ground for black female leadership. During the sixties, many young females rejected many of the traditional organizations for ambitious black women as being too middle class. Although black women found a lot of meaning in the black protest and civil rights movements and seemed to have fewer social conformists among their ranks, they did not occupy prominent leadership positions. They were often caught up with black men in that hydraulic principle that forced them to take only those roles that would enable their men to go forward. Many black women with outstanding leadership abilities held their skills in abeyance lest they might undermine the security and threaten the masculinity of the black men. Bound by the fear of the strong, uppity, castrating black woman, the full range of the black female's leadership was never fully exploited. There were, of course, exceptions. A small number of black women did not permit themselves to be bound by these dynamics all of the time.

It is significant to repeat that while white males were being trained for leadership of both sexes, and some few black males were sometimes provided opportunities for leadership in racially mixed groups, black females were limited to the leadership of other black females. Furthermore, when they dared to turn their attention from service-oriented programs to the political arena, they had to struggle against strong opposition in both the white and black communities. Despite these obstacles, many black women have cleverly combined political, civic, social goals and strategies, and some gains have been visible in each generation. But there is still a long way to go. Despite the outstanding achievements of some black women in many fields of endeavor, the mass of black women in America are still at the bottom of the heap, among this country's underdogs. Although increasing numbers of black women are beginning to occupy important positions of authority and prestige in organizations within and outside black communities, there are forces at work today, as in the past, that tax the physical and emotional stamina of these women. Their authority is undermined, their competence is compromised and the power they might conceivably exercise is united thus limiting their opportunities for rewards and mobility in the organization. I contend that this problem has its roots in myths about the privileged position and role of black women in slavery. The mythical image of the strong, powerful, castrating black matriarch pervades contemporary organizations and poses a critical dilemma for black females that makes competition for, and competent performance in, leadership positions at best a costly endeavor. There are increasing efforts to resurrect the Black Mammy in today's ambitious black women who aspire to move up the socioeconomic ladder or into political arenas. There are negative consequences for those who succumb as well as for those who dare to resist. The remainder of this paper is devoted to an elaboration of this thesis. In preparing the following section, I have utilized data compiled for a more extensive study of this topic. Many historical sources were utilized, most of which are the works of secondary authorities, but narratives of slaves and witnesses and black autobiographies were examined.

Very little of the literature is addressed to the problems of black women leaders, or to those of women in general. Therefore, I have utilized my own experiences as an appointed city official, an associate professor and department head of a professional training program in a prestigious Ivy League university, a Federal executive and a member of a consultant staff for group relations training in the Tavistock tradition. I have relied more heavily upon the experiences of numerous other black women leaders around the country. Some of them described their dilemmas during informal discussions at social gatherings or during professional meetings, others (totaling over 500 during the period of data gathering) while participating in institutes, workshops, or group relations training conferences. I have supplemented these sources with descriptions in the literature, particularly, biographies and autobiographies of black women. These were valuable although sparse resources. The most telling autobiographies were those of Ida B. Wells Barnett (Dusier, 1970) and Mary Church Terrell (1940).

The data derived from these experiences are naturally less structured and more casual than those that come from a more rigorously designed approach. Nevertheless, there are advantages in the intimacy of detail and the breadth of exposure that this approach permits, especially at such a rudimentary stage of inquiry. Keeping in mind then that the data are soft, I hope that the observations and thoughts presented here will at least stimulate the commitment toward a more intensive approach to this very critical area of study.

The presence of black women in leadership positions takes on highly significant meanings in organizational life. Myths of the superiority of black women over white women and black men emphasize their tremendous power and strength, and their unique capacity for warm, soothing interpersonal relationships. These myths prompt others to press black women into symbolic roles that circumscribe the nature and scope of their functions and limit their options and power in the organizations in which they live and work.

The black woman leader is often torn between the expectations and demands born of her mythical image and those that are inherent in her official status and tasks in the formal organization. The pressures to conform to the roles of her earlier predecessors are often irresistible. Whether she likes it or not, the black woman has come to represent the kind of person, a style of life, a set of attitudes and behaviors through which individuals and groups seek to fulfill their own socio-emotional needs in organizations. It is not surprising, therefore, that there is a great deal more interest in the *personal* qualities of black women administrators than in their skill and competence for formal leadership roles.

There is general resistance to having black women perform competently in formal, high-status positions. Rather, the preference is to have the black woman assume a variety of functions that resemble those described for the black mammy during the plantation era. In performing these functions, however, the power of the black woman leader is as illusory as was Mammy's. It is derived from her relationship in the *informal* system, her willingness to put her *person* at the disposal of those around her. It can be maintained only as long as she is willing or able to provide what is demanded of her.

The demands very often go beyond the responsibilities of her formal position. For example, the black woman in leadership is expected to comfort the weary and oppressed, intercede on behalf of those who feel abused, champion the cause for equality and justice—often as a lone crusader. She is expected to compensate for the deficits of other members of her group, speaking up for those who are unable or unwilling to speak for themselves, making demands on behalf of the weak or frightened, doing more than her share of the work to make up for people who dawdle or fail to complete their assigned tasks. Expected to be mother confessor, she counsels and advises her superiors and peers as well as her subordinates, often on matters unrelated to the tasks at hand. She is called upon to fill in for her boss in dealing with problems of sex and race, to mediate in situations of conflict, quiet the "natives," curb the aggression of black males, dampen the impact of other aggressive black women, and to maintain stability or restore order in the organization or one of its sectors.

Black women who are pressed into such positions are faced with problems that challenge their own identity and threaten their inner security. For example, they are often caught in the struggles between the boss and subordinates, blacks and whites, men and women, between units in the organization, and between the organization and the community in which it is located. Sometimes they are unclear who or what they are representing and find themselves trying to manage certain organizational boundaries without adequate authority and hence without appropriate backing and support. They are subject to high levels of tension as they become the repository of the problems, conflicts, and secrets of individuals and groups on both sides of the boundary.

Because of the myths about the strength and courage of their predecessors, black women today are also expected to have unlimited internal resources to cope with any problem that conceivably might confront them. Consequently, people around them are likely to be insensitive to their needs for socio-psychological support, reassurance, or some relief from the heavy demands on their time and energy.

Many of them work long hours in activities related to these symbolic roles, leaving less time and energy available for task performance. Consequently, doubts may be raised as to their competence for the positions they hold. Some black women in this predicament come to doubt their own ability and are disillusioned with their newly acquired status and prestige. Unfortunately, efforts to alter these situations are met with strong resistance from people who value their performance in the informal network of relationships. Such people are likely to subvert the leader's attempts to effect a more realistic distribution of time and effort between the informal and formal roles. If they persist, such situations not only undermine the upward mobility of the black woman, but also have important implications for her physical and emotional health. She takes the risk of being "used up" or "burnt out" rapidly. The trouble with symbolic leaders is that they often cannot tell where their personal lives end and where their organizational roles begin. They are treated as if they belong to the people around them, and they feel as though they do. Black women who succumb to these symbolic roles do not actually lead; they offer themselves to be used. Hence the danger of overcommitment to activities of this nature.

Case 1

> Dr. A. holds an executive position in a large and prestigious organization in the Mid-West. Her academic and professional credentials are impressive. In her present position she is the person on whom everybody depends. She is overworked because the people in her department believe they can't do without her, and she behaves as if they really can't.

Application: Dumas

She is the one who sees that visitors and clients are properly entertained. Most of the luncheon or dinner parties are held at her apartment, and it is she who makes the necessary preparations. At her office she has an open-door policy and people drop in at all hours during the day to seek her counsel and guidance or just to sit and talk. She is called upon to support the causes of the low-status groups in the organization and sometimes works with them after office hours to plan strategies and aid them in presenting their grievances to top management. She is called by local and national groups to recommend blacks to serve on special committees and boards of directors. In discussing these requests, she is often talked into serving on the boards or committees. In addition, she is assigned to several inter-organizational committees and task forces to represent her department. She is given the tiresome travel assignments that others do not wish to take. She is frequently called at the last minute to cover commitments that another member of the staff is unable to keep, including those of her boss. Her boss continues to redefine her job to take up slack created by staff attrition. In all of this, the responsibilities that comprise the job for which she was hired are compromised and she is beginning to receive criticism. Her clients are complaining that she does not return their telephone calls or follow through on commitments. Her colleagues are complaining that she does not provide feedback from the meetings she attends. The fact is that she frequently arrives at those meetings late and leaves early, so she neither gets much information from them, nor does she seem to contribute very much either. However, the people don't seem to mind. They comment on what a warm and pleasant person she is and how much they enjoy having her there for however long she is able to stay. Her friends and colleagues outside her organization have observed a downward trend in her communications and performance at professional meetings. She appears to be tired; her presentations are superficial and often confused. She touches on a variety of topics but never seems to get into any one in depth. Her family complains that she does not spend enough time at home. When she is not traveling, she works late at her office. Her friends in the community complain that she makes no social overtures, and they have begun to limit their contacts. Dr. A. complains bitterly that she never seems to get to those tasks that she is supposed to do because of all the interruptions and the extra responsibilities that are forced on her. Her boss doesn't seem to understand the pressures that she is working under. He is not satisfied with her performance in the role for which she was hired and has refused to recommend her for promotion.

She is growing more disillusioned with her job and plans to retire earlier than she anticipated. The popularity she once enjoyed is diminishing; she is not able to deliver all that people expect of her, and she still is unable to say no. She has much less influence than she had during the first year or so on the job. She has been in her current position for a little over three years and is looking forward to getting out within a couple of years.

Realizing this vulnerability, some black women refuse to assume symbolic roles. They try hard to focus exclusively on formal tasks and become rigid in their avoidance of personal involvement with their colleagues. They are likely to interpret invitations to participate in informal relationships as bids to behave according to stereotypes of earlier black women. Intent on avoiding that image, they isolate themselves, which makes them unavailable for those informal contacts that might well enhance their executive effectiveness. The more impersonal they are, the more curious people are to know them better, and the more they will challenge the boundary that the leader endeavors to maintain between her person and her role. Of course, the more this boundary is challenged the more rigid it becomes, which unfortunately leads to the image of a cold, inflexible authority. Thus, in the effort to avoid becoming the symbol of the good and willing resource for the satisfaction of the needs of people in the organization, these leaders develop an image that can be equally destructive. By their aloofness they are distinguished from the symbolic benevolent black mammy, but they become instead the wicked malevolent mammy. The negative consequences of this image are no less injurious than those endured by the executives who assume the caring, nurturing, protective roles.

In his analysis of the archetype of the Great Mother, Erich Neumann (1972) calls attention to the fantastic and chimerical images elicited by the symbolism of the Terrible Mother:

> In the myths and tales of all peoples, ages, and countries—and even in the nightmares of our own nights—witches and vampires, ghouls and specters assail us, all terrifyingly alike. The dark half of the black-and-white cosmic egg representing the Archetypal Feminine engenders terrible figures that manifest the black, abysmal side of life and the human psyche. Just as world, life, nature, and soul have been experienced as a generative and nourishing, protecting and warming Femininity, so their opposites are also perceived in the image of the Feminine; death and destruction, danger and distress, hunger and nakedness, appears as helplessness in the presence of the Dark and Terrible Mother.

Although males in authority may be symbolized as good or bad mothers, the implications are more severe for females. Feminine authority cast against a black background thus becomes the most haunting of all symbolic mothers. Bad mothers who are white seem to be more easily tolerated than bad mothers who are black; bad mothers who are black and female border on the intolerable. Indeed the rich imagery evoked by black women comes as close to the Great Mother as one might imagine. When the black woman leader fails to give people what they believe they need, she is perceived to be deliberately depriving and rejecting, and therefore, hostile and potentially destructive. Just as she is believed to be capable of providing generative, nourishing, protective Femininity of the most powerful order, she is also imagined to have the capacity to withhold or destroy resources necessary to life and safety in the organization's symbolic world. The forceful exercise of her authority thus arouses intense irrationality and creates one crisis after another with which she must deal.

The black woman leader who is perceived as a bad mother, bad black mammy, must deal with the dependency, fear, and rage that often are expressed covertly and undermine the effectiveness of all involved. Stubborn resistance to work is a frequent manifestation of anger in such situations. The leader finds herself deluged by requests for clarification of procedures or special instructions for the most simple tasks. Indeed, those who feel deprived by her will frequently relinquish their authority and behave as if only she has the knowledge and skill required for a particular task. This type of dependency leads many executives to take on themselves the responsibilities that should be delegated or shared by others.

Sometimes the anger and hostility find as targets people who are close to or supportive of the black woman in question. In these and other ways, the black woman in such situations is kept busy mediating staff conflicts, dealing with hostile confrontations, having to rush to meet deadlines for work that should have been completed long before and having to persist against covert resistance to get information she needs to do her job well. The following case illustrates this point.

Case 2

> Dr. B. has recently resigned from her position as dean of a professional school in a large private university. She held the position for three years. When she took the position her faculty, all white women, seemed very happy to have her, and wanted to get to know her better. She spent a great deal of time with them in social gatherings and orientation meetings.
>
> However, when the time came to turn her attention to work, she began to have problems. The faculty that seemed so eager to work with her and who appeared from the academic and professional credentials to be well qualified for their jobs began to appear more and more insecure and immature. The dean found herself giving more direction than she believed was warranted by the nature of their tasks, and had to be careful lest she arouse their anxiety. Her time was often spent in individual conferences to discuss plans

or to check completed work. In general most of the faculty seemed reluctant to work independently of her guidance and approval.

Dr. B. described the behavior of her faculty as a desire to be spoon fed by her, which she finally decided would not be in her best interest or theirs. So she challenged them to take more responsibility for their own assignments and to exercise the authority that had been delegated to them in their respective roles. She suggested that they might use each other to check out ideas and work through problems; she would continue to meet with them periodically but was unable to continue to give them the time they demanded. Later she found herself having to deal with a number of conflicts among the faculty and between faculty and students. It seemed that simple problems escalated rapidly into crises. It was difficult for her to get away from her school to attend to issues critical to its survival and its relationship with other parts of the university. The faculty complained when she was away and invariable some mishap would occur in her absence. With one exception, the faculty were becoming more and more dissatisfied with their jobs and were generally uncooperative. At a time when it was doubtful that she could recruit replacements, several of them gave notice of their intention to resign at the end of that academic year.

The only faculty member who seemed to work independently and on whom the dean had to rely very heavily became the target for hostility from her colleagues. The crowning blow to her and to the dean was a cruel joke: a C.O.D. package that contained an Afro wig.

These are but a few examples of the difficulties that Dean B. reported that no doubt figured significantly in her decision to resign the deanship.

The black woman executive, perceived to be either good or bad, becomes a kind of superstar among some individuals or groups in the organization. People love her when she gives what is desired and hate her when she fails to perform as expected. In either case people are moved by an image they have constructed of the black person in the leadership role—how they imagine her life style, attitudes, values, and what they symbolize for the beholder. When she is good, she becomes their heroine. When she is not good, she becomes their villain, but always an object for them to identify with, positively or negatively.

The leader who objects to being Mammy may not be subject to all the honors bestowed on her benevolent counterpart. Nevertheless, she does not suffer from want of attention from the people around her who seem to enjoy the experience of hating her. They want their friends and family to witness the bad person, especially in situations where she will be embarrassed, made into a fool, symbolically "killed off." So she is given invitations that set the stage for the kill. If she is not careful she may even do the job for them. Other blacks are often recruited for the dirty work in predominantly white organizations, or other women in predominantly male-oriented situations.

For example, the first black woman superintendent of public schools in a middle-sized urban community had held the position less than three years when she became involved in a series of angry disagreements with the Board of Education. From the reports of their conflicts in the public news, I was impressed by the fact that the one board member who consistently led the confrontation was also a black woman. No other voices on the board seemed to equal hers in opposition to the superintendent's handling of the business of public education or in support of her leadership.

I suspect that the board member who levied the harsh criticisms was doing so on behalf of at least the majority of the board. She was delegated to set the stage for the embarrassment of the superintendent, and for even more drastic action in the future. I am proposing that it was not by accident that the leadership for the opposition was assumed by a black female.

This situation reminds me of an incident that occurred after I refused to recommend reappointment of a member of the faculty in a program I administered. It was not my decision alone that determined the action; the committee voted unanimously to deny reappointment, although people behaved as if I had forced the committee to that action. I was challenged by the woman in question and several individuals and groups advocated that I change my recommendation, which they felt would lead the committee to reverse the decision. I refused to change my recommendation. However, the committee was persuaded to review the decision and a second vote was taken because some members felt that I had exerted an overwhelming influence on their votes, and they wanted an opportunity to reopen the case. This was done and the decision of the committee again was to deny reappointment, although the vote was not unanimous. The aggrieved applicant elicited the support of blacks in the community who led several angry protest marches into the school and the clinical agency where she and I held joint appointments. I found myself on the boundary between the school and the angry black leaders who yelled obscenities at me for allowing myself to be taken in by "the system" that was "kicking out" the only member of the faculty who cared anything about the black community. The one other black faculty member was on leave of absence; therefore I was the only black faculty member around at that time, and I felt totally alone. I became the target for a great deal of hostility over a period of several months. I must admit that I discovered in retrospect how much I had participated in my election to the post of "flak-catcher." People had treated me as if I were so powerful that I single-handedly forced the committee to deny reappointment; as if even those who might have protected the unfortunate woman's job were helpless against my wishes. I felt confident in my reasons for refusing to recommend her appointment. However, I came to believe that in exercising my responsibility to maintain the level of quality in the program that the faculty and I had agreed upon,

I had pushed the school into a terrible crisis. While I was not willing to change my vote, I did feel unusually responsible for the disturbance. Unwittingly, I was behaving as if I really did have all that power. And no one in the school objected to my taking the front line between them and the malcontents from outside. The dean was relieved to have me perform that role for her and for the school. The director of the clinical agency refused to have me assume that position in his organization. One might speculate about his reasons: being a white male and a good administrator, he was not about to relinquish his authority to me. Being a colleague and a friend, he wanted to protect me. Being a male chauvinist pig, he *had* to protect me. Regardless of the real motivations at the time, I have come to appreciate the soundness of the organizational principles that he later espoused as the major determinants for his position during that series of tense and stressful episodes.

Indeed these types of incidents are not limited to black women leaders. Nevertheless, blacks are particularly vulnerable, and black males are spared more often than black females.

The die seems to have been cast by the group of historians and other writers who chose from among all the black women in history the roles of the black mammy, Sojourner Truth, and Harriet Tubman as exemplary models. Descriptions of Harriet Tubman are particularly pertinent to this discussion. Note the following:

> There were many who in the years prior to 1860 undertook the Mosaic mission and appealed to the plantation owners to abandon the system of chattel slavery. There were those too who, tiring of the apparent fruitlessness of these diplomatic missions, took up the mantle of the deliverer. Some of these were notably unsuccessful (Nat Turner and John Brown, for example), while others, relying upon more devious means, were notably successful. Among these latter none was more daring or individually successful than Harriet Tubman . . . Harriet Tubman was not only an illiterate, highly visible runaway slave but . . . she was engaged in an illegal activity . . . And though the results of her unexampled heroism were not to free a whole nation of bondmen and bond-women, yet this object was as much the desire of her heart as it was the great leader of Israel. Her cry to the slave-holders was ever like his to Pharoah, "Let my people go," and not even he imperiled life and limb more willingly than did our courageous and self-sacrificing friend . . . Her name deserves to be handed down to posterity, side-by-side with the names of Jeanne d'Arc, Grace Darling, and Florence Nightingale, for not one of these women, noble and brave as they were, has shown more courage and more power of endurance, in facing danger and death to relieve human suffering, than this black woman . . . After her almost superhuman efforts in making her own escape from

slavery, and then returning . . . nine times, and bringing . . . away . . . over three hundred fugitives . . . her shrewdness . . . her courage in every emergency, and her willingness to endure hardship and face any danger for the sake of her poor followers was phenomenal . . . She had often risked her own life for her people, and she thought nothing of that (Bradford, 1974).

I know firsthand the tremendous hardships and anguish inherent in attempts to live up to this model in the symbolism of contemporary organizations that represent in microcosm the society at large. I have felt the pangs of guilt evoked by those who would lead me to believe that to protect myself and promote my general welfare is to let my people down. I am now beginning to see how it is possible to let my people down by *failing* to protect myself and my interests and to seek fulfillment of my own needs. Indeed in modern organizations, racism and sexism dictate that I AM MY PEOPLE. I AM BLACK. I AM WOMAN.

Numerous other black women executives know the pain and anguish to which I refer. Some of them are discovering, as I am, when and how *not* to be Mammy, Miss Truth, Miss Tubman, and still survive. This does not mean that they will be able to avoid becoming symbols in the organizations. It does mean that they are trying to have some part in the development of their symbolic images. It means that they are finding ways to balance the caring, nurturing, protective functions and those that are task-directed. There is at least one writer who argues that it is not possible for the same persons to fulfill the socio-emotional and task needs in organizations simultaneously. Perhaps the success of black women executives lies in their ability to move back and forth between socio-emotional and task-directed functions. The pendulum rarely stays in the center, and when it moves too far to either extreme there is trouble. But even the most successful black woman executive finds her life hectic at best and pays a high price for competent performance. Yet, her struggles yield greater and more lasting achievements and satisfaction than those of her black sisters who are locked into symbolic roles most of the time.

It is often difficult to separate the influence of race from that of sex; there is no doubt in my mind that the *combination* levies a heavy toll on the black woman who exercises authority and responsibility in groups and organizations. Herein lies the most significant challenge to black women executives, to those who claim an interest in promoting the upward social mobility of minority groups and women in America, and to all who are concerned with the development of social and psychological theories of organizational leadership.

23.

THE PSYCHODYNAMICS OF TAKING THE ROLE

Larry Hirschhorn

"No other technique for the conduct of life attaches the individual so firmly to reality as laying emphasis on work; for his work at least gives him a secure place in a portion of reality, in the human community. The possibility it offers of displacing a large amount of libidinal components, whether narcissistic, aggressive or even erotic, on to professional work and on to the human relations connected with it lends it a value by no means second to what it enjoys as something indispensable to the preservation and justification of existence in society. . . . And yet, as a path to happiness, work is not highly prized by men. They do not strive after it as they do after other possibilities of satisfaction. The great majority of people only work under stress of necessity, and this natural human aversion to work raises most difficult social problems."
      Sigmund Freud,
      Civilization and its Discontents, James Strachey ed,
      footnote (1), page 27

Freud raises a central question. If work can provide such satisfaction why do we dislike it so much? How can it be libidinized so that in working with others we grow to appreciate them rather than dislike them. Howard Schwartz has brilliantly argued that the text of *Civilization and Discontents* answers this footnote and that this footnote is in the thematic spine of the text.

In the text, Freud suggests that civilization is so demanding and provides such little gratification because it integrates people into large wholes by making them feel increasingly guilty. We internalize civilization's codes through the dictates of our superego—our moral conscience—that then punishes us whenever and wherever we fantasize taking pleasures that violate cultural or familial norms. In turn, the superego takes hold of the aggression we might deploy against others and directs it against ourselves. To lead a civilized existence, thus is to live in a guilt-ridden world. We punish ourselves both for our imagined deed and for our failure to meet the highest standards of our community. This is why success so rarely brings pleasure. All we have succeeded in doing is discharging an obligation. (Schwartz, 1983)

Since work is an integral part of our civilized life, it too must be organized through the mechanisms of guilt and punishment. The question that Freud asked can then be rephrased: How can we reduce the role that the superego plays in shaping our relationships at work? How can we libidinize work?

In the following paper I explore this question by examining the psychodynamics of taking a work role, of stating to self and others "this is my role, these are its bounds, this is its relationship to the tasks we face together." In the first section, I examine the consequences of failing to take a role by studying a critical incident in my own consulting work. In section two, I examine the psychodynamics of taking a role successfully and show how the relationship of superego to ego is changed in the process. Finally, in the third section I examine the consequence of this analysis for a general critique of work.

A PERSONAL EXPERIENCE

Consider the following: The county office of a state welfare department had to develop new criteria for determining old people's eligibility for home health services. These criteria would be used to channel a sizeable increase in service money to various providers throughout the county. My colleagues, Jane and Henry, contacted Robert B., the deputy of the office, and offered their consulting services. They argued that the office faced a complex political and policy problem. What planning process could the office use so that the resulting criteria were both technically and politically credible to hospital administrators, mental health centers and interest groups that represented the elderly?

Robert B. was frustrating to deal with. At first, he said he was very interested in our center's service but then failed to return successive phone calls and answer letters. After a month of silence, he contacted Jane and Henry, and the two met with him to discuss a possible scope of work. The conversation was a difficult one. Robert B. was aggressive and indirectly demeaning. How could the consultants really be of help to him? What could they do that social workers couldn't do? What was their distinctive competence? Unspecified "others" believed that they had none. He then told Jane and Henry of his plans. He was going to establish two committees, one technical and one policy, to establish and legitimate the new criteria. He was going to set up the former first, since the latter committee would have to deal with the more complex issues of interorganizational and interest group politics. Experts on aging throughout the city would sit on it. Could the consultants really help here? If they were simply good at "process" and "planning," what contributions could they make to the technical committee?

My colleagues returned from the meeting uncertain what to do next. They asked me to consult with them. As they described their meeting, I was struck by their depression. They had been hurt by Robert's attack and felt vulnerable, anxious and deskilled.

I suggested that Robert's plan was inadequate. He was dividing the work between two committees, technical and policy. But could the two be so clearly differentiated? First, if technical committee members came from organizations that served the aging, would they be representing just themselves or their home agencies? How would this be clarified? Wouldn't Robert have to consult initially with the directors of these organizations so that the status of technical experts on the committee could be clarified? Constituting a technical committee was a political process. Second, could the work of the two committees be differentiated in their substance? Robert imagined that the technical committee might create sample eligibility forms containing an array of medical and social service information. But the questions asked and unasked had policy, and therefore political, implications. For example, if the questionnaire emphasized medical status rather than the old persons' relationships to relatives and neighbors, the resulting service and funding patterns might favor hospital rather than social work services. I argued that perhaps Robert himself was quite anxious about the process and had created a fictitious division between policy and technical matters as a way of avoiding the difficult political tasks he faced.

Jane and Henry took my comments uneasily. I seemed to be depressing them more. Jane protested; the technical committee could be composed without regard to political considerations. Perhaps I didn't appreciate that the field of aging services was a "mushy" one in which people frequently crossed between roles. I replied that if this were true, people would then be even more confused about their role, mandate and delegation on the technical policy committee.

Jane asked what they should do. I advised that they write Robert B. a letter, which reflected on his plan to create two committees. The letter could highlight the risks that Robert faced in separating the two without at first negotiating with key stakeholders in the aging field. Such a letter, if thoughtful and supportive, would show Robert how the center could deploy its skills in planning and process to help him. The letter should end with a sketch of a work plan and an estimate of the contract cost.

Jane remained anxious. She worried that if they wrote a letter, Robert could ignore it as he had previous ones. They had to carry the letter by hand and make an appointment with him on the spot. I advised that they not try to "trap him." They were outsiders and could not scheme against him as if they were insiders. Since the process of entering and contracting with an organization so centrally shaped the consultation itself, it was important for them to negotiate with Robert in a direct manner. If they got a contract, they would get it with terms and conditions that would facilitate good work.

Jane and Henry appeared even more depressed. They seemed resigned to my advice in particular and my authority in general. My emerging authority had undermined theirs. More importantly, their depression stimulated feelings of "victory" in me as if I had conquered them by revealing their flaws. These feelings were further stimulated when Jane, noting that

Henry had to leave for another appointment, suggested that the two of us wrap up the meeting. I demurred, feeling that Jane was somehow aligning with me, the stronger male, against Henry. This was, after all, Henry's project not mine. But in protecting Henry, I felt again victorious, as if I had once again exposed Jane's weaknesses.

We ended the meeting, and upon leaving Henry's office my feelings of competence and mastery soured. I felt guilty and concerned. Had I paradoxically hurt my colleagues by helping them? I turned to Jane and asked her if she had read the draft report for a different project we were working on together. She looked at me quizically, "which report?" she asked. I described it to her. "Oh yes," she replied tepidly. I felt punished. She "obviously" did not like my report.

A LEARNING FROM EXPERIENCE

This case vignette highlights several interconnected processes. First, anxiety about work can lead people to step out of their work roles. They do this to turn away from work realities and create a surreal world in which threats can be met with fantasies of omnipotence, dependence or defensive denial. Second, when people depend on one another to do effective work, when they must collaborate, one person's anxiety may trigger an <u>anxiety chain</u>, through which anxiety becomes general and helps shape what Bion called a "basic assumption" group. In such a group, people deploy collective fantasies to deny risks. Third, such fantasies are filled with violence as people both punish themselves for their own failings and imagine that others are their persecutors. Finally, as people step out of role they also step away from one another. They experience real others as if they embodied the characteristics of fantasy figures, particularly "fragmented" or caricatured figures who are either all good and beautiful or all bad and evil. Such "part object" images, stimulated by fresh experiences of anxiety, draw on both infantile experiences of parents and siblings as well as juvenile memories of fairy tales and fantasies. Let us examine these propositions in greater detail.

ROBERT: AN HYPOTHESIS

I did not meet and experience Robert directly, but surely his behavior toward Jane and Henry was peculiar. They were potential resources for him, yet he terrorized him. Jane and Henry's obvious anxiety and sense of incompetence was surely some measure of Robert's aggression against them. Why did he act this way? Let me propose the following hypotheses about his behavior.

Robert faced a difficult political problem—how to create an eligibility system that met the test of technical and political credibility. He faced real risks, for in constructing a policy he would have to manage many interest groups so that they produced a consensus that did not undermine his own agency's position and credibility. His behavior suggests that he could not directly face those risks and take the role of a convenor and manager of a political process. Instead, he created a fiction of two separate processes, one called technical, one called policy, hoping that the former might limit his risks when facing the latter. This fiction, I suggest, enabled him to create an unconscious fantasy of "control." He could control a corp of free-floating technicians (who might be manipulable in a "mushy" social service field) and so deny his actual dependence on unpredictable political processes. In fact of course, his control over the technicians would be limited as well. As he stepped away from reality and out of role, as he failed to supply leadership, the technicians themselves would be thoroughly confused about their roles on the committee. This confusion would quickly reintroduce the interest group politics he sought to avoid.

Melanie Klein speaks of the "manic defense" as a psychological system for avoiding feelings of dependence on others. People repress these feelings when they evoke memories of earlier dependence on punishing and often hated parents. The manic defense cloaks these memories of injury and violence in the fantasy of control and omnipotence. However, the renewed experience of early punishment does not simply disappear. Rather, as in all defense systems, the feeling is transposed, and the anxious and, in fact, overly dependent person tries to punish other people in his setting. In so doing he feels "triumphant" over them and so secure in his once threatening and risky environment.

Klein's description of the manic defense may explain Robert's peculiar behavior toward Henry and Jane. I hypothesized that he was anxious when facing his work and developed a two-committee strategy, which in fantasy limited his dependence on potentially hostile others. Henry and Jane were two consultants who "depended" on him to make a sale. They consequently became ready targets for his fantasies of omnipotence and feelings of punishment. He terrorized them because he was feeling punished by the real risks he faced.

Now consider the ways in which Jane and I interacted. When I entered Henry's office Jane seemed anxious. As I advised the two, Jane seemed increasingly depressed, suggesting that I was punishing her by advising her. At the same time her punished look stimulated feelings of victory and contempt in me. What is going on?

Melanie Klein (1975) talks of the process of "projective identification," a psychological interaction in which one person deposits unwanted feelings into another's feeling system. The first person wishing to get rid of an unwanted feeling treats the other as if they had or embodied the feeling state. For example, someone burdened with intolerable sorrow may imagine that it is others who are sorrowful and may treat them as people to be pitied. By pitying others he may deny his own feelings of misery. The second person may respond in two ways. First, he may experience the projection consciously and feel uncomfortable that he has been given a part in the first's internal drama. He may resist being pitied. In contrast, he may respond unconsciously to the projection, may take the imported feeling as if it was his own, thus confirming the first person's projection. The latter possibility is most likely when the second has an emotional valence for the first's projected feeling state. Those who value being pitied may welcome the projections of those who cannot face their sorrow.

Jane and I were engaged in just such a psychological "dance." Let me propose the following hypothesis. Jane was feeling punished. She had internalized Robert's attack on her personal competence, she "took it personally." This stimulated her own "superego" voices, those voices within all of us that evoke the early reprimands of our parents who upbraded us for our failings, for "being bad." Such voices are frightening, because they lie within us. They can "spy" on us and hold us accountable for failings we hide from everyone else. These are the voices that shame us in front of ourselves alone. Jane projected these punishing voices onto me to diminish their power within her. The voice made concrete in a real other, particularly one who is a friend, becomes less terrifying, even if more real. I therefore became her persecutory agent, the source of her misery. This is why I began to feel unaccountably victorious and triumphant over her and Henry. As a persecutory agent, my job was to catch others in their failings.

But I also had a valence for this role, for such feelings of triumph. I believe that upon first entering Henry's room, the pain and discomfort of my colleagues made me uncomfortable. Their pain evoked all too painful feelings in me of past professional failures. Like Robert, I consequently deployed a manic defense, a defense against feelings of vulnerability by accepting Jane's projection. By feeling triumphant I could deny past and current feelings of pain and injury.

My behavior after the meeting, asking Jane to evaluate my report, is telling here. As I left the meeting, I once again became aware of Jane's pain and felt guilty and ashamed for having triumphed over her. I then asked her to judge my work, just as I had judged her, but clearly I was less interested in her opinion and more in simply "submitting" to her. After all, I only inferred from her tepid response that she thought little of my work. I did not engage her in conversation. By submitting to her, by offering myself up to her for evaluation, I hoped to relieve my guilt. I would sacrifice myself. It is possible of course, that my wish to submit stimulated a symmetrical wish in Jane to punish. She could take back her punishing voice, for now it could punish me for my failings rather than her for her felt limitations. In such a case, her tepid response <u>was</u> meant to punish, but clearly I had "asked for it."

The sequela of this incident is revealing. I returned to my office to begin work on another project. I and another colleague had contracted to work with a legal firm composed of six partners, numerous associates and many staff. One partner had just had a heart attack and others complained that the work was difficult, killing and frequently gave no pleasure. We were to begin by interviewing the six partners. I sat down to write a letter to the six explaining the interview format. Peculiarly, I stumbled on the problem of confidentiality. While I had interviewed clients in preparation for work on other projects numerous times, the problem of confidentiality suddenly loomed large. What would be the rules, what should they tell us or not tell us? Would they hamstring us, by revealing secrets in private that we could not therefore use at the retreat itself?

I composed a letter. It was written starkly as if I were pronouncing upon a set of logical propositions or laws of behavior. I reproduce the relevant part of the draft here.

". . . Our ground rules for confidentiality are based on the following assumptions:
—to be effective as consultants to the group we need to understand the processes, choices, preferences and values that are affecting firm X's development
—to be effective we need to share our learnings and data with the group
—therefore, individual partners should share that information with us that they feel the group of partners should know and understand."

The letter is bizarre. In content, it is strikingly noncollaborative, asking clients whom I barely knew to take on the full burden of revealing and concealing information. I would provide no assistance, nor could I be trusted; this despite the fact that in most other consulting activities, I found it relatively easy to take "organizational secrets" and present them back so that no single person was identified as the source. Moreover, as my colleague pointed out, what was the point of private interviews, if not to get information that was not readily revealed in public. He wondered if I was being too uncollaborative and had not carefully thought about the problems of "entry" into the organization.

The tone of the letter is even more suggestive. It is strikingly nonemotional, nonaffective. Its format—a set of logical propositions—is a sign that it emanates from an overly rational or rationalized mind, as if affect and feeling were too dangerous. The term "merciless logic" is suggestive, since no mercy or consideration was shown for the burden I was placing on the partners. Yet peculiarly, as I composed the letter, I felt strikingly strong, even proud, that I was so clearly defining my role and now they had to define theirs.

The manic defenses are once again evident. The pain of my last interaction with Jane spilled over into my other work. I retrieved my triumphant feelings, this time by demanding that my potential clients submit to my logical rules for conducting interviews. A chain of punishment and guilt extended from Robert's initial anxiety to my hapless letter to the lawyers.

THEMES FROM THE CASE

Let me examine some key themes that emerge from this case. First, real uncertainty and risk underlie this entire dynamic. The vicissitudes of work are ultimately grounded in the fact that people have to undertake tasks that present risks and pose threats. People's anxiety is not simply rooted in their internal voices or private preoccupations but reflects real threats to professional identity. Robert faced a real threat to himself and the interests of his organization in trying to coordinate politically a diverse set of political interests. Jane and Henry faced real uncertainties in trying to collaborate with a difficult client who might refuse to give them a contract. Finally, I faced real uncertainties in my role as an advisor and teacher. If I could not help Jane and Henry understand their situation I would fail as their consultant.

Second, if the anxiety grounded in work is too great, too difficult to bear, people will escape by <u>stepping out of role</u>. The role shapes their vision so that they see the work reality for what it is. But if they cannot bear the latter, they need to step out of role, so that they can step away from reality. Jane confused her role as a consultant who stands outside the organizational boundary with that of an employee or member who stands within it. This was why she could scheme against Robert and plan to trap him. But the fantasy of entrapment enabled her to turn away from the real uncertainty she faced—that as an outsider Robert had no commitments to her and might not give her a contract. Her fantasy enabled her to deny her essential dependence on the unpredictable behavior of others.

Similarly, in response to Jane and Henry's pain I stepped out of role twice. Jane and Henry engaged me as a consultant and teacher, but instead of focusing my efforts so that I could help them, I used my skill to undermine them. My skill became my "cleverness," the counterpoint voice to their failings. Thus the more I helped them, the more I deskilled them. I exploited their vulnerability as people asking for help. Similarly, when Jane and I left the room, I went "one down," even though I was her adviser at the moment, to relieve my guilt. Finally, Robert too stepped out of role. His capacity to operate in the social field surrounding his organization depended ultimately on his negotiating and political skills. Yet he imagined that he had the authority to convene and direct a committee composed of people from other organizations without negotiating with their supervisors and directors. He stepped out of his political role.

Note that in each case, stepping out of role means <u>violating a boundary in the social or interpersonal field</u>. Thus Robert violated the organizational boundaries in the field of aging services, Jane violated the consultant-client boundary, and I violated the teacher-student boundary. The boundary expresses the limiting conditions of reality itself, the constraints of operating in <u>reality</u> and of taking risks within it. When people find reality too frightening, however, they construct a counter-world in fantasy in which such boundaries disappear.

Third, anxiety is transmitted along a chain of interaction through the psychological process of projection and introjection. Robert begins the process by punishing my colleagues; I end it by punishing the lawyers. This chain is the analogue of Bion's "basic assumption" groups (Bion, 1961), a group in which people collude to ignore their task and indulge in anxiety relieving group fantasy. The basic assumption group unfolds through face to face interactions, the anxiety chain emerges through time and over space. Like the id therefore, it admits to the constraint of neither. In each case people's unconscious and near-instantaneous reactivity to the projections of others creates a protected channel for the transmission of anxiety. Such groups, as Turquet writes, "come into existence spontaneously, with no preparatory formulation, no expectations to be fulfilled. . . No effort seems to be required for their emergence and they have a full dynamic energy of their own." (Gibbard, et al., 1973)

Fourth, psychological violence frequently forges the links in the anxiety chain. This happens because of the interplay between anxiety created by real uncertainty and anxiety created by threatening voices within. The latter "superego" voices are mobilized when the real uncertainty evokes memories of having been "bad" children, of having failed in the eyes of our parents. Unconsciously we link the threat from without with a feeling of our worthlessness, as if "good" people would or should never face such a threat. These parental voices are punishing ones, and paradoxically we can feel bad even before we have failed in reality.

To be sure, some people can use these inner voices as prods for action. The verdict "you are bad," is translated into the injunction "you must become. . ." We then act to satisfy our parents, so that they will stop punishing us. But frequently, if the threat is severe enough or the superego strong enough, we will project out these punishing feelings onto others, we will punish our colleagues, clients and consultants as a way of escaping our self-punishment. Thus the anxiety chain leads people to violate both boundaries and persons. Indeed, each violation implies the other. Each springs from the same source—the real threat.

Finally, when anxiety mobilizes our behavior, we experience other people not as they are but as we _need_ them to be, so that they can play roles in our internal drama. In Abraham's terms (Segal, 1979, p. 50), we see them as "part objects" rather than "whole objects." When I triumphed over Jane and Henry I did not see them as whole people who periodically suffer and make mistakes, who are both "good" and "bad," but rather as weak enemies unworthy of my support because of their inadequacies. They become extensions of my internal psychological drama, a drama shaped by my need to deny the existence of pain and suffering in others. Thus paradoxically, we depersonalize others when we step out of role. By implication, we personalize our relationships when we take our role.

TAKING THE ROLE: AN INCIDENT

Thus far I have analyzed the dynamics of stepping out of role. Let me now explore the dynamics of taking it. Consider the following: I was working with an architectural and engineering company (AE Inc.), which built and serviced nuclear power plants. They helped utilities set up monitoring and control systems, called "quality assurance systems," for ensuring that workers followed safety procedures, when maintaining, inspecting or operating the power plant. It became apparent after Three Mile Island that "behavioral" or "psychological" processes limited the impact of such systems. Managers and supervisors resented doing the paper work required to demonstrate compliance with required procedures, and many workers and supervisors felt that quality assurance monitors were busybodies who did not understand the technical dynamics of a power plant. They were just "nit-picky" bureaucrats.

A senior manager at AE asked if I would work with them to develop training and intervention modules based on a behavioral approach to quality assurance. They would joint-venture with my center and with us sell these consultation services to utilities.

I was assigned to work with John and his subordinate Jim. Not surprisingly, the concept of a behavioral approach was a strange one to most of the engineers at AE. (My senior manager contact was an exception.) In speaking with engineers there, it seemed that many believed that psychology was primarily a science for influencing others, that it was a subspecialty of marketing and advertising. John in particular was nervous and decided that after I became familiar with the issues (through interviews) I should make three presentations: first to the internal Quality Assurance Group, then to a broader cross-section of mid-level managers and finally to the divisional vice presidents and president. If the presentation was accepted by each audience in succession he would feel comfortable developing a training and consulting package to be marketed to utilities.

The first two presentations went extremely well. "Behavior" as a frame of reference was acceptable, even stimulating. But John became very nervous when the time came to present to the vice-presidents. He had a very difficult time scheduling the meeting but finally set a date. I met with Jim, his subordinate, two weeks prior to the meeting to discuss the content of the presentation.

Jim told me that John was worried that I "not be too theoretical," that I give the vice presidents some behavioral "tools," so that they could "walk away with something." I became nervous. I told Jim that my success in the first two meetings was proof that an overview of key behavioral issues, based on theory as well as data, had worked. I felt that I had really contacted the audience's reality. They felt that I understood them. Jim countered that the vice presidents were particularly busy and had to feel that their time was used productively.

An anxiety chain was in the making. John's anxiety in presenting novel material to people with little time had been transmitted to me. The phrase "too theoretical" had particular personal meanings for me. It did not simply convey that I was not in touch with facts, but more significantly that I appeared as an "absent-minded professor," as a man who had little contact with reality and was passive in relationship to other men. Thus despite two experiences of success, the phrase evoked old but still operating self-concepts that made me feel weak and bad.

We continued to talk, and Jim, perhaps out of his own anxiety of making a decision and actually directing me, suggested that I "do a little bit of both," that I give them both a "diagnosis" and some "behavioral tools." I felt tempted to compromise, but then remembered that such compromises frequently served neither end—diagnosis or training—very well. In retrospect the phrase "a little bit" was telling and may have put me in touch with my anxiety. To do "a little bit" of anything was to do not much of anything. If I agreed with Jim, I would be colluding with him to not take a risk. But I knew as a professional consultant that I had to take risks—the process of establishing a collaborative relationship with a client was always uncertain.

When I recognized that Jim and I might be avoiding rather than taking risks, I was able to step back into my professional persona, my role. I told Jim that I thought my "primary task" (and I used this very professional word with him) was to establish a working alliance with the vice presidents, that as a result of the presentation they had to trust me as one who could understand their reality. "Training" them would not only divert me from this task, but in all likelihood communicate that I was not a collaborator. Surprisingly, Jim agreed. He thought that I could not do both and should therefore use my experience in the first two successful talks to shape my presentation to the vice-presidents. We agreed to take the risk. My presentation was successful.

CASE ANALYSIS

John believed that the vice presidents were important people who needed to leave my presentation with something concrete, with "tools." I suspect that his preoccupation with "tools" was based on the common though unconscious belief that senior managers are not collaborators, that as bosses they ask for much but give little. Similarly, his belief that their time was "valuable" and could not be wasted may have been a projection of his own feelings that he could not be of much value to his bosses. (I later found out that the vice presidents' meetings were run loosely and frequently went over the allotted time. They functioned in part as socializing occasions, since several flew in from different parts of the country.)

Finally, the engineering culture at AE did not support attention to "behavioral factors" at work. I had the feeling that engineers there believed that psychologists actually read minds. Early on, I had asked Jim and his colleagues if I might attend and observe a quality assurance division meeting in which auditing and monitoring issues were discussed.

They were uncomfortable with the prospect of a stranger observing their colleagues. Wouldn't the attendees feel that I was evaluating and scrutinizing them? I dropped the request. I concluded provisionally that their's was a culture in which people rarely disclosed difficult thoughts and feelings. (This hypothesis was confirmed many times over in my later work with the company.) Consequently, a behavioral scientist or psychologist became a projective screen for the guilt individuals felt when they did not say what they mean or mean what they said. The psychologist would "smoke" them out, would uncover the crime of nondisclosure. I suspect that John, as a member of this culture, shared these same fears. The discussion of behavioral issues at the vice president's meeting may have come to represent the danger of disclosure in general. If disclosure were a taboo and I represented disclosure, then John would be bringing a tabooed person and subject to the central "law-making" body of the company, the body that sanctioned taboos. John would be guilty by association for violating the taboo.

But what happened between Jim and me to limit the reach of the anxiety chain? Two affective moments stand out for me. First, when I took hold of my professional persona, when I took my role, I felt aggressive and commanding. Second, when Jim agreed with me, I felt a certain sweetness toward him. I appreciated him. These two moments of aggression and sweetness hold the key to the psychodynamics of taking the role.

Consider the aggression. Where did it come from? Why did I feel commanding in making my claim to Jim? I suggest that the aggression had two sources, one that we can call "bio-psychological" and one that was strictly psychological. Clearly, I faced a real threat. Jim's request made me aware, or at least more consciously aware, of the stakes of the up-coming meeting. If I failed, the contract was over. Such real threats mobilize flight-fight reactions, fundamentally a desire or wish to <u>move</u> physically and to do so aggressively. The bio-psychological roots of aggression are thus based on an appreciation of reality, on the dangers "out there."

But my ambivalance, my hesitation and my anxiety, all of which together suggest that I was for the moment paralyzed, i.e., I could <u>not</u> move, point to a psychological source of aggression, <u>not</u> focused on reality. In his essay on anxiety, Freud (1977) argued that anxiety feelings can function as signals of <u>impending</u> threats. Such threats emerge when a person has forbidden fantasies of sex or aggression. The sequence is as follows: he has the fantasy, he feels anxious for having the fantasy, he punishes himself for having the fantasy (e.g., he berates himself) and so relieves his anxiety. Under these conditions the anxiety is the signal of the up-coming self-punishment.

I suggest that my vulnerability to the anxiety chain was triggered by my sense of <u>impending</u> failure. I believed unconsciously that I would fail because, the phrase "too theoretical" triggered feelings of worthlessness. These feelings in turn were amplified by the voice of self-punishment, by superego voices, that punished me for failing to live up to the requirements of manliness and success. Thus, feelings of aggression were rooted in my experience of aggressing against myself.

This suggests that aggression at the moment of taking—or not taking—the role is shaped by two processes that pull in opposite directions: one toward reality and the external threat, and one away from it, toward the threats rooted in one's infantile past. The question is how will this admixture of aggression be directed? In psychodynamic terms <u>will it be placed in the service of the ego, as a ground for acting upon reality, or will it be placed in the service of the superego, as a vehicle for escaping from reality?</u> I faced a branch point. To escape my punishing voices I could turn away from reality, collude with Jim, by forming a "basic assumption" dyad with him, and ignore the real risks and real work we faced. We might, for example, have formed a "victim's" group, and gained emotional sympathy from one another for being at the mercy of such rigid bosses like John. This victim's group could have provided enough immediate gratification to stave off the experience of both real and superego threats.

We could have redirected the anger we deployed against ourselves onto our horrible bosses.

I suggest that the concept of my role provided me with an "observing ego" for reviewing the meaning of my anxiety. I could step back from my immediate emotional setting, because I could step into a role. It is telling that at the moment I stepped into role and disagreed with Jim, I used the very professional consulting term, "primary task." It was as though I were talking out loud to myself, to create, within myself, a countervoice to my superego voice. The resulting deployment of aggression was then shaped by the relative strength of the two voices. My professional voice, represented concretely by my skills, enabled me to stay in contact with reality. My ego could escape significant punishment and deploy both the bio-psychological and psychological roots of aggression in the service of taking a risk and mastering a threat. Looked at psychodynamically, we can say that the role enabled me to sublimate my aggression. It was no longer used to punish myself or others (e.g., bosses) but was used rather to master an objective reality.

Clearly, Jim's behavior, his willingness to follow my advice, was central here as well. When he brought John's objections to me I found him to be thoughtful rather than apprehensive. He had not reacted to John's anxiety. In general, he struck me as a person and professional who had come to an emotional understanding of his limits. While initially he appeared to me to be self-deprecating and without ambition, I gradually saw him as someone who had come to terms with ambition. He suffered little from omnipotent fantasies and professional restlessness. Perhaps this is why he could take the role of "advisee," of seriously listening to a consultant, with little conflict. He could be a good "follower." (Other clients in my experience hire consultants to argue with them.) I hypothesize that at bottom he could take risks because he was without ambition, at least that quality of ambition that is produced by the superego "you must become" injunction. (This link between ambition and the superego explains why certain people fail just when they get to the top. When they finally must be responsible for the risks their organization faces, they can no longer rely on their counterdependent stance to drive them. Their omnipotence gets the better of them and they feel paralyzed.)

But why the sweetness? Typically, we think of sublimation as delibidinizing our ties to others. We love people less (or less intensely) and love material objects and activities more. But here sublimation increased my loving feelings for Jim. The key to the difference lies in the relationship the ego has to the superego when compared to its relationship to the id. Through the latter, we sublimate sexual feeling to generate more abstracted and less physical expressions of love. This gives love its continuity and stability. Through the former by contrast, we reduce the punishing quality of the superego, by turning aggression outward toward tasks and through roles. We can then experience other people as whole objects. As we have seen, when we form relationships through an anxiety chain we use others as "part-objects." People become depersonalized vehicles for the management of our own anger and pain. I devalued Henry and Jane to deny my own pain; Robert devalued Jane and Henry to deny his own anxiety; and Jane turned me into a punishing agent to limit the strength of her punishing voices. We hated one another.

This suggests that when we take a role, face reality, and step out of the anxiety chain we see each other's "whole objects," as real people. This is the moment when we appreciate them and want to collaborate with them.

People who share a near-disaster with one another are familiar with this process. In the moment of an acute and pervasive threat, they overcome their neurotic uses of one another and experience each other intensely, as they really are. That is why people have reunions to "celebrate" the near disaster. The risks of work are modified or sublimated versions of such disasters. They are less life threatening and more chronic. That is why it is more difficult for people to personalize their relationships to one another at work. When we take our roles, however, we appreciate others because rather than use them, we share a common and problematic reality with them. We have faced outward, through our roles, toward a shared and risky world. Thus in taking the role we libidinize our relationships to our co-workers. Thus by sublimating sexual feelings we can love abstractions, and by sublimating aggression we can appreciate specific, concrete others. This complementary sublimation of sex and aggression together create a more secure and stable world of relationships.

We are now in a position to return to our original question. If work can potentially provide people with satisfaction by "displacing a large amount of libidinal components whether narcissistic, aggressive or even erotic," if work "like no other technique for the conduct of life attaches the individual so firmly to reality," (Freud, 1959) why do people so dislike it? The answer lies in peoples' inability to take their roles, to limit superego anxiety by sublimating aggression through roles and consequently appreciate co-workers as whole rather than part objects.

TRADITIONAL CRITICISMS OF WORK

Traditional critics of work and work designs may not appreciate the relationship between the role and the psychodynamics of working. Indeed some traditions directly, or indirectly criticize the role as the building block of work. For example, some Marxists as well as organizational development practitioners argue that "work should become playful." Yet work is not playful precisely because people face real threats. The role as a vehicle for sublimating aggression would be unnecessary if work posed no risks.

Similarly, those who criticize bureaucracies as depersonalizing may assume that roles as well as rules limit the depth of our relationships to co-workers. As we have seen, roles personalize work relationships. The critics of bureaucracy may be confounding the potential intimacy of family life with the potential for collaborative experiences at work. The former is based upon limiting aggression, sexualizing relationships and loving others precisely because they play no role in an overriding "project" or purpose. The latter, by contrast, is based on the mobilizing of aggression, desexualizing relationships and valuing others precisely because they share in a project or larger purpose. Perhaps the critique of bureaucracy masks an underlying wish to deny aggression's centrality to work.

Finally, those who argue that roles overspecialize people may be engaged in the "omnipotent" fantasy. Certainly people should be able to take on new roles at work and learn new skills. But at any given moment a person must make a commitment to a particular role, a particular position, a particular conception of reality. Those who see roles as overconstraining may be denying the necessary dependence of one worker on another. People must coordinate their efforts at work.

In sum, the critique of work may inadvertently become a critique of the role, so that roles are seen as depersonalizing, overconstraining and obstacles to fun. Yet such criticisms are ultimately utopian. They are based on the assumptions that the stakes at work are minimal, that aggression is unnecessary and the coordination is superfluous. But the work as a problem emerges precisely because, the stakes are real, coordination a must, and aggression the vehicle for mastering reality.

A NEW APPROACH TO THE CRITIQUE OF WORK

The perspective developed here provides a fresh starting point for criticizing work. It suggests that work will be hateful and hated when the severity of the threat and the severity of the superego combine to overwhelm the ego. In such cases, a person will either fail at his work or succeed only by responding to his inner guilt, only by responding to the commanding inner voice "you must become." Yet as we have seen, the role as a vehicle for sublimation plays a critical part in this see-saw drama between ego and superego. If it is appropriately designed, if its boundaries are appropriate, and the authority invested in it adequate, so that a role occupant can coordinate with others, face reality and understand the fit between his task and the organization's task, then the ego can more effectively navigate between reality and the superego. The stakes in appropriately designing organizations are thus great. A good configuration of roles not only means that the organization is efficient. More importantly, people within the organization can face their tasks with a relatively smaller burden of superego anxiety, self-punishment and hatred. The <u>intrapsychic</u> organization of aggression is shaped by the coherence of the <u>interpersonal</u> system of roles.

Finally, such a framework enables us to critique both the broader political economy of work as well as a particular work setting. On the one side, we can study how threats are shaped by technologies (e.g., nuclear power plants, toxic waste disposal) and by market structures. On the other side, we can examine how the broad culture of authority in family life and schools shape the strength and valence of superego anxiety.

Indeed, Freud's analysis of civilization and discontents may be given an added dimension. If modern technology poses more extreme threats, guilt and superego anxiety may indeed grow. The danger of post-industrial civilization is apparent. The confluence of superego forces and modern technology can lead to great destruction. This danger can be softened in two ways: first, if family life and schooling produce a new culture of authority based on ego as against superego authority, and second if we develop a more self-conscious and more psychodynamically sensitive traditon of organization design. Changes in culture and work design must parallel changes in technology.

TAKING THE ROLE AS A CREATIVE PROCESS

The temptation of the omnipotent fantasy is strong today, precisely because organizational environments are so threatening. We live, as many organizational theorists say, in "turbulent environments." The omnipotent fantasy, whether expressed in the ideal of proactivity (e.g., "take control and ignore constraints") or in the fantasy of nonspecialization, helps us deny our dependence on others. We cannot be omnipotent, but we can be creative. I suggest that the psychodynamics of taking a role provide the most secure psychological framework for learning new roles. <u>To take a role is to be creative</u>. In taking a role we "enact" it. We make it come alive by publicly setting its limits and boundary. Simultaneously we lay claim to some hypothesis about the real world. We interpret reality, we give it coherence by placing bounds on our own potential and rejecting our fantasies of omnipotence. Indeed leaders fail most frequently to take the leadership role when they insist on "keeping their options open." Behind the apparent conservatism of this strategy lies the omnipotent fantasy that the leader is prepared for anything.

CREATIVITY AND REPARATION

The link between creativity and the psychodynamics of role-taking runs deeper. Melanie Klein (Segal, 1979) writes that when we experience a person as "whole" for the first time, when we stop using that person as a part-object in our fantasies, we become depressed. We realize that we have hurt someone we now love as well. We wish to make up for this hurt, to repair the disrupted relationship, to both ask for forgiveness as well as forgive. In so doing, we actually make the other whole (in our fantasy) by giving back to them the goodness we tore from them.

Klein (Segal, 1979) argues that, in repairing relationships, we augment our ability to symbolize, to look at the unknown through the prism of the known, to use metaphors so that they might clarify a new situation. In short we become more creative. This happens because we no longer experience relevant others as actual extensions of our internal objects, our parental images but rather "as if" they were. We can observe our past transferences to others and so understand our once unconscious symbol making and symbol using activity. But our symbols and metaphors are ultimately about our relationships to others (this is the basis for dream analysis). Thus as we reduce the weight and power of our projections, we augment the flexibility and reach of our symbol making capacity.

Reparation can embrace work. When work is libidinized, it both produces and is nourished by reparation. Each time we take a role we must aggress against our co-workers. But if we successfully take the role, then we also come to appreciate our co-workers. Seeing them whole we want to forgive and be forgiven. I have little doubt that such a climate of forgiveness is fundamental to work group creativity. Only in such a climate do people feel free to take risks, to try something new, difficult and uncertain. But in a way I do not yet fully understand, this climate of forgiveness undoubtedly helps each individual extend the reach and grasp of his skills, to apply his knowledge to new problems by using and transforming the terms and conditions of old ones.

24.

UNCONSCIOUS PROCESS IN AN ORGANIZATION: A SERENDIPITOUS INVESTIGATION[1]

Edward R. Shapiro[2]

An organization, like a group, exists in rational and irrational forms. In rational form, it exists in its concrete structures (buildings, regulations, by-laws, etc.); in its irrational form, it is created consciously and unconsciously in the minds of the people who work within it. For purposes of investigation of unconscious process in organizations, the Tavistock/A.K. Rice Group Relations work uses a number of concepts. Chief among these are "projective identification" (Zinner and Shapiro, 1972), "the institution in the mind" (Turquet, 1975) and the "primary task" (Miller and Rice, 1977).

Projective identification is a psychological mechanism by which an individual creates apparent "knowledge" about other people from inadequate external data. From bits of evidence on which projections are superimposed, a fantasy is created that another person is known (Shapiro, 1982). Such a process that blurs boundaries between individuals is inevitable in organizations, since the complexity and distance of work life makes in-depth knowledge of the personalities of one's working colleagues unlikely. Complex fantasies are particularly powerful in relation to people in authority, since authority and task boundaries interfere with personal intimacy and call forth intense responses. It is of such fantasies and unconscious assumptions that the "institution in the mind" is created.

Each worker in an institution belongs to a different "institution in the mind." The pressures of these personalized notions contribute to the frequent aberrant responses of individuals to work stresses. Often, fantasies about the institution are collaboratively developed in subgroups and around work events. Only occasionally, through the study of particular roles or structures within institutions, can a more general picture of the organization be revealed.

Such a study often focuses around the "primary task"; the task that must be performed for the institution to survive. This concept is a tool for examining an institution's changing activities and is central to the understanding of unconscious organizational life. Lack of clarity about this task

Application: Shapiro

within an institution can contribute to heightened irrationality and work difficulties.

In the work of Tavistock Group Relations Conferences, these concepts can provide guidelines for the work of both members and staff as they attempt to sort through the individual and interactive complexities that both contribute to and interfere with the study of authority. Each individual who has learned from the experience of such conferences has, in different ways, attempted to apply these insights to the various organizational settings in which he or she works. This paper is in the service of such an application.

In this paper, I will discuss the experience I had when I became involved serendipitously in an unauthorized organizational consultation. The unplanned consultation occurred because of a confluence of organizational process and my interest in its interpretation, at a time when I was in a central, symbolic, confusingly defined and time-limited role. The analysis of the symbolic significance of this role provided an insight into the workings of the organization. The parallels between this experience and my experiences in Group Relations Conferences provided support for the following ideas:

1. Once a process consultant generates a hypothesis about authority relations in an organization, all data internal and external, as it is experienced, may be considered as relevant to its elaboration.
2. An outsider whose role requires him to relate to the organization as a whole will be exposed to and filled with data about the organization's authority problems. He will also be filled with other data as a convenient receptacle/carrying away container and must learn therefore to calibrate his personal experience in order to focus on the task of studying authority issues.
3. An event consciously designed to represent an organization will do exactly that, including representation of organizational problems in unconsciously determined symbolic and metaphoric form.

Singer, et.al. (1979) note that the task of management of internal boundaries in an organization includes a monitoring of the relationship between the overall task of the enterprise and its internal structures, so that form is appropriate to function. Nonetheless, they add, other factors in an organization such as personal needs, covert tasks, and shared defenses against anxiety (Menzies, 1975) may result in the formation of structures, internal to the organization, which do not facilitate task performance.

The internal structures of an organization (departments, formal events, task groups, regulations, etc.) develop from a variety of factors, including alterations in the external environment, internal pressures from the organizational process, and management views of the organization's needs. When these structures detract from the stated primary task, it may not be evident to personnel working within the organization because of their immersion in the process. An outside consultant attempting to relate to the organization and its task, however, may be more readily able to recognize incongruous structures because of his separation from the organizational pressures.

The following will illustrate my understanding of such a defensive internal organizational structure that both impeded work and symbolized organization-wide difficulties. I will describe the process of reaching this understanding through the analysis of my experience of my allotted role within the structure.

THE SETTING, THE STRUCTURE AND THE PROCESS

In the organization I will describe, the stated primary task was "to promote the study and development of the technique of group psychotherapy." The organization, which had been in existence for several decades, had developed a structure called an "Annual Institute." This event was a three day gathering designed to represent the organization, to provide an educational forum, to advertise the organization and attract new members, and to respond to the affiliative needs of the membership. A major feature of this event was the presence of an "outside resource person," who was to give a series of workshops around a relevant research or technical theme. I was contacted and invited to be the outside person to present a workshop on adolescents and families.

In my invitation, I was asked to accept the title of "Institute Leader." The task was defined as the presentation over two days of a series of lectures around a theme. I was told that between these lectures, faculty from the organization would conduct structured and unstructured (so called) "paratherapeutic" groups on the basis of their own individual interests.

The specific meaning of the word "leader" was not clarified, except that my seminars would be the "leading issue" of the event. Indeed, my name and topic figured prominently on the promotional brochure with the diverse groups elaborated within. I was flattered by the offer and pleased by the opportunity to present my work. I did not pursue my curiosity about the title of "leader."

The brochure suggested no relationship between the group activities and my lectures. Further, it became clear that I was not invited to attend the final day of the Institute when various members of the faculty were to discuss my presentations on a panel. When I asked about extending my stay in order to participate in the discussion, I was told quite firmly that it was not necessary.

On my arrival, I was met by one of the organizers of the Institute. I was introduced to some of the officers of the organization (not the president), but received neither briefing by nor an introduction to the group leaders. It seemed as though I had been invited as a guest lecturer, and my title of "Institute Leader" appeared unconnected to my task.

My lectures were well received and the membership (of about 300 persons) was responsive, participating actively in the discussion. My apparent role as guest lecturer carried with it the experience of distance from the membership, with my only connection being a formal one, from a stage. Encounters with members off the stage left me feeling somewhat idealized and kept at arms length. The warm, open response I experienced during the lectures was in sharp contrast to the tension I witnessed both between members and the organization's leadership as well as in the work of the boundary keepers of the various events, who appeared hassled, overworked, and irritated. (It is worth noting that this last observation represented my fantasy and denoted an internal comparison I was making at the time between myself and other "leaders.")

One aspect of my presentation was to be a demonstration family interview with a family selected by one of the organization's members. Shortly before the interview, one member pointed out the president of the organization, referring to him (somewhat contemptuously, I thought) as "crippled." He did, on close scrutiny, have a mildly deforming arthritis.

The family presented to me for the interview consisted of a mother and two teenage daughters. The parents were separated and despite some confusing attempts to invite the father for the consultation, he did not appear. His absence was discussed by the therapist as evidence of his inadequacy. The focus of the interview was on the theme of ambivalence toward the absent and possibly emotionally impaired father whose wounded narcissism had kept him from the interview. His separation from his wife and children had resulted in his being idealized, longed for and, covertly, devalued. Part of the discussion following the interview focused on issues of boundary formation in families and the complexities of providing an adequate framework for family therapy that would allow the therapeutic task to proceed. The question was raised from the audience as to whether an interview structure that excluded the father would make the task of family therapy (in this case, focusing on the parenting of the children) impossible.

This discussion about the framework for family work made me more acutely aware of problems in the framework of the Institute itself. I found myself feeling somewhat identified with the missing father, in that I, too, was a leader in name only. I began to think about my lack of connection to the process groups that would be occurring between my presentations. The family interview had been so moving, the audience so affected, and the issues so directly approached, that I anticipated some reaction and response carried over into the intervening group sessions. When I asked members of the Program Committee why there was no link between the structure of the lectures and that of the groups and suggested that they might be missing a learning opportunity, no one seemed to have thought of connecting the two. There was no one in the role of managing the interface and it appeared to be an unexamined internal structure that impeded learning, and, it seemed, interfered with my role as teacher. I began to feel more like the impaired and excluded father in the family interview who could not participate in the children's development. I realized that my own narcissism had interfered with my taking on the framework issues more directly at the beginning, and that I had been participating, like the father, in my own exclusion.

On the evening of the first day, following some of my lectures, the family interview and the beginning of the process groups, there was an event designed to honor the founders of the organization. This ceremony, which included a lengthy historical review by new officers and the presentation of awards, was held at a cocktail party. I was surprised at the atmosphere of chaos and apparent disrespect shown by younger members toward the older generation, manifest in their continuing to drink and talk as the speeches were given. I found myself again thinking about the day's theme of ambivalence toward absent fathers.

The following morning, I was greeted by one of the founding members, who offered me a paper he had written some years previously on the origins of the organization. The paper indicated that the organization had initially been formed around the attempt to integrate didactic material and group experience. The Annual Institutes had initially been developed as a forum to bring in an outside "Institute Leader" who was given authority to work with this integration both as a form of teaching and as an organizational consultation and reevaluation. The paper described this process as follows:

> "The evening before the Institute formally began, an informal meeting between the instructors and the resource person was arranged so that he would not enter the Institute as an individual standing against the group. (It) developed into a "free exchange" discussion . . . a means of systems integration. The Institute began with a talk by the resource person. . . Small group interaction was the primary focus. The instructors and the resource person met together again over lunch for feedback and a continuing learning experience. . . with the resource person serving as leader and contributor until resolution and integration was achieved." (Mendell, 1975, pg. 296)
>
> "The overall flow of information at the Institute was thus from the originating instructor group to the resource person to the instructors to the registrants back to the instructors and then to the resource person . . . focusing on the here-and-now interaction of people and circumstances . . . (with) the resource person serving as leader and arbiter. . ." (ibid, pg. 303).

The contrast between this description and my experience as a 'lecturer' at the current Institute was striking. I felt a strong temporal and symbolic link between myself (as the unauthorized current "Leader") and the author of the paper (as the retired and unheard founder). I developed a hypothesis that the emergence of the "Institute Leader" role as I was experiencing it might represent the confluence of organizational dynamics. I speculated that the role symbolically captured an organizational dilemma, and that there were problems in this organization of authorization, task and role definition, and boundary management that could be studied from the perspective of this Annual Institute. Specifically, it appeared to me that the structure of the Institute had defined a teaching role that was incorrectly titled and inadequately authorized. I recognized that my awareness of the problem was leading me in the direction of examining the organization.

Concepts derived from systems theory and Tavistock experience led me to think that the process groups might each be elaborating a piece of the organizational dilemma as reflected in their relatedness to my role, but I had no data to test this hypothesis. As if by chance, as I decided to study the emerging process, two members of separate groups approached me to discuss their group experiences.

One young woman told me of her experience of telling her group she would have to leave before their last meeting. Her group had spent the entire session in a fury about her limited commitment. I thought of my own limited time commitment and my departure, scheduled one day before the end of the conference (a fact that was known to the membership). I wondered about the possibility that her group was working on that aspect of their relatedness to me, through displacement onto her. I thought that the issue of limited commitment of leaders in this part-time organization might be important to the understanding of the systems difficulties.

The second group member, a young man, reported his group's dissatisfaction with their consultants. Members talked of a formlessness in the group's work and speculated openly about whether I was involved at all in the group aspect of the Institute. Several members had asked their consultants if I could be asked to consult to the group. I considered the possibility that this data might reflect members' awareness (in displacement) of the severed links between poorly authorized leaders and the task of the organization.

Following my morning's lecture, I was invited to meet with half of the faculty (while the other half continued their group work). I was given neither task nor agenda for these meetings and the faculty group present was unstructured. The time was spent in a focused discussion about my formal presentation.

At the end of my lectures, I met with the rest of the faculty, including the president and several members of the older generation. In my lectures, I had included some discussion of Bion's group theories and mentioned my experience as a Tavistock consultant. One of the older members opened the discussion by asking me if I had any observations about the organization itself. I told him that I had a number of thoughts about it in relationship to my peculiar role as "Institute Leader," but that since I had not been authorized formally to study the institution, I was lacking coherent and collaborative data. The president told me that he would be quite interested in my observations and the rest of the group agreed.

As I reviewed my experience with them, the group joined me in an active exploration of the authority dilemmas I had uncovered. Data were immediately forthcoming from the officers, the members, and the older generation in support of the following themes:

1. There had been a gradual loss of focus on the primary task of the organization. Economic and social pressures in a geographically isolated environment had left members feeling socially as well as professionally alone. There was some discussion about a possible shift in the primary task of the organization from an intellectual task to a social task, an idea that was supported by the presence of process groups at the Annual Institute without clear content. Loss of links

between cognitive and affective work within the organization paralleled the separation between my role and that of the groups. Faculty members felt disconnected, unguided, unclear about and unsupported in their group work, with no clear place to develop collaborative thinking and new ideas.
2. There was a sense of a loss of continuity with the past, with marked ambivalence toward the "founding fathers," who felt unneeded and patronized.
3. Deep splits existed within the organization. Leaders felt impaired, unauthorized and limited in their roles. They spoke of feeling that they, like I, held only a token function that was contested by others and unsupported by the membership.
4. There were feelings of loss of direction, depression, and despair about the future of the organization that had not previously been voiced or examined.

The work of this discussion was intense and active. Faculty members found my experience of my role to be directly representative of their organizational experience and confirming data were readily presented. It became clear that in this organization, the anxiety mobilized around open scrutiny (built into the original design of the Institute) had contributed to the defensive construction of barriers to scrutiny captured in the separation of the Leader from the groups and their process. Changes in the external world had led to an unwitting shift within the task of the organization in the direction of forming sentient ties and away from a search for integrated learning. In the absence of an open agreement on such a shift, work leadership was impaired.

Shared, unconscious meanings of the impairment of competent work leadership were elaborated for me in symbolic form over the course of the weekend. These metaphorical guideposts included barring the "Leader" from the wrap-up summary; the image of a "crippled" leader; contempt for the founding fathers; the presentation and intense discussion of a family with an absent father; the longing for the leader's presence; the lack of depth in the relationship to the Institute Leader; and the separation of the affects of idealization (of the lecturer) and fury (in the groups). The data strongly suggested that these unfolding events, capped by the gift to me of the paper describing the origins of the organization, were unconscious group communications presented for interpretation.

Despite the demonstration of the need for a more formally structured organizational consultation, however, such a request was not forthcoming. The problems of leadership had been articulated and demonstrated, and the question about a shift in the primary task raised, but the anxiety about outside scrutiny had not been addressed. The ongoing division in the organization between the need for integration of various aspects of the work, and the sentient need for internal good feelings persisted.

Several months later, in follow-up letters from the two people who had initially invited me, these differences were still evident. In one letter, the comment was, "I am rather hoping that the organization will ask you to return in two or three years for a real "leadership" function during an annual institute."

The second letter (a copy of which was forwarded by the writer of the first letter) read as follows:

> "We made several errors, including . . . not informing Ed of the format in advance. I have recommended (for the future) . . . that the presentor should:
>
> 1. Meet with the fellows and executive committee in advance.
> 2. A committee member should invite him to breakfast.
> 3. He should be given an invitation to the dinner.
>
> . . . We can easily call the "leader" the "presentor" and that should eliminate the problem because, in actuality, Shapiro is accurate, we have never allowed the "leader" to lead the Institute. . ."

Neither writer was present at the final faculty discussion, though each had seen a draft of this manuscript. The letters reflected the limitations of the consultation and the pacification response elicited. Though the first writer suggested the possibility of a "real leadership function," she did not recommend a consultation. The second writer ignored the organizational issues and recommended a more polite response for the next "presentor," in which he will be invited to dinner. The study of the organizational problems revealed by this serendipitous intervention was neither continued nor deepened.

DISCUSSION

A central focus for the work of a Tavistock consultant is the nature of authority. The consultant's study of authority in organizations requires that he or she pay serious attention to internal fantasies and associations. These are data not only about the inner workings of impulse and defense but also about the possible internal reflections of interactive pressures and projections from the group in relation to the person and role of the consultant. From this perspective, the distinction between the person in the role (with his grandiosity, aggression and other conflicts) and the role itself (with its symbolic and organizational meanings) can be scrutinized.

The initial impetus for examining this organization came from my own confusion about my role. Though called "Institute Leader," I was authorized only to lecture. Therefore, the only authorized work I could have done in relation to the data of this paper was to use my experience to broaden my lectures about projective identification and the meaning of unconscious interaction in groups and families. Any speculations about the organization were not authorized as a consultation.

It is this fact that I believe explains the limitations of this "serendipitous" consultation and raises an additional speculation about my role and its meaning for the organization. Specifically, why did I decide to share my observations with the faculty at the last moment in a framework that was unclearly authorized?

From the 'person' side of the equation, it is relatively easy for someone in a 'helping profession' to be seduced into offering 'help.' The stimulation of the "Leader" title and the flattery involved in the event itself contributed to an easy seduction out of role. As always, however, it soon became clear that such a seduction interfered with developing the work.

In this institution, I was authorized to teach. What I did not think to do was to speak to the faculty about the way in which my preoccupations about the process and the limitations of the structure were interfering with my teaching. The relevant issue might have been for me to discuss with the faculty what happens to a teacher whose links with his students are blocked.[3] In retrospect, it appears to me that the structure threatened my survival in my teaching role and contributed to my taking up an additional unauthorized role.

From the symbolic side, it seems to me that this role shift in this symbolic role can also be understood as an additional manifestation of organizational difficulty. My speculation is that in this organization, persons in formal roles are subject to pressures to take on unauthorized roles that interfere with work leadership. I suspect that these pressures are, in part, a consequence of threats to the organization's survival and a defensive hostility within the organization to the possibility of studying itself. My hypothesis is that these threats and the defensive response may be, in part, the consequences of a shared unwillingness to face a changing environment and an altered primary task.

In addition, my invitation into this organization can be understood as an example of the organization's efforts to deal with the outside environment.[4] From this perspective, I was the representative of that environment. I was treated with respect, but kept at a distance. The preparation of my observations into a published manuscript is one form of learning derived from this interaction and, while the process left something to be desired, it may be seen as one representative product of a focused interaction between the organization and an aspect of the outside world.

SUMMARY

This paper is an attempt to illustrate aspects of the confusing experience of an individual outsider at the interface with a system. The effort is to describe the phenomena as a first step in understanding the processes involved.

In addition to providing a limited but coherent opportunity to learn about symbolic structures in organizations, this experience underlined the need to take seriously the constrictions of an authorized role. The data from the follow-up letters suggest that it might have been more useful for this organization had I used my expertise to withhold my formulations until a clear contract for a consultation had been negotiated. My shifting out of

Application: Shapiro

role allowed the group to hear my observations without having to take me seriously as an authorized consultant.

Though the ideas generated in this process appeared to be of interest to members of the organization, it remained to be seen whether this serendipitous "consultation" would evoke reexamination and organizational change.

D. Evaluation

Why I Work as a Consultants in the Conferences of the A. K. Rice
 Institute 365
Margaret J. Rioch

The Politics of Involvement 383
Eric J. Miller

The Couch at Sea: Psychoanalytic Studies of Groups and Organizational Leadership 399
Otto F. Kernberg

25.

WHY I WORK AS A CONSULTANT IN THE CONFERENCES OF THE A. K. RICE INSTITUTE

Margaret J. Rioch

It is part of the A. K. Rice Credo that we should think about what we do, preferably before doing it, but at least afterward. Sometimes it seems that the most heinous crimes in consultation, either at conferences or not, can be forgiven if only one can think of a good interpretation to go with them. The interpretation should include both the group with which one is dealing as well as oneself. It should include deep and fundamental matters. Preferably it should deal with two questions, which I think are of paramount importance in our work: one, the relationship of person to role and two, the question of "Why do I do this work at all?"

The most poignant embodiment of this last question was given by Kenneth Rice, himself, who, a propos of several conferences, particularly the first American Conference, described sitting on the side of his bed at two o'clock in the morning, asking himself agonizingly "Why do I do this work?"

I have often since thought that not enough of this agony is felt now-a-days since everyone is so comfortable and confident. I have thought sometimes that the trouble with conferences is that we, the staff, do not suffer enough. I have seen examples of a director, particularly, suffering more than enough when he had to deal with an especially difficult member. And I have thought the rewards in terms of member learning were sure to be forthcoming. But it is a high price and we are not always willing to pay it. Happily we are not always forced to.

I should like to deal with these two problems as interrelated, the question of the role versus the person, and the question of why we do this work at all. The question of the role versus the person is one that has been around for a long time. There is a passage from "The Fifth Business" by Robertson Davies (1977) that I found very illuminating and that puts the whole situation of person-role better than I can. The person telling the story is being decorated in this passage by the King of England with the Victoria Cross for outstanding bravery in World War I.

"There was a moment, however, when the King and I were looking directly into each other's eyes, and in that instant I had a revelation that takes much longer to explain than to experience. Here am I, I reflected, being decorated as a hero; but I know that my heroic act was rather a dirty job I did when I was dreadfully frightened; I could just as easily have muddled it and been ingloriously killed. But it doesn't matter, because people seem to need heroes; so long as I don't lose sight of the truth, it might as well be me as anyone else.

"And here before me stands a marvellously groomed little man who is pinning a hero's medal on me because some of his forbears were Alfred the Great, and Charles the First, and even King Arthur, for anything I know to the contrary. But I shouldn't be surprised if inside he feels as puzzled about the fate that brings him here as I. We are public icons, we two: he, an icon of kingship, and I an icon of heroism, unreal yet very necessary; we have obligations above what is merely personal, and to let personal feelings obscure the obligations would be failing in one's duty.

"Ever since, I have tried to think charitably of people in prominent positions of one kind or another; we cast them in roles and it is only right to consider them as players, without trying to discredit them with knowledge of their off-stage life—unless they drag it into the middle of the stage themselves."

Not everyone is as aware as the person in this passage that "it doesn't much matter. It might as well be me as anyone else" who gets the Victoria Cross. Davies ascribes to his character a clear idea that the "People need heroes." In other words, the heroic role as well as the king role is created by the people, not so much by the person who plays the role. I think we mean something like this when we say that the group needs a scapegoat or a clown, or whatever it is that they need.

And so we have not only the person and the role, which always used to seem to me to be a clear kind of duality, but we also have the role created by the need of the group. We have the person and the role as perceived not only from the inside of the *person* playing the *role*, but also from the outside. What are "*they*," the *people*, the *group*, making of this *person* and this role? And do not their perceptions influence how the person perceives himself and his role?

I should like to suggest that it is because of a possible resolution of these seeming opposites, the person and the role, seen from inside and from outside, and also of the individual and the group, that some of us find reason for enduring the agony of staff membership, and it is still even now to some extent an agony for all of us.

The mysterious question of person-role starts at the very beginning of life, probably in the womb if the truth were known. Each person, as he is born, becomes the first, second or 16th child of his parents, a social role that must be filled. I do not know of any studies demonstrating that a person *dies* if he cannot in *some* measure fill the role he is born into. But it is said that "Among the Australian aborigines, if a boy in the course of his initiation seriously misbehaves, he is killed and eaten—which is an efficient way, of course, to get rid of juvenile delinquents, but deprives the community, on the other hand, of the gifts of original thought." (Roheim, 1945)

Later in life a child in *our* culture becomes more clearly a carrier of a certain role. Roger Shapiro (1976) calls these roles delineations and has shown how a young person suffers if he does not fill the role or delineation that his parents have set for him. We all know how difficult it is for a member of a group to get out of the role that the group members want him to be in. How much more difficult if the group is not merely a relatively transient one, but the family group to which the member belongs and with which he has to live everyday!

The difficulty in filling a role that *seems* unsuitable is at the root of many of the tragedies and sorrows of adult life when persons feel that they cannot or *will not* fill the role of old man or old woman, of even just middle aged, after having in youth been very beautiful or powerful physically or mentally.

So we see that role is often something like birth order, which is forced upon one, not chosen freely. One hears often that it would have been nice not to be an *only* child, or what a nuisance the siblings were who were always around being too big or too little. But surely as one grows up, one has or imagines one has more choice about the roles that one will fill.

One is first a student and then a young, beginning professional, or whatever one decides to be. After a while one becomes a mature professional, or something else. Sometimes one has the great good fortune, perhaps in middle age, to find an adjunct to one's profession that enriches it, gives it special meaning, and fits well with what one is already doing. This is what happened to me when I first went to Leicester in 1963 and became acquainted with the Group Relations Conference. This was for me an eye opening and heart opening experience. I think I did not learn exactly the lessons that the staff, Kenneth Rice, Pierre Turquet and others, thought they were teaching. I learned what was suitable and useful for me. As a result of my having been especially tuned to my own wave length, I have been very sympathetic to the new approach of James Gustafson and Lowell Cooper for many reasons, but especially because the new approach indicates something personal that the method means to them. If it does not have these variations of personal meaning, which indeed one may try to generalize and make scientific, the method dies, as Gustafson and Cooper point out.

We say, in fact, that members may learn new things at a conference that we have not even dreamed of and that the conferences are open-ended. We do not prescribe what should be learned. But sometimes we do *act* as if we knew what members should learn. After my first experience of a conference in England, it seemed clear to me why I had to go to England, for only there did the very road signs say "No right turn." In America they would say "No left turn." The thing that seemed clear to me was that there was "no right turn," no correct way. Whatever I did was both right and wrong, and at some deeper level it did not matter which it was. What I did could be interpreted by some as benevolent, and by some as destructive, and probably it was. The need to "make the right turn" can be a terrible burden. Members at conferences, for all their apparent rebelliousness, are very sensitive to what they think the staff members think is "the right way." We can stand on our heads and shout that we do not know and are not prescribing a correct solution. People are so eager to believe that *someone* knows the answers that they will probably not hear us shout.

To come back to the matter of the various roles that we fill in our lives, how lucky we are if we find something like the Group Relations Conferences to fill out the profession of psychologist and psychotherapist, or whatever else one is! I think that playing the role of consultant at such conferences has an important effect on the person who plays the role. I am here consciously using the phrase, "playing a role." I think that this role, as well as others that one plays in one's life, affects the person who plays the role so that he/she is no longer the same after playing it over a period of time.

The whole Women's movement surely has to do with a shift in the perception of the roles that women can or should fill. Has not this shift affected women as persons? Have not women become different since they are expected to fill different roles? And have not women found that the most dangerous enemies are not primarily the male chauvinist pigs, but the false images that they themselves carry within them of themselves as fragile, helpless, and dependent? In other words, the most potent aspect of the role-person dichotomy is often the picture one has as a person of one's role.

And is not old age, to take another and different example, not only the fact of biologically and chronologically growing older, but also the fact of having filled a number of different roles? Even though I may feel myself on the inside to be in many ways still a child, helpless, needing guidance and support, still I am different from the way I was as a real child of 6 or 8. I have filled the role of student, of young, perhaps already mature or old professional. I am surely not the same person as that inexperienced child of 8. The roles that I have played have molded me as a person at least as much as I as a person have molded the roles.

In the West it is not fashionable to think of one's Karma or Destiny. I am I, an individual, who can impress himself upon the raw material of the world as the potter molds the clay that is *his* raw material. I do not wish to argue this point tonight. But as each one of us looks back upon his life, whether long or short, a pattern emerges that one may or may not like. The question of whether I make the pattern or the pattern makes me is as futile as the hen and the egg problem. You have probably guessed that I am inclined to think that the pattern makes me, and that therefore death means simply the dissolution of the pattern, unbearable if it is indissolubly linked with the destruction of I-Me, an individual who made it, but not so unbearable if it is simply the dissolution of a pattern, like a cloud-shape. A wise old man, Bernard Berenson, the art critic, once said near the end of his life: "Now I am in the decline of my eighth decade and live so much more in the people, the books, the works of art, the landscape than in my own skin that of self . . . . little is left over. A complete life may be one ending in so full an identification with the not self that there is no self left to die." (1958)

To come back to the question of the person and the role, there are, I think, two extremes. One is where the person and the role do not fit at all. The sooner the person recognizes this or is helped to recognize this, the better for everyone concerned. Then there is the opposite case of the person who seems to fit his role so naturally and neatly that one says he was born to it or that one cannot imagine his doing anything else. Most of us belong somewhere between the two. And most of us go through phases or stages of development in which one role seems more fitting than others. If we hold for a moment to the example of consultancy, the typical inexperienced consultant has to mold his face or discipline it not to show emotion, and one of the favorite ways, which is not at all bad, is to stare at the floor in the middle of the room. Then he can surely not be accused of exchanging glances with a particular individual. He is not distracted from the group by a pretty or even by an ugly face. I am well aware of Bion's dictum often quoted by Kenneth Rice, that if one's attention is caught by one individual, one has lost sight of the task. But as one becomes more experienced, one relaxes more, and allows members to see the struggle. One may even look around to see the expressions on members' faces. This is not necessarily losing sight of the task. The essence of what one is doing and the seriousness of how one does it are bound to show through, even if one does look around and show some emotion.

The task has now become second nature so that one is less concerned with how one may appear to the group. The mask, which one formerly had to assume in order to play the role adequately, is no longer necessary. The role has become one with the person. The consultant role is not assumed lightly, nor cast off at the first possible opportunity. It allows one to be oneself, perhaps more than ever before when *not* playing the consultant role.

A third term has now insinuated itself into this paper, in addition to person and role, and that is "task." The person and role are united when one really accepts or embodies the task. Then the person and the role really become one. Perhaps we prefer not to do a particular task. We find it uncongenial or even against our principles. If we do accept it, then what follows may not always be what we wish, but we have accepted it whatever may come. A conference, for instance, may be uneventful, or it may be rocked by storms. One member may become psychotic. It will have become clear to members by the time the conference is well underway that if a fellow member becomes psychotic, all are in some way responsible. Each one has his own part in the psychosis. Thus there is a general upset, for not only is there a member in distress, but also everyone is guilty.

Application: Rioch

Members often say the staff is being not only rigid, but is also playing parts, or roles, quite consciously in order to manipulate them. I remember when this used to make me angry. "Don't they know that I do not play games with them?" I thought, and may even have said, "This is the most serious business possible." As I have become older, and I hope more mellow, I am no longer angered by this accusation. It seems fair and natural enough that people should think such outrageous behavior that they see in consultants must be planned with some ulterior motive; it must be manipulative.

But why do we go out of our way to assume this role of consultant? And what is this role anyway? It does seem to be a prize, even though apparently there is not the same eagerness for consultant slots that there used to be. Most of us have had to do some learning, have had to make some effort before fitting into the role of consultant. That is the rationale of supervision, training workshops, co-consultancies, and various methods that people have developed to help others to learn this difficult job.

What has it done to the *persons* who have often played the role of consultant? The first thing that comes to mind, and that I think you will recognize (all those of you who have been consultants), is that it provides deep friendship and good companionship. Even if the people who have worked together on staffs never see each other again, there has been among them a fine spirit of camaraderie that one rarely finds elsewhere. And that in itself is sufficient reason to treasure staff experience. But is that all?

A very simple, but very important thing often happens to those who have been consultants. Persons become more courageous. I do not know exactly how or why that happens. It would be significant if one could investigate it. I cannot believe that it is simply that one has had practice in taking risks that turn out all right. But I do know and I have experienced it myself that persons gain more courage. They do not lightly meet tigers in their lairs. But neither do they avoid them when the path leads through a jungle. I do not think this is just an aspect of the role taken as a consultant. Persons have changed when they have taken this role many times, so that the change is noticeable in other aspects of their lives.

One other way in which the role of consultant has affected many people as persons has to do with tasks altogether, not just the task of staff consultant. When they undertake a task, they tend to *do* it. They are not necessarily more perfect in this than others. But I think they, as persons, have stopped dragging their feet in their ordinary lives. Either they take on a task and do it, or they do not take it on. This means that they can live more in the present and actually be more present, rather than living in apprehension, regret, worry, or hope.

These things that I have mentioned so far as being the ways in which the persons of consultants have been affected by having taken the role are all considered to be "good" things by and large. But there are also shadow sides.

Consultants underline the difference between themselves and members. One way they do this is by sitting in a row up front facing the members in Openings and Conference Reviews. It was Kenneth Rice's contention that this underlined the difference in role although he also maintained that one *could* work no matter where one was sitting. When members wish to be particularly rebellious, they occupy the chairs of the staff up front, objecting to the separate seating. Perhaps we have not given enough thought to what it does to the *persons* of staff members to have the difference in their role marked out this unmistakably. This underlining of the difference is certainly engineered by the staff itself. This is one place where the members' perception of staff surely affects the way the staff members perceive and feel about themselves. Surely they must have something of the experience that I described earlier in the words of Robertson Davies. If they do not keep their eyes open very sharply, they will think they really are *icons*, if not of heroism, then of something special. This is emphasized by their having a special meeting place. This has not only practical reasons, but also symbolic significance to the staff *and* to members. It is emphasized by the staff's feeling about itself that it is set apart. Since we all have difficulty in thinking about apartness without assigning an up or down value to it, the staff members tend to think they are better than members and develop an attitude of arrogance and contempt for members that has often been commented on as a grave weakness in our staff.

But all of these things, both good and bad, may vary a great deal from one individual to another. Can we say something that will hold true in general, and for everyone, about this particular role of consultant and this particular task?

We can all say in our sleep that the task of the consultant is to help the group in its task of studying the nature of authority and the problems encountered in its exercise. The role of the consultant is to facilitate this task in a special way. It seems to me that what this means is a curious blend of activity and passivity. The consultant must be a mirror, wiped as clean as possible of personal concerns, giving back to each member what his projections are of authority figures, embodied, as the case may be, in an *old* man or a *young* woman, of the same race, or of a different one. At the same time the consultant does *act*, and surely his interpretations do guide the group; sometimes this is resented and sometimes welcomed. Thus he is anything but a passive reflection of everything that passes before him. We say that he continues to be a "work leader" even when the group no longer so avidly and clamorously needs him as they do when they are functioning in basic assumption, dependency.

He is not a leader in the sense of directing the group to do or not do something. He is a work leader only in the sense of a "primus inter pares." He is the first and the foremost in studying the group as a group, but he is not necessarily the only one, and he is never the only one by choice. He is a leader in that he shows a way, guides, points out a possible desirable direction.

Thus his role is two-fold, "active and passive." He is in this sense hermaphroditic and must allow for both traditionally masculine and traditionally feminine qualities to be projected upon him. He is a leader, certainly a work leader, without appearing to lead. I think that the fascination that this role has for many people, and, of course I include myself, is this kind of ambiguity, this secret power that is never flaunted and can therefore never be rebelled against, for if one rebels one is met not by opposition, but simply by an interpretation. There is something of the Zen Master in this, the master who has no real power to make his disciples do anything, but who nevertheless exercises enormous influence over them, so that they supposedly stand and literally freeze waiting in front of his door for admission. His power seems to lie in the fact that he refuses to exercise power. He tells the disciple to go away; he does not want to be bothered with him. This is not unlike the power of the psychotherapist, who in real life has no authority over the patient and does not need a particular patient and whose opinion supposedly carries no "real" weight. But the patient finds himself hanging on every word for signs of approval or disapproval. When a society, like our Western society, sponsors and backs psychoanalysis and group relations conferences and, like Eastern societies, backs Zen monasteries, they do indeed seem to have from society itself the awesome power to declare what is acceptable and what is not. Without this backing, whether it be overt or covert, it is doubtful if either psychoanalysis or group relations conferences or Zen Masters and disciples could long exist.

When things are going well, one likes to affirm the power that the role of consultant bestows. One thinks, and indeed one may even brag to one's colleagues, "I really did a great job in that group." When things are not going so well, one can with equal truth deny the power, for one is unable to "make" members do anything. One has no actual power over them. There is no police force and no army to back up the word of a consultant. One can only interpret. And members, of course, do not always wish to learn nor to follow the consultant's lead, especially if they are essentially being told that they are fools.

They are followers of a non-leader. When it suits him, he will shout them down. When it does not, he will be quiet. This must seem very arbitrary from the outside and maybe occasionally it is. It is hard for members to see (and it is hard sometimes for consultants to see, too) where the task lies. The consultant is not, if he is at his best, following an impulsive whim, but rather his interpretation of a general principle. But the distinction is not always easy to make.

But be that as it may, this is perhaps sufficient reason to explain why we do this work and what we get from it. Consultants have a secret power that they can exercise while at the same time denying it. But I think it is not the *deepest* reason. The deepest secret and the deepest reason why we engage in this work and in similar pursuits is, I think, mystical and spiritual.

I vividly remember a conference member who has since become a respected staff member saying in a conference review: "Whenever I look for the group I find myself, and when I look for myself I find the group."

I suspect that we are inarticulate about this most of the time because we are shy about saying these things openly. Most of us are still caught up in the rebellious struggle against formal religion, which we have identified with stuffiness, sanctimoniousness, and hypocrisy. Heaven forbid that we should have anything to do with anything that might be soft, or a cover-up for hostility or for angry feelings, more genuine than the soft, pleasant, superficial gobbledy gook that some of us were brought up on. And yet, what on earth is our "systems theory" all about, if not the merging of the one in the all? We teach that the whole is affected by each part, even the most inarticulate and silent parts, to say nothing of the parts being affected by the whole. But we would perhaps not be pleased to think that this is a religious as much as a purely scientific doctrine. It is a long time ago that "No man is an island" became so popular that one could not quote it without being sneered at for being so common. But since it is so long ago, we might remember it again, and including the lines "Ask not for whom the bell tolls. It tolls for thee." It has sometimes seemed to me that the conferences are a marvelous way to demonstrate the interrelatedness of events and to demonstrate that nothing happens in a vacuum. We are at pains to show this especially in "The Institutional Event" but it is probably demonstrable in other places as well.

It is perhaps no accident that our longest conference is 10 days or 2 weeks in duration. Perhaps we cannot stand the strain of a longer time span than that, and perhaps this explains why some of our best people are no longer to be found within, or close to the centers of institutions. It may be too much to ask to maintain the integrity, honesty, and openness of communication that conferences demand for longer than 2 weeks or in the midst of institutional life. But however that may be, the rewards of this behavior are clear, though fleeting and unpredictable. It is perhaps only in death that one finds a complete merging of the self with the other or others, but conferences give brief moments of insight into what that might be like, when the I of the consultant is really the same as the entity called the group. There is then no longer any conflict between me and the group and no bad choice between mine and thine, no question of my sacrificing myself for the group, for I am the group. When this really happens it is felt as uncanny. I remember one time when a woman, the only woman in a group, found herself crying. She did not know why; in fact she did not feel like crying, she said, but she thought she was crying for the group. Occasionally a group shudders at the place where it has found itself. I think we might say it is a place without the boundaries that we are used to in our every day skins. Occasionally I have been moved myself to say that I am the group and the group is me. Sometimes I have known that I went down into a deep tunnel like death and the reward was deeper and greater communication between me and the group. It is this last, I think, which Christian religious people speak of as The Way of the Cross. It is not felt as a sacrifice about which I have any choice, but it is a kind of inevitability that I take on myself in accepting the task and the role of a consultant.

To illumine these last thoughts, I should like you to hear a story. I wrote this story about ten years ago; then I did not think it had anything to do with groups, but on reading it lately, it seemed to me it had.

The telling of tales is an old and honorable occupation. It stands at the beginning of many cultures. The tale as a symbol of a truth is certainly

Application: Rioch

not a new idea. It is behind the Chassidic tradition of tales, and it is in the Sufi tradition of story telling.

The story I want you to hear is called "Marius." That is the name of the hero of the story. It is a kind of fairy tale. You should not expect realism from it. It is a tale that happened a long time ago, in a place far distant from any which any of us has ever known. It is a "once upon a time" story.

MARIUS

On Feast Days the folk of the Island gathered in the village square where the old men told tales learned from their fathers and their fathers' fathers. They told of glistening hosts of fish swimming in the forbidden harbor which lay deserted on the Island's southern shore, fish so delicate in flavor that in ancient times the gods chose them as their favorite repast. Once in each generation a young man, more daring than his fellows, attempted to penetrate into the bay and catch one, but not even the eldest of the elders could recount a success. High hills covered by torch thistles cut off the approach by land and, although access from the sea appeared to be easy, the old men told that no boat sailing into the bay ever returned or the boatman either.

Now there was a young fisherman named Marius who had listened intently throughout his boyhood to the old men's tales and he determined to brave the danger of the forbidden waters and to catch one of the fabulous fish. Marius excelled all the men of the Island in running and wrestling; he was strong-hearted and strong-willed. Not all the advice of the elders of the village would deter him; nor would he allow his two staunchest friends to share the adventure. The most he would permit was that they sail their boat alongside his up to the entrance of the bay and there wait and watch what would befall him. He made them promise and give it to him with an oath on the Holy Stone, that no matter what happened they would not enter the bay.

The sun shone and a following wind blew steadily as the two small boats sailed up to the narrow entrance into the harbor. On either side high rocky promontories looked down upon the fishermen. No living thing stirred along the shore. Marius dropped his sails, called goodbye to his friends, and edged into the bay. He stopped only once to turn to them again and remind them of their oath.

Roberto and Ricardo waved to him with forced cheerfulness. Wishing in their hearts that they had never embarked upon this adventure, they watched him row away. While he was still within hailing distance his friends saw him stop, put the oars inside the gunwale, and peer over the side of the boat. He stared so long and so concentratedly that they wondered whether he had forgotten them.

"Marius," called Roberto, "What do you see?"

"It is sufficient," added Ricardo. "Come back and tell us. You will be hero enough."

Why I Work as a Consultant

Without lifting his gaze from the water, Marius called to his friends, "I see a fish so beautiful that I shall have no peace until I have possessed her. She is three feet long, gold like the setting sun, and her eyes are as blue as the bluest sky."

"He speaks as one might speak of a woman!" Roberto said to Ricardo. "Is he bewitched?" and he lifted his voice to call over the water. "Marius, come back. It is a sin to speak thus of a fish. Come back before it is too late."

Now the two friends could not believe what they saw but both bore witness to it later in the same words: "Marius took his rod and cast the line. No sooner had it struck the water than the bow of the boat was lifted straight up into the air. We saw a flash of gold as dazzling as if the sun itself rose up out of the bay. The light blinded us and by the time we could see again the boat had overturned and Marius was gone. The next moment the boat too disappeared as if it had been sucked down into the water."

Roberto and Ricardo looked at each other. They rowed a little closer to the harbor entrance. No oars floated on the surface; no fishing gear was to be seen. It was as if Marius had never really been there. After a time they sailed silently back to their village where they recounted the strange tale. The elders nodded sadly and retold all their stories. Marius' parents were bitterly grief-stricken for he was their only child whom they loved dearly and they mourned for him as for one who has died.

Now in fact Marius was neither living nor dead. After he cast his line into the water to catch the beautiful fish he had been aware of a sudden convulsive movement of his boat, a flash of light, and then nothing. He did not know how much time had elapsed before he realized that he was walking along the bottom of the sea and that ahead of him, with his fishing rod in her mouth, swam the golden fish. His own hook was caught in his belt and the tug of the line towed him along behind her. Just ahead the sea floor declined sharply and Marius saw that they were descending into a cavern. The bright sun had illumined the path he was travelling but now, as they descended, huge rocks threw their shadows so that all forms became vague. For an instant Marius took for such shadows the six young men seated in a half-circle at the bottom of the cavern. Their faces were expressionless and their bodies as motionless as the coral stools on which they sat. An empty stool completed the semi-circle. In a moment the fish had towed him to it and, with a twitch of the line at his belt, he found himself sitting down.

Now Marius perceived that his fish was not the only one but that six others like her, yet not like her, swam in and out among the coral rocks. Of all of them his was the brightest gold and had the bluest eyes. While he watched she dropped the fishing rod from her mouth, swam past him, and looked at him with an expression of such longing in her blue eyes that Marius thought his heart would break. And it might have broken too if just then he had not seen one of the other fish approach the man on the stool next to him, snap at his hand, and calmly swim off. Marius noticed now with horror that the fingers of all six young men had been nibbled away so that only stumps of varying lengths were left. As his own fish again swam up to him he felt his blood run cold. He wanted to run or at least to hide his hands in his pockets but he could not move. The fish had his forefinger in her mouth. He felt her teeth press on it, but swiftly she glided away. For an instant he believed he had seen a tear in her blue eye but surely this was the strange effect of the light at the bottom of the sea which made everything look watery.

"What next?" thought Marius and, as his fish swam back and forth, he alternated between pity and fear. She seemed so wistful, but might she not eat up his fingers as the others did? The six young men appeared to be completely paralyzed but he could still move the muscles of his face and throat. It occurred to him to see whether he could speak.

"Oh fish," he began politely, "Will you be as kind as you are beautiful? Will you spare me my fingers or must they be nibbled like these others?"

"Hush!" whispered the fish quickly. "Here she comes."

And out of a tunnel which issued into the darkest corner of the cavern emerged an ugly black-robed figure, a witch with pointed cap and a nose so long and thin that in the shimmering light it looked like a snake.

"Oh," thought Marius, "so that's the way things stand here. She's the mistress and my fish is afraid of her. And good reason too. Did ever anyone see such a beak?"

As if the witch had read his thoughts she wrinkled up her nose and then let it out to its full length; it darted toward him like a sea serpent and before it, Marius withdrew his thought and inwardly tried to placate her with appeasing phrases.

"So you are the new hero," she sneered as she removed the hook from his belt and tossed it with the rod into a corner. "You wanted a delicate morsel of fish, didn't you? And you thought to brag to young and old of your village what a fine, daring fellow you are, eh? So now you sit and you will sit till kingdome come or till you're eaten yourself." And she laughed as only a witch can laugh. "Let me feel, young man, what fresh young human flesh is like. These here," and she pointed disparagingly to the six others, "have grown hard as coral." And she felt with her thin hands over Marius' body till he thought he would die of seasickness, but he could not escape her and he dared not speak. Finally she had her fill of him and withdrew into the tunnel.

The next day she appeared once more, once more pinched the soft parts of Marius' body, then set to work with her broom, sweeping the floor which overnight had become cluttered with sea nettles and bits of broken sponge. When she had finished, she gathered the seven golden fish about her at the far edge of the cavern. As she spoke to them her voice became as sweet as the lyre of Orpheus. Marius could scarcely believe that this was the witch who sneered at him so contemptuously.

"Come, my cherished ones," she called to the fish. And they circled about her like golden spokes of light. "Ah, Slither-tail," she said, "you are pale. Go play in the sun. And you, Rainbow-fin, I shall bring you some sea-grapes for your appetite. Amuse yourselves, my piscian darlings, with the six coral men and the new one of the soft flesh. I shall take leave of you now."

And the fish danced in sinuous curves, caressing her with their lithe tails. When she had gone they swam about as before. Sometimes they left the cavern for hours on end but Marius' fish, the bluest-eyed, was never absent from him very long.

This went on day after day; in fact Marius could not remember how many days. He had ceased to fear for his fingers for the fish always did the same thing, pressed gently, and glided away. He had come to like the feel of her mouth on his skin, and it seemed to him that now she smiled at him as she swam off. But he had never again mustered courage enough to speak to her. He simply sat and sat.

And yet a change was taking place in him. Was it that he too was turning into coral or was something within him hardening into resolute action? He was not sure. But he realized that he was observng the witch's habits more closely. He knew now that on one day out of seven she came early in the morning and did not appear again the whole day. "The Witch's Sabbath!" he thought to himself. "I will do it."

The Sabbath came and the witch's visit was over. Marius waited until his fish swam up to him and had his left forefinger in her mouth. With a tremendous effort of will, as if he were lifting a huge boulder, he stretched out his right hand and grasped the fish firmly through the gills. Once he had made the first move it was, as he had anticipated, much easier. Still holding her fast, he stood and said determinedly, "Now you will get the fishing line and tow me to shore as you towed me here." The fish had made no attempt to escape and, as he spoke, she seemed to blink assent. He let her go and in a moment she returned with the rod and line. He made the hook fast to his belt and off they went, not daring to look back to see whether the witch was following.

Marius found himself exhausted from the effort of moving his limbs and let himself be carried along by the strength of the fish. Even this motion was strenuous, however, after his long paralysis and presently he called to the fish, "I must stop a moment to rest. And it now occurs to me that I am desperately hungry. I have eaten nothing for months."

The fish turned; for the first time since the day of his arrival under the sea she spoke to him.

"It is just a little farther," she said earnestly. "You will find everything ready: an iron pot with water boiling over a fire and a sharp knife with which to cut off my head before you cook me."

Marius was so startled he almost stopped breathing.

"Cook *you*?" he gasped. "Are you mad?"

"Not at all," she said. "Isn't that why you came to the forbidden harbor, to catch me and eat my flesh?"

"But then I did not know you," he replied.

"You mean that now you like me less?" she asked half sadly.

Marius stammered and blushed a little.

"No, but I had thought to take you home with me," he told her.

"That is not possible," she replied. Her blue eyes fastened on his unblinking. "I cannot live out of water and you will die if you do not soon have food. There is nothing to eat but me."

Marius leaned against a giant sea fan and put his head in his hands. "You mean I must eat you or go back to the cavern?" he asked.

"That is it," she answered.

Marius stood for a long time pondering the question. "I cannot," he said finally.

The fish swam up against him. "Marius," she said seductively, "Eat me. I promise you, my flesh is sweet." And without giving him time for refusal, she tugged at the line. "Come," she said. "It is not far now."

The sea floor inclined upward so sharply that Marius had to concentrate all his effort to follow the fish; he had no time to think. Suddenly his head was above water. Still the fish swam on and Marius stumbled after her, half blind from the sun, half deaf from the pressure in his ears. They were fast approaching a white sandy beach where tall cocoanut palms waved in the breeze. And there indeed was an iron pot hung on a tripod over a fire with a sharp knife lying on the sand nearby. In the shallow water the golden fish became playful.

"Catch me, Marius," she laughed. "Catch me, as you did this morning. Put your hand once more through my gills and I am yours forever."

Then she slithered between his legs and was gone, only to return a moment later calling, "Marius, aren't you hungry?"

Now Marius was so confused by all that had happened that morning, his sudden arrival at shore, his love for the fish, but above all by his ravenous hunger, that he no longer knew what he was doing. The next time the fish flicked her tail before him he grasped her quickly through the gills, with a tremendous effort lifted her out of the water, waded to the shore, and cut off her head. Wild tears blinded him as he tossed her into the simmering water of the pot. Then he threw himself upon the sand shaking from head to foot.

But soon the pangs of hunger became so severe that he literally fell upon the fish as he pulled her from the boiling water and he ate as he had never eaten before. At first he was too hungry to taste, but after a time he became aware of a delicate sweetness which flowed from his palate through his whole body. His chin lifted and he rose to his feet refreshed and invigorated. As the strength from his fish grew within him a single thought took possession of his mind.

"The witch! I must get her," he said to himself.

And with the last morsel in his mouth he walked steadfastly back into the water.

The way to the cavern was long and arduous but he found it easily. On the six stools the six stony men still sat. At the entrance to the tunnel lay a black robe and pointed cap; beside them, an ugly mask with a long nose.

"Marius!" a voice called.

And Marius recognized the melodious tones the witch had used when she talked to the golden fish. He stepped into the tunnel and the voice called once more, apparently from a deeper level. Marius felt along the walls until he heard it again right at his feet.

"Lift me up," the voice said.

Marius hesitated, trembling with uncertainty, but then he stooped, lifted up a light form which he could not see, and retraced his steps into the cavern. He held in his arms a maiden, fair as a goddess, with hair as gold as his fish and eyes as blue as the bluest sky.

"Are you the witch or are you my golden fish?" he asked in bewilderment.

"I am Lucina," she said and the light of her almost dazzled him.

Marius laid her on a soft spot in the sea floor and quickly turned away.

"What am I to do with her?" he wondered aloud. "Eat her as I did the fish, choke her sweet voice to death in her throat as I wanted to do to the witch, or carry her in my arms always?"

"Marius!" The sound rolled on huge waves through the cavern.

Marius started and looked in the direction of the open sea. "The water has turned to gold!" he exclaimed. "But it is alive. Tiers upon tiers of golden fish! Like the seven, like my own fish!"

"Marius!" the chorus repeated. "Take her to the cottage on the shore where the fish became your flesh. She will bear you sons and daughters. You shall be the elder of a new village in the old forbidden harbor. That will be your life and we, the fish, will be your livelihood."

The water seemed to be filled with shooting stars as the golden chorus circled the cavern and swam out toward the sea. Now in the distance Marius heard them chanting:

> "Seven heroes sailed to the harbor.
> Only Marius broke the spell.
> Seven waited, enduring in silence.
> Only Marius loved the fish.
> Freed from her bondage, she died but to live again.
> Only he was loved by the fish."

Once more the strength and sweetness which had come to him after eating his beloved fish streamed through Marius' body. He turned to the blue-eyed girl who lay waiting on the sea floor and lifted her gently in his arms.

"We shall all go together," he said.

As they passed before the six stony youths he let the golden hair of Lucina fall in turn upon the forehead of every one. At the touch each man trembled, rose slowly to his feet, and followed Marius as he carried the maiden out of the cavern and through the water to the sandy beach where he had eaten the golden fish.

Seven boats lay in a row upon the sand; seven white cottages stood in a semi-circle among the palm trees. Marius approached the one nearest the shore and motioned to his companions who arranged themselves in the order in which they had sat on the seven stools, one at the door of each cottage.

"These are our homes," said Marius, and already he spoke with the authority becoming an elder. "Let us rest the night here. Tomorrow we shall take the boats and visit our old village."

And with that Marius carried his golden-haired bride over the threshhold of their cottage and laid her on the nuptual bed.

Early the next morning Marius, Lucina, and the six companions launched their boats and set forth. The men had all become less stony; they were talking and laughing with one another. Except that their fingers were a bit short and stumpy they had suffered no harm from their sojurn under the sea.

The sail was brief. In a few hours Marius and his companions landed at the wharf where he had always kept his boat.

"It is strange," he commented, "that no one at all is on the beach. Over yonder hill lies the village. Let us go quickly."

As the little band arrived at the summit Lucina exclaimed, "What a great crowd of people! What are they all doing there before that enormous rock? And look, there are more coming, two by two. Marius, why do you shudder?"

"I know not," he replied. "But that is our Holy Stone. Perhaps it is a Feast Day. Hurry, do hurry," he cried, pulling Lucina after him.

The eight arrived in the village square just as the slow moving procession halted before the Holy Stone.

"It is Marius!" someone shouted. The procession broke up and the villagers crowded upon him. "Marius!" they cried, but somberly, touching him, questioning, gaping, shaking their heads. Roberto and Ricardo pressed through the throng and embraced him.

"You are alive, truly!" muttered Roberto over and over again.

"Where have you been? Who are your companions?" asked Ricardo. "And who is the maiden with hair of gold like the setting sun and eyes as blue as the bluest sky?"

Marius tried to say everything at once. "She is my bride who bears the name of the ancient goddess of birth. I found her at the bottom of the sea. My fish, my golden fish saved us all." He paused a moment. "No, let me tell it slowly and in order as befits a tale of the enchanted harbor. But first we must seek the blessing of the Chief Elder and of my—." Marius turned to the white bearded Elder who stood motionless before the Holy Stone. "Where are my parents?" he asked.

For answer the old man pointed to the other side of the Holy Stone. Two biers rested there, each beside an open grave. Marius walked toward them and lifted the black cloth. "Could they not wait for me?" he asked as the crowd drew back.

"Your parents grieved for you as for one who has died," said the Elder. "For eight months and thirty days they performed the mourning rites but yesterday they did not come to the Holy Stone. When we went to their hut we found them dead. They wore such joyful expressions that I said at once, 'It must have been made known to them that all is well with Marius. What other thing could have filled their dying faces with such radiant light?'"

"Yesterday," Marius murmured, "the day when I ate my fish and the witch became Lucina." And stooping, he kissed the forehead of his father and the lips of his mother. Lucina took his hand and said quietly, "The shadow of death lies everywhere, Marius, on the earth and in the depths of the sea."

Then Marius addressed the Elder and his voice was large and deep with authority. "Speak the benediction upon the dead, Father, for the journey on which they now embark, and upon us who have returned from the depths of the sea. Consecrate my marriage to Lucina. Give to each of these six a faithful wife. And bless the village which we shall found."

The ceremonies lasted throughout the day. And after Marius had told his tale from beginning to end the Elder spoke his final blessing.

"Nine months ago," he concluded, "Marius went from us as a daring youth to brave the dangers of the forbidden waters. Today he goes from us again as an elder, with a bride from the depths of the sea, to bring life to the harbor of death."

EPILOGUE

Marius in his tale can be thought of as a consultant. No matter how many times he has been a consultant before, each time it is a new and dangerous thing to enter the forbidden harbor of our outrageous method of studying the nature of authority, of one's own authority in groups. But what fantastic and beautiful creatures inhabit the depths! The golden fish represents, among other things, the fascination that we feel with this work. She also represents our most beloved preconceptions, our unquestioned attachments and beliefs, which we must devour and destroy to attain new life and strength. Here it does not greatly matter whether the consultant devours the fish or whether he, as in the old Jonah story, is devoured by the fish. In any case, he is reborn from having become one with the fish and also from being willing to be destroyed. To be sure this venture is dangerous. Marius finds that his boat is capsized. He finds himself walking in unexplored regions at the bottom of the sea. But he is resolute. Even when he beholds the frightening witch and the motionless young men who, like inexperienced consultants, sit paralyzed while the fish have their way with them, *he* maintains his power to think and reflect. He remains passive for a long time, but he does not turn to coral. He becomes very active though it requires enormous effort. He takes the lead and frees himself and the six young men from paralysis. The witch is transformed, even as the often destructive basic assumption group may be transformed into one functioning at a higher level. Marius is transformed. He has lost himself to find himself again. He and the others have "suffered a sea change into something rich and strange." Since this is a fairy tale, not real life, you can be sure that "they all lived happily ever after."

26.

THE POLITICS OF INVOLVEMENT[1]

Eric J. Miller

My presence here tonight—regardless of my intentions, regardless of what I say and almost regardless of whether I open my mouth or not—is a political act. It involves me in a system of political relationships and relatedness that is created by those of us who are in this room in the here and now—in other words, the micro-politics of this very temporary institution in itself. But it is not only the task and roles of this occasion that connect us: this system is contending with, and having to mediate, roles in other political systems beyond this room that each one of you may perceive and that I may perceive (and the perceptions may or may not be reciprocal) as connecting us in a past or future relationship.

At a macro level, for example, this occasion may be interpreted as a miniature element in a set of international relationships. I am conscious of being part of a small foreign minority and perhaps the only Briton in a predominantly American assembly. Something as simple and obvious as the way I speak marks me out: my English accent may be judged elegant, quaint or just incomprehensible. And so, even if I had not raised the issue, I would expect that at least some of you for some part of the time would be mobilizing feelings, attitudes and stereotypes that derive from the roles that you have in your own particular constructs of this international system. Note too that there is a wide variety of constructs, each with its own implications for my relatedness to you. For example, for one of you I may be perceived as representing the colonial power that exploited this country until just over 200 years ago; for another I may be an ally in the North Atlantic Treaty Organization, aligned against a common enemy; another again may identify me as sharing a cultural heritage that goes back to Greek and Roman times; and this cultural identification might well be given a special political meaning by some Black Americans who would disavow such a heritage and lay greater stress on ethnic background than on nationality.

A second level of political system within which we may perceive ourselves to be related is the inter-institutional. This would mobilize me in my role as a member of the Tavistock Institute as distinct from the A. K. Rice Institute to which so many of you are affiliated. Given that the Rice Institute has a history of ideological and methodological dependence on the older and foreign institution, is organizationally and financially independent, has expanded rapidly and succeeded in "colonizing" substantial regions of North America (not to mention forays into, for example, Sweden and Ireland), we can safely predict that this inter-institutional relatedness will be evoking a considerable range of feelings—certainly many more than could be encompassed by the word "ambivalence."

This second level is complicated on this occasion by a third—the intra-institutional political system. Here I have at least two relevant roles. I have been a Board Member of the A. K. Rice Institute since its foundation; and very recently I have had the privilege of being made an Honorary Fellow of the Institute. Am I identified with a Board that I know is believed at times to levy harsh taxes on struggling regional centres and to spend the proceeds on beer and bureaucracy? Or am I in some people's minds split off from the rest of the Board—for better or worse? And what image, if any, is being constructed for this new role of Honorary Fellow? Is he expected to be an exceptionally potent source of wisdom and enlightenment? Or is it a token role for an old soldier no longer fit for active service?

I have mentioned three levels of the wider political systems that connect you and me within this room; but this classification does not pretend to be exhaustive. I am sure that, consciously or unconsciously, others are in your heads. For example, I have alluded to the politics of race but not of gender. Some women here may be wondering why these three new honorary fellows are all men. (This question was once addressed to an all-male staff group of which one of my fellow honorary fellows, Dick Herrick, and I were both members. Dick's reply was succinct: "Speaking for myself," he said, "I had no choice.") Operating here also, no doubt, are the political systems of one or more academic disciplines, each with its single-minded devotion to the advancement of knowledge—and also its lively competition for publication, prestige and professorial appointments.

Each of us, of course, uses constructs like this all the time as a way of imposing order and meaning on the world we perceive around us. They are related to personal myths and shared myths about the social order and the place of the individual within it. Although I have spoken as if the different constructs might be distributed among different people, it is probable that each of you is using more than one construct as a means of classifying me. You may move from one to another at a leisurely pace; or you may oscillate among them so rapidly that you are holding several different constructs almost—through never completely—simultaneously. At that point you have settled on an image of me that locates me, to your satisfaction, on several different dimensions; and this image will persist for a time until something I say or do, or some re-ordering that occurs inside you, dislodges me from my position on one dimension and leads you to reformulate the picture.

The systems I have identified are external to, and impinging upon, the micro-political system that belongs to this occasion itself. We have here the familiar social structure and defence mechanism of the chairman, the speaker and the suitably deferential audience. This provides you and me with understood roles and a role relationship, which for the moment are suppose to have priority over others. It is defensive insofar as it helps you to hold feelings at bay—feelings derived from your constructs of me or

The Politics of Involvement

feelings evoked by your experience of me here and now—that, if expressed, would in fantasy lead to chaos. (I find myself assuming that it is destructive feelings that would be unleashed, though it is a theoretical possibility that they might be warm, loving feelings. Unbridled expression of these, however, would probably have equally chaotic consequences.) When I sit down, we shall have the ritual of question and discussion time, which, under the supervision of the chairman, will permit some outlet for feelings provided they are couched in suitably polite language.[2]

This structure that we have here gives me an advantage in a fourth level of political activity that is a constant element in our lives—the interpersonal level. We can call it the "politics of identity." I need not in this company expound on the processes of splitting, projection and introjection and on the Kleinian theory of object relations. These are the processes through which the biological condition of individuality gets transformed into consciousness of individuality: an awareness of a boundary between "me" and "not me" and a sense of self. As Eliot puts it,

". . . . . human kind
Cannot bear very much reality"(Burnt Norton, I);

And hence we use these processes to attain some coherence in the construct or model of what is "me." We get rid of the bits that don't fit, the inconsistent and conflicting bits, and attach them to our constructs of the various "not mes" with which we populate our environment. Some of these "not mes," of course, we have not met and may never meet—for example, a president, a film star or a notorious criminal—but they are nevertheless significant receptacles for certain projections. To use the language of open systems, the individual exports chaos from inside and imports order from outside. So long as this import-export process is conducted in fantasy it is safe: there can be a satisfactory fit between the picture of self and the picture of other. But, as Rice and I have pointed out (e.g., Miller and Rice, 1967, p. 268; Rice, 1969, p. 573, p. 582), every transaction across the boundary has the potentiality for disaster: the fantasied boundary between "me" and "not me" may not stand the test of reality; I risk being forced to re-introject the bad bits that I have projected and to surrender the good bits that I have introjected.

An associate of mine, Andrew Szmidla, has developed a valuable conceptualization of boundary transactions between systems using a perspective that is different from but complementary to the conception of the boundary region of a system proposed by Rice and myself.

". . . The boundary [of $\underline{A}$ as a system] is in effect made up of two parts. . . . . The inside line represents the way $\underline{A}$ sees itself—call this the inline. The inline is under the control of $\underline{A}$. $\underline{A}$ can say where the boundary is to be drawn, what will be included and what will be excluded from its activities, and how interactions will occur across the boundary. The outside line represents how $\underline{B}$ sees $\underline{A}$—call this the outline. The outline is under the control of $\underline{B}$ and similarly can, by the way it is defined, allow A to do certain things and stop it from doing others. It is clearly extremely important that the inline and the outline are broadly congruent—that is, that the way A sees itself and its role is also the way B sees A. Without this shared frame of reference there will not only be problems of communication but, much more seriously, expectations by either or both parties working together may not be met and may even work against each other, leading to a breakdown in the relationship." (Szmidla and Khaleelee, 1975)[3]

In this formulation, identity is not the property of a system (say an individual). My inline is only one partial rendering of it. To quote my wife: "What you know as you is just an arrogant figment of your imagination." The outline is another part. Identity, therefore, is constantly being negotiated and renegotiated in intersystemic relationships of A with B (and also with C, D, E, etc.). We simplify such a relationship, however temporary, by drawing a boundary around it, which demarcates this AB from what is not AB (including other possible ABs). This supra-system that A and B create together defines the roles that A and B will and will not take up in the transaction. (For example, if A and B are professional colleagues of the opposite sex, they may agree to leave gender out of the transaction.) But that definition is seldom stable, and within the AB system A still has the task of negotiating his inline with B's outline of him (and vice versa). No relationship is immune to this process. Even long-term relationships, such as marriages, are best thought of as intermittent, rather than continuous. Each party is engaged in other relationships, involving renegotiation of his inline, and this experience is repeatedly re-imported into AB. . . . . I could elaborate on this; but I think the point is sufficiently made that every interpersonal relationship is a political relationship, involving continual negotiation of the boundary between me and not me, of inline and outline.

My advantage at the moment at this fourth, interpersonal level—the level of the politics of identity—is that for the time being I can present an inline without receiving overt messages from you that would indicate you have formulated an outline that is discrepant from my inline. The other party to this negotiation is silent. But the respite is only temporary. I have to guard against your developing an outline of me that is too uncomfortably discrepant from my inline; and to do this I have to try to manage your outline. I attempt this by anticipating your criticisms of what I have said so far. I can think of three such criticisms:

1. that it is unoriginal—an amalgam of the micro-sociology of, say, Goffman (e.g., in The Presentation of Self in Everyday Life) and the dynamic psychology of Melanie Klein;[4]
2. that, for what I am talking about, the term "politics" is a misnomer; and
3. that it has no relevance to the theme of group relations training.

The Politics of Involvement

Against the first criticism I will offer no counter-arguments. To acknowledge that your adversary is right is a well-tried disarming gambit in negotiations.

I will, however, defend the notion that the relationships I am discussing are political. There is no shortage of definitions of politics. One paper, by Paige (1967), for example, quotes Lenin's "who does what to whom" and Mao's "war without bloodshed," reminds us of the more familiar formulations of Lasswell (1936)—"who gets what, when, and how,"—Easton (1953)—"the authoritative allocation of values,"—Levy (1952)—"the allocation of power and responsibility," and Snyder (1958)—"the making of authoritative social decisions," and throws in for good measure a definition by a Japanese political scientist, Masao Maruyama—"the organization of control by man over man." Paige himself emphasizes the element of "purposive organizational behaviour, the object of which is to formulate and to achieve social goals by means of consensus and coercion." J.D.B. Miller states that politics "is about disagreement or conflict; and political activity is that which is intended to bring about or resist change, in face of possible resistance. . . . . .Conflict lies at the heart of politics" (J.D.B. Miller, 1962, p. 14). Barber defines international politics as being "concerned with interaction involving conflict or potential conflict between the actors in international relations. From the interaction emerge structures, processes and patterns which involve power and coercion on one hand but bargaining and cooperation on the other" (Barber, 1975, p. 22). I suggest that the same principle could apply to interpersonal and intergroup relations. In the way I use the term in this paper, relations between two systems are political where one system is consciously or unconsciously attempting, or is perceived as attempting, to impose its goals and values on another.

As to the question of relevance, I want to argue that the political dimension of group relations conferences, at both the micro and macro levels, has been relatively neglected, to the detriment of our understanding both of the processes that occur within the conferences themselves and also of the processes involved in the transition of members to their roles in external institutions. In recent conferences sponsored by the Tavistock Institute in Britain and France we have begun to tackle this issue. Thus for the "Leicester Conference" that my colleague, Gordon Lawrence, directed last September he used the title: "Individual and Organization: The Politics of Relatedness." My own attention to this dimension has been increasingly focused in recent years by consultancy in industry (Miller, 1977b), in health care systems (Miller, 1979a) and above all on rural development in Third World countries (Miller, 1976c, 1977a, 1979b); but the credit for pressing the implications for group relations training must go to Gordon Lawrence (cf. Lawrence, 1977, 1979; Lawrence and Miller, 1976).

I said at the opening of this address that my presence here tonight could be understood as a political act, regardless of any political intentions that I might have. I now want to acknowledge my conscious political intention, which is to promote scrutiny of the political dimensions of the conferences themselves as institutions and of their relatedness to the institutions from which members come, and also to begin to look at the responsibility that this understanding may place on those of us who sponsor, direct and staff these events. In doing so I am consciously putting forward a perspective that is partly counterposed to that of Margaret Rioch, in her address to last year's Scientific Meeting, entitled "Why I Work as a Consultant in the Conferences of the A.K. Rice Institute" (Rioch, 1978), and also to that of Garrett O'Connor in his "Commentary on Dr. Rioch's Presentation" (O'Connor, 1978). At the same time I want to pick up the recent critique of group relations conferences by Jim Gustafson and Lowell Cooper (Gustafson and Cooper, 1978), which they describe as an antithesis to the thesis of Rioch and others. I welcome their explicit acknowledgment of a political stance but question the conclusions to which it leads them. I shall not propound clear-cut solutions—the synthesis that Gustafson and Cooper are looking for; but I hope at least to sharpen our understanding of some of the dilemmas we face.

A convenient starting point is the issue of manipulation. Margaret Rioch has this to say:

> "Members often say the staff is being not only rigid, but is also playing parts, or roles, quite consciously in order to manipulate them. I remember when this used to make me angry. 'Don't they know that I do not play games with them?'. . . . .'This is the most serious business possible.'"

She goes on:

> ". . . . .I am no longer angered by this accusation. It seems fair and natural enough that people should think such outrageous behaviour that they see in consultants must be planned with some ulterior motive; it must be manipulation" (Rioch, 1978, p. 38).

I can identify with these sentiments; I have experienced that self-righteous anger myself and also prided myself on "growing out of it." But Margaret Rioch stops at that point; from manipulation she passes to another theme. She does not ask the questions that I believe we must address. Why the self-righteous anger? Surely that is an indication of denial? What is it that is being denied?

The obvious inference is that we are angered in manipulation that we are reluctant to acknowledge. "Manipulation," of course, is a dirty word. Let me substitute the phrase, "covert political activity," which might be marginally less disreputable—though only marginally—and examine some of the evidence.

The experience of a member arriving at a conference, as in arriving in any unfamiliar situation, is not dissimilar to my own in arriving here. He or she can expect to be perceived at a number of different levels, in a number of different roles. A few people may have some prior direct or indirect knowledge of him, but for the most part he will be at the receiving end of various stereotypes, based on ethnic origin, nationality, gender, institutional affiliation, occupation and so forth. Those furnish a preliminary "outline" against which he presents his "inline"; and he can reasonably look forward to a sequence of inter-personal transactions through which outline and inline will be brought into greater congruence. He also has available the alternative strategy of noninvolvement; that is, he attaches minimal value to the outlines conferred by this set of people and is not impelled to set the record straight—"I don't care what they think of me." But if he moves towards involvement he finds that the dominant group in this conference institution—the staff oligarchy—are not only refusing to confer an individual outline on him but apparently trying actively to destroy his inline by treating him as belonging to an alien category—conference member or group member. Moreover, it is a category about which staff appear to have certain stereotypes: members are ignorant, stupid, resistant, defended, unwilling to learn, and so on. Margaret Rioch comments on the complementary posture of staff:

> "The staff members tend to think they are better than members and develop an attitude of arrogance and contempt for members" (Rioch, 1978, p. 39).

If he persists in his involvement—and he may do this willingly or be sucked in without intending it—he will be subjected to a process of socialization towards the role of "a good member." It is a complex role, made all the more difficult to attain by the fact the definition is never explicit; the cues are always oblique. Thus the good member attends sessions on time, is serious and reflective, says "I," not "we," and doesn't ask the consultant questions; but he should also display that he is not dependent on staff, not compliant, not conformist. If he learns to press the right levers, he may earn the distinction of being referred to by staff (in the privacy of their common room) as "a work leader." Ultimately he may even have the privilege of being invited to join the ruling elite in a future conference—though I understand that this final accolade is a little less highly valued nowadays than it used to be.

I have painted a selective picture to make my point; but I think there is evidence enough in the experience of this audience to confirm the proposition that conference staffs are engaged in a political activity. In this respect, group relations conferences do not differ greatly from psychoanalysis and other therapies. To quote one analyst, Elliott Jaques:

> "Everytime an analyst interprets his patient's behaviour, the interpretation is made against a conception of what the patient would be like if he or she were not subject to the unconscious play of unresolved early conflict. As the analysis progresses and conflict is reduced, types of behaviour are noted that are accepted as more normal. And finally as the analysis reaches the point of possible termination, the so-called criteria of termination are used by the analyst in judging when a stopping point is appropriate."

He goes on to give examples of termination criteria:

"Sexual potency, the capacity to comprehend verbal communication, control of murderous impulses, capacity to love and recognize the needs and abilities of others, capacity to utilize abilities to the full in work, and so on" (Jaques, 1970, p. 12).

Whatever one may think of Jaques's criteria, at least they are explicit: to that extent the political activity is not covert. The patient who has read the book may still find his analyst's interpretation obscure or outrageous, but he knows that it is, or is intended to be, "made against a conception of what the patient would be like if. . . . ." This would not prevent the patient from accusing Jaques of manipulation, but within this context I would expect such a charge to be examinable as a phenomenon rather than to arouse defensive anger in the analyst.

In fact, we can be almost as explicit about the basis for conference design and consultant behaviour and we try in various ways to state this in conference brochures. We are intentionally exposing members to the experience of covert processes in groups and organizations—for example, the experience of being immersed in basic assumption thinking and of emerging from it. This is not something that—consciously at least—I feel ashamed or guilty about. I believe there is something here worth learning about and it is the essence of my contract with members to provide them with a setting in which this learning can take place. I uphold the value of personal insight, as an aspect of a wider value that knowledge is preferable to ignorance. To that extent, in directing a conference I am engaging in overt political activity in pursuit of an explicit value. I am also quite conscious, as I indicated just now, that I am initiating a process of socialization, the members' experience of which will itself generate data for us to examine together.

Why then should I and others be so sensitive to the charge of manipulation? What is being denied? We need a "because clause."

Margaret Rioch's paper itself offers us an initial clue. Immediately after raising and then dropping the issue of manipulation, she goes on to discuss the rewards and satisfactions of the consultant role:

"The first thing that comes to mind. . . . .is that it provides deep friendship and good companionship. Even if the people who have worked together on staffs never see each other again, there has been among them a fine spirit of comaradarie that one rarely finds elsewhere" (Rioch, 1978, p. 38).

Rarely but not never. Perhaps the obvious equivalence is with war—and indeed Margaret Rioch in this passage proceeds immediately to talk about courage and risk-taking. There are many examples of this kind of imagery that will be familiar to members of conference staffs. I myself used the metaphor of the old soldier just now. Gustafson and Cooper quote an earlier paper by Rioch with an echo of war-time Churchill.

"The staff sweats and bleeds and works for members. . . . ." (Rioch, 1971).

They use this as evidence that "the staff tends to take upon themselves a Christlike responsibility" (Gustafson and Cooper, 1978, p. 849). While that is a phenomenon that I have certainly observed, the imagery of crusaders is for me more compelling. (If I remember rightly, the crusader's death in battle was defined as martyrdom, which gave him an automatic entry visa to heaven.) And the heathen enemy of course is the membership—or, more specifically, as Gustafson and Cooper (1978, p. 844) indicate, "the baser tendencies of conference members."

It is tempting to pursue the image—the armour of the consultant role, with task as the banner and interpretation as both sword and shield—but for the moment I want to pursue the phenomenon of solidarity and the meaning it may have. Indeed this audience is sophisticated enough without my having to spell out the relatedness of intergroup conflict and intragroup cohesiveness. The fact that the crusades were able to mobilize—at least for short periods—quite disparate bands of soldiers from all over Europe suggests that their shared projections onto the heathen must have been quite powerful. What then are the differences and conflicts within staffs that necessitate this mobilization of solidarity and projection onto the members of ignorance, stupidity, resistance and other baser tendencies?

I can perhaps best answer this by trying to expose uncertainties and conflicts within myself. Jaques can offer indicators of normality as criteria for termination of an analysis. The method is existential, and includes the obscure or outrageous interpretation, but the output is defined: the task is to make patients normal. In our conferences the means is the end: the task itself is existentially defined—to study what is happening in the here and now. What about the output? May I quote something I wrote some three years ago:

> ". . . . .In terms of values, I see the conferences as vitally concerned with 'helping the individual to develop greater maturity in understanding and managing the boundary between his own inner world and the realities of his external environment' (Miller and Rice, 1967, p. 269). It is on his own authority that he decides what to do with his understanding in his roles in other institutions, whether as manager or managed. . . . ."

And then I prevaricated:

> "However, I acknowledge that I personally hope that he will acquire greater potency to question and perhaps change his relationship with his working environment" (Miller, 1977b, pp. 43-44).

That qualifying sentence gives the game away. Ostensibly, I fly the banner of the existential primary task and support the associated values, for which we have all sorts of good phrases: "exercising one's own authority," "moving from heteronomy towards autonomy," "managing one's own development," "managing oneself in role." Under this banner, I need not be defensive about the political nature of conferences: the goals and values I am trying to impose are overt and morally above reproach. My latent goal, however, is clearly to induce members to become agents of scrutiny and change in their own external institutions. This is more difficult to acknowledge; and it is of course at variance with the ostensible goal, which would give each member freedom to act or not to act. Yet this latent goal must, at least unconsciously, affect my behavior in my staff roles, and that behaviour in turn must be experienced, at least unconsciously, by members in the form of conflicting messages. My defensive response to the charge of manipulation then becomes much more explicable: I am in fact engaged in "covert political activity" that I would prefer to deny.

I can claim responsibilty only for my own conflicting goals. I would postulate, however, that in every staff group there are similar conflicts within and among individual staff members. Sometimes they surface and are worked at, painfully. Very rarely indeed, however, do they lead to the resignation or dismissal of a staff member. Usually there is agreement to differ, or the differences disappear underground, and camaraderie is resumed in the common cause against the common enemy.

Divergent external political affiliations among staff—marxist and capitalist, radical and conservative, black power, women's lib—are in my experience less problematic, simply because they are less easy to hide. Agreement to differ works not too badly. Members of a staff group that achieves such agreement in face of the diversity tend to experience a somewhat smug self-satisfaction—the lion has lain down with the lamb—and this suggests that some of the difference and potential chaos has been projected from the staff into the membership; but this projection is taken back insofar as some staff members can speak in the presence of members—in the institutional event or in plenaries—about the problems of reconciling these external affiliations with their staff roles.

Indeed, I would postulate that such obvious divergences help to cover and conceal a more fundamental contradiction in the task and design of conferences. I begin to pin down this contradiction more specifically in a recent paper on open system theory (Miller, 1979b). The theory leads to the following proposition:

> Significant changes within a system cannot be sustained unless consistent changes occur in the relatedness of the system to its environment.

All of us working in this field would, I believe, agree that we want members to acquire new insights at an intra-personal level, i.e., significant changes within the individual as a system that will find expression in the roles they take and the relationships they make. The conference as a temporary institution provides a space within which these new modalities can be explored and begin to be implemented. But if the systemic proposition is correct, this intra-personal learning will be only temporary unless it is reinforced by consistent changes in the immediate institutional environment to which members return. If that environment remains as before, we can predict that the learning will be lost, trivialized or submerged. So the returning member has to engage in the political process of renegotiating his revised inline, a process involving shifts in values and shifts in power, with the inevitable attendant conflicts. There is some evidence to suggest that the determined ex-member who finds his work-setting intractable will take the conflict into another institution, such as his marriage. And you may be familiar with the one elegant solution to sustaining the learning without risking any established institutional relationships at all—the solution being to become a perpetual staff member.

The dilemma therefore is this: If as staff members we have a private political agenda concerned with effecting change externally, our efforts to cling to the conference task and its associated ideology of "managing oneself in role," and our efforts to maintain unity within the staff group will inevitably lead to some projection onto the members of our uncertainty, conflict and chaos. On the other hand, if we cling as single-mindedly and objectively as we can to the conference task, what is our moral responsibility if we re-export members to intractable work-settings in which we know that their learning is unlikely to be sustained? To be sure, there are some institutions that have sent numerous members and are therefore likely to provide benign environments for negotiating revised roles and relationships, for example, the Menninger Foundation (Menninger, 1972). But in other cases are we not selling a shirt in the foreknowledge that it will shrink the first time it is laundered?

And there is a further complication. Those who uphold the purist conception of the conference task may be over-inclined to believe that they are dealing in absolute values. But the notion of exercising one's own authority or managing oneself in role is itself no more than an ideology or myth. It is a useful myth, to be sure, in that it helps us to identify and pin down other myths about authority and dependency; but its usefulness should not seduce us into elevating to a level where it is unexaminable; it is simply a case of "set a myth to catch a myth."

Therefore whether intentionally or by default, whether directly or vicariously, all of us who run conferences are involved in a political activity, in that we are consciously or unconsciously attempting to impose our goals and values on others, whether those others be the members themselves or the institutions to which they belong.

I have suggested that one resolution of the dilemma is to deny the charge of manipulation and to assert the basic virtue and purity of the approach. This leads typically to what might be called "flight into the inner world," or "flight into mysticism," which I perceive in parts of Margaret Rioch's 1978 paper and still more in Garrett O'Connor's. To quote from the latter:

> "In talking about the relationship of the part to the whole, or the whole to the part, and the mutuality of influence between them, Margaret admits, rather shyly I think, that the idea is a 'religious' [one] as much as [being] a purely scientific doctrine. It is in this area that she finds the deepest reasons for her involvement in this work. This corresponds to my experience, and I would like to expand the point,

because I think that the path to understanding more about human behaviour, and therefore more about what it is we try to do in conferences, lies in the direction of bridging the gap between religion and science—between intuition and mystical experience, on the one hand, and rational, logical thought on the other" (O'Connor, 1978, pp. 52-53).

Let me make it quite clear that in describing this pattern as "flight" I am in no way impugning the integrity or competence of the individuals concerned. I have worked with both of them over too long a period to have any doubts on that score. Moreover, as I must shyly admit, part of me too is very much identified with this way of thinking about the work we do.

Equally, however, another part of me is very much identified with the approach of Jim Gustafson and Lowell Cooper. I am not sure what to make of their statement that "the material basis of this tradition in England had been aristocratic and managerial interests, upper and middle class" (Gustafson and Cooper, 1978, p. 859), since both Ken Rice and I came from artisan and lower middle class backgrounds and we always seemed more skillful at making enemies than making money. But I am certainly in tune with their explicitly political stance and with their concern about the obstacles to making these conferences available to a wider clientele. (They may be pleased to know that in a three-day intergroup event that I directed last month—February 1979—nearly a third of the members were shop-floor workers and most of the rest were from clerical, secretarial and junior supervisory positions.) My hesitation is that in the approach they describe, certain essential features of conference learning may be short-circuited or eliminated. Have the members who have been through these experimental conferences gained some insight that might lead to a significant re-drawing of their inlines? Or has the learning been predominantly cognitive? My reading of their paper leads me to the second view. So whereas Rioch and O'Connor seem to be taking flight from the political into the mystical, perhaps Gustafson and Cooper are dealing with the political dimension by taking flight from the unconscious, or, more specifically, flight from the transference.

If I am anywhere near right in this analysis, over-simple though it is, then we have a strange convergence. In the traditional conferences which, as Gustafson and Cooper describe them, are identified with managerial interests, participants learn, through the transference, to question their assumptions about authority; but they often re-enter their institutions unequipped to apply their learning in change. In the Gustafson and Cooper model, on the other hand, members learn how to work collaboratively in groups and are probably able to transfer much of this learning; but they have had little experiential learning about authority relationships. In either case, therefore, the ruling authority—whether it is in a capitalist or socialist institution—is relatively immune from scrutiny and challenge.

Certainly it seems extremely difficult to hold on to the notion that the relationship between individual and group is both a part-whole relationship between sub-system and system <u>and</u> an inter-systemic relationship between two systems of different levels. We repeatedly get ensnared by the polarizations that we derive from our infantile two-breast, two-parent experiences. The same applies to the dichotomies of unconscious/conscious, intra-psychic/political, not to mention female/male, black/white and the rest. This affects, for example, perspectives on conflict. The reductionist view, which seems to be implied for instance by Jaques (1970), is that ultimately all conflict is internal: if intra-psychic conflicts are resolved and the individual ceases to be a net exporter of chaos, then conflict at other levels will die away. The marxist perspective on the other hand focuses on structural conflict: if that is dealt with, the individual should be released from his internal stress.

Although, as I warned you earlier, I do not have the synthesis that Gustafson and Cooper are asking for, I want at least to declare my intention of trying to resist these polarizations and to suggest three ways of tackling some of the issues raised here.

First, I believe that we must take much more seriously our responsibility for the post-conference experiences of members. Even if one sets the moral issue aside, there is the question of proper use of resources. There is a limit to the number of seeds one can afford to let fall by the wayside or onto stony places. My experience of rural development in Mexico indicates that <u>both</u> individual development <u>and</u> structural changes are required, and that they are interdependent: neither can move very far without the other. I suggest that this is also relevant to conference work. In fact, my colleagues and I at the Tavistock attempted this strategy on a small scale a few years ago with two client systems. One was the United States Dependents' Schools System in the European Area and the other were staffs, academic and administrators, from several English universities. In each case, we mounted a programme extending over 6-9 months. It started with an intensive one-week residential conference. In the second phase, participants met in what we called "implementation groups." These were locally based groups usually from one institution, which met regularly over several months, with support from consultants. The groups were designed to help their individual members, separately and jointly, to analyze their specific work-settings and to devise and implement strategies for development and change. All participants then reconvened in a third and final phase for further experiential work, review and onward planning. The university programme was not particularly successful. Experiential learning does not sit easily with the university culture of research and teaching, and only one of the implementation groups seemed to make effective use of the programme. With the Dependents' School System, the programme showed more positive outcomes: it apparently impacted on the structure and culture of the organization as a whole as well as on local schools. Although this particular design has not been repeated—mainly because of lack of opportunity—something similar is being attempted in the conferences that my colleague Gordon Lawrence has been directing in France, in association with the Fondation Internationale de l'Innovation Sociale, Paris. These provide opportunities for follow-up consultancy to participants.

One difficulty about such a programme design is that in the initial 'conference' phase, one can no longer cling to the myth of ending. Hence the future may be used as a defence against engaging with the present; and the primary task in the present may become: to make a future relationship. The consultant who is protecting prospective relationships with clients is less available for rigorous scrutiny of the here and now.

One point that emerges clearly from these programmes, and still more from organizational consultancy, but that remains less visible within conferences, is the political power attached to the consultant role. Whatever he may do or say in the guise of a professional, the fact that he is collaborating with certain members of an organization and not with others, and is perceived as in coalition with them, has an impact of its own.

The second thing we can do is to try to remove some of the protective boundaries around the staff role. This occurs in the "Praxis Event," which Gordon Lawrence introduced at the September 1978 Leicester Conference. Instead of starting from the notion of 'institution' or 'group' and trying to explicate the role of the individual within that, the Praxis Event explores what institutional forms may emerge when one starts from the notion of the individual and a task. Staff therefore relinquished both their managerial and their consultant roles. For both members and staff this was a challenging and daunting experience. Each was deprived of the customary role of the "other"—to rub up against, to project into, to set outline against inline—and we were forced back on our internal resources, and perhaps on latent, more primitive identities. The primary relationship was now between the individual, with his inline, and the task. It then seems that 'the other' and the myth of the group have very quickly to be evoked. I personally discovered how much I customarily use role as an armour, to defend me from exposure and from the making of choices.

My third point is related. In that conference, which had as its title "Individual and Organization: the Politics of Relatedness," we tried to work more than previously at what one might call the "meta-interpretation." That is to say, the consultant not only interprets in the usual way what is going on in the group in relation to him, and why he thinks this is happening, but he also attempts to elucidate the function—and it is a political function—of his making the interpretation at that time or in that way: to control, to defend his role or his person, to re-establish a damaged identity, and so on. Thus in the 'conference' phase of a programme, he might try to identify how his prospective relationships are affecting his interpretations of the here and now. This is not a startling new idea, but it does seem to me that staffs need to work much more assiduously at elucidating their own countertransferences, their projections, their manipulations and their collusions. It is interesting and valuable to join Gustafson and Cooper in tackling with members the problems of group development; but unless we can work with members in the here and now at elucidating the political nature of our involvement with them and theirs with us, and accept the pain and the responsibility that flow from that, I fear that our conferences will have about as much influence on contemporary institutions as a fly on an elephant's back. Of course, the fly can always try another elephant—a Canadian elephant, a French elephant, a Swedish elephant—but the fly tends to have a shorter lifespan than the elephant, so that unless he can evolve an effective set of teeth he might as well give up and go back to his dung-hill.

27.

THE COUCH AT SEA: PSYCHOANALYTIC STUDIES OF GROUP AND ORGANIZATIONAL LEADERSHIP

Otto F. Kernberg

Psychoanalytic contributions to the theory of group and organizational psychology have a puzzling quality. A few key theoretical contributions in this area occupy a territory somewhat peripheral to the mainstream of psychoanalysis, and most psychoanalysts tend to shy away from them. These contributions have nevertheless had a significant impact on the intellectual, scientific, and even political scenes. Their impact, however, has been limited in the field of organizational intervention, and there are good reasons for that: More about this later.

In what follows I present a brief overview of this field, with an emphasis on an area that seems to have received less attention than it merits—that of leaders of groups and organizations. The title of my article is intended to convey the sense of uncertainty and even danger that I have come to associate with attempts to apply psychoanalytically gained knowledge to large groups and organizations.

FREUD AND LEADERSHIP

Freud (1955b) initiated the psychoanalytic study of group processes, explaining them in terms of his then newly developed ego psychology. Freud understood the immediate sense of intimacy that individuals established with each other in mobs as derived from the projection of their ego ideal onto the leader, and their identification with him as well as with each other. The projection of the ego ideal onto the idealized leader eliminates moral constraints and the higher functions of self-criticism and responsibility that are so importantly mediated by the superego. The sense of unity and belonging protects the members of the mob from losing their sense of identity, but it is accompanied by a severe reduction in ego functioning. As a result of all these developments, primitive, ordinarily unconscious needs take over and the mob functions under the sway of drives and affects, excitement and rage, stimulated and directed by the leader.

Freud linked these concepts with his hypotheses regarding the historical origin of the primal horde (1955a). The leader who is idealized is both the oedipal hero who killed his father and who symbolically represents the alliance of all the sons, and also the father and his law, obeyed as the result of unconscious guilt for the parricide.

These formulations have been very influential in the history of contemporary thought, not only in the fields of psychology and sociology but even in political theory. As Lasch (1981) pointed out, these formulations have provided a theoretical underpinning for generations of Marxists and other socialist philosophers from Wilhelm Reich (1962) to Louis Althusser (1976). The patriarchal bourgeois family was seen as the place where the repressive ideology of capitalism was introjected and linked with the sexual prohibitions of the oedipal father.

Whereas Freud thought that the repression of sexuality was the price paid for cultural evolution, Reich thought that the repression of sexuality represented the effects of a pathological superego determined by the social structure of capitalism. Soviet Russia's sexual repressiveness, Reich explained, reflected the development of a Soviet authoritarian power structure.

In illustrating his theories of group psychology, Freud used the organization of the church and the army as examples of the relation of the group or, rather, the total organization, to its leader. But, Francois Roustang reminds us in his book *Dire Mastery* (1982) that Freud was never actually in the army, nor was he a member of any church. His personal experience of leadership came from the psychoanalytic movement. Roustang points to the paradox that Freud, who critically described the irrational relations between leaders and followers in organized institutions, should have been the author of "On the History of the Psychoanalytic Movement," written in 1914. Freud's paper clearly indicates, according to Roustang, his conviction that a truly scientific commitment to psychoanalysis coincided with loyalty to his (Freud's) ideas, whereas any questioning of key psychoanalytic concepts represented unconsciously determined resistances to truth. The ad hominem nature of the arguments Freud advanced against Jung and Adler is painful reading for any admirer of Freud's genius. One could dismiss Freud's relations to his immediate followers as an irrelevant historical curiosity, were it not so intimately linked with subsequent psychoanalytic history. Roustang, in his study of the relation between master and disciple, calls attention to a contradiction inherent to psychoanalytic movements: The goal of psychoanalysis is to resolve the transference. But psychoanalytic education attempts to maintain the transference that psychoanalysis tries to resolve. If fidelity to Freud, the charismatic founder of psychoanalysis, were required, the members of the societies could not be scientifically independent. The tradition has persisted, as Roustang makes clear in his discussion of Lacan.

Was Freud describing his psychoanalytic movement or unconsciously using it as a model while writing "Group Psychology and the Analysis of the Ego"? And how can one explain his lack of interest in examining the personality of the organizational leader itself? Freud seems to consider the nature of the leader mostly in terms of the leader's symbolic function as the youngest son of the symbolically murdered father. Freud simply attributes to the leader characteristics of self-assuredness and narcissistic self-investment, in contrast to the libido the group invests in him.

BION AND LEADERSHIP

Bion's contributions to small group processes, summarized in his book *Experiences in Groups* (1961), are sufficiently well known not to warrant their summary here. I consider his psychoanalytic explanation of the regressive processes that occur in small groups in terms of the three basic emotional assumptions of dependency, fight/flight, and pairing, and I consider their activation when the task structure of the group (Bion's "work group") breaks down the most important single contribution psychoanalysis has made to small group psychology. I hasten to add, however, that, whereas Bion's method of exploring primitive defenses, object relations, and anxieties in small unstructured groups may be of great value in learning about small group psychology and group processes, even in large organizations and large unstructured groups, I find the therapeutic value of his technique questionable.

In fact, inherent in Bion's method is the refusal of the leader to participate in the group. The leader observes and interprets all transactions, even those directed toward himself, in terms of group processes as if the leader were a cipher. This strategy reduces the ordinary social role relation between the members and the leader. The attempt to eliminate the leader as a distinct personality not only prevents the ordinary structuring of the group situation by means of socially accepted and reassuring roles and interactions, it creates—when applied to group psychotherapy—an artificiality in the posture of the leader. It results in making a mockery of the psychoanalyst seated unobserved behind the couch.

Confusing the psychoanalyst's technical neutrality with "disgruntled indifference," to which Freud himself (1963a) objected, is still prevalent today. Some analysts think that to be technically neutral requires not only not sharing their inner life with the patient (which is entirely appropriate), but the creation of the illusion that the analyst has *no* personality at all, which is hardly being realistic. I doubt whether it could have been said of Freud that he appeared to his patients as a "man without qualities."

This issue is related to the current analytic controversy regarding the extent to which the transference is based in the reality of what the patient observes in the analyst or belongs to the patient's past. This discussion neglects the fact that the transference usually crystallizes around realistic aspects of the analyst's personality, exaggerated and distorted as a consequence of the patient's unconscious transfer from experiences in the past. To differentiate the reality of the stimulus for the transference from the transference per se as a distortion or an exaggeration of that stimulus has always been a primary technical task. My point is that the fantasy or wish to erase *any* reality stimulus derived from the analyst only serves the patient's unconscious need for idealization.

There are advantages and dangers in Bion's technique. Among the advantages are the sharp highlighting of primitive modes of mental operations and the possibility of examining unconscious processes that influence group behavior. On the negative side, questions have been raised (Scheidlinger, 1960; Malan, Balfour, Hood, and Shooter, 1976) to what extent the artificial distancing of the group leader, the elimination of ordinary supportive features of group interactions, and the failure to provide cognitive instruments for self-understanding to individual patients regarding their particular psychopathology may be too strenuously demanding on the individual patient and thus be therapeutically counterproductive. I think Bion's technique may also artificially foster the idealization of the therapist.

Bion stresses the basic assumption that group leaders are sucked into their leadership role by the very nature of the regression in the group. Hence, Bion's leader is really a prisoner of the group atmosphere, or rather the group utilizes his personality characteristics for its own purposes. In contrast, the leader of the work group has a rational approach to reality and an awareness of the boundaries of the group. This rational leader has the capacity for reality testing, an awareness of time, and the capacity to stand up to the hatred of rationality activated under basic assumptions conditions. The distinctions Bion draws between the two types of leaders offer seminal concepts for the understanding of the ascendency of narcissistic and paranoid personalities under basic assumptions group conditions; but they also convey a strange failure to consider the reality of the person who is the work group leader. Did Bion assume that his own extremely powerful personality (obvious to everybody who met him) was submerged by his refusal to fulfill the ordinary role expectations in the group?

Again, this might appear to be a trivial issue, if it were not that, after many years of silence regarding group issues, the theme of the group and its leadership reemerges in Bion's book *Attention and Interpretation* (1977). Here Bion refers to the "exceptional individual" who may be a genius, a messiah, a mystic, or a scientist. Bion offers Isaac Newton as an outstanding example, pointing to Newton's mystical and religious preoccupations as the matrix from which his mathematical formulations evolved. It is hard to avoid the impression that Bion is referring here not only to the work group leader and his creativity but also to a very special type of leader whose convictions have a religious core, and whose behavior, as indicated by the collective term "mystic" with which Bion frames this category, implies the secrecy of one initiated, an obscure or occult character, someone mysterious or enigmatic.

Bion, I think, is here referring to himself, and the question of whether he was aware of it resonates with the question of whether Freud was aware of the nature of the model of the unmentioned leaders of the army or the church. Be that as it may, there is a sense Bion conveys of the impotence of rationality, a fragility in the creative mystic, which is endangered by the envious, paranoid, pedestrian, conventional, and limited nature of what Bion calls the establishment. Bion describes three types of interaction between mystic and establishment; a mutually enriching or "symbiotic" one, a mutually destructive or "parasitic" one, and a mutual ignoring or "commensal" one. His emphasis is on the risk of the destruction of the mystic who cannot be "contained" by the establishment, or vice versa, on the risk that the disruptive creativity of the mystic will destroy the establishment.

KENNETH RICE'S SCHOOL

Kenneth Rice's systems theory of organizations treats the individual, the group, and the social organization as a continuum of open systems. Rice (1965) integrates Bion's theories of small group functioning with his own and with Turquet's (1975) understanding of large group functioning and an open systems theory of social organizations.

Within this model, psychopathology may be conceptualized as a breakdown of the control function, a failure to carry out the primary task, and a threat to the survival of the system. In the individual we see breakdown of the ego and emotional regression; in the group, breakdown of leadership and paralysis in basic assumptions; and in the institution, breakdown of the administration, failure to carry out the institutional tasks, and loss of morale. Breakdown of boundary control is the principal manifestation of breakdown in the control function.

Rice's theories form the background to the Tavistock Clinic group relations conferences in Leicester and the A. K. Rice group relations conferences in this country. These are time-limited conferences for learning about group, organizational, administrative, and leadership functions. The conferences include small group meetings conducted according to a strictly Bionian technique, large group meetings applying this same technique as described by Rice and Turquet, intergroup exercises, theoretical conferences, and "application groups" to discuss problems of home organizations.

Rice and Turquet studied the behavior of large unstructured groups—of 40 to 120 persons—in ways similar to Bion's study of small group processes. Turquet stressed the individual member's sense of total loss of identity in large group situations, and the simultaneous dramatic diminution in the ability to evaluate realistically the effects of one's own acts or the acts of others within such a group setting. The individual is thrown into a void, even projective mechanisms fail, because it is impossible to evaluate realistically the behavior of anyone else; projections therefore become multiple and unstable, and the individual desperately tries to find some means of differentiating himself from the others.

Turquet also described how the individuals in the large group feared aggression, loss of control, and the emergence of violent behavior. The fear is the counterpart to provocative behaviors among the individuals, behaviors expressed in part randomly but mostly directed at the leader. It gradually becomes evident that it is those individuals who try to stand up to this atmosphere and maintain some semblance of individuality who are most subject to attack. At the same time, efforts at homogenization are prevalent, and any simplistic generalization or ideology that permeates the group may be easily picked up and transformed into an experience of absolute truth. In contrast to the simple rationalization of the violence that permeates the mob, in the large group a vulgar or "common-sense" philosophy functions as a calming, reassuring doctrine that reduces all thinking to obvious cliches. One cannot escape the impression that in the large group aggression largely takes the form of envy of thinking, of individuality, and of rationality.

In my experience with both large and small groups, including group relations conferences, several phenomena emerge with impressive regularity and intensity: First, the activation of intense anxieties and primitive fantasies in the small study groups, and, second, the activation of a primitive quality to both group functioning and potential individual aggression in the large group. The rapid development of ad hoc myths about the leadership or about the conference, and the search for a comprehensive and simplistic ideology in contrast to discriminating reasoning, illustrates in one stroke what happens during the breakdown of organizational functioning. The crucial function of boundary control in task performance and of the role of task-oriented leadership emerges in contrast to the dramatic temptations, at points of regressions, to select the most dysfunctional members of subgroups to basic assumptions group leadership and to blur all boundaries in the emotional turmoil that pervades the group.

One important drawback to group relations conferences is the relative failure to consider the effects of their temporary nature. Katz and Kahn (1966) pointed out that the learning of new attitudes on the part of staffs of social and industrial organizations, in the context of exploring the irrational aspects of group processes in an experiential setting, frequently fails. This failure results from their neglecting to analyze the stable features of the organizational structure and the relation between that structure and the real (in contrast to fantasied or irrational) conflicts of interests that such organizational structures mediate.

I think that short-term learning experiences in groups do not allow time for studying the impact of personality structures on members of organizations, particularly the personality of key leaders.

Here we are touching again, now at the level of the relation between large groups and organizational structure, the same, almost unnoticeable, neglect of the impact of the personality of the leader on organizational conflicts. Rice has the great merit of having fully developed a theory of organizational functioning that permits the diagnosis of both organizational regression—"loss of morale"—and of administrative distortions that facilitate such regressive group processes, a theoretically elegant and eminently practical approach to organizational dynamics. But, once again, the effects of the distorted personality on stable social organizations are missing here. It is almost as if the optimal, rational leader were a "man without qualities," or perhaps *should* be a man without qualities?

I think that the more severe the leader's personality pathology and the tighter the organizational structure, the greater are the destructive effects of the leader on the organization. It might be that, under extreme circumstances, the paranoid regression of an entire society maintains the sanity of the tyrant, and, when his control over that society breaks down he becomes psychotic: The final months of Hitler point to this possibility.

Under less extreme circumstances, the effort to "correct" organizational distortions by changing the behavior of the leader may have disastrous consequences for him as well as for those in the next hierarchy. If the organization has to live with a characterologically dysfunctional leader, it may be preferable to adapt the administrative structure to an optimal balance between task requirements and the leader's needs—a solution remarkably opposite to Rice's model.

But how is one to know where to draw the line between restructuring the organization to protect it from the leader's pathology and acknowledging that the organization requires a different leader?

The application of a combined psychoanalytic and open systems theory model of institutional functioning to therapeutic community models (see Main, 1946) illustrates the limits of the therapeutic use of large group analysis. (For a critique of therapeutic community models see Kernberg, 1982.)

I would like to stress that there is an enormous danger within a therapeutic community setting. The danger is that the open exploration of the total social field, wherein patients and staff interact by analyzing the content of the communications that emerge in the community meeting, may be transformed into a messianic denial of reality should the group come under the sway of a leadership characterized by narcissistic and paranoid features. To view the content of large group meetings as a reflection of the unconscious of the organization, and to trace the origin of distortions in the social system to its administrative structure or to the psychopathology of individual patients, or to conflicts at the boundary between patients and staff or of a particular service with the total hospital is exciting and potentially helpful. By the same token, the transformation of trust and openness into the messianic spirit of the dependent or pairing group or, rather, the large group that has found a narcissistic leader and a soothing simplistic ideology is a great and constant temptation for the group and the leader alike. The threat to rational evaluation of task boundaries and constraints, to the ordinary political negotiation around boundaries, is enormous. The proverbial disillusionment and burning out of staff involved in this process who overextend themselves in a messianic overevaluation of what can and should be accomplished need no illustrations.

Here, we find a paradoxical effect of psychoanalytic illumination of the unconscious in institutions: The deepest, hidden agendas of the institution appear at the surface in verbal communication at large group meetings. But this is an illusion: The immediate availability of understanding basic issues is no guarantee that they will be resolved. Unlike individual psychoanalysis, there is no direct link between emotional reality in groups and their resolution by actual institutional mechanisms of change. The neglect of the personality issues of leadership in the psychoanalytic contributions to group and organizational functioning mentioned before is compounded by the underestimation of the risk for disruption of all rationality by the snowballing effects of expanding small group and large group regressions in the process of self-exploration. The diagnostic instrument self-destructs, the collective patient becomes psychotic.

DIDIER ANZIEU AND JANINE CHASSEGUET-SMIRGEL

We come now to one more field of application of psychoanalytic theory to group and organizational processes, namely, the study of group processes as the breeding ground for social ideologies, perhaps the most exciting, but also the most controversial and most explosive application of psychoanalytic thinking to social phenomena. I am referring here to the work of French analysts, particularly Didier Anzieu (1971, 1981), Rene Kaes (1980), Janine Chasseguet-Smirgel (1975), and Denise Braunschweig and Michel Fain (1971).

Anzieu (1971) proposed that, under conditions of regression in the unstructured group, the relationship of individuals to the group as an entity acquires characteristics of fusion of their individual instinctual needs with a fantastic conception of the group as a primitive ego ideal equated to an all-gratifying primary object, the mother of the earliest stages of development. The psychology of the group, at that point, reflects the shared illusions (1) that the group is constituted by individuals who are all equal (thus denying sexual differences and castration anxiety); (2) that the group is self-engendered, that is, a powerful mother in itself; and (3) that the group itself might solve all narcissistic lesions (the group becomes an idealized "breast-mother").

Chasseguet-Smirgel (1975), expanding on Anzieu's observations, suggests that under such conditions groups (both small and large) tend to select leadership that represents not the paternal aspects of the prohibitive superego, but a pseudopaternal "merchant of illusions" who provides the group with an ideology (defined as a system of ideas shared by a group and serving to unify the group), which confirms the narcissistic aspirations of fusion of the individual with the group as a primitive ego ideal—the all-powerful and all-gratifying preoedipal mother. Basically, the identification with each other of the members of the small or large group permits them to experience a primitive narcissistic gratification of greatness and power. The violence of groups operating under the influence of ideologies adopted under such psychological conditions reflects the need to destroy any external reality that interferes with this group illusion. The loss of personal identity, of cognitive discrimination, of any individuality within such a group is compensated for by the shared sense of omnipotence of all its members. The regressed ego, the id, and the primitive (preoedipal) ego ideal of each individual are fused in this group illusion.

Writing earlier under the pseudonym "Andre Stephane," Chasseguet-Smirgel and Grunberger (1969) subjected the social psychology of both French fascism and the new left in light of the student rebellion of 1968, describing infantile characteristics common to both movements. Given the heated political atmosphere in France in 1968, Chasseguet-Smirgel and Bela Grunberger decided to publish their probing and disturbing analysis under a pseudonym. Here, we might say, rationality went into hiding; the observers of the social scene start from an acknowledgment of the (at least temporary) impotence of reason.

RATIONAL LEADERSHIP

Combining the psychoanalytic observations made of mobs, large groups, and small groups, I earlier proposed (1980) that group processes pose a basic threat to personal identity, linked to a proclivity in group situations for the activation of primitive object relations, primitive defensive operations, and primitive aggression with predominantly pregenital features. I proposed that Turquet's description of what happens in large groups constitutes the basic situation against which (1) the idealization of the leader in the horde, described by Freud; (2) the idealization of the group ideology and of leadership that promotes narcissistic self-aggrandizement of the group, described by Anzieu and Chasseguet-Smirgel; and (3) the small group processes described by Bion are all defending. Obviously, large group processes can be obscured or controlled by rigid social structuring. Bureaucratization, ritualization, and well-organized task performance are different methods with similar immediate effects.

Large group processes also highlight the intimate connection between threats to retaining one's identity and fear that primitive aggression and aggressively infiltrated sexuality will emerge. The point is that an important part of nonintegrated and unsublimated aggression is expressed in vicarious ways throughout group and organizational processes. The exercise of power in organizational and institutional life constitutes an important channel for the expression of aggression in group processes that would ordinarily be under control in dyadic or triadic relations.

I would now modify these earlier formulations. I still believe that large group processes threaten individual identity and therefore activate defenses against identity diffusion and a defensive idealization of the leader. But this formulation underestimates the primary gratification to be found in dissolving in fantasy the boundaries between the self and the primitive forerunners of the ego ideal, in what Freud (1955b) (referring to falling in love) called the fusion of ego and ego ideal in mania, in hypnosis, and in the excitement of identifying with others in the group. Anzieu and Chasseguet-Smirgel clarified this illusion of merger more fully when they pointed to its preoedipal nature, in contradistinction to the illusion of merger with a cruel but morally sophisticated superego that characterizes Freud's group member. To put it differently, the messianic characteristic of small and large group regression, with its pregenital features and its denial of intragroup aggression, has to be differentiated from the spirit of the mob, which satisfies every member's need to eliminate a sense of separateness in a common, powerfully self-righteous, emotionally laden movement forward, the destructive expansion of a rioting mob (Canetti, 1978).

But these two levels of regressive temptation (of the small and large group as opposed to that of the crowd) also call for two layers of regressive leadership. At one extreme we find the self-indulgent narcissist who can lead the small dependent assumption group or pacify the large group with a simplistic ideology that soothes while preventing envy of the leader, or, in a more "sophisticated" combination, the sexually "liberated" narcissist who preaches sexual liberation in the group's (symbolic or actual) bathtub and condenses polymorphous preoedipal sexuality with messianic merger. At the other extreme, and more disturbingly, we find the sadistic psychopath, with a well-rationalized cruelty, who energizes the mob into destructive action against a common enemy and frees it from responsibility for murder.

In an earlier work (1980, Chapter 13), I attempted to describe the effects on organizational regression of personality characteristics of the leader, with particular reference to schizoid, obsessive, paranoid, and narcissistic personalities, and I shall not repeat these characteristics here. In my earlier description, however, I limited my observations to small organizations, such as psychiatric hospitals and university departments, where there are usually no more than three levels of hierarchies and where, therefore, there is still some semblance or possibility of leader and followers knowing each other.

The question is to what extent such small, self-contained types of social organization surround the leader with a structure of rationality that would avoid the takeover by a sadistic or narcissistic leader or neutralize his regressive effects over an extended period of time. The possibility that the leader will be personally acquainted with those at the grass roots level of the organization protects the reality aspects of the total institution. But larger organizations, such as national bureaucracies or international corporations, where four to seven hierarchic levels of leadership are the rule, may no longer offer such a possibility of ordinary social control. In such large organizations, any direct contact between all levels of staff becomes impossible or unreal, and the replacement of reality by projective mechanisms increases.

Elliot Jaques (1976) has made a systematic analysis of bureaucracy. He finds that well-functioning bureaucracies have merit. They provide the social system with rationally determined hierarchies, public delineation of responsibility and accountability, stable delegation of authority, and an overall accountability of the organization to its social environment by both legal and political means and a parallel organization of employees and/or labor unions. Bureaucracies may thus provide an optimal balance between the potentially regressive consequences of hierarchically determined relations between individuals, on the one hand, and the possibility of redress of grievances and protection from arbitrariness, on the other.

Jaques's assumption is that the leaders of large social institutions are accountable to, or controlled by, the state or by law. The implicit counterpart to this assumption is that when such social controls are unavailable, the distortions at the top will go unchecked and will be communicated throughout the entire organization. A well-functioning bureaucracy in a democratic system may be one ideal model of organizational structure. In contrast, a tightly organized bureaucracy, controlled by a totalitarian state with a paranoid psychotic or sadistic psychopath at the head of it, would necessarily represent a social nightmare into which the regression of all included groups would very easily fit, without any possibility of rational correction from anywhere. The totalitarian bureaucracies of Nazi Germany and the Soviet Union were able to murder millions of people without any internal convulsions. These examples suggest that the authoritarian power generated within organizations, stemming from both individual psychopathology and from organizational regression, not to mention the ordinary discharge into the organization of unacknowledged narcissistic and aggressive needs by all individuals, may rapidly escalate, given certain social and political conditions, into socially sanctioned cruelty and dehumanization. The distinction between an ordinary dictatorship in which the right to privacy is preserved as long as no direct actions are taken against the regime and a totalitarian system in which all social interactions are regulated by an imposed ideology may be one of the painful discoveries of our time.

Elias Canetti, in his book *Crowds and Power* (1978), describes the universal temptation to become part of a crowd and of assuring personal survival and immortality by killing others as a basic unconscious motive for wanting the leadership of the crowd.

The psychoanalytic study of a particular subgroup of narcissistic patients with aggressive infiltration of their pathological grandiose self elaborated by Herbert Rosenfeld (1971) provides a counterpart to Canetti's description.

Psychoanalytically oriented consultants for institutional problems, whether they follow the model of Rice, Jaques, Harry Levinson (1972), or Abraham Zaleznik (1979), assume that regressive manifestations in group processes indicate institutional malfunctioning and that these group processes potentially point to the nature of the conflicts affecting the system. The usual procedure is to study the primary tasks of the organization, its administrative structure, how authority is distributed and delegated, whether the system has checks and balances, and whether it provides for a redress of grievances. With the possible exception of Levinson's, all these approaches focus on the leadership only after other factors have been studied, by the process, as it were, of elimination. Personality problems always appear at first in the foreground, but can only be diagnosed as causal features once all the other institutional issues have been analyzed and discarded.

Jaques's (1976, 1982) findings regarding an individual's capacity for work as measured by his capacity to estimate the time it will take to accomplish certain tasks and his effective capacity to organize and carry out such tasks (the maximum time span of discretion in his work) are a truly important contribution to organizational psychology and to selection criteria for leadership. Yet the psychoanalytically oriented consultant may be averse or reluctant to take this factor into consideration, and would more likely think in terms of psychopathology than in terms of the inequalities of a leader's capacity for performing his various tasks. In fact, it may be more difficult to assess this quality than to assess or even to sift out the aspects of personality that produce optimal leadership functioning. The leader of an organization as well as the consultant must be constantly alert to the danger of giving rein to their own narcissism and aggression and therefore may have difficulty in acknowledging that managerial leaders do differ in their administrative capabilities. The leader (and the consultant) must also resist any tendency to allow themselves to be influenced by fears of arousing unconscious envy by exposing the differences between people. The leader's task is to judge. Perhaps the best he can do is to maintain an alertness to the implications of standing in judgment of others.

On the basis of my experience as psychoanalyst, leader of groups (including therapeutic communities), medical director of psychiatric hospitals, and consultant to mental health institutions, I can attempt to describe the desirable personality characteristics for rational task leadership. First is high intelligence, which is necessary for strategic conceptual thinking; second is personal honesty and noncorruptibility by the political process; third is the capacity for establishing and maintaining object relations in depth, which is essential for evaluating others realistically; fourth is what might be called healthy narcissism in the sense of being self-assertive rather than self-effacing; and fifth is a sense of caution and alertness to the world rather than a naive credulousness—what someone I once knew called justifiable anticipatory paranoia.

The need for high intelligence, expressed in the capacity for strategic conceptual thinking, and probably also in creative imagination, may seem self-evident. The need for honesty and noncorruptibility may also seem self-evident, but requires testing under conditions of stress and political constraints. In practice, to be fair and just to those the leader knows personally is still possible; but to be fair and just to those who depend on him without his knowing them personally is the test of an integrity that transcends personal commitments to others. The fairness to many will necessarily appear as rigidity to the few; the leader's incorruptibility faced with the temptations of leadership will be experienced as sadistic rejection by the tempters, as may the leader's maintenance of fair rules applying to all. Here the narcissistic investment in moral righteousness may protect rational leadership, together with the paranoid distrust of temptations from the surrounding group. These functions require a well-integrated and mature superego, which assumes the sublimatory nature of ideals and value systems and signifies the preconditions for normal (in contrast to pathological) narcissism.

Under optimal conditions, the leader's narcissistic and paranoid features may neutralize each other's potentially negative effects on the organization and on the leader himself. The paranoid implications of suspiciousness toward subordinate efforts of kowtowing may prevent the disastrous consequences of a narcissistic leader's needs to be obeyed *and* loved at the same time. The narcissistic enjoyment of success in leadership may prevent the erosion of self-confidence that derives from paranoid fears about potential attacks or criticism from others. In stark contrast to such optimal combinations, severe character pathology in the leader in the form of pathological narcissism complicated by paranoid features may prove disastrous (see Kernberg, 1980, Chapter 13).

What is the "right" dosage of normal narcissism and paranoia required for rational leadership? Is it firmness without sadism, incorruptibility without rigidity, warmth without manipulativeness, or emotional depth without the loss of distance required to focus on the total gestalt of the group and on the task as contrasted with its human constraints? The optimal leader of an organization might have to blind himself to the awareness of the impact of his own personality on the organization sufficiently so to be able to resonate with the needs of the group, but not so much as to lose his capacity for using his personality in the leadership role.

A small dose of narcissism and paranoid traits may reinforce the power of rationality and honesty, and a small dose of sadism in the leader may protect the task systems from regression. Yet, an excess of these ingredients may suddenly trigger regression in leaders: A sense of justice and fairness may become self-righteousness and sadistic control. Regression in the leader may trigger regression in the organization.

In the psychoanalytic situation, the psychoanalyst has sufficient boundary control to help a patient discover his unconscious and, by the same token, to permit the development and potential resolution of the patient's unconscious conflicts around sex and aggression in the transference. In transferring the psychoanalytic investigation to group processes an easy activation of primitive processes may occur, which would immediately exceed the boundary control of the exploring psychoanalyst. By the same token, the psychoanalytic consultant exploring organizational issues that deal with the personality of the leader may trigger off a storm that would destroy not only the consultative process but the very capacity of the organization to tolerate it. The complexities of the technique of communication of organizational dynamics may be one factor limiting the consultant's task. But, it is not, in my view, the dominant one. The discrepancy between the analytic instrument—group shared unconscious fantasies, basic assumptions groups and system theory of organizations, and the capacity for containment on the part of the institution may provide a more important, and perhaps intimidating barrier to advances in this field.

I hope I have made clear why I think a nebulous ambiguity surrounds the subject of leadership in Freud, Bion, and others. I also hope my metaphoric title, The Couch at Sea, has communicated some of the excitement I find in exploring the social unconscious, even if the uncertainties still facing us mean having to navigate in troubled waters—and on the couch rather than behind it.

NOTES

Part One—Theory

Projective Identification in Dyads and Groups, pages 21-35

1. In a recent contribution, Ogden (1979) emphasized that projective identification has the special feature of providing a bridge or integrating conception between the intrapsychic and the interpersonal.

2. The language most often used to describe the interpersonal occurrence is that certain mental contents are "put into" the other person. The quotes are used to recognize that the phrase is a metaphor of an end product and is neither a valid description nor an explanation of what occurred. Rather, the person behaves *as if* the mental contents had been put into him. A dynamic explanation of that behavior is given in the final section of this article.

3. In a personal communication Martin Grotjahn suggested the term "invasive identification" to capture the intrusive effect on the target.

4. Ganzarain (1977) also noted the relationship between projective identification and scapegoating.

5. I am indebted to Dr. Donald Colson for suggesting this formulation.

Some Psychodynamics of Large Groups, pages 49-69

1. An earlier version of this paper was read as the Kincardine Foundation Lecture to the University of Edinburgh, March 1971.

2. P.M. Turquet has described a similar state in large unstructured groups of executives on study courses as *homogenisation*. It appears to be the same phenomenon and to have similar underlying dynamics. See 'Threats to Identity in the Large Group.' Winter Lecture of the British Psycho-Analytical Society (Unpublished, 1969).

Leadership: The Individual and the Group, pages 71-87

1. This chapter is based on a lecture given to the Paris Society of Psychosomatic Medicine in November 1967. The writer is much indebted to the work of Bion (1959), Rice (1963), and Miller and Rice (1967).

The Group-as-a-Whole Perspective and Its Theoretical Roots, pages 109-126

1. I wish to express my gratitude to James Krantz for his encouragement and to all the groups that have taught me. To Alison Mayas who provided editorial assistance and great support, a thousand thanks. The limitations of this paper are solely mine.

2. This paper is explicitly written for *Group Relations Reader 2*. For a more detailed treatment of the group-as-a-whole perspective, see Wells (1980).

3. The term 'phantasies' as in the Kleinian tradition represents unconscious fantasies.

4. Splitting as defined here occurs in degrees. It is considered that acts of splitting or fission are needed to divide ambivalent objects as a precursor

for projection or projective identification. Excessive splitting in the adult world has pathological outcomes; for the individual, pathological narcissism and for groups, extreme ethnocentrism.

5. Projective identification has been used primarily to describe intrapersonal and interpersonal dynamics. But evidence suggests that projective identification operates in part in determining the quality of intergroup relations. Hence, we include that level here.

6. This pattern of organization has characteristics of the Batesonian concept of 'mind,' a necessary characteristic of all living systems. Bates declares, "Mind is the essence of being alive." (Capra, 1982, p. 290)

Container and Contained, pages 127-133

1. I shall include psychoanalysis itself in the category of 'action' for reasons given under the heading of Language of Achievement in Chapter 13, *Seven Servants: Four Works by Wilfred Bion*.

Part Two—Method

Collaboration in Small Groups: Theory and Technique for Small Group Processes, pages 139-150

1. By "study groups" we refer to groups met to study their own (group) process. We discuss the tradition begun by Bion (1961) and continued by Rice (1965) and the Tavistock Institute of Human Relations in England and the A. K. Rice Institute in America (Rioch, 1970) primarily. Closely related is the tradition begun in the Harvard Department of Social Relations (Slater, 1966; Mills, 1967; Mann, 1975; Gibbard and Hartman, 1973). These two traditions, and group dynamics contributions from group therapists and group leaders of National Training Labs (NTL), are brought together in the recent book *Analysis of Groups* (Gibbard, Hartman, & Mann, 1974).

2. See Rice (1951) for a discussion of improving the organization of the main assembly line in a factory. Production is to be improved, but the needs of the workers hardly matter except insofar as they might disturb production.

3. The historical, political, and economic influences on study group process have been almost entirely neglected in the preoccupation with the so-called "laboratory conditions" of experimental small groups. (See Frankfort Institute for Social Research, 1973.)

4. For descriptions of the Small Study Group in the context of the Group Relations Conference, see Rice (1965) and Rioch (1970).

5. A third category of error is that of being muddled, which can be experienced by group members (and children) as abandoning or intruding or both. Bion does avoid this kind of error nicely. A muddled relation is very similar to a pseudo-mutual one (Gustafson, 1976b).

6. Balint is aware of the problems of the depressive and paranoid positions and the need to counter them when he states: "In psychiatric terms, the depression caused by the realization of one's shortcomings must be fully accepted; identification with the common group ideal must remain

now as before a desirable and attainable aim, but the group leader must watch very carefully when and how one or the other member is forced or allowed to slide into a paranoid position of the one who has been singled out" (p. 40).

7. See Cooper (1976) for description of how disturbances in the cotherapy relationship of group therapists are brought about by the patients in order to communicate the relationship difficulties the patients are having with each other.

8. The concept of making difficulties prominent in order to overcome them is borrowed from the (individual) psychoanalytic work of Weiss (unpublished) and Sampson (1976).

9. Other noteworthy writings concerning collaborative possibilities and phenomena in groups are Mann (1975), Main (1975), and Richardson (1975).

10. The exceptions to this have been noted earlier in the paper. Some individuals can learn under taxing conditions and others require more than we are allowing for in usual collaborative relations. We refer to a "good enough" average environment for learning.

A Study of Very Small Groups, pages 151-161

1. It may be that this faculty for having simultaneous multiple relationships without raising persecutory anxiety to a serious level is related to the personality characteristic termed Capacity by Jaques (1961).

Men and Women at Work: A Group Relations Conference on Person and Role, pages 163-172

1. Necessarily, my thanks go first to all of the people who attended the conferences described in this paper. Without their participation these conferences would not have continued evolving. Thanks also go to my many staff colleagues. The ideas in this paper are as much their collective contribution as they are mine. Finally, I would like to thank Dr. Daniel Levinson, whose research in the area of adult development has made an important contribution to my thinking about these conferences.

Much of the material in those sections introducing and describing the group relations conferences come from a variety of conference brochures. Since many of my colleagues have produced copy, which we freely borrow and exchange, I can only gratefully acknowledge these, by now anonymous, contributions.

Part Three—Application

Organizational Development and Industrial Democracy: A Current Case Study, pages 243-271

1. This and subsequent quotations, along with the survey findings summarized here, are taken from working papers prepared by AS and OK.

2. Six papers were discussed in detail: Jaques (1970), Money Kyrle (1961), Menzies (1960), Rice (1969), Main (1975), and Hopper and Weyman (1975). The group also looked at work by Schein (1965), Rice (1965), Miller and Rice (1967), Bion (1961), and Etzioni (1964).

Notes

3. Andrew Szmidla, in designing the questionnaire, had previously developed and adopted an important conception of boundary transactions between systems, using a perspective that is different but complementary to the conception of the boundary region of a system that I described in Part I. Since his formulation is not yet published, I will quote here from an explanation given in the report by OK and AS to the ECG:

> ... The boundary [of the ECG as a system] is in effect made up of two parts ... The inside line represents the way the ECG sees itself—call this the inline. The inline is under the control of the members of the ECG. They can say where the boundary is to be drawn, what will be included and what will be excluded from its activities, and how interactions will occur across the boundary. The outside line represents how the site sees the ECG—call this the outline. The outline is under the control of the site and similarly can, by the way it is defined, allow the ECG to do certain things and stop it from doing others. It is clearly extremely important that the inline and the outline are broadly congruent—that is, that the way the ECG sees itself and its role, is also the way the site sees the ECG. Without this shared frame of reference there will not only be problems of communication, but much more seriously, expectations by either or both parts working together may not be met and may even work against each other, leading to a breakdown in the relationship.

Hence the report fell into four main sections:

1. how the ECG saw itself
2. how the site saw the ECG
3. how the representative saw his role on the ECG
4. how the constituents saw the representatives' role on the ECG.

The Assisted Independent Living Program: A New Model for Community Care, pages 273-283

1. The authors want to acknowledge the help and assistance of Robert Gordon, M.F.C.C., current Director of the San Francisco AIL program and Carol Roberts, M.F.C.C., for their contributions to the development of the program.

2. A component of the program's ongoing evaluation was the use of a relatively simple instrument called the Group Environment Scale, developed by R. Moos, Consulting Psychologists Press, Palo Alto, Ca. Comparing the scores of households during the first month in the program with those taken following eighteen months in the program showed, among other things, a major shift in the clients' view of themselves in relation to authority figures. Initially clients perceived their coordinator as exercising significant control over the household, 80 percent on the scale, although they only wanted the coordinator to have a 20 percent impact on the household's decisions. Eighteen months later clients perceived the coor-

dinator as having a 35 percent impact while they wanted 45 percent. This data suggests movement in clients' projections onto authority and in their own sense of ability.
    3. Personal communication with Jim Illig, Ph.D., Executive Director, Baker Places, Inc., San Francisco, CA.

A Retrospective View of a Hospital-wide Group Relations Training Program: Costs, Consequences and Conclusions, pages 285-298
    1. Delivered April 22, 1983 at the 6th Scientific Meeting of the A. K. Rice Institute, San Francisco, CA.
    2. My grateful appreciation is due Leonard Horwitz, Ph.D. of The Menninger Foundation for his advice, counsel and assistance in the preparation of this paper, and to Virginia Eicholtz for her indefatigable editorial assistance.
    3. This renewed emphasis on the therapeutic potential of the environment is historically ironic, since more than 35 years ago Dr. Will Menninger introduced the concept of a therapeutic milieu into hospital treatment. (W. Menninger, 1982).

Belfast Communities Intervention, pages 299-306
    1. I would like to thank Dr. Margaret Rioch and Ms. Lorna Volk for their help.
    2. The original team was Leonard Doob and William Foltz who served as researchers and Edward Klein and James Miller, who were Tavistock consultants. We added Daniel Alevy, Barbara Bunker and Nancy French who had NTL training.

Unconscious Process in an Organization: A Serendipitous Investigation, pages 353-362
    1. A version of this chapter was presented at the Sixth Scientific Meeting of the A.K. Rice Institute in San Francisco and at Academic Conference, McLean Hospital, Belmont, Massachusetts.
    2. The author would like to thank Wesley Carr, Ph.D. for his helpful comments on an early draft of this chapter.
    3. I am grateful to Dr. Judith Freedman for this idea.
    4. I am grateful to Dr. William Pollack for this formulation.

The Politics of Involvement, pages 383-397
    1. An address to the Fourth Annual Scientific Meeting of the A.K. Rice Institute, "Group Relations in Transition: A Look to the Future," in Houston, Texas, March 22-24, 1979.
    2. It may be of passing interest to note that although the words "polite" and "politic" carry similar overtones of dissimulation and possibly, hypocrisy, they derive from quite different roots: "politic" from the Greek politikos, meaning "citizen" (politeia = "state") and "polite" from the Latin polire, meaning "to polish."
    3. This is quoted from a document prepared by the authors as consultants for a client organization. I have substituted A and B for the specific subsystems named in the document.

Notes

4. Also of course Laing (e.g. Laing, 1967; Laing et al., 1966), who was omitted in my original version. Garrett O'Connor, in reminding me of this, rightly pointed out that the inclusion or exclusion of references may itself be politically motivated.

BIBLIOGRAPHY

Adorno, T.W., et al. *The Authoritarian Personality.* New York: Harper, 1950.

Alderfer, C.P. "Understanding laboratory education: An Overview". *Monthly Labor Review* 93(1970):18-27.

Alderfer, C.P. "Group and intergroup relations". In *Improving Life and Work: Behavioral Sciences Approaches to Organizational Change*, edited by J.R. Hackman and J.L. Suttle. Santa Monica, CA: Goodyear, 1977.

Alevy, D., Bunker, B., Doob, L., Foltz, W., French, N., Klein, E., and Miller, J. "Rational, research and role relations in the Stirling workshop". *Journal of Conflict Resolution* 18(1974):276-284.

Althusser, L. *Positions.* Paris: Editions Sociales, 1976.

Anzieu, D. "L'illusion groupal". Nouvelle Revue de Psychanalyse 4(1971):73-93.

Anzieu, D. *Le groupe et l'inconscient: L'imaginaire groupal.* Paris: Dunod, 1981.

Argyris, C. *Personality and organization.* New York: Harper & Row, 1957.

Argyris, C. *Interpersonal competence and organizational effectiveness.* Homeward, Illinois: Irwin Dorsey, 1962.

Argyris, C. *Integrating the individual and the organization.* New York: Wiley, 1964.

Argyris, C. "Conditions for competence acquisition and therapy". *Journal of Applied Behavioral Science* 4(1968):147-177.

Argyris, C. *Intervention Theory and Method.* Reading, Mass: Addison-Wesley, 1970.

Arsenian, J., Semrad, E.V., and Shapiro, D. "An analysis of integral functions in small groups". *International Journal of Group Psychotherapy* 12(1962):421-434.

Back, K. *Beyond words: The story of sensitivity training and the encounter movement.* New York: Russell Sage, 1971.

Balint, M. "Method and technique in the teaching of medical psychology. II. Training general practitioners in psychotherapy". *British Journal of Medical Psychology* 27(1954):37-41.

Balint, M. *Thrills and regressions.* New York: International Universities Press, 1959.

Balint, M. *The basic fault, therapeutic aspects of regression.* London: Tavistock Publications, 1968.

Bannister, K., and Pincus, L. *Shared Phantasy in Marital Problems. Therapy in a 4-person relationship.* Hitchin, Hart: Codicote Press, 1965.

Barber, J. "The scope of international politics and foreign policy". In *The analysis of international politics* edited by J. Barber, J. Negro and M. Smith. Milton Keynes: Open University Press, 1975.

Bibliography

Bayes, M., and Newton, P. "Women in authority: A sociopsychological analysis". Presented at the Scientific Meetings of the A. K. Rice Institute, April 1976.

Bayes, M., Wisnent, L.; and Wilk, L.A. "The Mental Health Center and the Women's Liberation Group: An intergroup encounter". *Psychiatry* 40(1977):66-78.

Beard, J.H. "The Rehabilitation Services of Fountain House". *Alternatives to Mental Hospital Treatment*. New York: Plenum Press, 1978.

Beauvais, C. "The family and the work group: dilemmas for women in authority". Unpublished doctoral dissertation, City University of New York, 1976.

Beck, Robert L. "The Use of the Self Study Group in Social Work Education". Presented at the Scientific Meeting of the A.K. Rice Institute, 1983, San Francisco, California.

Bennis, W.G. "A funny thing happened on the way to the future". *American Psychologist* 25(1970):595-608.

Bennis, W.G. and Slater, P.E. "Democracy is inevitable"'. *Harvard Business Review* 42(1964):51-59.

Benson, M. Christina and Lundgren, John T. "The Dynamics of Groups and Organizations". In *Teaching Psychiatry and Behavioral Science*, edited by Joel Yager. New York: Grune and Stratton, Inc., 1982.

Berenson, Bernard "Editorial on the occasion of Berenson's death". *The Washington Post*, October 8, 1958.

Berkowitz, D., Shapiro R., Zinner, J, and Shapiro, E. "Concurrent family treatment of narcissistic disorders in adolescence". *International Journal of Psychoanalytic Psychotherapy* 3(1974a):370-396.

Berkowitz, D., Shapiro, R., Zinner, J., and Shapiro, E. "Family contributions to narcissistic disturbances in adolescence". *International Review of Psychoanalysis* 1(1974b):353-362.

Berman, M. *The Re-enchantment of the World*. New York: Bantam Books, 1984.

Bertalanffy, L. von. "The theory of open systems in physics and biology", *Science* 3(1950a):23-9.

Bertalanffy, L. von. "An outline of general system theory", *British Journal of the Philosophy of Science* 1(1950b):134-65.

Bion, W.R. *Experiences in groups*. New York: Basic Books, 1961.

Bion, W.R. "Attention and Interpretation". In *Seven Servants: Four Works by Wilfred Bion*. New York: Jason Aronson, 1977.

Blos, P. "The second individuation process of adolescence". *Psychoanalytic Study of the Child* 22(1961):162-186.

Boehringer, G.H., Zeruolis, V., Bayley, J., and Boehringer, K. "Stirling: The destructive application of Group techniques to a conflict". *Journal of Conflict Resolution* 18(1974):257-275.

Boorstin, D. *The Image*. New York: Pelican Books, 1963.

Bower, M. *The Development of Executive Leadership*. Cambridge, Mass: Harvard University Press, 1949.

Bibliography

Bradford, Sarah. *Harriet Tubman*. Secaucus, New Jersey: 1974. Quote is composite statement from Introduction by Butler A. Jones, preface containing several testimonial letters, and author's text.

Braunschweig, D., and Fain, M. *Eros et Anteros*. Paris: Petite Bibliotheque Payot, 1971.

Braxton, Earl. "Systemic Intervention Strategies for Managing the Casualty Syndrome in Organizational Life"'. Presented at the Scientific Meeting of the A.K. Rice Institute, 1983, San Francisco, California.

Broverman, I.K., Broverman, D.M., Clarkson, F.E., Rosenkrantz, P.S., and Vogel, S.R. "Sex-role stereotypes and clinical judgments of mental health". *Journal of Consulting and Clinical Psychology* 34(1970):1-7.

Brzezinski, Z. *Power and Principle*. New York: Farrar, Straus, Giroux, Inc., 1983.

Canetti, E. *Crowds and Power*. New York: Seabury Press, 1978.

Capra, F. *The Turning Point*. New York: Bantam Books, 1982.

Carter, J. *Keeping the Faith: Memoirs of a President*. New York: Bantam Books, 1982.

Chandler, E. "Choosing to work in groups: A naturalistic study of four women". Unpublished doctoral dissertation, City University of New York, 1975.

Chasseguet-Smirgel, J. *L'Ideal du Moi*. Paris: Claude Tchou, 1975.

Colman, A.D. "Group consciousness as a developmental phase". In *Group Relations Reader*, edited by A.D. Colman and W.H. Bexton. Washington, D.C.: A.K. Rice Institute, 1975.

Colman, A.D. and Bexton, W., eds. *Group Relations Reader 1*. Washington, D.C.: A.K. Rice Institute, 1975.

Cooper, L. "Co-therapy relationships in groups". *Small Group Behavior* 7(1976):473-498.

Cooper, L. and Gustafson, J. "Supervision In a Group: An Application of Group Theory". (Unpublished).

Correa, M.E., Klein, E.B., Howe, S.R. and Stone, W.N. "A bridge between training and practice: mental health professionals' learning in group relations conferences". *Social Psychiatry* 16(1981):137-142.

Cumming, J., and Cumming, E. *Ego and Milieu*. New York: Atherton Press, 1967.

Dalton, G.W., et al. *The Distribution of Authority in Formal Organizations*. Cambridge, Mass: Harvard University Press, 1968.

Davies, Robertson. *Fifth Business*. New York: Penguin Books, 1977.

Dicks, H. *Marital Tensions*. London: Tavistock, 1967.

Doob, L. *Resolving Conflict in Africa: The Fermada Workshop*. New Haven: Yale University Press, 1970.

Doob, L., and Foltz, W. "The impact of a workshop on grassroots leaders in Belfast". *Journal of Conflict Resolution* 18(1974):237-156.

Drucker, P.F. *The Practice of Management*. London: Heinemann, 1955.

Bibliography

Durkin, H.E. *The Group in Depth*. New York: International Universities Press 1964.

Dusier, Elfreda, ed. *Crusade for Freedom: Autobiography of Ida B. Wells*. Chicago University of Chicago Press, 1970.

Easton, D. *The Political System*. New York: Knopf, 1953.

Eissler, K.R. *Medical orthodoxy and the future of psychoanalysis*. New York: International Universities Press, 1965.

Emery, F.E. and Trist, E.L. "Sociotechnical systems". In *Management Science, models and techniques, Vol. 2*, edited by C.W. Churchman and M. Verhulst. Oxford: Permagon Press, 1960.

Emery, F.E., and Trist, E.L. *Towards a Social Ecology*. New York: Plenum Press, 1973.

Erikson, E. *Childhood and Society*. New York: Norton, 1950.

Erikson, E. "The problem of ego identity". *Journal of the American Psychoanalytic Association* 4(1956):56-121.

Etzioni, A. *Modern organizations*. Englewood Cliffs, N.J.: Prentice-Hall, 1964.

Ezriel, H. "Notes on psychoanalytic group therapy: II interpretation and research". *Psychiatry* 15(1952):119-126.

Fabian, J.J. "The hazards of being a professional woman". *Professional Psychology* 3(1972):324-325.

Faulkner, L.R., Terwilliger, W.B., Cutler, D.L. "Integrating Productive Activities into Aftercare Programs for Chronic Patients: The Oregon LINC Model". *Effective Aftercare for the 1980s*, edited by David L. Cutler. San Francisco: Jossey-Bass, 1983.

Foulkes, S.H. "Group analytic dynamics with special references to psychoanalytic concepts". *International Journal of Group Psychotherapy* 7(1957):40-52.

Frankfurt Institute for Social Research. *Aspects of sociology*. Boston: Beacon Press, 1973.

Freud, S. "Female sexuality". *International Journal of Psychoanalysis* 13(1932):281-297.

Freud, S. "Group psychology and the analysis of the ego". *Standard Edition, 18*. London: Hogarth Press, 1955a.

Freud, S. "Totem and Taboo". *Standard Edition, 13*. London: Hogarth Press, 1955b.

Freud, S. "On the History of the Psychoanalytic Movement". *Standard Edition, 14*. London: Hogarth Press, 1957a.

Freud, S. "Thoughts for the Times on War and Death". *Standard Edition, 14*. London: Hogarth Press, 1957b.

Freud, S. *Civilization and Its Discontents*. Edited by James Strachey. New York: W. W. Norton, 1959.

Freud, S. "The ego and the id". *Standard Edition, 19*. London: Hogarth, 1961.

Bibliography

Freud, S. "Letter to Oskar Pfister of 10-22-1927". *Sigmund Freud Oskar Pfister Briefe 1909-1939*. Frankfurt am Main: Fischer Verlag. (English Translation: Psychoanalysis and Faith: The Letters of Sigmund Freud and Oskar Pfister, eds. H. Meng and E. L. Freud.) New York: Basic Books, 1963a.

Freud, S. "Introductory lectures on psychoanalysis". *Standard Edition, 16*. London: Hogarth, 1963b.

Freud, S. *Inhibitions, Symptoms and Anxiety*. Edited by James Strachey. New York: W.W. Norton, 1977.

Friere, P. *Pedagogy of the oppressed*. New York: Herder and Herder, 1970.

Friere, P. *Cultural action for freedom*. London: Penguin, 1972.

Ganzarain, R. "General systems and object-relations theories: Their usefulness in group psychotherapy". *International Journal of Group Psychotherapy* 27(1977):441-456.

Gibbard, G. "Bion's Group Psychology: A Reconsideration". Unpublished, Veterans Hospital, West Haven, Conn., 1975.

Gibbard, G.S., and Hartman, J.J. "The significance of utopian fantasies in small groups". *International Journal of Group Psychotherapy* 23(1973):125-147.

Gibbard, G.S., Hartmann, J.J., and Mann, R.D., eds. *Analysis of groups*. San Francisco: Jossey-Bass, 1974.

Gillette, Jack and Van Steenberg, Vicki. "A Group - on Group Design for Teaching Group Dynamics in a Management School Setting". Presented at the Scientific Meeting of the A.K. Rice Institute, 1983, San Francisco, California.

Ginzberg, E. and Yohalem, A., eds. *Corporate lib: Women's challenge to management*. Baltimore: The Johns Hopkins University Press, 1973.

Goffman, E. *The presentation of self in everyday life*. New York: Doubleday, 1956.

Goffman, E. *Asylums: essays on the social situation of mental patients and other inmates*. Harmondsworth, Middlesex: Penguin, 1968.

Goldman, H.H., Gottozzi, A.A., Taube, C.A. "Defining and Counting the Chronically Mentally Ill". *Hospital and Community Psychiatry* 32(1981):21-27.

Gosling, R. Personal Communication.

Gould, L.J. "Attitudes toward women in authority". In *Women and Men—Roles, Attitudes and Power Relationships*, edited by E. Zuckerman. Radcliffe Club of New York, 1975.

Gould, L.J. "'Male-female work relations in group and organizational settings". Conference brochure, Washington-Baltimore Center of the A. K. Rice Institute, 1976.

Gould, L.J. "Men and women at work". Conference brochure, Washington-Baltimore Center of the A. K. Rice Institute, 1977.

Grinberg, L. "Countertransference and projective counteridentification". *Contemporary Psychoanalysis* 15(1979):226-247.

Grinberg, L., Gear, M.C., and Liendo, E.C. "Group dynamics according to a semiotic model based on projective identification and counteridentification".

In *Group Therapy*, edited by L.R. Wolberg and M. Aronson. New York: Stratton Intercontinental, 1976.

Gustafson, J.P. "The passive small group: Working concepts". *Human Relations* 29(1976a):793-803.

Gustafson, J.P. "The pseudo-mutual small group or institution". *Human Relations* 29(1976b):989-997.

Gustafson, J. "Crossed Purposes of Medical Residents and Their Patients: A New Problem Area for the Balint (G.P.) Seminar Method". (Unpublished).

Gustafson, J.P. and Cooper, L. "Towards the study of society in microcosm: critical problems of group relations conferences". *Human Relations* 31(1978):843-862.

Gustafson, J.P. and Cooper, L. "Collaboration in small groups: theory and technique for the study of small group processes". *Human Relations* 31(1979):155-171.

Gustafson, J.P. and Hausman, W. "The phenomenon of splitting in a small psychiatric organization". *Social Psychiatry* 10(1975):199-203.

Hammer, M. "Social Supports, Social Networks, and Schizophrenia". *Schizophrenia Bulletin* 7(1981):45-75.

Harrow, M., Astrachan, B.M., Tucker, G.J., Klein, E.B. and Miller, J.C. "The T-group and study group laboratory experiences". *Journal of Social Psychology* 85(1971):225-237.

Heath, E.S. and Bacal, H.A. "A method of group psychotherapy at the Tavistock Clinic". In *Progress in Group and Family Therapy*, edited by E.J. Sajar and H.S. Kaplan. New York: Brunner/Mazel, 1972.

Heimburger, E.M. and Baxter, R.F. "Physician Training in Group Relations". Paper presented at the Scientific Meeting of the A. K. Rice Institute, April, 1976, Minneapolis.

Heimburger, Elizabeth M. and Baxter, Robert F. "The Group Relations Conference as a Supplemental Training Experience for Physicians and other Health Care Professionals". *Journal of Personality and Social Systems* 2(1979):43-52.

Hennig, M. and Jardim, A. *The managerial woman*. Garden City, New York: Doubleday, 1977.

Higgin, G.W. and Bridger, H. *The psychodynamics of an intergroup experience*, Tavistock Pamphlet no. 10. London: Tavistock Publications, 1964.

Hodgson, R.C., Levinson, D.J., and Zaleznik, A. *The Executive Role Constellation: An Analysis of Personality and Role-Relations in Management*. Cambridge, Mass: Harvard University Press, 1965.

Hopper, E. and Weyman, A. "A sociological view of large groups". In *The Large Group: Therapy and Dynamics*, edited by L. Kreeger. London: Constable, 1975.

Horkheimer, M. "Authority and the family". In *Critical Theory*. New York: The Seabury Press, 1972.

Horney, K. *Feminine psychology*. New York: W.W. Norton, 1967.

Horwitz, L. *Clinical Prediction in Psychotherapy*. New York: Jason Aronson, 1974.

Horwitz, L. "Projective identification in dyads and groups". *International Journal of Group Psychotherapy* 33(1983):259-279.

Bibliography

Huber, J., ed. *Changing women in a changing society*. Chicago: University of Chicago Press, 1973.

Isaacs, S. "The Nature and Functions of Phantasy". In *Developments in Psycho-Analysis*, edited by M. Klein, P. Heimann, S. Isaacs and J. Riviere. London: Hogarth Press, 1952.

Jackson, S. "The lottery". In *Come Along With Me*, edited by S.E. Hyman. New York: Viking Press, 1968.

Jacobson, E. "Adolescent moods and the remodeling of psychic structure in adolescence". *Psychoanalytic study of the Child* 16(1961):164-183.

Jacobson, E. *The Self and the Object World*. New York: International Universities Press, 1964.

Janis, I. *Victims of Group Think*. Boston: Houghton, Mifflin, 1972.

Jaques, E. "Interpretive group discussion as a method of facilitating social change". *Human Relations* 1(1948):533-549.

Jaques, E. "On the dynamics of social structure". *Human Relations* 6(1953):3-24.

Jaques, E. *The Changing Culture of a Factory: a study of authority and participation in an industrial setting*. London: Tavistock, 1961.

Jaques, E. *Equitable Payment*. London: Heinemann, 1961.

Jaques, E. *Work, creativity and social justice*. London: Heinemann, 1970.

Jaques, E. "Social systems as defence against persecutory and depressive anxiety". In *Analysis of Groups*, edited by G.S. Gibbard, J.J. Hartmann, and R.D. Mann. San Francisco: Jossey-Bass, 1974.

Jaques, E. *A General Theory of Bureaucracy*. New York: Halsted, 1976.

Jaques, E. *The Form of Time*. New York: Crane, Russak, 1982.

Johnson, John L. and Fleisher, Kristine. "Reactions of Teachers of Emotionally Disturbed Children to Group Relations Conferences: A New Application of Tavistock Training. *Journal of Personality and Social Systems* 2(1980):11-25.

Joseph, D.I., Klein, E.B. and Astrachan, B.M. "Mental health students' reactions to a group training conference: Understanding from a system's perspective". *Social Psychiatry* 10(1975):79-85.

Kaes, R. *L'ideologie: Etudes psychoanalytiques*. Paris: Dunod, 1980.

Kaplan, R.E. "The dynamics of injury in encounter groups: power, splitting and the management of resistance". *International Journal of Group Psychotherapy* 32(1982):163-187.

Katz, D., and Kahn, R.L. *The Social Psychology of Organizations*. New York: Wiley, 1966.

Kernberg, O.F. "Borderline Personality Organization". *Journal of the American Psychoanalytic Association* 15(1967):641-685.

Kernberg, O.F. "Factors in the Psychoanalytic Treatment of Narcissistic Personalities". *Journal of the American Psychoanalytic Association* 18(1970):51-85.

Bibliography

Kernberg, O.F. "Psychoanalytic object-relations theory, group processes, and administration: toward an integrative theory of hospital treatment". *Annual of Psychoanalysis* 1(1973):363-388.

Kernberg, O.F. "Further Contributions to the Treatment of Narcissistic Personalities". *International Journal of Psychoanalysis* 55(1974):215-240.

Kernberg, O. *Borderline Conditions and Pathological Narcissism.* New York: Jason Aronson, 1975.

Kernberg, O. *Object Relations Theory and Clinical Psychoanalysis.* New York: Jason Aronson, 1976.

Kernberg, O.F. "Leadership and Organizational Functioning: Organizational Regression". *International Journal of Group Psychotherapy* 28(1978):3-25.

Kernberg, O.F. "Regression in leadership". *Psychiatry* 42(1979):24-39.

Kernberg, O. *Internal World and External Reality: Object Relations Theory Applied.* New York: Jason Aronson, 1980.

Kernberg, O. "Advantages and liabilities of therapeutic community models". In *The Individual and the Group, Vol. 1*, edited by M. Pine and L. Rafaelsen. London: Plenum Publishing Corp., 1982.

Kernberg, O.F. Personal communication, 1983.

Klein, E.B. "Transference in training groups". *Journal of Personality and Social Systems* 1(1977):53-64.

Klein, E.B. "An Overview of Recent Tavistock Work in the United States". In *Advances in Experiential Social Processes*, edited by C.L. Cooper and C. Alderfer. New York: Wiley, 1978.

Klein, E.B. Personal communication, 1983.

Klein, E.B. and Astrachan, B.M. "Learning in groups: A comparison of study groups and T-groups". *Journal of Applied Behavioral Science* 7(1971):659-683.

Klein, E.B., Correa, M.E., Howe, S.R., and Stone, W.N. "The effect of social systems on group relations training". *Social Psychiatry* 18(1983):7-12.

Klein, E.B. and Gould, L.J. "Boundary issues and organizational dynamics: a case study". *Social Psychiatry* 4(1973):204-211.

Klein, M. "Notes on some schizoid mechanisms". In *Developments in Psychoanalysis*, edited by M. Klein. London: Hogarth, 1946.

Klein, M. *Envy and Gratitude.* London: Tavistock Publications, 1957.

Klein, M. "Our adult world and its roots in infancy". *Human Relations* 12(1959):291-303.

Klein, M. "Notes on Some Schizoid Mechanisms". *The Writings of Melanie Klein.* London: Hogarth Press, 1975.

Knox, R.A. *Enthusiasm.* London: Oxford University Press, 1950.

Laing, R.D. *The politics of experience.* Harmondsworth, Middlesex: Penguin, 1967.

Laing, R.D., and Cooper, D. *Reason and violence: A decade of Sartre's philosophy, 1950-1960.* London: Tavistock Publications, 1964.

Bibliography

Laing, R.D., Phillipson, H., and Lee, A.R. *Inter-personal perception: a theory and a method of research*. New York: Springer, 1966.

Lamb, H.R. "What Did We Really Expect from Deinstitutionalization". *Hospital and Community Psychiatry* 32(1981):105-109.

Lasch, C. "The Freudian left and cultural revolution". *New Left Review* 129(1981):23-34.

Lasswell, H.D. *Politics: who gets what, when, how*. New York: Smith, 1936.

Laufer, M. "Assessment of adolescent disturbances: the application of Anna Freud's diagnostic profile". *Psychoanalytic Study of the Child* 20(1965):99-123.

Lawrence, W.G. "Management development . . . some ideals, images and realities". *Journal of European Industrial Training* 1(1977):21-25.

Lawrence, W.G. "A concept for today: the management of oneself in role". In *Exploring individual and organizational boundaries: a Tavistock open systems approach*, edited by W.G. Lawrence. London: Wiley, 1979.

Lawrence, W.G. et al. *Towards Managerial Development for Tomorrow*. Tavistock Institute of Human Relations Document No. 1119, (unpublished) 1975.

Lawrence, W.G. and Miller, E.J. "Epilogue". In *Task and Organization*, edited by E.J. Miller. London: Wiley, 1976.

Lawrence, W.G. and Robinson, P. "An innovation and its implementation: issues of evaluation". Tavistock Institute of Human Relations Document no. CASR 1069 (unpublished) 1975.

Lerner, H. "Early origins of envy and devaluation of women: Implications for sex role stereotypes". *Bulletin of the Menninger Clinic* 38(1974):538-553.

Levinson, D.J. and Klerman, G. "The clinician-executive: Some problematic issues for the psychiatrist in mental health organizations". *Psychiatry* 30(1967):3-15.

Levinson, D.J., Darrow, C.M., Klein, E.B., Levinson, M.H., and McKee, B. "The psychosocial development of men in early adulthood and the mid-life transition". In *Life History Research in Psychopathology*, vol. III, edited by D. Ricks, 1974.

Levinson, H. *The Exceptional Executive: A Psychological Conception*. Cambridge, Mass: Harvard University Press, 1968.

Levinson, H. *Organizational Diagnosis*. Cambridge, Mass: Harvard University Press, 1972.

Levy, M.J. *The structure of society*. Princeton: Princeton University Press, 1952.

Lewin, K. *Principles in topological psychology*. New York: McGraw Hill, 1936.

Lewin, K. "Frontiers in group dynamics. Concept, method and reality in social science; social equilibria and social change". *Human Relations* 1(1948):5-41.

Lewin, K. *Field theory in social science* New York: Harper Bros., 1950.

Loewald, H. "Therapeutic action of psychoanalysis". *International Journal Psychoanalysis* 1(1960):16-33.

Loewald, H. "Review of psychoanalytic concepts and the structural theory by J. Arlow and C. Brenner". *Psychoanalytic Quarterly* 35(1966):430-436.

Lupton, T. "Best fit in the design of organizations". In *Task and Organization*, edited by E.J. Miller. London: Wiley, 1976.

Mahler, M. "A study of the separation-individuation process and its possible application to borderline phenomena in the psychoanalytic situation". *Psychoanalytic Study of the Child* 26(1971):403-424.

Mahler, M., Pine, F., and Bergman, A. *The Psychological Birth of the Human Infant: Symbiosis and Individuation.* New York: Basic, 1975.

Main, T.F. "The hospital as a therapeutic institution". *Bulletin of the Menninger Clinic* 10(1946):66-70.

Main, T.F. "The Ailment". *British Journal of Medical Psychology* 30(1957):129-145.

Main, T.F. "Mutual Projection in a Marriage". *Comp. Psych.* 7(1966).

Main, T. "Some psychodynamics of large groups". In *The large group, dynamics and therapy*, edited by L. Kreeger. London: Constable, 1975.

Malan, D.H., Balfour, F.H.G., Hood, V.G., and Shooter, A.M.N. "Group psychotherapy: A long-term follow-up study". *Arch. Gen. Psychiat.* 33(1976):1303-1315.

Malin, A. and Grotstein, J.S. "Projective identification in the therapeutic process". *International Journal of Psychoanalysis* 47(1966):26-31.

Mandelbaum, A. "A family-centered approach to residential treatment". *Bulletin of the Menninger Clinic* 41(1977):27-39.

Mann, R.D. "Winners, losers and the search for equality in groups". In *Theories of group processes*, edited by C. Cooper. London: Wiley, 1975.

Marrow, A.J., Bowers, D. and Seashore, S. *Management by participation.* New York: Harper & Row, 1967.

Masler, E. "Interpretation of projective identification in group psychotherapy". *International Journal of Group Psychotherapy* 19(1969):441-447.

Maslow, A.H. *Eupsychian management.* Homewood, Illinois: Dorsey, 1965.

Masterson, J. *Treatment of the Borderline Adolescent: A Developmental Approach.* New York: Wiley, 1972.

Maux, A.J., Test, M.A., Stein, L.I. "Extrohospital Management of Severe Mental Illness". *Archives of General Psychiatry* 29(1973):505-511.

McGregor, D. "Conditions of effective leadership in the industrial organization". *Journal of Consulting Psychology* 8(1944):55-63.

McGregor, D. "On leadership". *Antioch Notes* 31(1954):9.

McGregor, D. *The human side of enterprise.* New York: McGraw-Hill, 1960.

Meissner, W.W. "A note on projective identification". *Journal of the American Psychoanalytic Association* 28(1980):43-68.

Mendell, D. "A paratherapeutic system". *International Journal of Group Psychotherapy* 25(1975):291-304.

Menninger, R.W. "The impact of group relations conferences on organizational growth". *International Journal of Group Psychotherapy* 22(1972):415-432.

Reprinted in *Group Relations Reader 1*, edited by A.D. Colman and W. Bexton. Washington, D.C.: A.K. Rice Institute, 1975.

Menninger, W.C. "The Menninger Hospital's guide to the order sheet". *Bulletin of The Menninger Clinic* 46(1982):21-112.

Menzies, I.E.P. "A case study in the functioning of social systems as a defense against anxiety". Tavistock Pamphlet No. 3, 1961. Also in *Group Relations Reader 1*, edited by A.D. Colman and W. Bexton. Washington, D.C.: A.K. Rice Institute, 1975.

Menzies, Isabel. "Staff Support Systems: Task and Anti-Task in Adolescent Institutions". In *Therapeutic Communities*, edited by R.D. Hinschelwood and N. McManning. London: Rutledge, Kegan and Paul, 1979.

Miller, E.J. "Technology, territory and time: the internal differentiation of complex production systems". *Human Relations* 12(1959):243-272.

Miller, E.J. "Socio-technical systems in weaving, 1953-70: a follow-up study". *Human Relations* 28(1975):349-386.

Miller, E.J. "The open-system approach to organizational analysis, with special reference to the work of A.K. Rice". In *European contributions to organization theory*, edited by G. Hofstede and M. Sami Kassem. Assen/Amsterdam: Van Gorcum, 1976a.

Miller, E.J. "Introductory essay: role perspectives and the understanding of organizational behaviour". In *Task and Organization*. London: Wiley, 1976b.

Miller, E.J. *Desarrollo Integral del Medio Rural: un experimento en Mexico*. Mexico, D. F.: Fondo de Cultura Economica, 1976a.

Miller, E. Preface. In *Task and Organization*. London: Wiley, 1976d.

Miller, E.J. "Towards a model for integrated rural development in Latin America". *Linkage* 2(1977a):8-9.

Miller, E.J. "Organizational development and industrial democracy: a current case-study". In *Organizational development in the UK and USA: a joint evaluation*, edited by C.L. Cooper. London: Macmillan Press, 1977b.

Miller, E.J. "Autonomy, dependency and organizational change". In *Innovation in patient care*, edited by D. Towell and C. Harries. London: Croom Helm, 1979a.

Miller, E.J. "Open systems revisited: a proposition about development and change". In *Exploring individual and organizational boundaries: a Tavistock open systems approach*, edited by W.G. Lawrence. London: Wiley, 1979b.

Miller, E.J. and Gwynne, G.V. *A life apart: a pilot study of residential institutions for the physically handicapped and the young chronic sick*. London: Tavistock Publications, 1972.

Miller, E.J. and Gwynne, G.V. "Dependence, interdependence, and counterdependence in residential institutions for incurables". In *Support, innovation, and autonomy: Tavistock Clinic golden jubilee papers*, edited by R. Gosling. London: Tavistock Publications, 1973.

Miller, E.J. and Rice, A.K. *Systems of organization*. London: Tavistock, 1967.

Miller, J.C. "The psychology of conflict in Belfast: Conferences as microcosm". *Journal of Personality and Social Systems* 1(1977):17-38.

Bibliography

Miller, J.D.B. *The nature of politics*. Harmondsworth: Penguin, 1962.

Mills, T. *The sociology of small groups*. Englewood Cliffs, N. J.: Prentice-Hall, 1967.

Modell, A. "The holding environment and the therapeutic action of psychoanalysis". *Journal of the American Psychoanalytic Association* 24(1976):285-307.

Neumann, E. *The origins and history of consciousness*. New York: Pantheon Books, 1954.

Neumann, E. *The great mother*. Princeton: Princeton University Press, 1955.

Newton, P.M. "Social structure and process in psychotherapy: A socio-psychological analysis of transference, resistance and change". *International Journal of Psychiatry* 11(1973):480-512.

Newton, P.M. and Levinson, D.J. "The work group within the organization: A sociopsychological approach". *Psychiatry* 36(1973):115-142.

O'Connor, G. "The Tavistock method of group study". *Science and Psychoanalysis* 18(1971):100-115.

O'Connor, G. "Commentary on Dr. Rioch's presentation". *Journal of Personality and Social Systems* 1(1978): 51-61.

Ogden, T.H. "On projective identification". *International Journal of Psychoanalysis* 60(1979):357-373.

Ollmann, B. *Alienation, Marx's conception of man in capitalist society*. Cambridge, Mass: Cambridge University Press, 1971.

Paige, G.D. "The rediscovery of politics". In *Approaches to development: politics, administration and change*, edited by J.D. Montgomery and W.J. Siffin. New York: McGraw-Hill, 1967.

Palmer, B. "Learning and the group experience". In *Exploring individual and organizational boundaries*, edited by W.G. Lawrence. New York: Wiley & Sons, 1979.

Parsons, T. "The incest taboo in relation to social structure and the socialization of the child". *British Journal of Sociology* 5(1954):101-117.

Pattison, E.M. DeFranciso, D., Wood, P., Frazer, H., Crowder, J. "A Psycholosocial Kinship Model for Family Therapy". *American Journal of Psychiatry* 45(1975):1246-1251.

Planty, E.G., and Freeston, J.T. *Developing Management Ability*. New York: Ronald Press, 1954.

Racker, H. *Transference and Countertransference*. New York: International Universities Press, 1968.

Redl, F. "Psychoanalysis and group therapy: A developmental point of view". *American Journal of Orthopsychiatry* 33(1963):135-142.

Reich, W. *The Sexual Revolution: Toward a Self-Governing Character Structure*. New York: The Noonday Press, 1962.

Rice, A.K. "The Use of unrecognized cultural mechanisms in an expanding machineshop". *Human Relations* 4(1951):143-160.

Bibliography

Rice, A.K. *Productivity and social organization.* London: Tavistock, 1958.

Rice, A.K. *The enterprise and its environment.* London: Tavistock, 1963.

Rice, A.K. *Learning for leadership.* London: Tavistock, 1965.

Rice, A.K. "Individual, Group and Intergroup Processes". *Human Relations* 22(1969):565-584.

Rice, A.K. *The modern university: A model organization.* London: Tavistock, 1970.

Richardson, E. Selections from: "The environment of learning". In *Group Relations Reader 1,* edited by A.D. Colman and W. Bexton. Washington, D.C.: A.K. Rice Institute, 1975.

Rioch, M. "A method for advanced learning and training in consulting to small groups". (Unpublished).

Rioch, M.J. "The work of Wilfred Bion on groups". *Psychiatry* 33(1970a):56-66. Reprinted in: *Group Relations Reader 1*, edited by A.D. Colman and W. Bexton. Washington, D.C.: A.K. Rice Institute, 1975.

Rioch, M. J. "Group relations: rationale and technique". *International Journal of Group Psychotherapy* 20(1970b):340-355. Reprinted in *Group Relations Reader 1*, edited by A.D. Colman and W. Bexton. Washington, D.C.: A.K. Rice Institute, 1975.

Rioch, M. "All we like sheep (Isaiah 53:6): followers and leaders". *Psychiatry* 34(1971):258-272.

Rioch, M.J. "The A. K. Rice group relations conference as a reflection of society". *Journal of Personality and Social Systems* 1(1977):1-16.

Rioch, M. "Why I work as a consultant in the conferences of the A. K. Rice Institute". *Journal of Personality and Social Systems* 1(1978):33-50.

Rioch, M.J. "A Method for Training for Consultancy in Small Groups". Paper presented at the Scientific Meeting of the A.K. Rice Institute, March, 1979, Houston, Texas.

Rioch, M.J. and Geller, M.H. "Training Methods for Small Group Consultants". Panel presented at the Scientific Meeting of the A. K. Rice Institute, April, 1977, Washington, D.C.

Rogers, K. "Notes on Organizational Consulting to Mental Hospitals". *Bulletin of the Menninger Clinic* 37(1973):211-231.

Roheim, Geza. *The Eternal Ones of the Dream.* New York: International Universities Press, 1945.

Rosenfeld, H. *Psychotic States.* New York: International Universities Press, 1965.

Rosenfeld, H. "A clinical approach to the psychoanalytic theory of the life and death instincts: An investigation into the aggressive aspects of narcissism". *International Journal of Psychoanalysis* 52(1971):169-178.

Roustang, F. *Dire Mastery. Discipleship from Freud to Lacan.* Baltimore: The Johns Hopkins University Press, 1982.

Sampson, H. "A critique of certain traditional concepts in the psychoanalytic theory of therapy". *Bulletin of the Menninger Clinic* 40(1976):255-262.

Bibliography

San Francisco Community Mental Health System Budget. 1983-84 Fiscal Year.

Sandler, J. "The background of safety". *International Journal of Psychoanalysis* 41(1960):352-356.

Sanford, N. "The Approach of the Authoritarian Personality". In *Psychology of Personality*, edited by J.L. McCary. New York: Logos Press, 1956.

Saravay, S.M. "Group psychology and the structural theory: a revised psychoanalytic model of group psychology". *Journal of the American Psychoanalytic Association* 23(1975):69-89.

Scheidlinger, S. "The concept of identification in group psychotherapy". *American Journal of Group Psychotherapy* 9(1955):661-672.

Scheidlinger, S. "Group process in group psychotherapy". *American Journal of Psychotherapy* 14(1960):104-120; 346-363.

Scheidlinger, S. "Identification, the sense of belonging and of identity in small groups". *International Journal of Group Psychotherapy* 14(1964):291-306.

Scheidlinger, S. "On the concept of the 'mother-group'". *International Journal of Group Psychotherapy* 24(1974):417-428.

Schindler, W. "The role of the mother in group psycho-therapy". *International Journal of Group Psychotherapy* 16(1966):198-202.

Schneider, M. *Neurosis and civilization, a Marxist-Freudian synthesis* (M. Roloff, Trans.). New York: Seabury Press, 1975.

Schwartz, Howard. "A Theory of Deontic Motivation". *Journal of Applied Behavioral Science* 19(1983).

Searles, H.F. "Psychotherapy of Schizophrenia". *British Journal of Medical Psychiatry* 34(1961):169-193.

Searles, H.F. "Transference psychosis in the psycho-therapy of schizophrenia". *International Journal of Psychoanalysis* 44(1963):249-281.

Segal, H. *Introduction to the Work of Melanie Klein*. New York: Basic Books, 1973.

Segal, H. *Melanie Klein*. New York: The Viking Press, 1979.

Settlage, C. "The technique of defense analysis in the psychoanalysis of an early adolescent". In *The Analyst and the Adolescent at Work*, edited by M. Harley. New York: Quadrangle, 1974.

Shapiro, E.R. "On curiosity: intrapsychic and inter-personal boundary formation in family life". *International Journal of Family Psychiatry* 3(1982):69-89.

Shapiro, R. "Adolescence and the psychology of the ego". *Psychiatry* 26(1963):77-87.

Shapiro, R. "Adolescent ego autonomy and the family". In *Adolescence: Psychosocial Perspectives*, edited by G. Caplan and S. Lebovici. New York: Basic, 1969.

Shapiro, R. "The Origin of Adolescent disturbances in the family: some considerations in theory and implications for therapy". In *Family Therapy and Disturbed Families*, edited by G. Zuk and I. Boxzormenyi. Palo Alto, Calif.: Science & Behavior Books, 1967.

Bibliography

Shapiro, R. "Ego psychology: its relation to Sullivan, Erikson, and object relations theory". In *American Psychoanalysis*, edited by J. Quen and E. Carlson. New York: Brunner/Mazel, 1978.

Shapiro, R., and Zinner, J. "Family organization and adolescent development". In *Task and Organization*, edited by E. Miller. London: Wiley, 1976.

Shapiro, E., Shapiro, R., Zinner, J., and Berkowitz, D. "The borderline ego and the working alliance: indications for family and individual treatment in adolescence". *International Journal of Psychoanalysis* 58(1977):77-89.

Shapiro, E., Zinner, J., Shapiro, R., and Berkowitz, D. "The influence of family experience on borderline personality development". *International Review of Psychoanalysis* 2(1975):399-411.

Sheffel, I. "Administration—a point of view for psychiatrists". *Bulletin of The Menninger Clinic* 15(1951):131-140.

Sheldrake, R. *A New Science of Life: The Hypothesis of Formative Causation*. Los Angeles: J. P. Tarche, 1982.

Singer, D.L., Astrachan, B.M., Gould, L.J., Klein, E.B. "Boundary management in psychological work with groups". In *Exploring individual and Organizational Boundaries*, edited by W.G. Lawrence. New York: Wiley, 1979.

Skertchley, A. *Tomorrow's Managers*. London: Staples Press, 1968.

Slater, P. *Microcosm, structural, psychological and religious evolution in groups*. New York: Wiley, 1966.

Snyder, R.C. "A decision-making approach to the study of political phenomena". In *New approaches to the study of politics*, edited by R.D Young. Chicago: Northwestern University Press, 1958.

Sokolvsky, J., Cohen, C., Berger, D., Geiger, J. "Personal Networks of Ex-Mental Patients in a Manhattan SRO Hotel." *Human Organization* 37(1978):5-15.

Special Task Force to the Secretary of Health, Education and Welfare. Work in America. Springfield, Virginia: National Technical Information Service, U.S. Department of Commerce, 1972.

Spitz, R. *The First Year of Life*. New York: IUP, 1965.

Stanton, A.M., and Schwartz, M. *The Mental Hospital*. New York: Basic Books, 1954.

Stephane, A. *L'Univers contestationnaire*. Paris: Petite Bibliotheque Payot, 1969.

Strachey, J. "The nature of the therapeutic action of psychoanalysis". *International Journal of Psychoanalysis* 15(1934):127-159.

Szmidla, A. and Khaleelee, O. Unpublished memorandum, 1975.

Taylor, S., Bogdanoff, M., Brown, D., Hillman, L., Kurash, C., Spain, J., Thatcher, B., and Weinstein, L. "By women, for women: A group relations conference". In *Exploring Individual and Organizational Boundaries*, edited by W.G. Lawrence. New York: Wiley, 1979.

Terrell, Mary Church. *A Colored Woman in a White World*. Washington, D.C.: Ransdell Publishers, 1940.

Bibliography

Tolsdorf, C.C. "Social Networks, Support and Coping: An Explanatory Study". *Family Process* 4(1976):407-417.

Trist, E.L. and Branforth, K.W. "Some social and psychological consequences of the long-wall method of coal getting". *Human Relations* 5(1951):6-24.

Trist, E.L. and Soffr, C. *Explorations in Group Relations*. Leicester: Leicester University Press, 1959.

Trist, E.L., Higgin, G.W., Murray, H. and Pollock, A. *Organizational choice*. London: Tavistock, 1963.

Trop, Jeffrey. "Group Dynamics and Psychiatric Inpatient Treatment: A Case Study". *Journal of Personality and Social Systems* 2(1980):3-10.

Turquet, P.M. "Leadership: the individual and the group". In *Analysis of Groups*, edited by G. Gibbard. San Francisco: Jossey-Bass, 1974.

Turquet, P. "Threats to identity in the large group". In *The Large Group: Dynamics and Therapy*, edited by L. Kreeger. London: Constable, 1975.

U.S. Bureau of the Census, Statistical abstract of the U.S.: 1976 (97th edition). Washington, D.C., 1976.

Vance, C. *Hard Choices: Critical Years in American Foreign Policy*. New York: Simon and Schuster, 1983.

Weiss, J. "The emergence of new themes: A contribution to the psychoanalytic theory of therapy". *International Journal of Psychoanalysis* 52(1971):459-467.

Weiss, J. "A new psychoanalytic theory of therapy and technique" (Unpublished).

Wells, L. "The group-as-a-whole: a systemic socioanalytic perspective on interpersonal and group relations". In *Advances in Social Experiential Processes*, edited by C.P. Alderfer and C. Cooper. London: John Wiley and Sons, Ltd., 1980.

Wells, L. "Effects of Ethnicity on the Quality of Student Life: An Embedded Intergroup Analysis". Doctoral dissertation, Yale University, 1982.

Willet, R.S. "Working in 'A Man's World': The woman executive". In *Woman in sexist society: Studies in power and powerlessness*, edited by V. Gornick and B. Moran. New York: Basic Books, 1971.

Winnicott, D.W. *The maturational process and the facilitating environment*. New York: International Universities Press, 1965.

Women's Bureau, Employment Standards Administration. U.S. Department of Labor. Women workers today. Washington, D.C.: U.S. Government Printing Office, 1975.

Women's Bureau, Employment Standards Administration. U.S. Department of Labor. The myth and the reality. Washington, D.C.: U.S. Government Printing Office, 1974 (revised).

Woodson, Carter. *History of the Negro Church*. Washington, D.C. 1921.

Wright, F. "The effects of style and sex of consultants and sex of members in self-study groups". *Small Group Behaviour* 7(1976).

Wright, F., and Gould, L.J. "Recent research on sex-linked aspects of group behavior: Implications for group psychotherapy". In *Group Therapy 1977: An Overview*. New York: Stratton Intercontinental Medical Book Corporation, 1977.

Yalom, I. *The Theory and practice of group psychotherapy*. New York: Basic Books, 1970.

Zaleznik, A. "Charismatic and Consensus Leaders: A Psychological Comparison". *Bulletin of the Menninger Clinic* 38(1974):222-238.

Zaleznik, A. "Psychoanalytic knowledge of group processes. Panel Report". *Journal of the American Psychoanalytic Association* 27(1979):146-147; 149-150.

Zinner, J., and Shapiro, R. "Projective identification as a mode of perception and behavior in families of adolescents". *International Journal of Psychoanalysis* 52(1972):523-530.

Zinner, J., and Shapiro, R. "The family group as a single psychic entity: implications for acting out in adolescence". *International Review of Psychoanalysis* 1(1974):179-186.

INDEX

A

Abandonment, 44, 135, 145, 414
   and intrusion, 149
Acculturation process, 205
Acting-out, 127, 130
Adaption, 39, 46
Admiration, 16
Adolescents
   and character pathology, 221
   and theory of unconscious assumptions, 220-224
   disturbed, 218-220
Adorno, T.W., 95
Adult development
   stages of, 165, 166, 168, 170
After-groups, 64, 66
Age
   -related issues, 163, 165, 169, 170-172
   See also Adult development, stages of
Ageism
   as defense mechanism, 301
Aggression, 7, 9, 22, 24, 26, 49, 99, 119, 250, 310, 316, 321, 327, 335, 346-349, 403, 407
A. K. Rice Institute, 1, 21, 30, 141, 152-153, 173-174, 183, 185-186, 190, 365, 383-384, 388, 403, 414, 417
Alderfer, C.P., i, 109, 135, 197
Alevy, D., 305, 417
Alienation, 144, 313
Althusser, L., 400
Ambition, 17
Ambivalence, 115-117, 120, 234-235, 237, 356-357
American University, 173
Anake, 86-87
Anonymisation, 61, 63, 66
Anxiety, 6-7, 11-12, 22, 40, 42-47, 65, 69, 82, 115-117, 122-123, 178, 222, 224, 229, 238-239, 247, 251, 263, 281, 287, 338, 341, 347, 401, 404
   -chain, 338, 342-344, 346-348
Anzieu, D., 406-407
Application groups, 189, 194, 288, 403
Appraisal terms, 83
Argyris, C., 197
Arsenian, J., 29
Assisted Independent Living Program (AIL), 273-283, 416
Astrachan, B.M., 197, 301
Authoritarian
   administrative structure, 96
   behavior in leadership roles, 95, 286
   organizational structure, 95-96, 357
   personality, 95-96
   role, 316
Authority, 209, 244, 254, 256, 263-264, 267, 293-294, 305, 353-354, 360, 371-372, 381, 393-394
   and leadership, 152, 166
   and learning, 181-182
   and staff, 168
   black women in, 325-334
   delegation of, 91, 97, 193, 409
   family, 311, 349
   -figure, 31, 63-64, 94, 101, 170, 172, 249
   in AIL program, 275, 280-281
   in work setting, 163, 165-166, 240, 260-261, 269-271, 310, 314-317, 342, 349-350
   issues of, 191, 301-302
   linkages, 305
   maternal, 311
   of males, 315-316
   structure, 204, 274
   -to-learn, 173
   women in, 164, 303, 309-322
Autonomy, 34
Avoidance mechanism, 281

Index

B

Bacal, H.A., 38
Back, K., 198
Baker Places, Inc., 273
Balfour, F.H.G., 402
Balint, M., 141-142, 145-146, 149-150, 414
Balloon
    as Very Small Group model, 159
Bannister, K., 50
Barber, J., 387
Barnett, I.B.W., 326
Basic assumption behavior, 45, 146
Basic assumption groups, 47, 74, 76-81, 86, 94, 99, 142, 145, 222, 338, 342, 404, 411
    dependency group (BD), 76, 78, 83-85
    fight/flight group (BF), 76-78, 80, 83-85
    oneness group (BO), 76, 78-79
    pairing group (BP), 76, 78-79, 84-85, 346
Basic assumptions, 29, 37, 40, 43, 85, 87, 223, 246, 319, 371, 401-403
Basic groups, 246
Baxter, R.F., i, 135, 185, 188, 213
Bayes, M., i, 172, 214, 309
Beard, J.H., 273
Beauvais, C., 172
Beck, R.L., 213
Belfast, Northern Ireland, 301-306
Bennis, W.G., 200, 202
Benson, M., 213
Berenson, B., 369
Bergman, A., 220
Berkowitz, D., 220, 227-228
Berman, M., 124
Bernard, H.S., i
Bertalanffy, L. von, 1, 247
Bexton, W., 286-287
Billet, 29
Binocular vision, 43, 48
Bion, W., i, 1-2, 21-23, 25, 28-29, 32, 34, 37-48, 74, 76, 87, 89, 94, 114-115, 127, 129, 135, 139, 141, 143-146, 149, 151-153, 161, 171, 199, 221-224, 226, 231, 246, 250, 253, 274, 288-289, 302, 310, 319, 338, 342, 358, 369, 407, 411, 414
    and leadership, 401-403
Birth order, 367
Blos, P., 220-221
Boehringer, G.H., 305
Boomer, D., 173
Boorstein, D., 233
Bouchet, E.A., 324
Boundaries, 21, 73-75, 82, 85, 99-100, 123, 142, 171, 235, 239, 248, 252, 255-256, 260, 349, 407
    between systems, 385, 416
    between tasks, 72
    control, 76, 91-92, 103-104, 245, 257, 268, 270, 296, 298, 332, 350, 354, 357, 403-404, 411
    -crossing, 201
    emotional, 46
    external, 201, 299, 311, 313-314, 317, 321
    family, 228, 310-311, 356
    group, 169, 199, 259, 262, 289, 293, 402
    of tasks, 170, 190, 194, 250
    of the individual, 391
    of Very Small Groups, 155
    organizational, 197, 249, 265, 327, 342
    person/role, 169-170, 270, 329
    plant/community, 209, 211
    racial, 324
    role-, 189, 192
    sub-group, 199
    violation of, 342-343
    See also Inline, Outline
Bower, M., 232
Bowers, D., 197
Bradford, S., 334
Branforth, K.W., 119, 247
Braunschweig, D., 406
Braxton, E., 213
Bridger, H., 254
Broverman, I.K., 310
Brown, J., 333
Brzezinski, Z., 120
Buckelew Houses, 283
Bullock Committee, 243
Bureaucracy

Index

analysis of, 408-409
Burnt Norton (Eliot), 385

C

Cambor, G., 173
Camus, A., 86
Canalize, 119-120, 124
Canetti, E., 407, 409
Capacity, 415
Capitalism, 400
Capra, F., 124, 414
CARS Labs, 113
Carter, J.E., 120
Cassel Hospital, 52-56
Catholic religious group, 301-306
Census, U.S. Bureau of, 309
Chandler, E., 172
Channels functions, 139
Chasseguet-Smirgel, J., 406-407
Chekov, A., 79
Childrearing, 311
Christian Church, 132-133
Chronic passivity, 98
Churchill, W., 73
Civil rights movement, 324
Civilising, 236-238
Clarkson, F.E., 310
Class antagonism, 142
Cluster meeting, 278
Collaboration, 139-150, 319, 338
Collective responsibility, 77
Collusive arrogation
    cycle of, 240
Colman, A.D., i, 43, 173, 176-177, 213, 273-274, 286-287, 299
Commensal relationship, 130, 161, 403
Common-sense philosophy, 404
Communication
    nonverbal in Very Small Groups, 155
Community care model, 273-283
Community intervention
    Belfast, 301-306
Community meeting, 278
Compassion, 86
Competence acquisition
    and therapy, 200
Competition, 318-319

in small groups, 175, 178
Complementary reactions, 27-28
    and identification, 33
Concordant identifications, 27, 33
Conference design, 166-168, 194
Conference plenaries, 167, 194
Confessional
    as Very Small Group model, 158
Consciousness raising groups, 305
Consultants, 90, 92-93, 139-140, 142, 146, 148, 175, 177, 181, 186, 192-193, 291, 365-381, 391, 395-396, 410
    and authority, 159
    and small groups, 173
    and behavior, 390
    in AIL program, 279-280, 283
    in Very Small Groups, 155
    team-, 190
    women as, 302, 315, 317
Containment, 2, 65, 127-133, 161, 247, 403, 411
Control
    fantasy of, 339
Cooper, L., i, 38, 135, 139, 143, 213, 367, 388, 390-391, 394-396, 415
Correa, M.E., 288, 305
Countertransference, 27, 30-33, 35, 296, 396
    complementary-, 28
Creativity, 350-351
Cross-training, 203, 209
Culture circles, 147
Culture of silence, 147
Cults, 54
Cumming, E., 274
Cumming, J., 274
Cybernetics, 1, 124
Cycle of degeneration, 161

D

Dalton, G.W., 89
Davien, R., 365-366
Day-dreams, 8
Day treatment programs, 276
Death, 368, 373
    of career, 238
    real, 238
Decision-making, 292

Index

centralized, 94
managerial, 244
organizational, 286, 290, 295
-process, 96-98, 105
Decompensation, 282-283
Dedifferentiation
of the super-ego, 44
Defense mechanism, 21-22, 98, 239, 246-247, 338-339, 384, 407
identification as a, 217
of systems, 306
Defenses, 52, 53, 58, 93, 169, 224, 252, 360, 401
of adolescents, 222
Defensive delineations, 225-226, 229
Deities, 129, 132
Delphic motto, 86
Democracy, 201
Democratisation, 62, 96
Dependency, 40, 94, 98, 159, 193-194, 201, 219, 223, 239-240, 246, 250, 252-254, 264, 271, 274, 282, 294, 319-322, 330, 338-339, 371, 393, 401
issues, 187
Depersonalization, 54, 343
Depressive
anxiety, 12-13, 148
position, 12-13, 39, 142, 200, 222, 414
Deprivation
of dependent needs, 320-321
Depth-psychological perspective, 147-150
Destruction, 44
Devaluation, 104
Dicks, H., 22, 25-26
Director culture, 147
Discharge terms, 83
Discipline, 13
Disclosure, 38
Discrimination, 129, 309
Disintegration,
of the super-ego, 44
Divine origin, 130
Doob, L., 301, 305, 417
Drucker, P.F., 232
Dumas, R.G., i, 214, 323
Durkin, H.E., 43
Dusier, E., 326

Dyads, 21, 23, 25, 27, 32, 35, 78, 171, 407

E

Easton, D., 387
Ego, 7-10, 27-28, 30, 44-45, 53, 73, 104, 129, 150, 217
and psychodynamics of role-taking, 336-351
autonomy, 222
boundaries, 22, 24-27, 33
breakdown, 403
defensive processes, 200
discrimination, 225
functioning, 219, 223
-goals, 102
-id maturation, 226
ideals, 58, 399, 406-407
introjection by the-, 226
psychology, 399
regression, 224
structure, 26
Eisold, K., i, 1, 37
Eissler, K.R., 131
Eliot, T.S., 385
Emery, F.E., 89, 247
Empathy, 24, 26
Enemy
external, 140
internal, 140
Entrapment
fantasy of, 342
Envied
fear of being, 63
Envy, 11, 15-18, 22-23, 27, 34, 39, 57, 62-64, 67, 91, 101-102, 104, 131, 142-143, 199, 404, 408, 410
Erikson, E., 222
EST training, 111
Establishment, 48, 127, 129, 131, 132
Evans, F.B., i
Executive development. *See* Management development
External object, 28, 34, 35
Externalization, 63
Ezriel, H., 29

440

F

Fabian, J.J., 314
Fain, M., 406
Family, 310-311
   as Very Small Group model, 158-159
   boundaries, 313
   dynamics, 217-229, 314
   group, 367
   -systems theory, 221
Family therapy, 217-229, 295, 356
   conjoint, 219-221, 228-229
   dynamics, 72
   fantasies, 72
   transactions, 26, 35
Fantasy, 6, 8-9, 11, 23-25, 29, 31, 34, 37-40, 43-45, 51, 55-56, 58, 69, 114-115, 146, 149, 151, 175, 180-181, 194, 221, 223-224, 229, 239, 251, 254, 275, 338-339, 342, 346, 349-350, 360, 385, 404, 411, 413
   absence of, 303
   mutual projective, 50, 59, 289
   of schizoid personalities, 96
   of womens' roles, 310, 319-320
   projective, 49, 54, 353
   unconscious, 18
Faulkner, L.R., 273
Fear, 44
   of abandonment, 27
Ferster, C., 173-178
Field theory, 246
Fight/flight, 40-41, 86, 94, 98-100, 120, 145, 246, 303, 319, 346, 401
Figure/ground phenomena, 169, 171
Fitz, A., 197
Fleisher, K., 213
Flight, 49, 54, 86, 223, 393-394
Foltz, W., 301, 305, 417
Fondation Internationale de l'Innovation Sociale, 395
Formative causation, 124
Foulkes, S.H., 43
Freeston, J.T., 232
Freud, S., 5-7, 12-13, 16, 22, 37, 43-44, 50, 77, 128-130, 132, 161, 217, 219, 226, 238, 311, 335-336, 346, 348-349, 399-401, 407, 411
   and leadership, 399-401
Friere, P., 143, 147, 149, 252
Functional administrative structure, 96, 294

G

Galbraith, J.K., 74
Games
   theory of, 1
Gate functions, 139
Gear, M.C., 21
Geller, M.H., i, 173, 176-177, 185
Gender
   conference plenaries, 167, 169
   fantasy about-, 165
   groups, 303-306
   -related issues, 163, 166, 168-170, 172, 312, 314, 321, 386
Generalisation, 61, 66
General systems theory, 1
Genius, 48, 128, 130, 402
   See also Messiah, Mystic
Gestalt, 114, 116
   dyadic-, 158
   of group, 119-121, 411
   of human systems, 246
   therapy, 111
Gibbard, G.S., 43, 114-115, 343, 414
Gillette, J., 213
Ginzberg, E., 309
Goffman, E., 250, 386
Goldman, H.H., 275
Gosling, R., i, 38, 135
Gould, L.J., i, 135, 163, 165, 167, 172, 293
Goya, F., 78
Gratification, 104-106, 335, 346, 407
   narcissistic, 102-103, 406
Greed, 11-12, 17-18, 39, 142-143
Grinberg, L., 21, 28
Grotstein, J.S., 21, 33, 188
Group
   analysis, 38-39, 46, 48
   as-mother, 114-116
   behavior, 22, 30, 310

Index

boundaries, 47
definition of, 5
dispersion, 145
dynamics, 38-39, 285, 296
formation, 193
functioning, 2
instinct, 37
leaders, 40
member as spokesman, 29-32, 35
membership, 45-46, 48
mentality, 22, 28
psychology, 37, 210
psychotherapy, 21
reality, 38
rebellion, 145
relations conference, 38, 185-196, 285-298, 305, 354, 367-368, 372, 387-389, 414
relations training, 1-2, 274
task-, 47, 159
tension, 29
theory, 37
therapists, 22-23, 28, 47
therapy, 37-38, 48, 145
training, 185-198
unconscious, 147
work settings, 163
Group-as-a-whole, 1-2, 23, 37, 109-126, 413
emotion, 34
level, 112
root and derivatives, 116
Group Environment Scale, 416
Group functioning
mature level, 222-223
regressed level, 222-223
Group-individual balance, 291
Group processes, 91-92, 109, 139, 165, 169, 177, 182, 290, 297
regressive-, 107
Group relations training, 152, 386-387
organization wide-, 285-298
Groups
as multi-level systems, 109-113
closed-system-, 73, 77-78
consciousness raising-, 305
five levels of, 110-113
open-system-, 73-75
projection, 51
projective processes in large-, 55
projective processes in small-, 55
psychodynamics of large-, 49-69
therapeutic powers of, 295
See also After-groups, Application groups, Basic groups, Consciousness raising groups, Implementation groups, Large groups, Small groups, Study groups, Work groups
Grubb Institute for Behavioral Studies, 152-153
Grunberger, B., 406
Guilt, 10, 12-15, 67, 281, 321, 335-336, 340-341, 349, 400
Gustafson, J.P., ii, 38, 135, 139, 143, 145, 213, 291, 367, 388, 390-391, 394-396
Gwynne, G.V., 251

H

Hamlet, 86
Hammer, M., 282
Hartman, J.J., 43, 414
Harrow, M., 197
Hausman, W., 291
Heath, E.S., 38
Heimburger, E.M., ii, 135, 185, 188, 191, 213
Herd instinct, 37
Here and now situation, 146, 152, 154, 169, 173, 175, 254, 260, 288, 291, 297
Herrick, D., 384
Higgin, G.W., 254
Hirschhorn, L., ii, 214, 335
History of the Peloponnesian War (Thucydides), 89
Hitler, A., 50, 405
Hodgson, R.C., 89
Holding environment, 142-145, 148, 150
Holographic paradigm, 124
Homogenisation, 413
Homosexuality, 9
Hood, V.G., 402
Horkheimer, M., 311
Horney, K., 311
Horticultural model, 251-252

Horwitz, L., ii, 2, 21, 34, 115, 417
Hostility, 14, 41, 61-62, 64, 66, 99, 131, 148, 201, 238, 330
  projected, 60, 62
Household management structure, 277-278
Howe, S.R., 305
Huber, J., 309
Human nature
  assumptions about, 198-199, 202-204, 210
Human origin, 130
Human relations school, 247
Hydraulic system principle of male/female relationships, 324

I

Id, 7, 27, 342, 347, 406
Idealization, 129-130
Identification, 9-10, 15-16, 23, 25, 27, 105, 143, 145, 190, 203, 217, 226, 311, 369, 399, 406
  and learning, 177
  processes, 28
  with the leader, 85
Identity, 45, 386
  formation, 222
Implementation groups, 395
Import-conversion-export process, 235-236, 385
Impulse life, 146
Independent community living, 273, 280
Individual
  and the group, 85
  behavior, 37
Individuation *See* Separation-individuation
Industrial democracy, 243-271
Infancy, 5-6, 8-9, 18, 24
Information theory, 1
Inheritance, 238-239
Inline, 385-386, 388-389, 393, 396, 416
Instinctual
  impulses, 7, 8
  knowledge, 6
Institutional
  collusive projection, 52
  event, 167, 185, 193, 373
Integration, 53
  personality-, 67
Integrity, 18
Inter-group
  conflict, 391
  events in Belfast, 302-306
  processes, 153, 179, 189
  relations, 387
Inter-institutional relationships, 384
Internal
  processes, 73
  relationships, 202, 210
Inter-organizational level, 113
Interpersonal
  competence, 301
  level, 2, 111, 118, 123-124, 385
  relations, 217, 314, 386-387, 413-414
  system of roles, 349
  transaction, 23, 25, 28, 34, 389
Interpretation, 65-67, 80, 127, 131, 140, 144, 146, 148, 169, 177-179, 359, 365, 389, 391, 396
Inter-system relationships, 260, 386
Intimacy, 26-27, 139-140, 159, 311, 348, 353, 399
  in Very Small Groups, 157
Intragroup
  cohesion, 391
  relations, 119
Intra-institutional political system, 384
Intrapersonal level, 111, 122-124, 392
Intra-psychic, 1, 2
  conflicts, 395
  organization of aggression, 349
  processes, 118, 413-414
  theory of pathogenesis and treatment, 291
  transformations, 22-23, 25, 28, 34
Introjection, 7-9, 13, 24, 28, 35, 342, 385
  by the ego, 226
Intrusion, 135
  protection from, 313
Involvement
  politics of, 383-397
Isaacs, S., 8
Isolation, 86, 314

443

Index

J

Jackson, S., 30
Jacobson, E., 44, 219, 222
Janis, I., 121
Jaques, E., 51, 140, 142, 150, 197, 200, 210, 247, 251, 389-391, 395, 408-409, 415
Jardim, A., 309
Johnson, J.L., 213
Joseph, D.I., 197
Jung, C., 400

K

Kabbalah, 129
Kaes, R., 406
Kahn, R.L., 404
Kaplan, R.E., 118
Karl Menninger School of Psychiatry, 295
Karma, 368
Katz, D., 404
Kernberg, O.F., ii, 2, 21, 24, 28, 44, 47, 101-103, 214, 217, 220, 287, 292, 294, 296, 399, 405, 410
Khaleelee, I., 256, 258-261, 263-265, 267, 386, 415-416
Klein, E.B., ii, 135, 185, 197, 213, 289, 293-294, 299, 301, 305, 417
Klein, M., ii, 1, 5, 21, 39-40, 44, 50, 115, 141-143, 199, 248, 288, 339, 350, 386
Kleinian theory, 222, 385, 413
Klerman, G., 312
Knox, R.A., 132
Krantz, J., ii

L

Labor, U.S. Dept. of, 309
Laing, R.D., 143, 418
Lamb, H.R., 273

Large groups, 56, 78, 153, 166, 254
  behavior of, 260-265, 267
  events in Belfast, 302-306
  psychodynamics of, 49-69
Lasch, C., 400
Lasswell, H.D., 387
Laufer, M., 219
Law and order, 299
Lawrence, W.G., ii, 213, 231-232, 236, 249, 387, 395-396
Leader-follower relations, 201
Leadership, 17, 89, 92, 140, 146, 148, 164, 170, 172, 193, 202, 205, 283, 293, 302, 305
  and authority, 95-96, 152, 163, 166
  and power, 198, 200-202, 204, 210
  and staff, 168
  and teamwork, 199
  and the individual, 85
  as a relationship, 201
  black women in, 323-334
  boundaries, 197, 289
  charismatic-, 105-106
  choice of, 106-107, 263, 406
  collaborative-, 140-141, 311, 317
  conferences, 197
  consensus, 105-106
  idealization, 407
  in basic assumption groups, 77, 78
  in work settings, 163, 165-166, 264, 316-319, 359, 361
  males in-, 315
  organizational-, 334
  personal-, 74
  personality features of, 90, 101
  psychoanalytic studies of group-, 399-411
  psychoanalytic studies of organizational-, 399-411
  rational-, 407-411
  role, 29, 43-44, 46-48, 73
  skills, 301
  small group-, 74
  women in-, 309, 312-322
Learning, 189
  advanced, 178
  experiential, 190, 395
  in a small group, 173-183

Index

passive, 186, 190
short-term, 404
Leicester Conference, 160, 387, 396, 403
Lenin, 387
Lerner, H., 310-311
Levinson, D.J., 165, 310, 312, 317, 415
Levinson, H., 89, 257, 409
Levy, M.J., 387
Lewin, K., 139, 152, 246-248
Liendo, E.C., 21
Loewald, H., 34, 217
Lofgren, L., 173, 176-177, 180
Loneliness, 86
Lundgren, J.T., 213
Lupton, T., 247
Luria, I., 129

M

Macro-systems, 200-201
Mahler, M., 44, 220
Main, T.F., ii, 2, 49-51, 89, 405, 415
Malan, D.H., 402
Male/female dynamics, 166, 169, 171
Malin, A., 21, 33, 118
Management
 assumptions, 202
 development, 231-240
 dynamics, 205-207
 neutrality of, 237
 philosophy, 203, 208, 210
 positions, 309
 relationships, 202
 scientific-, 247
 structure of household, 277
Managerial theory, 292
Mandala House, 273-274
Mandelbaum, A., 22
Manic defense, 339-341
Mann, R.D., 139, 414-415
Mao, 387
Marital
 therapy, 22
 transactions, 26-27, 35
"Marius," 374-381
Marrow, A.J., 197
Marxism, 129, 348, 395, 400

Masao Maruyama, 387
Masler, E., 21, 32-33
Maslow, A.H., 198-199, 202
Masterson, J., 220
Maternal object, 39
Maux, A.J., 273
McGregor, D., 198-199, 201-203, 247
Medders, N.M., ii, 213
Meissner, W.W., 26
Membership criteria, 193
Mendell, D., 357
Menninger Foundation, 285-287, 289, 293, 393, 417
Menninger, R.W., ii, 213, 285-287, 290, 393, 417
Menzies, I., 51, 171, 200, 213, 247, 251, 354, 415
Messiah, 48, 128, 402
 See also Genius, Mystic
Micro-systems, 200-201
Miller, B., 197
Miller, E.J., ii, 89, 140, 169, 197, 213-214, 231, 235-236, 243, 245, 247, 249-251, 285, 288, 293, 301, 310, 353, 383-385, 387, 391-392, 415, 417
Minorities, 63, 207, 209
Modell, A., 140-142
Monopolist, 29-32
Moos, R., 416
Morale *See* Group processes
Mossell, S.T., 324
Mother, 6, 8-9, 11, 15, 19, 23, 39, 199, 313, 320-321, 329-330
 -child relations, 141, 311
Mount Holyoke College, 185
Mystic, 48, 128-133, 402
 creative-, 132
 nihilist-, 128, 132
 See also Genius, Messiah
Myths, 78, 86, 325-327, 384
 of authority, 393
 of groups, 396

N

Narcissism, 57-59, 62, 100-106, 401, 405-411, 414
 in relationships, 53-54

Index

pathological, 102-103, 106, 120, 218, 220, 227-229
withdrawals by, 66
National Association of Colored Women, 324
National Labor Relations Board, 208
National Training Laboratory, 135, 152, 197-200, 202, 210-211, 295, 299-303, 414
Nazism, 50, 409
Negotiation, 98, 193-195, 386-387, 393, 405
as Very Small Group model, 159
skills, 303
Neumann, E., 310, 329
New Industrial State (Galbraith), 74
Newton, I., 402
Newton, P.M., iii, 172, 214, 309-310, 317
Nietzche, 128
Noninterpretive therapeutic intervention, 66-67
Nuremberg Trials, 50
Nurturance, 42, 117, 201, 296, 310, 320

O

"O," 48, 133
Object relations, 401, 407, 410
internalized, 103, 105
part-, 103
total-, 103
Object relations theory, 1, 21, 39, 43, 46
and family dynamics, 217-229
Object relationship, 21, 44, 46, 50, 54, 248-249
representation, 28
Objective judgement, 14
Obsessive personality, 97-98
O'Connor, G., 166, 299, 388, 393-394, 418
Odysseus, 78
Oedipal dynamics, 43, 318
pre-, 37-38, 46, 406-408
Oedipus complex, 6, 9-10, 15, 107, 161
Oedipus myth, 79, 86, 133, 400

Ogden, T.H., 33, 413
Ollman, B., 144
Open systems, 235, 247-249, 288, 305, 385
framework, 109, 255
theory, 2, 90, 392, 403, 405
Opening plenary session, 166
Organizational
administration, 195
behavior, 172, 387
boundaries, 197, 327, 342
consultation, 195, 197
development, 243-271
leadership, 334
management, 90
processes, 165, 302, 305
regression, 408-409
tasks, 90, 99, 104, 106, 313
theory, classical, 247, 404
work settings, 163
Oshry Power Labs, 113
Outline, 385-386, 388-389, 396, 416

P

Paige, G.D., 387
Pairing, 40, 94, 158, 246, 319, 401
Palmer, B., 289
Paranoia, 11, 13, 98-100, 405, 410-411
Paranoid-schizoid position, 11, 21, 39, 142-143, 200, 408, 414
in adolescents, 222
Parasitic relationships, 23, 130-131, 161, 402
Parsons, T., 311
Part-object relationships, 43-44, 248-249, 338
Part vs whole, 246-247, 343, 348, 394
Participatory management, 94, 269, 287
Pattison, E.M., 282
Peer support network, 278
Persecution, 44, 99, 415
Persecutory anxiety, 9-14, 17-18, 23
Person-role dichotomy, 365-366, 368-369

Personalisation
  loss of, 61
Personality, 5, 7-9, 13, 15, 18
  invasion, 54-55
  reorganization, 219
PET, 111
Phantasy *See* Fantasy
Physical proximity
  in Very Small Groups, 155
Pincus, L., 50
Pine, F., 52, 220
Plant-community
  boundaries, 209, 211
  dynamics, 207-209
Planty, E.G., 232
Play technique, 5, 6
Plenaries
  conference, 167
  gender conference, 167
  opening, 166
  total conference, 167
Political management, 96
Political relationships, 383-384, 386
Politics
  academic, 384
  gender, 384
  international, 387
  of identity, 385-386
  racial, 384
Power, 94, 128
  and leadership, 198, 200-202, 204, 210, 312
  and work groups, 314-317
  of therapist, 42
"Praxis Event," 396
Predictions, 83
Primary task, 2, 72-77, 82, 140, 166, 169, 172, 200, 271, 345, 347, 353, 355, 358, 361, 401, 403, 409
  analysis, 235-236
  existential-, 236-237, 239, 249
  implementation of, 79, 81, 84, 252
  normative-, 236-237, 249
  phenomenal-, 236-239, 249, 251
Prisons, 72
Process
  and social structure, 199-200
  groups, 173-174, 176
Projected introjection, 28

Projection, 7, 8, 10, 14, 21-22, 24, 53, 55, 57, 85, 155, 171, 221, 255, 342-343, 345, 350, 360, 385, 391-393, 396, 417
  collusive, 59, 69
  multiple-, 59
  of self, 59
  trial-, 53-54
Projective counteridentification, 28
Projective identification, 2, 21-35, 40, 49-51, 53, 63, 116, 118-126, 130, 226-227, 339, 353, 360, 413-414
  and study groups, 146
  benign-, 65
  of parents, 225
Projective processes, 49-53, 55, 57, 62, 66, 68, 403
  benign-, 56
  in groups, 55
  in Very Small Groups, 157
  malignant, 53-55
Protestant religious group, 300-306
Psychoanalysis, 5, 21, 127, 129-130, 132, 140, 218, 372, 389, 414
  applied-, 131
Psychoanalytic theory, 79, 127
Psychological universalism, 247
Psychology of growth, 210
Psychotic anxiety, 40, 44

Q

Quantum physics, 124
Quasi-stable equilibria functions, 139
Queens University, 302

R

Rabbinical directorate, 132-133
Racial antagonism, 142
Racism, 323, 334
Racker, H., 27-28, 33
Reality-testing, 53-59, 63-65, 85, 385
Redl, F., 29
Reductionist view of conflict, 395

Index

Regression, 2, 22-24, 34, 39-40, 43-44, 46-47, 52, 94, 96, 115-116, 142, 194, 297, 402-403, 406-407, 411
   in organizational leadership, 89-107, 404
   of adolescents, 221-223, 227
   of family, 218, 224-225, 228
   paranoid-, 100, 404
Regressive-adaptive process, 44, 401
Reich, W., 400
Reintrojection, 24-25, 28, 33-35
Reparation, 350-351
Repression, 7, 13, 400
Resentment, 9, 14
Residential treatment program, 273-276, 279-281, 283
Resignation, 75
Resistance
   counterdependent-, 187
   depth-psychological, 149
   external, 219-221, 228
   internal, 219-220, 228
   sociopolitical, 149, 387
   to therapy, 218
Responsibility, 128, 316-317, 321
   issues of, 191
Rice, A.K., 22, 72, 89, 140, 152, 166, 168-170, 185, 197, 200-202, 204, 235-236, 245-247, 249-250, 253, 285, 288-289, 293, 310, 353, 365, 367, 369, 385, 391, 394, 403-405, 409, 414-415
Rioch, M., iii, 22, 90, 135, 147, 166, 168, 173, 185, 198, 214, 274, 289, 365, 388-390, 393-394, 414, 417
Risk-taking, 38, 342, 344-345, 347, 390
Rivalry, 9, 15, 17, 34
Robinson, P., 236
Rogers, K., 90, 95
Roheim, G., 367
Role
   analysis groups, 288
   assignment, 22, 226, 311
   boundaries, 189, 192
   changes, 179-180, 183
   collusion, 22
   competition, 78
   definition, 192, 357
   differentiation, 71, 120
   -fit, 50-51, 62
   heroic-, 366
   institutional-, 269
   managerial-, 269
   of staff, 168, 396
   -play, 304
   psychodynamics of taking the-, 335-351
   -relations consultation groups, 167
   simplicity, 82
   stepping out of, 342-343
   -suction, 29-31, 35
Roles, 52, 175-176, 384
   at group relations conferences, 186, 393
   of men and women at work, 163-172, 312-322
   sex-, 309
   symbolic-, 329, 334
   total-, 309
Rosenfeld, H., 21, 409
Rosenkrantz, P.S., 310
Roustang, F., 400
Rules, 128, 131

S

Sadism, 22, 98-99, 411
Safety
   conditions of, 144-147
Salient image, 233-235
Sampson, H., 149-150, 415
Sandler, J., 141
Sanford, N., 90, 95
Saravay, S.M., 43
Sartre, 143
Satellite housing programs, 274-275, 280
Scapegoating, 29-32, 35, 42, 120, 122, 125, 179, 291, 294, 306, 366, 413
   in Very Small Groups, 157
Scarcity, 143
   conditions of, 144-147
Scheidlinger, S., 43, 46, 115, 402
Schindler, W., 43
Schizoid personality, 96-97, 408
Schizophrenia, 11, 21, 26, 55, 276
Schneider, M., 144

Schwartz, H., 90, 335-336
Searles, H.F., 21, 55
Seashore, S., 197
Sectarianism as a defense, 304
Segal, H., 25, 222, 288, 343, 350
Self, 7, 16, 21-25, 28, 34-35, 45
  -awareness, 75
  -containment, 83
  -criticism, 399
  -esteem, 45
  -evaluation, 82
  -expression, 13-14
  -image, 45
  -object differentiation, 26, 226
  recovery of the, 64
  representations, 28, 45
Semrad, E.V., 29
Sensitivity training, 111
Sentience, 192, 202, 250, 298
Sentient
  groups, 250, 296
  tasks, 206
  ties, 189, 209, 289, 305, 359
Separation, 129-130
  anxiety, 23
  -individuation, 220, 227-229
Settlage, C., 218
Sex roles, 309-310, 321
Sexism, 170, 323, 334
  as a defense system, 306
  non-, 170-171
Sexuality, 24, 163, 166, 168-170
  fantasies about, 165
Shapiro, E.R., iii, 214, 353
Shapiro, R.L., iii, 213, 217, 219-220, 222, 227-228, 367
Shaw, G.B., 132
Sheffel, I., 293
Sheldrake, R., 119, 124
Shooter, A.M.N., 402
Singer, D.L., 289, 354
Skertchley, A., 237
Skills development, 234
Slater, P., 142, 144-145, 150, 200, 414
Slavery, 323, 325, 333-334
Small group, 31, 78, 173
  advanced learning in, 173-183
  behavior, 71, 260
  collaboration in, 139-150
  consultant, 135, 185
  dynamics, 152
  events in Belfast, 302-306
  of same gender, 166
  plenaries, 169
  processes, 139-150
  theory, 221
  very-, 135, 151-161, 254
Snell, B., 86
Snyder, R.C., 387
Social structure
  and process, 198-200, 202, 210
Social systems theory, 1
Socio-technical system, 247, 288
Socrates, 74
Sofer, C., 152, 254
Sokolvsky, J., 282
Sophisticated groups *See* Work groups
Spitz, R., 157
Splitting, 7, 10-12, 25, 39, 50-51, 53, 56, 59, 67, 85, 104, 116-118, 120, 122, 124-125, 170, 221, 227-228, 385, 413-414
  in Very Small Groups, 155, 157
Staff
  group, 179, 312
  in-training, 188-195
  role, 185, 190
Stanton, A.M., 90
Star Power, 113
Stephane, Andre *See* Chasseguet-Smirgel, J.
Stereotyping, 155
  of sex roles, 310-311
Stirling University, 301, 304-306
Stone, W.N., 305
Strachey, J., 34, 335
Strategic management training, 113
Structural theory, 217-218
Structural universalism, 247
Study groups, 139, 143-144, 146, 197, 414
Sublimation, 347-349
Submissiveness, 16, 103
Sufism, 129
Superego, 7, 12, 16, 27-28, 33-34, 44, 50, 129, 217, 335-336, 340, 343, 346, 349-350, 399, 406, 410
Superior-subordinate relationship, 263
Symbiotic relationship, 130-131, 161, 402
Symmetry *See* Pairing
System processes, 109, 395

Index

Systemic thinking, 247
Systems theory, 357, 373, 403, 411
Szesody, I., 173
Szmidla, A., 256-265, 267, 385-386, 415-416

T

Task
  boundaries, 96, 170, 194, 250, 353, 405
  definition, 90, 92, 189, 193, 293, 296, 312, 357, 369
  demands, 124, 334
  groupings, 169, 204
  groups, 143, 195, 204
  leadership, 95, 410
  organization, 169
  performance, 92, 125, 319, 320, 327, 404, 407
  See also Primary Task
Task system, 249, 411
  dominant-, 235
  related-, 235
Tasks
  and structure, 200
  of role-relations consultation groups, 167
  of staff members, 168
Tavistock Institute of Human Relations, 1, 21, 25, 30, 34, 38, 112, 140, 141, 144, 173, 231, 245-247, 249, 253-254, 259, 263, 383-384, 387, 395, 414, 417
  model, 28, 135, 152, 177, 185, 198-210, 204, 210, 274, 287-288, 295, 301-303, 325, 353-354, 357-358, 360, 403
Taylor, S., 164
Termination
  criteria for, 389-391
Terrell, M.C., 326
T-group encounter, 111, 197, 295, 302
Theory X management, 205-206, 209-210
Theory Y management, 198, 201, 204-210
Therapeutic
  alliance, 141
  community technique, 51-52, 291, 295-296, 405
  relationship, 34
Therapy and competence
  acquisition, 200
  depth-oriented-, 200
Thompson, D., iii
Thucydides, 84
Tolerance, 16
Topology, 246
Total conference plenary, 167
Training
  -in-service, 320
  model, 135
  programs, 186, 188, 190, 301-306
  vs therapy, 170-171
Transference, 6, 24, 26, 31, 33, 35, 47, 119, 130, 247, 255, 401
  cocoon-, 142
  counter-, 27-28, 30-33, 35, 247, 296
  flight from, 394
  neurosis, 142
  situation, 5, 15
Treatment facilities, 273
Treatment processes
  and managerial theory, 292
Trist, E.L., 89, 119, 152, 200, 247, 254
Trop, J., 213
Truth, S., 333-334
Tubman, H., 333-334
Turner, N., 333
Turquet, P., iii, 2, 71, 80, 152, 158, 223, 246, 253-254, 343, 353, 367, 403, 407, 413

U

Unconscious assumptions, 225-229
  theory of, 220-224
Unconscious motivation, 200
Unconscious processes, 5, 152, 274, 402
  in an organization, 353-362
Unions, 207, 209-210
United States Dependents' Schools System, 395

University of Missouri-Columbia, 185
University of Pennsylvania, 324

V

Valency, 47, 85
Van Steenberg, V., 213
Vance, C., 120
Violence
  psychological, 343
Vogel, S.R., 310

W

War and war games, 113, 390
Warehousing model, 251
Washington School of Psychiatry, 177, 181
Weiss, J., 141, 150
Wells, L., Jr., iii, 109, 114-115, 117, 120
West, K.L., iii
We/they situations, 60-61
Willett, R.S., 309
Winnicott, D.W., 34, 141
Withdrawal
  social, 187
Women
  black, 323-334
  in authority, 164, 303, 309-322
  role of, 303-304, 309

Women's movement, 163, 368
Woodson, C., 323
Work
  critique of, 349-350
Work groups, 47, 50-51, 74-75, 79, 81, 84-85, 129, 176, 194-195, 222, 312, 317, 319, 401
  autonomous-, 199
  functioning-, 223
  leadership in, 81-82, 310, 359, 361, 402
  primary-, 247, 271
  sophisticated, 81-83, 246
Work organization, 170
Work role, 165, 250, 270, 310, 317, 336, 338
Working through, 12-13
Wright, F., 172

Y

Yale University, 112, 197, 301, 324
Yalom, I., 38, 145
Yohalem, A., 309

Z

Zaleznik, A., 105, 409
Zen, 372
Zinner, J., 219-220, 227, 353